Programming with Microsoft Foundation Class Library

Microsoft® Visual C++™

Development System for Windows™ and Windows NT™
Version 2.0

Microsoft Corporation

PUBLISHED BY
Microsoft Press
A Division of Microsoft Corporation
One Microsoft Way
Redmond, Washington 98052-6399

Copyright © 1994 by Microsoft Corporation

Library of Congress Cataloging-in-Publication Data
Programming with MFC / Microsoft Corporation.
     p.   cm.
    Includes index.
    ISBN 1-55615-802-5
    1. C++ (Computer program language) 2. Microsoft C++.
  I. Microsoft Corporation.
  QA76.73.C153P76   1994
  005.26--dc20   94-30463
                                    CIP

Printed and bound in the United States of America.

1 2 3 4 5 6 7 8 9 MLML 9 8 7 6 5 4

Distributed to the book trade in Canada by Macmillan of Canada, a division of Canada
Publishing Corporation.

A CIP catalogue record for this book is available from the British Library.

Microsoft Press books are available through booksellers and distributors worldwide.
For further information about international editions, contact your local Microsoft
Corporation office. Or contact Microsoft Press International directly at fax (206) 936-7329.

Information in this document is subject to change without notice. Companies, names, and data used in examples herein
are fictitious unless otherwise noted. No part of this document may be reproduced or transmitted in any form or by any
means, electronic or mechanical, for any purpose, without the express written permission of Microsoft Corporation.

U.S. Patent No. 4955066

For Programming with the Microsoft Foundation Class Library: Macintosh is a registered trademark of Apple
Computer, Inc. dBASE is a registered trademark and Paradox is a trademark of Borland International, Inc. CompuServe
is a registered trademark of CompuServe, Inc. Intel is a registered trademark of Intel Corporation. FoxPro, Microsoft,
Microsoft Access, MS-DOS, Visual Basic, and Win32 are registered trademarks and Visual C++, Win32s, Windows, and
Windows NT are trademarks of Microsoft Corporation in the U.S. and other countries. MIPS is a registered trademark of
MIPS Computer Systems, Inc. Btrieve is a registered trademark of Novell, Inc. Unicode is a trademark of Unicode,
Incorporated. Paintbrush is a trademark of ZSoft Corporation.

Document No. DB57160-0794

For Programming Techniques: Intel is a registered trademark of Intel Corporation. IBM is a registered trademark of
International Business Machines Corporation. Lotus is a registered trademark of Lotus Development Corporation.
CodeView, Microsoft, MS, MS-DOS, QuickC, Win32, and XENIX are registered trademarks and Visual C++, Win32s,
Windows, and Windows NT are trademarks of Microsoft Corporation in the U.S. and other countries. MIPS is a
registered trademark of MIPS Computer Systems, Inc. Tandy is a registered trademark of Tandy Corporation.

Document No. DB57162-0694

Contents

Part 2   MFC Encyclopedia

Part 3   Appendix

Figures and Tables

Figures (*continued*)

Tables

Tables (*continued*)

Introduction

This book contains information on programming with the Microsoft® Foundation Class Library (MFC). The class library is a set of C++ classes that encapsulate the functionality of applications written for the Microsoft Windows™ operating system. This version of MFC supports programming for Win32® platforms, including Microsoft Windows NT™.

Part 1, meant to be read sequentially, is an overview of the class library, designed to help you understand the major components of an MFC application and how they work together. Part 1 explains the following topics:

- The key components of an MFC application:
  - An application object, which represents your application
  - Document template objects, which create document, frame window, and view objects
  - Document objects, which store data and serialize it to persistent storage
  - View objects, which display a document's data and manage the user's interaction with the data
  - Frame window objects, which contain views
  - Thread objects, which let you program multiple threads of execution using MFC classes
- Dialog boxes, controls, and control bars, such as toolbars and status bars.
- Object Linking and Embedding (OLE) Visual Editing and OLE Automation.
- Database support using Open Database Connectivity (ODBC).
- Useful general-purpose classes, such as strings, collections, exceptions, and date/time objects.

Part 2, designed for random access, presents an encyclopedia—an alphabetical collection of articles on programming with MFC. You can use these articles to follow many different threads of information. For an overview of how the articles work with each other, see the first article "Using the Encyclopedia" on page 123. Articles that begin particularly important threads include:

- "MFC" on page 323

- "OLE Overview" on page 360
- "Database Overview" on page 210

Document Conventions

This book uses the following typographic conventions:

Example	Description
STDIO.H	Uppercase letters indicate filenames, registers, and terms used at the operating-system command level
char, _setcolor, __far	Bold type indicates C and C++ keywords, operators, language-specific characters, and library routines. Within discussions of syntax, bold type indicates that the text must be entered exactly as shown.
	Many constants, functions, and keywords begin with either a single or double underscore. These are required as part of the name. For example, the compiler recognizes the **__cplusplus** manifest constant only when the leading double underscore is included.
expression	Words in italics indicate placeholders for information you must supply, such as a filename. Italic type is also used occasionally for emphasis in the text.
[[*option*]]	Items inside double square brackets are optional.
**#pragma pack {1	2}**	Braces and a vertical bar indicate a choice among two or more items. You must choose one of these items unless double square brackets ([[ ]]) surround the braces.
`#include <io.h>`	This font is used for examples, user input, program output, and error messages in text.
CL [[*option*...]] *file*...	Three dots (an ellipsis) following an item indicate that more items having the same form may appear.

`while()`
`{`
.
.
.
`}`
	A column or row of three dots tells you that part of an example program has been intentionally omitted.

CTRL+ENTER	Small capital letters are used to indicate the names of keys on the keyboard. When you see a plus sign (+) between two key names, you should hold down the first key while pressing the second.
	The carriage-return key, sometimes marked as a bent arrow on the keyboard, is called ENTER.

Example	Description
"argument"	Quotation marks enclose a new term the first time it is defined in text.
`"C string"`	Some C constructs, such as strings, require quotation marks. Quotation marks required by the language have the form `"` `"` and `'` `'` rather than " " and ' '.
Dynamic-Link Library (DLL)	The first time an acronym is used, it is usually spelled out.
Microsoft Specific →	Some features documented in this book have special usage constraints. A heading identifying the nature of the exception, followed by an arrow, marks the beginning of these exception features.
END Microsoft Specific	**END** followed by the exception heading marks the end of text about a feature which has a usage constraint.
▶ `CEnterDlg;`	The arrow adjacent to the code indicates that it has been altered from a previous example, usually because you are being instructed to edit it.

PART 1

Overview of the MFC Library

C H A P T E R   1

Using the Classes to Write Applications for Windows

Taken together, the classes in the Microsoft Foundation Class Library (MFC) make up an "application framework"—the framework on which you build an application for Windows. At a very general level, the framework defines the skeleton of an application and supplies standard user-interface implementations that can be placed onto the skeleton. Your job as programmer is to fill in the rest of the skeleton—those things that are specific to your application. You can get a head start by using AppWizard to create the files for a very thorough starter application. You use the Microsoft Visual C++™ resource editors to design your user-interface elements visually, ClassWizard to connect those elements to code, and the class library to implement your application-specific logic.

Version 3.0 of the MFC framework supports 32-bit programming for Win32 platforms, including Microsoft Windows NT version 3.5 and later. MFC Win32 support includes multithreading.

This chapter presents a broad overview of the application framework. It also explores the major objects that make up your application and how they are created. Among the topics covered in this chapter are the following:

- The major objects in a running application
- Division of labor between the framework and your code
- The application class, which encapsulates application-level functionality
- How document templates create and manage documents and their associated views and frame windows
- Class **CWnd**, the root base class of all windows
- Graphic objects, such as pens and brushes

Subsequent chapters continue the framework story, covering:

- Messages and commands: Chapter 2, "Working with Messages and Commands"
- Documents, views, and frame windows: Chapter 3, "Working with Frame Windows, Documents, and Views"

- Chapter 4, "Working with Dialog Boxes, Controls, and Control Bars"
- Chapter 5, "Working with Object Linking and Embedding"

  Besides giving you a considerable head start in writing applications for Windows, MFC also makes it much easier to write applications that specifically use Object Linking and Embedding (OLE). You can make your application an OLE Visual Editing container, an OLE Visual Editing server, or both, and you can add OLE Automation so that other applications can use objects from your application or even drive it remotely.

- Chapter 6, "Working with Databases"

  MFC also supplies a set of database classes that simplify writing data-access applications. Using the database classes, you can connect to databases via an Open Database Connectivity (ODBC) driver, select records from tables, and display record information in an on-screen form.

- Chapter 7, "Using the General-Purpose Classes"

  In addition, MFC is fully enabled for writing applications that use Unicode™ and multibyte character sets (MBCS), specifically double-byte character sets (DBCS).

For a step-by-step tutorial in which you build an application with the framework, read *Introducing Visual C++*, Chapters 6 through 15. The following table directs you to other documents:

Where to Find More Information

Topic	Book	Chapters
Classes mentioned in this book	*Class Library Reference*	Alphabetic reference
AppWizard	*Visual C++ User's Guide*	Chapter 1
ClassWizard	*Visual C++ User's Guide*	Chapter 12
Development environment	*Visual C++ User's Guide*	Chapters 1–21
Tutorials	*Introducing Visual C++*	Chapters 5–27
Diagnostics, exceptions	*Programming with the Microsoft Foundation Class Library* (this book)	Part 2 (see "Diagnostics" and "Exceptions"
Macros and globals	*Class Library Reference*	Alphabetic reference
Resources	*Visual C++ User's Guide*	Chapters 4–11

The Framework

Your work with the framework is based largely on a few major classes and several Visual C++ tools. Some of the classes encapsulate a large portion of the Win32 application programming interface (API). Other classes encapsulate application concepts such as documents, views, and the application itself. Still others encapsulate OLE features and ODBC data-access functionality.

SDI and MDI

MFC makes it easy to work with both single document interface (SDI) and multiple document interface (MDI) applications.

SDI applications allow only one open document frame window at a time. MDI applications allow multiple document frame windows to be open in the same instance of an application. An MDI application has a window within which multiple MDI child windows, which are frame windows themselves, can be opened, each containing a separate document. In some applications, the child windows can be of different types, such as chart windows and spreadsheet windows. In that case, the menu bar can change as MDI child windows of different types are activated.

Documents, Views, and the Framework

At the heart of the framework are the concepts of document and view. A document is a data object with which the user interacts in an editing session. It is created by the New or Open commands on the File menu and is typically saved in a file. A view is a window object through which the user interacts with a document.

The key objects in a running application are:

- The document(s)

  Your document class (derived from **CDocument**) specifies your application's data.

  If you want OLE functionality in your application, derive your document class from **COleDocument** or one of its derived classes, depending on the type of functionality you need.

- The view(s)

  Your view class (derived from **CView**) is the user's "window on the data." The view class specifies how the user sees your document's data and interacts with it. In some cases, you may want a document to have multiple views of the data.

  If you need scrolling, derive from **CScrollView**. If your view has a user interface that is laid out in a dialog-template resource, derive from **CFormView**. For simple text data, use or derive from **CEditView**. For a form-based data-access application, such as a data-entry program, derive from **CRecordView**.

- The frame windows

  Views are displayed inside "document frame windows." In an SDI application, the document frame window is also the "main frame window" for the application. In an MDI application, document windows are child windows displayed inside a main frame window. Your derived main frame-window class specifies the styles and other characteristics of the frame windows that contain your views. Derive from **CFrameWnd** to customize the document frame window for SDI applications. Derive from **CMDIFrameWnd** to customize the main frame window for MDI applications. Also derive a class from **CMDIChildWnd** to customize each of the distinct kinds of MDI document frame windows that your application supports.

- The document template(s)

  A document template orchestrates the creation of documents, views, and frame windows. A particular document-template class creates and manages all open documents of one type. Applications that support more than one type of document have multiple document templates. Use class **CSingleDocTemplate** for SDI applications, or use class **CMultiDocTemplate** for MDI applications.

- The application object

  Your application class (derived from **CWinApp**) controls all of the objects above and specifies application behavior such as initialization and cleanup. The application's one and only application object creates and manages the document templates for any document types the application supports.

- Thread objects

  If your application creates separate threads of execution—for example, to perform calculations in the background—you'll use classes derived from **CWinThread**. **CWinApp** itself is derived from **CWinThread** and represents the primary thread of execution (or the main process) in your application. You can also use MFC in secondary threads.

In a running application, these objects cooperatively respond to user actions, bound together by commands and other messages. A single application object manages one or more document templates. Each document template creates and manages one or more documents (depending on whether the application is SDI or MDI). The user views and manipulates a document through a view contained inside a frame window. Figure 1.1 shows the relationships among these objects for an SDI application.

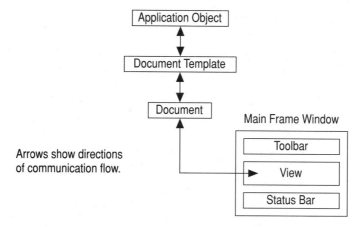

Figure 1.1   Objects in a Running SDI Application

The rest of this chapter explains how the framework tools, AppWizard, ClassWizard and the resource editors, create these objects, how they work together, and how you use them in your programming. Documents, views, and frame windows are discussed in more detail in Chapter 3, "Working with Frame Windows, Documents, and Views."

AppWizard, ClassWizard, and the Resource Editors

Visual C++ includes two wizards for use in MFC programming, along with many integrated resource editors. While you can write MFC applications without most of these tools, the tools greatly simplify and speed your work.

Use AppWizard to Create an MFC Application

Use AppWizard to create an MFC project in Visual C++—which can include OLE and database support. Files in the project contain your application, document, view, and frame-window classes; standard resources, including menus and an optional toolbar; other required Windows files; and optional .RTF files containing standard Windows Help topics.

Use ClassWizard to Manage Classes and Windows Messages

ClassWizard helps you create handler functions for Windows messages and commands; create and manage classes; create class member variables; create OLE Automation methods and properties; create database classes; and more.

Tip   ClassWizard also helps you to override virtual functions in the MFC classes. Select the class and select the virtual function to override. The rest of the process is similar to message handling, as described in the following paragraphs.

Applications running under Windows are "message driven." User actions and other events that occur in the running program cause Windows to send messages to the windows in the program. For example, if the user clicks the mouse in a window, Windows sends a **WM_LBUTTONDOWN** message when the left mouse button is pressed and a **WM_LBUTTONUP** message when the button is released. Windows also sends **WM_COMMAND** messages when the user selects commands from the menu bar.

In the framework, various objects—documents, views, frame windows, document templates, the application object—can "handle" messages. Such an object provides a "handler function" as one of its member functions, and the framework maps the incoming message to its handler.

A large part of your programming task is choosing which messages to map to which objects and then implementing that mapping. To do so, you use the ClassWizard tool.

ClassWizard will create empty message-handler member functions, and you use the source code editor to implement the body of the handler.

Use the Resource Editors to Create and Edit Resources

Use the Visual C++ resource editors to create and edit menus, dialog boxes, custom controls, accelerator keys, bitmaps, icons, cursors, strings, and version resources. ClassWizard works with the editors: for example, when you create a dialog-template resource, you can run ClassWizard to connect the resource to a dialog class.

To help you even more, the Microsoft Foundation Class Library provides a file called COMMON.RC, which contains "clip art" resources that you can copy from COMMON.RC and paste into your own resource file. COMMON.RC includes toolbar buttons, common cursors, icons, and more. You can use, modify, and redistribute these resources in your application. For more information about COMMON.RC, see the article "COMMON.RC Sample Resources" in Part 2.

For more information about the tools and how they work together, see the article "Tools for MFC Programming."

Building on the Framework

Your role in configuring an application with the framework is to supply the application-specific source code and to connect the components by defining what messages and commands they respond to. You use the C++ language and standard C++ techniques to derive your own application-specific classes from those supplied by the class library and to override and augment the base class's behavior.

Table 1.1 shows what you do in relation to what the framework does. Table 1.2 shows your role and the framework's role in creating OLE applications. For the most part, you can follow these tables as a sequence of steps for creating an MFC application, although some of the steps are alternative options. For example, most applications use one type of view class from the several types available.

Table 1.1   Sequence for Building an Application with the Framework

Task	You do	The framework does
Create a skeleton application.	Run AppWizard. Specify the options you want in the options pages. Options include making the application an OLE server, container, or both; adding OLE Automation; and making the application database-aware.	AppWizard creates the files for a skeleton application, including source files for your application, document, view, and frame windows; a resource file; a project file (.MAK); and others—all tailored to your specifications.
See what the framework and AppWizard offer without adding a line of your own code.	Build the skeleton application and run it in Visual C++.	The running skeleton application derives many standard File, Edit, View, and Help menu commands from the framework. For MDI applications, you also get a fully functional Window menu, and the framework manages creation, arrangement, and destruction of MDI child windows.
Construct your application's user interface.	Use the Visual C++ resource editors to visually edit the application's user interface: ▪ Create menus. ▪ Define accelerators. ▪ Create dialog boxes. ▪ Create and edit bitmaps, icons, and cursors. ▪ Edit the toolbar bitmap created for you by AppWizard. ▪ Create and edit other resources. You can also test the dialog boxes in the dialog editor.	The default resource file created by AppWizard supplies many of the resources you need. Visual C++ lets you edit existing resources and add new resources, easily and visually.

Table 1.1   Sequence for Building an Application with the Framework (*continued*)

Task	You do	The framework does
Map menus to handler functions.	Use ClassWizard to connect menus and accelerators to handler functions in your code.	ClassWizard inserts message-map entries and empty function templates in the source files you specify and manages many manual coding tasks.
Write your handler code.	Use ClassWizard to jump directly to the code in the source code editor. Fill in the code for your handler functions.	ClassWizard brings up the editor, scrolls to the empty function template, and positions the cursor for you.
Map toolbar buttons to commands.	Map each button on your toolbar to a menu or accelerator command by assigning the button the appropriate command ID.	The framework controls the drawing, enabling, disabling, checking, and other visual aspects of the toolbar buttons.
Test your handler functions.	Rebuild the program and use the built-in debugging tools to test that your handlers work correctly.	You can step or trace through the code to see how your handlers are called. If you've filled out the handler code, the handlers carry out commands. The framework will automatically disable menu items and toolbar buttons that are not handled.
Add dialog boxes.	Design dialog-template resources with the dialog editor. Then use ClassWizard to create a dialog class and the code that handles the dialog box.	The framework manages the dialog box and facilitates retrieving information entered by the user.
Initialize, validate, and retrieve dialog-box data.	You can also define how the dialog box's controls are to be initialized and validated. Use ClassWizard to add member variables to the dialog class and map them to dialog controls. Specify validation rules to be applied to each control as the user enters data. Provide your own custom validations if you wish.	The framework manages dialog-box initialization and validation. If the user enters invalid information, the framework displays a message box and lets the user reenter the data.

Table 1.1   Sequence for Building an Application with the Framework (*continued*)

Task	You do	The framework does
Create additional classes.	Use ClassWizard to create additional document, view, and frame-window classes beyond those created automatically by AppWizard. You can create additional database recordset classes, dialog classes, and so on.	ClassWizard adds these classes to your source files and helps you define their connections to any commands they handle.
Implement your document class.	Implement your application-specific document class(es). Add member variables to hold data structures. Add member functions to provide an interface to the data.	The framework already knows how to interact with document data files. It can open and close document files, read and write the document's data, and handle other user interfaces. You can focus on how the document's data is manipulated.
Implement Open, Save, and Save As commands.	Write code for the document's `Serialize` member function.	The framework displays dialog boxes for the Open, Save, and Save As commands on the File menu. It writes and reads back a document using the data format specified in your `Serialize` member function.
Implement your view class.	Implement one or more view classes corresponding to your documents. Implement the view's member functions that you mapped to the user interface with ClassWizard.	The framework manages most of the relationship between a document and its view. The view's member functions access the view's document to render its image on the screen or printed page and to update the document's data structures in response to user editing commands.
Enhance default printing.	If you need to support multipage printing, override view member functions.	The framework supports the Print, Print Setup, and Print Preview commands on the File menu. You must tell it how to break your document into multiple pages.

Table 1.1   Sequence for Building an Application with the Framework (*continued*)

Task	You do	The framework does
Add scrolling.	If you need to support scrolling, derive your view class(es) from **CScrollView**.	The view automatically adds scroll bars when the view window becomes too small.
Create form views.	If you want to base your views on dialog-template resources, derive your view class(es) from **CFormView**.	The view uses the dialog-template resource to display controls. The user can tab from control to control in the view.
Create database forms.	If you want a form-based data-access application, derive your view class from **CRecordView**.	The view works like a form view, but its controls are connected to the fields of a **CRecordset** object representing a database table. MFC moves data between the controls and the recordset for you.
Create a simple text editor.	If you want your view to be a simple text editor, derive your view class(es) from **CEditView**.	The view provides editing functions, Clipboard support, and file input/output.
Add splitter windows.	If you want to support window splitting, add a **CSplitterWnd** object to your SDI frame window or MDI child window and hook it up in the window's **OnCreateClient** member function.	The framework supplies splitter-box controls next to the scroll bars and manages splitting your view into multiple panes. If the user splits a window, the framework creates and attaches additional view objects to the document.
Build, test, and debug your application.	Use the facilities of Visual C++ to build, test, and debug your application.	Visual C++ lets you adjust compile, link, and other options. And it lets you browse your source code and class structure.

Table 1.2 shows your role and the framework's role in creating OLE applications. These represent options available rather than a sequence of steps to perform.

Table 1.2   Creating OLE Applications

Task	You do	The framework does
Create an OLE Visual Editing server.	Run AppWizard. Choose OLE Full Server or OLE Mini-server in the OLE options. (From an existing application, emulate Step 7 in the Scribble tutorial.)	The framework generates a skeleton application with OLE server capability enabled. All of the OLE capability can be transferred to your existing application with only slight modification.
Create an OLE Visual Editing container application from scratch.	Run AppWizard. Choose OLE Container in the OLE options. In ClassWizard, jump to the source code editor. Fill in code for your OLE handler functions.	The framework generates a skeleton application that can insert OLE objects created by OLE Server applications.
Create an application that supports OLE Automation from scratch.	Run AppWizard. Choose Automation Support in the OLE options. Use ClassWizard to expose methods and properties in your application for automation.	The framework generates a skeleton application that can be activated and automated by other applications.

As you can see, AppWizard, the Visual C++ resource editors, ClassWizard, and the framework do a lot of work for you and make managing your code much easier. The bulk of your application-specific code is in your document and view classes. For a tour of this process with real applications, see *Introducing Visual C++*:

- Chapters 6 through 15 show you how to use the basic MFC framework.

- Chapters 16 through 23 teach OLE programming techniques.

- Chapters 24 through 27 explain database programming techniques.

While it is possible to do these tasks by hand or using other tools, your savings in time, energy, and errors suggest that using the tools and framework is greatly to your benefit.

How the Framework Calls Your Code

It is crucial to understand the relationship between your source code and the code in the framework. When your application runs, most of the flow of control resides in the framework's code. The framework manages the message loop that gets messages from Windows as the user chooses commands and edits data in a view. Events that the framework can handle by itself don't rely on your code at all. For example, the framework knows how to close windows and how to exit the application in response to user commands. As it handles these tasks, the framework uses message handlers and C++ virtual functions to give you opportunities to respond to these events as well. But your code is not in the driver's seat, the framework is.

Your code is called by the framework for application-specific events. For example, when the user chooses a menu command, the framework routes the command along a sequence of C++ objects: the current view and frame window, the document associated with the view, the document's document template, and the application object. If one of these objects can handle the command, it does so, calling the appropriate message-handler function. For any given command, the code called may be yours or it may be the framework's.

This arrangement is somewhat familiar to programmers experienced with traditional programming for Windows or event-driven programming.

In the next few sections, you'll see what the framework does as it initializes and runs the application and then cleans up as the application terminates. You'll also get a clearer picture of where the code you write fits in.

CWinApp: The Application Class

The main application class encapsulates the initialization, running, and termination of an application for Windows. An application built on the framework must have one (and only one) object of a class derived from **CWinApp**. This object is constructed before windows are created.

Note Your application class constitutes your application's primary thread of execution. Using Win32 API functions, you can also create secondary threads of execution. These threads can use the MFC library. For more information, see the article "Multithreading" in Part 2.

Like any program for Windows, your framework application has a **WinMain** function. In a framework application, however, you don't write **WinMain**. It is supplied by the class library and is called when the application starts up. **WinMain** performs standard services such as registering window classes. Then it calls member functions of the application object to initialize and run the application.

To initialize the application, **WinMain** calls your application object's InitApplication and InitInstance member functions. To run the application's message loop, **WinMain** calls the **Run** member function. On termination, **WinMain** calls the application object's ExitInstance member function. Figure 1.2 shows the sequence of execution in a framework application.

WinMain   Standard function supplied by framework
  calls

         InitInstance   Initializes current instance of the application

calls

         Run   Runs the message loop and **OnIdle**
           calls

                  ExitInstance   Cleans up after the application

Figure 1.2   Sequence of Execution

Note   Names shown in bold type indicate elements supplied by the Microsoft Foundation Class Library and Visual C++. Names shown in monospaced type indicate elements that you create or override.

CWinApp and AppWizard

When it creates a skeleton application, AppWizard declares an application class derived from **CWinApp**. AppWizard also generates an implementation file that contains the following items:

- A message map for the application class
- An empty class constructor
- A variable that declares the one and only object of the class
- A standard implementation of your InitInstance member function

The application class is placed in the project header and main source files. The names of the class and files created are based on the project name you supply in AppWizard.

The standard implementations and message map supplied are adequate for many purposes, but you can modify them as needed. The most interesting of these implementations is the InitInstance member function. Typically you will add code to the skeletal implementation of InitInstance.

Overridable CWinApp Member Functions

CWinApp provides several key overridable member functions:

- **InitInstance**
- **Run**
- **ExitInstance**

- **OnIdle**

The only **CWinApp** member function that you must override is **InitInstance**.

InitInstance

Windows allows you to run more than one copy, or "instance," of the same application. **WinMain** calls **InitInstance** every time a new instance of the application starts.

The standard `InitInstance` implementation created by AppWizard performs the following tasks:

- As its central action, creates the document templates that, in turn, create documents, views, and frame windows. For a description of this process, see "Document Templates" on page 19.
- Loads standard file options from an .INI file, including the names of the most recently used files.
- Registers one or more document templates.
- For an MDI application, creates a main frame window.
- Processes the command line to open a document specified on the command line or to open a new, empty document.

Run

A framework application spends most of its time in the **Run** member function of class **CWinApp**. After initialization, **WinMain** calls **Run** to process the message loop.

Run cycles through a message loop, checking the message queue for available messages. If a message is available, **Run** dispatches it for action. If no messages are available—often the case—**Run** calls **OnIdle** to do any idle-time processing that you or the framework may need done. If there are no messages and no idle processing to do, the application waits until something happens. When the application terminates, **Run** calls **ExitInstance**. Figure 1.3 shows the sequence of actions in the message loop.

Message dispatching depends on the kind of message. For more information, see Chapter 2, "Working with Messages and Commands."

ExitInstance

The **ExitInstance** member function of class **CWinApp** is called each time a copy of your application terminates, usually as a result of the user quitting the application. Override **ExitInstance** if you need special cleanup processing, such as freeing graphics device interface (GDI) resources or deallocating memory used during program execution. Cleanup of standard items such as documents and views, however, is provided by the framework, with other overridable functions for doing special cleanup specific to those objects.

OnIdle

When no Windows messages are being processed, the framework calls the **CWinApp** member function **OnIdle** (described in the *Class Library Reference*). Override **OnIdle** to perform background tasks. The default version updates the state of user-interface objects such as toolbar buttons and performs cleanup of temporary objects created by the framework in the course of its operations. Figure 1.3 illustrates how the message loop calls **OnIdle** when there are no messages in the queue.

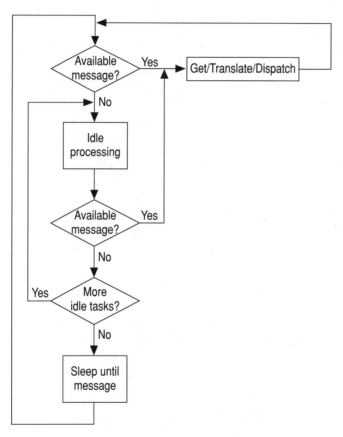

Figure 1.3   The Message Loop

Special CWinApp Services

Besides running the message loop and giving you an opportunity to initialize the application and clean up after it, **CWinApp** provides several other services.

Shell Registration

By default, AppWizard makes it possible for the user to open data files that your application has created by double-clicking them in the Windows File Manager. If your application is an MDI application and you specify an extension for the files your application creates, AppWizard adds calls to the **EnableShellOpen** and **RegisterShellFileTypes** member functions of **CWinApp** to the InitInstance override that it writes for you.

RegisterShellFileTypes registers your application's document types with File Manager. The function adds entries to the registration database that Windows maintains. The entries register each document type, associate a file extension with the file type, specify a command line to open the application, and specify a dynamic data exchange (DDE) command to open a document of that type.

EnableShellOpen completes the process by allowing your application to receive DDE commands from File Manager to open the file chosen by the user.

This automatic registration support in **CWinApp** eliminates the need to ship an .REG file with your application or to do special installation work.

File Manager Drag and Drop

Windows versions 3.1 and later allow the user to drag filenames from the file view window in the File Manager and drop them into a window in your application. You might, for example, allow the user to drag one or more filenames into an MDI application's main window, where the application could retrieve the filenames and open MDI child windows for those files.

To enable file drag and drop in your application, AppWizard writes a call to the **CWnd** member function **DragAcceptFiles** for your main frame window in your InitInstance. You can remove that call if you do not want to implement the drag-and-drop feature.

Note You can also implement more general drag-and-drop capabilities—dragging data between or within documents—using OLE. For information, see the article "Drag and Drop (OLE)" in Part 2.

Keeping Track of the Most Recently Used Documents

As the user opens and closes files, the application object keeps track of the four most recently used files. The names of these files are added to the File menu and updated when they change. The framework stores these filenames in an .INI file with the same name as your project and reads them from the file when your application starts up. The `InitInstance` override that AppWizard creates for you includes a call to the **CWinApp** member function **LoadStdProfileSettings**, which loads information from the .INI file, including the most recently used filenames.

Document Templates

To manage the complex process of creating documents with their associated views and frame windows, the framework uses two document template classes: **CSingleDocTemplate** for SDI applications and **CMultiDocTemplate** for MDI applications. A **CSingleDocTemplate** can create and store one document of one type at a time. A **CMultiDocTemplate** keeps a list of many open documents of one type.

Some applications support multiple document types. For example, an application might support text documents and graphics documents. In such an application, when the user chooses the New command on the File menu, a dialog box shows a list of possible new document types to open. For each supported document type, the application uses a distinct document template object. Figure 1.4 illustrates the configuration of an MDI application that supports two document types. The figure shows several open documents.

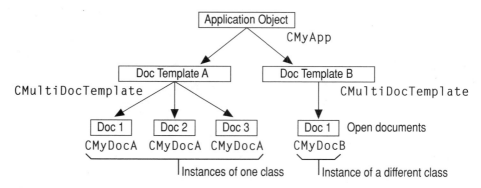

Figure 1.4   An MDI Application with Two Document Types

Document templates are created and maintained by the application object. One of the key tasks performed during your application's `InitInstance` function is to construct one or more document templates of the appropriate kind. This feature is described in "Document Template Creation" below. The application object stores a pointer to each document template in its template list and provides an interface for adding document templates.

If you need to support two or more document types, you must add an extra call to **AddDocTemplate** for each document type.

Document Template Creation

While creating a new document in response to a New or Open command from the File menu, the document template also creates a new frame window through which to view the document.

The document-template constructor specifies what types of documents, windows, and views the template will be able to create. This is determined by the arguments you pass to the document-template constructor. The following code illustrates creation of a **CMultiDocTemplate** for a sample application:

```
AddDocTemplate( new CMultiDocTemplate( IDR_SCRIBTYPE,
        RUNTIME_CLASS( CScribDoc ),
        RUNTIME_CLASS( CMDIChildWnd ),
        RUNTIME_CLASS( CScribView ) ) );
```

The pointer to a new **CMultiDocTemplate** object is used as an argument to **AddDocTemplate**. Arguments to the **CMultiDocTemplate** constructor include the resource ID associated with the document type's menus and accelerators, and three uses of the **RUNTIME_CLASS** macro. **RUNTIME_CLASS** returns the **CRuntimeClass** object for the C++ class named as its argument. The three **CRuntimeClass** objects passed to the document-template constructor supply the information needed to create new objects of the specified classes during the document creation process. The example shows creation of a document template that creates CScribDoc objects with CScribView objects attached. The views are framed by standard MDI child frame windows.

Document/View Creation

The framework supplies implementations of the New and Open commands (among others) on the File menu. Creation of a new document and its associated view and frame window is a cooperative effort among the application object, a document template, the newly created document, and the newly created frame window. Table 1.3 summarizes which objects create what.

Table 1.3   Object Creators

Creator	Creates
Application object	Document template
Document template	Document
Document template	Frame window
Frame window	View

Relationships Among MFC Objects

To help put the document/view creation process in perspective, first consider a running program: a document, the frame window used to contain the view, and the view associated with the document.

- A document keeps a list of the views of that document and a pointer to the document template that created the document.
- A view keeps a pointer to its document and is a child of its parent frame window.
- A document frame window keeps a pointer to its current active view.
- A document template keeps a list of its open documents.
- The application keeps a list of its document templates.
- Windows keeps track of all open windows so it can send messages to them.

These relationships are established during document/view creation. Table 1.4 shows how objects in a running program can access other objects. Any object can obtain a pointer to the application object by calling the global function **AfxGetApp**.

Table 1.4   Gaining Access to Other Objects in Your Application

From object	How to access other objects
Document	Use **GetFirstViewPosition** and **GetNextView** to access the document's view list.
	Call **GetDocTemplate** to get the document template.
View	Call **GetDocument** to get the document.
	Call **GetParentFrame** to get the frame window.
Document frame window	Call **GetActiveView** to get the current view.
	Call **GetActiveDocument** to get the document attached to the current view.
MDI frame window	Call **MDIGetActive** to get the currently active **CMDIChildWnd**.

Typically, a frame window has one view, but sometimes, as in splitter windows, the same frame window contains multiple views. The frame window keeps a pointer to the currently active view; the pointer is updated any time another view is activated.

> **Note** A pointer to the main frame window is stored in the **m_pMainWnd** member
> variable of the application object. A call to **OnFileNew** in your override of the
> **InitInstance** member function of **CWinApp** sets **m_pMainWnd** for you. If you
> don't call **OnFileNew**, you must set the variable's value in **InitInstance** yourself.
> (SDI OLE server applications may not set the variable if /Embedding is on the
> command line.) Note that **m_pMainWnd** is now a member of class **CWinThread**
> rather than **CWinApp**.

Creating New Documents, Windows, and Views

Figures 1.5, 1.6, and 1.7 give an overview of the creation process for documents,
views, and frame windows. Later chapters that focus on the participating objects
provide further details.

Upon completion of this process, the cooperating objects exist and store pointers to
each other. These figures show the sequence in which objects are created. You can
follow the sequence from figure to figure.

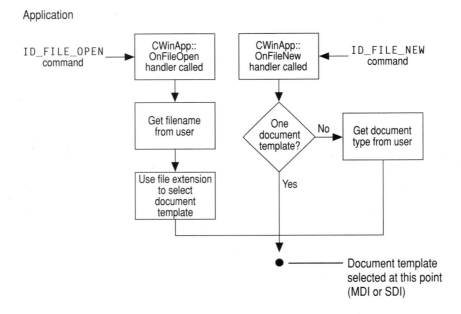

Figure 1.5   Sequence in Creating a Document

Document Template: OpenDocumentFile

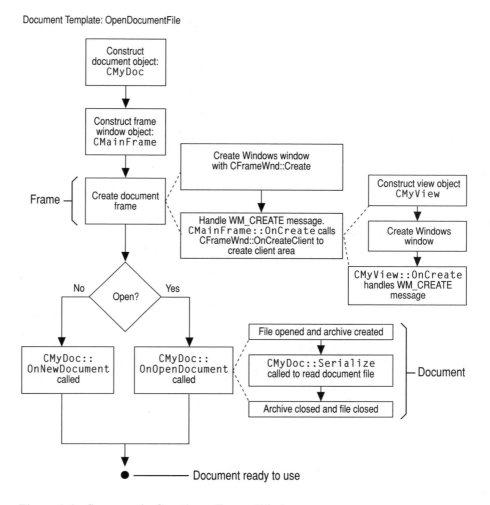

Figure 1.6   Sequence in Creating a Frame Window

View

Figure 1.7   Sequence in Creating a View

For information about how the framework initializes the new document, view, and frame-window objects, see classes **CDocument**, **CView**, **CFrameWnd**, **CMDIFrameWnd**, and **CMDIChildWnd** in the *Class Library Reference*. Also see Technical Note 22 under MFC in Books Online, which explains the creation and initialization processes further under its discussion of the framework's standard commands for the New and Open items on the File menu.

Initializing Your Own Additions to These Classes

Figures 1.5, 1.6, and 1.7 also suggest the points at which you can override member functions to initialize your application's objects. An override of **OnInitialUpdate** in your view class is the best place to initialize the view. The **OnInitialUpdate** call occurs immediately after the frame window is created and the view within the frame window is attached to its document. For example, if your view is a scroll view (derived from **CScrollView** rather than **CView**), you should set the view size based on the document size in your OnInitialUpdate override. (This process is described in the description of class **CScrollView**.) You can override the **CDocument** member functions **OnNewDocument** and **OnOpenDocument** to provide application-specific initialization of the document. Typically, you must override both since a document can be created in two ways.

In most cases, your override should call the base class version. For more information, see the named member functions of classes **CDocument**, **CView**, **CFrameWnd**, and **CWinApp** in the *Class Library Reference*.

Windows of Your Own with CWnd

Although the framework provides windows on your documents, you may at times want to create your own windows, particularly child windows. Keeping in mind how much the framework does for you, the present discussion focuses on windows in a more general way, with particular emphasis on creating windows of your own. For more information about the frame windows that the framework creates, see Chapter 3, "Working with Frame Windows, Documents, and Views."

In MFC, all windows are ultimately derived from class **CWnd**. This includes dialog boxes, controls, control bars, and views as well as frame windows and your own child windows, as shown in the MFC hierarchy diagram in the *Class Library Reference*.

Window Objects

A C++ window object (whether for a frame window or some other kind of window) is distinct from its corresponding Windows window (the **HWND**), but the two are tightly linked. A good understanding of this relationship is crucial for effective programming with MFC.

The window *object* is an object of the C++ **CWnd** class (or a derived class) that your program creates directly. It comes and goes in response to your program's constructor and destructor calls. The Windows *window*, on the other hand, is an opaque handle to an internal Windows data structure that corresponds to a window and consumes system resources when present. A Windows window is identified by a "window handle" (**HWND**) and is created after the **CWnd** object is created by a call to the **Create** member function of class **CWnd**. The window may be destroyed either by a program call or by a user's action. The window handle is stored in the window object's **m_hWnd** member variable. Figure 1.8 shows the relationship between the C++ window object and the Windows window. Creating windows is discussed in "Creating Windows" on page 28. Destroying windows is discussed in "Destroying Windows" on page 29.

C++ Window object (CWnd)   Windows window

Figure 1.8   Window Object and Windows Window

CWnd and its derived classes provide constructors, destructors, and member functions to initialize the object, create the underlying Windows structures, and access the encapsulated **HWND**. **CWnd** also provides member functions that encapsulate Windows APIs for sending messages, accessing the window's state, converting coordinates, updating, scrolling, accessing the Clipboard, and many other tasks. Most Windows window-management APIs that take an **HWND** argument are encapsulated as member functions of **CWnd**. The names of the functions and their parameters are preserved in the **CWnd** member function. For details about the Windows APIs encapsulated by **CWnd**, see class **CWnd** in the *Class Library Reference*.

The general literature on programming for Windows is a good resource for learning how to use the **CWnd** member functions, which typically encapsulate the **HWND** APIs. For example, see Charles Petzold's *Programming Windows 3.1*, third edition, and Jeffrey Richter's *Advanced Windows NT*.

One of the primary purposes of **CWnd** is to provide an interface for handling Windows messages, such as **WM_PAINT** or **WM_MOUSEMOVE**. Many of the member functions of **CWnd** are handlers for standard messages—those beginning with the identifier **afx_msg** and the prefix "On," such as **OnPaint** and **OnMouseMove**. Chapter 2, "Working with Messages and Commands," covers messages and message handling in detail. The information there applies equally to the framework's windows and those that you create yourself for special purposes.

Derived Window Classes

Although you can create windows directly from **CWnd**, or derive new window classes from **CWnd**, most windows used in a framework program are instead created from one of the **CWnd**-derived frame-window classes supplied by MFC:

CFrameWnd
Used for SDI frame windows that frame a single document and its view. The frame window is both the main frame window for the application and the frame window for the current document.

CMDIFrameWnd
Used as the main frame window for MDI applications. The main frame window is a container for all MDI document windows and shares its menu bar with them. An MDI frame window is a top-level window that appears on the desktop.

CMDIChildWnd
Used for individual documents opened in an MDI main frame window. Each document and its view are framed by an MDI child frame window contained by the MDI main frame window. An MDI child window looks much like a typical frame window but is contained inside an MDI frame window instead of sitting on the desktop. However, the MDI child window lacks a menu bar of its own and must share the menu bar of the MDI frame window that contains it. Figure 1.9 shows an MDI application whose main frame window contains two MDI document windows. Each document window contains a document and its view.

Figure 1.9   An MDI Frame Window with Children

In addition to frame windows, several other major categories of windows are derived from **CWnd**:

Views

Views are created using the **CWnd**-derived class **CView** (or one of its derived classes). A view is attached to a document and acts as an intermediary between the document and the user. A view is a child window (not an MDI child) that typically fills the client area of an SDI frame window or an MDI child frame window.

Dialog Boxes

Dialog boxes are created using the **CWnd**-derived class **CDialog**.

Forms

Form views based on dialog-template resources, like dialog boxes, are created using classes **CFormView** and **CRecordView**.

Controls

Controls such as buttons, list boxes, and combo boxes are created using other classes derived from **CWnd**.

Control Bars

Child windows that contain controls. Examples include toolbars and status bars.

Refer again to the MFC hierarchy diagram in the *Class Library Reference*. Views are explained in Chapter 3, "Working with Frame Windows, Documents, and Views." Dialog boxes, controls, and control bars are explained in Chapter 4.

In addition to the window classes provided by the class library, you may need special-purpose child windows. To create such a window, write your own **CWnd**-derived class and make it a child window of a frame or view. Bear in mind that the framework manages the extent of the client area of a document frame window. Most of the client area is managed by a view, but other windows, such as control bars or your own custom windows, may share the space with the view. You may need to interact with the mechanisms in classes **CView** and **CControlBar** for positioning child windows in a frame window's client area.

The next section, "Creating Windows," discusses creation of window objects and the Windows windows they manage.

Creating Windows

Most of the windows you need in a framework program are created automatically by the framework. You have already seen, in this chapter, how the framework creates the frame windows associated with documents and views. But you can create your own windows—in addition to the windows supplied by the framework —for special purposes.

Registering Window "Classes"

In a traditional program for Windows, you process all messages to a window in its "window procedure" or "**WndProc**." A **WndProc** is associated with a window by means of a "window class registration" process. The main window is registered in the **WinMain** function, but other classes of windows can be registered anywhere in the application. Registration depends on a structure that contains a pointer to the **WndProc** function together with specifications for the cursor, background brush, and so forth. The structure is passed as a parameter, along with the string name of the class, in a prior call to the **RegisterClass** function. Thus a registration class can be shared by multiple windows.

In contrast, most window class registration activity is done automatically in a framework program. If you are using MFC, you typically derive a C++ window class from an existing library class using the normal C++ syntax for class inheritance. The framework still uses traditional "registration classes," and it provides several standard ones, registered for you in the standard application initialization function. You can register additional registration classes by calling the **AfxRegisterWndClass** global function and then pass the registered class to the **Create** member function of **CWnd**. As described here, the traditional "registration class" in Windows is not to be confused with a C++ class.

For more information, see Technical Note 1 under MFC in Books Online.

General Creation Sequence

If you are creating a window of your own, such as a child window, this section describes what you need to know. The framework uses much the same process to create windows for your documents as that described earlier in the chapter.

All the window classes provided by the Microsoft Foundation Class Library employ two-phase construction. That is, during an invocation of the C++ **new** operator, the constructor allocates and initializes a C++ object but does not create a corresponding Windows window. That is done afterwards by calling the **Create** member function of the window object.

The **Create** member function makes the Windows window and stores its **HWND** in the C++ object's public data member **m_hWnd**. **Create** gives complete flexibility over the creation parameters. Before calling **Create**, you may want to register a window class with **AfxRegisterWndClass** in order to set the icon and class styles for the frame.

For frame windows, you can use the **LoadFrame** member function instead of **Create**. **LoadFrame** makes the Windows window using fewer parameters. It gets many default values from resources, including the frame's caption, icon, accelerator table, and menu.

Note   Your icon, accelerator table, and menu resources must have a common resource ID, such as **IDR_MAINFRAME**.

Destroying Windows

Care must be taken with your own child windows to destroy the C++ window object when the user is finished with the window. If these objects are not destroyed, your application will not recover their memory. Fortunately, the framework manages window destruction as well as creation for frame windows, views, and dialog boxes. If you create additional windows, you are responsible for destroying them.

In the framework, when the user closes the frame window, the window's default **OnClose** handler calls **DestroyWindow**. The last member function called when the Windows window is destroyed is **OnNcDestroy**, which does some cleanup, calls the **Default** member function to perform Windows cleanup, and lastly calls the virtual member function **PostNcDestroy**. The **CFrameWnd** implementation of **PostNcDestroy** deletes the C++ window object.

Do not use the C++ **delete** operator to destroy a frame window or view. Instead, call the **CWnd** member function **DestroyWindow**. Frame windows, therefore, should be allocated on the heap with operator **new**. Care must be taken when allocating frame windows on the stack frame or globally. Other windows should be allocated on the stack frame whenever possible.

If you need to circumvent the object-**HWND** relationship, MFC provides another **CWnd** member function, **Detach**, which disconnects the C++ window object from the Windows window. This prevents the destructor from destroying the Windows window when the object is destroyed.

Working with Windows

Working with windows calls for two kinds of activity:

- Handling Windows messages

- Drawing in the window

To handle Windows messages in any window, including your own child windows, use ClassWizard to map the messages to your window class. Then write message-handler member functions in your class. Chapter 2, "Working with Messages and Commands," details message handling.

Most drawing in a framework application occurs in the view, whose OnDraw member function is called whenever the window's contents must be drawn. If your window is a child of the view, you might delegate some of the view's drawing to your child window by having OnDraw call one of your window's member functions.

In any case, you will need a device context for drawing.

Device Contexts

A device context is a Windows data structure that contains information about the drawing attributes of a device such as a display or a printer. All drawing calls are made through a device-context object, which encapsulates the Windows APIs for drawing lines, shapes, and text. Device contexts allow device-independent drawing in Windows. Device contexts can be used to draw to the screen, to the printer, or to a metafile.

CPaintDC objects encapsulate the common idiom of Windows calling the **BeginPaint** function, then drawing in the device context, then calling the **EndPaint** function. The **CPaintDC** constructor calls **BeginPaint** for you, and the destructor calls **EndPaint**. The simplified process is to create the **CDC** object, draw, and destroy the **CDC** object. In the framework, much of even this process is automated. In particular, your OnDraw function is passed a **CPaintDC** already prepared (via **OnPrepareDC**), and you simply draw into it. It is destroyed by the framework and the underlying device context is released to Windows upon return from the call to your OnDraw function.

CClientDC objects encapsulate working with a device context that represents only the client area of a window. The **CClientDC** constructor calls the **GetDC** function, and the destructor calls the **ReleaseDC** function. **CWindowDC** objects encapsulate a device context that represents the whole window, including its frame.

CMetaFileDC objects encapsulate drawing into a Windows metafile. In contrast to the **CPaintDC** passed to OnDraw, you must in this case call **OnPrepareDC** yourself. For more information about these classes, see the *Class Library Reference*.

Drawing is discussed in greater detail in Chapter 3, "Working with Frame Windows, Documents, and Views."

Although most drawing—and thus most device-context work—in a framework program is done in the view's OnDraw member function, as described in Chapter 3, you can still use device-context objects for other purposes. For example, to provide tracking feedback for mouse movement in a view, you need to draw directly into the view without waiting for OnDraw to be called.

In such a case, you can use a **CClientDC** device-context object to draw directly into the view. For more information about mouse drawing, see "Interpreting User Input Through a View" on page 71 in Chapter 3.

Graphic Objects

Windows provides a variety of drawing tools to use in device contexts. It provides pens to draw lines, brushes to fill interiors, and fonts to draw text. The Microsoft Foundation Class Library provides graphic-object classes equivalent to the drawing tools in Windows. Table 1.5 shows the available classes and the equivalent Windows GDI handle types.

The general literature on programming for the Windows GDI applies to the Microsoft Foundation classes that encapsulate GDI graphic objects. This section explains the use of these graphic-object classes:

Table 1.5   Classes for Windows GDI Objects

Class	Windows handle type
CPen	HPEN
CBrush	HBRUSH
CFont	HFONT
CBitmap	HBITMAP
CPalette	HPALETTE
CRgn	HRGN

Each of the graphic-object classes in the class library has a constructor that allows you to create graphic objects of that class, which you must then initialize with the appropriate create function, such as **CreatePen**.

The following four steps are typically used when you need a graphic object for a drawing operation:

1. Define a graphic object on the stack frame. Initialize the object with the type-specific create function, such as **CreatePen**. Alternatively, initialize the object in the constructor. See the discussion of one-stage and two-stage creation below.

2. Select the object into the current device context, saving the old graphic object that was selected before.

3. When done with the current graphic object, select the old graphic object back into the device context to restore its state.

4. Allow the frame-allocated graphic object to be deleted automatically when the scope is exited.

Note If you will be using a graphic object repeatedly, you can allocate it once and select it into a device context each time it is needed. Be sure to delete such an object when you no longer need it.

You have a choice between two techniques for creating graphic objects:

- One-stage construction: Construct and initialize the object in one stage, all with the constructor.

- Two-stage construction: Construct and initialize the object in two separate stages. The constructor creates the object and an initialization function initializes it.

Two-stage construction is always safer. In one-stage construction, the constructor could throw an exception if you provide incorrect arguments or memory allocation fails. That problem is avoided by two-stage construction, although you do have to check for failure. In either case, destroying the object is the same process.

The following brief example shows both methods of constructing a pen object:

```
void CMyView::OnDraw( CDC* pDC )
{
    CPen myPen1( PS_DOT, 5, RGB(0,0,0) );    // One-stage
    // Two-stage: first construct the pen
    CPen myPen2;
    // Then initialize it
    if( myPen2.CreatePen( PS_DOT, 5, RGB(0,0,0) ) )
        // Use the pen
}
```

After you create a drawing object, you must select it into the device context in place of the default pen stored there:

```
void CMyView::OnDraw( CDC* pDC )
{
    CPen penBlack;  // Construct it, then initialize
    if( newPen.CreatePen( PS_SOLID, 2, RGB(0,0,0) ) )
    {
        // Select it into the device context
        // Save the old pen at the same time
        CPen* pOldPen = pDC->SelectObject( &penBlack );

        // Draw with the pen
        pDC->MoveTo(...);
        pDC->LineTo(...);

        // Restore the old pen to the device context
        pDC->SelectObject( pOldPen );
    }
    else
    {
        // Alert the user that resources are low
    }
}
```

The graphic object returned by **SelectObject** is a "temporary" object. That is, it will be deleted by the **OnIdle** member function of class **CWinApp** the next time the program gets idle time. As long as you use the object returned by **SelectObject** in a single function without returning control to the main message loop, you will have no problem.

In Chapter 2

So far you have seen how the framework creates its major component objects. In Chapter 2, you will see:

- How the framework dispatches Windows messages, including commands, to those objects.

- How the objects "handle" the messages and commands to do the application's work.

Commands are a new category of messages introduced by the Microsoft Foundation Class Library.

CHAPTER 2

Working with Messages and Commands

Chapter 1 introduced the major objects in a running framework application written with the Microsoft Foundation Class Library (MFC). This chapter describes how messages and commands are processed by the framework and how you connect them to their handler functions using the ClassWizard tool. Topics covered include:

- Messages and commands
- Message categories
- How the framework calls a message handler
- Message maps
- Managing messages and commands with ClassWizard
- Dynamic update of user-interface objects
- Dynamic display of command information in the status bar

Messages and Commands in the Framework

Applications written for Microsoft Windows are "message driven." In response to events such as mouse clicks, keystrokes, window movements, and so on, Windows sends messages to the proper window. Framework applications process Windows messages like any other application for Windows. But the framework also provides some enhancements that make processing messages easier, more maintainable, and better encapsulated.

The following sections introduce the key terms used in the rest of the chapter to discuss messages and commands:

- Messages
- Message handlers
- Message categories
- Windows messages and control-notification messages
- Command messages

- Message maps
- User-interface objects and command IDs
- Command targets

Messages

The message loop in the **Run** member function of class **CWinApp** retrieves queued messages generated by various events. For example, when the user clicks the mouse, Windows sends several mouse-related messages, such as **WM_LBUTTONDOWN** when the left mouse button is pressed and **WM_LBUTTONUP** when the left mouse button is released. The framework's implementation of the application message loop dispatches the message to the appropriate window.

The important categories of messages are described in "Message Categories" on page 36.

Message Handlers

In MFC, a dedicated "handler" function processes each separate message. Message-handler functions are member functions of a class. This book uses the terms "message-handler member function," "message-handler function," "message handler," and "handler" interchangeably. Some kinds of message handlers are also called "command handlers."

Writing message handlers accounts for a large proportion of your work in writing a framework application. This chapter describes how the message-processing mechanism works.

What does the handler for a message do? The answer is that it does whatever you want done in response to that message. ClassWizard will create the handlers for you and allow you to implement them. You can jump directly from ClassWizard to the handler function's definition in your source files and fill in the handler's code using the Visual C++ source code editor. Or you can create all of your handlers with ClassWizard, then move to the editor to fill in all functions at once. For details on using ClassWizard, see "How to Manage Commands and Messages with ClassWizard" on page 51.

You can use all of the facilities of Microsoft Visual C++ and the Microsoft Foundation Class Library to write your handlers. For a list of all classes, see the "Class Summary" in the *Class Library Reference*.

Message Categories

What kinds of messages do you write handlers for? There are three main categories:

1. Windows messages

   This includes primarily those messages beginning with the **WM_** prefix, except for **WM_COMMAND**. Windows messages are handled by windows and views. These messages often have parameters that are used in determining how to handle the message.

2. Control notifications

   This includes **WM_COMMAND** notification messages from controls and other child windows to their parent windows. For example, an edit control sends its parent a **WM_COMMAND** message containing the **EN_CHANGE** control-notification code when the user has taken an action that may have altered text in the edit control. The window's handler for the message responds to the notification message in some appropriate way, such as retrieving the text in the control.

   The framework routes control-notification messages like other **WM_** messages. One exception, however, is the **BN_CLICKED** control-notification message sent by buttons when the user clicks them. This message is treated specially as a command message and routed like other commands.

3. Command messages

   This includes **WM_COMMAND** notification messages from user-interface objects: menus, toolbar buttons, and accelerator keys. The framework processes commands differently from other messages, and they can be handled by more kinds of objects, as explained below.

Windows Messages and Control-Notification Messages

Messages in categories 1 and 2—Windows messages and control notifications—are handled by windows: objects of classes derived from class **CWnd**. This includes **CFrameWnd**, **CMDIFrameWnd**, **CMDIChildWnd**, **CView**, **CDialog**, and your own classes derived from these base classes. Such objects encapsulate an **HWND**, a handle to a Windows window.

Command Messages

Messages in category 3—commands—can be handled by a wider variety of objects: documents, document templates, and the application object itself in addition to windows and views. When a command directly affects some particular object, it makes sense to have that object handle the command. For example, the Open command on the File menu is logically associated with the application: the application opens a specified document upon receiving the command. So the handler for the Open command is a member function of the application class. For more about commands and how they are routed to objects, see "How the Framework Calls a Handler" on page 40.

Message Maps

Each framework class that can receive messages or commands has its own "message map." The framework uses message maps to connect messages and commands to their handler functions. Any class derived from class **CCmdTarget** can have a message map. Later sections of this chapter explain message maps in detail and describe how to use them.

In spite of the name "message map," message maps handle both messages and commands—all three categories of messages listed in "Message Categories" on page 36.

User-Interface Objects and Command IDs

Menu items, toolbar buttons, and accelerator keys are "user-interface objects" capable of generating commands. Each such user-interface object has an ID. You associate a user-interface object with a command by assigning the same ID to the object and the command. As explained in "Messages," commands are implemented as special messages. Figure 2.1 shows how the framework manages commands. When a user-interface object generates a command, such as ID_EDIT_CLEAR_ALL, one of the objects in your application handles the command —in the figure, the document object's OnEditClearAll function is called via the document's message map.

Figure 2.1   Commands in the Framework

Figure 2.2 shows how MFC updates user-interface objects such as menu items and toolbar buttons. Before a menu drops down, or during the idle loop in the case of toolbar buttons, MFC routes an update command. In the figure, the document object calls its update command handler, OnUpdateEditClearAll, to enable or disable the user-interface object.

Figure 2.2   Command Updating in the Framework

Command IDs

A command is fully described by its command ID alone (encoded in the **WM_COMMAND** message). This ID is assigned to the user-interface object that generates the command. Typically, IDs are named for the functionality of the user-interface object they are assigned to.

For example, a Clear All item in the Edit menu might be assigned an ID such as **ID_EDIT_CLEAR_ALL**. The class library predefines some IDs, particularly for commands that the framework handles itself, such as **ID_EDIT_CLEAR_ALL** or **ID_FILE_OPEN**. You will create other command IDs yourself.

When you create your own menus in the Visual C++ menu editor, it is a good idea to follow the class library's naming convention as illustrated by **ID_FILE_OPEN**. The next section, "Standard Commands," explains the standard commands defined by the class library.

Standard Commands

The framework defines many standard command messages. The IDs for these commands typically take the form:

ID_*Source*_*Item*

where *Source* is usually a menu name and *Item* is a menu item. For example, the command ID for the New command on the File menu is **ID_FILE_NEW**. Standard command IDs are shown in bold type in the documentation. Programmer-defined IDs are shown in a font that is different from the surrounding text.

The following is a list of some of the most important commands supported:

File Menu Commands
    New, Open, Close, Save, Save As, Page Setup, Print Setup, Print, Print Preview, Exit, and most-recently-used files.

Edit Menu Commands
Clear, Clear All, Copy, Cut, Find, Paste, Repeat, Replace, Select All, Undo, and Redo.

View Menu Commands
Toolbar and Status Bar.

Window Menu Commands
New, Arrange, Cascade, Tile Horizontal, Tile Vertical, and Split.

Help Menu Commands
Index, Using Help, and About.

Object Linking and Embedding (OLE) Commands (Edit Menu)
Insert New Object, Edit Links, Paste Link, Paste Special, and *typename* Object (verb commands).

The framework provides varying levels of support for these commands. Some commands are supported only as defined command IDs, while others are supported with thorough implementations. For example, the framework implements the Open command on the File menu by creating a new document object, displaying an Open dialog box, and opening and reading the file. In contrast, you must implement commands on the Edit menu yourself, since commands like **ID_EDIT_COPY** depend on the nature of the data you are copying.

For more information about the commands supported and the level of implementation provided, see Technical Note 22 under MFC in Books Online. The standard commands are defined in the file AFXRES.H.

Command Targets

Figure 2.1 (shown earlier in this chapter) shows the connection between a user-interface object, such as a menu item, and the handler function that the framework calls to carry out the resulting command when the object is clicked.

Windows sends messages that are not command messages directly to a window whose handler for the message is then called. However, the framework routes commands to a number of candidate objects—called "command targets"—one of which normally invokes a handler for the command. The handler functions work the same way for both commands and standard Windows messages, but the mechanism by which they are called is different, as explained in the next section, "How the Framework Calls a Handler."

How the Framework Calls a Handler

The following sections first examine how the framework routes commands, then examine how other messages and control notifications are sent to windows:

- Message sending and receiving

- How noncommand messages reach their handlers
- Command routing

Message Sending and Receiving

Consider the sending part of the process and how the framework responds.

Most messages result from user interaction with the program. Commands are generated by mouse clicks in menu items or toolbar buttons or by accelerator keystrokes. The user also generates Windows messages by, for example, moving or resizing a window. Other Windows messages are sent when events such as program startup or termination occur, as windows get or lose the focus, and so on. Control-notification messages are generated by mouse clicks or other user interactions with a control, such as a button or list-box control in a dialog box.

The **Run** member function of class **CWinApp** retrieves messages and dispatches them to the appropriate window. Most command messages are sent to the main frame window of the application. The **WindowProc** predefined by the class library gets the messages and routes them differently, depending on the category of message received.

Now consider the receiving part of the process.

The initial receiver of a message must be a window object. Windows messages are usually handled directly by that window object. Command messages, usually originating in the application's main frame window, get routed to the command-target chain described in "Command Routing" on page 42.

Each object capable of receiving messages or commands has its own message map that pairs a message or command with the name of its handler.

When a command-target object receives a message or command, it searches its message map for a match. If it finds a handler for the message, it calls the handler. For more information about how message maps are searched, see "How the Framework Searches Message Maps" on page 44. Refer again to Figure 2.1 (shown earlier in this chapter).

How Noncommand Messages Reach Their Handlers

Unlike commands, standard Windows messages do not get routed through a chain of command targets but are usually handled by the window to which Windows sends the message. The window might be a main frame window, an MDI child window, a standard control, a dialog box, a view, or some other kind of child window.

At run time, each Windows window is attached to a window object (derived directly or indirectly from **CWnd**) that has its own associated message map and handler functions. The framework uses the message map—as for a command—to map incoming messages to handlers.

Command Routing

Your responsibility in working with commands is limited to making message-map connections between commands and their handler functions, a task for which you use ClassWizard. You must also write most command handlers.

All messages are usually sent to the main frame window, but command messages are then routed to other objects. The framework routes commands through a standard sequence of command-target objects, one of which is expected to have a handler for the command. Each command-target object checks its message map to see if it can handle the incoming message.

Different command-target classes check their own message maps at different times. Typically, a class routes the command to certain other objects to give them first chance at the command. If none of those objects handles the command, the original class checks its own message map. Then, if it can't supply a handler itself, it may route the command to yet more command targets. Table 2.1 shows how each of the classes structures this sequence. The general order in which a command target routes a command is:

1. To its currently active child command-target object.
2. To itself.
3. To other command targets.

How expensive is this routing mechanism? Compared to what your handler does in response to a command, the cost of the routing is low. Bear in mind that the framework generates commands only when the user interacts with a user-interface object.

Table 2.1   Standard Command Route

When an object of this type receives a command . . .	It gives itself and other command-target objects a chance to handle the command in this order:
MDI frame window (**CMDIFrameWnd**)	1. Active **CMDIChildWnd**
	2. This frame window
	3. Application (**CWinApp** object)
Document frame window (**CFrameWnd, CMDIChildWnd**)	1. Active view
	2. This frame window
	3. Application (**CWinApp** object)

Table 2.1   Standard Command Route (*continued*)

When an object of this type receives a command . . .	It gives itself and other command-target objects a chance to handle the command in this order:
View	1. This view
	2. Document attached to the view
Document	1. This document
	2. Document template attached to the document
Dialog box	1. This dialog box
	2. Window that owns the dialog box
	3. Application (**CWinApp** object)

Where numbered entries in the second column of Table 2.1 mention other objects, such as a document, see the corresponding item in the first column. For instance, when you read in the second column that the view forwards a command to its document, see the "Document" entry in the first column to follow the routing further.

An Example

To illustrate, consider a command message from a Clear All menu item in an MDI application's Edit menu. Suppose the handler function for this command happens to be a member function of the application's document class. Here's how that command reaches its handler after the user chooses the menu item:

1. The main frame window receives the command message first.
2. The main MDI frame window gives the currently active MDI child window a chance to handle the command.
3. The standard routing of an MDI child frame window gives its view a chance at the command before checking its own message map.
4. The view checks its own message map first and, finding no handler, next routes the command to its associated document.
5. The document checks its message map and finds a handler. This document member function is called and the routing stops.

If the document did not have a handler, it would next route the command to its document template. Then the command would return to the view and then the frame window. Finally, the frame window would check its message map. If that check failed as well, the command would be routed back to the main MDI frame window and then to the application object—the ultimate destination of unhandled commands.

OnCmdMsg

To accomplish this routing of commands, each command target calls the **OnCmdMsg** member function of the next command target in the sequence. Command targets use **OnCmdMsg** to determine whether they can handle a command and to route it to another command target if they cannot handle it.

Each command-target class may override the **OnCmdMsg** member function. The overrides let each class route commands to a particular next target. A frame window, for example, always routes commands to its current child window or view, as shown in Table 2.1 (shown earlier in this chapter).

The default **CCmdTarget** implementation of **OnCmdMsg** uses the message map of the command-target class to search for a handler function for each command message it receives—in the same way that standard messages are searched. If it finds a match, it calls the handler. Message-map searching is explained in "How the Framework Searches Message Maps" below.

Overriding the Standard Routing

In rare cases when you must implement some variation of the standard framework routing, you can override it. The idea is to change the routing in one or more classes by overriding **OnCmdMsg** in those classes. Do so:

- In the class that breaks the order to pass to a nondefault object.
- In the new nondefault object or in command targets it might in turn pass commands to.

If you insert some new object into the routing, its class must be a command-target class. In your overriding versions of **OnCmdMsg**, be sure to call the version that you're overriding. See the **OnCmdMsg** member function of class **CCmdTarget** in the *Class Library Reference* and the versions in such classes as **CView** and **CDocument** in the supplied source code for examples.

How the Framework Searches Message Maps

The framework searches the message-map table for matches with incoming messages. Once you use ClassWizard to write a message-map entry for each message you want a class to handle and to write the corresponding handlers, the framework calls your handlers automatically. The following sections explain message-map searching:

- Where to find message maps
- Derived message maps

Where to Find Message Maps

When you create a new skeleton application with AppWizard, AppWizard writes a message map for each command-target class it creates for you. This includes your derived application, document, view, and frame-window classes. Some of these message maps already have AppWizard-supplied entries for certain messages and predefined commands, and some are just placeholders for handlers that you will add.

A class's message map is located in the .CPP file for the class. Working with the basic message maps that AppWizard creates, you use ClassWizard to add entries for the messages and commands that each class will handle. A typical message map might look like the following after you add some entries:

```
BEGIN_MESSAGE_MAP(CMyView, CView)
    //{{AFX_MSG_MAP(CMyView)
    ON_WM_MOUSEACTIVATE()
    ON_COMMAND(ID_EDIT_CLEAR_ALL, OnEditClearAll)
    ON_UPDATE_COMMAND_UI(ID_EDIT_CLEAR_ALL, OnUpdateEditClearAll)
    ON_BN_CLICKED(ID_MY_BUTTON, OnMyButton)
    //}}AFX_MSG_MAP
END_MESSAGE_MAP()
```

The message map consists of a collection of macros. Two macros, **BEGIN_MESSAGE_MAP** and **END_MESSAGE_MAP**, bracket the message map. Other macros, such as **ON_COMMAND**, fill in the message map's contents. These macros are explained later in this chapter.

Note   The message-map macros are not followed by semicolons.

The message map also includes comments of the form

```
//{{AFX_MSG_MAP(CMyView)
//}}AFX_MSG_MAP
```

that bracket many of the entries (but not necessarily all of them). ClassWizard uses these special comments when it writes entries for you. All ClassWizard entries go between the comment lines.

When you use ClassWizard to create a new class, it provides a message map for the class. Alternatively, you can create a message map manually using the source code editor.

Derived Message Maps

During message handling, checking a class's own message map is not the end of the message-map story. What happens if class CMyView (derived from **CView**) has no matching entry for a message?

Keep in mind that **CView**, the base class of CMyView, is derived in turn from **CWnd**. Thus CMyView *is* a **CView** and *is* a **CWnd**. Each of those classes has its own message map. Figure 2.3 shows the hierarchical relationship of the classes, but keep in mind that a CMyView object is a single object that has the characteristics of all three classes.

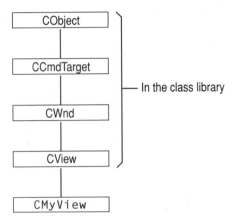

Figure 2.3   A View Hierarchy

So if a message can't be matched in class CMyView's message map, the framework also searches the message map of its immediate base class. The **BEGIN_MESSAGE_MAP** macro at the start of the message map specifies two class names as its arguments:

```
BEGIN_MESSAGE_MAP(CMyView, CView)
```

The first argument names the class to which the message map belongs. The second argument provides a connection with the immediate base class—**CView** here—so the framework can search its message map too.

The message handlers provided in a base class are thus inherited by the derived class. This is very similar to normal virtual member functions without needing to make all handler member functions virtual.

If no handler is found in any of the base-class message maps, default processing of the message is performed. If the message is a command, the framework routes it to the next command target. If it is a standard Windows message, the message is passed to the appropriate default window procedure.

To speed message-map matching, the framework caches recent matches on the likelihood that it will receive the same message again. One consequence of this is that the framework processes unhandled messages quite efficiently. Message maps are also more space-efficient than implementations that use virtual functions.

Message-Map Structure

In your source files, a message map consists of a sequence of predefined macros. The macros inside the message map are called "entry macros." The entry macros used in a message map depend upon the category of the message to be handled. The following sample shows a message map with several common entries (given in the same order as the items in Table 2.2):

```
BEGIN_MESSAGE_MAP(CMyView, CView)
    //{{AFX_MSG_MAP(CMyView)
    ON_WM_MOUSEACTIVATE()
    ON_COMMAND(ID_EDIT_CLEAR_ALL, OnEditClearAll)
    ON_UPDATE_COMMAND_UI(ID_EDIT_CLEAR_ALL, OnUpdateEditClearAll)
    ON_BN_CLICKED(ID_MY_BUTTON, OnMyButton)
    ON_MESSAGE(WM_MYMESSAGE, OnMyMessage)
    ON_REGISTERED_MESSAGE(WM_FIND, OnFind)
    //}}AFX_MSG_MAP
END_MESSAGE_MAP()
```

Table 2.2 summarizes the various kinds of entries. Each entry consists of a macro with zero or more arguments. The macros are predefined by the class library. For examples of the macros, see the message map above.

Table 2.2   Message-Map Entry Macros

Message type	Macro form	Arguments
Predefined Windows messages	**ON_WM_XXXX**	None
Commands	**ON_COMMAND**	Command ID, Handler name
Update commands	**ON_UPDATE_COMMAND_UI**	Command ID, Handler name
Control notifications	**ON_XXXX**	Control ID, Handler name
User-defined message	**ON_MESSAGE**	User-defined message ID, Handler name (see Technical Note 6 under MFC in Books Online)
Registered Windows message	**ON_REGISTERED_MESSAGE**	Registered message ID variable, Handler name (see Technical Note 6 under MFC in Books Online)
A range of command IDs	**ON_COMMAND_RANGE**	Start and end of a contiguous range of command IDs. See "Message-Map Ranges" on page 48.
A range of command IDs for updating	**ON_UPDATE_COMMAND_UI_RANGE**	Start and end of a contiguous range of command IDs. See "Message-Map Ranges" on page 48.

Table 2.2   Message-Map Entry Macros (*continued*)

Message type	Macro form	Arguments
A range of control IDs	**ON_CONTROL_RANGE**	A control-notification code and the start and end of a contiguous range of command IDs. See "Message-Map Ranges" on page 48.

Names in the table with the notation **_XXX** represent groups of messages whose names are based on standard message names or control-notification codes in Windows. For example: **ON_WM_PAINT**, **ON_WM_LBUTTONDOWN**, **ON_EN_CHANGE**, **ON_LB_GETSEL**. Even though the **ON_WM_XXX** macros take no arguments, the corresponding handler functions often do take arguments, passed to them by the framework.

Message-Map Ranges

MFC also supports mapping ranges of messages to a single message-handler function. You can map:

- Ranges of command IDs to:
    - A command handler function.
    - A command update handler function.
- A control-notification message for a range of control IDs to a message-handler function.

Mapping a range of messages is useful in a variety of situations. For example, to handle the "zoom" command in the HIERSVR sample application, a range of menu command IDs is mapped to a single handler function. You might also map a range of command IDs to a single update handler function so that all of the commands are either enabled or disabled together. (Update handlers are explained in "How to Update User-Interface Objects" on page 52.)

Note ClassWizard does not support message-map ranges. You must write these message-map entries yourself.

For more information about message-map ranges, see the article "Message Map: Ranges of Messages" in Part 2.

Declaring Handler Functions

Certain rules and conventions govern the names of your message-handler functions. These depend on the message category, as described in the following sections:

- Standard Windows messages
- Commands and control notifications

Standard Windows Messages

Default handlers for standard Windows messages (**WM_**) are predefined in class **CWnd**. The class library bases names for these handlers on the message name. For example, the handler for the **WM_PAINT** message is declared in **CWnd** as:

```
afx_msg void OnPaint( );
```

The **afx_msg** keyword suggests the effect of the C++ **virtual** keyword by distinguishing the handlers from other **CWnd** member functions. Note, however, that these functions are not actually virtual; they are instead implemented through message maps. Message maps depend solely on standard preprocessor macros, not on any extensions to the C++ language. The **afx_msg** keyword resolves to white space after preprocessing.

To override a handler defined in a base class, simply use ClassWizard to define a function with the same prototype in your derived class and to make a message-map entry for the handler. Your handler "overrides" any handler of the same name in any of your class's base classes.

In some cases, your handler should call the overridden handler in the base class so the base class(es) and Windows can operate on the message. Where you call the base-class handler in your override depends on the circumstances. Sometimes you must call the base-class handler first and sometimes last. Sometimes you call the base-class handler conditionally, if you choose not to handle the message yourself. Sometimes you should call the base-class handler, then conditionally execute your own handler code, depending on the value or state returned by the base-class handler.

Important It is not safe to modify the arguments passed into a handler if you intend to pass them to a base-class handler. For example, you might be tempted to modify the *nChar* argument of the OnChar handler (to convert to uppercase, for example). This behavior is fairly obscure, but if you need to accomplish this effect, use the **CWnd** member function **SendMessage** instead.

How do you determine the proper way to override a given message? ClassWizard helps with this decision. When ClassWizard writes the skeleton of the handler function for a given message—an OnCreate handler for **WM_CREATE**, for example—it sketches in the form of the recommended overridden member function. The following example recommends that the handler first call the base-class handler and proceed only on condition that it does not return –1.

```
int CMyView::OnCreate(LPCREATESTRUCT lpCreateStruct)
{
    if (CView::OnCreate(lpCreateStruct) == -1)
        return -1;
    // TODO: Add your specialized creation code here
    return 0;
}
```

By convention, the names of these handlers begin with the prefix "On." Some of these handlers take no arguments, while others take several. Some also have a return type other than **void**. The default handlers for all **WM_** messages are documented in the *Class Library Reference* as member functions of class **CWnd** whose names begin with "On." The member function declarations in **CWnd** are prefixed with **afx_msg**.

Commands and Control Notifications

There are no default handlers for commands or control-notification messages. Therefore, you are bound only by convention in naming your handlers for these categories of messages. When you map the command or control notification to a handler, ClassWizard proposes a name based on the command ID or control-notification code. You can accept the proposed name, change it, or replace it.

Convention suggests that you name handlers in both categories for the user-interface object they represent. Thus a handler for the Cut command on the Edit menu might be named

```
afx_msg void OnEditCut();
```

Because the Cut command is so commonly implemented in applications, the framework predefines the command ID for the Cut command as **ID_EDIT_CUT**. For a list of all predefined command IDs, see the file AFXRES.H. For more information, see "Standard Commands" on page 39.

In addition, convention suggests a handler for the **BN_CLICKED** notification message from a button labeled "Use As Default" might be named

```
afx_msg void OnClickedUseAsDefault();
```

You might assign this command an ID of IDC_USE_AS_DEFAULT since it is equivalent to an application-specific user-interface object.

Both categories of messages take no arguments and return no value.

How to Manage Commands and Messages with ClassWizard

ClassWizard is a tool is designed specifically to connect Windows messages and user-interface objects such as menus to their handlers. Figure 2.4 shows ClassWizard being used to map a message to a handler.

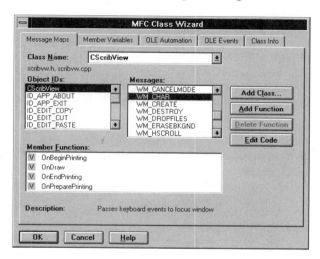

Figure 2.4   ClassWizard

The typical development scenarios are as follows:

- You determine that one of your classes must handle a certain Windows message, so you run ClassWizard and make the connection.

- You create a menu or accelerator resource, then invoke ClassWizard to connect the command associated with that object to a handler.

As you work with the framework, you'll find that ClassWizard greatly simplifies your message-management tasks.

ClassWizard writes the following information to your source files:

- The appropriate message-map entry for the connection

- A declaration of the handler as a member function of the class

- An empty function template for you to fill in with the handler's code

For detailed information about using ClassWizard to connect messages to handlers, see Chapter 12 in the *Visual C++ User's Guide*. For examples, see Chapters 11 and 12 in *Introducing Visual C++*.

Important   Use ClassWizard to create and edit all message-map entries. If you add them manually, you may not be able to edit them with ClassWizard later. If you add them outside the bracketing comments, `//{{AFX_MSG_MAP(classname)` and `//}}AFX_MSG_MAP`, ClassWizard cannot edit them at all. Note that by the same token ClassWizard will not touch any entries you add outside the comments, so feel free to add messages outside the comments if you do not want them to be modified. Some messages, such as message-map ranges, must be added outside the comments.

How to Update User-Interface Objects

Typically, menu items and toolbar buttons have more than one state. For example, a menu item is grayed (dimmed) if it is unavailable in the present context. Menu items can also be checked or unchecked. A toolbar button can also be disabled if unavailable, or it can be checked.

Who updates the state of these items as program conditions change? Logically, if a menu item generates a command that is handled by, say, a document, it makes sense to have the document update the menu item. The document probably contains the information on which the update is based.

If a command has multiple user-interface objects (perhaps a menu item and a toolbar button), both are routed to the same handler function. This encapsulates your user-interface update code for all of the equivalent user-interface objects in a single place.

The framework provides a convenient interface for automatically updating user-interface objects. You can choose to do the updating in some other way, but the interface provided is efficient and easy to use.

The following sections explain the use of update handlers:

- When update handlers are called
- The **ON_UPDATE_COMMAND_UI** macro
- The **CCmdUI** class

When Update Handlers Are Called

Suppose the user clicks the mouse in the File menu, which generates a **WM_INITMENUPOPUP** message. The framework's update mechanism collectively updates all items on the File menu before the menu drops down so the user can see it.

To do this, the framework routes update commands for all menu items in the pop-up menu along the standard command routing. Command targets on the routing have an opportunity to update any menu items by matching the update command with an appropriate message-map entry (of the form **ON_UPDATE_COMMAND_UI**) and calling an "update handler" function. Thus, for a menu with six menu items, six update commands are sent out. If an update handler exists for the command ID of the menu item, it is called to do the updating. If not, the framework checks for the existence of a handler for that command ID and enables or disables the menu item as appropriate.

If the framework does not find an **ON_UPDATE_COMMAND_UI** entry during command routing, it automatically enables the user-interface object if there is an **ON_COMMAND** entry somewhere with the same command ID. Otherwise, it disables the user-interface object. Therefore, to ensure that a user-interface object is enabled, supply a handler for the command the object generates or supply an update handler for it. See Figure 2.2 (shown earlier in this chapter).

It is possible to disable the default disabling of user-interface objects. For more information, see the **m_bAutoMenuEnable** member of class **CFrameWnd** in the *Class Library Reference*.

Menu initialization is automatic in the framework, occurring when the application receives a **WM_INITMENUPOPUP** message. During the idle loop, the framework searches the command routing for button update handlers in much the same way as it does for menus.

The ON_UPDATE_COMMAND_UI Macro

Use ClassWizard to connect a user-interface object to a command-update handler in a command-target object. It will automatically connect the user-interface object's ID to the **ON_UPDATE_COMMAND_UI** macro and create a handler in the object that will handle the update.

For example, the Scribble tutorial in *Introducing Visual C++* updates a Clear All command in its Edit menu. In the tutorial, ClassWizard adds a message-map entry in the chosen class, a function declaration for a command-update handler called OnUpdateEditClearAll in the class declaration, and an empty function template in the class's implementation file. The function prototype looks like this:

```
afx_msg void OnUpdateEditClearAll( CCmdUI* pCmdUI );
```

Like all handlers, the function shows the **afx_msg** keyword. Like all update handlers, it takes one argument, a pointer to a **CCmdUI** object.

The CCmdUI Class

When it routes the update command to the handler, the framework passes the handler a pointer to a **CCmdUI** object (or to an object of a **CCmdUI**-derived class). This object represents the menu item or toolbar button or other user-interface object that generated the command. The update handler calls member functions of the **CCmdUI** structure through the pointer to update the user-interface object. For example, here is an update handler for the Clear All menu item:

```
void CMyClass::OnUpdateToolsMyTool( CCmdUI* pCmdUI )
{
    if( ToolAvailable() )
        pCmdUI->Enable( TRUE );
}
```

This handler calls the **Enable** member function of an object with access to the menu item. **Enable** makes the item available for use.

How to Display Command Information In the Status Bar

When you run AppWizard to create the skeleton of your application, you can easily support a toolbar and a status bar. A single option in AppWizard supports both together. When a status bar is present, the framework automatically gives helpful feedback as the user of your application moves the mouse through items in the menus. The framework automatically displays a prompt string in the status bar when the menu item is being selected. For example, when the user drags the mouse over the Cut item on the Edit menu, the framework might display "Cut the selection and put it on the Clipboard" in the message area of the status bar. The prompt helps the user grasp the menu item's purpose. This also works when the user clicks a toolbar button. Figure 2.5 shows a status bar displaying a command prompt string.

Figure 2.5   A Command Prompt in the Status Bar

You can easily add to this status-bar help by defining prompt strings for the menu items that you add to the program. To do so, provide the prompt strings when you edit the properties of the menu item in the menu editor. The strings you define this way are stored in your application's resource file; they have the same IDs as the commands they explain.

By default, AppWizard adds the ID for a standard prompt, "Ready," which is displayed when the program is waiting for new messages. If you specify the Context-Sensitive Help option in AppWizard, the ID for a help prompt, "For Help, press F1," is added to your application. This ID is **AFX_IDS_IDLEMESSAGE**.

In Chapter 3

So far you have seen how the framework creates its major component objects and how those objects communicate through Windows messages and user-initiated commands. In Chapter 3, you will learn more about documents, views, frame windows, drawing, and printing.

CHAPTER 3

Working with Frame Windows, Documents, and Views

Previous chapters introduced the primary objects in an application built upon the framework of the Microsoft Foundation Class Library (MFC) and showed how these objects communicate via messages and commands.

This chapter takes you deeper into three of the most important objects in a framework application:

- Frame windows, which contain and manage your views
- Documents, which define your application's data
- Views, which display your documents and manage user interaction with them

The chapter also explains how the framework manages printing and print preview since printing functionality is intimately tied to the view.

One of the most important features of the framework is the division of labor among frame windows, documents, and views. The document manages your data. The view displays it and takes user input. And the frame window puts a frame around the view. Code that defines and manipulates data resides in the document class. Code that displays the data and interprets user input resides in the view class.

Frame Windows

When an application runs under Microsoft Windows, the user interacts with documents displayed in frame windows. A document frame window has two major components: the frame and the contents that it frames. A document frame window can be a single document interface (SDI) frame window or a multiple document interface (MDI) child window. Windows manages most of the user's interaction with the frame window: moving and resizing the window, closing it, and minimizing and maximizing it. You manage the contents inside the frame.

The framework uses frame windows to contain views. The two components—frame and contents—are represented and managed by two different classes in MFC. A frame-window class manages the frame, and a view class manages the contents.

The view window is a child of the frame window. Drawing and other user interaction with the document take place in the view's client area, not the frame window's client area. The frame window provides a visible frame around a view, complete with a caption bar and standard window controls such as a control menu, buttons to minimize and maximize the window, and controls for resizing the window. The "contents" consist of the window's client area, which is fully occupied by a child window—the view. Figure 3.1 shows the relationship between a frame window and a view.

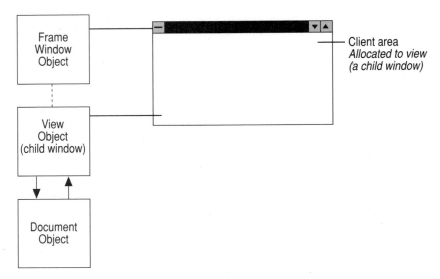

Figure 3.1   Frame Window and View

This chapter also discusses splitter windows. In a splitter window, the frame window's client area is occupied by a splitter window, which in turn has multiple child windows, called panes, which are views.

The following sections explain about frame windows:

- Window classes
- The frame-window classes created by AppWizard
- Managing child windows
- Managing the current view
- Managing menus, control bars, and accelerators
- Working with the File Manager
- Orchestrating other window actions

Window Classes

Each application has one "main frame window," a desktop window that usually has the application name in its caption. Each document usually has one "document frame window." A document frame window contains at least one view, which presents the document's data. For an SDI application, there is one frame window derived from class **CFrameWnd**. This window is both the main frame window and the document frame window. For an MDI application, the main frame window is derived from class **CMDIFrameWnd**, and the document frame windows, which are MDI child windows, are derived from class **CMDIChildWnd**.

These classes provide most of the frame-window functionality you need for your applications. Under normal circumstances, the default behavior and appearance they provide will suit your needs. If you need additional functionality, derive from these classes.

The Frame-Window Classes Created by AppWizard

When you use AppWizard to create a skeleton application, in addition to application, document, and view classes, AppWizard creates a derived frame-window class for your application's main frame window. The class is called CMainFrame by default, and the files that contain it are named MAINFRM.H and MAINFRM.CPP.

If your application is SDI, your CMainFrame class is derived from class **CFrameWnd**. If your application is MDI, CMainFrame is derived from class **CMDIFrameWnd**. If you choose to support a toolbar, the class also has member variables of type **CToolBar** and **CStatusBar** and an OnCreate message-handler function to initialize the two control bars.

If your application is MDI, AppWizard does not derive a new document frame-window class for you. Instead, it uses the default implementation in **CMDIChildWnd**. Later on, if you need to customize your document frame window, you can use ClassWizard to create a new document frame-window class.

These frame-window classes work as created, but to enhance their functionality, you must add member variables and member functions. You may also want to have your window classes handle other Windows messages.

Using Frame Windows

The framework creates document frame windows—and their views and documents —as part of its implementation of the New and Open commands on the File menu. Because the framework does most of the frame-window work for you, you play only a small role in creating, using, and destroying those windows. You can, however, explicitly create your own frame windows and child windows for special purposes.

Creating Document Frame Windows

As you saw in "Document/View Creation" on page 20 in Chapter 1, the **CDocTemplate** object orchestrates creating the frame window, document, and view and connecting them all together. Three **CRuntimeClass** arguments to the **CDocTemplate** constructor specify the frame window, document, and view classes that the document template creates dynamically in response to user commands such as the New command on the File menu or the New Window command on an MDI Window menu. The document template stores this information for later use when it creates a frame window for a view and document.

In order for the **RUNTIME_CLASS** mechanism to work correctly, your derived frame-window classes must be declared with the **DECLARE_DYNCREATE** macro. This is because the framework needs to create document frame windows using the dynamic construction mechanism of class **CObject**. For details about **DECLARE_DYNCREATE**, see the article "CObject Class: Deriving a Class from CObject" in Part 2 and the "Macros and Globals" section in the *Class Library Reference*.

When the user chooses a command that creates a document, the framework calls upon the document template to create the document object, its view, and the frame window that will display the view. Chapter 1, "Using the Classes to Write Applications for Windows," describes this creation process. When it creates the document frame window, the document template creates an object of the appropriate class—a class derived from **CFrameWnd** for an SDI application or from **CMDIChildWnd** for an MDI application. The framework then calls the frame-window object's **LoadFrame** member function to get creation information from resources and to create the Windows window. The framework attaches the window handle to the frame-window object. Then it creates the view as a child window of the document frame window.

Note You cannot create your own child windows or call any Windows API functions in the constructor of a **CWnd**-derived object. This is because the **HWND** for the **CWnd** object has not been created yet. Most Windows-specific initialization, such as adding child windows, must be done in an **OnCreate** message handler.

Destroying Frame Windows

The framework manages window destruction as well as creation for those windows associated with framework documents and views. If you create additional windows, you are responsible for destroying them.

In the framework, when the user closes the frame window, the window's default **OnClose** handler calls **DestroyWindow**. The last member function called when the Windows window is destroyed is **OnNcDestroy**, which does some cleanup, calls the **Default** member function to perform Windows cleanup, and lastly calls the virtual member function **PostNcDestroy**. The **CFrameWnd** implementation of **PostNcDestroy** deletes the C++ window object. You should never use the C++ **delete** operator on a frame window. Use **DestroyWindow** instead.

When the main window closes, the application closes. If there are modified unsaved documents, the framework displays a message box to ask if the documents should be saved and ensures that the appropriate documents are saved if necessary.

What Frame Windows Do

Besides simply framing a view, frame windows are responsible for numerous tasks involved in coordinating the frame with its view and with the application. **CMDIFrameWnd** and **CMDIChildWnd** inherit from **CFrameWnd**, so they have **CFrameWnd** capabilities as well as new capabilities that they add. Examples of child windows include views, controls such as buttons and list boxes, and control bars, including toolbars, status bars, and dialog bars. The frame window is responsible for managing the layout of its child windows. In the framework, a frame window positions any control bars, views, and other child windows inside its client area. The frame window also forwards commands to its views and can respond to notification messages from control windows. Chapter 1, "Using the Classes to Write Applications for Windows," shows how commands are routed from the frame window to its view and other command targets.

Managing Child Windows

MDI main frame windows (one per application) contain a special child window called the **MDICLIENT** window. The **MDICLIENT** window manages the client area of the main frame window, and itself has child windows: the document windows, derived from **CMDIChildWnd**. Because the document windows are frame windows themselves (MDI child windows), they can also have their own children. In all of these cases, the parent window manages its child windows and forwards some commands to them.

In an MDI frame window, the frame window manages the **MDICLIENT** window, repositioning it in conjunction with control bars. The **MDICLIENT** window, in turn, manages all MDI child frame windows. Figure 3.2 shows the relationship between an MDI frame window, its **MDICLIENT** window, and its child document frame windows.

Figure 3.2   MDI Frame Windows and Children

An MDI frame window also works in conjunction with the current MDI child window, if there is one. The MDI frame window delegates command messages to the MDI child before it tries to handle them itself.

Managing the Current View

As part of the default implementation of frame windows, a frame window keeps track of a currently active view. If the frame window contains more than one view, as for example in a splitter window, the current view is the most recent view in use. The active view is independent of the active window in Windows or the current input focus.

When the active view changes, the framework notifies the current view by calling its **OnActivateView** member function. You can tell whether the view is being activated or deactivated by examining **OnActivateView**'s *bActivate* parameter. By default, **OnActivateView** sets the focus to the current view on activation. You can override **OnActivateView** to perform any special processing when the view is deactivated or reactivated. For example, you might want to provide special visual cues to distinguish the active view from other, inactive views. For more information, see the **OnActivateView** member function of class **CView** in the *Class Library Reference*.

A frame window forwards commands to its current (active) view, as described in Chapter 1, "Using the Classes to Write Applications for Windows," as part of the standard command routing.

Managing Menus, Control Bars, and Accelerators

The frame window manages updating user-interface objects, including menus, toolbar buttons, and the status bar. It also manages sharing the menu bar in MDI applications.

The frame window participates in updating user-interface items using the **ON_UPDATE_COMMAND_UI** mechanism described in "How to Update User-Interface Objects" on page 52 in Chapter 2. Buttons on toolbars and other control bars are updated during the idle loop. Menu items in drop-down menus on the menu bar are updated just before the menu drops down.

The frame window also positions the status bar within its client area and manages the status bar's indicators. The frame window clears and updates the message area in the status bar as needed and displays prompt strings as the user selects menu items or toolbar buttons, as described in Chapter 2.

For MDI applications, the MDI frame window manages the menu bar and caption. An MDI frame window owns one default menu that is used as the menu bar when there are no active MDI child windows. When there are active children, the MDI frame window's menu bar is taken over by the menu for the active MDI child window. If an MDI application supports multiple document types, such as chart and worksheet documents, each type puts its own menus into the menu bar and changes the main frame window's caption.

CMDIFrameWnd provides default implementations for the standard commands on the Window menu that appears for MDI applications. In particular, the New Window command (**ID_WINDOW_NEW**) is implemented to create a new frame window and view on the current document. You need to override these implementations only if you need advanced customization.

Multiple MDI child windows of the same document type share menu resources. If several MDI child windows are created by the same document template, they can all use the same menu resource, saving on system resources in Windows.

Each frame window maintains an optional accelerator table that does keyboard accelerator translation for you automatically. This mechanism makes it easy to define accelerator keys (also called shortcut keys) that invoke menu commands.

Frame-Window Styles

The frame windows you get with the framework are suitable for most programs, but you can gain additional flexibility by using the advanced functions **PreCreateWindow** and **AfxRegisterWindowClass**. **PreCreateWindow** is a member function of **CWnd**. **AfxRegisterWindowClass** is a global function documented in "Macros and Globals" in the *Class Library Reference*.

If you apply the **WS_HSCROLL** and **WS_VSCROLL** styles to the main frame window, they are instead applied to the **MDICLIENT** window so users can scroll the **MDICLIENT** area.

If the window's **FWS_ADDTOTITLE** style bit is set (which it is by default), the view tells the frame window what title to display in the window's title bar based on the view's document name.

Working with the File Manager

The frame window manages a relationship with the Windows File Manager.

By adding a few initializing calls in your override of the **CWinApp** member function **InitInstance**, as described in Chapter 1, you can have your frame window indirectly open files dragged from the Windows File Manager and dropped in the frame window. See "File Manager Drag and Drop" on page 18 in Chapter 1.

The frame window can also respond to dynamic data exchange (DDE) requests to open files from the File Manager (if the file extension is registered or associated with the application). See "Shell Registration" on page 18 in Chapter 1.

Orchestrating Other Window Actions

The frame window orchestrates semimodal states such as context-sensitive help and print preview. The framework's role in managing context-sensitive help is described in the article "Help" in Part 2. For a description of the frame window's role in print preview, see "Printing and Print Preview" on page 77.

Documents and Views

The parts of the framework most visible both to the user and to you, the programmer, are the document and view. Most of your work in developing an application with the framework goes into writing your document and view classes. This section describes:

- The purposes of documents and views and how they interact in the framework.
- What you must do to implement them.

The **CDocument** class provides the basic functionality for programmer-defined document classes. A document represents the unit of data that the user typically opens with the Open command on the File menu and saves with the Save command on the File menu.

The **CView** class provides the basic functionality for programmer-defined view classes. A view is attached to a document and acts as an intermediary between the document and the user: the view renders an image of the document on the screen and interprets user input as operations upon the document. The view also renders the image for both printing and print preview.

Figure 3.3 shows the relationship between a document and its view.

Figure 3.3   Document and View

The document/view implementation in the class library separates the data itself from its display and from user operations on the data. All changes to the data are managed through the document class. The view calls this interface to access and update the data.

Documents, their associated views, and the frame windows that frame the views are created by a document template, as described in "Document/View Creation" on page 20 in Chapter 1. The document template is responsible for creating and managing all documents of one document type.

Document and View Classes Created by AppWizard

AppWizard gives you a head start on your program development by creating skeletal document and view classes for you. You can then use ClassWizard to map commands and messages to these classes and the Visual C++ source code editor to write their member functions.

The document class created by AppWizard is derived from class **CDocument**. The view class is derived from **CView**. The names that AppWizard gives these classes and the files that contain them are based on the project name you supply in the AppWizard dialog box. From AppWizard, you can use the Classes dialog box to alter the default names.

Some applications might need more than one document class, view class, or frame-window class. For more information, see "Multiple Document Types, Views, and Frame Windows" on page 73.

Using Documents and Views

Working together, documents and views:

- Contain, manage, and display your application-specific data.
- Provide an interface for manipulating the data.
- Participate in writing and reading files.
- Participate in printing.
- Handle most of your application's commands and messages.

Managing Data

Documents contain and manage your application's data. To use the AppWizard-supplied document class, you must do the following:

- Derive a class from **CDocument** for each type of document.
- Add member variables to store each document's data.
- Override **CDocument**'s **Serialize** member function in your document class. **Serialize** writes and reads the document's data to and from disk.

You may also want to override other **CDocument** member functions. In particular, you will often need to override **OnNewDocument** and **OnOpenDocument** to initialize the document's data members and **DeleteContents** to destroy dynamically allocated data. For information about overridable members, see class **CDocument** in the *Class Library Reference*.

Document Data Variables

Implement your document's data as member variables of your document class. For example, the Scribble tutorial program declares a data member of type **CObList**—a linked list that stores pointers to **CObject** objects. This list is used to store arrays of points that make up a freehand line drawing.

How you implement your document's member data depends on the nature of your application. To help you out, MFC supplies a group of "collection classes"—arrays, lists, and maps (dictionaries), including collections based on C++ templates—along with classes that encapsulate a variety of common data types such as **CString**, **CRect**, **CPoint**, **CSize**, and **CTime**. For more information about these classes, see the "Class Library Overview" in the *Class Library Reference*.

When you define your document's member data, you will usually add member functions to the document class to set and get data items and perform other useful operations on them.

Your views access the document object by using the view's pointer to the document, installed in the view at creation time. You can retrieve this pointer in a view's member functions by calling the **CView** member function **GetDocument**.

Be sure to cast this pointer to your own document type. Then you can access public document members through the pointer.

If frequent data transfer requires direct access, or you wish to use the nonpublic members of the document class, you may want to make your view class a friend (in C++ terms) of the document class.

Serializing Data to and from Files

The basic idea of persistence is that an object should be able to write its current state, indicated by the values of its member variables, to persistent storage. Later, the object can be re-created by reading, or "deserializing," the object's state from persistent storage. A key point here is that the object itself is responsible for reading and writing its own state. Thus, for a class to be persistent, it must implement the basic serialization operations.

The framework provides a default implementation for saving documents to disk files in response to the Save and Save As commands on the File menu and for loading documents from disk files in response to the Open command. With very little work, you can implement a document's ability to write and read its data to and from a file. The main thing you must do is override **CDocument**'s **Serialize** member function in your document class.

AppWizard places a skeletal override of the **CDocument** member function **Serialize** in the document class it creates for you. After you have implemented your application's member variables, you can fill in your `Serialize` override with code that sends the data to an "archive object" connected to a file. A **CArchive** object is similar to the **cin** and **cout** input/output objects from the C++ iostream library. However, **CArchive** writes and reads binary format, not formatted text.

The Document's Role

The framework responds automatically to the File menu's Open, Save, and Save As commands by calling the document's `Serialize` member function if it is implemented. An **ID_FILE_OPEN** command, for example, calls a handler function in the application object. During this process, the user sees and responds to the File Open dialog box and the framework obtains the filename the user chooses. The framework creates a **CArchive** object set up for loading data into the document and passes the archive to `Serialize`. The framework has already opened the file. The code in your document's `Serialize` member function reads the data in through the archive, reconstructing data objects as needed. For more information about serialization, see the article "Serialization (Object Persistence)" in Part 2.

The Data's Role

In general, class-type data should be able to serialize itself. That is, when you pass an object to an archive, the object should know how to write itself to the archive and how to read itself from the archive. MFC provides support for making classes serializable in this way. If you design a class to define a data type and you intend to serialize data of that type, design for serialization.

Bypassing the Archive Mechanism

As you have seen, the framework provides a default way to read and write data to and from files. Serializing through an archive object suits the needs of a great many applications. Such an application reads a file entirely into memory, lets the user update the file, and then writes the updated version to disk again.

However, some applications operate on data very differently, and for these applications serialization through an archive is not suitable. Examples include database programs, programs that edit only parts of large files, programs that write text-only files, and programs that share data files.

In these cases, you can override the **Serialize** member function of **CDocument** in a different way to mediate file actions through a **CFile** object rather than a **CArchive** object.

You can use the **Open**, **Read**, **Write**, **Close**, and **Seek** member functions of class **CFile** to open a file, move the file pointer (seek) to a specific point in the file, read a record (a specified number of bytes) at that point, let the user update the record, then seek to the same point again and write the record back to the file. The framework will open the file for you, and you can use the **GetFile** member function of class **CArchive** to obtain a pointer to the **CFile** object. For even more sophisticated and flexible use, you can override the **OnOpenDocument** and **OnSaveDocument** member functions of class **CWinApp**. For more information, see class **CFile** in the *Class Library Reference*.

In this scenario, your Serialize override does nothing, unless, for example, you want to have it read and write a file header to keep it up to date when the document closes.

For an example of such nonarchived processing, see the CHKBOOK sample program in MFC Samples under MFC in Books Online.

Handling Commands in the Document

Your document class may also handle certain commands generated by menu items, toolbar buttons, or accelerator keys. By default, **CDocument** handles the Save and Save As commands on the File menu, using serialization. Other commands that affect the data may also be handled by member functions of your document. For example, in the Scribble tutorial program, class CScribDoc provides a handler for the Edit Clear All command, which deletes all of the data currently stored in the document. Unlike views, documents cannot handle standard Windows messages.

Displaying Data in a View and Interacting with the User

The view's responsibilities are to display the document's data graphically to the user and to accept and interpret user input as operations on the document. Your tasks in writing your view class are to:

- Write your view class's `OnDraw` member function, which renders the document's data.

- Connect appropriate Windows messages and user-interface objects such as menu items to message-handler member functions in the view class.

- Implement those handlers to interpret user input.

In addition, you may need to override other **CView** member functions in your derived view class. In particular, you may want to override **OnInitialUpdate** to perform special initialization for the view and **OnUpdate** to do any special processing needed just before the view redraws itself. For multipage documents, you also must override **OnPreparePrinting** to initialize the Print dialog box with the number of pages to print and other information. For more information on overriding **CView** member functions, see class **CView** in the *Class Library Reference*.

The Microsoft Foundation Class Library also provides several derived view classes for special purposes:

- **CScrollView**, which provides automatic scrolling and view scaling.

- **CFormView**, which provides a scrollable view useful for displaying a form made up of dialog controls. A **CFormView** object is created from a dialog-template resource.

- **CRecordView**, a form view whose controls are connected to the fields of a **CRecordset** object representing a database table.

- **CEditView**, which provides a view with the characteristics of an editable-text control with enhanced editing features. You can use a **CEditView** object to implement a simple text editor.

To take advantage of these special classes, derive your view classes from them. For more information, see "Scrolling and Scaling Views" on page 72 and "Special View Classes" on page 77. For more information on the database classes, including **CRecordView** and **CRecordset**, see Chapter 6, "Working with Databases."

Drawing in a View

Nearly all drawing in your application occurs in the view's `OnDraw` member function, which you must override in your view class. (The exception is mouse drawing, discussed in the next section, "Interpreting User Input Through a View.") Your `OnDraw` override:

1. Gets data by calling the document member functions you provide.

2. Displays the data by calling member functions of a device-context object that the framework passes to OnDraw.

When a document's data changes in some way, the view must be redrawn to reflect the changes. Typically, this happens when the user makes a change through a view on the document. In this case, the view calls the document's **UpdateAllViews** member function to notify all views on the same document to update themselves. **UpdateAllViews** calls each view's **OnUpdate** member function. The default implementation of **OnUpdate** invalidates the view's entire client area. You can override it to invalidate only those regions of the client area that map to the modified portions of the document.

The **UpdateAllViews** member function of class **CDocument** and the **OnUpdate** member function of class **CView** let you pass information describing what parts of the document were modified. This "hint" mechanism lets you limit the area that the view must redraw. **OnUpdate** takes two "hint" arguments. The first, *lHint*, of type **LPARAM**, lets you pass any data you like, while the second, *pHint*, of type **CObject***, lets you pass a pointer to any object derived from **CObject**.

When a view becomes invalid, Windows sends it a **WM_PAINT** message. The view's **OnPaint** handler function responds to the message by creating a device-context object of class **CPaintDC** and calls your view's OnDraw member function. You do not normally have to write an overriding OnPaint handler function.

Recall from Chapter 1 that a device context is a Windows data structure that contains information about the drawing attributes of a device such as a display or a printer. All drawing calls are made through a device-context object. For drawing on the screen, OnDraw is passed a **CPaintDC** object. For drawing on a printer, it is passed a **CDC** object set up for the current printer.

Your code for drawing in the view first retrieves a pointer to the document, then makes drawing calls through the device context. The following simple OnDraw example illustrates the process:

```
void CMyView::OnDraw( CDC* pDC )
{
    CMyDoc* pDoc = GetDocument();
    CString s = pDoc->GetData();    // Returns a CString
    CRect rect;

    GetClientRect( &rect );
    pDC->SetTextAlign( TA_BASELINE | TA_CENTER );
    pDC->TextOut( rect.right / 2, rect.bottom / 2,
                  s, s.GetLength() );
}
```

In this example, you would define the GetData function as a member of your derived document class.

The example prints whatever string it gets from the document, centered in the view. If the OnDraw call is for screen drawing, the **CDC** object passed in *pDC* is a **CPaintDC** whose constructor has already called **BeginPaint**. Calls to drawing functions are made through the device-context pointer. For information about device contexts and drawing calls, see class **CDC** in the *Class Library Reference* and "Working with Windows" on page 29 in Chapter 1.

For more examples of how to write OnDraw, see the MFC sample programs, which you can access under MFC in Books Online.

Interpreting User Input Through a View

Other member functions of the view handle and interpret all user input. You will usually define message-handler member functions in your view class to process:

- Windows messages generated by mouse and keyboard actions.
- Commands from menus, toolbar buttons, and accelerator keys.

These message-handler member functions interpret the following actions as data input, selection, or editing, including moving data to and from the Clipboard:

- Mouse movements and clicks, drags, and double-clicks
- Keystrokes
- Menu commands

Which Windows messages your view handles depends on your application's needs.

You saw earlier, in "Messages and Commands in the Framework" on page 35 in Chapter 2, how to assign menu items and other user-interface objects to commands and how to bind the commands to handler functions with ClassWizard. You have also seen how the framework routes such commands and sends standard Windows messages to the objects that contain handlers for them.

For example, your application might need to implement direct mouse drawing in the view. The Scribble tutorial example shows how to handle the **WM_LBUTTONDOWN**, **WM_MOUSEMOVE**, and **WM_LBUTTONUP** messages respectively to begin, continue, and end the drawing of a line segment. On the other hand, you might sometimes need to interpret a mouse click in your view as a selection. Your view's OnLButtonDown handler function would determine whether the user was drawing or selecting. If selecting, the handler would determine whether the click was within the bounds of some object in the view and, if so, alter the display to show the object as selected.

Your view might also handle certain menu commands, such as those from the Edit menu to cut, copy, paste, or delete selected data using the Clipboard. Such a handler would call some of the Clipboard-related member functions of class **CWnd** to transfer a selected data item to or from the Clipboard.

Printing and the View

Your view also plays two important roles in printing its associated document. The view:

- Uses the same `OnDraw` code to draw on the printer as to draw on the screen.

- Manages dividing the document into pages for printing.

For more information about printing and about the view's role in printing, see "Printing and Print Preview" on page 77.

Scrolling and Scaling Views

MFC supports views that scroll and views that are automatically scaled to the size of the frame window that displays them. Class **CScrollView** supports both kinds of views.

For more information about scrolling and scaling, see class **CScrollView** in the *Class Library Reference*. For a scrolling example, see Chapter 13, "Enhancing Views," in *Introducing Visual C++*.

Scrolling

Frequently the size of a document is greater than the size its view can display. This may occur because the document's data increases or the user shrinks the window that frames the view. In such cases, the view must support scrolling.

Any view can handle scroll-bar messages in its **OnHScroll** and **OnVScroll** member functions. You can either implement scroll-bar message handling in these functions, doing all the work yourself, or you can use the **CScrollView** class to handle scrolling for you.

CScrollView does the following:

- Manages window and viewport sizes and mapping modes
- Scrolls automatically in response to scroll-bar messages

You can specify how much to scroll for a "page" (when the user clicks in a scroll-bar shaft) and a "line" (when the user clicks in a scroll arrow). Plan these values to suit the nature of your view. For example, you might want to scroll in 1-pixel increments for a graphics view but in increments based on the line height in text documents.

Scaling

When you want the view to automatically fit the size of its frame window, you can use **CScrollView** for scaling instead of scrolling. The logical view is stretched or shrunk to fit the window's client area exactly. A scaled view has no scroll bars.

Multiple Document Types, Views, and Frame Windows

The standard relationship among a document, its view, and its frame window is described in "Document/View Creation" on page 20 in Chapter 1. Many applications support a single document type (but possibly multiple open documents of that type) with a single view on the document and only one frame window per document. But some applications may need to alter one or more of those defaults.

Multiple Document Types

AppWizard creates a single document class for you. In some cases, though, you may need to support more than one document type. For example, your application may need worksheet and chart documents. Each document type is represented by its own document class and probably by its own view class as well. When the user chooses the File New command, the framework displays a dialog box that lists the supported document types. Then it creates a document of the type that the user chooses. Each document type is managed by its own document-template object.

To create extra document classes, use the Add Class button in the ClassWizard dialog box. Choose **CDocument** as the Class Type to derive from and supply the requested document information. Then implement the new class's data.

To let the framework know about your extra document class, you must add a second call to **AddDocTemplate** in your application class's InitInstance override. For more information, see "Document Templates" on page 19 in Chapter 1.

Multiple Views

Many documents require only a single view, but it is possible to support more than one view of a single document. To help you implement multiple views, a document object keeps a list of its views, provides member functions for adding and removing views, and supplies the **UpdateAllViews** member function for letting multiple views know when the document's data has changed.

MFC supports three common user interfaces requiring multiple views on the same document. These models are:

- View objects of the same class, each in a separate MDI document frame window.

  You might want to support creating a second frame window on a document. The user could choose a New Window command to open a second frame with a view of the same document and then use the two frames to view different portions of the document simultaneously. The framework supports the New Window command on the Window menu for MDI applications by duplicating the initial frame window and view attached to the document.

- View objects of the same class in the same document frame window.

  Splitter windows split the view space of a single document window into multiple separate views of the document. The framework creates multiple view objects from the same view class. For more information, see "Splitter Windows" on page 75.

- View objects of different classes in a single frame window.

  In this model, a variation of the splitter window, multiple views share a single frame window. The views are constructed from different classes, each view providing a different way to view the same document. For example, one view might show a word-processing document in normal mode while the other view shows it in outline mode. A splitter control allows the user to adjust the relative sizes of the views.

Figure 3.4 shows the three user-interface models in the order presented above.

Figure 3.4   Multiple-View User Interfaces

The framework provides these models by implementing the New Window command and by providing class **CSplitterWnd**, as discussed in the next section, "Splitter Windows." You can implement other models using these as your starting point. For sample programs that illustrate different configurations of views, frame windows, and splitters, see MFC Samples under MFC in Books Online.

For more information about **UpdateAllViews**, see class **CView** in the *Class Library Reference* and Chapter 13 in *Introducing Visual C++*.

Splitter Windows

In a splitter window, the window is, or can be, split into two or more scrollable panes. A splitter control (or "split box") in the window frame next to the scroll bars allows the user to adjust the relative sizes of the panes. Each pane is a view on the same document. In "dynamic" splitters, the views are of the same class, as shown in Figure 3.4(b). In "static" splitters, the views can be of different classes. Splitter windows of both kinds are supported by class **CSplitterWnd**.

Dynamic splitter windows, with views of the same class, allow the user to split a window into multiple panes at will and then scroll different panes to see different parts of the document. The user can also unsplit the window to remove the additional views. The splitter windows added to the Scribble application in Chapter 13 of *Introducing Visual C++* are an example. That chapter describes the technique for creating dynamic splitter windows. A dynamic splitter window is shown in Figure 3.4(b).

Static splitter windows, with views of different classes, start with the window split into multiple panes, each with a different purpose. For example, in the Visual C++ bitmap editor, the image window shows two panes side by side. The left-hand pane displays a life-sized image of the bitmap. The right-hand pane displays a zoomed or magnified image of the same bitmap. The panes are separated by a "splitter bar" that the user can drag to change the relative sizes of the panes. A static splitter window is shown in Figure 3.4(c).

For more information, see class **CSplitterWnd** in the *Class Library Reference* and MFC Samples under MFC in Books Online.

Initializing and Cleaning Up Documents and Views

Use the following guidelines for initializing and cleaning up after your documents and views:

- The framework initializes documents and views; you initialize any data you add to them.

- The framework cleans up as documents and views close; you must deallocate any memory that you allocated on the heap from within the member functions of those documents and views.

Note Recall that initialization for the whole application is best done in your override of the **InitInstance** member function of class **CWinApp**, and cleanup for the whole application is best done in your override of the **CWinApp** member function **ExitInstance**.

The life cycle of a document (and its frame window and view or views) in an MDI application is as follows:

1. During dynamic creation, the document constructor is called.
2. For each new document, the document's **OnNewDocument** or **OnOpenDocument** is called.
3. The user interacts with the document throughout its lifetime.
4. The framework calls **DeleteContents** to delete data specific to a document.
5. The document's destructor is called.

In an SDI application, step 1 is performed once, when the document is first created. Then steps 2 through 4 are performed repeatedly each time a new document is opened. The new document reuses the existing document object. Finally, step 5 is performed when the application ends.

Initializing

Documents are created in two different ways, so your document class must support both ways. First, the user can create a new, empty document with the File New command. In that case, initialize the document in your override of the **OnNewDocument** member function of class **CDocument**. Second, the user can use the Open command on the File menu to create a new document whose contents are read from a file. In that case, initialize the document in your override of the **OnOpenDocument** member function of class **CDocument**. If both initializations are the same, you can call a common member function from both overrides, or **OnOpenDocument** can call **OnNewDocument** to initialize a clean document and then finish the open operation.

Views are created after their documents are created. The best time to initialize a view is after the framework has finished creating the document, frame window, and view. You can initialize your view by overriding the **OnInitialUpdate** member function of **CView**. If you need to reinitialize or adjust anything each time the document changes, you can override **OnUpdate**.

Cleaning Up

When a document is closing, the framework first calls its **DeleteContents** member function. If you allocated any memory on the heap during the course of the document's operation, **DeleteContents** is the best place to deallocate it.

Note You should not deallocate document data in the document's destructor. In the case of an SDI application, the document object might be reused.

You can override a view's destructor to deallocate any memory you allocated on the heap.

Special View Classes

Besides **CScrollView**, the Microsoft Foundation Class Library provides three other classes derived from **CView**:

- **CFormView**, a view with attributes of a dialog box and a scrolling view. A **CFormView** is created from a dialog-template resource. You can create the dialog-template resource with the Visual C++ dialog editor.

- **CRecordView**, a form view whose controls are connected to fields of a **CRecordset** object that represents a database table.

- **CEditView**, a view that uses the Windows edit control as a simple multiline text editor. You can use a **CEditView** as the view on a document.

About CFormView

CFormView provides a view based on a dialog-template resource. You can use it to create formlike views with edit boxes and other dialog controls. The user can scroll the form view and tab among its controls. Form views support scrolling using the **CScrollView** functionality. For more information, see class **CFormView** in the *Class Library Reference*.

About CRecordView

CRecordView provides database forms. You can use AppWizard or ClassWizard to create a form whose controls exchange data directly with the fields data members of a **CRecordset** object. The **CRecordset** object selects data for a "current record" in an associated table in a database. For more information, see classes **CRecordView** and **CRecordset** in the *Class Library Reference* and Chapter 6, "Working with Databases."

About CEditView

CEditView provides the functionality of a **CEdit** control with enhanced editing features: printing; find and replace; cut, copy, paste, clear, and undo commands; and File Save and File Open commands. You can use a **CEditView** to implement a simple text-editor view. See classes **CEditView** and **CEdit** in the *Class Library Reference*.

Printing and Print Preview

Microsoft Windows implements device-independent display. This means that the same drawing calls, made through a device context passed to your view's OnDraw member function, are used to draw on the screen and on other devices, such as printers. You use the device context to call graphics device interface (GDI) functions, and the device driver associated with the particular device translates the calls into calls that the device can understand.

When your framework document prints, `OnDraw` receives a different kind of device-context object as its argument; instead of a **CPaintDC** object, it gets a **CDC** object associated with the current printer. `OnDraw` makes exactly the same calls through the device context as it does for rendering your document on the screen.

The framework also provides an implementation of the File Print Preview command as described in "Print Preview" on page 78.

The article "Printing" in Part 2 describes in detail the partnership between you and the framework during printing and print preview. In particular, see Figure 1 in the article. Chapter 14 in *Introducing Visual C++* provides an example.

Printing the Document

To print, the framework calls member functions of the view object to set up the Print dialog box, allocate fonts and other resources needed, set the printer mode for a given page, print a given page, and deallocate resources. Once the document as a whole is set up, the process iteratively prints each page. When all pages have been printed, the framework cleans up and deallocates resources. You can, and sometimes must, override some view member functions to facilitate printing. For information, see class **CView** in the *Class Library Reference*.

When the view's **OnPrint** member function is called, it must calculate what part of the document image to draw for the given page number. Typically, **OnPrint** adjusts the viewport origin or the clipping region of the device context to specify what should be drawn. Then **OnPrint** calls the view's **OnDraw** member function to draw that portion of the image.

Print Preview

The framework also implements print-preview functionality and makes it easy for you to use this functionality in your applications. Print preview shows a reduced image of either one or two pages of the document as it would appear when printed. The implementation also provides controls for printing the displayed page(s), moving to the next or the previous page, toggling the display between one and two pages, zooming the display in and out to view it at different sizes, and closing the display. If the framework knows how long the document is, it can also display a scroll bar for moving from page to page.

To implement print preview, instead of directly drawing an image on a device, the framework must simulate the printer using the screen. To do this, the Microsoft Foundation Class Library implements the **CPreviewDC** class, which is used in conjunction with the implementation class **CPreviewView**. All **CDC** objects contain two device contexts. In a **CPreviewDC** object, the first device context represents the printer being simulated; the second represents the screen on which output is actually displayed.

In response to a Print Preview command from the File menu, the framework creates a **CPreviewDC** object. Then when your application performs an operation that sets a characteristic of the printer device context, the framework performs a similar operation on the screen device context. For example, if your application selects a font for printing, the framework selects a font for screen display that simulates the printer font. When your application sends output that would go to the printer, the framework instead sends it to the screen.

The order and manner in which pages of a document are displayed are also different for print preview. Instead of printing a range of pages from start to finish, print preview displays one or two pages at a time and waits for a cue from the user before it displays different pages.

You are not required to do anything to provide print preview, other than to make sure the Print Preview command is in the File menu for your application. However, if you choose, you can modify the behavior of print preview in a number of ways. For more information about making such modifications to print preview in your application, see Technical Note 30 under MFC in Books Online.

In Chapter 4

In this and previous chapters, you have seen how the framework's application, frame window, document, and view classes work, bound together by messages and commands mapped to handler functions in the program's run-time objects. In Chapter 4, you will learn about dialog boxes and the controls that appear in them and about control bars, such as toolbars, status bars, and dialog bars.

CHAPTER 4

Working with Dialog Boxes, Controls, and Control Bars

The previous chapter explained windows, particularly the frame windows used to display views of documents. As you saw briefly in that chapter, class **CWnd** is the base class of many other window classes besides the frame windows.

This chapter covers the following topics, including several additional categories of window classes:

- Dialog boxes
- Control windows
- Control bars

Dialog boxes are used to retrieve input from the user. Inside a dialog box, the user interacts with controls, such as buttons, list boxes, combo boxes, and edit boxes. You can also place controls in a frame window, a view, or a control bar. Using "property sheets," your MFC dialog boxes can also use the "tab dialog box" look used in many dialog boxes in Microsoft Word, Excel, and Visual C++ itself.

A toolbar is a control bar that contains bitmapped buttons; these buttons can be configured to appear and behave as pushbuttons, radio buttons, or check boxes. An MFC toolbar can "dock" to any side of its parent window or float in its own mini-frame window. A status bar is a control bar that contains text-output panes, or "indicators." A dialog bar is a control bar based on a dialog-template resource; as in a dialog box, the user can tab among the controls.

Dialog Boxes

Applications for Windows frequently communicate with the user through dialog boxes. Class **CDialog** provides an interface for managing dialog boxes, the Visual C++ dialog editor makes it easy to design dialog boxes and create their dialog-template resources, and ClassWizard simplifies the process of initializing and validating the controls in a dialog box and of gathering the values entered by the user.

The following sections provide details about dialog boxes:

- Dialog components
- Modal and modeless dialog boxes
- Property sheets and property pages in a dialog box
- Creating a dialog resource template
- The life cycle of a dialog box
- Dialog data exchange and validation
- Type-safe access to controls in a dialog box
- Mapping windows messages to your class
- Common dialog classes

Dialog-Box Components in the Framework

In the framework, a dialog box has two components:

- A dialog-template resource that specifies the dialog box's controls and their placement.

    The dialog resource stores a dialog template from which Windows creates the dialog window and displays it. The template specifies the dialog box's characteristics, including its size, location, style, and the types and positions of the dialog box's controls. You will usually use a dialog template stored as a resource, but you can also create your own template in memory.

- A dialog class, derived from **CDialog**, to provide a programmatic interface for managing the dialog box.

    A dialog box is a window and will be attached to a Windows window when visible. When the dialog window is created, the dialog-template resource is used as a template for creating child window controls for the dialog box.

Modal and Modeless Dialog Boxes

You can use class **CDialog** to manage two kinds of dialog boxes:

- Modal dialog boxes, which require the user to respond before continuing the program
- Modeless dialog boxes, which stay on the screen and are available for use at any time but permit other user activities

The resource editing and ClassWizard procedures for creating a dialog template are the same for modal and modeless dialog boxes.

Creating a dialog box for your program requires the following steps:

1. Use the dialog editor to design the dialog box and create its dialog-template resource.

2. Use ClassWizard to create a dialog class.

3. Connect the dialog resource's controls to message handlers in the dialog class.

4. Use ClassWizard to add data members associated with the dialog box's controls and to specify dialog data exchange and dialog data validations for the controls.

Property Sheets and Property Pages

An MFC dialog box can take on a "tab dialog" look by incorporating property sheets and property pages. Called a "property sheet" in MFC, this kind of dialog box, similar to many dialog boxes in Microsoft Word, Excel, and Visual C++, appears to contain a stack of tabbed sheets, much like a stack of file folders seen from front to back, or a group of cascaded windows. Controls on the front tab are visible; only the labeled tab is visible on the rear tabs. Property sheets are particularly useful for managing large numbers of properties or settings that fall fairly neatly into several groups. Typically, one property sheet can simplify a user interface by replacing several separate dialog boxes.

Property sheets are implemented with classes **CPropertySheet** and **CPropertyPage** (described in the *Class Library Reference*). **CPropertySheet** defines the overall dialog box, which can contain multiple "pages" based on **CPropertyPage**.

For information on creating and working with property sheets, see the article "Property Sheets" in Part 2.

Creating the Dialog Resource

To design the dialog box and create the dialog resource, you use the Visual C++ dialog editor. In the dialog editor, you can:

- Adjust the size and location your dialog box will have when it appears.

- Drag various kinds of controls from a controls palette and drop them where you want them in the dialog box.

- Position the controls with alignment buttons on the toolbar.

- Test your dialog box by simulating the appearance and behavior it will have in your program. In Test mode, you can manipulate the dialog box's controls by typing text in text boxes, clicking pushbuttons, and so on.

When you finish, your dialog-template resource is stored in your application's resource script file. You can edit it later if needed. For a full description of how to create and edit dialog resources, see Chapter 5 in the *Visual C++ User's Guide*.

This technique is also used to create the dialog-template resources for **CFormView** and **CRecordView** classes.

When the dialog box's appearance suits you, use ClassWizard to create a dialog class and map its messages, as discussed in the next section, "Creating a Dialog Class with ClassWizard."

Creating a Dialog Class with ClassWizard

Table 4.1 lists dialog-related tasks that ClassWizard helps you manage.

Table 4.1   Dialog-Related Tasks

Task	Apply to . . .
Create a new **CDialog**-derived class to manage your dialog box.	Each dialog box.
Map Windows messages to your dialog class.	Each message you want handled.
Declare class member variables to represent the controls in the dialog box.	Each control that yields a text or numeric value you want to access from your program.
Specify how data is to be exchanged between the controls and the member variables.	Each control you want to access from your program.
Specify validation rules for the member variables.	Each control that yields a text or numeric value, if desired.

Mapping dialog-class member variables to dialog-box controls and specifying data exchange and validation are explained in "Dialog Data Exchange and Validation" on page 87.

Creating Your Dialog Class

For each dialog box in your program, create a new dialog class to work with the dialog resource.

Chapter 12 in the *Visual C++ User's Guide* explains how to create a new dialog class. When you create a dialog class with ClassWizard, ClassWizard writes the following items in the .H and .CPP files you specify:

In the .H file:

- A class declaration for the dialog class. The class is derived from **CDialog**.

In the .CPP file:

- A message map for the class.

- A standard constructor for the dialog box.

- An override of the **DoDataExchange** member function. Edit this function with ClassWizard. It is used for dialog data exchange and validation capabilities as described later in this chapter.

Life Cycle of a Dialog Box

During the life cycle of a dialog box, the user invokes the dialog box, typically inside a command handler that creates and initializes the dialog object; the user interacts with the dialog box; and the dialog box closes.

For modal dialog boxes, your handler gathers any data the user entered once the dialog box closes. Since the dialog object exists after its dialog window has closed, you can simply use the member variables of your dialog class to extract the data.

For modeless dialog boxes, you may often extract data from the dialog object while the dialog box is still visible. At some point, the dialog object is destroyed; when this happens depends on your code.

Creating and Displaying Dialog Boxes

Creating a dialog object is a two-phase operation. First, construct the dialog object. Then create the dialog window. Modal and modeless dialog boxes differ somewhat in the process used to create and display them. Table 4.2 lists how modal and modeless dialog boxes are normally constructed and displayed.

Table 4.2   Dialog Creation

Dialog type	How to create it
Modeless	Construct **CDialog**, then call **Create** member function.
Modal	Construct **CDialog**, then call **DoModal** member function.

Creating Modal Dialog Boxes

To create a modal dialog box, call either of the two public constructors declared in **CDialog** and then call the dialog object's **DoModal** member function to display the dialog box and manage interaction with it until the user chooses OK or Cancel. This management by **DoModal** is what makes the dialog box "modal." For modal dialog boxes, **DoModal** loads the dialog resource.

Creating Modeless Dialog Boxes

For a modeless dialog box, you must provide your own public constructor in your dialog class. To create a modeless dialog box, call your public constructor and then call the dialog object's **Create** member function to load the dialog resource. You can call **Create** either during or after the constructor call. If the dialog resource has the property **WS_VISIBLE**, the dialog box appears immediately. If not, you must call its **ShowWindow** member function.

Using a Dialog Template in Memory

Instead of using the methods given in Table 4.2, you can create either kind of dialog box indirectly from a dialog template in memory. For more information, see class **CDialog** in the *Class Library Reference*.

Setting the Dialog Box's Background Color

You can set the background color of your dialog boxes by calling the **CWinApp** member function **SetDialogBkColor** in your InitInstance override. The color you set is used for all dialog boxes and message boxes.

Initializing the Dialog Box

After the dialog box and all of its controls are created but just before the dialog box (of either type) appears on the screen, the dialog object's **OnInitDialog** member function is called. For a modal dialog box, this occurs during the **DoModal** call. For a modeless dialog box, **OnInitDialog** is called when **Create** is called. You typically override **OnInitDialog** to initialize the dialog box's controls, such as setting the initial text of an edit box. You must call the **OnInitDialog** member function of the base class, **CDialog**, from your OnInitDialog override.

Handling Windows Messages

Dialog boxes are windows, so they can handle Windows messages if you supply the appropriate handler functions.

Retrieving Data from the Dialog Object

The framework provides an easy way to initialize the values of controls in a dialog box and to retrieve values from the controls. The more laborious manual approach is to call functions such as the **SetDlgItemText** and **GetDlgItemText** member functions of class **CWnd**, which apply to control windows. With these functions, you access each control individually to set or get its value, calling functions such as **SetWindowText** and **GetWindowText**. The framework's approach automates both initialization and retrieval.

Dialog data exchange (DDX) lets you exchange data between the controls in the dialog box and member variables in the dialog object more easily. This exchange works both ways. To initialize the controls in the dialog box, you can set the values of data members in the dialog object, and the framework will transfer the values to the controls before the dialog box is displayed. Then you can at any time update the dialog data members with data entered by the user. At that point, you can use the data by referring to the data member variables.

You can also arrange for the values of dialog controls to be validated automatically with dialog data validation (DDV).

Use ClassWizard to add DDX and DDV capabilities to a dialog class. DDX and DDV are explained in more detail in "Dialog Data Exchange and Validation" on page 87.

For a modal dialog box, you can retrieve any data the user entered when **DoModal** returns **IDOK** but before the dialog object is destroyed. For a modeless dialog box, you can retrieve data from the dialog object at any time by calling **UpdateData** with the argument **TRUE** and then accessing dialog class member variables. This subject is discussed in more detail in "Dialog Data Exchange and Validation" on page 87.

Closing the Dialog Box

A modal dialog box closes when the user chooses one of its buttons, typically the OK button or the Cancel button. Choosing the OK or Cancel button causes Windows to send the dialog object a **BN_CLICKED** control-notification message with the button's ID, either **IDOK** or **IDCANCEL**. **CDialog** provides default handler functions for these messages: **OnOK** and **OnCancel**. The default handlers call the **EndDialog** member function to close the dialog window. You can also call **EndDialog** from your own code. For more information, see the **EndDialog** member function of class **CDialog** in the *Class Library Reference*.

To arrange for closing and deleting a modeless dialog box, override **PostNcDestroy** and invoke the **delete** operator on the **this** pointer. The next section, "Destroying the Dialog Box," explains what happens next.

Destroying the Dialog Box

Modal dialog boxes are normally created on the stack frame and destroyed when the function that created them ends. The dialog object's destructor is called when the object goes out of scope.

Modeless dialog boxes are normally created and "owned" by a parent view or frame window—the application's main frame window or a document frame window. The default **OnClose** handler calls **DestroyWindow**, which destroys the dialog-box window. If the dialog box stands alone, with no pointers to it or other special ownership semantics, you should override **PostNcDestroy** to destroy the C++ dialog object. You should also override **OnCancel** and call **DestroyWindow** from within it. If not, the "owner" of the dialog box should destroy the C++ object when it is no longer necessary.

Dialog Data Exchange and Validation

Dialog data exchange (DDX) is an easy way to initialize the controls in your dialog box and to gather data input by the user. Dialog data validation (DDV) is an easy way to validate data entry in a dialog box. To take advantage of DDX and DDV in your dialog boxes, use ClassWizard to create the data members and set their data types and specify validation rules. For additional information about DDX/DDV and for examples, see Chapter 12 in the *Visual C++ User's Guide* and Chapter 12 in *Introducing Visual C++*.

Data Exchange

If you use the DDX mechanism, you set the initial values of the dialog object's member variables, typically in your **OnInitDialog** handler or the dialog constructor. Immediately before the dialog is displayed, the framework's DDX mechanism transfers the values of the member variables to the controls in the dialog box, where they appear when the dialog box itself appears in response to **DoModal** or **Create**. The default implementation of **OnInitDialog** in **CDialog** calls the **UpdateData** member function of class **CWnd** to initialize the controls in the dialog box.

The same mechanism transfers values from the controls to the member variables when the user clicks the OK button (or whenever you call the **UpdateData** member function with the argument **TRUE**). The dialog data validation mechanism validates any data items for which you specified validation rules.

Figure 4.1 illustrates dialog data exchange.

Figure 4.1   Dialog Data Exchange

UpdateData works in both directions, as specified by the **BOOL** parameter passed to it. To carry out the exchange, **UpdateData** sets up a **CDataExchange** object and calls your dialog class's override of **CDialog**'s **DoDataExchange** member function. **DoDataExchange** takes an argument of type **CDataExchange**. The **CDataExchange** object passed to **UpdateData** represents the context of the exchange, defining such information as the direction of the exchange.

When you (or ClassWizard) override **DoDataExchange**, you specify a call to one DDX function per data member (control). Each DDX function knows how to exchange data in both directions based on the context supplied by the **CDataExchange** argument passed to your DoDataExchange by **UpdateData**.

MFC provides many DDX functions for different kinds of exchange. The following example shows a DoDataExchange override in which two DDX functions and one DDV function are called:

```
void CMyDialog::DoDataExchange(CDataExchange* pDX)
{
    CDialog::DoDataExchange(pDX);      // Call base class version
    //{{AFX_DATA_MAP(CMyDialog)
    DDX_Check(pDX, IDC_MY_CHECKBOX, m_bVar);
    DDX_Text(pDX, IDC_MY_TEXTBOX, m_strName);
    DDV_MaxChars(pDX, IDC_MY_TEXTBOX, m_strName, 20);
    //}}AFX_DATA_MAP
}
```

The DDX_ and DDV_ lines between the //{{AFX_DATA_MAP and //}}AFX_DATA_MAP delimiters are a "data map." The sample DDX and DDV functions shown are for a check-box control and an edit-box control, respectively.

If the user cancels a modal dialog box, the **OnCancel** member function terminates the dialog box and **DoModal** returns the value **IDCANCEL**. In that case, no data is exchanged between the dialog box and the dialog object.

Data Validation

You can specify validation in addition to data exchange by calling DDV functions, as shown in the example in the previous section, "Data Exchange." The **DDV_MaxChars** call in the example validates that the string entered in the text-box control is not longer than 20 characters. The DDV function typically alerts the user with a message box if the validation fails and puts the focus on the offending control so the user can reenter the data. A DDV function for a given control must be called immediately after the DDX function for the same control.

You can also define your own custom DDX and DDV routines. For details on this and other aspects of DDX and DDV, see Technical Note 26 under MFC in Books Online.

ClassWizard will write all of the DDX and DDV calls in the data map for you. Do not manually edit the lines in the data map between the delimiting comments.

Type-Safe Access to Controls in a Dialog Box

The controls in a dialog box can use the interfaces of MFC control classes such as **CListBox** and **CEdit**. You can create a control object and attach it to a dialog control. Then you can access the control through its class interface, calling member functions to operate on the control, as shown below. The methods described here are designed to give you type-safe access to a control. This is especially useful for controls such as edit boxes and list boxes.

There are two approaches to making a connection between a control in a dialog box and a C++ control member variable in a **CDialog**-derived class.

Without ClassWizard

The first approach uses an inline member function to cast the return type of class **CWnd**'s **GetDlgItem** member function to the appropriate C++ control type, as in this example:

```
// Declared inline in class CMyDialog
CButton* GetMyCheckbox()
{
    return (CButton*)GetDlgItem(ID_MYCHECKBOX);
}
```

You can then use this member function to access the control in a type-safe manner with code similar to the following:

```
GetMyCheckbox()->SetState(TRUE);
```

With ClassWizard

However, there is a much easier way to accomplish the same effect if you are familiar with the DDX features. You can use the Control property in ClassWizard.

If you simply want access to a control's value, DDX provides it. If you want to do more than access a control's value, use ClassWizard to add a member variable of the appropriate class to your dialog class. Attach this member variable to the Control property.

Member variables can have a Control property instead of a Value property. The Value property refers to the type of data returned from the control, such as **CString** or **int**. The Control property enables direct access to the control through a data member whose type is one of the control classes in MFC, such as **CButton** or **CEdit**.

Note For a given control, you can, if you wish, have multiple member variables with the Value property and at most one member variable with the Control property. You can have only one MFC object mapped to a control because multiple objects attached to a control, or any other window, would lead to an ambiguity in the message map.

You can use this object to call any member functions for the control object. Such calls affect the control in the dialog box. For example, for a check-box control represented by a variable m_checkboxDefault, of type **CButton**, you could call:

```
m_checkboxDefault.SetState(TRUE);
```

Here the member variable m_checkboxDefault serves the same purpose as the member function GetMyCheckbox shown above in the "Without ClassWizard" discussion. If the check box is not an auto check box, you would still need a handler in your dialog class for the **BN_CLICKED** control-notification message when the button is clicked.

For more information about controls, see "Controls" on page 92.

Mapping Windows Messages to Your Class

If you need your dialog box to handle Windows messages, override the appropriate handler functions. To do so, use ClassWizard to map the messages to the dialog class. This writes a message-map entry for each message and adds the message-handler member functions to the class. Use the Visual C++ source code editor to write code in the message handlers. Chapter 2, "Working with Messages and Commands," describes message maps and message-handler functions in detail.

Commonly Overridden Member Functions

Table 4.3 list the most likely member functions to override in your **CDialog**-derived class.

Table 4.3   Commonly Overridden Member Functions of Class CDialog

Member function	Message it responds to	Purpose of the override
OnInitDialog	**WM_INITDIALOG**	Initialize the dialog box's controls
OnOK	**BN_CLICKED** for button **IDOK**	Respond when the user clicks the OK button
OnCancel	**BN_CLICKED** for button **IDCANCEL**	Respond when the user clicks the Cancel button

OnInitDialog, **OnOK**, and **OnCancel** are virtual functions. To override them, you declare an overriding function in your derived dialog class using ClassWizard; in these cases, ClassWizard will not add any message-map entries because they are not necessary.

OnInitDialog is called just before the dialog box is displayed. You must call the default **OnInitDialog** handler from your override—usually as the first action in the handler. By default, **OnInitDialog** returns **TRUE** to indicate that the focus should be set to the first control in the dialog box.

OnOK is typically overridden for modeless but not modal dialog boxes. If you override this handler for a modal dialog box, call the base class version from your override—to ensure that **EndDialog** is called—or call **EndDialog** yourself.

OnCancel is usually overridden for modeless dialog boxes.

For more information about these member functions, see class **CDialog** in the *Class Library Reference* and the discussion on "Life Cycle of a Dialog Box" on page 85.

Commonly Added Member Functions

If your dialog box contains pushbuttons other than OK or Cancel, you need to write message-handler member functions in your dialog class to respond to the control-notification messages they generate. For an example, see Chapter 12, "Adding a Dialog Box," in *Introducing Visual C++*. You can also handle control-notification messages from other controls in your dialog box.

Common Dialog Classes

In addition to class **CDialog**, MFC supplies several classes derived from **CDialog** that encapsulate commonly used dialog boxes, as shown in Table 4.4. The dialog boxes encapsulated are called the "common dialog boxes" and are part of the Windows common dialog library (COMMDLG.DLL). The dialog-template resources and code for these classes are provided in the Windows common dialog boxes that are part of Windows versions 3.1 and later.

Table 4.4　Common Dialog Classes

Derived dialog class	Purpose
CColorDialog	Lets user select colors
CFileDialog	Lets user select a filename to open or to save
CFindReplaceDialog	Lets user initiate a find or replace operation in a text file
CFontDialog	Lets user specify a font
CPrintDialog	Lets user specify information for a print job

For more information about the common dialog classes, see the individual class names in the *Class Library Reference*. MFC also supplies a number of standard dialog classes used for OLE. For information about these classes, see the base class, **COleDialog**, in the *Class Library Reference*.

Three other classes in MFC have dialog-like characteristics. For information about classes **CFormView** and **CRecordView**, see "About CFormView" and "About CRecordView" on page 77 in Chapter 3. For information about class **CDialogBar**, see "Control Bars" on page 97.

Controls

MFC supplies a set of classes that correspond to the standard control windows provided by Microsoft Windows. These include buttons of several kinds, static- and editable-text controls, scroll bars, list boxes, and combo boxes. Table 4.5 lists the classes and the corresponding standard controls. The next section, "Additional Controls," describes new kinds of controls.

Table 4.5   Standard Control Window Classes

Class	Windows control
CStatic	Static-text control
CButton	Button control: pushbutton, check box, radio button, or group-box control
CListBox	List-box control
CComboBox	Combo-box control
CEdit	Edit control
CScrollBar	Scroll-bar control

Each control class encapsulates a Windows control and provides a member-function user interface to the underlying control. Using a control object's member functions, you can get and set the value or state of the control and respond to various standard messages sent by the control to its parent window (usually a dialog box). For additional control classes, see "Additional Controls," which follows.

You can create control objects in a window or dialog box. You can also use a control class as an interface to a control created in a dialog box from a dialog-template resource.

Additional Controls

In addition to the standard Windows controls, MFC provides several other control classes. These provide buttons labeled with bitmaps instead of text, control bars, and splitter-window controls. Splitter windows are discussed in Chapter 3, "Working with Frame Windows, Documents, and Views."

Table 4.6 lists the the additional classes and their purposes.

Table 4.6   Additional Control Classes

Class	Purpose
CBitmapButton	Button labeled with a bitmap instead of text
CToolBar	Toolbar arranged along a border of a frame window and containing other controls
CStatusBar	Status bar arranged along a border of a frame window and containing panes, or indicators
CDialogBar	Control bar created from a dialog-template resource and arranged along a border of a frame window

Note VBX controls are not supported in 32-bit versions of Visual C++.

Control bars, including toolbars, status bars, and dialog bars, are discussed in "Control Bars" on page 97.

Bitmap Buttons

Class **CBitmapButton** allows you to have button controls labeled with bitmaps instead of text. An object of this class stores four **CBitmap** objects that represent various states of the button: up (active), down (pushed), focused, and disabled. Bitmap buttons can be used in dialog boxes. For more information, see class **CBitmapButton** in the *Class Library Reference*. Figure 4.2 shows bitmap buttons in a dialog box.

Figure 4.2   Bitmap Buttons

Controls and Dialog Boxes

Normally the controls in a dialog box are created from the dialog template at the time the dialog box is created. Use ClassWizard to manage the controls in your dialog box. For details, see "Dialog Data Exchange and Validation" on page 87, "Type-Safe Access to Controls in a Dialog Box" on page 89, and "Mapping Windows Messages to Your Class" on page 91.

Making and Using Controls

You make most controls for dialog boxes in the Visual C++ dialog editor. But you can also create controls in any dialog box or window. The following sections explain how to add controls to a dialog box:

- Using the dialog editor.
- By hand.
- Deriving control classes from existing MFC control classes.

Using the Dialog Editor

When you create your dialog-template resource with the dialog editor, you drag controls from a controls palette and drop them into the dialog box. This adds the specifications for that control type to the dialog-template resource. When you construct a dialog object and call its **Create** or **DoModal** member function, the framework creates a Windows control and places it in the dialog window on screen.

Doing It By Hand

To create a control object yourself, you will usually embed the C++ control object in a C++ dialog or frame-window object. Like many other objects in the framework, controls require two-stage construction. You should call the control's **Create** member function as part of creating the parent dialog box or frame window. For dialog boxes, this is usually done in **OnInitDialog**, and for frame windows, in **OnCreate**.

The following example shows how you might declare a **CEdit** object in the class declaration of a derived dialog class and then call the **Create** member function in **OnInitDialog**. Because the **CEdit** object is declared as an embedded object, it is automatically constructed when the dialog object is constructed, but it must still be initialized with its own **Create** member function.

```
class CMyDialog : public CDialog
{
protected:
    CEdit m_edit;    // Embedded edit object
public:
    virtual BOOL OnInitDialog();
};
```

The following OnInitDialog function sets up a rectangle, then calls **Create** to create the Windows edit control and attach it to the uninitialized **CEdit** object.

```
BOOL CMyDialog::OnInitDialog()
{
    CDialog::OnInitDialog();
    CRect rect(85, 110, 180, 210);

    m_edit.Create(WS_CHILD | WS_VISIBLE | WS_TABSTOP |
            ES_AUTOHSCROLL | WS_BORDER, rect, this, ID_EXTRA_EDIT);
    m_edit.SetFocus();
    return FALSE;
}
```

After creating the edit object, you can also set the input focus to the control by calling the **SetFocus** member function. Finally, you return 0 from **OnInitDialog** to show that you set the focus. If you return a nonzero value, the dialog manager sets the focus to the first control item in the dialog item list. In most cases, you'll want to add controls to your dialog boxes with the dialog editor.

Deriving Controls from a Standard Control

As with any **CWnd**-derived class, you can modify a control's behavior by deriving a new class from an existing control class.

To create a derived control class, follow these steps:

1. Derive your class from an existing control class and optionally override the **Create** member function so that it provides the necessary arguments to the base-class **Create** function.

2. Use ClassWizard to provide message-handler member functions and message-map entries to modify the control's behavior in response to specific Windows messages.

3. Provide new member functions to extend the functionality of the control (optional).

Using a derived control in a dialog box requires extra work. The types and positions of controls in a dialog box are normally specified in a dialog-template resource. If you create a derived control class, you cannot specify it in a dialog template since the resource compiler knows nothing about your derived class. To place your derived control in a dialog box, follow these steps:

1. Embed an object of the derived control class in the declaration of your derived dialog class.

2. Override the **OnInitDialog** member function in your dialog class to call the **SubclassDlgItem** member function for the derived control.

SubclassDlgItem "dynamically subclasses" a control created from a dialog template. When a control is dynamically subclassed, you hook into Windows, process some messages within your own application, then pass the remaining messages on to Windows. For more information, see the **SubclassDlgItem** member function of class **CWnd** in the *Class Library Reference*. The following example shows how you might write an override of **OnInitDialog** to call **SubclassDlgItem**:

```
BOOL CMyDialog::OnInitDialog()
{
    CDialog::OnInitDialog();
    m_wndMyBtn.SubclassDlgItem(IDC_MYBTN, this);
    return TRUE;
}
```

Because the derived control is embedded in the dialog class, it will be constructed when the dialog box is constructed, and it will be destroyed when the dialog box is destroyed. Compare this code to the example in "Doing It By Hand" on page 95.

Control Bars

Control bars greatly enhance a program's usability by providing quick, one-step command actions. Control bars include toolbars, status bars, and dialog bars. The base class of all control bars is **CControlBar**.

- A toolbar is a control bar that displays a row of bitmapped buttons that activate commands. Pressing a toolbar button is similar to choosing a menu item. The buttons can act like pushbuttons, check boxes, or radio buttons. A toolbar is usually aligned to the top of a frame window, but an MFC toolbar can also be dragged and "docked" to any other side of its parent window, and it can be "floated"—placed in a floating mini-frame window. A toolbar can also display "tool tips" as the user moves the mouse over the toolbar's buttons. A tool tip is a tiny popup window that presents a short description of the button's purpose.

- A status bar is a control bar with a row of text output panes, or "indicators." The output panes are commonly used as message lines and as status indicators. Examples include the command help-message lines that briefly explain the selected menu or toolbar command and the indicators that indicate the status of the SCROLL LOCK, NUM LOCK, and other keys. Status bars are usually aligned to the bottom of a frame window.

- A dialog bar is a control bar with the functionality of a modeless dialog box. Dialog bars are created from dialog templates and can contain any Windows control. Dialog bars support tabbing among controls and can be aligned to the top, bottom, left, or right side of a frame window.

The basic functionality of all three control-bar types is similar. The base class, **CControlBar**, provides the functionality for positioning the control bar in its parent frame window. Because a control bar is usually a child window of a parent frame window, it is a "sibling" to the client view or MDI client of the frame window. A control-bar object uses information about its parent window's client rectangle to position itself. Then it alters the parent's remaining client-window rectangle so that the client view or MDI client window fills the rest of the client window.

Note If a button on the control bar doesn't have a **COMMAND** or **UPDATE_COMMAND_UI** handler, the button is automatically disabled by the framework.

Toolbars

Toolbars display a collection of easy-to-use buttons that represent commands. AppWizard makes it easy to add a toolbar to your application. Moreover, the toolbar can:

- Remain stationary along one side of its parent window.

- Be dragged and "docked" by the user on any side or sides of the parent window you specify.
- Be "floated" in its own mini-frame window so the user can move it around to any convenient position.

MFC toolbars can also be made to display "tool tips"—tiny popup windows containing a short text description of a toolbar button's purpose. As the user moves the mouse over a toolbar button, the tool tip window pops up to offer a hint.

For more information about "dockable" toolbars, see the article "Toolbars: Docking and Floating." For more information about tool tips, see the article "Toolbars: Tool Tips." Both articles are in Part 2.

The buttons in a toolbar are analogous to the items in a menu. Both kinds of user-interface objects generate commands, which your program handles by providing handler functions. Often toolbar buttons duplicate the functionality of menu commands, providing an alternative user interface to the same functionality. Such duplication is arranged by giving the button and the menu item the same ID.

Once constructed, a **CToolBar** object creates the toolbar image by loading a single bitmap that contains one image for each button. AppWizard creates a standard toolbar bitmap, in file TOOLBAR.BMP, that you can customize with the Visual C++ graphics editor. Figure 4.3 shows that bitmap as it appears in the graphics editor.

Figure 4.3   The Standard Toolbar Bitmap

Figure 4.4 shows a toolbar as it appears in a running application, including separators between groups of buttons.

Figure 4.4   A Toolbar with Separators

The buttons in a toolbar are only bitmaps, but the toolbar object processes mouse clicks in the toolbar and generates the appropriate command based on the clicked button's position in the toolbar.

Buttons are correlated with the commands they generate by an array of command IDs, in which the position of an ID in the array is the same as the position of a button image in the toolbar bitmap. If you choose the Initial Toolbar option in AppWizard, AppWizard adds a "buttons" array to the source file for your main frame-window class. The array also contains **ID_SEPARATOR** elements used to space the buttons into groups. The separators are ignored in determining button positions. For an example of using the Visual C++ graphics editor and the array to modify the default toolbar provided by AppWizard, see Chapter 10 in *Introducing Visual C++*.

You can make the buttons in a toolbar appear and behave as pushbuttons, check boxes, or radio buttons.

For more information, see class **CToolBar** in the *Class Library Reference*.

Status Bars

As with toolbars, a **CStatusBar** object is based on an array of IDs for its indicator panes. If you select the Initial Toolbar option in AppWizard, AppWizard creates the array for a status bar as well as the array for a toolbar in the source file for your main frame-window class. The array looks like this:

```
static UINT BASED_CODE indicators[] =
{
    ID_SEPARATOR,          // message line indicator
    ID_INDICATOR_CAPS,
    ID_INDICATOR_NUM,
    ID_INDICATOR_SCRL,
};
```

These indicators are arranged horizontally along the status bar from left to right. You can add more indicators by adding more IDs to the array. You can size these indicators as needed. You can also add separators by adding **ID_SEPARATOR** elements. The leftmost indicator, at position 0, takes up all space remaining after the other panes are placed. This indicator is most often used as a message area in which to display text strings such as command prompts. Figure 4.5 shows a status bar that displays several indicators.

| Save the active document | CAP NUM SCRL |

Figure 4.5   A Status Bar

Like the toolbar, the status-bar object is embedded in its parent frame window and is constructed automatically when the frame window is constructed. During creation, a call to the **SetIndicators** member function of class **CStatusBar** associates an ID from the array with each indicator. The status bar, like all control bars, is destroyed automatically as well.

For an example of using a status bar, see the Scribble tutorial program in *Introducing Visual C++*. For more information, see class **CStatusBar** in the *Class Library Reference*.

Dialog Bars

Because it has the characteristics of a modeless dialog box, a **CDialogBar** object provides a more powerful toolbar. There are several key differences between a toolbar and a **CDialogBar** object. A **CDialogBar** object is created from a dialog-template resource, which you can create with the Visual C++ dialog editor and which can contain any kind of Windows control. The user can tab from control to control. And you can specify an alignment style to align the dialog bar with any part of the parent frame window or even to leave it in place if the parent is resized. Figure 4.6 shows a dialog bar with a variety of controls.

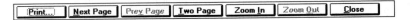

Figure 4.6   A Dialog Bar

In other respects, working with a **CDialogBar** object is like working with a modeless dialog box. Use the dialog editor to design and create the dialog resource.

One of the virtues of dialog bars is that they can include controls other than buttons.

While it is normal to derive your own dialog classes from **CDialog**, you do not typically derive your own class for a dialog bar. Dialog bars are extensions to a main window and any dialog-bar control-notification messages, such as **BN_CLICKED** or **EN_CHANGE**, will be sent to the parent of the dialog bar— the main window.

For more information about dialog bars, see class **CDialogBar** in the *Class Library Reference*.

In Chapter 5

Chapters 1 through 4 have explained how the framework functions and given you some insight into its use. The next chapter, Chapter 5, explains MFC support for programming with OLE.

C H A P T E R   5

Working with Object Linking and Embedding

The OLE classes of the Microsoft Foundation Class Library (MFC) are a set of C++ classes that provide an object-oriented interface to the Object Linking and Embedding version 2 (OLE) application programming interface (API). The OLE classes leverage the class library framework, making it easy to use OLE with the remainder of the class library, although you can use portions of the OLE classes without using all of the class library. With Visual C++ version 2.0, the OLE classes have been ported to Win32.

The OLE classes add the following components to the class library:

- C++ classes that provide an object-oriented interface to the OLE API
- Extensions to AppWizard for creating programs that use OLE
- Extensions to ClassWizard for creating and editing automated classes
- Sample programs that illustrate use of the classes and wizards
- Online documentation that includes overview material, tutorials, programming articles, and a class reference

In this chapter, you'll find information on:

- Features of the OLE classes
- Requirements for using the OLE classes
- Installing the OLE classes
- Distributing your application
- Getting started with the OLE classes

Features of the OLE Classes

The MFC OLE classes supply the following features:

- They are integrated with other parts of the Microsoft Foundation Class Library.

- They encapsulate much of the complexity of the OLE API in a small set of C++ classes that provide a higher-level interface to OLE.

- They allow you to call C-language OLE API functions directly wherever the OLE classes don't meet your needs.

The OLE classes support visual editing containers, servers, drag and drop, automation, message filters, compound files, and automatic registration. Explanations of these terms can be found in the "OLE Overview" article in Part 2. If you need access to other portions of the OLE API, you can work with it directly. A number of tools and sample applications are also available to help you test your OLE applications. For more information, see the article "Debugging OLE Applications: Tools" in Part 2.

Visual C++ combines key OLE components, including the required header files, libraries, DLLs, tools, and documentation. A number of sample programs are also included for testing your applications.

Requirements for Using the OLE Classes

This product assumes that you are familiar with C++. It is also helpful if you are familiar with writing applications for Windows and know how to use the Microsoft Foundation Class Library. Some understanding of OLE architecture will help, but is not required; for any OLE information you do need, Visual C++ provides the OLE Software Development Kit (SDK). Additional information about OLE is available in Kraig Brockschmidt's book *Inside OLE 2* (Microsoft Press, 1994).

Installing the OLE Classes

If you choose "MFC OLE" when you run Setup to install Visual C++, the MFC OLE classes and retail OLE DLLs from the OLE Software Development Kit (SDK) are automatically installed. If you choose the OLE SDK button, you can install additional portions of the OLE SDK: debugging and retail DLLs, OLE SDK help files, sample source files, and tools. Only the retail DLLs are installed by default.

Note In addition to static link libraries, the class library supplies the OLE classes in DLL form. The release version is MFCO30.DLL. The debugging version of the DLL is MFCO30D.DLL. For more information, see the articles "Library Versions" and "DLLs: Naming Conventions" in Part 2. Also see Technical Note 33 under MFC in Books Online.

Distributing Your Application

When you write an application with the OLE classes and distribute it to your customers, you may also need to distribute some DLL components of the OLE SDK —and the Microsoft Foundation Class Library. Which DLLs are required depends on how you write your application with the class library.

Distributable Components

Your Visual C++ license authorizes you to freely distribute the release mode OLE and MFC DLLs that are needed to support an OLE application developed using Visual C++. Both the license and the file \MSVC20\REDIST\REDISTRB.WRI on the Visual C++ CD-ROM disc list the files that are redistributable. Should there be a discrepancy between these two lists, assume that the list in REDISTRB.WRI is correct.

Getting Started with the MFC OLE Classes

The best place to begin reading about the OLE classes is the article "OLE Overview" in Part 2. "OLE Overview" introduces the classes and points to related articles about the concepts, components, and procedures of the OLE classes. These articles are presented in alphabetical order in Part 2. For information about how the articles are structured and how to get the most from them, see the first article, "Using the Encyclopedia."

For hands-on experience, see the three tutorials for the OLE classes:

- OLE Container Tutorial, which builds an OLE visual editing container application. The container tutorial begins in Chapter 17 of *Introducing Visual C++*.

- OLE Server Tutorial, which builds a new "Step 7" onto the Scribble tutorial presented in Chapters 6 through 15 in *Introducing Visual C++*. The server tutorial begins in Chapter 16.

   Note The OLE server tutorial is a continuation of the general MFC tutorial, called Scribble. If you are familiar with MFC programming already, you can begin the server tutorial based on the Scribble Step 6 files. See the tutorial for details.

- OLE Automation Server Tutorial, which creates an application that can be driven by other applications. The Autoclik tutorial begins in Chapter 20 of *Introducing Visual C++*.

The "Class Library Overview" of the *Class Library Reference* lists MFC classes by category, including OLE classes, with brief descriptions designed to help you locate the class you need.

Note The OLE documentation refers to embedded and linked items as "objects" and refers to types of items as "classes." To avoid confusion with C++ terminology, the Visual C++ *Class Library Reference* uses the term "item" to distinguish the OLE entity from the corresponding C++ object, and the term "type" to distinguish the OLE category from the C++ class.

In Chapter 6

In this chapter, you were introduced to the MFC OLE classes. Chapter 6 introduces the MFC database classes, which help you write applications to manipulate databases for which you have a 32-bit Open Database Connectivity (ODBC) driver.

C H A P T E R   6

Working with Databases

The database classes in the Microsoft Foundation Class Library (MFC) are a set of C++ classes that provide a high-level application programming interface (API) for access to databases from C++ and Microsoft Windows. Although you can use the database classes without some parts of the class library application framework, such as documents and views, in most cases you'll probably want to take advantage of the full class library.

The database classes add the following components to the class library:

- C++ database classes that provide a high-level API for accessing databases compatible with Open Database Connectivity (ODBC).

- Extensions to AppWizard and ClassWizard for creating application-specific database classes.

- Sample programs that illustrate use of the classes and the wizards.

- Online documentation that includes overview material, a tutorial, a set of programming articles, and a class reference.

Important To use the MFC database classes for targeting a Win32 platform (such as Windows NT) you must have the 32-bit ODBC driver for your data source. Visual C++ supplies a 32-bit ODBC driver for Microsoft SQL Server. Other drivers can be obtained from Microsoft and other vendors. Visual C++ provides a coupon for ordering the Microsoft ODBC Driver Fulfillment Kit (32-Bit). You should contact other driver vendors directly.

In this chapter, you'll find information on:

- Features of the database classes
- Similarity to the Microsoft Access and Microsoft Visual Basic data-access API
- The database classes and ODBC
- Requirements for using the database classes
- Installing the database classes

- Distributing your application
- Getting started with the database classes

Features of the Database Classes

The MFC database classes supply the following features:

- They are integrated with other parts of the Microsoft Foundation Class Library.
- They support form-based data-access applications via class **CRecordView**, which, like its base class, **CFormView**, is based on a dialog-template resource.
- They supply the record field exchange (RFX) mechanism for transferring data between a table in a data source and a **CRecordset** object, and between the "recordset" and a **CRecordView**.
- They require only a small part of the class library, so you can write applications without the class library's document/view architecture if you prefer.
- They provide a C++ database programming model very similar to the Basic-language data-manipulation models of Microsoft Access and Microsoft Visual Basic.
- They encapsulate much of the complexity of the ODBC API in a small set of C++ classes that provide a higher-level interface to ODBC.
- They allow you to call C-language ODBC API functions directly wherever the database classes don't meet your needs.

The database classes support data manipulation, such as selecting records from a table on a data source; adding, updating, and deleting records; scrolling through a recordset; and parameterizing a recordset with information obtained or calculated at run time. If you need data design language (DDL) functionality, you can work directly with SQL and the ODBC API.

The database classes do not yet provide functionality specific to Indexed Sequential Access Method (ISAM) databases. The version of ODBC that the database classes use does not directly support ISAM, but ODBC drivers exist for many popular ISAM databases. For more information, see the article "Recordset" in Part 2.

Note The availability of some features of the database classes depends on the availability of suitable 32-bit ODBC drivers. To use MFC "dynasets," your ODBC driver must support keyset-driven cursors. For more information, see the articles "Dynaset" and "ODBC" in Part 2.

Similarity to the Microsoft Access and Microsoft Visual Basic Data-Access API

The goal of the MFC database classes is to provide programmers a high-level C++ and Microsoft Windows API for accessing ODBC data sources. These high-level abstractions are the C++ equivalent of the Microsoft Access and Microsoft Visual Basic data-access objects, so the programming model is simple and familiar for programmers who have used either of those products but who want to work in C++.

For example, the database class **CRecordset** has member functions such as **MoveNext**, which are equivalent to the **MoveNext** method of a Dynaset in Microsoft Visual Basic or of a Recordset in Microsoft Access.

The default programming model for the database classes makes the key assumption that the programmer knows the structure of the database (its "schema") at design time and that the structure won't change in any way that would affect the application. A type-safe C++ class is then created to supply a high-performance way to access and manipulate data in that structure. The database classes don't directly support the ability to determine database schema information at run time, although they allow you to do so by calling the underlying SQL and ODBC API functions directly.

The Database Classes and ODBC

The MFC database classes are based on ODBC to ensure maximum interoperability. Normally, you won't need to call ODBC API functions directly (although you can if you need to). You need the 32-bit ODBC Driver Manager dynamic-link libraries (DLLs) and 32-bit ODBC drivers for your target database management systems (DBMSs) during development, and your end user needs the 32-bit Driver Manager DLLs and driver(s) for the DBMS(s) he or she uses.

Visual C++ incorporates many key ODBC components, including the required header files, libraries, and DLLs. It also supplies tools, including the ODBC Driver Manager, the ODBC Cursor Library, and the ODBC Administrator control panel application, which you use to configure data sources. Visual C++ also supplies a 32-bit ODBC driver for Microsoft SQL Server.

ODBC is an industry standard and a component of the Microsoft Windows Open Services Architecture (WOSA). For more information about ODBC and about obtaining the ODBC Driver Catalog, see the article "ODBC" in Part 2.

Figure 6.1 shows the relationships among an application, the database classes, ODBC, and a DBMS.

Figure 6.1   The Database Classes and ODBC

Requirements for Using the Database Classes

This product assumes you are familiar with C++. It will also be helpful if you are familiar with writing applications for Windows and know how to use the Microsoft Foundation Class Library. You should understand the structure of databases, but for most purposes, you won't need to know much about ODBC or Structured Query Language (SQL).

Installing the Database Classes

If you choose "MFC Libraries" when you run Setup to install Visual C++, Setup automatically installs the class library, including the database classes. Setup installs the ODBC Driver Manager and the 32-bit ODBC driver for Microsoft SQL Server. If you have the Microsoft SQL Server product, you can use it to work through the MFC database tutorial in *Introducing Visual C++*. If you don't have SQL Server, you'll need the DBMS you want to target along with the appropriate 32-bit ODBC driver for that DBMS. Setup also installs a tool called STDREG to help you configure a tutorial data source on any DBMS. For details, see Chapter 24, "Creating a Database Application," in *Introducing Visual C++*.

Visual C++ also includes the ODBC Software Development Kit (SDK), which gives you additional information and tools for writing and testing ODBC drivers.

> **Note** In addition to static link libraries, the class library supplies the database classes in DLL form. The release version is MFCD30.DLL. The debugging version of the DLL is MFCD30D.DLL. For more information about AFXDLL, see the articles "Library Versions" and "Dynamic-Link Libraries (DLLs)" in Part 2. Also see Technical Note 33 under MFC in Books Online.

Distributing Your Application

When you write an application with the database classes and distribute it to your customers, you may also need to distribute some components of the ODBC SDK—and possibly a Microsoft Foundation Class Library DLL, depending on how you write your application with the class library.

Distributable Microsoft Foundation Class Library Components

If you choose to write your application using the AFXDLL version of the Microsoft Foundation Class Library, you must distribute the files MFC30.DLL, MFCO30.DLL (for OLE), and MFCD30.DLL (for database) with your application.

Distributable ODBC Components

ODBC applications usually ship with an ODBC setup program, an ODBC administration control panel application, and possibly one or more ODBC drivers and related files. Each driver is designed to allow ODBC access to a specific DBMS.

For information about the ODBC components you can redistribute with your program, see "Redistributing ODBC Components to Your Customers" in the article "ODBC" in Part 2.

Getting Started with the Database Classes

The best place to begin reading about the database classes is the article "Database Overview" in Part 2. "Database Overview" introduces the classes and points to related articles about the concepts, components, and procedures of the database classes. These articles are presented in alphabetical order in Part 2. For information about how the articles are structured and how to get the most from them, see the first article, "Using the Encyclopedia."

For hands-on experience, see the database tutorial, which begins in Chapter 24 of *Introducing Visual C++*. The tutorial uses a student registration database, similar to one a college might use for maintaining student and course records (although simpler).

The class reference for the database classes is in the *Class Library Reference*. The "Class Library Overview" of the *Class Library Reference* lists MFC classes by category, with brief descriptions designed to help you locate the class you need.

In Chapter 7

Chapter 7 completes this overview of the Microsoft Foundation Class Library by explaining the "general-purpose" classes and facilities of MFC. These classes, global functions, and macros help you diagnose problems with your application, manage file input/output, handle exceptional conditions, use collection classes, and more.

C H A P T E R   7

Using the General-Purpose Classes

This chapter summarizes the use of the general-purpose classes in the Microsoft Foundation Class Library (MFC). These classes provide useful services, including:

- Services provided by deriving your classes from class **CObject**
- File input/output with class **CFile**
- Collection classes for storing aggregate data
- Strings
- Time and date
- Diagnostic services
- Exception handling

CObject Services

The **CObject** base class provides the following services to objects of its derived classes:

- Object diagnostics
- Run-time class information
- Object persistence

Some of these services are available only if you use certain macros in derived class declarations and implementations. To make use of the services listed above and explained in the following sections, you should seriously consider deriving most of your nontrivial classes from **CObject**. Many of the MFC classes are so derived, including almost all of the application architecture classes that make up the framework. (The various categories of classes that make up the framework are listed in the MFC hierarchy diagrams and in the "Class Library Overview" in the *Class Library Reference*.)

Object Diagnostics

MFC provides many diagnostic features. Some object diagnostics include diagnostic dump context and supplied by the **CObject** class. For global diagnostic features, see "Memory Diagnostics" on page 117.

Diagnostic Dump Context

The **CDumpContext** class works in conjunction with the **Dump** member function of the **CObject** class to provide formatted diagnostic printing of internal object data. **CDumpContext** provides an insertion (**<<**) operator that accepts, among other types, **CObject** pointers; standard types, such as **BYTE** and **WORD**; and **CString** and **CTime** objects.

A predefined **CDumpContext** object, **afxDump**, is available in the Debug version of the Microsoft Foundation classes (**#define_DEBUG** is required in your source code). The **afxDump** object allows you to send **CDumpContext** information to the debugger output window or to a debug terminal. For more information about **afxDump**, see "Macros and Globals" in the *Class Library Reference*, and Technical Note 12 under MFC in Books Online.

Object Validity Checking

You override the base class **AssertValid** member function in your derived class to perform a specific test of your object's internal consistency. Call the **ASSERT_VALID** macro, passing it a pointer to any **CObject**, to call that object's AssertValid function. The implementation of an AssertValid function usually includes calls to the **ASSERT** macro. For more information about **AssertValid**, see in the article "Diagnostics: Detecting Memory Leaks" in Part 2.

Run-Time Class Information

MFC offers the developer some optional features that make it possible to do run-time type checking. If you derive a class from **CObject** and include one of three macros (**IMPLEMENT_DYNAMIC**, **IMPLEMENT_DYNCREATE**, or **IMPLEMENT_SERIAL**), you can use member functions to:

- Access the class name at run time.
- Safely cast a generic **CObject** pointer to a derived class pointer.

Run-time class information is particularly valuable in the Debug environment because it can be used to detect incorrect casts and to produce object dumps with class names included. For more information, see the article "CObject Class: Accessing Run-Time Class Information" in Part 2.

Note To access run-time type information, you must use the **DECLARE_DYNAMIC**, **DECLARE_DYNCREATE**, or **DECLARE_SERIAL** macro in your class declaration, and you must use the corresponding **IMPLEMENT_DYNAMIC**, **IMPLEMENT_DYNCREATE**, or **IMPLEMENT_SERIAL** macro in your class implementation.

Run-time class information is, of course, available in the Release environment. During serialization, the run-time class information is used to store the object's type with the object data.

Run-time class testing is not meant to be a substitute for using virtual functions added in a common base class. Use the run-time type information only when virtual functions are not appropriate.

Object Persistence

Class **CObject**, in conjunction with class **CArchive**, supports "object persistence" through a process called serialization. Object persistence allows you to save a complex network of objects in a permanent binary form (usually disk storage) that persists after those objects are deleted from memory. Later you can load the objects from persistent storage and reconstruct them in memory. Loading and saving serializable data is mediated by an "archive" object of class **CArchive**.

To create your own serializable **CObject**-derived class, you must use the **DECLARE_SERIAL** macro in the class declaration, and you must use the corresponding **IMPLEMENT_SERIAL** macro in the class implementation. If you have added new data members in your derived class, you must override the base class'**Serialize** member function to store object data to the archive object and load object data from it. Once you have a serializable class, you can serialize objects of that class to and from a file via a **CArchive** object.

A **CArchive** object provides a type-safe buffering mechanism for writing or reading serializable objects to or from a **CFile** object. Usually the **CFile** object represents a disk file; however, it can be also be a memory file (**CMemFile** object), perhaps representing the Clipboard. A given **CArchive** object either stores (writes, serializes) data or loads (reads, deserializes) data, but never both. Thus two successively created **CArchive** objects are required to serialize data to a file and then deserialize it back from the file. The life of a **CArchive** object is limited to one pass—either writing an object to a file or reading an object from a file.

When storing an object to a file, an archive attaches the **CRuntimeClass** name to the object. Then, when another archive loads the object from a file, the archive uses the **CRuntimeClass** name of the object to dynamically reconstruct the object in memory. A given object may be referenced more than once as it is written to the file by the storing archive. The loading archive, however, will reconstruct the object only once. The details about how an archive attaches **CRuntimeClass** information to objects and reconstructs objects, taking into account possible multiple references, are described in Technical Note 2 under MFC in Books Online.

As you serialize data to an archive, the archive accumulates the data until its buffer is full. When the buffer is full, the archive then writes its buffer to the **CFile** object pointed to by the **CArchive** object. Similarly, as you read data from an archive, the archive reads data from the file to its buffer, and then from the buffer to your deserialized object. This buffering reduces the number of times a hard disk is physically read, thus improving your application's performance.

There are two ways to create a **CArchive** object. The most common way, and the easiest, is to let the framework create one for your document on behalf of the Save, Save As, and Open commands on the File menu. The other way is to explicitly create the **CArchive** object yourself.

To let the framework create the **CArchive** object for your document, simply implement the document's Serialize function, which writes and reads to and from the archive. You also have to implement Serialize for any **CObject**-derived objects that the document's Serialize function in turn serializes directly or indirectly.

There are other occasions besides serializing a document via the framework when you may need a **CArchive** object. For example, you might want to serialize data to and from the Clipboard, represented by a **CMemFile** object. Or, you might want to develop a user interface for saving files that is different from the one offered by the framework. In this case, you can explicitly create a **CArchive** object. You do this the same way the framework does. For more detailed information, see the articles "Files" and "Serialization (Object Persistence)" in Part 2.

The File Classes

The **CFile** family of classes provides a C++ programming interface to files. The **CFile** class itself gives access to low-level binary files, and the **CStdioFile** class gives access to buffered "standard I/O" files. **CStdioFile** files are often processed in "text mode," which means that newline characters are converted to carriage return–linefeed pairs on output.

CMemFile supports "in-memory files." The files behave like disk files except that bytes are stored in RAM. An in-memory file is a useful means of transferring raw bytes or serialized objects between independent processes.

Because **CFile** is the base class for all file classes, it provides a polymorphic programming interface. If a **CStdioFile** file is opened, for example, its object pointer can be used by the virtual **Read** and **Write** member functions defined for the **CFile** class. The **CDumpContext** and **CArchive** classes, described previously, depend on the **CFile** class for input and output. For more information, see the article "Files" in Part 2.

The Collection Classes

MFC contains a number of ready-to-use lists, arrays, and maps that are referred to as "collection classes." A collection is a very useful programming idiom for holding and processing groups of class objects or groups of standard types. A collection object appears as a single object. Class member functions can operate on all elements of the collection.

MFC supplies two kinds of collection classes:

- Collection templates
- Nontemplate collections

The collection template classes are based on C++ templates, but the original collection classes released with MFC version 1.0—not based on templates—are still available.

Most collections can be archived or sent to a dump context. The **Dump** and **Serialize** member functions for **CObject** pointer collections call the corresponding functions for each of their elements. Some collections cannot be archived—for example, pointer collections.

Note   The collection classes **CObArray**, **CObList**, **CMapStringToOb**, and **CMapWordToOb** accept **CObject** pointer elements and thus are useful for storing collections of objects of **CObject**-derived classes. If such a collection is archived or sent to a diagnostic dump context, then the element objects are automatically archived or dumped as well. For more about collection classes, including details about which classes can be serialized and dumped, see the article "Collections: Choosing a Collection Class" in Part 2.

When you program with the application framework, the collection classes will be especially useful for implementing data structures in your document class. For an example, see the document implementation in the Scribble tutorial contained in *Introducing Visual C++*.

Lists

In addition to "list" class templates, MFC supplies predefined list classes for **CString** objects, **CObject** pointers, and void pointers. A list is an ordered grouping of elements. New elements can be added at the head or tail of the list, or before or after a specified element. The list can be traversed in forward or reverse sequence, and elements can be retrieved or removed during the traversal.

Arrays

In addition to "array" class templates, MFC supplies predefined array classes for bytes, words, doublewords, **CString** objects, **CObject** pointers, and void pointers. An array implemented this way is a dynamically sized grouping of elements that is directly accessible through a zero-based integer subscript. The subscript ([ ]) operator can be used to set or retrieve array elements. If an element above the current array bound is to be set, you can specify whether the array is to grow automatically. When growing is not required, array collection access is as fast as standard C array access.

Maps

A "map" is a dictionary that maps keys to values. In addition to map class templates, predefined map classes support **CString** objects, words, **CObject** pointers, and void pointers. Consider the **CMapWordToOb** class as an example. A **WORD** variable is used as a key to find the corresponding **CObject** pointer. Duplicate key values are not allowed. A key-pointer pair can be inserted only if the key is not already contained in the map. Key lookups are fast because they rely on a hashing technique.

The CString Class

The **CString** class supports dynamic character strings. **CString** objects can grow and shrink automatically, and they can be serialized. Member functions and overloaded operators add Basic-like string-processing capability. These features make **CString** objects easier to use than C-style fixed-length character arrays. Conversion functions allow **CString** objects to be used interchangeably with C-style strings. Thus a **CString** object can be passed to a function that expects a pointer to a constant string (**const char***) parameter.

CString is enabled for both multibyte character sets (MBCS, also known as double-byte character sets, DBCS) and Unicode. **CString** now also supplies functionality similar to **sprintf** with the **Format** member function and supports reducing string storage overhead with the **FreeExtra** member function.

Note   Class **CString** is not derived from class **CObject**.

Like other Microsoft Foundation classes, the **CString** class allocates memory on the heap. You must be sure that **CString** destructors are called at appropriate times to free unneeded memory. There is no automatic "garbage collection" as there is in Basic. For more information about **CString**, see the *Class Library Reference* and the article "Strings" in Part 2.

The CTime and CTimeSpan Classes

The **CTime** class encapsulates the run-time **time_t** data type. Thus it represents absolute time values in the range 1970 to 2036, approximately. There are member functions that convert a time value to years, months, days, hours, minutes, and seconds. The class has overloaded insertion and extraction operators for archiving and for diagnostic dumping. For Win32 support, there are also **CTime** constructors based on the Win32 **SYSTEMTIME** and **FILETIME** structures. The **SYSTEMTIME**-based constructor is the most convenient to use with Win32.

The **CTimeSpan** class extends **time_t** by representing relative time values. When one **CTime** object is subtracted from another one, the result is a **CTimeSpan** object. A **CTimeSpan** object can be added to or subtracted from a **CTime** object. A **CTimeSpan** value is limited to the range of ± 68 years, approximately. For more information about **CTime** and **CTimeSpan**, see the *Class Library Reference* and the article "Date and Time" in Part 2.

Note   Classes **CTime** and **CTimeSpan** are not derived from class **CObject**.

Diagnostic Services

The Microsoft Foundation Class Library provides diagnostic services that make it easier to debug your programs. These services include macros and global functions that allow you to trace your program's memory allocations, dump the contents of objects during run time, and print debugging messages during run time. Most of these services require the Debug version of the library and thus should not be used in released applications. For a detailed description of the functions and macros available, see the article "Diagnostics" in Part 2 and the overview of "Macros and Globals" in the *Class Library Reference*.

Memory Diagnostics

Many applications use the C++ **new** operator to allocate memory on the heap. MFC provides a special Debug version of **new** that inserts extra control bytes in allocated memory blocks. These control bytes, together with the run-time class information that results from **CObject** derivation, allow you to analyze memory-allocation statistics and detect memory-block bounds violations. A memory dump can include the source filename and the line number of the allocated memory and, in the case of objects from **CObject**-derived classes, the name of the class and the output from its **Dump** function. For more information, see "Memory Diagnostics" in the article "Diagnostics: Detecting Memory Leaks" in Part 2.

> **Tip** You can activate the debug version of **new** on a per-CPP file basis by #defining **DEBUG_NEW**.

Diagnostic Output

Many programmers want diagnostic output statements in their programs, particularly during the early stages of development. The **TRACE** statement acts like **printf** except that the **TRACE** code is not generated by the compiler with the Release version of the library. In the Windows environment, debugging output goes to the debugger if it is present.

> **Important** For important information on using **TRACE**, see the "Macros and Globals" section of the *Class Library Reference* and Technical Note 7 under MFC in Books Online.

You can use the **afxDump** dump context object for stream-style dumping of standard types as well as MFC objects. If you use **afxDump**, be sure to bracket references with **#ifdef _DEBUG** and **#endif** statements. For more information on **afxDump**, see the article "Diagnostics: Dumping Object Contents" in Part 2.

Assertions

In the Debug environment, the **ASSERT** macro evaluates a specified condition. If the condition is false, the macro displays a message in a message box that gives the source filename and the line number and then terminates the program. In the Release environment, the **ASSERT** statement has no effect.

VERIFY, a companion macro, evaluates the condition in both the Debug and Release environments. It prints and terminates only in the Debug environment.

Classes derived from **CObject**, directly or indirectly, can also override the **AssertValid** member function to test the internal validity of objects of the class. For an example, see "Object Validity Checking" on page 112.

Exception Handling

MFC uses C++ exceptions as proposed by the ANSI C++ standard. The MFC exception macros used in previous versions of MFC are provided for backward compatibility with existing MFC applications. You can choose to use either C++ exceptions or the original MFC exception mechanism. These macros allow you to deal with abnormal conditions that are outside the program's control. Abnormal conditions include low memory, I/O errors, and attempted use of an unsupported feature. They do not include programming errors or normally expected conditions such as an end-of-file condition. In general, you can consider an uncaught exception to be a bug that remains in your program after shipping.

In most cases, you should use the C++ exception mechanism rather than MFC's original macro-based mechanism. If you are programming for Windows NT, you should use C++ exceptions instead of Windows NT structured exceptions (SEH).

Exception handling in the Microsoft Foundation classes relies on "exception objects" and uses standard C++ exceptions. The process starts with the interruption of normal program execution in response to a **throw** expression. Execution resumes at the appropriate **catch** statement leading into code that presumably deals with the abnormal condition. Exception objects can include standard C++ data types as well as objects of classes derived from **CException**. **CException**-based exception objects differentiate the various kinds of exceptions and are used for communication.

Note   MFC now supports C++ exceptions and the **try**, **catch**, and **throw** keywords. For more information, see the article "Exceptions" in Part 2.

This exception-handling scheme eliminates the need for extensive error testing after every library function call. If, for example, you enclose your entire program in an exception-handling block, then you don't have to test for low memory after each statement that contains the **new** operator.

If you don't provide **try** and **catch** exception-processing code in your classes, exceptions will be caught in the Microsoft Foundation code. This results in termination of the program through the global function **AfxTerminate**, which normally calls the run-time function **abort**. However, if you use the **AfxSetTerminate** function, the effect of **AfxTerminate** is changed. When programming for Windows, it is important to remember that exceptions cannot cross the boundary of a "callback." In other words, if an exception occurs within the scope of a message or command handler, it must be caught there, before the next message is processed. If you do not catch an exception, the **CWinApp** member function **ProcessWndProcException** is called as a last resort. This function displays an error message and then continues processing. You can customize the default handling of uncaught exceptions by overriding **CWinApp::ProcessWndProcException**.

For exception-processing examples and a more detailed explanation of error categories, see the article "Exceptions" in Part 2. For a detailed description of the MFC-specific functions and macros available, see the "Macros and Globals" section in the *Class Library Reference*. For a general discussion of C++ exception handling, see Chapter 7, "C++ Exception Handling," in *Programming Techniques*.

In Part 2

This concludes the overview of the Microsoft Foundation Class Library. Part 2 contains programming articles in an "enyclopedia" format, covering an expanding body of topics in MFC programming. For an introduction to the contents of Part 2 and to its format, see the first article, "Using the Encyclopedia."

PART 2

MFC Encyclopedia

Main Articles:

Using the Encyclopedia

The programming articles in Part 2 show you how to accomplish specific tasks and explain important topics in more detail than is possible in the reference or the tutorial. The articles are available both online and in print. Online, they are linked with the reference and with each other, to make browsing easy and to let you find your own path through the topics. In print, the articles are cross-referenced in the index.

This article explains:

- How the articles are structured
- What the articles contain
- Where to start

How the Articles Are Structured

The enyclopedia in Part 2 is hierarchical, with the following structure:

- At the top level, there are main articles arranged in alphabetical order.
- Below most of the main articles are clusters of related "child" articles. Child articles are arranged logically—following their main article—rather than alphabetically.

The title of each child article begins with the name of its parent main article so you can always find your way back. For example, the article "ClassWizard: OLE Support" is a child article of a main "ClassWizard" article.

Articles also have the following helpful navigation features:

- Each main article usually ends with a list of its child articles.
- Online, these are "jumps" for easy access to the articles.
- Most articles contain numerous cross-references to other articles and to related information in the reference.
- Books Online provides scrollbars and browse buttons (<< and >>) so you can easily read an article or group of articles straight through.

What the Articles Contain

Article content is of two types:

- Architectural information
- Procedural information

Architectural articles explain how some part of the class library works. Each article covers a conceptual topic, such as "how documents and views are created," "how

OLE servers and containers interact," or "how database updates work." Conceptual articles give you a foundation as you work out your own solution using the many facilities of the Microsoft Foundation Class Library.

Procedural articles detail the steps for performing a task. Each article explains starting conditions, steps to follow, and the results you can expect at the end. Procedural articles mark out the "beaten path"—the common tasks that most programmers will need to perform. Most such tasks are of a beginning or intermediate level of difficulty.

Where to Start

If you are primarily interested in OLE topics, begin with the article titled "OLE Overview." If you are primarily interested in database topics, begin with the article titled "Database Overview." These articles are listed alphabetically, under "O" and "D" respectively. For articles about MFC, 32-bit programming, and porting to 32 bit, see the article "MFC." For other MFC programming topics, look up the topic you are interested in. For example, if you are interested in how to use ClassWizard, begin with the article titled "ClassWizard."

Activation

This article explains the role of "activation" in the visual editing of OLE items. After a user has embedded a new OLE item in a container application, it may need to be modified. To do this, the user double-clicks the item, which causes the menus and toolbars in the current frame window to change to reflect those belonging to the server application that created this item. This behavior, known as "in-place activation," allows the user to edit any embedded item in a compound document without leaving the container document's window.

It is also possible to edit embedded OLE items in a separate window. This will happen if either the container or server application does not support in-place activation. In this case, when the user double-clicks an embedded item, the server application is launched in a separate window and the embedded item appears as its own document. The user edits the item in this window. When editing is complete, the user closes the server application and returns to the container application.

As an alternative, the user can choose "open editing" with the *<object>* Open command on the Edit menu. This opens the object in a separate window.

Note Editing embedded items in a separate window is standard behavior in version 1 of OLE, and some OLE applications may support only this style of editing.

In-place activation promotes a "document-centric" approach to document creation. The user can treat a compound document as a single entity, working on it without switching between applications. However, in-place activation is used only for embedded items, not for linked items: they must be edited in a separate window. This is because a linked item is actually stored in a different document. Editing a linked item in a separate window reminds the user that the item is owned by another document.

See Also   Articles: "Containers," "Servers"

Activation: Verbs

This article explains the role primary and secondary verbs play in OLE activation.

Usually, double-clicking an embedded item allows the user to edit it. However, certain items don't behave this way. For example, double-clicking an item created with the Sound Recorder application does not open the server in a separate window; instead, it plays the sound.

The reason for this behavior difference is that Sound Recorder items have a different "primary verb." The primary verb is the action performed when the user double-clicks an OLE item. For most types of OLE items, the primary verb is Edit, which launches the server that created the item. For some types of items, such as Sound Recorder items, the primary verb is Play.

Many types of OLE items support only one verb, and Edit is the most common one. However, some types of items support multiple verbs. For example, Sound Recorder items support Edit as a secondary verb.

Another verb used frequently is Open. The Open verb is identical to Edit, except the server application is launched in a separate window. This verb should be used when either the container application or the server application does not support in-place activation.

Any verbs other than the primary verb must be invoked through a submenu command when the item is selected. This submenu contains all the verbs supported by the item and is usually reached by the *typename* Object command on the Edit menu. For information on the *typename* Object command, see the article "Menus and Resources: Container Additions."

The verbs a server application supports are listed in the Windows registration database. If your server application is written with the Microsoft Foundation Class Library, it will automatically register all verbs when the server is started. If not, you should register them during the server application's initialization phase. For more information, see the article "Registration."

See Also   Articles: "Activation," "Containers," "Servers"

Administrator, ODBC

See the articles "Data Source: Managing Connections" and "ODBC Administrator."

Application Framework

The Microsoft Foundation Class Library (MFC). For more information, see the article "MFC."

AppWizard

AppWizard lets you configure the skeleton of a new C++ application that uses the Microsoft Foundation Class Library (MFC).

To run AppWizard, choose the New command from the File menu in Visual C++. In the New dialog box, select the file type "Project." In the New Project dialog box, choose MFC AppWizard (exe) in the Project-type drop-down list. (If you're building an MFC extension DLL, choose MFC AppWizard (dll) instead.)

AppWizard Features

AppWizard lets you configure the skeleton application with the following options:

- Specify a Visual C++ project name and directory.

New Feature
- Specify an application type: single document interface (SDI), multiple document interface (MDI), or dialog-based. The new dialog-based option lets you easily use a dialog box as your application's user interface.

- Specify database options. You can:

  - Specify minimal support by including the correct header files and link libraries, or you can derive your view class from **CRecordView** for a form-based application.

  - Provide a user interface for opening and saving disk files in addition to accessing a database from the same application.

  - Specify a data source to connect to and which table and columns you want to access.

- Specify Object Linking and Embedding (OLE) options: your application can be a container, a mini-server, a full server, or both a container and a server, and it can have OLE Automation support.

- Specify whether you want:

New Feature
  - A toolbar or a status bar. By default, the toolbar is an MFC "dockable" toolbar, a new feature in MFC version 3.0.

  - An About dialog box (in dialog-based applications).

  - Support for printing and print preview or context-sensitive help.

New Feature
  - Support for 3D controls.

  - Helpful source-file comments to guide where you add your own code.

  - A Visual C++ makefile or an external makefile that you can edit directly.

New Feature
- Specify which styles and captions you want for the main frame and child window.

New Feature
- Specify whether you want splitter window support.

New Feature
- Specify the number of files listed in the most-recently-used (MRU) file list on the File menu.

- Specify whether you want to link with the MFC libraries statically or dynamically. Linking dynamically with AFXDLL (MFC in a DLL) reduces the size of your executable file and lets several applications share a single copy of MFC at run time. By default, AppWizard provides the dynamic linking support.

- Specify the names of your application's classes and what class you derive your view class from.

For a description of the most commonly used AppWizard features, see Chapter 1 in the *Visual C++ User's Guide*.

The following articles explain other aspects of using AppWizard, including database and OLE support:

- AppWizard: Files Created
- AppWizard: Database Support
- AppWizard: OLE Support

AppWizard: Files Created

This article describes the files that AppWizard creates for you, depending on which options you've chosen.

The article first describes the core files common to all AppWizard-created applications and then describes files that are added when you select toolbar and Help support.

Tip   You'll undoubtedly want to examine the source code files you created. To orient you, AppWizard also creates a text file, README.TXT, in your new application directory. This file explains the contents and uses of the other new files created by AppWizard for *your* application, reflecting *your* option choices.

Standard AppWizard Files

The following categories of standard files created by AppWizard are described in this article:

- Project files and makefiles
- Application source and header files
- Resource files
- Precompiled header files
- Context-sensitive help files
- AppWizard files added by options

Project Files and Makefiles

PRJNAME.MAK

This is the project file for your MFC project. It is also an NMAKE-compatible file. If you select the External makefile option, you can edit the makefile manually, but you can't take advantage of many Visual C++ project editing features.

PRJNAME.CLW

This file contains information used by ClassWizard to edit existing classes or add new classes. ClassWizard also uses this file to store information needed to create and edit message maps and dialog data maps, and to create prototype member functions.

Application Source and Header Files

Depending on the type of application—single document, multiple document, or dialog-based—AppWizard creates some of the following application source and header files:

PRJNAME.H

This is the main include file for the application. It contains all global symbols and **#include** directives for other header files.

PRJNAME.CPP

This file is the main application source file. It creates one object of the class `CPrjnameApp` (which is derived from **CWinApp**) and overrides the **InitInstance** member function.

`CPrjnameApp::InitInstance` does several things. It registers document templates, which serve as a connection between documents and views, creates a main frame window, and creates an empty document (or opens a document if one is specified as a command-line argument to the application).

IPFRAME.CPP, IPFRAME.H

These files are created if the Mini-Server or Full-Server option is selected in AppWizard's OLE Options page (step 3 of 6). The files derive and implement the in-place frame window class, named **CInPlaceFrame**, used when the server is in-place activated by an OLE container application.

MAINFRM.CPP, MAINFRM.H

These files derive the **CMainFrame** class from either **CFrameWnd** (for SDI applications) or **CMDIFrameWnd** (for MDI applications). The **CMainFrame** class handles the creation of toolbar buttons and the status bar, if the corresponding options are selected in AppWizard's Application Options page (step 4 of 6). The MAINFRM.CPP file also contains the array of object IDs— called **buttons**—for the default toolbar buttons provided with an MFC application.

*PRJNA*DLG.CPP, *PRJNA*DLG.H

These files are created if you choose a dialog-based application. The files derive and implement the dialog class, named `CPrjnameDlg`, and include skeleton member functions to initialize a dialog and perform dialog data exchange (DDX). Your About dialog class is also placed in these files instead of in *PRJNAME*.CPP.

*PRJNA*DOC.CPP, *PRJNA*DOC.H

These files derive and implement the document class, named `CPrjnameDoc`, and include skeleton member functions to initialize a document, serialize (save and load) a document, and implement debugging diagnostics.

*PRJNA*VW.CPP, *PRJNA*VW.H

These files derive and implement the view class, named `CPrjnameView`, that is used to display and print the document data. The `CPrjnameView` class is derived from **CEditView**, **CFormView**, **CRecordView**, **CScrollView**, or **CView** and has skeleton member functions to draw the view and implement debugging diagnostics. If you have enabled support for printing, message-map entries are added for print, print setup, and print preview command messages. These entries call the corresponding member functions in the base view class.

Resource Files

AppWizard creates a number of resource-related files. If the project is for a DLL, the wizard also creates a .DEF file, which is available for your list of exports.

PRJNAME.RC, RESOURCE.H

This is the resource file for the project and its header file. The resource file contains the default menu definition and accelerator and string tables for a generic MFC·application. It also specifies a default About box and an icon file (RES*PRJNAME*.ICO). The resource file includes the file AFXRES.RC for standard Microsoft Foundation class resources. If toolbar support has been specified as an option, it also specifies the toolbar bitmap file (RES\\TOOLBAR.BMP).

RES*PRJNAME*.ICO

This is the icon file for the generic MFC application. This icon appears when the application is minimized and is also used in the About box.

RES\\TOOLBAR.BMP

This bitmap file is used to create tiled images for the toolbar. The initial toolbar and status bar are constructed in the **CMainFrame** class.

Precompiled Header Files

STDAFX.CPP, STDAFX.H

These files are used to build a precompiled header file *PRJNAME*.PCH and a precompiled types file STDAFX.OBJ.

Context-Sensitive Help Files

MAKEHELP.BAT

This batch file can be used to build the Help file for your application.

PRJNAME.HPJ

This is the Help project file used by the help compiler to create your application's help file.

HLP\\AFXCORE.RTF

This is the template help file for document-based (MDI/SDI) applications.

HLP\\AFXPRINT.RTF

This file, created if printing support is selected (which it is by default), describes the printing commands and dialog boxes.

Other .RTF files are created if you choose OLE or database options. See README.TXT in your project directory for a description of these files.

AppWizard Files Added by Options

Most of the options you can choose in AppWizard use the standard files to implement their features. This section describes additional nonstandard files created to support certain options.

Note For information about the files created when you choose database options, see the article "AppWizard: Database Source Files and Resources." For information about the files created when you choose OLE options, see the article describing the option. For example, for files related to an OLE server application, see the articles on OLE servers.

CHILDFRM.H/.CPP

These files are created only if you have chosen an MDI application and you either chose splitter window support or you chose any of the nondefault child frame-window styles. The files implement a class called CChildFrame, derived from **CMDIChildWnd**. CChildFrame is analogous to CMainFrame: AppWizard creates these classes because you must, under the appropriate circumstances, derive your own classes from **CFrameWnd** and **CMDIChildWnd**.

PRJNAME.ODL

This file is created if you have selected OLE Automation support. You can use this file as input to the Make Type Library utility, which creates a corresponding type library (.TLB) file.

PRJNAME.REG

This file is created in two cases. (1) You have selected any OLE server option or OLE Automation option. (2) You have selected a document file extension (one of the options available in the Advanced Options dialog box). The file demonstrates the kind of registration settings the framework will set for you.

RES\ITOOLBAR.BMP

This file is created only if you have chosen any OLE server support and have also chosen the Dockable Toolbar option. The file contains tiled images for the toolbar when the server application is in-place activated inside a container application. The file is similar to the standard RES\TOOLBAR.BMP except that many nonserver commands are removed.

See Also   Article: "AppWizard: Database Source Files and Resources"

AppWizard: Database Support

When you set options for your new skeleton application in AppWizard, you can specify database options in addition to the general AppWizard options. You can set database options from AppWizard's Database Options page (step 2 of 6) for a document-based application (MDI/SDI). This article explains the database options.

Figure 1 shows the AppWizard Database options page.

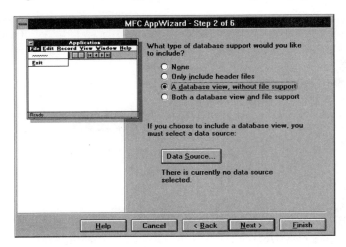

Figure 1.   AppWizard's Database Options

Important   You must have the Microsoft Open Database Connectivity (ODBC) software installed on your machine with at least one configured data source and the appropriate ODBC driver for that data source in order to use the database classes. *Visual C++* Setup installs the ODBC software. The Scribble tutorial in *Introducing Visual C++* describes how to configure a tutorial data source.

If you want database support in your application, use the following procedure. The procedure assumes you have read the introductory material on AppWizard in Chapter 1 in the *Visual C++ User's Guide*.

▶   **To create an application with database support**

1. Create an MFC AppWizard project.

Tip   You might want to consider creating a single document interface (SDI) application. A data-entry application, for example, probably doesn't require more than one view of the database.

---

2. On AppWizard's Database Options page (step 2 of 6), choose your database support option. The options are described in the article "AppWizard: Database Options."

3. If you chose either "A database view, without file support" or "Both a database view and file support" in step 2 of this procedure, a Data Source button is enabled. Choose Data Source.

   –Or–

   If you chose "Only include header files," choose Next and continue with step 6 of this procedure. You will have to create your recordset classes later with ClassWizard.

4. In the Data Sources dialog box, double-click the name of a data source already registered on your machine through the ODBC Administrator tool described in the article "ODBC Administrator."

5. In the Select a Table dialog box, double-click the name of a table in the data source whose columns you want to bind to your recordset.

   For some ODBC drivers, queries can be used as the source, but the wizards don't detect this.

6. Choose Next and complete your nondatabase AppWizard selections. When you finish, choose the Finish button, then OK.

   AppWizard creates files for your project.

AppWizard: Database Options

This article describes the MFC database options available in AppWizard. These options include:

- None
- Only include header files
- A database view, without file support
- Both a database view and file support

A record view—derived from class **CRecordView**—is a form view, based on a dialog template resource, that uses dialog data exchange (DDX) to exchange data between the view's controls and a **CRecordset**-derived object. You can map the form's controls to data members of a recordset. For more information about record views, see the article "Record Views." For more information about recordsets, see the article "Recordset."

No Database Support

AppWizard defaults to this option ("None" in the AppWizard dialog box) and adds no database support to your application.

Only Include Header Files

Choose this option for the minimum database support. AppWizard adds an **#include** directive for the header file that defines the database classes. The file AFXDB.H is included in STDAFX.H. With this support, you can use any of the database classes, related macros and global functions, and other items defined in AFXDB.H. AppWizard creates no database-related classes for you; you can create what you need later with ClassWizard.

In addition to the **#include** directive, AppWizard causes your application to link with the necessary libraries: ODBC32.LIB and, if you selected the "Use MFC in a shared dll" option (which AppWizard provides as the default), also MFCD30.LIB or MFCD30D.LIB.

A Database View, Without File Support

Choose this option when you want an application with the following characteristics:

- A view class derived from **CRecordView** rather than **CView**.

  This view class makes your application form-based. AppWizard creates an empty dialog template resource to which you must later add dialog controls with the Visual C++ dialog editor.

- A class derived from **CRecordset**.

  The **CRecordView**-derived class contains a pointer to a recordset object based on this class. Record view controls are mapped to recordset field data members via dialog data exchange (DDX).

- No disk-file user interface and serialization.

  A database application usually manages data record-by-record, interacting with the database, rather than managing whole data files.

- No document-related File-menu commands.

  This option also creates a menu resource whose File menu lacks document-related commands: New, Open, Save, and Save As. Without serialization, you probably don't need these commands.

Note Choosing this option makes the application single document interface (SDI). Choosing file support allows either SDI or MDI (multiple document interface).

This option creates a **CDocument**-derived class. In general, you'll use this class to store a **CRecordset** object, or a pointer to one. For more information on how to use this document class, see the article "MFC: Using Database Classes Without Documents and Views." The article discusses various document/view configurations, including applications with no document or view.

For more information about the files and resources AppWizard creates under this option, see the article "AppWizard: Database Source Files and Resources."

Both a Database View and File Support

Choose this option when you want an application with the following characteristics:

- A view class derived from **CRecordView** rather than **CView**.

  This view class makes your application form-based. AppWizard creates an empty dialog template resource to which you must later add dialog controls with the Visual C++ dialog editor.

- A class derived from **CRecordset**.

  The **CRecordView**-derived class contains a pointer to a recordset object based on this class. Record view controls are mapped to recordset field data members via dialog data exchange (DDX).

- A disk-file interface in addition to a record view on the database.

  This application opens a disk file in addition to a database. The disk file might store, for example, "style sheet" information, so the user can configure, save, and quickly restore alternative views of the database.

The document class that AppWizard creates under this option supports serialization, and the application includes support for document-related commands on the File menu: New, Open, Save, and Save As. For more information on how to use this document class, see the article "MFC: Using Database Classes Without Documents and Views."

Note For the last two options, AppWizard binds all columns of the table you select to the recordset. If you don't want all the columns, you can remove some of them later with ClassWizard. See the article "ClassWizard: Binding Recordset Fields to Table Columns."

For more details about using AppWizard, see Chapter 1 in the *Visual C++ User's Guide*.

The following article explains the files and resources that AppWizard creates, depending on the database options you select:

- AppWizard: Database Source Files and Resources

See Also   Article: "ClassWizard"

AppWizard: Database Source Files and Resources

This article explains:

- The database-related classes and files that AppWizard creates.
- The resources that AppWizard creates.

For information about the files and resources that AppWizard creates besides those for database options, see the article "AppWizard: Files Created."

Database Classes and Files

The classes and files that AppWizard creates depend on which option you choose. For details on the database options, see the article "AppWizard: Database Options."

If you choose the "None" or "Only include header files" option, AppWizard creates no special classes or files for database support.

If you choose the option "A database view, without file support" or the option "Both a database view and file support," AppWizard creates the following classes and files:

Classes Produced

AppWizard creates application, frame-window, document, and view classes. The view class is derived from **CRecordView**. It also creates a **CRecordset**-derived class associated with the record view class.

Class Names

AppWizard names the record view class and its associated recordset class as follows:

Record View Class Name

AppWizard names the record view class based on the name of your Visual C++ project, denoted here by *Prjname*. This name has the form "C*Prjname*View". If you change the default class name offered, the class is given the name you specify.

Recordset Class Name

The recordset class is named "C*Prjname*Set" or the base name you gave for the project with "Set" appended. By default, the name ends in "Set", but you can change the default name offered.

Filenames

As with other files created by AppWizard, the filenames for the record view class are based on the name of your Visual C++ project. AppWizard writes the view class in files *PRJNAME*VIEW.H/.CPP. If *prjname* has at least five characters, the first five characters are used, and the suffix is "VW" instead of "VIEW". The wizard writes the recordset class in files *PRJNAME*SET.H/.CPP. By default, the filenames end in "Set", preceded by up to five characters of *prjname*, but you can change the filenames.

Database Resources

If you choose the "A database view, without file support" or "Both a database view and file support" option, AppWizard creates not only the classes described above under "Database Classes and Files," but also the following resources:

- A dialog template resource whose resource ID is **IDD_*PRJNAME*_FORM**, where *PRJNAME* is based on your project name.

- A menu resource.

  The resource includes commands for moving from record to record in the record view. AppWizard also creates command-handler functions and user-interface update handlers in the **CRecordView**-derived class for these commands.

  If you choose "Both a database view and file support," the menu resource includes document-related commands on the File menu: New, Open, Save, and Save As.

  If you choose "A database view, without file support," the document-related File menu commands are omitted. General commands, such as Exit, remain on the menu.

  If the application is single document interface (SDI), the menu's resource ID is **IDR_MAINFRAME**. For a multiple document interface (MDI) application, AppWizard uses the document's menu resource, whose ID is **IDR_*DOCNAME*TYPE**, where *DOCNAME* is the document's type string.

Note Choosing the option "A database view, without file support" makes the application SDI. Choosing file support allows either SDI or MDI.

- A set of toolbar buttons for the navigational commands (if you choose the Dockable Toolbar option as well as a Database Support option).

Important The dialog template resource that AppWizard creates contains only the static text string "TODO: Place form controls on this dialog." You must use the Visual C++ dialog editor to delete the string and add controls that will map to your recordset data members. See the article "ClassWizard: Creating a Database Form."

See Also   Article: "ClassWizard"

AppWizard: OLE Support

AppWizard supports the following OLE features:

- OLE Visual Editing.

  AppWizard creates an entire project, including implementation and header files, that supports a variety of OLE Visual Editing application types. These types include different styles of container applications such as Visual Editing Container/Servers and simple Container applications. You can also create Visual Editing mini-servers and full-servers. For more information on OLE options, see the article "AppWizard: Creating an OLE Visual Editing Application."

- Ability to support Automation in your classes.

  Check the Automation support option if you want your application to have OLE Automation support. This means that your document class is exposed as a programmable object that can be used by any Automation client. You can also expose other classes you create as OLE Automation programmable objects. For more information on Automation, see the articles "ClassWizard: OLE Automation Support," "Automation Clients," and "Automation Servers."

For general information about using AppWizard, see Chapter 1 in the *Visual C++ User's Guide*.

See Also   Article: "OLE Overview"

In the *Class Library Reference*: **COleServerDoc**, **COleDocument**, **COleServerItem**, **COleClientItem**, **COleIPFrameWnd**

AppWizard: Creating an OLE Visual Editing Application

This article explains:

- The purpose of the OLE Options page.
- The creation of an OLE Visual Editing application.
- Classes and resources created by AppWizard.
- Filenames suggested by AppWizard.

The OLE Options Page

AppWizard's OLE Options page (step 3 of 6) allows you to access the many features of OLE that are implemented by the MFC OLE classes. These features include Visual Editing and OLE Automation. You access these features by choosing the Visual Editing options your application will support, creating an application of one of the following OLE Visual Editing types:

- Container
- Mini-Server
- Full-Server
- Both Container and Server

Creating an OLE Visual Editing Application

▶ **To create an OLE Visual Editing application**

1. Create a new MFC AppWizard project and specify the project name, the project path and drive, and the name of the subdirectory for project files.

2. Use the AppWizard OLE Options page (step 3 of 6).

3. Choose the form of OLE Visual Editing you want in your application:

   - None: Select if you do not want Visual Editing support. This is the default setting.

   - Container: Select if you want your application to visually contain OLE objects. For more information on containers, see the article "Containers."

   - Mini-Server: Select if you want your application to be visually embedded inside an OLE container. Note that mini-servers cannot run as stand-alone applications, and only support embedded items. For more information on servers, see the article "Servers."

   - Full-Server: Select if you want your application to be visually embedded inside an OLE container. Full-servers are able to run as stand-alone applications, and support both linked and embedded items. For more information on servers, see the article "Servers."

   - Both container and server: Select if you want your application to be both a Visual Editing container and a server.

4. Repeatedly choose Next to move to the next AppWizard Options page and set other options for your application.

5. When you have finished setting options, choose Finish. This displays your choices.

6. Confirm your choices by choosing the OK button.

AppWizard creates files for your classes in the directory you specified and opens the project. For more information, see "Classes and Resources Created" and "Filenames Suggested" below.

Classes and Resources Created

AppWizard creates application, document, view, and frame-window classes. The exact classes created will differ depending on which Visual Editing option you chose from the OLE Options page.

All document-based (non-dialog based) applications created with AppWizard, regardless of the type of OLE support, have an application class derived from **CWinApp**, an about dialog class created from **CDialog**, a view class derived from **CView** (or from one of its derived classes), and a frame-window class derived from **CMDIFrameWnd**. If your application uses a single document interface, your frame-window class is derived from **CFrameWnd**.

The class from which your application's document class is derived will vary depending on the Visual Editing options you selected. For non-Visual Editing applications, the class is derived from **CDocument**. For mini-, full-, and container-servers, the class is derived from **COleServerDoc**. For containers, the class is derived from **COleDocument**.

In addition to the above-mentioned classes, servers will have two additional classes: an in-place frame-window class derived from **COleFrameWnd** and a server item class derived from **COleServerItem**.

Containers will have a container class derived from **COleClientItem**.

Filenames Suggested

As with other files created by AppWizard, the suggested filenames for the document, view, frame window, server item, and container classes are based on the name of your Visual C++ project. For example, AppWizard writes the view class in files *prjname*VIEW.H/.CPP and the document class is found in files *prjname*DOC.H/.CPP. If the suggested filenames are too long, they are shortened. These suggested filenames can be changed by using AppWizard. For a complete description of the project created by AppWizard, see the file README.TXT created by AppWizard with the rest of your project, found in *dirname*.

Asynchronous Access

See classes **CDatabase** and **CRecordset** in the *Class Library Reference*.

Automation Clients

OLE Automation makes it possible for your application to manipulate objects implemented in another application, or to "expose" objects so they can be manipulated. An "automation client" is an application that can manipulate exposed objects belonging to another application. The application that exposes the objects is called the "OLE Automation server." The client manipulates the server application's objects by accessing those objects' properties and functions.

There are two types of OLE Automation clients:

- Clients that dynamically (at run time) acquire information about the properties and operations of the server.
- Clients that possess static information (provided at compile time) that specifies the properties and operations of the server.

Clients of the first kind acquire information about the server's methods and properties by means of queries to the OLE system's **IDispatch** mechanism. Although it is adequate to use for dynamic clients, **IDispatch** is difficult to use for static clients, where the objects being driven must be known at compile time. For static bound clients, the Microsoft Foundation classes provide the **COleDispatchDriver** class along with ClassWizard support.

Static bound clients use a "proxy class" that is statically linked with the client application. This class provides a type-safe C++ encapsulation of the server application's properties and operations.

The class **COleDispatchDriver** provides the principal support for the client side of OLE Automation. Using ClassWizard, you create a class derived from **COleDispatchDriver**.

You then specify the type-library file describing the properties and functions of the server application's object. ClassWizard reads this file and creates the **COleDispatchDriver**-derived class, with member functions that your application can call to access the server application's objects in C++ in a type-safe manner. Additional functionality inherited from **COleDispatchDriver** simplifies the process of calling the proper OLE Automation server.

See Also   Articles: "Automation Clients: Using Type Libraries," "AppWizard: OLE Support," "ClassWizard: OLE Automation Support," "ClassWizard: Adding Automation Properties and Methods"

Automation Clients: Using Type Libraries

Automation clients must have information about server objects' properties and methods if the clients are to manipulate the servers' objects. Properties have data types; methods often return values and accept parameters. The client requires information about the data types of all of these in order to statically bind to the server object type.

This type information can be made known in several ways. The recommended way is to create a "type library."

For information on Microsoft Object Description Language and MkTypLib, see Chapters 2 and 9 of *OLE Programmer's Reference, Volume 2.*

ClassWizard can read a type-library file and create a "dispatch class" derived from **COleDispatchDriver**. An object of that class has properties and operations duplicating those of the server object. Your application calls this object's properties and operations, and functionality inherited from **COleDispatchDriver** routes these calls to the OLE system, which in turn routes them to the server object.

ClassWizard automatically maintains this type-library file for you if you chose to include OLE Automation when the project was created. As part of each build, the .TLB file will be built with MkTypLib.

▶ **To create a dispatch class from a type-library (.TLB) file**

1. Start ClassWizard, and select the OLE Automation page.

2. Choose the Read Type Library button.

   The Type Library Tool dialog box appears.

3. Use the Type Library Tool dialog box to select the .TLB file.

   Tip Some type library information is stored in files with .DLL, .OCX, or .OLB file extensions.

   ---

4. Choose either the OK button or the Classes button.

   The Confirm Classes dialog box appears. The New Dispatch Classes list box lists the external names of the classes described in the type-library file. Other controls in the Confirm Classes dialog box show the proposed names for the dispatch classes and for the header and implementation files for those classes. As you select a class in the New Dispatch Classes list box, the Class Name box shows the name for the corresponding class.

   You can use the Browse buttons to select other files, if you prefer to have the header and implementation information written in existing files or in a directory other than the project directory.

5. In the Confirm Classes dialog box, edit the names of the new dispatch classes and their files.

6. Choose OK to close the Confirm Classes dialog box.

   The Type Library Tool writes header and implementation code for your dispatch class, using the class names and filenames you have supplied, and adds the .CPP file to your project.

See Also   Article: "ClassWizard: Adding Automation Properties and Methods"

Automation Servers

An automation server is an application that exposes programmable objects to other applications, which are called "automation clients." Exposing programmable objects enables clients to "automate" certain procedures by directly accessing the objects and functionality the server makes available.

Exposing objects in this way is beneficial when applications provide functionality that is useful for other applications. For example, a word processor might expose its spell-checking functionality so that other programs can use it. Exposure of objects thus enables vendors to improve their applications' functionality by using the "ready-made" functionality of other applications.

By exposing application functionality through a common, well-defined interface, OLE Automation makes it possible to build applications in a single general programming language like Microsoft Visual Basic instead of in diverse application-specific macro languages.

Support for Automation Servers

ClassWizard, AppWizard, and the framework all provide extensive support for automation servers. They handle much of the overhead involved in making an automation server, so you can focus your efforts on the functionality of your application.

The framework's principal mechanism for supporting OLE Automation is the dispatch map, a set of macros that expands into the declarations and calls needed to expose methods and properties for OLE. A typical dispatch map looks like this:

```
BEGIN_DISPATCH_MAP(CMyServerDoc, COleServerDoc)
    //{{AFX_DISPATCH_MAP(CMyServerDoc)
    DISP_PROPERTY(CMyServerDoc, "Msg", m_strMsg, VT_BSTR)
    DISP_FUNCTION(CMyServerDoc, "SetDirty", SetDirty, VT_EMPTY, VTS_I4)
    //}}AFX_DISPATCH_MAP
END_DISPATCH_MAP()
```

ClassWizard assists in maintaining dispatch maps. When you add a new method or property to a class, ClassWizard adds a corresponding DISP_FUNCTION or DISP_PROPERTY macro with parameters indicating the class name, external and internal names of the method or property, and data types.

ClassWizard also simplifies the declaration of OLE Automation classes and the management of their properties and operations. When you use ClassWizard to add a class to your project, you specify its base class. If the base class allows automation, ClassWizard displays controls you use to specify whether the new class should support OLE Automation, whether it is "OLE Createable" (that is, whether objects of the class can be created on a request from an OLE client), and the external name for the OLE client to use.

ClassWizard then creates a class declaration, including the appropriate macros for the OLE features you have specified. ClassWizard also adds the skeleton code for implementation of your class's member functions.

AppWizard simplifies the steps involved in getting your automation server application off the ground. If you select Automation support in AppWizard's OLE Options page, AppWizard adds to your application's **InitInstance** function the calls required to register your automation objects and run your application as an OLE Automation server.

See Also   Articles: "AppWizard: OLE Support," "Automation Clients," "ClassWizard: OLE Automation Support"

In *Introducing Visual C++*: Chapter 20, "Creating an OLE Automation Server"

In the *Class Library Reference*: **COleServerDoc, COleServerItem**

Automation Servers: Object-Lifetime Issues

When an automation client creates or activates an OLE item, the server passes the client a pointer to that object. The client establishes a reference to the object through a call to the OLE function **IUnknown::AddRef**. This reference is in effect until the client calls **IUnknown::Release**. (Client applications written with the Microsoft Foundation Class Library's OLE classes need not make these calls; the framework does so.) The OLE system and the server itself may establish references to the object. A server should not destroy an object as long as external references to the object remain in effect.

The framework maintains an internal count of the number of references to any server object derived from **CCmdTarget**. This count is updated when an automation client or other entity adds or releases a reference to the object.

When the reference count becomes 0, the framework calls the virtual function **CCmdTarget::OnFinalRelease**. The default implementation of this function calls the **delete** operator to delete this object.

The Microsoft Foundation Class Library provides additional facilities for controlling application behavior when external clients have references to the application's objects. Besides maintaining a count of references to each object, servers also maintain a global count of active objects. The global functions **AfxOleLockApp** and **AfxOleUnlockApp** update the application's count of active objects. If this count is nonzero, the application does not terminate when the user chooses Close from the system menu or Exit from the File menu. Instead, the application's main window is hidden (but not destroyed) until all pending client requests have been completed. Typically, **AfxOleLockApp** and **AfxOleUnlockApp** are called in the constructors and destructors, respectively, of classes that support OLE Automation.

Sometimes circumstances force the server to terminate while a client still has a reference to an object. For example, a resource on which the server depends may become unavailable, causing the server to encounter an error. Or the user may close a server document that contains objects to which other applications have references.

See Also   In the *Class Library Reference*: **AfxOleLockApp, AfxOleUnlockApp, AfxOleCanExitApp**

In the *OLE 2 Programmer's Reference, Volume 1*: **IUnknown::AddRef, IUnknown::Release**

Binary Large Object

See the article "Recordset: Working with Large Data Items."

BLOB

See the article "Recordset: Working with Large Data Items."

Catalog Information

Information about the tables in a data source can include the names of tables and the columns in them, table privileges, names of primary and foreign keys, information about predefined queries or stored procedures, information about indexes on tables, and statistics about tables.

See the article "Data Source: Determining the Schema of the Data Source."

See also information about the ODBC "catalog functions" in the ODBC SDK *Programmer's Reference* and the CATALOG sample program. For information about MFC samples, see MFC Samples under MFC in Books Online.

ClassWizard

ClassWizard helps you create additional classes beyond those you create with AppWizard. ClassWizard also lets you browse and edit your classes.

To run ClassWizard, choose the ClassWizard command from the Project menu in Visual C++.

ClassWizard supports the following features:

New Feature

- Support for creating and managing new classes derived from most of the MFC classes.

  For example, ClassWizard makes it easy to create classes for your owner-draw list boxes and other controls.

- Support for message maps. You can use ClassWizard to:

  - Map Windows messages to message-handler functions in your classes.

  - Map command messages from menu items, toolbar buttons, and accelerators to handler functions in your classes.

  - Map control-notification messages from dialog controls to your classes.

  - Provide "update handlers" to enable or disable user-interface objects, such as menus and toolbar buttons.

  - Jump from ClassWizard to the handler function for a particular message or command.

  - Specify a "filter" that determines which categories of Windows messages ClassWizard offers to map to handlers in your class.

- Support for mapping dialog controls to class member variables.

  This helps you enable dialog data exchange (DDX) and dialog data validation (DDV) for the controls in your dialog boxes. DDX exchanges data between dialog controls and their corresponding member variables in a dialog class. DDV validates this data.

- Support for OLE Automation You can use ClassWizard to:
  - Add classes that support OLE Automation.
  - Add properties and methods to your classes that support OLE Automation.
  - Create a C++ class for an existing OLE Automation object on your system, such as Microsoft Excel.

New Feature
- Support for OLE Controls. You can use ClassWizard to:
  - Specify properties and methods for OLE Controls.
  - Specify the events your OLE Control can fire.

  For more information, see the *OLE Custom Control Programmer's Guide* in the OLE Custom Control Developer's Kit (CDK).

- Support for database access. You can:
  - Create classes derived from **CRecordset**.
  - Specify a data source, table, and columns for a recordset.
  - Create database form classes derived from **CRecordView**.
  - Map controls of a record view database form to the fields of a recordset object.

New Feature
- Support for overriding many MFC virtual member functions. You can use ClassWizard to:
  - Browse virtual functions provided by MFC and choose the ones you want to override.
  - Jump to the code for editing.
- Foreign classes.

  Just as you can map dialog box controls to dialog class data members, you can map window controls to data members of class **CRecordset** (called a "foreign class" in this context). For more information, see the article "ClassWizard: Foreign Objects."

For general information about using ClassWizard, see Chapter 12 in the *Visual C++ User's Guide*.

The following articles describe ClassWizard tips and techniques:

- ClassWizard: Tips and Troubleshooting
- ClassWizard: Database Support
- ClassWizard: OLE Automation Support

See Also   Article: "AppWizard"

ClassWizard: Special-Format Comment Sections

This article explains where and how ClassWizard edits your source files.

When you add a new class using ClassWizard, special-format comments are placed in your code to mark the sections of the header and implementation files that ClassWizard edits. ClassWizard never modifies code that is outside these commented sections.

Message-Map Comments

For most classes, there are two related sections of code that ClassWizard edits: the member-function definitions in the class header file and the message-map entries in the class implementation file.

The ClassWizard comments in the header file look like this:

```
//{{AFX_MSG(<classname>)
    // NOTE: the ClassWizard will add member functions here
//}}AFX_MSG
```

The ClassWizard section in the implementation file is set off with comments that look like this:

```
//{{AFX_MSG_MAP(<classname>)
    // NOTE: the ClassWizard will add message map macros here
//}}AFX_MSG_MAP
```

The notes in the ClassWizard section act as placeholders. ClassWizard removes the note from any ClassWizard section in which it writes code.

Virtual Function Comments

As with message handlers, ClassWizard writes code to two locations when you use it to override a virtual function in one of your classes.

The ClassWizard comments in the header file look like the following example for virtual function overrides:

```
//{{AFX_VIRTUAL(<classname>)
    virtual BOOL OnPreparePrinting(CPrintInfo* pInfo);
//}}AFX_VIRTUAL
```

The ClassWizard section in the implementation file has no special comments. Virtual function definitions in the .CPP file look like other function definitions.

Data Map Comments

For dialog boxes, form views, and record views, ClassWizard creates and edits three other sections that are marked with special format comments:

- Member variable declarations in the class header file:

```
//{{AFX_DATA
...
//}}AFX_DATA
```

- Member variable initialization in the class implementation file:

```
//{{AFX_DATA_INIT
...
//}}AFX_DATA_INIT
```

- Data-exchange macros in the implementation file:

```
//{{AFX_DATA_MAP
...
//}}AFX_DATA_MAP
```

Field Map Comments

For record field exchange, ClassWizard creates and edits three other sections that are marked with special format comments:

- Member variable declarations in the class header file:

```
//{{AFX_FIELD
...
//}}AFX_FIELD
```

- Record exchange function calls in the implementation file:

```
//{{AFX_FIELD_MAP
...
//}}AFX_FIELD_MAP
```

- Member variable initializations in the class header file:

```
//{{AFX_FIELD_INIT
...
//}}AFX_FIELD_INIT
```

OLE Dispatch Map Comments

For OLE method dispatch, ClassWizard creates and edits four other sections that are marked with special format comments:

- OLE events in the class header file:

```
//{{AFX_EVENT
...
//}}AFX_EVENT
```

- OLE events in the class implementation file:

```
//{{AFX_EVENT_MAP
...
//}}AFX_EVENT_MAP
```

- OLE Automation declarations in the class header file:

```
//{{AFX_DISP
...
//}}AFX_DISP
```

- OLE Automation mapping in the class implementation file:

```
//{{AFX_DISP_MAP
...
//}}AFX_DISP_MAP
```

For more information see "Working with Dialog-Box Data" in Chapter 12, "Using ClassWizard," in the *Visual C++ User's Guide*.

ClassWizard: Tips and Troubleshooting

This article summarizes key tips and troubleshooting advice for using ClassWizard effectively. The following topics are covered:

- Using ClassWizard Tab Dialogs
- Adding Functions with ClassWizard
- Adding Variables with ClassWizard
- Adding Code from ClassWizard
- Importing Classes from Other Projects
- Opening Your .RC File

Using ClassWizard Tab Dialogs

ClassWizard has a "tab dialog" user interface: the ClassWizard dialog box contains "tabs" that resemble the tabs on a group of file folders. Each tab's label shows what kind of functionality you can edit on that tab. To select a tab, click its label. Use the following tips:

- Use the Message Maps tab to browse the messages that a class can handle or to create, edit, or delete the member functions mapped to the messages. Use the Edit Code button to jump to a message handler function's code in the Visual C++ source code editor.
- Use the Member Variables tab to bind member variables to dialog, form view, or record view controls. You can also bind record view member variables both to record view controls and to the columns of a table in your data source.

- Use the OLE Automation tab to create and edit the OLE Automation capabilities of your application. For example, you can create Automation properties and methods.

- Use the OLE Events tab to specify actions that will cause your OLE control to fire events. For example, you can specify that a mouse click on your control fires a particular event that the control's container responds to with a handler.

- Use the Class Info tab to browse and set general class options. You can set a class's message filter to determine what messages ClassWizard offers to map to handlers in your class. You can also view or set a "foreign object" associated with your dialog form view or record view class. For information about foreign objects, see the article "ClassWizard: Foreign Objects."

Adding Functions with ClassWizard

ClassWizard lets you create handler functions and connect them to the menu items, toolbar buttons, and accelerators whose commands they respond to. Use the following tips:

- To connect a dialog box or other user-interface object to a menu command or toolbar button with ClassWizard, you must first create the dialog box, menu entry, or toolbar button and its object ID using the appropriate Visual C++ resource editor.

- You can bind more than one user-interface object to a single function. You can bind both a menu command and a toolbar button to a single function, for instance. In this case, selecting either object in your application causes the same action.

- If you delete a member function in the ClassWizard dialog box, the declaration is deleted from the class in the header file, and the message-map entry is deleted from the implementation file. But you must delete the function code and any cross-references to the function manually.

- To add a function and edit its related code, you should make your selections in this order on the ClassWizard Message Maps tab:

  1. Select a class name.

  2. Select an Object ID.

  3. Select a Message.

  You can then select an associated function to edit or delete, or click the Add Function button to add a member function to the class.

  By convention, the names of all message-handling functions begin with the prefix **On**.

- Override virtual functions in much the same way, also on the Message Maps tab:

  1. Select a class name.

2. In the Object IDs box, select the class name again.

3. In the Messages box, select a virtual function to override.

4. Choose Add Function.

Adding Variables with ClassWizard

ClassWizard lets you add member variables to some classes. For example, you can add member variables to a dialog class to represent the dialog box's controls. Use the following tips:

- Edit Variables is available in the ClassWizard dialog box only in classes with a data map. This includes dialog, form view, and record view classes. For information about data maps, see Chapter 12 in the *Visual C++ User's Guide*.

- By convention, the names of all member variables in the class library begin with the prefix **m_**.

- By using ClassWizard to map a dialog control to a dialog-class member variable with the Value property (the default), you can use dialog data exchange (DDX) and dialog data validation (DDV). This eliminates the need to move data between the control and the member variable yourself. It also allows you to specify validation rules for the data. For more information about DDX and DDV, see Chapter 12 in the *Visual C++ User's Guide*.

- You can also map a dialog control to a dialog-class member variable with the Control property. This creates a member variable of an appropriate class, such as **CEdit**. You can then call the member functions of the control object through this variable.

Adding Code from ClassWizard

After you've added a new member function in the ClassWizard dialog box, choose Edit Code to add the implementation code for the function. A Visual C++ source code editor window opens with the file containing the class for the member function. A highlighted comment indicates where to add your code. Use the following tip:

- You can select a function in ClassWizard's Message Maps tab and then click Edit Code to locate and examine code quickly.

Importing Classes from Other Projects

Classes you created for another programming project can sometimes be reused in new projects. For information about how to "import" these classes into your new project so that ClassWizard is aware of them, see Chapter 12 in the *Visual C++ User's Guide*. Also use the following tip:

- If you are importing several message-handling classes from another project, you can save time by rebuilding the ClassWizard information file (project.CLW) rather than importing each class separately in the Add Class dialog box. You can completely rebuild the .CLW file by deleting the project's .CLW file and then, from the resource editor, opening ClassWizard. Answer Yes when asked if you want to rebuild the .CLW file. Then use the Select Source Files dialog box to provide ClassWizard with a list of files in your project.

Note The .H and .CPP files for the classes you import must have special-format comments, as described in the article "ClassWizard: Special-Format Comment Sections."

Opening Your .RC File

Visual C++ lets you open resources in two ways. You can open individual resources (in compiled form) in the Visual C++ resource editors. Or you can open the .RC file to edit it directly as a text file. Use the following tip:

- To open the .RC file as text, choose the Open command on the File menu and select the Open As option to Text.

ClassWizard: Database Support

You can use ClassWizard to work with two main database classes:

- **CRecordset**   Represents a set of records selected from a data source.
- **CRecordView**   Supplies a database form, based on a dialog resource template, whose controls map to the field data members of an associated recordset object.

DDX and Foreign Object Support

When you create a record view class, you associate it with a particular recordset class and map the record view's controls to field data members of the recordset class.

This close association between a record view and a recordset takes advantage of another feature you can use in ClassWizard: "foreign objects." Dialog data exchange (DDX) lets you simplify data transfer between the controls in a dialog box or form view and the data members in a corresponding class. With foreign objects, you can exchange data between the controls and the data members of a separate object—in this case, between the controls of a record view and the data members of a recordset.

When you specify the **CRecordset**-derived class to associate with a **CRecordView**-derived class, you can name an existing recordset class or create a new one. ClassWizard adds a member variable to the record view class named, by default, **m_pSet**. The data type of this variable is the recordset class. Figure 1 shows the relationships between a record view on the screen, a record view object, and a recordset object. The recordset is the foreign object. ClassWizard creates the record view and recordset classes and maps record view controls to recordset data members via **m_pSet**.

Figure 1   DDX and Foreign Objects

Database Source Files

When you create a **CRecordset** or **CRecordView** class with ClassWizard, the wizard creates the classes in the files you specify in the Add Class dialog box. The default filenames are based on the class name you enter. You can modify the default names, place the recordset and record view in the same files, or consolidate all recordsets in one set of files.

Browsing and Editing Database Classes

You can also browse and edit existing classes with ClassWizard. When you edit an existing recordset class, ClassWizard provides an SQL Data Sources dialog box that you can use to update the table columns bound to the recordset if the table's schema has changed since you created the class. You can also, with a little extra work, use this mechanism to specify the columns of additional tables for a join of tables. For more information about joins, see the article "Recordset: Performing a Join."

The following articles explain the details of using ClassWizard's database support:

- ClassWizard: Creating a Recordset Class
- ClassWizard: Binding Recordset Fields to Table Columns
- ClassWizard: Creating a Database Form
- ClassWizard: Mapping Form Controls to Recordset Fields
- ClassWizard: Foreign Objects

See Also   Articles: "ClassWizard: Creating a Recordset Class," "AppWizard"

ClassWizard: Creating a Recordset Class

This article explains how to create a recordset class with ClassWizard.

You'll need a new **CRecordset**-derived class for each table, join of tables, or predefined query you work with in your program. Each recordset class specifies a its own set of columns and may also specify parameters.

For information about mapping recordset field data members to columns in the table, see the article "ClassWizard: Binding Recordset Fields to Table Columns." For information about using a recordset for a join of tables, see the article "Recordset: Performing a Join." For information about using a recordset for a predefined query, see the article "Recordset: Declaring a Class for a Predefined Query."

Table 1 shows the major steps in creating a recordset class.

Table 1   Recordset Class Creation Summary

To	Do this
Create the class	Use the Add Class dialog box in ClassWizard
Select a data source and database table for the class	Select a data source in the SQL Data Sources dialog box, then use the Tables dialog box to select a table from those available on the data source
Remove any column mappings you don't want. By default, AppWizard and ClassWizard bind all columns in the table to recordset field data members	Select a column name on the Member Variables tab and choose Delete Variable
Optionally parameterize the underlying SQL statements	Manually add parameter data members
Optionally use dialog data exchange (DDX) to map recordset data members to controls in a record view	See the article "Record Views"

For more information about parameterizing your class, see the article "Recordset: Parameterizing a Recordset." For information about using DDX between record view controls and recordset data members, see the article "ClassWizard: Mapping Form Controls to Recordset Fields."

Creating the Recordset Class

You can add a new class derived from class **CRecordset** in ClassWizard's Add Class dialog box. This dialog box is available from any tab in ClassWizard.

▶ **To create the recordset class**

1. Run ClassWizard.

2. Choose the Add Class button to open the Add Class dialog box (Figure 1).

Figure 1   Specifying Information for a New Class

3. Select **CRecordset** as the class type of the new class.

4. Enter a name for the class and filenames for its .H and .CPP files.

5. Choose the Create Class button.

   The SQL Data Sources dialog box (Figure 2) opens, displaying a list of data sources already registered on your machine with ODBC Administrator.

Figure 2   Selecting a Data Source in ClassWizard

6. Double-click the name of your data source.

   The Tables dialog box (Figure 3) opens, displaying a list of the tables in your data source.

Figure 3   Selecting a Database Table in ClassWizard

7. Double-click the name of the table you want.

    ClassWizard's Member Variables tab appears again. Notice that ClassWizard binds all of the table's columns to recordset field data members. For information about removing bindings you don't want, see the article "ClassWizard: Binding Recordset Fields to Table Columns."

8. When you finish, choose OK to close ClassWizard. ClassWizard writes your class files in the specified directory and adds them to your project.

ClassWizard: Binding Recordset Fields to Table Columns

Both AppWizard and ClassWizard bind all columns of your selected table to the recordset. This article explains how to:

- Remove data members for any columns you don't want in the recordset.

  If you want only a subset of the columns bound by the wizards, use ClassWizard to remove the field data members for any columns you don't want.

- Select table columns and map them to recordset field data members.

  If you subsequently remove any of the bindings the wizards made, you can later rebind them with ClassWizard.

- Update columns in your recordset to reflect new columns in the table on the data source.

Removing Columns from Your Recordset

You might sometimes need to remove columns from a recordset. Both AppWizard and ClassWizard automatically bind all table columns to the recordset. If you want only a subset of the columns, use the following procedure.

▶ **To remove a column from a recordset**

1. In ClassWizard, choose the Member Variables tab.

2. Select a member variable name in the Members column of the Column Names box.

3. Choose Delete Variable.

   The member variable is removed from your recordset class. (The column in the data source to which the member variable was bound is not deleted.)

Warning Be careful not to remove any columns that are part of the table's primary key. In some tables, the primary key is a single column; in others, it's composed of two or more columns taken together. Removing these columns could damage your data on the data source.

Adding Columns to Your Recordset

Once you select a table, ClassWizard displays a list of all columns in the table. You can remove column bindings, and you can later rebind columns whose bindings have been removed. The following procedure explains how to bind an unbound column.

▶ **To add a column to the recordset**

1. Create the recordset class and associate it with a database table.

   If you create the class with ClassWizard, follow the procedure "To create the recordset class" in the article "ClassWizard: Creating a Recordset Class."

   If you create the class with AppWizard, follow the procedure in the article "AppWizard: Database Support."

2. On the Member Variables tab, select the recordset class name in the Class Name box if it is not already selected.

3. Select a column in the Column Names box.

4. Choose the Add Variable button to open the Add Member Variable dialog box.

5. Type a name for the recordset data member that will represent the selected column.

   ClassWizard supplies a standard data member prefix, m_, for the name. Append the rest of the name to this prefix or type over it.

   The variable's property and data type are already specified in the dialog box. The property for these variables is always "Value." The data type is based on the SQL data type of the column on the data source.

6. Choose OK to close the Add Member Variable dialog box.

7. Choose OK to close ClassWizard.

ClassWizard writes your class files to the specified directory and adds them to your project.

Tip Rather than binding columns to data members one at a time, you can choose the Bind All button to bind all columns. ClassWizard gives the data members default names based on the column names. Binding columns one at a time gives you more control over the columns bound and how they're named, but Bind All is quick and easy.

Figure 1 shows the Member Variables tab with a data member added for one of the available columns.

Figure 1   Adding a Data Member to the Recordset

Updating Your Recordset's Columns

Tables in a data source sometimes change—in particular, columns may be added to a table. To bring your recordset class up to date with respect to these changes, use the Update Columns button.

▶ **To update the columns in your recordset**

1. On the Member Variables tab, select your recordset class.

2. Choose the Update Columns button.

Any new columns are shown in the list but not yet bound to recordset field data members. To bind them, see the procedure "To add a column to the recordset" in "Adding Columns to Your Recordset" above.

When you use Update Columns, columns you've previously bound to recordset data members are left alone; to unbind a column, delete its data member. Any columns in the table that aren't bound to the recordset disappear from the refreshed recordset.

See Also   Articles: "ClassWizard: Creating a Database Form," "AppWizard"

ClassWizard: Creating a Database Form

The Microsoft Foundation Class Library database classes supply class **CRecordView** for implementing database forms with controls in which to display record fields. This article explains how to create a record view class with ClassWizard and associate it with a recordset class.

Important To use the MFC database classes, you must have specified at least minimum database support ("Only include header files") in AppWizard. If you didn't, open file STDAFX.H and add an **#include** directive for AFXDB.H.

The purpose of a record view class is to provide a form view whose controls are mapped directly to the field data members of a recordset object (and indirectly to the corresponding columns in a table on the data source). Setting up this mapping enables dialog data exchange (DDX) directly between the form's controls and the recordset's field data members. This article explains how to make the association.

Tip The easiest way to use a record view as your application's main view is to use AppWizard. See the article "AppWizard: Database Support."

The following procedure begins the process.

▶ **To create a record view associated with a recordset**

1. Create the recordset class.

   See the article "Recordset: Declaring a Class for a Table."

2. Create a dialog-template resource.

   See Chapter 5 in the *Visual C++ User's Guide*.

   In the Styles property page of your dialog template, set the following properties, as you would for a **CFormView** object:

   - In the Style box, select Child (**WS_CHILD** on).
   - In the Border box, select None (**WS_BORDER** off).
   - Clear the Visible check box (**WS_VISIBLE** off).
   - Clear the Titlebar check box (**WS_CAPTION** off).

Tip As you place controls on your dialog template, you can help ClassWizard be smarter. See the tips in the article "ClassWizard: Mapping Form Controls to Recordset Fields."

To continue from step 2, see the following procedure.

▶ **To create the record view class**

1. Run ClassWizard with the Visual C++ dialog editor open on your dialog-template resource.

    The Add Class dialog box opens.

2. Specify **CRecordView** as the base class for the new class.

3. Enter a name for the class and filenames for its .H and .CPP files.

4. Choose the Create Class button.

    The Select a Record Set dialog box opens.

5. Select the recordset class you created in step 1 of the procedure "To create a record view associated with a recordset."

    –Or–

    Choose New to create a new recordset class. In this case, select a data source and table for the recordset as prompted. Close the Select a Record Set dialog box. On returning to the Member Variables tab, select your new recordset class.

6. Bind columns to recordset field data members. See the article "ClassWizard: Binding Recordset Fields to Table Columns."

    Note If you next choose the Class Info tab, you'll see your recordset class listed in the Foreign Class box. For more information about "foreign" classes, see the article "ClassWizard: Foreign Objects."

7. Choose OK to exit ClassWizard.

For information about binding your record view controls to the recordset, see the article "ClassWizard: Mapping Form Controls to Recordset Fields."

ClassWizard: Mapping Form Controls to Recordset Fields

A database form based on class **CRecordView** uses dialog data exchange (DDX) to exchange data between the form's controls and the field data members of the form's associated recordset object. This article explains how to use ClassWizard to set up the DDX connection between the controls and the recordset.

This connection is different from the normal use of DDX, which connects the controls in a dialog box directly to the data members of the associated dialog class. DDX for a **CRecordView** object is indirect. The connection goes from form controls through the record view object to the field data members of the associated recordset object. For more information, see the articles "Record Views" and "ClassWizard: Foreign Objects." Table 1 summarizes the mapping process.

Table 1   Mapping Record View Controls to a Recordset

To	Do this
Specify the form control	Select the record view class on ClassWizard's Member Variables tab and select one of the form's control IDs
Specify the recordset data member to connect it to	Use the Add Variable dialog box to select a recordset data member indirectly

The following procedure assumes you have already followed the procedures in the article "ClassWizard: Creating a Database Form." Specifically, you've created a **CRecordset**-derived class and added some field data members to it, created a dialog-template resource, created a **CRecordView**-derived class, and associated the record view class with the recordset class. Your record view class is associated with the dialog-template resource, to which you've added controls with the Visual C++ dialog editor.

▶ **To map the form controls to the recordset**

1. Choose ClassWizard's Member Variables tab.

2. In the Class Name box, select the name of your record view class.

3. In the Control IDs box, select a control ID.

4. Choose the Add Variable button to name a variable associated with the control.

5. In the Add Member Variable dialog box, choose a variable name by selecting a recordset data member in the Member Variable Name drop-down list box.

   Important Use the drop-down list box to select a data member name from the associated recordset (a "foreign object"). The names that appear are of the form `m_pSet->m_recordsetVarName`. You can type the name instead, but selecting from the drop-down list is faster and more accurate.

   All variables of the recordset class appear in the box, not just variables of the currently selected data type.

6. Choose OK to close the Add Member Variable dialog box.

7. Repeat steps 3 through 6 for each control in the record view that you want to map to a recordset field data member.

8. Choose OK to close ClassWizard.

By selecting a name from the drop-down list, you specify a connection that passes through the record view object to a field data member of its associated recordset object.

Tip If you're running ClassWizard with the Visual C++ dialog editor open, the following shortcut is available. Choose a control on the form; then press CTRL and double-click the mouse. This opens ClassWizard's Add Member Variables dialog box, where you can bind a recordset field data member to the control. (If you use this shortcut before a class has been created for the dialog template, ClassWizard opens and displays its Add Class dialog box.)

If you follow a simple rule when placing controls on your record view form, ClassWizard is able to preselect the most likely recordset member in the dialog box. The rule is to place the static text label for the control ahead of the corresponding control in the tab order.

Tip You can use CTRL+Double-click for pushbuttons too. In these cases, ClassWizard creates a message handler function for the **BN_CLICKED** notification message in your record view class. You can edit its code to specify the button's action.

See Also   Article: "ClassWizard: Foreign Objects"

ClassWizard: Foreign Objects

ClassWizard extends dialog data exchange (DDX) by allowing you to map controls on a form or dialog box indirectly to a "foreign object"—a **CRecordset** object. This article explains:

- What foreign objects are.
- How to use foreign objects.

Foreign Objects

The best way to understand foreign objects is to consider DDX for a dialog box or form view and then see how it is extended. This discussion considers a form view, based on class **CFormView**.

DDX maps the controls in a form view to data members of the **CFormView**-derived class associated with the dialog-template resource. Controls in a form view correspond one-to-one with form view class data members. Two entities are connected: the form view on the screen and the form view class. (Dialog boxes work this way too.)

DDX for foreign objects connects not two entities but three. Figure 1 shows this connection, with a record view on screen at one end, a **CRecordView** class in the middle, and a third object—the foreign object—at the other end: a **CRecordset** object.

Figure 1   DDX for Foreign Objects

The record view class in Figure 1 contains a member variable, a pointer whose type matches the class of the foreign object. The DDX mapping is from three record view controls to members of the foreign object through the pointer, as illustrated by the following **DoDataExchange** function:

```
void CSectionForm::DoDataExchange(CDataExchange* pDX)
{
    CRecordView::DoDataExchange(pDX);
    //{{AFX_DATA_MAP(CSectionForm)
    DDX_FieldText(pDX, IDC_COURSE, m_pSet->m_strCourseID, m_pSet);
    DDX_FieldText(pDX, IDC_INSTRUCTOR, m_pSet->m_strInstructor, m_pSet);
    DDX_FieldText(pDX, IDC_ROOMNO, m_pSet->m_strRoomNo, m_pSet);
    //}}AFX_DATA_MAP
}
```

Notice the indirect reference to recordset fields, through the m_pSet pointer to a CSections recordset object:

```
m_pSet->m_strCourseID
```

Also notice that m_pSet is repeated as the fourth argument in each **DDX_FieldText** call.

ClassWizard and Foreign Objects

You set the foreign class and object on ClassWizard's Class Info tab. The Foreign Class box names the class of the foreign object (**CRecordset**). The Foreign Object box names the pointer variable that points to an object of that class. (You can specify only one foreign object per class.)

If you select a class based on a dialog-template resource on ClassWizard's Member Variables tab, ClassWizard locates the appropriate pointer variable in the class and puts its type into the Foreign Class box. It also puts the variable name into the Foreign Object box. You can change these values if you wish.

If you create a **CRecordView** class with AppWizard and then use ClassWizard to specify the DDX connections, ClassWizard automatically notes the presence in the view class of a pointer to a **CRecordset**-derived object. ClassWizard sets this as the value in the Foreign Class box. It puts the name of the pointer variable into the Foreign Object box.

See Also   Article: "ClassWizard: Mapping Form Controls to Recordset Fields"

ClassWizard: OLE Automation Support

ClassWizard supports the following OLE Automation features:

- Add classes that support OLE Automation. This makes your application an OLE Automation server. These classes will be exposed to OLE Automation clients such as Microsoft Visual Basic or Microsoft Excel.

- Add methods and properties to your classes that support OLE Automation.

- Create a C++ class for another OLE Automation object on your system, such as Microsoft Excel. For more information, see the article "ClassWizard: Accessing Automation Servers."

An OLE Automation class has a programming interface that other applications use to manipulate objects that your application implements. This is referred to as a "dispatch interface." For more information about dispatch interfaces, see the *OLE Programmer's Reference, Volume 2*.

ClassWizard's Add Class button now allows you to create classes supporting OLE Automation. Click this button to display a dialog box in which you can specify the name of your class, the filenames in which your class is implemented, and the type of framework class from which your class is derived. You can also choose whether your class supports OLE Automation.

▶ **To add an OLE Automation class**

1. Run ClassWizard from the Project menu.
2. Choose the OLE Automation tab.
3. Choose the Add Class button to open the Add Class dialog box.
4. Type a name for the class.

5. Specify **CCmdTarget**, or another class found in the list box, as the class type for the new class.

6. If you do not like the names specified by ClassWizard, enter new names for the class and its .H and .CPP files.

7. Choose the OLE Automation option, specifying an external name, to expose this class to OLE Automation clients. If you choose OLE Automation, you can also optionally choose OLE Creatable. The external name will then be used by the automation client to request an object of this class from the automation server.

    When you have entered all the necessary information, choose Create Class to create the necessary code.

To continue defining the dispatch interface for your OLE Automation class, see the article "ClassWizard: Adding Automation Properties and Methods."

A class that is OLE Creatable allows other applications to create a stand-alone object of the class, for example by using the Visual Basic function **CreateObject**, and to incorporate that Automation object into their application. In general, you should make only your top-level classes, such as documents, creatable from other OLE applications. Classes that are parts of these top-level classes are usually not OLE Creatable and are instead accessed from a member function in the top-level class.

For example, consider a list document, which contains a list of items. It's a good idea to make the top-level document class OLE Creatable, because this allows other applications to create a list from nothing. You then add/enumerate the items in the list, but you cannot create them as stand-alone objects because they depend on their position inside the list. For this reason only, stand-alone objects should be OLE Creatable. Notice that if you checked the Automation check box in AppWizard your document class is OLE Creatable. In other words, it can be accessed from other Automation clients.

Note OLE Creatable documents are made possible by class **COleTemplateServer**. When you choose OLE support in AppWizard, a **COleTemplateServer** object manages your documents. Such documents can be created by OLE Automation.

The following articles explain the details of using ClassWizard's OLE support:

- ClassWizard: Adding Automation Properties and Methods
- ClassWizard: Accessing Automation Servers

ClassWizard: Adding Automation Properties and Methods

This article explains how to use ClassWizard to add OLE Automation properties and methods to an OLE Automation class. Topics include:

- Adding a member variable property to your class
- Adding a Get/Set Methods property to your class
- Adding a method to your class

A class that supports OLE Automation exposes a set of functions (known as methods) and properties—the dispatch interface—for use by other applications. ClassWizard offers a simple, quick way to implement this ability in your classes.

Use member variable properties if you don't need to know when the values change. The most common case for member variables is when there is no user interface to be updated when changes occur.

▶ **To add a member variable property to your OLE Automation class**

1. In ClassWizard, choose the OLE Automation tab.
2. Select a class name that supports OLE Automation. You can also select the name of your document class if you checked the OLE Automation check box in AppWizard. Notice that the Add Property and Add Method buttons are unavailable for classes that do not support OLE Automation.
3. Click the Add Property button and supply the following information:
   - External Name: Name that automation clients use to refer to this property.
   - Type: Any of the choices found in the list box.
   - Implementation: Choose Member Variable.
   - Variable Name: Name of the C++ class data member.

   Tip You can also supply the name of a notification function that is called when the variable changes.

   ---

4. Choose OK to close ClassWizard.

Use Get/Set Methods properties if you need to know when the value changes, or when you are dealing with calculated properties. The most common use of Get/Set properties is to reflect changes in a user interface for calculated properties or items that are updated.

▶ **To add a Get/Set Methods property to your OLE Automation class**

1. In ClassWizard, choose the OLE Automation tab.

2. Select a class name that supports OLE Automation. You can also select the name of your document class if you checked the OLE Automation check box in AppWizard. Notice that the Add Property and Add Method buttons are unavailable for classes that do not support OLE Automation.

3. Click the Add Property button and supply the following information:
   - External Name: Name that automation clients use to refer to this property.
   - Type: Any of the choices found in the list box.
   - Implementation: Choose Get/Set Methods.
   - Variable Name: The C++ class member function names used to get and set the property.
   - Notification Function: The name of a member function, which you write, that will be called whenever the property value is changed.

4. Choose OK to create the necessary code.

Tip To create a read-only property, delete the name of the C++ member function used to set the peroperty's value.

▶ To add a method to your OLE Automation class

1. In ClassWizard, choose the OLE Automation tab.

2. Select a class name that supports OLE Automation. You can also select the name of your document class if you checked the OLE Automation check box in AppWizard. Notice that the Add Property and Add Method buttons are unavailable for classes that do not support OLE Automation.

3. Open the Add Method dialog box and supply the following information:
   - External Name: Name that automation clients use to refer to this method.
   - Internal Name: Name of the C++ member function to add to the class.
   - Return Type: Any choice found in the list box.

4. Add any method parameters you need, using the grid control:
   a. Double-click in the first empty row under the Name label to activate an edit control; then enter the parameter name.
   b. Double-click the row under the Type label to activate a drop-down list; then select the parameter's type.

   Continue this procedure until you have entered all the parameters you need. To delete a parameter, delete its row by clicking once in the row and pressing the DELETE key or the BACKSPACE key.

5. Choose OK in the Add Method dialog box to create the member function.

See Also   Article: "ClassWizard: Accessing Automation Servers"

ClassWizard: Accessing Automation Servers

OLE Automation allows other applications to expose objects and their interfaces to your application. You can make use of this feature by writing Automation Clients in C++, as well as in Visual Basic and other interpreted languages that support Automation.

For information and a procedure, see the article "Automation Clients: Using Type Libraries."

Client, OLE Automation

See the article "Automation Clients."

Clipboard

The Clipboard is the standard Windows method of transferring data between a source and a destination. It can also be very useful in OLE operations. With the advent of OLE, there are two Clipboard mechanisms in Windows. The standard Windows Clipboard API is still available, but it has been supplemented by the OLE data transfer mechanism. This mechanism uses the Clipboard for cut and paste and for drag-and-drop support. This article describes:

- When to use the OLE Clipboard mechanism and when to use the standard Clipboard mechanism.
- Using the OLE Clipboard mechanism.

For a brief introduction to the standard Windows Clipboard API, see the article "Clipboard: Using the Windows Clipboard."

When to Use Each Mechanism

Follow these guidelines in using the Clipboard:

- Use the OLE Clipboard mechanism now to enable new capabilities in the future. While the standard Clipboard API will be maintained, the OLE mechanism is the future of data transfer.
- Use the OLE Clipboard mechanism if you are writing an OLE application or you want any of the OLE features, such as drag and drop.
- Use the OLE Clipboard mechanism if you are providing OLE formats.
- Otherwise, use the standard Windows Clipboard API.

Using the OLE Clipboard Mechanism

OLE uses its own standard formats for transferring data through the Clipboard.

When you cut or copy data from an application, the data is stored on the Clipboard to be used later in paste operations. This data can be in a variety of formats. When a user chooses to paste data from the Clipboard, the application can choose which of these formats to use. The application should be written to choose the format that provides the most information, unless the user specifically asks for a certain format. Before continuing, you may want to read the "Data Objects and Data Sources (OLE)" family of articles. They describe the fundamentals of how data transfers work, and how to implement them in your applications.

OLE defines a number of standard formats that can be used for transferring data through the Clipboard. These include metafiles, text, bitmaps, and others. However, it is a good idea for applications that need more detail than given by the standard formats to register their own custom Clipboard formats.

For example, Microsoft Excel registers a custom format for spreadsheets. This format carries much more information than, for example, a bitmap does. When this data is pasted into an application that supports the spreadsheet format (any OLE application), all the formulas and values from the spreadsheet are retained and can be updated if necessary. In the case of a bitmap, however, there is no way to change the data short of totally re-creating it.

To retrieve the maximum amount of information from the Clipboard, applications should check for these custom formats before pasting data from the Clipboard.

For more detailed information, see the following articles:

- Clipboard: Copying and Pasting Data
- Clipboard: Adding Other Formats
- Clipboard: Using the Windows Clipboard

See Also   Articles: "Clipboard: Copying and Pasting Data," "OLE Overview," "Data Objects and Data Sources (OLE)," "Clipboard: Using the Windows Clipboard"

Clipboard: Using the Windows Clipboard

This article describes how to use the standard Windows Clipboard API within your MFC application.

Most applications for Windows support cutting or copying data to the Windows Clipboard and pasting data from the Clipboard. The Clipboard data formats vary among applications. The framework supports only a limited number of Clipboard formats for a limited number of classes. You will normally implement the Clipboard-related commands—Cut, Copy, and Paste—on the Edit menu for your view. The class library defines the command IDs for these commands: **ID_EDIT_CUT**, **ID_EDIT_COPY**, and **ID_EDIT_PASTE**. Their message-line prompts are also defined.

The Clipboard is a system service shared by the entire Windows session, so it does not have a handle or class of its own. You manage the Clipboard through member functions of class **CWnd**.

Chapter 2, "Working with Messages and Commands," explains how to handle menu commands in your application by mapping the menu command to a handler function. As long as your application does not define handler functions for the Clipboard commands on the Edit menu, they remain disabled. To write handler functions for the Cut and Copy commands, implement selection in your application. To write a handler function for the Paste command, query the Clipboard to see whether it contains data in a format your application can accept. For example, to enable the Copy command, you might write a handler something like the following:

```
void CMyView::OnEditCopy()
{
   if ( !OpenClipboard() )
   {
      AfxMessageBox( "Cannot open the Clipboard" );
      return;
   }
   // ...
   // Get the currently selected data
   // ...
   // For the appropriate data formats...
   if ( ::SetClipboardData( CF_??, hData ) == NULL )
   {
      AfxMessageBox( "Unable to set Clipboard data" );
      CloseClipboard();
      return;
   }
   // ...
   CloseClipboard();
}
```

The Cut, Copy, and Paste commands are only meaningful in certain contexts. The Cut and Copy commands should be enabled only when something is selected, and the Paste command only when something is in the Clipboard. You can provide this behavior by defining update handler functions that enable or disable these commands depending on the context. For more information, see "How to Update User-Interface Objects" on page 52 in Chapter 2.

The Microsoft Foundation Class Library does provide Clipboard support for text editing with the **CEdit** and **CEditView** classes. The OLE classes also simplify implementing Clipboard operations that involve OLE items. For more information on the OLE classes, see "Using the OLE Clipboard Mechanism" in the "Clipboard" article.

Implementing other Edit menu commands, such as Undo (**ID_EDIT_UNDO**) and Redo (**ID_EDIT_REDO**), is also left to you. If your application does not support these commands, you can easily delete them from your resource file using the Visual C++ resource editors.

See Also   Article: "Clipboard: Copying and Pasting Data"

Clipboard: **Copying and Pasting Data**

This article describes the minimum work necessary to implement copying to and pasting from the Clipboard in your OLE application. It is recommended that you read the "Data Objects and Data Sources (OLE)" family of articles before proceeding.

Before you can implement either copying or pasting, you must first provide functions to handle the Copy, Cut, and Paste options on the Edit menu.

Copying Data

▶ **To copy data to the Clipboard**

1. Determine whether the data to be copied is native data or is an embedded or linked item.

   - If the data is embedded or linked, obtain a pointer to the **COleClientItem** object that has been selected.

   - If the data is native and the application is a server, create a new object derived from **COleServerItem** containing the selected data. Otherwise, create a **COleDataSource** object for the data.

2. Call the selected item's **CopyToClipboard** member function.

3. If the user chose a Cut operation instead of Copy operation, delete the selected data from your application.

To see an example of this sequence, see the **OnEditCut** and **OnEditCopy** functions in the OCLIENT and HIERSVR sample programs. Note that these samples maintain a pointer to the currently selected data, so step 1 is already complete. For information about MFC samples, see MFC Samples under MFC in Books Online.

Pasting Data

Pasting data is more complicated than copying it because you need to choose the format to use in pasting the data into your application.

▶ **To paste data from the Clipboard**

1. In your view class, implement **OnEditPaste** to handle users choosing the Paste option from the Edit menu.

2. In the **OnEditPaste** function, create a **COleDataObject** object and call its **AttachClipboard** member function to link this object to the data on the Clipboard.

3. Call **COleDataObject::IsDataAvailable** to check whether a particular format is available. Use **COleDataObject::BeginEnumFormats** to look for other formats until you find one most suited to your application.

4. Perform the paste of the format.

For an example of how this works, see the implementation of the **OnEditPaste** member functions in the view classes defined in the OCLIENT and HIERSVR sample programs. For information about MFC samples, see MFC Samples under MFC in Books Online.

Tip   The main benefit of separating the paste operation into its own function is that the same paste code can be used when data is dropped in your application during a drag-and-drop operation. As in OCLIENT and HIERSVR, your **OnDrop** function can also call **DoPasteItem**, reusing the code written to implement Paste operations.

To handle the Paste Special option on the Edit menu, see the article "Dialog Boxes in OLE."

See Also   Articles: "Clipboard: Adding Other Formats," "Data Objects and Data Sources: Creation and Destruction," "OLE Overview"

Clipboard: Adding Other Formats

This article explains how to expand the list of supported formats, particularly for OLE support. The article "Clipboard: Copying and Pasting Data" describes the minimum implementation necessary to support copying and pasting from the Clipboard. If this is all you implement, the only formats placed on the Clipboard are **CF_METAFILEPICT**, **CF_EMBEDSOURCE**, and **CF_LINKSOURCE**. Most applications will need more formats on the Clipboard than these three.

Registering Custom Formats

To create your own custom formats, follow the same procedure you would use when registering any custom Clipboard format: pass the name of the format to the **::RegisterClipboardFormat** function and use its return value as the format ID.

Placing Formats on the Clipboard

To add more formats to those placed on the Clipboard, you must override the **OnGetClipboardData** function in the class you derived from either **COleClientItem** or **COleServerItem** (depending on whether the data to be copied is native). In this function, you should use the following procedure.

▶ **To place formats on the Clipboard**

1. Create a **COleDataSource** object.

2. Pass this data source to a function that adds your native data formats to the list of supported formats by calling **COleDataSource::CacheGlobalData**.

3. Add standard formats by calling **COleDataSource::CacheGlobalData** for each standard format you want to support.

This technique is used in the HIERSVR sample program (examine the **OnGetClipboardData** member function of the **CServerItem** class). The only difference in this sample is that step three is not implemented because HIERSVR supports no other standard formats. For information about MFC samples, see MFC Samples under MFC in Books Online.

See Also   Article: "Data Objects and Data Sources: Manipulation"

CObject Class

CObject is the root base class for most of the Microsoft Foundation Class Library (MFC). The **CObject** class contains many useful features that you may want to incorporate into your own program objects, including serialization support, run-time class information, and object diagnostic output. If you derive your class from **CObject**, your class can exploit these **CObject** features.

The cost of deriving your class from **CObject** is minimal. Your derived class will have the overhead of four virtual functions and a single **CRuntimeClass** object.

The following articles explain how to derive a class from **CObject** and how to access run-time class information using **CObject**:

- CObject Class: Deriving a Class from CObject
- CObject Class: Specifying Levels of Functionality
- CObject Class: Accessing Run-Time Class Information
- CObject Class: Dynamic Object Creation

See Also   Articles: "Files," "Serialization (Object Persistence)"

CObject Class: Deriving a Class from CObject

This article describes the minimum steps necessary to derive a class from **CObject**. Other CObject Class articles describe the steps needed to take advantage of specific **CObject** features, such as serialization and diagnostic debugging support.

In the discussions of **CObject**, the terms "interface file" and "implementation file" are used frequently. The interface file (often called the header file, or .H file) contains the class declaration and any other information needed to use the class. The implementation file (or .CPP file) contains the class definition as well the code that implements the class member functions. For example, for a class named CPerson, you would typically create an interface file named PERSON.H and an implementation file named PERSON.CPP. However, for some small classes that will not be shared among applications, it is sometimes easier to combine the interface and implementation into a single .CPP file.

You can choose from four levels of functionality when deriving a class from **CObject**:

- Basic functionality: No support for run-time class information or serialization but includes diagnostic memory management.
- Basic functionality plus support for run-time class information.
- Basic functionality plus support for run-time class information and dynamic creation.
- Basic functionality plus support for run-time class information, dynamic creation, and serialization.

Classes designed for reuse (those that will later serve as base classes) should at least include run-time class support and serialization support, if any future serialization need is anticipated.

You choose the level of functionality by using specific declaration and implementation macros in the declaration and implementation of the classes you derive from **CObject**.

Table 1 shows the relationship among the macros used to support serialization and run-time information.

Table 1   Macros Used for Serialization and Run-Time Information

Macro used	CObject::IsKindOf	CRuntimeClass::CreateObject	CArchive::operator>> CArchive::operator<<
Basic **CObject** functionality	No	No	No
DECLARE_DYNAMIC	Yes	No	No
DECLARE_DYNCREATE	Yes	Yes	No
DECLARE_SERIAL	Yes	Yes	Yes

▶ **To use basic CObject functionality**

- Use the normal C++ syntax to derive your class from **CObject** (or from a class derived from **CObject**).

  The following example shows the simplest case, the derivation of a class from **CObject**:

```
class CPerson : public CObject
{
    // add CPerson-specific members and functions...
}
```

Normally, however, you may want to override some of **CObject**'s member functions to handle the specifics of your new class. For example, you may usually want to override the **Dump** function of **CObject** to provide debugging output for the contents of your class. For details on how to override **Dump**, see the article "Diagnostics: Dumping Object Contents." You may also want to override the **AssertValid** function of **CObject** to provide customized testing to validate the consistency of the data members of class objects. For a description of how to override **AssertValid**, see "Overriding the AssertValid Function" in the article "Diagnostics: Checking Object Validity."

The article "CObject Class: Specifying Levels of Functionality" describes how to specify other levels of functionality, including run-time class information, dynamic object creation, and serialization.

CObject Class: Specifying Levels of Functionality

This article describes how to add the following levels of functionality to your **CObject**-derived class:

- Run-time class information
- Dynamic creation support
- Serialization support

For a general description of **CObject** functionality, see the article "CObject Class: Deriving a Class from CObject."

▶ To add run-time class information

CObject supports run-time class information through the **IsKindOf** function, which allows you to determine if an object belongs to or is derived from a specified class. For more detailed information, see the articles "Files" and "Serialization (Object Persistence)." This capability is not supported directly by the C++ language. The **IsKindOf** function permits you to do a type-safe cast down to a derived class.

Use the following steps to access run-time class information:

1. Derive your class from **CObject**, as described in the "CObject Class: Deriving a Class from CObject " article.

2. Use the **DECLARE_DYNAMIC** macro in your class declaration, as shown here:

```
class CPerson : public CObject
{
    DECLARE_DYNAMIC( CPerson )

    // rest of class declaration follows...
};
```

3. Use the **IMPLEMENT_DYNAMIC** macro in the implementation file (.CPP) of your class. This macro takes as arguments the name of the class and its base class, as follows:

```
IMPLEMENT_DYNAMIC( CPerson, CObject )
```

Note Always put **IMPLEMENT_DYNAMIC** in the implementation file (.CPP) for your class. The **IMPLEMENT_DYNAMIC** macro should be evaluated only once during a compilation and therefore should not be used in an interface file (.H) that could potentially be included in more than one file.

▶ **To add dynamic creation support**

CObject also supports dynamic creation, which is the process of creating an object of a specific class at run time. The object is created by the **CreateObject** member function of **CRuntimeClass.** Your document, view, and frame class should support dynamic creation because the framework (through the **CDocTemplate** class) needs to create them dynamically. Dynamic creation is not supported directly by the C++ language. To add dynamic creation, you must do the following:

1. Derive your class from **CObject.**

2. Use the **DECLARE_DYNCREATE** macro in the class declaration.

3. Define a constructor with no arguments (a default constructor).

4. Use the **IMPLEMENT_DYNCREATE** macro in the class implementation file.

▶ **To add serialization support**

"Serialization" is the process of writing or reading the contents of an object to and from a file. The Microsoft Foundation Class Library uses an object of the **CArchive** class as an intermediary between the object to be serialized and the storage medium. The **CArchive** object uses overloaded insertion (**<<**) and extraction (**>>**) operators to perform writing and reading operations.

The following steps are required to support serialization in your classes:

1. Derive your class from **CObject.**

2. Override the **Serialize** member function.

> **Note** If you call **Serialize** directly, that is, you do not want to serialize the object through a polymorphic pointer, omit steps 3 through 5.

3. Use the **DECLARE_SERIAL** macro in the class declaration.
4. Define a constructor with no arguments (a default constructor).
5. Use the **IMPLEMENT_SERIAL** macro in the class implementation file.

> **Note** A "polymorphic pointer" points to an object of a class (call it A) or to an object of any class derived from A (say, B). To serialize through a polymorphic pointer, the framework must determine the run-time class of the object it is serializing (B), since it might be an object of any class derived from some base class (A).

For more details on how to enable serialization when you derive your class from **CObject**, see the articles "Files" and "Serialization (Object Persistence)."

See Also   Article: "CObject Class: Accessing Run-Time Class Information"

CObject Class: Accessing Run-Time Class Information

This article explains how to access information about the class of an object at run time.

If you have derived your class from **CObject** and used the **DECLARE_DYNAMIC** and **IMPLEMENT_DYNAMIC**, the **DECLARE_DYNCREATE** and **IMPLEMENT_DYNCREATE**, or the **DECLARE_SERIAL** and **IMPLEMENT_SERIAL** macros explained in the article, "CObject Class: Deriving a Class from CObject," the **CObject** class has the ability to determine the exact class of an object at run time.

The ability to determine the class of an object at run time is most useful when extra type checking of function arguments is needed and when you must write special-purpose code based on the class of an object. However, this practice is not usually recommended because it duplicates the functionality of virtual functions.

The **CObject** member function **IsKindOf** can be used to determine if a particular object belongs to a specified class or if it is derived from a specific class. The argument to **IsKindOf** is a **CRuntimeClass** object, which you can get using the **RUNTIME_CLASS** macro with the name of the class. The use of the **RUNTIME_CLASS** macro is shown in this article.

▶ **To use the RUNTIME_CLASS macro**

- Use **RUNTIME_CLASS** with the name of the class, as shown here for the class **CObject**:

```
CRuntimeClass* pClass = RUNTIME_CLASS( CObject );
```

You will rarely need to access the run-time class object directly. A more common use is to pass the run-time class object to the **IsKindOf** function, as shown in the next procedure. The **IsKindOf** function tests an object to see if it belongs to a particular class.

▶   **To use the IsKindOf function**

1. Make sure the class has run-time class support. That is, the class must have been derived directly or indirectly from **CObject** and used the **DECLARE_DYNAMIC** and **IMPLEMENT_DYNAMIC**, the **DECLARE_DYNCREATE** and **IMPLEMENT_DYNCREATE**, or the **DECLARE_SERIAL** and **IMPLEMENT_SERIAL** macros explained in the article "CObject Class: Deriving a Class from CObject."

2. Call the **IsKindOf** member function for objects of that class, using the **RUNTIME_CLASS** macro to generate the **CRuntimeClass** argument, as shown here:

```
// in .H file
class CPerson : public CObject
{
    DECLARE_DYNAMIC( CPerson )
public:
    CPerson(){};

    // other declaration
};

// in .CPP file
IMPLEMENT_DYNAMIC( CPerson, CObject )

CObject* pMyObject = new CPerson;

if( myObject->IsKindOf( RUNTIME_CLASS( CPerson ) ) )
{
    //if IsKindOf is true, then cast is all right
    CPerson* pmyPerson = (CPerson*) pmyObject;
}
```

Note **IsKindOf** returns **TRUE** if the object is a member of the specified class or of a class derived from the specified class. **IsKindOf** does not support multiple inheritance or virtual base classes, although you can use multiple inheritance for your derived Microsoft Foundation classes if necessary.

One use of run-time class information is in the dynamic creation of objects. This process is discussed in the article "CObject Class: Dynamic Object Creation."

For more detailed information on serialization and run-time class information, see the articles "Files" and "Serialization (Object Persistence)."

CObject Class: Dynamic Object Creation

This article explains how to create an object dynamically at run time. The procedure uses run-time class information, as discussed in the article "CObject Class: Accessing Run-Time Class Information."

▶ **To dynamically create an object given its run-time class**

- Use the following code to dynamically create an object by using the **CreateObject** function of the **CRuntimeClass**. Note that on failure, **CreateObject** returns NULL instead of raising an exception:

```
CRuntimeClass* pRuntimeClass = RUNTIME_CLASS( CMyClass );
CObject* pObject = pRuntimeClass->CreateObject();
ASSERT( pObject->IsKindOf( RUNTIME_CLASS( CMyClass ) ) );
```

Collections

This group of articles explains the MFC collection classes.

The Microsoft Foundation Class Library provides collection classes to manage groups of objects. These classes are of two types:

- Collection classes created from C++ templates
- Collection classes not created from templates

Other topics covered in this article include:

- Collection shapes
- Further reading about collections

Tip The nontemplate collection classes are those provided by MFC since MFC version 1.0. If your code already uses these classes, you can continue to use them. If you write new type-safe collection classes for your own data types, consider using the newer template-based classes.

Collection Shapes

A collection class is characterized by its "shape" and by the types of its elements. The shape refers to the way the objects are organized and stored by the collection. MFC provides three basic collection shapes: lists, arrays, and maps (also known as dictionaries). You can pick the collection shape most suited to your particular programming problem.

Each of the three provided collection shapes is described briefly below. Table 1 in the article "Collections: Choosing a Collection Class" compares the features of the shapes to help you decide which is best for your program.

- List

  The list class provides an ordered, nonindexed list of elements, implemented as a doubly linked list. A list has a "head" and a "tail," and adding or removing elements from the head or tail, or inserting or deleting elements in the middle, is very fast.

- Array

  The array class provides a dynamically sized, ordered, and integer-indexed array of objects.

- Map (also known as a dictionary)

  A map is a collection that associates a key object with a value object.

The Template-Based Collection Classes

The easiest way to implement a type-safe collection that contains objects of any type is to use one of the MFC template-based classes. For examples of these classes, see the MFC COLLECT sample under MFC in Books Online.

Table 1 lists the MFC template-based collection classes.

Table 1   Collection Template Classes

Collection contents	Arrays	Lists	Maps
Collections of objects of any type	CArray	CList	CMap
Collections of pointers to objects of any type	CTypedPtrArray	CTypedPtrList	CTypedPtrMap

The Collection Classes Not Based on Templates

If your application already uses MFC nontemplate classes, you can continue to use them, although for new collections you should consider using the template-based classes. Table 2 lists the MFC collection classes not based on templates.

Table 2   Nontemplate Collection Classes

Arrays	Lists	Maps
CObArray	CObList	CMapPtrToWord
CByteArray	CPtrList	CMapPtrToPtr
CDWordArray	CStringList	CMapStringToOb

Table 2   Nontemplate Collection Classes (*continued*)

Arrays	Lists	Maps
CPtrArray		CMapStringToPtr
CStringArray		CMapStringToString
CWordArray		CMapWordToOb
CUIntArray		CMapWordToPtr

Table 2 in the article "Collections: Choosing a Collection Class" describes the MFC collection classes in terms of their characteristics (other than shape):

- Whether the class uses C++ templates
- Whether the elements stored in the collection can be serialized
- Whether the elements stored in the collection can be dumped for diagnostics
- Whether the collection is type-safe

Further Reading About Collections

The following articles describe how to use the collection classes to make type-safe collections and how to perform a number of other operations using collections:

- Collections: Choosing a Collection Class
- Collections: Template-Based Classes
- Collections: How to Make a Type-Safe Collection
- Collections: Accessing All Members of a Collection
- Collections: Deleting All Objects in a CObject Collection
- Collections: Creating Stack and Queue Collections

Collections: Choosing a Collection Class

This article contains detailed information designed to help you choose a collection class for your particular application needs.

Your choice of a collection class depends on a number of factors, including:

- The features of the class shape: order, indexing, and performance, as shown in Table 1
- Whether the class uses C++ templates
- Whether the elements stored in the collection can be serialized
- Whether the elements stored in the collection can be dumped for diagnostics
- Whether the collection is type-safe

Table 1 summarizes the characteristics of the available collection shapes.

- Columns 2 and 3 describe each shape's ordering and access characteristics. In the table, the term "ordered" means that the order in which items are inserted and deleted determines their order in the collection; it does not mean the items are sorted on their contents. The term "indexed" means that the items in the collection can be retrieved by an integer index, much like items in a typical array.

- Columns 4 and 5 describe each shape's performance. In applications that require many insertions into the collection, insertion speed might be especially important; for other applications, lookup speed may be more important.

- Column 6 describes whether each shape allows duplicate elements.

Table 1   Collection Shape Features

Shape	Ordered?	Indexed?	Insert an element	Search for specified element	Duplicate elements?
List	Yes	No	Fast	Slow	Yes
Array	Yes	By int	Slow	Slow	Yes
Map	No	By key	Fast	Fast	No (keys) Yes (values)

Table 2 summarizes other important characteristics of specific MFC collection classes as a guide to selection. Your choice may depend on whether the class is based on C++ templates, whether its elements can be serialized via MFC's document serialization mechanism, whether its elements can be dumped via MFC's diagnostic dumping mechanism, or whether the class is type-safe—that is, whether you can guarantee the type of elements stored in and retrieved from a collection based on the class.

Table 2   Characteristics of MFC Collection Classes

Class	Uses C++ templates	Can be serialized	Can be dumped	Is type-safe
CArray	Yes	Yes [1]	Yes [1]	No
CTypedPtrArray	Yes	Depends [2]	Yes	Yes
CByteArray	No	Yes	Yes	Yes [3]
CDWordArray	No	Yes	Yes	Yes [3]
CObArray	No	Yes	Yes	No
CPtrArray	No	No	Yes	No
CStringArray	No	Yes	Yes	Yes [3]
CWordArray	No	Yes	Yes	Yes [3]
CUIntArray	No	No	Yes	Yes [3]

Table 2 Characteristics of MFC Collection Classes (*continued*)

Class	Uses C++ templates	Can be serialized	Can be dumped	Is type-safe
CList	Yes	Yes [1]	Yes [1]	No
CTypedPtrList	Yes	Depends [2]	Yes	Yes
CObList	No	Yes	Yes	No
CPtrList	No	No	Yes	No
CStringList	No	Yes	Yes	Yes [3]
CMap	Yes	Yes [1]	Yes [1]	No
CTypedPtrMap	Yes	Depends [2]	Yes	Yes
CMapPtrToWord	No	No	Yes	No
CMapPtrToPtr	No	No	Yes	No
CMapStringToOb	No	Yes	Yes	No
CMapStringToPtr	No	No	Yes	No
CMapStringToString	No	Yes	Yes	Yes [3]
CMapWordToOb	No	Yes	Yes	No
CMapWordToPtr	No	No	Yes	No

[1] To serialize, you must explicitly call the collection object's **Serialize** function; to dump, you must explicitly call its **Dump** function. You cannot use the form `ar << collObj` to serialize or the form `dmp << collObj` to dump.

[2] Serializability depends on the underlying collection type. For example, if a typed pointer array is based on **CObArray**, it is serializable; if based on **CPtrArray**, it is not serializable. In general, the "Ptr" classes cannot be serialized.

[3] If marked Yes in this column, a nontemplate collection class is type-safe provided you use it as intended. That is, for example, if you store bytes in a **CByteArray**, the array is type-safe. But if you use it to store characters, its type safety is less certain.

See Also   Articles: "Collections: Template-Based Classes," "Collections: How to Make a Type-Safe Collection," "Collections: Accessing All Members of a Collection"

Collections: Template-Based Classes

This article explains the type-safe template-based collection classes in MFC version 3.0. Using these templates to create type-safe collections is more convenient and provides better type safety than using the collection classes not based on templates.

MFC predefines two categories of template-based collections:

- Simple array, list, and map classes

  CArray, CList, CMap

- Arrays, lists, and maps of typed pointers

  CTypedPtrArray, CTypedPtrList, CTypedPtrMap

The simple collection classes are all derived from class **CObject**, so they inherit the serialization, dynamic creation, and other properties of **CObject**. The typed pointer collection classes require you to specify the class you derive from—which must be one of the nontemplate pointer collections predefined by MFC, such as **CPtrList** or **CPtrArray**. Your new collection class inherits from the specified base class, and the new class's member functions use encapsulated calls to the base class members to enforce type safety.

For more information about Visual C++ templates, see Chapter 6 in *Programming Techniques*.

Using Simple Array, List, and Map Templates

To use the simple collection templates, you need to know what kind of data you can store in these collections and what parameters to use in your collection declarations.

Simple Array and List Usage

The simple array and list classes, **CArray** and **CList**, take two parameters: *TYPE* and *ARG_TYPE*. These classes can store any data type, which you specify in the *TYPE* parameter:

- Fundamental C++ data types, such as **int**, **char**, and **float**
- C++ structures and classes
- Other types that you define

For convenience and efficiency, you can use the *ARG_TYPE* parameter to specify the type of function arguments. Typically, you specify *ARG_TYPE* as a reference to the type you named in the *TYPE* parameter. For example:

```
CArray<int, int> myArray;
CList<CPerson, CPerson&> myList;
```

The first example declares an array collection, myArray, that contains **int**s. The second example declares a list collection, myList, that stores CPerson objects. Certain member functions of the collection classes take arguments whose type is specified by the *ARG_TYPE* template parameter. For example, the **Add** member function of class **CArray** takes an *ARG_TYPE* argument:

```
CArray<CPerson, CPerson&> myArray;
CPerson person;
myArray->Add( person );
```

Simple Map Usage

The simple map class, **CMap**, takes four parameters: *KEY*, *ARG_KEY*, *VALUE*, and *ARG_VALUE*. Like the array and list classes, the map classes can store any data type. Unlike arrays and lists, which index and order the data they store, maps associate keys and values: you access a value stored in a map by specifying the value's associated key. The *KEY* parameter specifies the data type of the keys used to access data stored in the map. If the type of *KEY* is a structure or class, the *ARG_KEY* parameter is typically a reference to the type specified in *KEY*. The *VALUE* parameter specifies the type of the items stored in the map. If the type of *ARG_VALUE* is a structure or class, the *ARG_VALUE* parameter is typically a reference to the type specified in *VALUE*. For example:

```
CMap< int, int, MY_STRUCT, MY_STRUCT& > myMap1;
CMap< CString, LPCSTR, CPerson, CPerson& > myMap2;
```

The first example stores MY_STRUCT values, accesses them by **int** keys, and returns accessed MY_STRUCT items by reference. The second example stores CPerson values, accesses them by **CString** keys, and returns references to accessed items. This example might represent a simple address book, in which you look up persons by last name.

Because the *KEY* parameter is of type **CString** and the *KEY_TYPE* parameter is of type **LPCSTR**, the keys are stored in the map as items of type **CString** but are referenced in functions such as **SetAt** through pointers of type **LPCSTR**. For example:

```
CMap< CString, LPCSTR, CPerson, CPerson& > myMap2;
CPerson person;
LPCSTR lpstrName = "Jones";
myMap2->SetAt( lpstrName, person );
```

Using Typed-Pointer Collection Templates

To use the typed-pointer collection templates, you need to know what kinds of data you can store in these collections and what parameters to use in your collection declarations.

Typed-Pointer Array and List Usage

The typed-pointer array and list classes, **CTypedPtrArray** and **CTypedPtrList**, take two parameters: *BASE_CLASS* and *TYPE*. These classes can store any data type, which you specify in the *TYPE* parameter. They are derived from one of the nontemplate collection classes that stores pointers; you specify this base class in *BASE_CLASS*. For arrays, use either **CObArray** or **CPtrArray**. For lists, use either **CObList** or **CPtrList**.

In effect, when you declare a collection based on, say **CObList**, the new class not only inherits the members of its base class, but it also declares a number of additional type-safe member functions and operators that provide type safety by encapsulating calls to the base class members. These encapsulations manage all necessary type conversion.

For example:

```
CTypedPtrArray<CObArray, CPerson*> myArray;
CTypedPtrList<CPtrList, MY_STRUCT*> myList;
```

The first example declares a typed-pointer array, myArray, derived from **CObArray**. The array stores and returns pointers to CPerson objects (where CPerson is a class derived from **CObject**). You can call any **CObArray** member function, or you can call the new type-safe **GetAt** and **ElementAt** functions or use the type-safe **[ ]** operator.

The second example declares a typed-pointer list, myList, derived from **CPtrList**. The list stores and returns pointers to MY_STRUCT objects. A class based on **CPtrList** is used for storing pointers to objects not derived from **CObject**. **CTypedPtrList** has a number of type-safe member functions: **GetHead**, **GetTail**, **RemoveHead**, **RemoveTail**, **GetNext**, **GetPrev**, and **GetAt**.

Typed-Pointer Map Usage

The typed-pointer map class, **CTypedPtrMap**, takes three parameters: *BASE_CLASS*, *KEY*, and *VALUE*. The *BASE_CLASS* parameter specifies the class from which to derive the new class: **CMapPtrToWord**, **CMapPtrToPtr**, **CMapStringToPtr**, **CMapWordToPtr**, **CMapStringToOb**, and so on. *KEY* is analogous to *KEY* in **CMap**: it specifies the type of the key used for lookups. *VALUE* is analogous to *VALUE* in **CMap**: it specifies the type of object stored in the map.

For example:

```
CTypedPtrMap<CMapPtrToPtr, CString, MY_STRUCT*> myPtrMap;
CTypedPtrMap<CMapStringToOb, CString, CMyObject*> myObjectMap;
```

The first example is a map based on **CMapPtrToPtr**—it uses **CString** keys mapped to pointers to MY_STRUCT. You can look up a stored pointer by calling a type-safe **Lookup** member function. You can use the **[ ]** operator to look up a stored pointer and add it if not found. And you can iterate the map using the type-safe **GetNextAssoc** function. You can also call other member functions of class **CMapPtrToPtr**.

The second example is a map based on **CMapStringToOb**—it uses string keys mapped to stored pointers to CMyObject objects. You can use the same type-safe members described in the previous paragraph, or you can call members of class **CMapStringToOb**.

Note If you specify a **class** or **struct** type for the *VALUE* parameter, rather than a pointer or reference to the type, the class or structure must have a copy constructor.

See Also   Article: "Collections: How to Make a Type-Safe Collection"

In the *Class Library Reference*: **CArray**, **CList**, **CMap**, **CTypedPtrArray**, **CTypedPtrList**, **CTypedPtrMap**

Collections: How to Make a Type-Safe Collection

This article explains how to make type-safe collections for your own data types. Topics include:

- Using template-based classes for type-safety
- Implementing helper functions
- Using nontemplate collection classes

The Microsoft Foundation Class Library provides predefined type-safe collections based on C++ templates. Because they are templates, these classes provide type safety and ease of use without the type-casting and other extra work involved in using a nontemplate class for this purpose. The COLLECT sample in MFC Samples under MFC in Books Online demonstrates the use of template-based collection classes in an MFC application. In general, use these classes any time you write new collections code.

Using Template-Based Classes for Type-Safety

▶ **To use template-based classes**

1. Declare a variable of the collection class type. For example:

   ```
   CList<int, int> m_intList;
   ```

2. Call the member functions of the collection object. For example:

   ```
   m_intList.AddTail( 100 );
   m_intList.RemoveAll( );
   ```

3. If necessary, implement the helper functions **SerializeElements**, **ConstructElements**, and **DestructElements**. For information on implementing these functions, see "Implementing Helper Functions" below.

This example shows the declaration of a list of integers. The first parameter in step 1 is the type of data stored as elements of the list. The second parameter specifies how the data is to be passed to and returned from member functions of the collection class, such as **Add** and **GetAt**.

Implementing Helper Functions

The template-based collection classes **CArray**, **CList**, and **CMap** use six global helper functions that you can customize as needed for your derived collection class. For information on these helper functions, see "Collection Class Helpers" in the *Class Library Reference*. Three of these helper functions are used in constructing, destructing, and serializing collection elements; implementations of these functions are necessary for most uses of the template-based collection classes.

Construction and Destruction

The helper functions **ConstructElements** and **DestructElements** are called by members that respectively add and remove elements from a collection.

Helper	Called directly by	Called indirectly by
ConstructElements	CArray::SetSize CArray::InsertAt	CList::AddHead CList::AddTail CList::InsertBefore CList::InsertAfter CMap::operator []
DestructElements	CArray::SetSize CArray::RemoveAt CList::RemoveAll CMap::RemoveAll	CList::RemoveHead CList::RemoveTail CList::RemoveAt CMap::RemoveKey

You should override these functions if their default action is not suitable for your collection class. The default implementation of **ConstructElements** sets to 0 the memory that is allocated for new elements of the collection; no constructors are called. The default implementation of **DestructElements** does nothing.

In general, overriding **ConstructElements** is necessary whenever the collection stores objects that require a call to a constructor (or other initializing function), or when the objects have members requiring such calls. Overriding **DestructElements** is necessary when an object requires special action, such as the freeing of memory allocated from the heap, when the object is destroyed.

For example, you might override **ConstructElements** for an array of **CPerson** objects as follows:

```
CPerson : public CObject { . . . };
CArray< CPerson, CPerson& > personArray;

void ConstructElements( CPerson* pNewPersons, int nCount )
{
    for ( int i = 0; i < nCount; i++, pNewPersons++ )
    {
        // call CPerson default constructor directly
        pNewPersons->CPerson::CPerson();
    }
}
```

This override iterates through the new **CPerson** objects, calling each object's constructor. Your override cannot call **new** for the objects; their memory already is allocated before the call to **ConstructElements**.

Serialization

The **CArray**, **CList**, and **CMap** classes call **SerializeElements** to store collection elements to or read them from an archive.

The default implementation of the **SerializeElements** helper function does a bitwise write from the objects to the archive, or a bitwise read from the archive to the objects, depending on whether the objects are being stored in or retrieved from the archive. Override **SerializeElements** if this action is not appropriate.

If your collection stores objects derived from **CObject** and you use the **IMPLEMENT_SERIAL** macro in the implementation of the collection element class, you can take advantage of the serialization functionality built into **CArchive** and **CObject**:

```
CPerson : public CObject { . . . };
CArray< CPerson, CPerson& > personArray;

void SerializeElements( CArchive& ar, CPerson* pNewPersons, int nCount )
{
    for ( int i = 0; i < nCount; i++, pNewPersons++ )
    {
        // Serialize each CPerson object
        if ( ar.IsStoring() )
            ar << pNewPersons;
        else
            ar >> pNewPersons;
    }
}
```

The overloaded insertion operators for **CArchive** call **CObject::Serialize** (or an override of that function) for each **CPerson** object.

Using Nontemplate Collection Classes

MFC also supports the collection classes introduced with MFC version 1.0. These classes are not based on templates. They can be used to contain data of the supported types **CObject***, **UINT**, **DWORD**, and **CString**. You can use these predefined collections (such as **CObList**) to hold collections of any objects derived from **CObject**. MFC also provides other predefined collections to hold primitive types such as **UINT** and void pointers (**void***). In general, however, it is often useful to define your own type-safe collections to hold objects of a more specific class and its derivatives. Note that doing so with the collection classes not based on templates is more work than using the template-based classes.

There are two ways to create type-safe collections with the nontemplate collections:

1. Use the nontemplate collections, with type casting if necessary. This is the easiest approach.

2. Derive from and extend a nontemplate type-safe collection.

▶ **To use the nontemplate collections with type casting.**

- Use one of the nontemplate classes, such as **CWordArray**, directly.

  For example, you can create a **CWordArray** and add any 32-bit values to it, then retrieve them. There is nothing more to do. You just use the predefined functionality.

  You can also use a predefined collection, such as **CObList**, to hold any objects derived from **CObject**. A **CObList** collection is defined to hold pointers to **CObject**. When you retrieve an object from the list, you may have to cast the result to the proper type since the **CObList** functions return pointers to **CObject**. For example, if you store CPerson objects in a **CObList** collection, you have to cast a retrieved element to be a pointer to a CPerson object. The following example uses a **CObList** collection to hold CPerson objects:

  ```
  class CPerson : public CObject {...};

  CPerson* p1 = new CPerson(...);
  CObList myList;

  myList.AddHead( p1 );    // No cast needed
  CPerson* p2 = ( CPerson* )myList.GetHead();
  ```

  This technique of using a predefined collection type and casting as necessary may be adequate for many of your collection needs. If you need further functionality or more type safety, use a template-based class, or read the next procedure.

▶ **To derive and extend a nontemplate type-safe collection**

- Derive your own collection class from one of the predefined nontemplate classes.

  When you derive your class, you can add type-safe wrapper functions to provide a type-safe interface to existing functions.

  For example, if you derived a list from **CObList** to hold CPerson objects, you might add the wrapper functions AddHeadPerson and GetHeadPerson, as shown below.

  ```
  class CPersonList : public CObList
  {
  public:
      void AddHeadPerson( CPerson* person )
          {AddHead( person );}

      const CPerson* GetHeadPerson()
          {return (CPerson*)GetHead();}
  };
  ```

These wrapper functions provide a type-safe way to add and retrieve `CPerson` objects from the derived list. You can see that for the `GetHeadPerson` function, you are simply encapsulating the type casting.

You can also add new functionality by defining new functions that extend the capabilities of the collection rather than just wrapping existing functionality in type-safe wrappers. For example, the article "Collections: Deleting All Objects in a CObject Collection" describes a function to delete all the objects contained in a list. This function could be added to the derived class as a member function.

See Also

Article: "Collections: Accessing All Members of a Collection"

Under MFC in Books Online: Technical Note 4

Collections: Accessing All Members of a Collection

The MFC array collection classes—both template-based and not—use indexes to access their elements. The MFC list and map collection classes—both template-based and not—use an indicator of type **POSITION** to describe a given position within the collection. To access one or more members of these collections, you first initialize the position indicator and then repeatedly pass that position to the collection and ask it to return the next element. The collection is not responsible for maintaining state information about the progress of the iteration. That information is kept in the position indicator. But, given a particular position, the collection is responsible for returning the next element.

The following procedures show how to iterate over the three main types of collections provided with MFC:

- Iterating an array
- Iterating a list
- Iterating a map

▶ **To iterate an array**

- Use sequential index numbers with the **GetAt** member function:

```
CTypedPtrArray<CObArray, CPerson*> myArray;

for( int i = 0; i < myArray.GetSize();i++ )
{
    CPerson* thePerson = myArray.GetAt( i );
    ...
}
```

This example uses a typed pointer array that contains pointers to `CPerson` objects. The array is derived from class **CObArray**, one of the nontemplate predefined classes. **GetAt** returns a pointer to a `CPerson` object. For typed pointer collection classes—arrays or lists—the first parameter specifies the base class; the second parameter specifies the type to store.

The **CTypedPtrArray** class also overloads the [ ] operator so that you can use the customary array-subscript syntax to access elements of an array. An alternative to the statement in the body of the for loop above is

```
CPerson* thePerson = myArray[ i ];
```

This operator exists in both **const** and non-**const** versions. The **const** version, which is invoked for **const** arrays, can appear only on the right side of an assignment statement.

▶ **To iterate a list**

- Use the member functions **GetHeadPosition** and **GetNext** to work your way through the list:

```
CTypedPtrList<CObList, CPerson*> myList;

POSITION pos = myList.GetHeadPosition();
while( pos != NULL )
{
    CPerson* thePerson = myList.GetNext( pos );
    ...
}
```

This example uses a typed pointer list to contain pointers to CPerson objects. The list declaration resembles the one for the array in the procedure "To iterate an array" (above) but is derived from class **CObList**. **GetNext** returns a pointer to a CPerson object.

▶ **To iterate a map**

- Use **GetStartPosition** to get to the beginning of the map and **GetNextAssoc** to repeatedly get the next key and value from the map, as shown by the following example:

```
CMap<CString, LPCTSTR, CPerson*, CPerson*> myMap;

POSITION pos = myMap.GetStartPosition();
while( pos != NULL )
{
    CPerson* pPerson;
    CString string;
    // Get key ( string ) and value ( pPerson )
    myMap.GetNextAssoc( pos, string, pPerson );
    // Use string and pPerson
}
```

This example uses a simple map template (rather than a typed pointer collection) that uses **CString** keys and stores pointers to CPerson objects. When you use access functions such as **GetNextAssoc**, the class provides pointers to CPerson objects. If you use one of the nontemplate map collections instead, you must cast the returned **CObject** pointer to a pointer to a CPerson. The template solution is cleaner and provides better type safety. The nontemplate code is more complicated, as you can see here:

```
CMapStringToOb myMap;     // A nontemplate collection class

POSITION pos = myMap.GetStartPosition( );
while( pos != NULL )
{
    CObject* pObject;
    CPerson* pPerson;
    CString string;
    // Gets key (string) and value (pObject)
    myMap.GetNextAssoc( pos, string, pObject );
    ASSERT( pObject->IsKindOf( RUNTIME_CLASS( CPerson ) ) );
    pPerson = (CPerson*)pObject;
    // Use string and pPerson
}
```

See Also   Article: "Collections: Deleting All Objects in a CObject Collection"

Collections: Deleting All Objects in a CObject Collection

This article explains how to delete all objects in a collection (without deleting the collection object itself).

To delete all the objects in a collection of **CObject**s (or of objects derived from **CObject**), you use one of the iteration techniques described in the article "Collections: Accessing All Members of a Collection" to delete each object in turn.

Caution   Objects in collections can be shared. That is, the collection keeps a pointer to the object, but other parts of the program may also have pointers to the same object. You must be careful not to delete an object that is shared until all the parts have finished using the object.

This article shows you how to delete the objects in:

- A list
- An array
- A map

▶ **To delete all objects in a list of pointers to CObject**

1. Use **GetHeadPosition** and **GetNext** to iterate through the list.

2. Use the **delete** operator to delete each object as it is encountered in the iteration.

3. Call the **RemoveAll** function to remove all elements from the list after the objects associated with those elements have been deleted.

The preceding technique deletes all objects in a list.

The following example shows how to delete all objects from a list of CPerson objects. Each object in the list is a pointer to a CPerson object that was originally allocated on the heap.

```
CTypedPtrList<CObList, CPerson*> myList;
POSITION pos = myList.GetHeadPosition();

while( pos != NULL )
{
    delete myList.GetNext( pos );
}
myList.RemoveAll();
```

The last function call, **RemoveAll**, is a list member function that removes all elements from the list. The member function **RemoveAt** removes a single element.

Notice the difference between deleting an element's object and removing the element itself. Removing an element from the list merely removes the list's reference to the object. The object still exists in memory. When you delete an object, it ceases to exist and its memory is reclaimed. Thus, it is important to remove an element immediately after the element's object has been deleted so that the list won't try to access objects that no longer exist.

▶ **To delete all elements in an array**

1. Use **GetSize** and integer index values to iterate through the array.

2. Use the **delete** operator to delete each element as it is encountered in the iteration.

3. Call the **RemoveAll** function to remove all elements from the array after they have been deleted.

The code for deleting all elements of an array is as follows:

```
CArray<CPerson*, CPerson*> myArray;

int i = 0;
while (i < myArray.GetSize() )
{
    delete myArray.GetAt( i++ );
}

myArray.RemoveAll();
```

Like the list example above, you can call **RemoveAll** to remove all elements in an array or **RemoveAt** to remove an individual element.

▶ **To delete all elements in a map**

1. Use **GetStartPosition** and **GetNextAssoc** to iterate through the array.

2. Use the **delete** operator to delete the key and/or value for each map element as it is encountered in the iteration.

3. Call the **RemoveAll** function to remove all elements from the map after they have been deleted.

    The code for deleting all elements of a **CMap** collection is as follows. Each element in the map has a string as the key and a CPerson object (derived from **CObject**) as the value.

```
CMap<CString, LPCSTR, CPerson*, CPerson*> myMap;
// ... Add some key-value elements ...
// Now delete the elements
POSITION pos = myMap.GetStartPosition();
while( pos != NULL )
{
    CPerson* pPerson;
    CString string;
    // Gets key (string) and value (pPerson)
    myMap.GetNextAssoc( pos, string, pPerson );
    delete pPerson;
}
// RemoveAll deletes the keys
myMap.RemoveAll();
```

You can call **RemoveAll** to remove all elements in a map or **RemoveKey** to remove an individual element with the specified key.

See Also   Article: "Collections: Creating Stack and Queue Collections"

Collections: Creating Stack and Queue Collections

This article explains how to create other data structures, such as stacks and queues, from MFC list classes. The examples use classes derived from **CList**, but you can use **CList** directly unless you need to add functionality.

Stacks

Because the standard list collection has both a head and a tail, it is easy to create a derived list collection that mimics the behavior of a last-in-first-out stack. A stack is like a stack of trays in a cafeteria. As trays are added to the stack, they go on top of the stack. The last tray added is the first to be removed. The list collection member functions **AddHead** and **RemoveHead** can be used to add and remove elements specifically from the head of the list; thus the most recently added element is the first to be removed.

▶ **To create a stack collection**

- Derive a new list class from one of the existing MFC list classes and add more member functions to support the functionality of stack operations.

  The following example shows how to add member functions to push elements on to the stack, peek at the top element of the stack, and pop the top element from the stack:

```
class CTray : public CObject { ... };

class CStack : public CTypedPtrList< CObList, CTray* >
{
public:
    // Add element to top of stack
    void Push( CTray* newTray )
        { AddHead( newTray ); }

    // Peek at top element of stack
    CTray* Peek()
        { return IsEmpty() ? NULL : GetHead(); }

    // Pop top element off stack
    CTray* Pop()
        { return RemoveHead(); }
};
```

Note that this approach exposes the underlying **CObList** class. The user can call any **CObList** member function, whether it makes sense for a stack or not.

Queues

Because the standard list collection has both a head and a tail, it is also easy to create a derived list collection that mimics the behavior of a first-in-first-out queue.

A queue is like a line of people in a cafeteria. The first person in line is the first to be served. As more people come, they go to the end of the line to wait their turn. The list collection member functions **AddTail** and **RemoveHead** can be used to add and remove elements specifically from the head or tail of the list; thus the most recently added element is always the last to be removed.

▶ **To create a queue collection**

- Derive a new list class from one of the predefined list classes provided with the Microsoft Foundation Class Library and add more member functions to support the semantics of queue operations.

  The following example shows how you can append member functions to add an element to the end of the queue and get the element from the front of the queue.

```
class CPerson : public CObject { ... };

class CQueue : public CTypedPtrList< CObList, CPerson* >
{
public:
    // Go to the end of the line
    void AddToEnd( CPerson* newPerson )
        { AddTail( newPerson ); }          // End of the queue

    // Get first element in line
    CPerson* GetFromFront()
        { return IsEmpty() ? NULL : RemoveHead(); }
};
```

Column

A column is a field in a table. For example, the first field in all the records in a table constitutes a vertical column in the table.

See the article "Recordset."

Commit

Completing an update to the data source.

See the article "Transaction."

COMMON.RC Sample Resources

Visual C++ includes sample resources that you can use in your own application. These include:

- A large number of icons that represent common business and data-processing tasks.

- Several commonly used cursors that are not included as predefined Windows resources.

- A selection of toolbar-button bitmaps.

These resources are located in a file called COMMON.RC in the \MSVC20\SAMPLES\MFC\CLIPART directory on the Visual C++ CD-ROM disc. Additional sample resources can be found in this directory.

▶ **To copy resources from COMMON.RC to your own resource script file**

1. Use the Visual C++ File menu to open both your .RC file and COMMON.RC at the same time.

2. Hold down the CTRL key and drag the resources you want from the COMMON.RC resource browser window to the resource browser window of your own application.

For more information about browsing and editing resources with Visual C++, see Chapter 4 in the *Visual C++ User's Guide*.

Connect String

A string containing the necessary information to connect to a data source.

See **CDatabase::Open** and **CRecordset::GetDefaultConnec**t in the *Class Library Reference*.

Containers

A "container application" is an application that can incorporate embedded or linked items into its own documents. The documents managed by a container application must be able to store and display OLE Visual Editing items as well as data created by the application itself. A container application must also allow users to insert new items or edit existing items. Chapters 17 through 19 in *Introducing Visual C++* take you through the process of creating a container application. You should complete that tutorial before reading this family of articles.

The following articles detail various issues you must address when writing container applications:

- Containers: Implementing a Container
- Containers: Client Items
- Containers: Compound Files

- Containers: User-Interface Issues
- Containers: Advanced Features

See Also   Articles: "Servers," "Activation," "Menus and Resources"

Containers: Implementing a Container

Chapters 17 through 19 in *Introducing Visual C++* describe the implementation of a simple Visual Editing container, explaining each step in detail. This article summarizes the tutorial procedure and points you to other articles that provide more detailed explanations of the various facets of implementing containers. It also lists some optional OLE features you may want to implement and the articles describing these features.

▶ **To prepare your CWinApp-derived class**

1. Initialize the OLE libraries by calling **AfxOleInit** in the **InitInstance** member function.

2. Call **CDocTemplate::SetContainerInfo** in **InitInstance** to assign the menu and accelerator resources used when an embedded item is activated in-place. For more information on this topic, see the "Activation" article.

These features are provided for you automatically when you use AppWizard to create a container application. See the article "AppWizard: OLE Support."

▶ **To prepare your view class**

1. Keep track of selected items by maintaining a pointer, or list of pointers if you support multiple selection, to the selected items. Your **OnDraw** function must draw all OLE items.

2. Override **IsSelected** to check whether the item passed to it is currently selected.

3. Implement an **OnInsertObject** message handler to display the Insert Object dialog box.

4. Implement an **OnSetFocus** message handler to transfer focus from the view to an in-place active OLE embedded item.

5. Implement an **OnSize** message handler to inform an OLE embedded item that it needs to change its rectangle to reflect the change in size of its containing view.

Because the implementation of these features varies dramatically from one application to the next, AppWizard provides only a basic implementation. You will likely have to customize these functions to get your application to function properly. For a more detailed explanation and an example of this, see Chapter 19 of *Introducing Visual C++* and the CONTAIN sample. For information about MFC samples, see MFC Samples under MFC in Books Online.

▶ **To handle embedded and linked items**

1. Derive a class from **COleClientItem**. Objects of this class represent items that have been embedded in or linked to your compound document.

2. Override **OnChange**, **OnChangeItemPosition**, and **OnGetItemPosition**. These functions handle sizing, positioning, and modifying embedded and linked items.

AppWizard will derive the class for you, but you will likely need to override **OnChange** and the other functions listed with it in step 2 in the preceding procedure. The skeleton implementations need to be customized for most applications, because these functions are implemented differently from one application to the next. For more information about this, see step 2 of the CONTAIN tutorial in *Introducing Visual C++* and the DRAWCLI sample. For information about MFC samples, see MFC Samples under MFC in Books Online.

You must add a number of items to the container application's menu structure to support OLE. For more information on these, see the article "Menus and Resources: Container Additions."

You may also want to support some of the following features in your container application:

- In-place activation when editing an embedded item.

  For more information, see the article "Activation."

- Creation of OLE items by dragging and dropping a selection from a server application.

  For more information, see the article "Drag and Drop."

- Links to embedded objects or combination container/server applications.

  For more information, see the article "Containers: Advanced Features."

See Also   Article: "Containers: Client Items"

Containers: Client Items

This article explains what client items are and from what classes your application should derive its client items.

"Client items" are data items belonging to another application that are either contained in or referenced by a container application's document. Client items whose data is contained within the document are "embedded"; those whose data is stored in another file referenced by the container document are "linked."

The document class in an OLE application is derived from the class **COleDocument** rather than **CDocument**. The **COleDocument** class inherits from **CDocument** all of the functionality necessary for using the document/view architecture on which Microsoft Foundation Class Library applications are based. **COleDocument** also defines an interface that treats a document as a collection of **CDocItem** objects. Several **COleDocument** member functions are provided for adding, retrieving, and deleting elements of that collection.

Every container application should derive at least one class from **COleClientItem**. Objects of this class represent items embedded in a compound document. These objects exist for the life of the document containing them, unless they are deleted from the document.

CDocItem is the base class for **COleClientItem** and **COleServerItem**. Objects of classes derived from these two act as intermediaries between the OLE item and the client and server applications, respectively. Each time a new OLE item is added to the document, the framework adds a new object of your client application's **COleClientItem**-derived class to the document's collection of **CDocItem** objects.

See Also   Articles: "Containers: Compound Files," "Containers: User-Interface Issues," "Containers: Advanced Features"

In the *Class Library Reference*: **COleClientItem**, **COleServerItem**

Containers: Client-Item Notifications

This article discusses the overridable functions that the framework calls when server applications modify items in your client application's document.

COleClientItem defines several overridable functions that are called in response to requests from the server application. These overridables usually act as notifications. They inform the container application of various events, such as scrolling, activation, or a change of position, and of changes that the user makes when editing or otherwise manipulating the item.

The framework notifies your container application of changes through a call to **COleClientItem::OnChange**, an overridable function whose implementation is required. This protected function receives two arguments. The first specifies the reason the server changed the item:

Notification	Meaning
OLE_CHANGED	The OLE item's appearance has changed.
OLE_SAVED	The OLE item has been saved.
OLE_CLOSED	The OLE item has been closed.
OLE_RENAMED	The server document containing the OLE item has been renamed.
OLE_CHANGED_STATE	The OLE item has changed from one state to another.
OLE_CHANGED_ASPECT	The OLE item's draw aspect has been changed by the framework.

These values are from the **OLE_NOTIFICATION** enumeration, which is defined in AFXOLE.H.

The second argument to this function specifies how the item has changed or what state it has entered:

When first argument is	Second argument
OLE_SAVED or **OLE_CLOSED**	Is not used.
OLE_CHANGED	Specifies the aspect of the OLE item that has changed.
OLE_CHANGED_STATE	Describes the state being entered (**emptyState**, **loadedState**, **openState**, **activeState**, or **activeUIState**).

For further information about the states a client item can assume, see the article "Containers: Client-Item States."

The framework calls **COleClientItem::OnGetItemPosition** when an item is being activated for in-place editing. Implementation is required for applications that support in-place editing. AppWizard provides a basic implementation, which assigns the item's coordinates to the **CRect** object that is passed as an argument to **OnGetItemPosition**.

If an OLE item's position or size changes during in-place editing, the container's information about the item's position and clipping rectangles must be updated and the server must receive information about the changes. The framework calls **COleClientItem::OnChangeItemPosition** for this purpose. AppWizard provides an override that calls the base class's function. You should edit the function AppWizard writes for your **COleClientItem**-derived class so that the function updates any information retained by your client-item object.

See Also   Article: "Containers: Client-Item States"

In the *Class Library Reference*: **COleClientItem::OnChangeItemPosition**

Containers: Client-Item States

This article explains the different states a client item passes through in its lifetime.

A client item passes through several states as it is created, activated, modified, and saved. Each time the item's state changes, the framework calls **COleClientItem::OnChange** with the **OLE_CHANGED_STATE** notification. The second parameter is a value from the **COleClientItem::ItemState** enumeration. It can be one of the following:

- **COleClientItem::emptyState**
- **COleClientItem::loadedState**

- **COleClientItem::openState**
- **COleClientItem::activeState**
- **COleClientItem::activeUIState**

In the "empty" state, a client item is not yet completely an item. Memory has been allocated for it, but it has not yet been initialized with the OLE item's data. This is the state a client item is in when it has been created through a call to **new** but has not yet undergone the second step of the typical two-step creation.

In the second step, performed through a call to **COleClientItem::CreateFromFile** or another **CreateFrom***xxxx* function, the item is completely created. The OLE data (from a file or some other source, such as the Clipboard) has been associated with the **COleClientItem**-derived object. Now the item is in the "loaded" state.

When an item has been opened in the server's window rather than opened in place in the container's document, it is in the "open" (or "fully open") state. In this state, a cross-hatch usually is drawn over the representation of the item in the container's window to indicate that the item is active elsewhere.

When an item has been activated in place, it passes, usually only briefly, through the "active" state. It then enters the "UI active" state, in which the server has merged its menus, toolbars, and other user-interface components with those of the container. The presence of these user-interface components distinguishes the UI active state from the active state. Otherwise, the active state resembles the UI active state. If the server supports Undo, the server is required to retain the OLE item's undo-state information until it reaches the loaded or open state.

See Also   Articles: "Activation," "Containers: Client-Item Notifications," "Trackers"

In the *Class Library Reference*: **CRectTracker**

Containers: Compound Files

This article explains the components and implementation of compound files and the advantages and disadvantages of using compound files in your OLE applications.

Compound files are an integral part of OLE. They are used to facilitate data transfer and compound document storage. Compound files are an implementation of the structured storage model. Consistent interfaces exist that support serialization to a "storage," a "stream," or a file object. Compound files are supported in the Microsoft Foundation Class Library by the classes **COleStreamFile** and **COleDocument**.

Note Using a compound file does not imply that the information comes from a compound document. Compound files are just one of the ways to store compound documents and other data.

Components of a Compound File

OLE's implementation of compound files uses three object types: stream objects, storage objects, and **ILockBytes** objects. These objects are similar to the components of a standard file system in the following manner:

- Stream objects, like files, store data of any type.
- Storage objects, like directories, can contain other storage and stream objects.
- **LockBytes** objects represent the interface between the storage objects and the physical hardware. They determine how the actual bytes are written to whatever storage device the **LockBytes** object is accessing, such as a hard drive or an area of global memory. For more information about **LockBytes** objects and the **ILockBytes** OLE 2 interface, see Chapter 6 in the *OLE 2 Programmer's Reference, Volume 1*.

Advantages and Disadvantages of Compound Files

Compound files provide benefits not available with earlier methods of file storage. They include:

- Incremental file accessing
- File access modes
- Standardization of file structure.

The potential disadvantages of compound files—large size and performance issues relating to storage on floppy disks—should be considered when deciding whether to use them in your application.

Incremental Access to Files

Incremental access to files is an automatic benefit of using compound files. Because a compound file can be viewed as a "file system within a file," individual object types, such as stream or storage, can be accessed without the need to load the entire file. This can drastically decrease the time an application needs to access new objects for editing by the user. Incremental updating, based on the same concept, offers similar benefits. Instead of saving the entire file just to save the changes made to one object, OLE saves only the stream or storage object edited by the user.

File Access Modes

Being able to determine when changes to objects in a compound file are committed to disk is another benefit of using compound files. The mode in which files are accessed, either transacted or direct, determines when changes are committed.

- Transacted mode uses a two-phase commit operation to make changes to objects in a compound file, thereby keeping both the old and the new copies of the document available until the user chooses to either save or undo the changes.

- Direct mode incorporates changes to the document as they are made, without the ability to later undo them.

For more information on access modes, see the *OLE 2 Programmer's Reference, Volume 1*.

Standardization

The standardized structure of compound files allows different OLE applications to browse through compound files created by your OLE application with no knowledge of the application that actually created the file.

Size and Performance Considerations

Due to the complexity of the compound file storage structure and the ability to save data incrementally, files using this format tend to be larger than other files using unstructured or "flat file" storage. If your application frequently loads and saves files, using compound files can cause the file size to increase much more quickly than noncompound files. Because compound files can get large, the access time for files stored on and loaded from floppy disks can also be affected, resulting in slower access to files.

Another issue that affects performance is compound-file fragmentation. The size of a compound file is determined by the difference between the first and last disk sectors used by the file. A fragmented file can contain many areas of free space that do not contain data, but are counted when calculating the size. During the lifetime of a compound file, these areas are created by the insertion or deletion of storage objects.

Using Compound Files Format for Your Data

After successfully creating an application that has a document class derived from **COleDocument**, ensure that your main document constructor calls **EnableCompoundFile**. When AppWizard creates OLE container applications, this call is inserted for you.

See Also

Article: "Containers: User-Interface Issues"

In the *Class Library Reference*: **COleStreamFile**, **COleDocument**

In the *OLE 2 Programmer's Reference, Volume 1*: **IStream**, **IStorage**, **ILockBytes**

Containers: User-Interface Issues

You must add a number of features to a container application's user interface to adequately manage linked and embedded items. These features involve changes to the menu structure and to the events that the application handles. For detailed information about them, see the following articles:

For information on	See
Menu additions for containers	"Menus and Resources: Container Additions"
Additional resources for containers	"Menus and Resources: Container Additions"
Painting linked or embedded items	*Introducing Visual C++*, Container Tutorial, Chapter 17
New dialog boxes for containers	"Dialog Boxes in OLE"

See Also   Articles: "Containers: Advanced Features," "Menus and Resources"

Containers: Advanced Features

This article describes the steps necessary to incorporate optional advanced features into existing container applications. These features are:

- An application that is both a container and a server
- An OLE link to an embedded object

Creating a Container/Server Application

A container/server application is an application that acts as both a container and a server. Microsoft Word for Windows is an example of this. You can embed Word for Windows documents in other applications, and you can also embed items in Word for Windows documents. The process for modifying your container application to be both a container and a full-server (you can't create a combination container/mini-server application) is similar to the process for creating a full-server.

The article "Servers: Implementing a Server" lists a number of tasks required to implement a server application. If you convert a container application to a container/server application, you'll need to perform some of those same tasks, adding code to the container. The following lists the important things to consider:

- The container code created by AppWizard already initializes the OLE 2 subsystem. You won't need to change or add anything for that support.
- Wherever the base class of a document class is **COleDocument**, change the base class to **COleServerDoc**.

- Override **COleClientItem::CanActivate** to avoid editing items in place while the server itself is being used to edit in place.

  For example: the OCLIENT sample application has embedded an item created by your container/server application. You open the OCLIENT application and in-place edit the item created by your container/server application. While editing your application's item, you decide you want to embed an item created by the HIERSVR sample application. To do this, you cannot use in-place activation. You must fully open HIERSVR to activate this item. Because the Microsoft Foundation Class Library does not support this OLE feature, overriding **COleClientItem::CanActivate** allows you to check for this situation and prevent a possible run-time error in your application.

If you are creating a new application and want it to function as a container/server application, choose that option in the OLE Options dialog box in AppWizard and this support will be created automatically. For more information, see the article "AppWizard: Creating an OLE Visual Editing Application." For information about MFC samples, see MFC Samples under MFC in Books Online.

Links to Embedded Objects

The Links to Embedded Objects feature enables a user to create a document with an OLE link to an embedded object inside your container application. For example, create a document in a word processor containing an embedded spreadsheet. If your application supports links to embedded objects, it could paste a link to the spreadsheet contained in the word processor's document. This feature allows your application to use the information contained in the spreadsheet without knowing where the word processor originally got it.

▶ **To link to embedded objects in your application**

1. Derive your document class from **COleLinkingDoc** instead of **COleDocument**.

2. Create an OLE class ID (**CLSID**) for your application by using the Class ID Generator included with the OLE 2 Toolkit.

3. Register the application with OLE.

4. Create a **COleTemplateServer** object as a member of your application class.

5. In your application class's **InitInstance** member function, do the following:

   - Connect your **COleTemplateServer** object to your document templates by calling the object's **ConnectTemplate** member function.

   - Call the **COleTemplateServer::RegisterAll** member function to register all class objects with the OLE system.

- Call **COleTemplateServer::UpdateRegistry**. The only parameter to **UpdateRegistry** should be **OAT_CONTAINER** if the application is not launched with the "/Embedded" switch. This registers the application as a container that can support links to embedded objects.

  If the application is launched with the "/Embedded" switch, it should not show its main window, similar to a server application.

The OCLIENT sample implements this feature. For an example of how this is done, see the **InitInstance** function in the OCLIENT.CPP file of this sample application. For information about MFC samples, see MFC Samples under MFC in Books Online.

See Also   Article: "Servers"

Current Record

The current record is the record currently stored in the field data members of a recordset.

See the article "Recordset."

Database

For a general overview of the MFC database classes, see Chapter 6, "Working with Databases."

See Also   Articles: "Database Overview," "Data Source (ODBC)"

Database Overview

> **Important** To use the MFC database classes for targeting a Win32 platform (such as Windows NT), you must have the 32-bit ODBC driver for your data source. Drivers can be obtained from Microsoft and other vendors. Visual C++ provides a way to order the Microsoft ODBC Driver Fulfillment Kit (32-Bit). You should contact other driver vendors directly.

This article introduces the main concepts of the Microsoft Foundation Class Library's database classes and provides an overview of how the classes work together. Topics covered in this article include:

- Similarity to Microsoft Access and Visual Basic
- Connecting to a data source
- Selecting and manipulating records
- Displaying and manipulating data in a form
- Working with documents and views
- Access to ODBC and SQL
- For further reading

The MFC database classes are designed to provide access to any database for which an ODBC driver is available. Because the classes use ODBC, your application can access data in many different data formats and different local/remote configurations. You do not have to write special-case code to handle different database management systems (DBMSs). As long as your users have an appropriate 32-bit ODBC driver for the data they wish to access, they can use your program to manipulate data in tables stored there.

Similarity to Microsoft Access and Visual Basic

MFC data access is very similar to the model used for data access in Microsoft Access and Microsoft Visual Basic. You connect to a data source through a "database" object. You select records through a "recordset" object. A recordset can be either:

- A "dynaset": a dynamic query that remains synchronized with the data source as other users update it.

  –Or–

- A "snapshot": a static query that reflects the state of the data at the moment of the snapshot.

If you are familiar with Microsoft Access or Microsoft Visual Basic, you will find the Visual C++ database-class programming model very similar. Using the model in conjunction with Visual C++ and MFC lets you build data-access solutions that can tap into the power and flexibility of C++.

Connecting to a Data Source

A data source is a specific set of data, the information required to access that data, and the location of the data source, which can be described using a data-source name. From your program's point of view, the data source includes the data, the DBMS, the network (if any), and ODBC.

To access data provided by a data source, your program must first establish a connection to the data source. All data access is managed through that connection.

Data-source connections are encapsulated by class **CDatabase**. Once a **CDatabase** object is connected to a data source, you can:

- Construct recordsets, which select records from tables or queries.
- Manage transactions, batching updates so all are "committed" to the data source at once (or the whole transaction is "rolled back" so the data source is unchanged)—if the data source supports the required level of transactions.
- Directly execute SQL statements.

When you finish working with a data-source connection, you close the **CDatabase** object and either destroy it or reuse it for a new connection. For more information about data-source connections, see the article "Data Source (ODBC)."

Selecting and Manipulating Records

Normally when you select records from a data source using a Structured Query Language (SQL) **SELECT** statement, you get a "result set"—a set of records from a table or a query. With the database classes, you use a "recordset" object to select and access the result set. This is an object of an application-specific class that you derive from class **CRecordset**. When you define a recordset class, you specify the data source to associate it with, the table to use, and the columns of the table. Either ClassWizard or AppWizard creates a class with a connection to a specific data source. The wizards write the **GetDefaultSQL** member function of class **CRecordset** to return the table name. For more information on using the wizards to create recordset classes, see the articles "AppWizard: Database Support" and "ClassWizard: Database Support."

Using a **CRecordset** object at run time, you can:

- Examine the data fields of the current record.
- Filter or sort the recordset.
- Customize the default SQL **SELECT** statement.
- Scroll through the selected records.
- Add, update, or delete records (if both the data source and the recordset are updatable).
- Test whether the recordset allows requerying, and refresh the recordset's contents.

When you finish using the recordset object, you close and destroy it. For more information about recordsets, see the article "Recordset."

Displaying and Manipulating Data in a Form

Many data-access applications select data and display it in fields in a form. The database class **CRecordView** gives you a **CFormView** object directly connected to a recordset object. The record view uses dialog data exchange (DDX) to move the values of the fields of the current record from the recordset to the controls on the form, and to move updated information back to the recordset. The recordset, in turn, uses record field exchange (RFX) to move data between its field data members and the corresponding columns in a table on the data source.

You can use AppWizard or ClassWizard to create the record view class and its associated recordset class in conjunction.

The record view and its recordset are destroyed when you close the document. For more information about record views, see the article "Record Views." For more information about RFX, see the article "Record Field Exchange."

Working with Documents and Views

The Microsoft Foundation Class Library relies on a document/view architecture for many of its features. Typically a document stores your data, and a view displays it within the client area of a frame window and manages user interaction with the data. The view communicates with the document to obtain and update the data. You can use the database classes with the framework or without it.

With the Framework

Normally, you use your record view in conjunction with the framework's document/view architecture. Your document class stores a **CDatabase** object—a connection to the data source—rather than the data itself. If you need a form-based user interface, the view object associated with the document is an object derived from the MFC **CRecordView** class. A **CRecordset**-derived class is associated both with the **CDatabase** object and with the record view. The record view communicates with the data source through its recordset, moving data between the record view and the recordset with DDX and between the recordset and the data source with RFX. For more information about using database classes in the framework, see the article "MFC: Using Database Classes with Documents and Views."

By default, AppWizard creates a skeleton application with no database support. But you can select options to include minimal database support or more complete form-based support. For more information about AppWizard options, see the article "AppWizard: Database Support."

Without the Framework

You can also use the database classes without using the full document/view architecture. For more information, see the article "MFC: Using Database Classes Without Documents and Views."

Access to ODBC and SQL

Just as the Microsoft Foundation Class Library encapsulates many Windows API calls but still lets you call any Windows API function directly, the database classes give you the same flexibility with regard to the ODBC API. While the database classes shield you from much of the complexity of ODBC, you can call ODBC API functions directly from anywhere in your program.

Similarly, the database classes shield you from having to work much with SQL, but you can use SQL directly if you wish. You can customize recordset objects by passing a custom SQL statement (or setting portions of the default statement) when you open the recordset. You can also make SQL calls directly using the **ExecuteSQL** member function of class **CDatabase**.

For Further Reading About Database Support

The following articles further explain the concepts and techniques introduced in this article:

- AppWizard: Database Support
- ClassWizard: Database Support
- Data Source (ODBC)
- Dynaset
- Exceptions: Database Exceptions
- MFC: Using Database Classes with Documents and Views
- MFC: Using Database Classes Without Documents and Views

- ODBC
- ODBC Administrator
- Record Field Exchange
- Recordset
- Record Views
- Serialization: Serialization vs. Database Input/Output
- Snapshot
- SQL
- Transaction

A good place to begin your reading is with the article "Recordset."

See Also   In *Introducing Visual C++*: the database tutorial in Chapters 25 through 27

In the *Class Library Reference*: **CDatabase**, **CRecordset**, **CRecordView**, **CFieldExchange**, **CDBException**, **CLongBinary**

Data Objects and Data Sources (OLE)

When you perform a data transfer, by using either the Clipboard or drag and drop, the data has a source and a destination. One application provides the data for copying and another application accepts it for pasting. Each side of the transfer needs to perform different operations on the same data for the transfer to succeed. The Microsoft Foundation Class Library (MFC) provides two classes that represent each side of this transfer:

- Data sources (as implemented by **COleDataSource** objects) represent the source side of the data transfer. They are created by the source application when data is to be copied to the Clipboard, or when data is provided for a drag-and-drop operation.
- Data objects (as implemented by **COleDataObject** objects) represent the destination side of the data transfer. They are created when the destination application has data dropped into it, or when it is asked to perform a paste operation from the Clipboard.

The following articles explain how to use data objects and data sources in your applications. This information applies to both container and server applications, because both may be called upon to copy and paste data.

- Data Objects and Data Sources: Creation and Destruction
- Data Objects and Data Sources: Manipulation

See Also   Articles: "Drag and Drop," "Clipboard"

In the *Class Library Reference*: **COleDataObject**, **COleDataSource**

Data Objects and Data Sources: Creation and Destruction

As explained in the article "Data Objects and Data Sources (OLE)," data objects and data sources represent both sides of a data transfer. This article explains when to create and destroy these objects and sources to perform your data transfers properly. Topics include:

- Creating data objects
- Destroying data objects
- Creating data sources
- Destroying data sources

Creating Data Objects

Data objects are used by the destination application—either the client or the server. A data object in the destination application is one end of a connection between the source application and the destination application. A data object in the destination application is used to access and interact with the data in the data source.

There are two common situations where a data object is needed. The first is when data is dropped in your application using drag and drop. The second is when Paste or Paste Special is chosen from the Edit Menu.

In a drag-and-drop situation, you do not need to create a data object. A pointer to an existing data object will be passed to your **OnDrop** function. This data object is created by the framework as part of the drag-and-drop operation and will also be destroyed by it. This is not always the case when pasting is done by another method. For more information, see "Destroying Data Objects" below.

If the application is performing a paste or paste special operation, you should create a **COleDataObject** object and call its **AttachClipboard** member function. This associates the data object with the data on the Clipboard. You can then use this data object in your paste function.

For an example of how this is done, see the **DoPasteItem** function in the MAINVIEW.CPP file that is part of the OCLIENT sample program. OCLIENT implements a function that performs all paste operations and calls **DoPasteItem** from its **OnDrop**, **OnPaste**, and **OnPasteLink** functions. Because **OnDrop** has a pointer to a data object passed to it, it passes the pointer on to **DoPasteItem**. **OnPaste** and **OnPasteLink** pass **NULL** for this parameter, telling **DoPasteItem** to create a data object and attach it to the Clipboard. This scheme separates your paste code so you only have to debug it in one place, but you can still use it for both kinds of paste operations. For information about MFC samples, see MFC Samples under MFC in Books Online.

Destroying Data Objects

If you follow the scheme described in "Creating Data Objects" above, destroying them is a trivial aspect of data transfers. The data object that was created in your paste function will be destroyed when your paste function returns.

If you follow another method of handling paste operations, make sure the data object is destroyed after your paste operation is complete. Until the data object is destroyed, it will be impossible for any application to successfully copy data to the Clipboard.

Creating Data Sources

Data sources are used by the source of the data transfer—which can be either the client or the server side of the data transfer. A data source in the source application is one end of a connection between the source application and the destination application. A data object in the destination application is used to interact with the data in the data source.

Data sources are created when an application needs to copy data to the Clipboard. A typical scenario runs like this:

1. The user selects some data.
2. The user chooses Copy (or Cut) from the Edit menu or begins a drag-and-drop operation.
3. Depending on the design of the program, the application creates either a **COleDataSource** object or an object from a class derived from **COleDataSource**.
4. The selected data is inserted into the data source by calling one of the functions in the **COleDataSource::CacheData** or **COleDataSource::DelayRenderData** groups.
5. The application calls the **SetClipboard** member function (or the **DoDragDrop** member function if this is a drag-and-drop operation) belonging to the object created in step 3.
6. If this is a Cut operation or **DoDragDrop** returns **DROPEFFECT_MOVE**, the data selected in step 1 is deleted from the document.

This scenario is implemented by the OCLIENT and HIERSVR sample programs. Look at the source for each application's **CView**-derived class for all but the **GetClipboardData** and **OnGetClipboardData** functions. These two functions are in either the **COleClientItem** or **COleServerItem**-derived class implementations. These sample programs provide a good example of how to implement these concepts. For information about MFC samples, see MFC Samples under MFC in Books Online.

One other situation in which you might want to create a **COleDataSource** object occurs if you are modifiying the default behavior of a drag-and-drop operation. For more information, see the "Drag and Drop: Customizing" article.

Destroying Data Sources

Data sources must be destroyed by the application currently responsible for them. In situations where you hand the data source to OLE, such as calling **COleDataSource::SetClipboard**, you do not have to worry about destroying it because it will be destroyed by OLE. If you do not hand your data source to OLE, then you are responsible for destroying it, as with any typical C++ object.

See Also   Article: "Data Objects and Data Sources: Manipulation"

In the *Class Library Reference*: **COleDataObject**, **COleDataSource**

Data Objects and Data Sources: Manipulation

After a data object or data source has been created, you can perform a number of common operations on the data, such as inserting and removing data, enumerating the formats the data is in, and more. This article describes the techniques necessary to complete the most common operations. Topics include:

- Inserting data into a data source
- Determining the formats available in a data object
- Retrieving data from a data object

Inserting Data into a Data Source

How data is inserted into a data source depends on whether the data is supplied immediately or on demand, and in which medium it is supplied. The possibilities are as follows:

Supplying Data Immediately (Immediate Rendering)

- Call **COleDataSource::CacheGlobalData** repeatedly for every Clipboard format in which you are supplying data. Pass the Clipboard format to be used, a handle to the memory containing the data and, optionally, a **FORMATETC** structure describing the data.

  –Or–

- If you want to work directly with **STGMEDIUM** structures, you call **COleDataSource::CacheData** instead of **COleDataSource::CacheGlobalData** in the option above.

Supplying Data on Demand (Delayed Rendering)

This is an advanced topic.

- Call **COleDataSource::DelayRenderData** repeatedly for every Clipboard format in which you are supplying data. Pass the Clipboard format to be used and, optionally, a **FORMATETC** structure describing the data. When the data is requested, the framework will call **COleDataSource::OnRenderData**, which you must override.

  −Or−

- If you use a **CFile** object to supply the data, call **COleDataSource::DelayRenderFileData** instead of **COleDataSource::DelayRenderData** in the option above. When the data is requested, the framework will call **COleDataSource::OnRenderFileData**, which you must override.

Determining the Formats Available in a Data Object

Before an application allows the user to paste data into it, it needs to know if there are formats on the Clipboard that it can handle. To do this, your application should do the following:

1. Create a **COleDataObject** object and a **FORMATETC** structure.
2. Call the data object's **AttachClipboard** member function to associate the data object with the data on the Clipboard.
3. Do one of the following:
   - Call the data object's **IsDataAvailable** member function if there are only one or two formats you need. This will save you time in cases where the data on the Clipboard supports significantly more formats than your application.

   −Or−

   - Call the data object's **BeginEnumFormats** member function to start enumerating the formats available on the Clipboard. Then call **GetNextFormat** until the Clipboard returns a format your application supports or there are no more formats.

If you are using **ON_UPDATE_COMMAND_UI**, you can now enable the Paste and, possibly, Paste Special items on the Edit menu. To do this, call either **CMenu::EnableMenuItem** or **CCmdUI::Enable**. For more information on what container applications should do with menu items and when, see the "Menus and Resources: Container Additions" article.

Retrieving Data from a Data Object

Once you have decided on a data format, all that's left is to retrieve the data from the data object. To do this, the user decides where he or she wants to put the data, and the application calls the appropriate function. The data will be available in one of the following mediums:

Medium	Function to call
Global Memory (**HGLOBAL**)	**COleDataObject::GetGlobalData**
File (**CFile**)	**COleDataObject::GetFileData**
STGMEDIUM structure (**IStorage**)	**COleDataObject::GetData**

Commonly, the medium will be specified along with its Clipboard format. For example, a **CF_EMBEDDEDSTRUCT** object is always in an **IStorage** medium which requires an **STGMEDIUM** structure; therefore, you would use **GetData** because it is the only one of these functions that can accept an **STGMEDIUM** structure.

For cases where the Clipboard format is in an **IStream** or **HGLOBAL** medium, the framework can provide a **CFile** pointer that references the data. The application can then use file read to get the data much as it might import data from a file. Essentially, this is the client-side interface to the **OnRenderData** and **OnRenderFileData** routines in the data source.

The data can then be inserted into your document just as you would handle any other data in the same format.

See Also   Articles: "Clipboard," "Drag and Drop"

In the *Class Library Reference*: **COleDataObject**, **COleDataSource**

Data Source (ODBC)

In database terms, a data source is a specific set of data, the information required to access that data, and the location of the data source, which can be described using a data-source name. To work with class **CDatabase**, the data source must be one that you have configured through Open Database Connectivity (ODBC) Administrator. Examples of data sources include a remote database running on Microsoft SQL Server across a network, or a Microsoft Access file in a local directory. From your application, you can access any data source for which you have an ODBC driver.

You can have one or more data sources active in your application at one time, each represented by a **CDatabase** object. You can also have multiple simultaneous connections to any data source. You can connect to remote as well as to local data sources, depending on the drivers you have installed and the capabilities of your ODBC drivers. For more information about data sources and ODBC Administrator, see the articles "ODBC" and "ODBC Administrator."

The following articles explain more about data sources:

- Data Source: Managing Connections
- Data Source: Determining the Schema of the Data Source

See Also   In the *Class Library Reference*: **CDatabase**

Data Source: Managing Connections

This article explains:

- How to configure a data source.
- How a multiuser environment affects a data source and its recordsets.
- Why you generalize a connection string to a data source.
- How to connect to a data source.
- How to disconnect from a data source.
- How to reuse a **CDatabase** object.

Connecting to a data source means establishing communications with a DBMS in order to access the data. When you connect to a data source from an application through an ODBC driver, the driver makes the connection for you, either locally or across a network.

You can connect to any data source for which you have an ODBC driver. Users of your application must also have the same ODBC driver for their data source. For more information about redistributing ODBC drivers, see "Redistributing ODBC Components to Your Customers" in the article "ODBC."

Configuring a Data Source

ODBC Administrator is used to configure your data sources. You can also use ODBC Administrator after installation to add or remove data sources. When you create applications, you can either direct your users to the ODBC Administrator to let them add data sources, or you can build this functionality into your application by making direct ODBC installation calls. For more information, see the "Setup DLL Function Reference" chapter in the ODBC *Programmer's Reference*, the article "ODBC Administrator," and the online ODBC API Reference help system.

Working in a Multiuser Environment

If multiple users are connected to a data source, they can change data while you are manipulating it in your recordsets. Similarly, your changes may affect other users' recordsets. For more information about how your updates affect other users, and how their updates affect you, see the articles "Recordset: How Recordsets Update Records" and "Transaction."

Generalizing the Connection String

ClassWizard uses a default connection string to establish a connection to a data source. You use this connection to view tables and columns while you are developing your application. However, this default connection string may not be appropriate for your users' connections to the data source through your application. For example, their data source and the path to its location may be different from the one used in developing your application. In that case, you should re-implement the **CRecordset::GetDefaultConnect** member function in a more generic fashion and discard ClassWizard's implementation. For example, use one of the following approaches:

- Register and manage the connect strings by using ODBC Administrator.

- Remove the data-source name completely. The framework supplies "ODBC" as the data source and ODBC will display a dialog box asking for the data-source name, and any other required connection information.

- Supply the data-source name only. ODBC will ask for the user ID and password, if required. For example, before generalizing, the connection string looks like this:

```
CString CApp1Set::GetDefaultConnect()
{
    return "ODBC;DSN=afx;UID=sa;PWD=Fred;";
}
```

To generalize it, rewrite **GetDefaultConnect** so that it returns one of the following values:

```
// Most general case. User must select data source and
// supply user and password
    return "ODBC;";
// User and password required
    return "ODBC;DSN=mydb;";
// Password required
    return "ODBC;DSN=mydb;UID=sa;";
// On most systems, will connect to server w/o any queries to user
    return "ODBC;DSN=mydb;UID=sa;PWD=Fred;";
```

Connecting to a Specific Data Source

To connect to a specific data source, your data source must already have been configured with ODBC Administrator.

▶ **To connect to a specific data source**

1. Construct a **CDatabase** object.

2. Call its **Open** member function.

For more information about how to specify the data source if it is something other than the one you specified with ClassWizard, see **CDatabase::Open** in the *Class Library Reference*.

Disconnecting from a Data Source

You must close any open recordsets before calling the **Close** member function of **CDatabase**. In recordsets associated with the **CDatabase** object you want to close, any pending **AddNew** or **Edit** statements are canceled, and all pending transactions are rolled back.

▶ **To disconnect from a data source**

1. Call the **CDatabase** object's **Close** member function.

2. Destroy the object unless you want to reuse it.

Reusing a CDatabase Object

You can reuse a **CDatabase** object after disconnecting from it, whether you use it to reconnect to the same data source or to connect to a different data source.

▶ **To reuse a CDatabase object**

1. Close the object's original connection.

2. Instead of destroying the object, call its **Open** member function again.

See Also   Article: "Data Source: Determining the Schema of the Data Source"

In the *Class Library Reference*: **CRecordset, CDatabase::Open, CDatabase::Close**

Data Source: Determining the Schema of the Data Source

To set up data members in your **CRecordset** objects, you need to know the schema of the data source to which you are connecting. Determining the schema of a data source involves obtaining a list of the tables in the data source, a list of the columns in each table, the data type of each column, and the existence of any indexes.

▶ **To determine the schema of a data source**

- See the CATALOG and DYNABIND sample applications, which use the ODBC API functions **::SQLTables** and **::SQLColumns**.

For information about MFC samples, see MFC Samples under MFC in Books Online.

See Also   Articles: "Data Source (ODBC)," "Data Source: Managing Connections"

Date and Time

This article describes how to take advantage of the class library general-purpose services related to time and date management. Procedures described include:

- Getting the current time
- Calculating elapsed time
- Formatting a string representation of a date/time

The **CTime** class provides a way to represent date and time information easily. The **CTimeSpan** class represents elapsed time, such as the difference between two **CTime** objects.

Note **CTime** objects can be used to represent dates between January 1, 1970, and February 5, 2036. **CTime** objects have a resolution of 1 second. **CTime** is based on the **time_t** data type, defined in the *Run-Time Library Reference*.

The following procedure shows how to create a **CTime** object and initialize it with the current time. The next procedure shows how to calculate the difference between two **CTime** objects and get a **CTimeSpan** result.

▶ **To get the current time**

1. Allocate a **CTime** object, as follows:

   ```
   CTime theTime;
   ```

   Note Uninitialized **CTime** objects are not initialized to a valid time.

   ---

2. Call the **CTime::GetCurrentTime** function to get the current time from the operating system. This function returns a **CTime** object that can be used to set the value of **CTime**, as follows:

   ```
   theTime = CTime::GetCurrentTime();
   ```

   Since **GetCurrentTime** is a static member function from the **CTime** class, you must qualify its name with the name of the class and the scope resolution operator (**::**), `CTime::GetCurrentTime()`.

Of course, the two steps outlined previously could be combined into a single program statement as follows:

```
CTime theTime = CTime::GetCurrentTime();
```

▶ **To calculate elapsed time**

- Use the **CTime** and **CTimeSpan** objects to calculate the elapsed time, as follows:

```
CTime startTime = CTime::GetCurrentTime();

// ... perform time-consuming task ...

CTime endTime = CTime::GetCurrentTime();

CTimeSpan elapsedTime = endTime - startTime;
```

Once you have calculated elapsedTime, you can use the member functions of **CTimeSpan** to extract the components of the elapsed-time value.

▶ **To format a string representation of a time or elapsed time**

- Use the **Format** member function from either the **CTime** or **CTimeSpan** classes to create a character string representation of the time or elapsed time, as shown by the following example.

```
CTime t( 1991, 3, 19, 22, 15, 0 ); // 10:15PM March 19, 1991
CString s = t.Format( "%A, %B %d, %Y" );
// s == "Tuesday, March 19, 1991"
```

See Also   Article: "Date and Time: SYSTEMTIME Support"

In the *Class Library Reference*: **CTime**, **CTimeSpan**

Date and Time: SYSTEMTIME Support

The **CTime** class has constructors that accept system and file times from Win32. If you use **CTime** objects for these purposes, you must modify their initialization accordingly, as described in this article.

MFC still provides **CTime** constructors that take time arguments of the MS-DOS® style, but the **CTime** class also supports a constructor that takes a Win32 **SYSTEMTIME** structure and another that takes a Win32 **FILETIME** structure.

The new **CTime** constructors are:

- **CTime(const SYSTEMTIME&** *sysTime* **);**
- **CTime(const FILETIME&** *fileTime* **);**

The *fileTime* parameter is a reference to a Win32 **FILETIME** structure, which represents time as a 64-bit value, a more convenient format for internal storage than a **SYSTEMTIME** structure and the format used by Win32 to represent the time of file creation.

If your code contains a **CTime** object initialized with the system time, you should use the **SYSTEMTIME** constructor in Win32.

You most likely will not use **CTime FILETIME** initialization directly. If you use a **CFile** object to manipulate a file, **CFile::GetStatus** retrieves the file timestamp for you via a **CTime** object initialized with a **FILETIME** structure.

See Also   Article: "Date and Time"

DBCS

Double-byte character set encoding—a form of Multibyte Character Set (MBCS) encoding in which characters are always either one or two bytes wide. MFC and Visual C++ support both DBCS and Unicode applications.

For information on using DBCS with MFC, see Chapter 12 in *Programming Techniques*.

DBMS

Database Management System.

See the article "Data Source (ODBC)."

Debugging

The Microsoft Foundation Class Library (MFC) and Visual C++ help you debug your applications in a variety of ways. This article presents a few useful general debugging techniques and refers you to other articles on related debugging topics.

For information about using the Visual C++ debugger, see Chapter 14, "Using the Debugger," in the *Visual C++ User's Guide*.

Following are several techniques for debugging your MFC application:

- Before you start a debugging session (or as soon as possible after you start), arrange the debugger and the program you are debugging on the screen so that neither overlaps the other. Otherwise, there may be situations in which the debugger completely obscures the program being debugged.

- Turn on Multi-App Debugging from the TRACER application when you are debugging an application and one or more DLLs. The Multi-App Debugging option prefixes each trace statement with the name of the application that generated it. TRACER can be found in the \MSVC20\BIN directory, and an icon for it is installed in the Microsoft Visual C++ program group in Program Manager with the name "MFC Trace Options."

- If you have trouble setting breakpoints with the debugger, you can hard-code them into your application with the following statement:

```
DebugBreak( );
```

which is platform independent. For MFC applications, you can also use:

```
AfxDebugBreak( );
```

This does an

```
_asm int 3
```

in Intel® versions and calls **DebugBreak** on other platforms. The advantage (on Intel) is that you break in source code rather than in kernel code.

Be sure to remove these statements when building release-mode applications or include them under **#ifdef _DEBUG**.

- If you run into limitations with the Visual C++ debugger, you can always use **TRACE** statements and the TRACER application. Activating the Multi-App Debugging option in TRACER can be very useful in tracking the order of events.

Note For Win32s™, you use "remote debugging"—the debugger is hosted on Windows NT, and the debuggee runs on another machine and is controlled through the serial port.

For additional information specific to MFC debugging, see the following articles:

- Diagnostics
- Debugging OLE Applications

Debugging OLE Applications

OLE applications perform a number of tasks outside of the programmer's direct control. Communication between DLLs, usage counts on objects, and Clipboard operations are just a few of the areas where you may encounter unexpected behavior. Usually when this happens, your first step is to track down the source of the problem. The difficulty with OLE applications is that it isn't always obvious how to debug a particular problem. This series of articles describes techniques you can use to track down problems, some of which are unique to OLE applications. It also introduces you to the special tools and testing aids available to help you write solid OLE applications.

Debugging OLE applications begins with the same general debugging techniques you use in other kinds of applications. For more information, see the article "Debugging."

Tip When you're debugging an OLE server and container, start up two instances of Visual C++, load the server and container projects, set appropriate breakpoints in each, and debug. When the container makes a call into the server that hits a breakpoint, the container will wait until the server code returns (that is, until you finish debugging it). You can also trace into calls that go across process boundaries. For more information on tracing into these calls, see "Debugging OLE2 Applications" in Chapter 14 of the *Visual C++ User's Guide*.

For more detailed information on debugging containers and servers, and for information on the tools available in Visual C++, see the following articles:

- Debugging OLE Applications: Containers
- Debugging OLE Applications: Servers
- Debugging OLE Applications: Tools

Debugging OLE Applications: Containers

This article briefly discusses an issue unique to OLE container applications. Debugging a container application is very similar to debugging a standard, non-OLE MFC program, except when you attempt to debug an event that generates a callback (such as dragging data over the container application). In this case, you must set a breakpoint in the callback function.

Note The Visual C++ debugger supports stepping across and into OLE containers and servers. This includes the ability to step across OLE Remote Procedure Calls (LRPC). For more information, see "Debugging OLE2 Applications" in Chapter 14 of the *Visual C++ User's Guide*.

See Also   Article: "Debugging OLE Applications: Servers"

Debugging OLE Applications: Servers

Debugging OLE server applications poses a unique set of problems that are not always easy to solve. This article details debugging tasks that might not behave the way you would expect when debugging a server application. Topics include:

- Starting to debug the server
- Debugging containers and servers simultaneously
- Debugging an SDI server

Starting to Debug the Server

If you do not have debugging information for your container application, or do not need to see symbolic information for the container, starting to debug the server application is a three-step process:

1. Start debugging the server as a normal application.
2. Set breakpoints as desired.
3. Start the container application from Program Manager or File Manager.

For information on viewing symbolic information for both the container and the server, see "Debugging Containers and Servers Simultaneously" below.

Debugging Containers and Servers Simultaneously

To debug both a container and a server at the same time, start a separate session of Visual C++ for each. That is, run multiple instances of Visual C++, one for the container and one for the server. See the Tip in the article "Debugging OLE Applications."

Debugging an SDI Server

If you are debugging an SDI server application, you should set the Program Arguments line of the Debug Options dialog box to "/Embedding" or "/Automation" so the debugger can launch the server application as though it were launched from a container. Starting the container from Program Manager or File Manager will now cause the container to use the instance of the server started in the debugger.

See Also   Article: "Debugging OLE Applications: Tools"

Debugging OLE Applications: Tools

Visual C++ supplies several tools that can help you find problems in your OLE applications. This article briefly summarizes the purpose of each tool. The tools include:

- Test Applications
- Viewers and Spy Programs

Test Applications

Test applications allow you to test various types of OLE applications against existing OLE applications. Visual C++ and the OLE SDK provide a number of samples to use for testing. These include:

Container and Server

CL2TEST and SR2TEST are applications you can use to test your OLE applications. Both CL2TEST and SR2TEST are full-featured OLE applications and allow testing particular OLE API calls. This can be helpful in reproducing a series of events, one call at a time.

Outline Series

This series of applications shows how to convert a non-OLE application to an OLE server and container.

Microsoft Foundation Class Samples

The CONTAIN, OCLIENT, SUPERPAD, HIERSVR, and SCRIBBLE (Step 7) samples are also available to test your applications against. Full source code for these samples is included. CONTAIN and SCRIBBLE are fully explained in the tutorials in *Introducing Visual C++*. For information about MFC samples, see MFC Samples under MFC in Books Online.

For more information on these programs, see the *OLE 2 Release Notes*.

Viewers and Spy Programs

Viewers and spy programs allow you to examine objects and events on your computer and in memory.

OLE2Viewer

OLE2VIEW displays the OLE objects installed on your computer and the interfaces they support. It also allows you to edit the registry and look at type libraries.

Docfile Viewer

DFVIEW displays the contents of any compound file. The sources for DFVIEW are included in the \MSVC20\OLE2\TOOLS\DFVIEW directory.

IDataObject Viewer

DOBJVIEW displays the list of data formats offered by OLE data objects created by the Clipboard or drag-and-drop operations.

Running Object Table Viewer

IROTVIEW displays information about OLE objects currently existing in memory.

Diagnostics

The Microsoft Foundation Class Library (MFC) contains many diagnostic features to help debug your program during development. These features, especially those that track memory allocations, will slow down your program. Others, such as assertion testing, will cause your program to halt when erroneous conditions are encountered.

In a retail product, slow performance and program interruption are clearly unacceptable. For this reason, MFC provides a method for turning the debugging and diagnostic features on or off. When you are developing your program, you typically build a debug version of your program and link with the Debug version of MFC. Once the program is completed and debugged, you build a release version and link with the Release version of MFC.

Note   Before you can use many of the MFC diagnostic features, you must enable diagnostic tracing by setting the **afxTraceEnabled** flag and customizing the **afxTraceFlags** to the level of detail you would like to see in trace messages. The easiest way to make these settings is with the TRACER.EXE utility.

In Program Manager, open the Microsoft Visual C++ program group and double-click the MFC Trace Options icon. For more information, see Technical Note 7 under MFC in Books Online.

The following articles describe the debugging and diagnostic features of the class library:

- Diagnostics: Debugging Features
- Diagnostics: Detecting Memory Leaks
- Diagnostics: Dumping All Objects
- Diagnostics: Tracking Memory Allocations

Diagnostics: Debugging Features

The following features are included for all classes derived from **CObject** in the Debug version of the Microsoft Foundation Class Library (MFC):

- **Dump** member function to dump object contents to debugging output

  See the articles "Diagnostics: Dumping Object Contents" and "Diagnostics: Dumping All Objects."

- Trace output to print or display debugging output to evaluate argument validity

  See the article "Diagnostics: The TRACE Macro."

- Assertions and **AssertValid** member function

  See the article "Diagnostics: Checking Object Validity."

- Memory diagnostics to detect memory leaks

  See the article "Diagnostics: Detecting Memory Leaks."

- **DEBUG_NEW** macro to show where objects were allocated

  See the article "Diagnostics: Tracking Memory Allocations."

▶ **To enable the debugging features**

1. Compile with the symbol **_DEBUG** defined. This is typically done by passing the **/D_DEBUG** flag on the compiler command line. To accomplish this in Visual C++, choose the Debug target in the Target box at the top of the Project Window. When you define the **_DEBUG** symbol, sections of code delimited by **#ifdef _DEBUG / #endif** are compiled.

2. Link with the Debug versions of MFC. Setting the Debug option in Visual C++ ensures linking with the Debug libraries. The Debug versions of the library have a "D" at the end of the library name. The Debug version of MFC is named NAFXCWD.LIB, and the Release version (non-debug) is named NAFXCW.LIB.

Note Pragmas in the MFC header files will automatically link the correct version of MFC. You don't need to explicitly specify the MFC library in Visual C++. Thus this step 2 is informational only. For more information, see the article "Library Versions."

Diagnostics: Dumping Object Contents

This article explains how to get a diagnostic dump of the contents of your objects.

When deriving a class from **CObject**, you have the option to override the **Dump** member function and write a textual representation of the object's member variables to a dump context which is similar to an I/O stream. Like an I/O stream, you can use the insertion (**<<**) operator to send data to a **CDumpContext**.

You do not have to override **Dump** when you derive a class from **CObject.** However, if you use other diagnostic features for debugging, providing the capability for dumping an object and viewing its contents is very helpful and highly recommended.

Note Before you can dump objects, you must enable diagnostic tracing so you can see the results of your dump in the debugger. See the Note in the article "Diagnostics."

▶ **To override the Dump member function**

1. Call the base class version of **Dump** to dump the contents of a base class object.

2. Write a textual description and value for each member variable of your derived class.

The declaration of the Dump function in the class declaration looks like:

```
class CPerson : public CObject
{
public:
#ifdef _DEBUG
    virtual void Dump( CDumpContext& dc ) const;
#endif

    CString m_firstName;
    CString m_lastName;
    // etc. ...
};
```

Note Since object dumping only makes sense when you are debugging your program, the declaration of the Dump function is bracketed with an **#ifdef _DEBUG / #endif** block.

In the following example from an implementation file for the class CPerson, the Dump function's first statement calls the **Dump** member function for its base class. It then writes a short description of each member variable along with the member's value to the diagnostic stream.

```
#ifdef _DEBUG
void CPerson::Dump( CDumpContext& dc ) const
{
    // call base class function first
    CObject::Dump( dc );

    // now do the stuff for our specific class
    dc << "last name: " << m_lastName << "\n"
        << "first name: " << m_firstName << "\n";
}
#endif
```

Note Again, notice that the definition of the Dump function is bracketed by **#ifdef _DEBUG / #endif** directives. If you refer to **afxDump** in a program linked with the nondebug libraries, you will get unresolved externals errors at link time.

▶ **To send Dump output to afxDump**

- You must supply a **CDumpContext** argument to specify where the dump output will go when you call the Dump function for an object. MFC supplies a predefined **CDumpContext** object named **afxDump** that you will normally use for routine object dumping. The following example shows how to use **afxDump**:

```
CPerson pMyPerson = new CPerson;
// set some fields of the CPerson object...
//...
```

```
                    // now dump the contents
                    #ifdef _DEBUG
                    pMyPerson->Dump( afxDump );
                    #endif
```

In Windows NT, **afxDump** output is sent to the debugger, if present. Otherwise, you will not get any **afxDump** output.

Note **afxDump** is defined only in the Debug version of MFC.

See Also   Article: "Diagnostics: The TRACE Macro"

Diagnostics: The TRACE Macro

This article explains how to use the **TRACE** macro during development to print or display debugging messages from a program. **TRACE** prints a string argument to your debugger.

Note With 32-bit MFC, the only way to get debug output is via the debugger.

The **TRACE** macro can handle a variable number of arguments, similar to the way **printf** operates. Following are examples of different ways to use **TRACE** macros:

```
int x = 1;
int y = 16;
float z = 32.0;
TRACE( "This is a TRACE statement\n" );

TRACE( "The value of x is %d\n", x );

TRACE( "x = %d and y = %d\n", x, y );

TRACE( "x = %d and y = %x and z = %f\n", x, y, z );
```

The **TRACE** macro is active only in the Debug version of the class library. After a program has been debugged, you can build a Release version to deactivate all **TRACE** calls in the program.

Tip When debugging Unicode, the **TRACE0**, **TRACE1**, **TRACE2**, and **TRACE3** macros are easier to use because the **_T** macro is not needed.

For important information on the **TRACE** macro, see "Macros and Globals" in the *Class Library Reference* and Technical Note 7 under MFC in Books Online.

See Also   Article: "Diagnostics: The ASSERT Macro"

Diagnostics: The ASSERT Macro

This article explains how to check assumptions made by your functions, using the **ASSERT** macro.

The most typical use of the **ASSERT** macro is to identify program errors during development. The argument given to **ASSERT** should be chosen so that it holds true only if the program is operating as intended. The macro evaluates the **ASSERT** argument and, if the argument expression is false (0), alerts the user and halts program execution. No action is taken if the argument is true (nonzero).

When an assertion fails, a message box appears with the following text:

```
assertion failed in file <name> in line <num>
Abort Retry Ignore
```

where `<name>` is the name of the source file and `<num>` is the line number of the assertion that failed.

If you choose Abort, program execution terminates. If you choose Ignore, program execution continues. It is possible to break into the debugger after an **ASSERT** by choosing the Retry button. Neither Abort nor Ignore will activate a debugger, so they provide no way to examine the call stack.

If you are running under the debugger and choose Retry, a call to **AfxDebugBreak** embedded in the code causes a break into the debugger. At this point, you can examine the call stack. In the Visual C++ debugger, you can do this by choosing the Call Stack command on the Debug menu. If you have enabled "Just-in-Time debugging" this will work even if the application is not being debugged. For more information about Just-in-Time debugging, see Chapter 14, "Using the Debugger," in the *Visual C++ User's Guide*.

The following example shows how the **ASSERT** macro could be used to check the validity of a function's return value:

```
int x = SomeFunc(y);
ASSERT(x >= 0);   // Assertion fails if x is negative
```

ASSERT can also be used in combination with the **IsKindOf** function to provide extra checking for function arguments, such as in the following example. (For a discussion of the **IsKindOf** function, see the article "CObject Class: Accessing Run-Time Class Information.")

```
ASSERT( pObject1->IsKindOf( RUNTIME_CLASS( CPerson ) ) );
```

The liberal use of assertions throughout your programs can catch errors during development. A good rule of thumb is that you should write assertions for any assumptions you make. For example, if you assume that an argument is not **NULL**, use an assertion statement to check for that condition.

The **ASSERT** macro will catch program errors only when you are using the Debug version of the Microsoft Foundation Class Library during development. It will be turned off (and produce no code) when you build your program with the Release version of the library.

Note The expression argument to **ASSERT** will not be evaluated in the release version of your program. If you want the expression to be evaluated in both debug and release environments, use the **VERIFY** macro instead of **ASSERT**. In debug versions, **VERIFY** is the same as **ASSERT**. In release environments, **VERIFY** evaluates the expression argument but does not check the result.

See Also   Article: "Diagnostics: Checking Object Validity"

Diagnostics: Checking Object Validity

This article explains how to check the internal consistency of the objects in your application. Topics include:

- Using the **ASSERT_VALID** macro
- Overriding the **AssertValid** function

Using the ASSERT_VALID Macro

Use the **ASSERT_VALID** macro to perform a run-time check of an object's internal consistency. The class of that object should override the **AssertValid** function of **CObject** as described in "Overriding the AssertValid Function" below. The **ASSERT_VALID** macro is a more robust way of accomplishing:

```
pObject->AssertValid();
```

Like the **ASSERT** macro, **ASSERT_VALID** is turned on in the debug version of your program, but turned off in the release version.

Overriding the AssertValid Function

The **AssertValid** member function is provided in **CObject** to allow run-time checks of an object's internal state. **AssertValid** typically performs assertions on all the object's member variables to see if they contain valid values. For example, **AssertValid** can check that all pointer member variables are not **NULL**. If the object is invalid, **AssertValid** halts the program.

Although you are not required to override **AssertValid** when you derive your class from **CObject**, you can make your class safer and more reliable by doing so. The following example shows how to declare the **AssertValid** function in the class declaration:

```
class CPerson : public CObject
{
protected:
    CString m_strName;
    float   m_salary;
public:
#ifdef _DEBUG
    virtual void AssertValid() const;      // Override
#endif
    // ...
};
```

When you override `AssertValid`, first call **AssertValid** for the base class. Then
use the **ASSERT** macro to check the validity of the members unique to your
derived class, as shown by the following example:

```
#ifdef _DEBUG
void CPerson::AssertValid()
{
    // call inherited AssertValid first
    CObject::AssertValid();

    // check CPerson members...
    ASSERT( !m_strName.IsEmpty()); // Must have a name
    ASSERT( m_salary > 0 ); // Must have an income
}
#endif
```

If any of the member variables of your class store objects, you can use the
ASSERT_VALID macro to test their internal validity (if their classes override
AssertValid). The following example shows how this is done.

Consider a class `CMyData`, which stores a **CObList** in one of its member variables.
The **CObList** variable, m_DataList, stores a collection of `CPerson` objects. An
abbreviated declaration of `CMyData` looks like this:

```
class CMyData : public CObject
{
    // Constructor and other members ...
    protected:
        CObList* m_pDataList;
    // Other declarations ...
    public:
#ifdef _DEBUG
        virtual void AssertValid( ) const; // Override
#endif
    // Etc. ...
};
```

The **AssertValid** override in `CMyData` looks like this:

```
#ifdef _DEBUG
void CMyData::AssertValid( )
{
    // Call inherited AssertValid
    CObject::AssertValid( );
    // Check validity of CMyData members
    ASSERT_VALID( m_pDataList );
    // ...
}
#endif
```

CMyData uses the **AssertValid** mechanism to add validity tests for the objects stored in its data member to the validity test of the CMyData object itself. The overriding **AssertValid** of CMyData invokes the **ASSERT_VALID** macro for its own **m_pDataList** member variable.

The chain of validity testing might stop at this level, but in this case class **CObList** overrides **AssertValid** too, and the **ASSERT_VALID** macro causes it to be called. This override performs additional validity testing on the internal state of the list. If an assertion failure occurs, diagnostic messages are printed, and the program halts.

Thus a validity test on a CMyData object leads to additional validity tests for the internal states of the stored **CObList** list object. With a little more work, the validity tests could include the CPerson objects stored in the list as well. You could derive a class CPersonList from **CObList** and override **AssertValid**. In the override, you would call **CObject::AssertValid** and then iterate through the list, calling AssertValid on each CPerson object stored in the list. The CPerson class shown at the beginning of this section already overrides **AssertValid**.

This is a powerful mechanism when you build for debugging, and when you subsequently build for release, the mechanism is turned off automatically.

Users of an AssertValid function of a given class should be aware of the limitations of this function. A triggered assertion indicates that the object is definitely bad and execution will halt. However, a lack of assertion only indicates that no problem was found, but the object isn't guaranteed to be good.

Diagnostics: Detecting Memory Leaks

This article explains the facilities that MFC provides for detecting memory leaks. Topics include:

- Memory diagnostics
- Detecting a memory leak
- Dumping memory statistics

A memory leak occurs when you allocate memory on the heap and never deallocate that memory to make it available for reuse, or if you mistakenly use memory that has already been allocated. This is a particular problem for programs that are intended to run for extended periods. In a long-lived program, even a small incremental memory leak can compound itself; eventually all available memory resources are exhausted and the program crashes. Traditionally, memory leaks have been very hard to detect.

The Microsoft Foundation Class Library (MFC) provides classes and functions you can use to detect memory leaks during development. Basically, these functions take a snapshot of all memory blocks before and after a particular set of operations. You can use these results to determine if all memory blocks allocated during the operation have been deallocated.

Note MFC automatically dumps all leaked objects when your program exits.

The size or length of the operation you choose to bracket with these diagnostic functions is arbitrary. It can be as small as a single program statement, or it can span the entry and exit from the entire program. Either way, these functions allow you to detect memory leaks and identify which memory blocks have not been deallocated properly.

Memory Diagnostics

Before you can use the memory diagnostics facilities, you must enable diagnostic tracing. See the Note at the end of the article "Diagnostics" as well as the rest of this discussion.

▶ **To enable or disable memory diagnostics**

- Call the global function **AfxEnableMemoryTracking** to enable or disable the diagnostic memory allocator. Since memory diagnostics are on by default in the Debug library, you will typically use this function to temporarily turn them off, which increases program execution speed and reduces diagnostic output.

▶ **To select specific memory diagnostic features with afxMemDF**

- If you want more precise control over the memory diagnostic features, you can selectively turn individual memory diagnostic features on and off by setting the value of the MFC global variable **afxMemDF**. This variable can have the following values as specified by the enumerated type **AfxMemDF**:

Value	Meaning
allocMemDF	Turn on diagnostic memory allocator (default).
delayFreeMemDF	Delay freeing memory when calling **delete** or **free** until program exits. This will cause your program to allocate the maximum possible amount of memory.
checkAlwaysMemDF	Call **AfxCheckMemory** every time memory is allocated or freed.

These values can be used in combination by performing a logical-OR operation:

```
afxMemDF |= delayFreeMemDF | checkAlwaysMemDF;
```

Detecting a Memory Leak

The following instructions and example show you how to detect a memory leak.

▶ **To detect a memory leak**

1. Create a **CMemoryState** object and call the **Checkpoint** member function to get the initial snapshot of memory.

2. After you perform the memory allocation and deallocation operations, create another **CMemoryState** object and call **Checkpoint** for that object to get a current snapshot of memory usage.

3. Create a third **CMemoryState** object, call the **Difference** member function, and supply the previous two **CMemoryState** objects as arguments. The return value for the **Difference** function will be nonzero if there is any difference between the two specified memory states, indicating that some memory blocks have not been deallocated.

The following example shows how to check for memory leaks:

```
// Declare the variables needed
#ifdef _DEBUG
    CMemoryState oldMemState, newMemState, diffMemState;
    oldMemState.Checkpoint();
#endif

    // do your memory allocations and deallocations...
    CString s = "This is a frame variable";
    // the next object is a heap object
    CPerson* p = new CPerson( "Smith", "Alan", "581-0215" );

#ifdef _DEBUG
    newMemState.Checkpoint();
    if( diffMemState.Difference( oldMemState, newMemState ) )
    {
        TRACE( "Memory leaked!\n" );
    }
#endif
```

Notice that the memory-checking statements are bracketed by **#ifdef _DEBUG / #endif** blocks so that they are only compiled in debug versions of your program.

Dumping Memory Statistics

The **CMemoryState** member function **Difference** determines the difference between two memory-state objects. It detects any objects that were not deallocated from the heap between the beginning and end memory-state snapshots.

▶ **To dump memory statistics**

- The following example (continuing the example from the previous section) shows how to call **DumpStatistics** to get information about the objects that have not been deallocated:

```
if( diffMemState.Difference( oldMemState, newMemState ) )
{
    TRACE( "Memory leaked!\n" );
    diffMemState.DumpStatistics();
}
```

A sample dump from the example above is shown here:

```
0 bytes in 0 Free Blocks
22 bytes in 1 Object Blocks
45 bytes in 4 Non-Object Blocks
Largest number used: 67 bytes
Total allocations: 67 bytes
```

- The first line describes the number of blocks whose deallocation was delayed if **afxMemDF** was set to **delayFreeMemDF**. For a description of **afxMemDF**, see the procedure "To select specific memory diagnostic features with afxMemDF" presented under "Memory Diagnostics" earlier in this article.

- The second line describes how many objects remain allocated on the heap.

- The third line describes how many non-object blocks (arrays or structures allocated with **new**) were allocated on the heap and not deallocated.

- The fourth line gives the maximum memory used by your program at any one time.

- The last line lists the total amount of memory used by your program.

See Also   Articles: "Diagnostics: Dumping All Objects," "Diagnostics: Tracking Memory Allocations"

In the *Class Library Reference*: **AfxEnableMemoryTracking**, **CMemoryState**

Diagnostics: Dumping All Objects

This article explains how to obtain a diagnostic dump of all objects in your program. Topics include:

- Performing an object dump
- Interpreting an object dump

DumpAllObjectsSince dumps out a description of all objects detected on the heap that have not been deallocated. As the name implies, **DumpAllObjectsSince** dumps all objects allocated since the last **Checkpoint**. However, if no **Checkpoint** has taken place, all objects and non-objects currently in memory are dumped.

Note Before you can use MFC object dumping, you must enable diagnostic tracing. See the Note in the article "Diagnostics."

Performing an Object Dump

▶ **To dump all objects**

- Expanding on the example shown in "Detecting a Memory Leak" in the "Diagnostics: Detecting Memory Leaks" article, the following code dumps all objects that have not been deallocated when a memory leak is detected:

```
if( diffMemState.Difference( oldMemState, newMemState ) )
{
    TRACE( "Memory leaked!\n" );
    diffMemState.DumpAllObjectsSince();
}
```

A sample dump from the preceding example is shown here:

```
Dumping objects ->

{5} strcore.cpp(80) : non-object block at $00A7521A, 9 bytes long
{4} strcore.cpp(80) : non-object block at $00A751F8, 5 bytes long
{3} strcore.cpp(80) : non-object block at $00A751D6, 6 bytes long
{2} a CPerson at $51A4

Last Name: Smith
First Name: Alan
Phone #: 581-0215

{1} strcore.cpp(80) : non-object block at $00A7516E, 25 bytes long
```

The numbers in braces at the beginning of most lines specify the order in which the objects were allocated. The most recently allocated object is displayed first. You can use these ordering numbers to help identify allocated objects.

To set a breakpoint when a particular allocation occurs, first start your application in the debugger. Set the global variable **_afxBreakAlloc** to the number in braces discussed earlier. This will set a conditional breakpoint in your application that will trigger when the allocation you specify is being made. Looking at the call stack at this point will tell you the path your program took to get to the specified allocation.

Interpreting an Object Dump

The preceding dump comes from the memory checkpoint example introduced in "Detecting a Memory Leak" in the "Diagnostics: Detecting Memory Leaks" article. Remember that there were only two explicit allocations in that program—one on the frame and one on the heap:

```
// do your memory allocations and deallocations ...
CString s = "This is a frame variable";
// the next object is a heap object
CPerson* p = new CPerson( "Smith", "Alan", "581-0215" );
```

Start with the CPerson object; its constructor takes three arguments that are pointers to **char**. The constructor uses these arguments to initialize **CString** member variables for the CPerson class. In the memory dump, you can see the CPerson object listed along with three non-object blocks (3, 4, and 5) that hold the characters for the **CString** member variables. These memory blocks will be deleted when the destructor for the CPerson object is invoked.

Block number 2 represents the CPerson object itself. After the CPerson address listing, the contents of the object are displayed. This is a result of **DumpAllObjectsSince** calling the Dump member function for the CPerson object.

You can guess that block number 1 is associated with the **CString** frame variable because of its sequence number and its size, which match the number of characters in the frame **CString** variable. The allocations associated with frame variables are automatically deallocated when the frame variable goes out of scope.

In general, you shouldn't worry about heap objects associated with frame variables because they are automatically deallocated when the frame variables go out of scope. In fact, you should position your calls to **Checkpoint** so that they are outside the scope of frame variables to avoid clutter in your memory diagnostic dumps. For example, place scope brackets around the previous allocation code, as shown here:

```
oldMemState.Checkpoint();
{
    // do your memory allocations and deallocations ...
    CString s = "This is a frame variable";
    // the next object is a heap object
    CPerson* p = new CPerson( "Smith", "Alan", "581-0215" );
}
newMemState.Checkpoint();
```

With the scope brackets in place, the memory dump for this example is as follows:

```
Dumping objects ->

{5} strcore.cpp(80) : non-object block at $00A7521A, 9 bytes long
{4} strcore.cpp(80) : non-object block at $00A751F8, 5 bytes long
{3} strcore.cpp(80) : non-object block at $00A751D6, 6 bytes long
{2} a CPerson at $51A4

Last Name: Smith
First Name: Alan
Phone #: 581-0215
```

Notice that some allocations are objects (such as `CPerson`) and some are non-object allocations. "Non-object allocations" are allocations for objects not derived from **CObject** or allocations of primitive C types such as **char**, **int**, or **long**. If the **CObject**-derived class allocates additional space, such as for internal buffers, those objects will show both object and non-object allocations.

Notice that the memory block associated with the **CString** frame variable has been deallocated automatically and does not show up as a memory leak. The automatic deallocation associated with scoping rules takes care of most memory leaks associated with frame variables.

For objects allocated on the heap, however, you must explicitly delete the object to prevent a memory leak. To clean up the last memory leak in the previous example, you can delete the `CPerson` object allocated on the heap, as follows:

```
{
    // do your memory allocations and deallocations ...
    CString s = "This is a frame variable";
    // the next object is a heap object
    CPerson* p = new CPerson( "Smith", "Alan", "581-0215" );
    delete p;
}
```

See Also   Article: "Diagnostics: Detecting Memory Leaks"

Diagnostics: Tracking Memory Allocations

The Microsoft Foundation Class Library (MFC) defines the macro **DEBUG_NEW** to assist you in locating memory leaks. You can use **DEBUG_NEW** everywhere in your program that you would ordinarily use the **new** operator.

When you compile a Debug version of your program, **DEBUG_NEW** keeps track of the filename and line number for each object that it allocates. Then, when you call **DumpAllObjectsSince**, as described in the article "Diagnostics: Dumping All Objects," each object allocated with **DEBUG_NEW** will be shown with the file and line number where it was allocated, thus allowing you to pinpoint the sources of memory leaks.

When you compile a Release version of your program, **DEBUG_NEW** resolves to a simple **new** operation without the filename and line number information. Thus, you pay no speed penalty in the Release version of your program.

▶   **To use DEBUG_NEW**

- Define a macro in your source files that replaces **new** with **DEBUG_NEW**, as shown here:

```
#define new DEBUG_NEW
```

Note   While the framework uses **DEBUG_NEW** in debug builds, your code does not. You must enable this feature as shown in this procedure.

You can then use **new** for all heap allocations. The preprocessor will substitute **DEBUG_NEW** when compiling your code. In the Debug version of the library, **DEBUG_NEW** will create debugging information for each heap block. In the Release version, **DEBUG_NEW** will resolve to a standard memory allocation without the extra debugging information.

Note   You must place the **#define** statement after all statements that use the **IMPLEMENT_DYNCREATE** or **IMPLEMENT_SERIAL** macros in your source module, or you will get a compile-time error.

See Also   Article: "Diagnostics: Detecting Memory Leaks"

Dialog Boxes in OLE

While a user runs an OLE-enabled application, there are times when the application needs information from the user in order to carry out the operation. The MFC OLE classes provide a number of dialog boxes to gather the required information. This article lists the tasks handled by the OLE dialog boxes and the classes needed to display those dialog boxes. For full details on OLE dialog boxes and the structures used to customize their behavior, see the *Class Library Reference* and see the *User Interface Dialog Help* (OLE2UI.HLP) file included with the OLE SDK.

Insert Object
> This dialog box allows the user to insert newly created or existing objects into the compound document. It also allows the user to choose to display the item as an icon and enables the Change Icon command button. Display this dialog box when the user chooses Insert Object from the Edit menu. Use the **COleInsertDialog** class to display this dialog box.

Paste Special

This dialog box allows the user to control the format used when pasting data into a compound document. The user can choose the format of the data, whether to embed or link the data, and whether to display it as an icon. Display this dialog box when the user chooses Paste Special from the Edit menu. Use the **COlePasteSpecialDialog** class to display this dialog box.

Change Icon

This dialog box allows the user to select which icon is displayed to represent the linked or embedded item. Display this dialog box when the user chooses Change Icon from the Edit menu or chooses the Change Icon button in either the Paste Special or Convert dialog boxes. Also display it when the user opens the Insert Object dialog box and chooses Display as Icon. Use the **COleChangeIconDialog** class to display this dialog box.

Convert

This dialog box allows the user to change the type of an embedded or linked item. For example, if you have embedded a metafile in a compound document and later want to use another application to modify the embedded metafile, you can use the Convert dialog box. This dialog box is usually displayed by choosing *item type* Object from the Edit menu and then, on the cascading menu, choosing Convert. Use the **COleConvertDialog** class to display this dialog box. For an example, run the OCLIENT sample program, which is available in the "MFC Samples on CDROM" program group.

Edit Links or Update Links

The Edit Links dialog box allows the user to change information about the source of a linked object. The Update Links dialog box verifies the sources of all the linked items in the current dialog box and displays the Edit Links dialog box if necessary. Display the Edit Links dialog box when the user chooses Links from the Edit menu. The Update Links dialog box is usually displayed when a compound document is first opened. Use either the **COleLinksDialog** or the **COleUpdateDialog** class depending on which dialog box you want to display.

Server Busy or Server Not Responding

The Server Busy dialog box is displayed when the user attempts to activate an item and the server is currently unable to handle the request, usually because the server is in use by another user or task. The Server Not Responding dialog box is displayed if the server does not respond to the activation request at all. These dialog boxes are displayed via **COleMessageFilter**, based on an implementation of the OLE interface IMessageFilter, and the user can decide whether to attempt the activation request again. Use the **COleBusyDialog** class to display this dialog box.

Document/View Architecture

For general information, see Chapters 1 and 3 in Part 1.

See Also   Articles: "MFC: Using Database Classes with Documents and Views," "MFC: Using Database Classes Without Documents and Views"

Drag and Drop (OLE)

The drag-and-drop feature of OLE is primarily a shortcut for copying and pasting data. When you use the Clipboard to copy or paste data, a number of steps are required. You select the data, choose Cut or Copy from the Edit menu, move to the destination file, window or application, place the cursor in the desired location, and choose Paste from the Edit menu.

OLE drag and drop is different from File Manager's drag-and-drop mechanism, which can only handle filenames and is designed specifically to pass filenames to applications. OLE drag and drop is much more general. It allows you to drag and drop any data that could also be placed on the Clipboard.

When you use OLE drag and drop, you remove two steps from the process. You select the data from the source window (the "drop source"), drag it to the desired destination (the "drop target"), and drop it by releasing the mouse button. The operation eliminates the need for menus and is quicker than the copy/paste sequence. The only requirement is that both the drop source and drop target must be open and at least partially visible on the screen.

Using OLE drag and drop, data can be transferred from one location to another within a document, between different documents, or between applications. It can be implemented in either a container or a server application, and any application can be a drop source, a drop target, or both. If an application has both drop-source and drop-target support implemented, drag and drop is enabled between child windows, or within one window. This feature can make your application much easier to use.

If you only want to use the drag-and-drop capabilities of OLE, see the article "Drag and Drop: Customizing." You can use the techniques explained in that article to make non-OLE applications drop sources. The article "Drag and Drop: Implementing a Drop Target" describes how to implement drop-target support for both OLE and non-OLE applications. It will also be helpful to to examine the OCLIENT and HIERSVR samples. For information about MFC samples, see MFC Samples under MFC in Books Online.

If you have not read the "Data Objects and Data Sources (OLE)" family of articles, you may want to do so now. These articles explain the fundamentals of data transfer, and how to implement it in your applications.

For more information about drag and drop, see the following articles:

- Drag and Drop: Implementing a Drop Source
- Drag and Drop: Implementing a Drop Target
- Drag and Drop: Customizing

See Also   Article: "Data Objects and Data Sources (OLE)"

Drag and Drop: Implementing a Drop Source

This article explains how to get your application to provide data to a drag-and-drop operation.

Basic implementation of a drop source is relatively simple. The first step is to determine what events begin a drag operation. Recommended user interface guidelines define the beginning of a drag operation as the selection of data and a **WM_LBUTTONDOWN** event occurring on a point inside the selected data. The OCLIENT and HIERSVR samples follow these guidelines. For information about MFC samples, see MFC Samples under MFC in Books Online.

If your application is a container and the selected data is a linked or an embedded object of type **COleClientItem**, call its **DoDragDrop** member function. Otherwise, construct a **COleDataSource** object, initialize it with the selection, and call the data source object's **DoDragDrop** member function. If your application is a server, use **COleServerItem::DoDragDrop**. For information about customizing standard drag-and-drop behavior, see the article "Drag and Drop: Customizing."

If **DoDragDrop** returns **DROPEFFECT_MOVE**, you should delete the source data from the source document immediately. No other return value from **DoDragDrop** has any effect on a drop source.

See Also   Articles: "Drag and Drop: Implementing a Drop Target," "Drag and Drop: Customizing," "Data Objects and Data Sources: Creation and Destruction," "Data Objects and Data Sources: Manipulation"

In the *Class Library Reference*: **COleDataSource::DoDragDrop**, **COleClientItem::DoDragDrop**, **CView::OnDragLeave**

Drag and Drop: Implementing a Drop Target

This article outlines how to make your application a drop target. Implementing a drop target takes slightly more work than implementing a drop source, but it's still relatively simple. These techniques also apply to non-OLE applications.

▶ **To implement a drop target**

1. Add a member variable to each view in the application that you want to be a drop target. This member variable must be of type **COleDropTarget** or a class derived from it.

2. From your view class's function that handles the **WM_CREATE** message (typically **OnCreate**), call the new member variable's **Register** member

function. **Revoke** will be called automatically for you when your view is destroyed.

3. Override the following functions. If you want the same behavior throughout your application, override these functions in your view class. If you want to modify behavior in isolated cases or want to enable dropping on non-**CView** windows, override these functions in your **COleDropTarget**-derived class.

Override	To allow
OnDragEnter	Drop operations to occur in the window. Called when the cursor first enters the window.
OnDragLeave	Special behavior when the drag operation leaves the specified window.
OnDragOver	Drop operations to occur in the window. Called when the cursor is being dragged across the window.
OnDrop	Handling of data being dropped into the specified window.
OnScrollBy	Special behavior for when scrolling is necessary in the target window.

See the MAINVIEW.CPP file that is part of the OCLIENT sample for an example of how these functions work together. For information about MFC samples, see MFC Samples under MFC in Books Online.

See Also   Articles: "Drag and Drop: Implementing a Drop Source," "Data Objects and Data Sources: Creation and Destruction," "Data Objects and Data Sources: Manipulation"

In the *Class Library Reference*: **COleDropTarget**

Drag and Drop: Customizing

The default implementation of the drag-and-drop feature is sufficient for most applications. However, some applications may require that this standard behavior be changed. This article explains the steps necessary to change these defaults. In addition, you can use this technique to establish applications that do not support compound documents as drop sources.

If you are customizing standard OLE drag-and-drop behavior, or you have a non-OLE application, you must create a **COleDataSource** object to contain the data. When the user starts a drag-and-drop operation, your code should call the **DoDragDrop** function from this object instead of from other classes that support drag-and-drop operations.

Optionally, you can create a **COleDropSource** object to control the drop and override some of its functions depending on the type of behavior you want to change. This drop-source object is then passed to **COleDataSource::DoDragDrop** to change the default behavior of these functions. These different options allow a great deal of flexibility in how you support drag-and-drop operations in your application. For more information about data sources, see the article "Data Objects and Data Sources (OLE)."

You can override the following functions to customize drag-and-drop operations:

Override	To customize
OnBeginDrag	How dragging is initiated after you call DoDragDrop.
GiveFeedback	Visual feedback, such as cursor appearance, for different drop results.
QueryContinueDrag	The termination of a drag-and-drop operation. This function enables you to check modifier key states during the drag operation.

See Also   Article: "Drag and Drop: Implementing a Drop Source"

In the *Class Library Reference*: **COleDropSource**, **COleDataSource**

Driver Manager, ODBC

See the article "ODBC."

Driver, ODBC

See the article "ODBC."

Drop Source

See the article "Drag and Drop: Implementing a Drop Source."

Drop Target

See the article "Drag and Drop: Implementing a Drop Target."

Dynamic-Link Libraries (DLLs)

A "dynamic-link library" (DLL) is a binary file that acts as a shared library of functions that can be used simultaneously by multiple applications. DLLs are used for a variety of reasons, primarily for either:

- Sharing common code between different executable files.

  – Or –

- Breaking an application into separate components, thus allowing easy upgrades.

The Microsoft Foundation Class Library (MFC) supports development of your DLLs in two different ways:

- Dynamically linking your DLL to the shared MFC DLL.
- Statically linking MFC into your DLL.

Dynamically Linking Your DLL to MFC

Use the AFXDLL version of MFC to dynamically link your DLL to MFC. AFXDLL refers to an **_AFXDLL** preprocessor symbol that is defined when building your DLL, as discussed in the article "DLLs: Building and Using an Extension DLL."

If your DLL is dynamically linked to MFC, it can be called only by MFC applications that also dynamically link to MFC. Such a DLL is called an "extension DLL" because it derives new custom classes from MFC in the shared DLL, and offers this "extended" version of MFC to applications that call your DLL.

The AFXDLL version of MFC is named according to the convention described in the article "DLLs: Naming Conventions." Visual C++ supplies prebuilt versions of the AFXDLL version of MFC, plus a number of non-MFC DLLs that you can use and distribute with your applications. These are documented in REDISTRB.WRI, which is found in the \MSVC20\REDIST directory on the Visual C++ CD-ROM disc.

Statically Linking Your DLL to MFC

Use the USRDLL version of MFC to statically link the MFC library into your DLL. USRDLL refers to a **_USRDLL** preprocessor symbol that is defined when building your DLL, as discussed in the article "DLLs: Building and Using the USRDLL Version."

If your DLL is statically linked to the MFC library, functions in your DLL can be called by any Win32 application, as well as by programs that use MFC.

The USRDLL version of MFC is named according to the convention described in the article "DLLs: Naming Conventions."

The remaining articles in this group explain how to build and use the various versions of MFC and the conventions used to name them.

- DLLs: Using the Shared DLL Version of MFC
- DLLs: Building and Using an Extension DLL
- DLLs: Building and Using the USRDLL Version
- DLLs: Programming Tips
- DLLs: Naming Conventions

See Also
In *Programming Techniques*: Chapter 4, "Creating DLLs for Windows NT"

In the *Win32 Programmer's Reference, Volume 2*: Chapter 50, "Dynamic Link Libraries"

DLLs: Using the Shared DLL Version of MFC

This article describes the shared DLL or "AFXDLL" version of MFC, and when and how to use it in your applications. For more information on using the shared DLL version of MFC with your DLL, see the article "DLLs: Building and Using an Extension DLL."

The entire Microsoft Foundation Class Library (MFC) is provided in a set of redistributable DLLs. This enables applications to access MFC functionality by dynamically linking to these DLLs. This architecture is particularly useful in two situations: sharing the class library between multiple executable files to save disk and memory usage and building MFC extension DLLs.

If you are building an application that consists of multiple executable files, all of which are written using MFC, you can save a significant amount of disk and memory space by using the shared version of the class library. The only disadvantage is that you must distribute the shared DLL MFC30.DLL (or another similar file) with your application. See the article "DLLs: Naming Conventions" for a complete list of AFXDLL libraries.

Note Applications created with AppWizard will use the shared DLL version of MFC by default.

If you are building an extension to MFC and wish to put it in a DLL, you must use the AFXDLL version of the class library. See the article "DLLs: Building and Using an Extension DLL."

Using the Shared MFC DLL with Your Application

Applications that use the shared DLL version of MFC have only one important restriction: they must be an MFC application. This means they must have a **CWinApp**-derived object.

In addition, you must choose "Use MFC in a shared DLL" in the Microsoft Foundation Classes list box on the General tab in the Project Settings dialog box. AppWizard automatically does this for you if you choose "Use MFC in a shared DLL" when creating an AppWizard executable.

Rebuilding the Shared DLL

The AFXDLL version of MFC can be rebuilt. Normally this would be done only if you modify the MFC source code, or if you need to build MFC with special compiler options. For information on how to do this, see the README.TXT and MAKEFILE files in the \MSVC20\MFC\SRC directory. If you modify and rebuild the AFXDLL version of MFC, you must rename the newly built DLL to something other than MFC30.DLL to reflect that it has been modified. Otherwise, applications that depend on this DLL could stop functioning correctly.

See Also   Article: "DLLs: Naming Conventions"

In *Programming Techniques*: Chapter 4, "Creating DLLs for Windows NT"

In the *Win32 Programmer's Reference, Volume 2*: Chapter 50, "Dynamic Link Libraries"

DLLs: Building and Using an Extension DLL

An MFC extension DLL is a DLL that typically implements reusable classes derived from the existing Microsoft Foundation Class Library classes. Extension DLLs can also be used for passing MFC-derived objects between the .EXE and the .DLL. This article describes how to build and use these DLLs. Topics include:

- Building an extension DLL
- Exporting classes without using decorated names
- Exporting symbols by ordinal
- Calling an extension DLL from your application

An MFC extension DLL uses the shared DLL version of MFC in the same way an application uses the shared version of MFC, as described in the article "DLLs: Using the Shared DLL Version of MFC," with a few additional considerations:

- It does not have a **CWinApp**-derived object.

- It calls **AfxInitExtensionModule** in its **DllMain** function. The return value of this function should be checked. If a zero value is returned from **AfxInitExtensionModule**, return 0 from your **DllMain** function.

- It will create a **CDynLinkLibrary** object during initialization if the extension DLL wishes to export **CRuntimeClass**es or resources to the application.

For an example of a DLL that fulfills the basic requirements for an extension DLL, see the DLLHUSK sample in the \MSVC20\SAMPLES\MFC\DLLHUSK directory. In particular, look at the TESTDLL1.CPP and TESTDLL2.CPP files.

Building an Extension DLL

To build an extension DLL, you must choose "Use MFC in a shared DLL" in the Microsoft Foundation Classes list box on the General tab in the Project Settings dialog box. AppWizard automatically does this for you if you create an AppWizard Win32 DLL from the New Project dialog box.

When you create your extension DLL, you must also create a C++ header file (.H) and a definitions file (.DEF) for the DLL so applications can access its contents. There are two methods for creating these two files. The first method exports entire classes without requiring decorated names for that class in the .DEF file. The second method requires putting decorated names in a .DEF file. This latter method is more efficient as you can export the symbols by ordinal. MFC uses this method.

Exporting Classes Without Using Decorated Names

In the header file for your DLL, add the **AFX_EXT_CLASS** keyword to the declaration of your class as follows:

```
class AFX_EXT_CLASS CMyClass : public CDocument
{
// <body of class>
};
```

This allows you to export entire classes without placing the decorated names for all that class's symbols in the .DEF file. This method is used by the DLLHUSK sample in the \MSVC20\SAMPLES\MFC\DLLHUSK directory.

Exporting Symbols by Ordinal

This method requires that you place the decorated names for all external symbols in your .DEF file. This is more efficient, but is useful if you only want to export a small percentage of the symbols in the DLL.

To use this method, place the following code at the beginning and end of your header file:

```
#undef AFX_DATA
#define AFX_DATA AFX_EXT_DATA
// <body of your header file>
#undef AFX_DATA
#define AFX_DATA
```

These four lines ensure that your code will be compiled correctly for an extension DLL. Leaving out these four lines may cause your DLL to either compile or link incorrectly.

For information on how to export symbols from your extension DLL, see Chapter 4, "Creating DLLs for Windows NT," in *Programming Techniques*.

Calling an Extension DLL from Your Application

Applications that use MFC extension DLLs have the same restrictions as applications that use the AFXDLL version of MFC: they must be an MFC application containing a **CWinApp**-derived object.

To build an application that uses an MFC extension DLL, you must choose "Use MFC in a shared DLL" in the Microsoft Foundation Classes list box on the General tab in the Project Settings dialog box.

After you have either run AppWizard or made the necessary change to your project, add the import library for the extension DLL to your list of libraries to link with in the Object/Library Modules edit box on the Linker tab in the Project Settings dialog box. Make sure you put the debug version of the import library in the debug settings and the release version in the release settings.

The only other change you must make is to add the include file for the DLL to any source files that use the DLL.

See Also   Article: "DLLs: Naming Conventions"

In the *Win32 Programmer's Reference, Volume 2*: Chapter 50, "Dynamic Link Libraries"

DLLs: Building and Using the USRDLL Version

To statically link MFC into your DLL, use the USRDLL version of MFC. This article explains how to build a DLL using the USRDLL version of the library and how to use it from your applications.

A DLL that links with the USRDLL version of MFC can be called by any Win32 application. Symbols are usually exported from a USRDLL using the standard "C" interface. The declaration of a function exported from a USRDLL would look something like this:

```
extern "C" EXPORT YourExportedFunction( );
```

Building a DLL Using the USRDLL Version of MFC

To create a DLL that statically links to the USRDLL version of MFC, do the following:

- When creating a new project, choose "Dynamic-Link Library" as your target type.

- Choose "Use MFC in a Static Library" in the Microsoft Foundation Classes list box on the General tab in the Project Settings dialog box. This will add NAFXDW.LIB (for release target) and NAFXDWD.LIB (for debug target) to your list of libraries.

A DLL statically linked to the USRDLL version of MFC cannot also dynamically link to the AFXDLL version of MFC. If you wish to dynamically link a DLL to the AFXDLL version of MFC, you must build an extension DLL. See the article "DLLs: Building and Using an Extension DLL."

Calling a DLL Statically Linked to the USRDLL Version of MFC

A DLL statically linked to the USRDLL version of MFC is dynamically bound to an application just like any other DLL. You must add the import library of the DLL to the list of libraries you link with the application. Or, you can dynamically link to the DLL by calling **LoadLibrary** (see the *Win32 Programmer's Reference, Volume 4*) from your application.

When you build your DLL, Visual C++ also builds an import library for you. This library has the same basename as your DLL, but has the extension .LIB. When you wish to implicitly link with your DLL, add the import library to the Object/Library Modules edit box on the Linker tab in the Project Settings dialog box.

For more information on using DLLs, see Chapter 4, "Creating DLLs for Windows NT," in *Programming Techniques*.

See Also   Article: "DLLs: Naming Conventions"

In the *Win32 Programmer's Reference, Volume 2*: Chapter 50, "Dynamic Link Libraries"

DLLs: Programming Tips

This article covers topics specific to writing and using DLLs with MFC. You should read Chapter 4, "Creating DLLs for Windows NT," in *Programming Techniques* before reading this article. The topics in this article build on information in that chapter. Topics include:

- Initialization and termination
- OLE

- Multithreading and DLLs
- Passing object pointers between applications and extension DLLs
- Sample programs

Initialization and Termination

The only special initialization case that you should be aware of is that MFC extension DLLs need to do two things in their **DllMain** function:

- Call **AfxInitExtensionModule**, and check the return value.
- Create a **CDynLinkLibrary** object if the DLL will be exporting **CRuntimeClass** objects or has its own custom resources.

DLLs statically linked to the USRDLL version of MFC should perform their initialization and termination tasks in the same location as an MFC application: in **InitInstance** and **ExitInstance**.

Object Linking and Embedding (OLE)

OLE allows object servers to be completely implemented inside a DLL. This type of server is called an "in-proc server." MFC does not completely support in-proc servers for all the features of Visual Editing, mainly because OLE does not provide a way for a server to hook into the container's main message loop. MFC requires access to the container application's message loop to handle accelerator keys and idle-time processing.

If you are writing an OLE Automation server and your server has no user interface, it is possible to make your server an in-proc server and put it completely into a DLL. For more information, see the article "Automation Servers."

Multithreading and DLLs

A USRDLL should keep track of multiple threads by calling **::TlsAlloc** and **::TlsGetValue** (see the *Win32 Programmer's Reference, Volume 4*) in its **InitInstance** function. This method allows the DLL to keep track of thread-specific data without worrying about what code was executed before the DLL was loaded. For more information on thread local storage (TLS) see Chapter 43, "Processes and Threads," in the *Win32 Programmer's Reference, Volume 2*.

Extension DLLs have another method available to handle multithreading in addition to the USRDLL method. The DLL can handle the **DLL_THREAD_ATTACH** and **DLL_THREAD_DETACH** cases in its **DllMain** function. These cases are passed to **DllMain** when threads attach and detach from the DLL. Calling **::TlsAlloc** when a DLL is attaching allows the DLL to maintain TLS indices for every thread attached to the DLL.

A sample initialization function that handles these cases is included in section 50.2.5, "Using Thread Local Storage in a Dynamic-Link Library," in the *Win32*

Programmer's Reference, Volume 2. (The sample actually names the function **LibMain**, but MFC requires that this function be named **DllMain**.)

Passing Object Pointers Between Applications and Extension DLLs

If you need to pass an MFC or MFC-derived object pointer to or from an MFC DLL, the DLL should be an extension DLL. The member functions associated with the passed object exist in the module where the object was created. Since these functions are properly exported when using the shared DLL version of MFC, you can freely pass MFC or MFC-derived object pointers between an application and the extension DLLs it loads.

Sample Programs

Two MFC DLL samples are included with Visual C++:

DLLHUSK
> Demonstrates how to write, build, and use extension DLLs. This sample can be found in the SAMPLES\MFC\DLLHUSK directory.

DLLTRACE
> Demonstrates how to write, build, and use USRDLLs. This sample can be found in the SAMPLES\MFC\DLLTRACE directory.

Examining the source code and makefiles for these samples can give you pointers for building your DLLs.

See Also   Articles: "Multithreading," "OLE Overview," "Dynamic-Link Libraries (DLLs)"

In *Programming Techniques*: Chapter 4, "Creating DLLs for Windows NT"

In the *Win32 Programmer's Reference, Volume 2*: Chapter 50, "Dynamic Link Libraries"

DLLs: Naming Conventions

The DLLs and libraries included in MFC version 3.0 follow a structured naming convention. This makes it easier to know which DLL or library you should be using for which purpose. The naming convention for libraries is fully described in the article "Library Versions." This article describes the naming conventions for files required to build and use DLLs with MFC version 3.0.

The AFXDLL version of MFC comes in a number of different forms. These forms are named according to the convention MFC[O|D]30[U][D].DLL as detailed in Table 1. The import libraries needed to build applications or extension DLLs that use these DLLs have the same base name as the DLL but have a .LIB extension.

Table 1   AFXDLL Naming Convention

DLL	Description
MFC30.DLL	Release version without Unicode support
MFC30D.DLL	Debug version without Unicode support
MFCO30.DLL	Release version for OLE support
MFCO30D.DLL	Debug version for OLE support
MFCD30.DLL	Release version for database support
MFCD30D.DLL	Debug version for database support
MFC30U.DLL	Release version with Unicode support
MFC30UD.DLL	Debug version with Unicode support
MFCO30U.DLL	Release version for OLE with Unicode support
MFCO30UD.DLL	Debug version for OLE with Unicode support

If you are dynamically linking to the AFXDLL version of MFC, whether it is from an application or from an extension DLL, you must include MFC30.DLL with your product. If your application has OLE or database support, you must also include MFCO30.DLL or MFCD30.DLL, respectively. If you require Unicode support in your application, include the versions of the DLLs with 'U's in their name.

Note   Unicode is not supported for the database classes.

If you are statically linking your DLL to MFC, you must link it with one of the USRDLL versions of MFC. These versions are named according to the convention [N|U]AFXDW[D].LIB as listed in Table 2.

Table 2   USRDLL Naming Conventions

DLL	Description
NAFXDW.LIB	Release USRDLL version
NAFXDWD.LIB	Debug USRDLL version
UAFXDW.LIB	Release USRDLL version with Unicode support
UAFXDWD.LIB	Debug USRDLL version with Unicode support

For a list of DLLs included with Visual C++ version 2.0 that can be distributed with your applications, see the file REDISTRB.WRI in the \MSVC20\REDIST directory on the Visual C++ CD-ROM disc.

See Also   Article: "Library Versions"

Dynaset

This article describes dynasets and discusses their availability.

A "dynaset" is a recordset with dynamic properties. During its lifetime, a recordset object in dynaset mode (usually called simply a "dynaset") stays synchronized with the data source in the following way. In a multiuser environment, other users may edit or delete records that are in your dynaset or add records to the table your dynaset represents. Records your application adds to or deletes from the recordset are reflected in your dynaset. Records that other users add to the table will not be reflected in your dynaset until you rebuild the dynaset by calling its **Requery** member function. When other users delete records, MFC code skips over the deletions in your recordset. Other users' editing changes to existing records are reflected in your dynaset as soon as you scroll to the affected record.

Similarly, edits you make to records in a dynaset are reflected in dynasets in use by other users. Records you add are not reflected in other users' dynasets until they requery their dynasets. Records you delete are marked as "deleted" in other users' recordsets. If you have multiple connections to the same database (multiple **CDatabase** objects), recordsets associated with those connections have the same status as the recordsets of other users.

Dynasets are most valuable when data must be dynamic, as, for example, in an airline reservation system.

Important   To use dynasets, you must have an ODBC driver for your data source that supports dynasets, and the ODBC cursor library must not be loaded. See "Availability of Dynasets" below.

To specify that a recordset is a dynaset, pass **CRecordset::dynaset** as the first parameter to the **Open** member function of your recordset object.

Note   For updatable dynasets, your ODBC driver must support either positioned update statements or the **::SQLSetPos** ODBC API function. If both are supported, MFC uses **::SQLSetPos** for efficiency.

Availability of Dynasets

The MFC database classes support dynasets if the following requirements are met:

- The ODBC cursor library DLL must not be in use for this data source.

  If the cursor library is used, it masks some functionality of the underlying ODBC driver that is necessary for dynaset support. If you want to use dynasets (and your ODBC driver has the functionality required for dynasets, as described in the rest of this section), you can cause MFC not to load the cursor library when you create a **CDatabase** object. For more information, see the article "ODBC" and the **Open** member function of class **CDatabase**.

In ODBC terminology, dynasets and snapshots are referred to as "cursors." A cursor is a mechanism used for keeping track of its position in a recordset. For more information about cursors, see the ODBC SDK *Programmer's Reference*.

- The ODBC driver for your data source must support keyset-driven cursors.

  Keyset-driven cursors manage data from a table by getting and storing a set of keys. The keys are used to obtain current data from the table when the user scrolls onto a particular record. To determine whether your driver provides this support, call the **::SQLGetInfo** ODBC API function with the **SQL_SCROLL_OPTIONS** parameter.

  If you try to open a dynaset without keyset support, you get a **CDBException** with the return code value **AFX_SQL_ERROR_DYNASET_NOT_SUPPORTED**.

- The ODBC driver for your data source must support extended fetching.

  "Extended fetching" is the ability to scroll backwards as well as forwards over the resulting records of your SQL query. To determine whether your driver supports this ability, call the **::SQLGetFunctions** ODBC API function with the **SQL_API_SQLEXTENDEDFETCH** parameter.

If you want updatable dynasets (or snapshots, for that matter), your ODBC driver must also support either:

- The **::SQLSetPos** ODBC API function.

  –Or–

- Positioned updates.

The **::SQLSetPos** function allows MFC to update the data source without sending SQL statements. If this support is available, MFC uses it in preference to making updates via SQL. To determine whether your driver supports **::SQLSetPos**, call **::SQLGetInfo** with the **SQL_POS_OPERATIONS** parameter.

Positioned updates use SQL syntax (of the form **WHERE CURRENT OF** <cursorname>) to identify a particular row in the table on the data source. To determine whether your driver supports positioned updates, call **::SQLGetInfo** with the **SQL_POSITIONED_STATEMENTS** parameter.

Generally, MFC dynasets (but not forward-only recordsets) require an ODBC driver with level 2 API conformance. If the driver for your data source conforms to the level 1 API set, you can still use both updatable and read-only snapshots and forward-only recordsets, but not dynasets. However, a level 1 driver can support dynasets if it supports extended fetching and keyset-driven cursors. For more information about ODBC conformance levels, see the article "ODBC."

Note If you want to use both snapshots and dynasets, you must base them on two different **CDatabase** objects (two different connections).

Unlike snapshots, which use intermediate storage maintained by the ODBC cursor library, dynasets fetch a record directly from the data source as soon as you scroll to it. This keeps the records originally selected by the dynaset synchronized with the data source. For more information about ODBC and about driver availability, see the article "ODBC."

Embedded OLE Item

See the article "Activation."

Exceptions

This article explains the exception-handling mechanisms available in the Microsoft Foundation Class Library. Two mechanisms are available:

- C++ exceptions, available in MFC version 3.0.
- The MFC exception macros, available in MFC versions 1.0 and later.

If you're writing a new application using MFC, you should use the C++ mechanism. You can use the macro-based mechanism if your existing application already uses that mechanism extensively.

You can readily convert existing code to use C++ exceptions instead of the MFC exception macros. Advantages of converting your code and guidelines for doing so are described in the article "Exceptions: Converting from MFC Exception Macros."

If you have already developed an application using the MFC exception macros, you can continue using the MFC exception macros in your existing code, while using C++ exceptions in your new code. The article "Exceptions: Changes to Exception Macros in Version 3.0" gives guidelines for doing so.

Note To enable C++ exception handling in your code, select Enable Exception Handling in the C++ Language category of the C/C++ tab of the Project Settings dialog box, or use the /GX compiler option. The default is /GX-, which disables exception handling.

This article covers the following topics:

- When to use exceptions
- MFC exception support
- Further reading about exceptions

When to Use Exceptions

Three categories of outcomes can occur when a function is called during program execution: normal execution, erroneous execution, or abnormal execution. Each category is described below.

- Normal execution

  The function may execute normally and return. Some functions return a result code to the caller, which indicates the outcome of the function. The possible result codes are strictly defined for the function and represent the range of possible outcomes of the function. The result code can indicate success or failure or can even indicate a particular type of failure that is within the normal range of expectations. For example, a file-status function can return a code that indicates that the file does not exist. Note that the term "error code" is not used since a result code represents one of many expected outcomes.

- Erroneous execution

  The caller makes some mistake in passing arguments to the function or calls the function in an inappropriate context. This situation causes an error, and it should be detected by an assertion during program development. (For more information on assertions, see the article "Diagnostics: The ASSERT Macro.")

- Abnormal execution

  Abnormal execution includes situations where conditions outside the program's control are influencing the outcome of the function, such as low memory or I/O errors. Abnormal situations should be handled by catching and throwing exceptions.

Using exceptions is especially appropriate for the third category: abnormal execution.

MFC Exception Support

Whether you use the C++ exceptions directly or use the MFC exception macros, you will use **CException** or **CException**-derived objects that may be thrown by the framework or by your application.

MFC provides several predefined kinds of exceptions:

Exception class	Meaning
CMemoryException	Out-of-memory
CFileException	File exception
CArchiveException	Archive/Serialization exception
CNotSupportedException	Response to request for unsupported service
CResourceException	Windows resource allocation exception
CDBException	Database exceptions
COleException	OLE exceptions
COleDispatchException	OLE dispatch (automation) exceptions
CUserException	Exception that alerts the user with a message box, then throws a generic **CException**

For a description of each MFC function and the exceptions that can possibly be thrown by that function, see the *Class Library Reference*.

> **Note** MFC supports both C++ exceptions and the MFC exception macros. MFC does not directly support Windows NT structured exception handlers (SEH) as discussed in Chapter 8 in *Programming Techniques*.

Further Reading About Exceptions

The following articles explain using the class library for exception handing:

- Exceptions: Catching and Deleting Exceptions
- Exceptions: Examining Exception Contents
- Exceptions: Freeing Heap Objects in Exceptions
- Exceptions: Throwing Exceptions from Your Own Functions
- Exceptions: Database Exceptions
- Exceptions: OLE Exceptions

The following articles compare the MFC exception macros and the C++ exception keywords and explain how you can adapt your code:

- Exceptions: Changes to Exception Macros in Version 3.0
- Exceptions: Converting from MFC Exception Macros
- Exceptions: Using MFC Macros and C++ Exceptions

See Also   In the *Class Library Reference*: **CException**

Exceptions: Changes to Exception Macros in Version 3.0

This is an advanced topic.

In Microsoft Foundation Class Library version 3.0, the exception-handling macros have been changed to use C++ exceptions. This article tells how those changes can affect the behavior of existing code that uses the macros.

This article covers the following topics:

- Exception types and the CATCH macro
- Re-throwing exceptions

Exception Types and the CATCH Macro

In earlier versions of MFC, the **CATCH** macro uses MFC run-time type information to determine an exception's type; the exception's type is determined, in other words, at the catch site. With C++ exceptions, however, the exception's type is always determined at the throw site by the type of the exception object that is thrown. This will cause incompatibilities in the rare case in which the type of the pointer to the thrown object differs from the type of the thrown object.

The following example illustrates the consequence of this difference between MFC version 3.0 and earlier versions:

```
TRY
{
    THROW( (CException*) new CCustomException() );
}
CATCH( CCustomException, e )
{
    TRACE( "MFC 2.x will land here\n" );
}
AND_CATCH( CException, e )
{
    TRACE( "MFC 3.0 will land here\n" );
}
END_CATCH
```

This code behaves differently in version 3.0 because control always passes to the first catch block with a matching exception-declaration. The result of the throw expression

```
THROW((CException*)new CCustomException());
```

is thrown as a **CException***, even though it is constructed as a **CCustomException**. The **CATCH** macro in MFC versions 2.5 and earlier uses **CObject::IsKindOf** to test the type at run time. Because the expression

```
e->IsKindOf( RUNTIME_CLASS( CException ) )
```

is true, the first catch block catches the exception. In version 3.0, which uses C++ exceptions to implement many of the exception-handling macro, the second catch block matches the thrown **CException**.

Code like this is not common. It usually appears when an exception object is passed to another function that accepts a generic **CException***, performs "pre-throw" processing, and finally throws the exception.

To work around this problem, move the throw expression from the function to the calling code and throw an exception of the actual type known to the compiler at the time the exception is generated.

Re-Throwing Exceptions

A catch block cannot throw the same exception pointer that it caught.

For example, this code was valid in previous versions, but will have unexpected results with version 3.0:

```
TRY
{
    // Do something to throw an exception.
}
CATCH( CSomeException, e )
{
    THROW( e );    // Wrong. Use THROW_LAST() instead
}
END_TRY
```

Using **THROW** in the catch block causes the pointer e to be deleted, so that the outer catch site will receive an invalid pointer. Use **THROW_LAST** to re-throw e.

See Also   Article: "Exceptions: Catching and Deleting Exceptions"

Exceptions: Catching and Deleting Exceptions

The following instructions and examples show you how to catch and delete exceptions. For more information on the **try**, **catch**, and **throw** keywords, see Chapter 7, "C++ Exception Handling," in *Programming Techniques*.

Your exception handlers must delete exception objects they handle, because failure to delete the exception causes a memory leak whenever that code catches an exception.

Your **catch** block must delete an exception when:

1. The **catch** block throws a new exception.

   Of course, you must not delete the exception if you throw the same exception again:

   ```
   catch(CException* e)
   {
       if (m_bThrowExceptionAgain)
           throw; // Do not delete e
   }
   ```

2. Execution returns from within the **catch** block.

Note When deleting a **CException**, use the **Delete** member function to delete the exception. Do not use the **delete** keyword, since it can fail if the exception is not on the heap.

▶ **To catch and delete exceptions**

- Use the **try** keyword to set up a **try** block. Execute any program statements that might throw an exception within a **try** block.

  Use the **catch** keyword to set up a **catch** block. Place exception-handling code in a **catch** block. The code in the **catch** block is executed only if the code within the **try** block throws an exception of the type specified in the **catch** statement.

  The following skeleton shows how **try** and **catch** blocks are normally arranged:

```
// Normal program statements
...

try
{
    // Execute some code that might throw an exception.
}
catch( CException* e )
{
    // Handle the exception here.
    // "e" contains information about the exception.
    e->Delete();
}

// Other normal program statements
...
```

  When an exception is thrown, control passes to the first **catch** block whose exception-declaration matches the type of the exception. You can selectively handle different types of exceptions with sequential **catch** blocks as listed below:

```
try
{
    // Execute some code that might throw an exception.
}
catch( CMemoryException* e )
{
    // Handle the out-of-memory exception here.
}
catch( CFileException* e )
{
    // Handle the file exceptions here.
}
catch( CException* e )
{
    // Handle all other types of exceptions here.
}
```

See Also   Article: "Exceptions: Converting from MFC Exception Macros"

Exceptions: Converting from MFC Exception Macros

This is an advanced topic.

This article explains how to convert existing code written with Microsoft Foundation Class macros—**TRY**, **CATCH**, **THROW**, and so on—to use the C++ exception-handling keywords **try**, **catch**, and **throw**. Topics include:

- Conversion advantages
- Converting code with exception macros to use C++ exceptions

Advantages of Converting

You probably do not need to convert existing code, although you should be aware of differences between the macro implementations in MFC version 3.0 and the implementations in earlier versions. These differences and subsequent changes in code behavior are discussed in "Exceptions: Changes to Exception Macros in Version 3.0."

The principal advantages of converting are:

- Code that uses the C++ exception-handling keywords compiles to a slightly smaller .EXE or .DLL.
- The C++ exception-handling keywords are more versatile: they can handle exceptions of any data type that can be copied (**int**, **float**, **char**, **and** so on), whereas the macros handle exceptions only of class **CException** and classes derived from it.

The major difference between the macros and the keywords is that code using the macros "automatically" deletes a caught exception when the exception goes out of scope. Code using the keywords does not, so you must explicitly delete a caught exception. For more information, see the article "Exceptions: Catching and Deleting Exceptions."

Another difference is syntax. The syntax for macros and keywords differs in three respects:

1. Macro arguments and exception declarations:

   A **CATCH** macro invocation has the following syntax:

   CATCH(*exception_class*, *exception_object_pointer_name*)

   Notice the comma between the class name and the object pointer name.

   The exception declaration for the **catch** keyword uses this syntax:

   catch(*exception_type exception_name*)

   This exception declaration statement indicates the type of exception the catch block handles.

2. Delimitation of catch blocks:

With the macros, the **CATCH** macro (with its arguments) begins the first catch block; the **AND_CATCH** macro begins subsequent catch blocks; and the **END_CATCH** macro terminates the sequence of catch blocks.

With the keywords, the **catch** keyword (with its exception declaration) begins each catch block. There is no counterpart to the **END_CATCH** macro; the catch block ends with its closing brace.

3. The throw expression:

The macros use **THROW_LAST** to re-throw the current exception. The **throw** keyword, with no argument, has the same effect.

Doing the Conversion

▶ **To convert code using macros to use the C++ exception-handling keywords**

1. Locate all occurrences of the Microsoft Foundation Class Library macros **TRY**, **CATCH**, **AND_CATCH**, **END_CATCH**, **THROW**, and **THROW_LAST**.

2. Replace or delete all occurrences of the macros:

For this macro:	Perform this action:
TRY	Replace with **try**
CATCH	Replace with **catch**
AND_CATCH	Replace with **catch**
END_CATCH	Delete
THROW	Replace with **throw**
THROW_LAST	Replace with **throw**

3. Modify the macro arguments so that they form valid exception declarations.

For example, change

```
CATCH( CException, e )
```

to

```
catch( CException* e )
```

4. Modify the code in the catch blocks so that it deletes exception objects as necessary. For more information, see the article "Exceptions: Catching and Deleting Exceptions."

Here is an example of exception-handling code using MFC exception macros. Note that because the code in the following example uses the macros, the exception e is deleted automatically:

```
TRY
{
    // Do something to throw an exception.
}
CATCH(CException, e)
{
    if (m_bPassExceptionsUp)
        THROW_LAST();

    if (m_bReturnFromThisFunction)
        return;

    // Not necessary to delete the exception e.
}
END_CATCH
```

The code in the next example uses the C++ exception keywords, so the exception must be explicitly deleted:

```
try
{
    // Do something to throw an exception.
}
catch(CException* e)
{
    if (m_bPassExceptionsUp)
        throw;

    if (m_bThrowDifferentException)
    {
        e->Delete();
        throw new CMyOtherException;
    }

    if (m_bReturnFromThisFunction)
    {
        e->Delete();
        return;
    }

    e->Delete();
}
```

See Also   Article: "Exceptions: Using MFC Macros and C++ Exceptions"

Exceptions: Using MFC Macros and C++ Exceptions

This article discusses considerations for writing code that uses both the Microsoft Foundation Class Library exception-handling macros and the C++ exception-handling keywords.

This article covers the following topics:

- Mixing exception keywords and macros
- Try blocks inside catch blocks

Mixing Exception Keywords and Macros

You can mix MFC exception macros and C++ exception keywords in the same program. But you cannot mix MFC macros with C++ exception keywords in the same block because the macros delete exception objects automatically when they go out of scope, whereas code using the exception-handling keywords does not. For more information, see the article "Exceptions: Catching and Deleting Exceptions."

The main difference between the macros and the keywords is that the macros "automatically" delete a caught exception when the exception goes out of scope. Code using the keywords does not do so; exceptions caught in a catch block must be explicitly deleted. Mixing macros and C++ exception keywords can cause memory leaks when an exception object is not deleted, or heap corruption when an exception is deleted twice.

The following code, for example, invalidates the exception pointer:

```
TRY
{
    TRY
    {
        // Do something to throw an exception.
    }
    CATCH(CException, e)  // The "inner" catch block
    {
        throw;  // Invalid attempt to throw exception
                // to the outer catch block below.
    }
    END_CATCH
}
CATCH(CException, e)  // The "outer" catch block
{
    // Pointer e is invalid because
    // it was deleted in the inner catch block.
}
END_CATCH
```

The problem occurs because e is deleted when execution passes out of the "inner" **CATCH** block. Using the **THROW_LAST** macro instead of the **THROW** statement will cause the "outer" **CATCH** block to receive a valid pointer:

```
TRY
{
    TRY
    {
        // Do something to throw an exception.
    }
    CATCH(CException, e)  // The "inner" catch block
    {
        THROW_LAST() // Throw exception to the outer catch block below.
    }
    END_CATCH
}
CATCH(CException, e)  // The "outer" catch block
{
    // Pointer e is valid because
    // THROW_LAST() was used.
}
END_CATCH
```

Try Blocks Inside Catch Blocks

You cannot re-throw the current exception from within a **try** block that is inside a **CATCH** block. The following example is invalid:

```
TRY
{
    // Do something to throw an exception.
}
CATCH(CException, e)
{
    try
    {
        throw;  // Wrong.  Causes e (the exception
                // being thrown) to be deleted.
    }
}
END_CATCH
```

See Also   Article: "Exceptions: Examining Exception Contents"

Exceptions: Examining Exception Contents

Although a **catch** block's argument can be of almost any data type, the Microsoft Foundation Class Library functions throw exceptions of types derived from the class **CException**. To catch an exception thrown by an MFC function, then, you write a **catch** block whose argument is a pointer to a **CException** object (or an object derived from **CException**, such as **CMemoryException**). Depending on the exact type of the exception, you can examine the data members of the exception object to gather information about the specific cause of the exception.

For example, the **CFileException** type has the **m_cause** data member, which contains an enumerated type that specifies the cause of the file exception. Some examples of the possible return values are **CFileException::fileNotFound** and **CFileException::readOnly**.

The following example shows how to examine the contents of a **CFileException**. Other exception types can be examined in a similar way.

```
try
{
    // Do something to throw a file exception.
}
catch( CFileException* theException )
{
    if( theException->m_cause == CFileException::fileNotFound )
        TRACE( "File not found\n" );
    theException->Delete();
}
```

See Also   Articles: "Exceptions: Freeing Objects in Exceptions," "Exceptions: Catching and Deleting Exceptions"

Exceptions: Freeing Objects in Exceptions

This article explains the need and the method of freeing objects when an exception occurs. Topics include:

- Handling the exception locally
- Throwing exceptions after destroying objects

Exceptions thrown by the framework or by your application interrupt normal program flow. Thus, it is very important to keep close track of objects so that you can properly dispose of them in case an exception is thrown.

There are two primary methods to do this.

- Handle exceptions locally using the **try** and **catch** keywords, then destroy all objects with one statement.
- Destroy any object in the **catch** block before throwing the exception outside the block for further handling.

These two approaches are illustrated below as solutions to the following problematic example:

```
void SomeFunc()          // Problematic code
{
    CPerson* myPerson = new CPerson;

    // Do something that might throw an exception.
    myPerson->SomeFunc();

    // Now destroy the object before exiting.
    delete myPerson;
}
```

As written above, myPerson will not be deleted if an exception is thrown by SomeFunc. Execution jumps directly to the next outer exception handler, bypassing the normal function exit and the code that deletes the object. The pointer to the object goes out of scope when the exception leaves the function, and the memory occupied by the object will never be recovered as long as the program is running. This is a memory leak; it would be detected by using the memory diagnostics.

Handling the Exception Locally

The **try/catch** paradigm provides a defensive programming method for avoiding memory leaks and ensuring that your objects are destroyed when exceptions occur. For instance, the example shown earlier in this article could be rewritten as follows:

```
void SomeFunc()
{
    CPerson* myPerson = new CPerson;

    try
    {
        // Do something that might throw an exception.
        myPerson->SomeFunc();
    }
    catch( CException* e )
    {
        // Handle the exception locally
        e->Delete();
    }

    // Now destroy the object before exiting.
    delete myPerson;
}
```

This new example sets up an exception handler to catch the exception and handle it locally. It then exits the function normally and destroys the object. The important aspect of this example is that a context to catch the exception is established with the **try/catch** blocks. Without a local exception frame, the function would never know that an exception had been thrown and would not have the chance to exit normally and destroy the object.

Throwing Exceptions After Destroying Objects

Another way to handle exceptions is to pass them on to the next outer exception-handling context. In your **catch** block, you can do some cleanup of your locally allocated objects and then throw the exception on for further processing.

The throwing function may or may not need to deallocate heap objects. If the function always deallocates the heap object before returning in the normal case, then the function should also deallocate the heap object before throwing the exception. On the other hand, if the function does not normally deallocate the object before returning in the normal case, then you must decided on a case-by-case basis whether the heap object should be deallocated.

The following example shows how locally allocated objects can be cleaned up:

```
void SomeFunc()
{
    CPerson* myPerson = new CPerson;

    try
    {
        // Do something that might throw an exception.
        myPerson->SomeFunc();
    }
    catch( CException, e )
    {
        // Destroy the object before passing exception on.
        delete myPerson;
        // Throw the exception to the next handler.
        throw;
    }

    // On normal exits, destroy the object.
    delete myPerson;
}
```

The exception mechanism automatically deallocates frame objects; the destructor of the frame object is also called.

If you call functions that can throw exceptions, you can use **try/catch** blocks to make sure that you catch the exceptions and have a chance to destroy any objects you have created. In particular, be aware that many Microsoft Foundation Class Library functions can throw exceptions.

See Also   Article: "Exceptions: Catching and Deleting Exceptions"

Exceptions: Throwing Exceptions from Your Own Functions

It is possible to use the Microsoft Foundation Class Library exception-handling paradigm solely to catch exceptions thrown by functions in MFC or other libraries. In addition to catching exceptions thrown by library code, you can throw exceptions from your own code if you are writing functions that can encounter exceptional conditions.

When an exception is thrown, execution of the current function is aborted and jumps directly to the **catch** block of the innermost exception frame. The exception mechanism bypasses the normal exit path from a function. Therefore, you must be sure to delete those memory blocks that would be deleted in a normal exit.

▶ **To throw an exception**

- Use one of the MFC helper functions, such as **AfxThrowMemoryException**. These functions throw a preallocated exception object of the appropriate type.

  In the following example, a function tries to allocate two memory blocks and throws an exception if either allocation fails:

```
{
    char* p1 = (char*)malloc( SIZE_FIRST );
    if( p1 == NULL )
        AfxThrowMemoryException();
    char* p2 = (char*)malloc( SIZE_SECOND );
    if( p2 == NULL )
    {
        free( p1 );
        AfxThrowMemoryException();
    }

    // ... Do something with allocated blocks ...

    // In normal exit, both blocks are deleted.
    free( p1 );
    free( p2 );
}
```

  If the first allocation fails, you can simply throw the memory exception. If the first allocation is successful but the second one fails, you must free the first allocation block before throwing the exception. If both allocations succeed, then you can proceed normally and free the blocks when exiting the function.

  –Or–

- Use a user-defined exception to indicate a problem condition. You can throw an item of any type, even an entire class, as your exception.

This example attempts to play a sound through a wave device and throws an exception if there is a failure.

```
#define WAVE_ERROR -5
{
    // This Win32 API returns 0 if the sound cannot be played.
    // Throw an integer constant if it fails.
    if( sndPlaySound("SIREN.WAV", SND_ASYNC) )
        throw WAVE_ERROR;
}
```

Note MFC's default handling of exceptions applies only to pointers to **CException** objects (and objects of **CException**-derived classes). The example above bypasses MFC's exception mechanism.

See Also   Article: "Exceptions: Exceptions in Constructors"

Exceptions: Exceptions in Constructors

When throwing an exception in a constructor, clean up whatever objects and memory allocations you have made prior to throwing the exception, as explained in "Exceptions: Throwing Exceptions from Your Own Functions."

Throwing an exception in a constructor is tricky, however, because the memory for the object itself has already been allocated by the time the constructor is called. There is no simple way to deallocate the memory occupied by the object from within the constructor for that object. Thus, you will find that throwing an exception in a constructor will result in the object remaining allocated. For a discussion of how to detect objects in your program that have not been deallocated, see the article "Diagnostics: Detecting Memory Leaks."

If you are performing operations in your constructor that can fail, it might be a better idea to put those operations into a separate initialization function rather than throwing an exception in the constructor. That way, you can safely construct the object and get a valid pointer to it. Then, you can call the initialization function for the object. If the initialization function fails, you can delete the object directly.

See Also   Article: "Exceptions: Freeing Objects in Exceptions"

Exceptions: Database Exceptions

This article explains how to handle database exceptions. Topics include:

- Approaches to exception handling
- A database exception-handling example

Approaches to Exception Handling

In addition to return codes defined by the framework, which have names of the form **AFX_SQL_ERROR_XXX**, some **CDBExceptions** are based on ODBC return codes. The return codes for such exceptions have names of the form **SQL_ERROR_XXX**.

The return codes—both framework-defined and ODBC-defined—that the database classes can return are documented under the **m_nRetCode** data member of class **CDBException**. Additional information about return codes defined by ODBC is available in the ODBC SDK *Programmer's Reference*.

You should always write exception handlers to handle exceptional conditions.

The most pragmatic approach to catching database exceptions is to test your application with exception scenarios. Determine the likely exceptions that might occur for an operation in your code, and force the exception to occur. Then examine the trace output to see what exception is thrown, or examine the return code (of type **RETCODE**) in the debugger. This lets you know which return codes you'll see for the exception scenarios you are using.

A Database Exception-Handling Example

The following example attempts to construct a **CRecordset**-derived object on the heap with the **new** operator, and then open the recordset. The **Open** member function could throw a **CDBException**, so this code brackets the **Open** call with a **try** block. The subsequent **catch** block will catch a **CDBException**. You could examine the exception object itself, called e, but in this case it's enough to know that the attempt to create a recordset has failed. The **catch** block displays a message box and cleans up by deleting the recordset object.

```
CRecordset* CSectionView::OnGetRecordset()
{
    if ( m_pSet != NULL )
        return m_pSet;          // Recordset already allocated

    m_pSet = new CSectionSet( NULL );
    try
    {
        m_pSet->Open( );
    }
    catch( CDBException* e )
    {
        AfxMessageBox( e->m_strError, MB_ICONEXCLAMATION );
        delete m_pSet;
        m_pSet = NULL;
        e->Delete();
    }
    return m_pSet;
}
```

See Also   Article: "Exceptions: OLE Exceptions"

In the *Class Library Reference*: **CDBException**

Exceptions: OLE Exceptions

The techniques and facilities for handling exceptions in OLE are the same as those for handling other exceptions. For further information on exception handling, see the article "Exceptions."

All exception objects are derived from the abstract base class **CException**. The MFC Library provides two classes for handling Object Linking and Embedding (OLE) exceptions:

- **COleException**   For handling general OLE exceptions.
- **COleDispatchException**   For generating and handling OLE dispatch (automation) exceptions.

The difference between these two classes is the amount of information they provide and where they are used. The class **COleException** has a public data member that contains the OLE status code for the exception. The class **COleDispatchException** supplies more information, including the following:

- An application-specific error code
- An error description, such as "Disk full"
- A help context that your application can use to provide additional information for the user
- The name of your application's help file
- The name of the application that generated the exception

The class **COleDispatchException** provides more information so that it can be used with products like Microsoft Visual Basic. The verbal error description can be used in a message box or other notification; the help information can be used to help the user respond to the conditions that caused the exception.

Two global functions correspond to the two OLE exception classes: **AfxThrowOleException** and **AfxThrowOleDispatchException**. Use them to throw general OLE exceptions and OLE dispatch exceptions, respectively.

See Also   In the *Class Library Reference*: **COleException**, **COleDispatchException**

Field

A single item of data in a record, such as a phone number field in a customer record.

See the article "Recordset."

Files

In the Microsoft Foundation Class Library (MFC), the **CFile** class handles normal file I/O operations. This article explains how to open and close files as well as read and write data to those files. It also discusses file status operations. For a description of how to use the object-based serialization features of MFC as an alternative way of reading and writing data in files, see the article "Serialization (Object Persistence)."

Note When you use MFC **CDocument** objects, the framework does much of the serialization work for you. In particular, the framework creates and uses the **CFile** object. You only have to write code in your override of the **Serialize** member function of class **CDocument**.

The **CFile** class provides an interface for general-purpose binary file operations. The **CStdioFile** and **CMemFile** classes are derived from **CFile** to supply more specialized file services.

This article covers the following topics:

- Opening files
- Reading and writing files
- Closing files
- Accessing file status

Opening Files

In MFC, the most common way to open a file is a two-stage process.

▶ **To open a file**

1. Create the file object without specifying a path or permission flags.

   You usually create a file object by declaring a **CFile** variable on the stack frame.

2. Call the **Open** member function for the file object, supplying a path and permission flags.

The return value for **Open** will be nonzero if the file was opened successfully or 0 if the specified file could not be opened. The **Open** member function is prototyped as follows:

```
virtual BOOL Open( LPCTSTR lpszFileName, UINT nOpenFlags,
CFileException* pError = NULL );
```

The open flags specify which permissions, such as read-only, you want for the file. The possible flag values are defined as enumerated constants within the **CFile** class, so they are qualified with "**CFile::**," as in **CFile::modeRead**. Use the **CFile::modeCreate** flag if you want to create the file.

The following example shows how to create a new file with read/write permission (replacing any previous file with the same path):

```
char* pszFileName = "c:\\test\\myfile.dat";
CFile myFile;
CFileException fileException;

if ( !myFile.Open( pszFileName, CFile::modeCreate |
        CFile::modeReadWrite ), &fileException )
{
    TRACE( "Can't open file %s, error = %u\n",
        pszFileName, fileException.m_cause );
}
```

Note This example creates and opens a file. If there are problems, the **Open** call can return a **CFileException** object in its last parameter, as shown here. The **TRACE** macro prints both the filename and a code indicating the reason for failure. You can call the **AfxThrowFileException** function if you require more detailed error reporting.

Reading and Writing Files

If you've used the C run-time library file-handling functions, MFC reading and writing operations will appear familiar. This section describes reading directly from and writing directly to a **CFile** object. You can also do buffered file I/O with the **CArchive** class.

▶ **To read from and write to the file**

- Use the **Read** and **Write** member functions to read and write data in the file.

  –Or–

- The **Seek** member function is also available for moving to a specific offset within the file.

Read takes a pointer to a buffer and the number of bytes to read and returns the actual number of bytes that were read. If the required number of bytes could not be read because end-of-file (EOF) is reached, the actual number of bytes read is returned. If any read error occurs, an exception is thrown. **Write** is similar to **Read**, but the number of bytes written is not returned. If a write error occurs, including not writing all the bytes specified, an exception is thrown. If you have a valid **CFile** object, you can read from it or write to it as shown in the following example:

```
char      szBuffer[256];
UINT      nActual = 0;
CFile myFile;

myFile.Write( szBuffer, sizeof( szBuffer ) );
myFile.Seek( 0, CFile::begin );
nActual = myFile.Read( szBuffer, sizeof( szBuffer ) );
```

Note You should normally carry out input/output operations within a **try/catch** exception handling block. For more information, see the article "Exceptions."

Closing Files

As usual in I/O operations, once you finish with a file, you must close it.

▶ **To close a file**

- Use the **Close** member function. This function closes the file-system file and flushes buffers if necessary.

If you allocated the **CFile** object on the frame (as in the examples shown earlier in this article), the object will automatically be closed and then destroyed when it goes out of scope. Note that deleting the **CFile** object does not delete the physical file in the file system.

Accessing File Status

CFile also supports getting file status, including whether the file exists, creation and modification dates and times, logical size, and path.

▶ **To get file status**

- Use the **CFile** class to get and set information about a file. One useful application is to use the **CFile** static member function **GetStatus** to determine if a file exists. **GetStatus** returns 0 if the specified file does not exist.

Thus, you could use the result of **GetStatus** to determine whether to use the **CFile::modeCreate** flag when opening a file, as shown by the following example:

```
CFile theFile;
char* szFileName = "c:\\test\\myfile.dat";
BOOL bOpenOK;

CFileStatus status;
if( CFile::GetStatus( szFileName, status ) )
{
    // Open the file without the Create flag
    bOpenOK = theFile.Open( szFileName,
                       CFile::modeWrite );
}
else
{
    // Open the file with the Create flag
    bOpenOK = theFile.Open( szFileName,
                       CFile::modeCreate | CFile::modeWrite );
}
```

See Also   Article: "Serialization (Object Persistence)"

In the *Class Library Reference*: **CFile**

Find

See the article "Recordset: Scrolling."

Forms

For information about form-based data-access programs, see the article "Record Views."

For information about MFC support for form-based programs in general, see classes **CRecordView**, **CDialog**, and **CFormView** in the *Class Library Reference*.

Framework

The Microsoft Foundation Class Library (MFC) is frequently referred to as "the framework" or "application framework." For an introduction and general information about the framework, see Part 1 of this book and the Scribble tutorial, Chapters 6 through 15 in *Introducing Visual C++*.

For further reading, see the article "MFC."

See Also   Articles: "CObject Class," "MFC: Using Database Classes with Documents and Views," "MFC: Using Database Classes Without Documents and Views"

Help

This group of articles describes support provided by the Microsoft Foundation Class Library (MFC) for context-senstive Windows Help for your applications.

Applications written for Windows usually provide context-sensitive Help, allowing the user to get Help on a particular window, dialog box, command, or toolbar button. MFC makes it simple to add context-sensitive Help to your application.

The user can access Help in three ways:

- Getting Help from the Help menu.
- Getting Help on the task at hand by pressing the F1 key. This kind of help is called "F1 Help."
- Getting Help by invoking a "help mode" with SHIFT+F1 and then selecting a user-interface object to get help about. This kind of help is called "SHIFT+F1 Help."

This article presents an overview of the MFC Help subsystem, in the following topics:

- Components of Help
- Help-menu support
- More precise context-sensitivity
- Help support tools
- Authoring and compiling Help

The following additional articles explain MFC Help support in more detail:

- Help: F1 and Shift+F1 Help
- Help: OLE Support for Help
- Help: Message-Map Support
- Help: The Help Project File
- Help: The MAKEHM and MAKEHELP.BAT Tools
- Help: Authoring Help Topics

For a detailed example, see Chapter 15 in *Introducing Visual C++*. For additional technical information, see Technical Note 28 under MFC in Books Online.

Components of Help

The Help subsystem in the MFC framework has the following components, many of which are supplied by AppWizard when you choose its Context-Sensitive Help option:

- A Help drop-down menu with several commands. For a new MDI application, there are two copies of this menu: one for an application with no open documents and one for each type of document that uses its own menu structure. AppWizard supplies these menus.

- Several message-map entries in your **CWinApp**-derived application class. These entries bind F1 and SHIFT+F1 commands to their respective command handlers. AppWizard supplies these message-map entries.

- Message handlers for F1 and SHIFT+F1. Class **CWinApp** supplies these handlers, and AppWizard supplies the message-map entries for them.

- The **CWinApp::WinHelp** member function, which calls the Windows help program.

- Additional AppWizard support for Help, including several Help-related files. The files include skeleton .RTF files that contain Help entries for the common elements of the Windows user interface, such as the File and Edit menus. You can edit these files to revise the supplied text and add your own application-specific Help information.

- A mechanism and tool for mapping resource and command IDs in your application to "help contexts" in Windows Help. The MAKEHM tool is introduced in "Using MAKEHM and MAKEHELP.BAT" later in this article.

Help-Menu Support

The framework implements the following Help menu commands:

Help Index
   Opens Help on your application's contents screen.
Using Help
   Opens Help on an explanation of how to use Windows Help.

For a description of this support and its effect on the message map in your application class, see the article "Help: Message-Map Support."

More Precise Context-Sensitivity

F1 Help and SHIFT+F1 Help are activated based on help context IDs. The standard Help implementation in the framework can obtain a Help context from a window, dialog box, message box, menu item, or toolbar button. If you need more precise control over this mechanism, you can override parts of the mechanism.

For additional information, see Technical Note 28 under MFC in Books Online.

Help Support Tools

You will use three main tools to develop your application's Help system: AppWizard, MAKEHM, and the Windows Help Compiler. You also need an editor, such as Microsoft Word for Windows, that can edit rich text format (.RTF) files. You can use the Visual C++ graphics editor to create bitmaps to include in your Help files.

Choosing the Help Option in AppWizard

AppWizard is your first tool for implementing context-sensitive Help. Set the Context-Sensitive Help option in AppWizard. AppWizard then provides the message-map entries in your **CWinApp**-derived class that connect the whole help mechanism. AppWizard also creates a set of skeletal starter files, as shown in Table 1. The bitmap and .RTF files are in an HLP subdirectory that AppWizard creates in your project directory.

Table 1   AppWizard-Supplied Help Files

File	Description
[Yourproject].HPJ	A Windows Help project file that the Windows Help Compiler uses to compile your Help
MAKEHELP.BAT	A batch file that manages Help ID mapping and calls the Help Compiler
HLP*.BMP	Various bitmap files used with the supplied Help files
HLP*.RTF	Skeleton Help files in .RTF format that contain starter Help for the application components supplied by the framework

The help project file (.HPJ) and MAKEHELP.BAT are in your project directory. The other files are in an HLP subdirectory of your project directory.

You can edit these files as described in "Authoring and Compiling Help" later in this article to fill in application-specific Help information.

Using MAKEHM and MAKEHELP.BAT

Once you've created the Help support files with AppWizard and are ready to prepare context-sensitive Help files, run MAKEHELP.BAT from the command line to create a "Help mapping" file (.HM extension) and to compile your Help file. MAKEHELP.BAT calls the MAKEHM tool, which translates the contents of your RESOURCE.H file to a Help mapping file, which is then included in the [MAP] section of your .HPJ file. The [MAP] section associates context strings (or aliases) with context numbers used by the Help Compiler.

When you create a new resource or object within a resource, Visual C++ assigns it an identifier consisting of a C preprocessor macro name mapped to an integer value. Visual C++ writes these symbols as **#define** statements in a file called RESOURCE.H.

MAKEHM reads your RESOURCE.H file, locates all applicable **#define** statements (defining various IDs, including those for dialog boxes, menus, and toolbar buttons), and adds an appropriate number to each ID number, using certain rules that depend on the kind of ID (dialog box, menu, and so on). The new "Help IDs" are written to an .HM file, which the Help Compiler uses to define contexts.

After MAKEHELP.BAT runs the MAKEHM tool, it then runs the Windows Help Compiler to create the .HLP file. The Help Compiler creates the .HLP file in your application's main source code directory. If a WINDEBUG and/or WINREL subdirectory already exists, the MAKEHELP.BAT tool also copies the .HLP file to that subdirectory. This is useful because when you run either the debug or release version of your application, it will expect to find the .HLP file in the same directory as the debug or release executable file.

If you build a debug or release version of the application after you have already run MAKEHELP.BAT, and you don't need or care to rebuild the .HLP file, copy the .HLP file manually from the application source directory to the WINDEBUG or WINREL subdirectory.

If you add new resources for which you wish to implement help contexts, run MAKEHELP.BAT again.

Authoring and Compiling Help

For details about authoring and compiling Windows Help, see the *Help Compiler User's Guide*.

The preferred way to build Help for your framework application is to run MAKEHELP.BAT. You must have the Microsoft Windows Help Compiler in your path.

Figure 1 shows the general process for creating a Help system for your application.

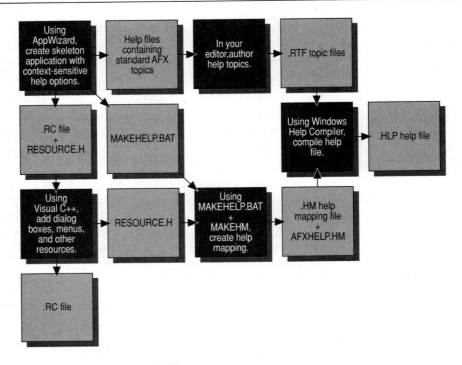

Figure 1   Preparing Help Files

For an example of preparing Help files, see Chapter 15 in *Introducing Visual C++*.

See Also   Article: "Help: F1 and SHIFT+F1 Help"

Help: F1 and SHIFT+F1 Help

This article describes the two forms of context-sensitive Windows Help supported by MFC.

F1 Help opens Help on a topic associated with the currently selected item in your application. MFC supplies F1 Help for windows, dialog boxes, message boxes, menus, and toolbar buttons.

SHIFT+F1 Help invokes a special "Help mode" in which the cursor turns into a Help cursor. The user can then select a visible object in the user interface, such as a menu item, toolbar button, or window. This opens Help on a topic that describes the selected item.

F1 Help Support

The framework implements F1 Help for windows, dialog boxes, message boxes, menus, and toolbar buttons. If the cursor is over a window, dialog box, or message box when the user presses the F1 key, the framework opens Windows Help for that window. If a menu item is highlighted, the framework opens Windows Help for that menu item. And if a toolbar button has been pressed (but the mouse not released yet), the framework opens Windows Help for that toolbar button. (With extra work, you can implement F1 Help for other things.)

When the user presses the F1 key, the framework processes the keystroke as a Help request as follows, using a variation on the normal command routing. Pressing F1 causes a **WM_COMMAND** message to be sent for the **ID_HELP** command. If the application supports Help, this command is mapped to the **OnHelp** message handler of class **CWinApp** and is routed directly there. **OnHelp** uses the ID of the current frame window or dialog box to determine the appropriate Help topic to display. If no specific Help topic is found, **OnHelp** displays default Help, which is usually mapped to **CWinApp** member function **OnHelpIndex** in the application object's message map—the same handler as for the Help Index menu command.

SHIFT+F1 Help Support

If the user presses SHIFT+F1 at any time the application is active, the framework puts the application into Help mode and changes the cursor to a Help cursor (arrow + question mark). The next thing the user clicks determines what Help context the framework opens in Windows Help.

If the user presses SHIFT+F1, the framework routes the command **ID_CONTEXT_HELP** through the normal command routing. The command is mapped to the **CWinApp** member function **OnContextHelp**, which captures the mouse, changes the cursor to a Help cursor, and puts the application into Help mode. The Help cursor is maintained as long as the application is in Help mode but reverts to a normal arrow cursor if it is not over the application that is in Help mode. Activating a different application cancels Help mode in the original application. While in Help mode, the application determines what object the user clicks and calls the **CWinApp** member function **WinHelp** with the appropriate context, determined from the object clicked upon. Once an object has been selected, Help mode ends and the cursor is restored to the normal arrow.

Note For information about how context-sensitive help is managed in OLE applications, see the article "Help: OLE Support for Help."

For more information, see Technical Note 28 under MFC in Books Online.

See Also   Article: "Help: Message-Map Support"

Help: OLE Support for Help

This article describes the requirements for Help support in Object Linking and Embedding (OLE) Visual Editing applications.

For SHIFT+F1 support, some special coordination is required between OLE containers and in-place active servers. When the user chooses to activate SHIFT+F1 Help mode, both applications need to enter the mode. Whichever application gets the message to enter the mode notifies the other application. Then either application is prepared to respond when the user clicks the mouse on an item for which he or she wants help. Likewise, when the user terminates Help mode, the application that gets the message notifies the other application. Note that the Microsoft Foundation Class Library automatically handles this notification process between the container and the in-place server.

Caution Neither the container nor the server can enter SHIFT+F1 Help mode unless the other application also supports the mode.

For F1 Help support, by contrast, whichever application gets the message when F1 is pressed handles the help request.

See Also   Article: "Help: Message-Map Support"

Help: Message-Map Support

MFC supports two Help menu commands: Help Index and Using Help. These commands and the support for F1 and SHIFT+F1 Help work through the message map. Topics covered in this article include:

- Help commands in the message map
- About the Help commands
- Completing your application's Help

Help Commands in the Message Map

To support the Help menu commands, F1 help, and SHIFT+F1 help, AppWizard adds five entries to the message map for your **CFrameWnd**-derived or **CMDIFrameWnd**-derived class. This message map is in the MAINFRM.CPP file. After you run AppWizard, choosing the Context-Sensitive Help option, the message map for class CMainFrame will look like the following for an MDI application:

```
// CMainFrame

BEGIN_MESSAGE_MAP(CMainFrame, CMDIFrameWnd)
    //{{AFX_MSG_MAP(CMainFrame)

    // NOTE - the ClassWizard will add and remove mapping macros here.
    //  DO NOT EDIT what you see in these blocks of generated code !
    ON_WM_CREATE()
    //}}AFX_MSG_MAP
```

```
        // Global help commands
        ON_COMMAND( ID_HELP_INDEX, CMDIFrameWnd::OnHelpIndex)
        ON_COMMAND( ID_HELP_USING, CMDIFrameWnd::OnHelpUsing)
        ON_COMMAND( ID_HELP, CMDIFrameWnd::OnHelp)
        ON_COMMAND( ID_CONTEXT_HELP, CMDIFrameWnd::OnContextHelp)
        ON_COMMAND( ID_DEFAULT_HELP, CMDIFrameWnd::OnHelpIndex)
END_MESSAGE_MAP( )
```

For an SDI application, references to **CMDIFrameWnd** in this code are replaced by references to **CFrameWnd**.

About the Help Commands

The five help-related message-map entries follow the comment `// Global help commands`. Table 1 explains the purpose of each command ID used in these entries.

Table 1   Help-Related Command IDs

Command ID	Purpose
ID_HELP_INDEX	Responds to the Index item on the Help menu by displaying the Windows Help index
ID_HELP_USING	Responds to the Using Help item on the Help menu by displaying information about using Windows Help
ID_HELP	Responds to F1 by displaying a specific topic in Windows Help
ID_CONTEXT_HELP	Responds to SHIFT+F1 by putting the application into help mode
ID_DEFAULT_HELP	Used when a specific help context cannot be found

Notice that all of these commands are mapped to member functions of class **CMDIFrameWnd** (in the case of an MDI application; or to **CFrameWnd** in the case of an SDI application). Unlike most of the other commands you place into the message map, these have handler functions predefined by the class library. Making the message-map entry enables the command.

The application's accelerator table defines F1 for **ID_HELP** and SHIFT+F1 for **ID_CONTEXT_HELP**. You can change the keys used for these help functions by using Visual C++ to change the key values in the accelerator table.

When the user chooses a Help menu command (or uses one of the context-sensitive Help techniques described in "F1 Help Support" and "SHIFT+F1 Help Support" in the article "Help: F1 and SHIFT+F1 Help"), the framework calls **CWinApp**'s **WinHelp** member function. This action, in turn, starts the Windows help program and passes context information to it.

Completing Your Application's Help

Once you have activated the Help menu commands with ClassWizard, you can complete your help by:

1. Running MAKEHELP.BAT.

   Once you use Visual C++ to create your application's dialog boxes, menus, and other resources, run the MAKEHELP.BAT file created by AppWizard to produce a help map (.HM) file. The help map file defines help context IDs corresponding to the IDs of dialog boxes, menu commands, and other resources in your application.

2. Authoring Help topics.

   Starting with the .RTF files supplied by AppWizard in the HLP subdirectory of your project, remove topics you don't need, edit the remaining material, and add new topics for the menu commands, dialog boxes, toolbar buttons, and so on, that you added to your program. Each help topic requires a help context ID. Use the *symbol* of the menu command, dialog box, and so on, that you supplied when you created the resource. This is the symbol that is defined in the application's RESOURCE.H file: for example, `IDD_MY_DIALOG`.

   In the .RTF file, the context ID is a string, not a number, yet the application and the framework refer to the context ID as a number, not a string. The .HM file created by the MAKEHM tool establishes the association between the context ID number and the context ID topic screen. The article "Help: Authoring Help Topics" describes the process of mapping these IDs to Help topics and writing the topics in your .RTF files.

3. Compiling Help.

   When you finish authoring Help topics, you can run MAKEHELP.BAT to create a Help map file and then run the Windows Help Compiler. The article "Help: The MAKEHM and MAKEHELP.BAT Tools" describes this process.

See Also   Articles: "Help: The Help Project File," "Example Help Contexts" in the article "Help: The MAKEHM and MAKEHELP.BAT Tools"

Help: The Help Project File

This article describes the Help project (.HPJ) file that AppWizard creates for you.

The Help project file provides coordinating information used by the Windows Help Compiler. When you create your project with AppWizard and choose the Context-Sensitive Help option, your application's help project file will look like the following .HPJ file from the Scribble tutorial application:

```
[OPTIONS]
CONTENTS=main_index
TITLE=SCRIBBLE Application Help
COMPRESS=true
WARNING=2

[FILES]
hlp\afxcore.rtf
hlp\afxprint.rtf

[BITMAPS]
; toolbar buttons for File commands
hlp\filenew.bmp
hlp\fileopen.bmp
hlp\fileprnt.bmp
hlp\filesave.bmp

; toolbar buttons for Edit commands
hlp\editcopy.bmp
hlp\editcut.bmp
hlp\editpast.bmp
hlp\editundo.bmp

...

[ALIAS]
HIDR_MAINFRAME = main_index
HIDR_SCRIBHTYPE = HIDR_DOC1TYPE
HIDD_ABOUTBOX = HID_APP_ABOUT

HID_HT_SIZE = HID_SC_SIZE
HID_HT_HSCROLL = scrollbars
HID_HT_VSCROLL = scrollbars
HID_HT_MINBUTTON = HID_SC_MINIMIZE
HID_HT_MAXBUTTON = HID_SC_MAXIMIZE
AFX_HIDP_INVALID_FILENAME    = AFX_HIDP_default
AFX_HIDP_FAILED_TO_OPEN_DOC = AFX_HIDP_default

...

[MAP]
#include <C:\MSVC20\MFC\include\afxhelp.hm>
#include <hlp\scribble.hm>
```

This file describes options used by the Windows Help Compiler, topic files with the
.RTF extension to be included in the help build, bitmap files to be included in the
build, a mapping of context strings to context numbers, and more.

Of particular interest is the [MAP] section, which in this example points to two included files with the .HM (help mapping) extension. The article "Help: The MAKEHM and MAKEHELP.BAT Tools" explains more about help-context mapping. For more information about Windows Help project files, see the *Tools User's Guide* for Microsoft Win32.

See Also   Article: "Help: The MAKEHM and MAKEHELP.BAT Tools"

Help: The MAKEHM and MAKEHELP.BAT Tools

This article describes the tools you use to map Help context IDs in your application to Help topics in your Help file. Topics covered include:

- Help context IDs
- Preferred resource ID prefixes
- Example help contexts
- Running the tools

In Windows Help, a "help context" consists of a string and a number. The help context string is what the help text author uses to identify help topics. The help context number is what the programmer uses to identify help topics. Help author and programmer come together in the [MAP] section of the .HPJ file, which associates the help context string and number. When your application calls Windows Help, Windows Help uses the context your application passes to locate and display the help topic denoted by that context. At run time, the framework manages supplying the appropriate help context.

To facilitate relating the windows, dialog boxes, and commands in your application to Windows Help contexts, the Microsoft Foundation Class Library provides the MAKEHM.EXE tool, which creates the information used in the [MAP] section of the .HPJ file.

AppWizard creates a MAKEHELP.BAT file that you'll use to compile your help. MAKEHELP.BAT calls MAKEHM.EXE and then the Windows Help Compiler.

Help Context IDs

When you use Visual C++ to create dialog-template resources, menu commands, and the like, Visual C++ writes **#define** statements in a file named RESOURCE.H (by default). For example, there might be **#define** statements for such symbols as `IDD_MY_DIALOG` and `ID_PEN_WIDTHS`.

The following illustrates what Visual C++ creates in your RESOURCE.H file and the Help contexts that the MAKEHM tool maps the IDs to. The RESOURCE.H IDs

```
#define IDD_MY_DIALOG    2000
#define ID_MY_COMMAND     150
```

would be translated by MAKEHM into

```
HIDD_MY_DIALOG    0x207d0
HID_MY_COMMAND    0x10096
```

Dialog-box IDs are translated to values beginning at 0x20000. Command and resource IDs are translated to values beginning at 0x10000. That is, the framework reserves specific ranges of values for different kinds of objects. For details, see the contents of MAKEHELP.BAT and Technical Note 28 under MFC in Books Online.

This format is compatible with the Help Compiler, which maps context IDs (the numbers on the right side) to topic names (the symbols on the left). Use these topic names in the .RTF Help files to identify contexts.

For more information about how Visual C++ adds symbols to RESOURCE.H and how you can view and manipulate them with the Visual C++ Symbol Browser, see Chapter 4 in the *Visual C++ User's Guide*.

Preferred Resource ID Prefixes

To facilitate using MAKEHELP.BAT and MAKEHM, observe the conventions in specifying IDs for your resource objects, as shown in Table 1. It is important that different kinds of resource objects have different ID prefixes.

Table 1   Preferred Resource ID Naming Conventions

Predefined ID	Object
IDP_	Message-box prompt
IDD_	Dialog-box ID
ID_	Toolbar or menu command (**IDM_** is okay too)
IDR_	Frame-related resources
IDW_	Control bar

For example, here's a call to the MAKEHM tool in the MAKEHELP.BAT file for the Scribble tutorial application:

```
makehm IDD_,HIDD_,0x20000 resource.h >> hlp\scribble.hm
```

MAKEHELP.BAT expects dialog resources to be named with **IDD_** prefixes. The corresponding help contexts will be named with **HIDD_** prefixes.

Note The Scribble tutorial teaches MFC programming techniques. See *Introducing Visual C++.*

Use the **IDS_** prefix for normal string resources, and do not write Help topics for them. For string resources used in message boxes, use the **IDP_** prefix and write Help topics for them so the user can get context-sensitive Help by pressing F1 while the message box is displayed.

Example Help Contexts

As your application grows, you'll define a number of new IDs (symbols). For example, the following lists the RESOURCE.H file for the Scribble tutorial application after Step 6 of the tutorial:

```
//{{NO_DEPENDENCIES}}
// Visual C++ generated include file.
// Used by SCRIBBLE.RC
//
#define IDR_MAINFRAME                  2
#define IDR_SCRIBTYPE                  3
#define IDD_ABOUTBOX                   100
#define ID_PEN_THICK_OR_THIN           32768
#define ID_PEN_WIDTHS                  32769
#define IDD_PEN_WIDTHS                 101
#define IDC_THIN_PEN_WIDTH             104
#define IDC_THICK_PEN_WIDTH            105
#define IDC_DEFAULT_PEN_WIDTHS         106
```

Symbols defined for the Scribble tutorial include IDR_SCRIBTYPE (Scribble's menus and other application-specific resources), IDD_PEN_WIDTHS (a Pen Widths dialog box), ID_PEN_THICK_OR_THIN (a Thick Line command), and so on. Notice that one Scribble command, **ID_EDIT_CLEAR_ALL**, doesn't appear in RESOURCE.H because it's a predefined ID in the class library. AppWizard will already have generated a Help topic for it in the .RTF files it creates to get you started.

MAKEHM will map these symbols to Windows help contexts when you run MAKEHELP.BAT. The following excerpt from a MAKEHELP.BAT file for the Scribble tutorial shows how MAKEHELP.BAT calls MAKEHM:

```
...
echo // Commands (ID_* and IDM_*) >>hlp\scribble.hm
makehm ID_,HID_,0x10000 IDM_,HIDM_,0x10000 resource.h >>hlp\scribble.hm
echo. >>hlp\scribble.hm
echo // Prompts (IDP_*) >>hlp\scribble.hm
makehm IDP_,HIDP_,0x30000 resource.h >>hlp\scribble.hm
echo. >>hlp\scribble.hm
echo // Resources (IDR_*) >>hlp\scribble.hm
```

```
makehm IDR_,HIDR_,0x20000 resource.h >>hlp\scribble.hm
 .
 .
 .
REM -- Make help for Project SCRIBBLE
call hc32 scribble.hpj
echo.
```

After you run MAKEHELP.BAT, the SCRIBBLE.HM file looks like the following:

```
// MAKEHELP.BAT generated Help Map file.  Used by SCRIBBLE.HPJ.

// Commands (ID_* and IDM_*)
HID_PEN_THICK_OR_THIN        0x18000
HID_PEN_WIDTHS               0x18001

// Prompts (IDP_*)

// Resources (IDR_*)
HIDR_MAINFRAME               0x20002
HIDR_SCRIBTYPE               0x20003

// Dialogs (IDD_*)
HIDD_ABOUTBOX                0x20064
HIDD_PEN_WIDTHS              0x20065

// Frame Controls (IDW_*)
```

This file contains help contexts for two commands, two resources (menus and other application resources), and two dialog boxes.

Running the Tools

When you run MAKEHELP.BAT from the command line, it calls the MAKEHM tool to map the **#define** statements in RESOURCE.H to Windows Help strings in an .HM file. The MAKEHM tool collects **#define** statements from RESOURCE.H and uses the command-line parameters passed to MAKEHM to map defined symbols to help strings in a .HM file. For the example IDs in the previous paragraph, it would create help strings such as HIDD_MY_DIALOG and HID_PEN_WIDTHS. These context strings are formed by prefixing an "H" to the symbol found in RESOURCE.H. MAKEHM also maps the ID's numeric value to a corresponding number for the help context. An example is shown in "Example Help Contexts" above.

When MAKEHELP.BAT runs the Windows Help Compiler, the compiler uses the .HM files pointed to by the .HPJ file to set up the help contexts in your new help file. Once you finish compiling your .HLP file, you can use it from your application.

See Also   Article: "Help: Authoring Help Topics"

Help: Authoring Help Topics

The framework manages navigation from application user interfaces to help contexts. Implementing further navigation within the help file is the domain of help authoring rather than programming. The purpose of this article is to describe the general process of authoring and editing help topic files. Topics covered include:

- Editing the starter .RTF files
- Help topics in the .RTF file
- Example topics
- Compiling and testing your help file

Editing the help topics for any application is too big a task to work through in just one article; however a few examples will help you get started. The examples in this article were edited with Microsoft Word for Windows, but you can use any application that can edit rich text format (.RTF) files. To make the following discussion concrete, the examples are drawn from the Scribble tutorial program, presented in Chapters 6 through 16 of *Introducing Visual C++*. If you want to see how help is prepared for Scribble, look at Chapter 15 in that book.

When you run AppWizard to start the Scribble tutorial, the wizard creates not only source code files but also a set of files in rich text format (.RTF) containing starter help topics for many of the user-interface elements that Scribble will have, including its menu commands. To complete a help file for Scribble, follow the steps outlined in this group of Help articles. Then edit the .RTF files to fill in Help material that AppWizard couldn't supply.

The discussion in the rest of this article takes you through part of that process to illustrate the techniques and to point out some guidelines and tips. Scribble is used here merely as an example.

Editing the Starter .RTF Files

The .RTF files that AppWizard creates for an application—such as Scribble—contain starter help topics for many elements of the Windows user interface. Some of them are fairly complete, while others are skeletal and must be filled out.

If you want to customize the help topics supplied by AppWizard, you must do the following, using all of the .RTF files in your project's HLP subdirectory (for example, MYSCRIB\HLP):

- Globally replace the placeholder string "<<YourApp>>" in the .RTF files with the name of the application: for example, replace "<<YourApp>>" with "Scribble".
- From the help topics, remove any references to menu items absent in your application.

For example, file PEN.RTF contains a topic for the Edit Links command, which Scribble doesn't support.

- Replace the helpful directives in the help topics with your own information. These directives are bracketed by << and >> symbols.

Notice that because the class library predefines **ID_EDIT_CLEAR_ALL**, Scribble's file PEN.RTF already contains a help topic for the Clear All command added to the Edit menu in the Scribble tutorial. However, the skeletal directive for such commands, "<< Write application-specific help here. >>," needs to be replaced with a real description.

- Add topics for new commands and dialog boxes.

Examine the listing of RESOURCE.H in "Example Help Contexts" in the article "Help: The MAKEHM and MAKEHELP.BAT Tools." It lists the following help topics (as seen in Scribble):

- Two resource-related HIDs (**HIDR_**), for menus and related resources
- Two dialog-box HIDs (**HIDD_**), for About and Pen Widths dialog boxes
- Two command HIDs (**HID_**), for Thick Line and Pen Widths commands

In the Scribble tutorial, the Pen Widths dialog box is new, so new help topics are needed for the dialog box and for two new commands. (The About dialog box is created by AppWizard, so it already has a topic in PEN.RTF.)

Help Topics in the .RTF File

Help topics in an .RTF file are separated by hard page breaks. Each topic has a name and a "footnote" symbol (#).

The footnote symbol # identifies context strings. Other possible footnote symbols identify keywords for searching (K) and topic names ($). Topic text can contain "popups" and "jumps." A popup displays a small window with extra information when its "hot spot" is clicked. A jump takes the user to another topic screen in the help system when its button is clicked. Hot spots for popups and jumps are text strings with special formatting. For more information, see the *Tools User's Guide* for Microsoft Win32. If you're using Word for Windows for .RTF files, you can examine the file PEN.RTF with hidden text displayed.

Example Topics

To illustrate the process of adding topics, this section shows the structure needed for a user to jump from the main index screen in help to a screen showing general information about the new Pen menu, and from there to screens that describe the Scribble tutorial application's two Pen menu commands. These items are added to the PEN.RTF file.

The Main Index Screen

Figure 1 shows the main index screen as it appears in compiled help. This is what the screen looks like after the Pen menu entry has been added to Scribble.

Figure 1   The Main Index Screen in Compiled Help

Figure 2 shows the help topic for the main index screen as it appears in Microsoft Word for Windows (with hidden text displayed). The screen contains entries for six menus: File, Edit, View, Pen, Window, and Help. The Pen menu is Scribble-specific, so this jump has been added. The others are created by AppWizard.

Each of the menu names on this screen is a "hot spot" that links to another topic. By clicking this hot spot, the user can jump to another screen in the help system. If you examine this screen in the PEN.RTF file using Word for Windows, you see that the menu names—such as "Pen Menu"— are formatted with double underlining. (This might be represented differently by another RTF editor.) Each menu name is followed immediately by a context name formatted as hidden text. For the Pen menu, this text reads "menu_pen."

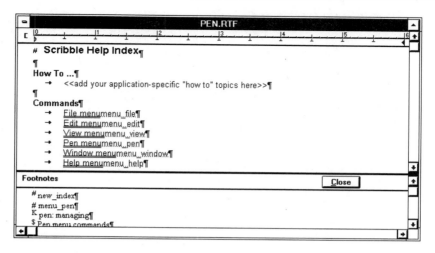

Figure 2   The Main Index Screen in PEN.RTF

The Pen Menu Screen

Figure 3 shows the text in PEN.RTF for a help screen on the Pen Menu topic. The upper part of the figure shows the text of the file; the lower part shows footnote text. All formatting and hidden text are displayed.

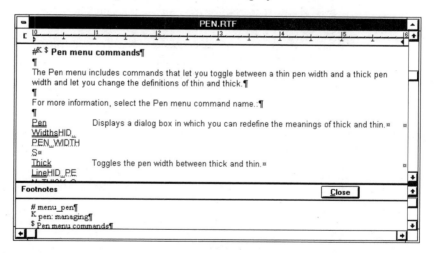

Figure 3   The Pen Menu Topic in the PEN.RTF File

The topic screen begins with a hard page break. The next line shows the footnote character, #, followed by the title to be displayed on the user's screen, "Pen menu commands." The rest of the screen contains descriptive text and two more hot spots for jumping to screens about the individual menu items.

The footnote text associated with the # footnote for the Pen menu is "menu_pen," which names the context—the destination of jumps to this screen of the help system.

Setting up this screen requires entering the hard page break and the footnote, then writing the text. In Word for Windows, for example, you'd use the Break command on the Insert menu to enter a hard page break. Then you'd use the Footnote entry on the Insert menu to specify a footnote with the special footnote character #.

Next, you'd type the footnote text in the footnote window. Finally, you'd type the descriptive text and format the hot spots.

The jumps to screens for individual menu items consist of:

- Visible text, such as "Pen Widths," formatted as double underlined, to designate the hot spot on the screen for the jump.

- Hidden text, such as "HID_PEN_WIDTHS," to designate the destination help topic.

In the RTF files that AppWizard supplies, tables (as in Word for Windows) are used to present groups of jumps, but help authors are not required to use tables.

A Screen for a Menu Item

Figure 4 shows a screen for the Pen Widths and Thick Line menu items.

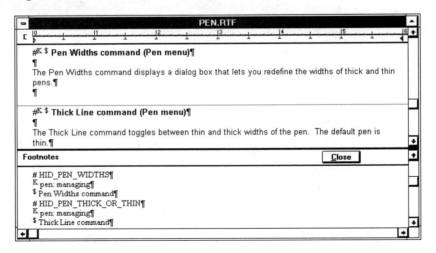

Figure 4   The Pen Widths and Thick Line Topics in the PEN.RTF File

The screen is set up similarly to its parent screen for the Pen menu as a whole. Notice the text used for the footnotes in the lower part of Figure 4.

Compiling and Testing Your Help File

Once your help authoring is finished, you can compile your help file. If you're trying out the techniques described in these articles, perhaps by working through the Scribble tutorial in *Introducing Visual C++*, and you've chosen to author the application's help files, use the following procedure to see the results.

▶ **To compile and test the application's help**

1. To compile help, run MAKEHELP.BAT from the command line.

   ```
   c:>makehelp
   ```

   The .HLP file is placed in your project directory (for example, MYSCRIB).

2. To prepare the application for testing your help, build it from the Visual C++ Project menu.

3. To test help, run the application and try out the help features.

See Also   Articles: "Help: The Help Project File," "Help: The MAKEHM and MAKEHELP.BAT Tools"

In-Place Activation

See the article "Servers: Implementing In-Place Frame Windows."

In-Place Editing

See the article "Servers: Implementing In-Place Frame Windows."

Library Versions

This article provides information on available versions of the Microsoft Foundation Class Library. Topics covered include:

- Automatic linking of MFC library version
- Library naming conventions.
- AFXDLL versions
- Dynamic-link library (DLL) support
- Selecting a library

Automatic Linking of MFC Library Version

In versions of MFC prior to version 3.0 (prior to Visual C++ version 2.0), you had to manually specify the correct version of the MFC library in the input list of libraries for the linker. As of MFC version 3.0, it is no longer necessary to manually specify the version of the MFC library. Instead, the MFC header files automatically determine the correct version of the MFC library, based on values defined with **#define**, such as **_DEBUG** or **_UNICODE**. The MFC header files add "/defaultlib" directives instructing the linker to link in a specific version of the MFC library.

For example, the following code fragment from the AFX.H header file instructs the linker to link in either the NAFXCWD.LIB or NAFXCW.LIB version of MFC, depending on whether you are using the debug version of MFC:

```
...
#ifndef _UNICODE
    #ifdef _DEBUG
        #pragma comment(lib, "nafxcwd.lib")
    #else
        #pragma comment(lib, "nafxcw.lib")
    #endif
#else
    #ifdef _DEBUG
        #pragma comment(lib, "uafxcwd.lib")
    #else
        #pragma comment(lib, "uafxcw.lib")
    #endif
#endif...
```

MFC header files also link in all required libraries, including MFC libraries, Win32 libraries, OLE libraries, OLE libraries built from samples, ODBC libraries, and so on. The Win32 libraries include KERNEL32.LIB, USER32.LIB, and GDI32.LIB.

Library Naming Conventions

Object-code libraries for MFC use the following naming conventions. The library names have the form

*u*AFX*c*W*d*.LIB

where the letters shown in italic lowercase are placeholders for specifiers whose meanings are shown in Table 1:

Table 1   Library Naming Conventions

Specifier	Values and Meanings
u	ANSI (N) or Unicode (U)
c	Type of program to create: C=EXE, D=USRDLL
d	Debug or Release: D=Debug; omit specifier for Release

The default is to build a debug Windows ANSI application for the Intel® platform: NAFXCWD.LIB. All libraries—listed in Table 2—are included prebuilt in the \MSVC20\MFC\LIB directory on the Visual C++ CD-ROM disc.

Table 2   Static Library Versions

Library	Description
NAFXCW.LIB	Release version: Windows EXE
NAFXCWD.LIB	Debug version: Windows EXE (default)
NAFXDWD.LIB	Debug USRDLL version
NAFXDW.LIB	Release USRDLL version
UAFXCWD.LIB	Debug version: Windows EXE with Unicode support
UAFXCW.LIB	Release version: Windows EXE with Unicode support
UAFXDW.LIB	Release version: DLL with Unicode support
UAFXDWD.LIB	Debug version: DLL with Unicode support

Note If you need to build a library version, see the README.TXT file in \MSVC20\MFC\SRC directory. This file describes using the supplied MAKEFILE with NMAKE.

If you are building a console application and wish to link with the MFC libraries, use NAFXCW.LIB or NAFXCW.LIB instead of NAFXCRD.LIB or NAFXCR.LIB.

AFXDLL Versions

Instead of building your application by statically linking to the MFC object-code libraries, you can build your application to use one of the AFXDLL libraries— which contain MFC in a DLL that multiple running applications can share. For a table of AFXDLL names, see the article "DLLs: Naming Conventions."

Note By default, AppWizard creates an AFXDLL project. To use static linking of MFC code instead, set the "Use MFC in a static library" option in AppWizard.

Dynamic-Link Library Support

The NAFXDWD.LIB and NAFXDW.LIB libraries create your application as a dynamic-link library (called a USRDLL) that can be used with applications not built with the class library. Don't confuse this DLL support with MFC30.DLL and MFC30D.DLL (known as AFXDLL), which contain the entire 32-bit class library in a DLL. For more information, see the article "Dynamic-Link Libraries (DLLs)." For a table of USRDLL names, see the article "DLLs: Naming Conventions."

Selecting a Library

By default, AppWizard creates an application that uses the NAFXCWD.LIB library, which builds a Windows debug application.

▶ **To change the current object-code library used by Visual C++**

- See the procedure "To define a new target" in "Using Targets" in Chapter 2 of the *Visual C++ User's Guide.*

See Also   Article: "Dynamic-Link Libraries (DLLs)"

Linked OLE Item

See the article "Activation."

MBCS

Multibyte Character Set encoding. In Visual C++, MBCS support is limited to double byte character set (DBCS) encoding. MFC supports both DBCS and Unicode.

For information about using DBCS with MFC, see Chapter 12 in *Programming Techniques*.

Memory Management

This group of articles describes how to take advantage of the general-purpose services of the Microsoft Foundation Class Library (MFC) related to memory management. Memory allocation can be divided into two main categories: frame allocations and heap allocations.

One main difference between the two allocation techniques is that with frame allocation you typically work with the actual memory block itself, whereas with heap allocation you are always given a pointer to the memory block. Another major difference between the two schemes is that frame objects are automatically deleted, while heap objects must be explicitly deleted by the programmer.

The following articles describe how to use the capabilities of C and C++ to accomplish memory allocations on the frame and on the heap:

- Memory Management: Frame Allocation
- Memory Management: Heap Allocation
- Memory Management: Memory Allocation on the Frame and on the Heap
- Memory Management: Resizable Memory Blocks

The third article above demonstrates MFC memory allocation techniques.

Memory Management: Frame Allocation

Allocation on the frame takes its name from the "stack frame" that is set up whenever a function is called. The stack frame is an area of memory that temporarily holds the arguments to the function as well as any variables that are defined local to the function. Frame variables are often called "automatic" variables because the compiler automatically allocates the space for them.

There are two key characteristics of frame allocations. First, when you define a local variable, enough space is allocated on the stack frame to hold the entire variable, even if it is a large array or data structure. Second, frame variables are automatically deleted when they go out of scope:

```
void MyFunction( )
{
    // Local object created on the stack
    CString strName;
    ...
    // Object goes out of scope and is deleted as function ends
}
```

For local function variables, this scope transition happens when the function exits, but the scope of a frame variable can be smaller than a function if nested braces are used. This automatic deletion of frame variables is very important. In the case of simple primitive types (such as **int** or **byte**), arrays, or data structures, the automatic deletion simply reclaims the memory used by the variable. Since the variable has gone out of scope, it cannot be accessed anyway. In the case of C++ objects, however, the process of automatic deletion is a bit more complicated.

When an object is defined as a frame variable, its constructor is automatically invoked at the point where the definition is encountered. When the object goes out of scope, its destructor is automatically invoked before the memory for the object is reclaimed. This automatic construction and destruction can be very handy, but you must be aware of the automatic calls, especially to the destructor.

The key advantage of allocating objects on the frame is that they are automatically deleted. When you allocate your objects on the frame, you don't have to worry about forgotten objects causing memory leaks. (For details on memory leaks, see the article "Diagnostics: Detecting Memory Leaks.") A disadvantage of frame allocation is that frame variables cannot be used outside their scope. Another factor in choosing frame allocation versus heap allocation is that for large structures and objects, it is often better to use the heap instead of the stack for storage since stack space is often limited.

Memory Management: Heap Allocation

The heap is reserved for the memory allocation needs of the program. It is an area apart from the program code and from the stack. Typical C programs use the functions **malloc** and **free** to allocate and deallocate heap memory. The Debug version of the Microsoft Foundation Class Library provides modified versions of the C++ built-in operators **new** and **delete** to allocate and deallocate objects in heap memory.

When you use **new** and **delete** instead of **malloc** and **free**, you are able to take advantage of the class library's memory-management debugging enhancements, which can be useful in detecting memory leaks. When you build your program with the Release version of the Microsoft Foundation Class Library, the standard versions of the **new** and **delete** operators provide an efficient way to allocate and deallocate memory (the Release version of the Microsoft Foundation Class Library does not provide modified versions of these operators).

Note that the total size of objects allocated on the heap is limited only by your system's available virtual memory.

Memory Management: Allocation on the Frame and on the Heap

This article describes how MFC performs frame allocations and heap allocations for each of the three typical kinds of memory allocations:

- An array of bytes
- A data structure
- An object

Allocation of an Array of Bytes

▶ **To allocate an array of bytes on the frame**

- Define the array as shown by the following code. The array is automatically deleted and its memory reclaimed when the array variable exits its scope.

```
{
    const int BUFF_SIZE = 128;

    // Allocate on the frame
    char myCharArray[BUFF_SIZE];
    int myIntArray[BUFF_SIZE];
    // Reclaimed when exiting scope
}
```

▶ **To allocate an array of bytes (or any primitive data type) on the heap**

- Use the **new** operator with the array syntax shown in this example:

```
const int BUFF_SIZE = 128;

// Allocate on the heap
char* myCharArray = new char[BUFF_SIZE];
int* myIntArray = new int[BUFF_SIZE];
```

▶ **To deallocate the arrays from the heap**

- Use the **delete** operator as follows:

```
delete [] myCharArray;
delete [] myIntArray;
```

Allocation of a Data Structure

▶ **To allocate a data structure on the frame**

- Define the structure variable as follows:

```
struct MyStructType {...};
void SomeFunc(void)
{
    // Frame allocation
    MyStructType myStruct;

    // Use the struct
    myStruct.topScore = 297;

    // Reclaimed when exiting scope
}
```

The memory occupied by the structure is reclaimed when it exits its scope.

▶ **To allocate data structures on the heap**

- Use **new** to allocate data structures on the heap and **delete** to deallocate them, as shown by the following examples:

```
// Heap allocation
MyStructType* myStruct = new MyStructType;

// Use the struct through the pointer ...
myStruct->topScore = 297;

delete myStruct;
```

Allocation of an Object

▶ **To allocate an object on the frame**

- Declare the object as follows:

```
{
    CPerson myPerson;      // Automatic constructor call here

    myPerson.SomeMemberFunction();     // Use the object

}
```

The destructor for the object is automatically invoked when the object exits its scope.

▶ **To allocate an object on the heap**

- Use the **new** operator, which returns a pointer to the object, to allocate objects on the heap. Use the **delete** operator to delete them.

The following heap and frame examples assume that the `CPerson` constructor takes no arguments.

```
// Automatic constructor call here
CPerson* myPerson = new CPerson;

myPerson->SomeMemberFunction();          // Use the object

delete myPerson;                    // Destructor invoked during delete
```

If the argument for the `CPerson` constructor is a pointer to **char**, the statement for frame allocation is:

```
CPerson myPerson( "Joe Smith" );
```

The statement for heap allocation is:

```
CPerson* MyPerson = new CPerson( "Joe Smith" );
```

Memory Management: Resizable Memory Blocks

The **new** and **delete** operators, described in the article "Memory Management: Allocation on the Frame and on the Heap," are good for allocating and deallocating fixed-size memory blocks and objects. Occasionally, your application may need resizable memory blocks. You must use the standard C run-time library functions **malloc**, **realloc**, and **free** to manage resizable memory blocks on the heap.

Mixing the **new** and **delete** operators with the resizable memory-allocation functions on the same memory block will result in corrupted memory in the Debug version of the Microsoft Foundation Class Library. You should not use **realloc** on a memory block allocated with **new**. Likewise, you should not allocate a memory block with the **new** operator and delete it with **free**, or use the **delete** operator on a block of memory allocated with **malloc**.

Menus and Resources

This group of articles explains the use of menus and resources in MFC OLE applications.

OLE Visual Editing places additional requirements on the menu layout and resources provided by OLE applications because there are a number of modes in which both container and server applications can be started and used. For example, a full-server application can be started in any of these three modes:

- Stand-alone
- In place, for editing an item in the context of a container
- Open, for editing an item outside the context of its container

This requires three separate menu layouts, one for each possible mode of the application. Accelerator tables are also necessary for each new mode. A container application may or may not support in-place activation; if it does, it needs a new menu structure and associated accelerator tables.

In-place activation requires that the container and server applications must negotiate for menu, toolbar, and status bar space. All resources must be designed with this in mind. The article "Menus and Resources: Menu Merging" covers this topic in detail.

Because of these issues, OLE applications created with AppWizard can have up to four separate menus and accelerator table resources. These are used for the following reasons:

Resource name	Use
IDR_MAINFRAME	Used in an MDI application if no file is open, or in an SDI application regardless of open files. This is the standard menu used in non-OLE applications.
IDR_<project>TYPE	Used in an MDI application if files are open. Used when an application is running stand-alone.
IDR_<project>TYPE_SRVR_IP	Used by the server or container when an object is open in place.
IDR_<project>TYPE_SRVR_EMB	Used by a server application if an object is opened without using in-place activation.

Each of these resource names represents a menu and, usually, an accelerator table. A similar scheme should be used in MFC applications that are not created with AppWizard.

The following articles discuss topics related to containers, servers, and the menu merging necessary to implement in-place activation:

- Menus and Resources: Container Additions
- Menus and Resources: Server Additions
- Menus and Resources: Menu Merging

Menus and Resources: Container Additions

This article explains the changes that need to be made to the menus and other resources in a Visual Editing container application. In container applications, two types of changes need to be made: modifications to existing resources to support OLE Visual Editing and addition of new resources used for in-place activation. If you use AppWizard to create your container application, these steps will be done for you, but they may require some customization.

If you don't use AppWizard, you may want to look at OCLIENT.RC, the resource script for the OCLIENT sample application, to see how these changes are implemented. This sample is located in \MSVC20\SAMPLES\MFC\OCLIENT.

Topics covered in this article include:

- Container menu additions
- Accelerator table additions
- String table additions

Container Menu Additions

You must add a number of items to the Edit menu:

Item	Purpose
Insert New Object...	Opens the OLE Insert Object dialog box to insert a linked or embedded item into the document. This may be placed in the Insert menu if applicable to your application.
Paste Link	Pastes a link to the item on the Clipboard into the document.
OLE Verb	Calls the selected item's primary verb. The text of this menu item changes to reflect the primary verb of the selected item.
Links...	Opens the OLE Edit Links dialog box to change existing linked items.

In addition to the changes listed in this article, your source file must include AFXOLECL.RC, which is required for the Microsoft Foundation Class Library implementation. Insert New Object is the only required menu addition. Other items can be added, but these listed are the most common.

You must create a new menu for your container application if you want to support in-place activation of contained objects. This menu consists of the same File menu and Window pop-up menus used when files are open, but it has two separators placed between them. These separators are used to indicate where the server object should place its menus when activated in place. For more information on this menu-merging technique, see the article "Menus and Resources: Menu Merging."

Accelerator Table Additions

Small changes to a container application's accelerator table resources are necessary if you are supporting in-place activation. The first change allows the user to press the escape key (ESC) to cancel the in-place editing mode. Add the following entry to the main accelerator table using Visual C++ :

ID	Key	Type
ID_CANCEL_INPLACE	**VK_ESCAPE**	**VIRTKEY**

The second change is to create a new accelerator table that corresponds to the new menu resource created for in-place activation. This table has entries for the File and Window menus in addition to the **VK_ESCAPE** entry above. The following example is the accelerator table created for in-place activation in step 2 of the CONTAIN tutorial sample:

```
IDR_CONTRTYPE_CNTR_IP ACCELERATORS PRELOAD MOVEABLE PURE
BEGIN
    "N",            ID_FILE_NEW,            VIRTKEY, CONTROL
    "O",            ID_FILE_OPEN,           VIRTKEY, CONTROL
    "S",            ID_FILE_SAVE,           VIRTKEY, CONTROL
    "P",            ID_FILE_PRINT,          VIRTKEY, CONTROL
    VK_F6,          ID_NEXT_PANE,           VIRTKEY
    VK_F6,          ID_PREV_PANE,           VIRTKEY, SHIFT
    VK_ESCAPE,      ID_CANCEL_EDIT,         VIRTKEY, NOINVERT
END
```

String Table Additions

Most of the changes to string tables for container applications correspond to the additional menu items mentioned in "Container Menu Additions" earlier in this article. They supply the text displayed in the status bar when each menu item is displayed. As an example, here are the string-table entries AppWizard generates:

```
STRINGTABLE DISCARDABLE
BEGIN
    IDP_OLE_INIT_FAILED      "OLE initialization failed.  Make sure that
    the OLE libraries are the correct version."
    IDP_FAILED_TO_CREATE     "Failed to create object.  Make sure that
    the object is entered in the system registry."
END
```

Note In the above example, the string literals have been split over two lines. Be sure to enter this text on one line. Using the Visual C++ string editor will ensure these are entered on one line.

See Also   Article: "Menus and Resources: Server Additions"

Menus and Resources: Server Additions

This article explains the changes that need to be made to the menus and other resources in a Visual Editing server application. A server application requires many additions to the menu structure and other resources because it can be started in one of three modes: stand-alone, embedded, or in place. As described in the "Menus and Resources" article, there are a maximum of four sets of menus. All four are used for a full-server application, while only three are used for a mini-server. AppWizard will create the menu layout necessary for the type of server you want. Some customization may be necessary.

If you don't use AppWizard, you may want to look at HIERSVR.RC, the resource script for the HIERSVR sample application, to see how these changes are implemented. This sample can be found in the \MSVC20\SAMPLES\MFC\HIERSVR subdirectory.

Topics covered in this article include:

- Server menu additions
- Accelerator table additions
- String table additions
- Mini-Server additions

Server Menu Additions

Server applications must have menu resources added to fully support OLE Visual Editing. The menus used when the application is run in stand-alone mode do not have to be changed, but you must add two new menu resources before building the application; one to support in-place activation and one to support the server being fully open. Both menu resources are used by full- and mini-server applications.

- To support in-place activation, you must create a menu resource that is very similar to the menu resource used when run in stand-alone mode. The difference in this menu is that the File and Window items (and any other menu items that deal with the application, and not the data) are missing. The container application will supply these menu items. For more information on, and an example of, this menu-merging technique, see the article "Menus and Resources: Menu Merging."

- To support fully open activation, you must create a menu resource nearly identical to the menu resource used when run in stand-alone mode. The only modification to this menu resource is that some items are reworded to reflect the fact that the server is operating on an item embedded in a compound document. For example, in step 7 of the Scribble tutorial, when the application is open in-place, the Save command on the File menu changes to Save Copy As.

In addition to the changes listed in this article, your resource file needs to include AFXOLESV.RC, which is required for the Microsoft Foundation Class Library implementation. This file is in the \MSVC20\MFC\INCLUDE subdirectory.

Accelerator Table Additions

Two new accelerator table resources must be added to server applications; they correspond directly to the new menu resources described above. The first accelerator table is used when the server application is activated in place. It consists of all the entries in the view's accelerator table except those tied to the File and Window menus.

The second table is nearly an exact copy of the view's accelerator table. Any differences parallel changes made in the fully open menu mentioned in "Server Menu Additions" above.

For an example of these accelerator table changes, compare the IDR_HIERSVRTYPE_SRVR_IP and IDR_HIERSVRTYPE_SRVR_EMB accelerator tables with **IDR_MAINFRAME** in the HIERSVR.RC file included in the HIERSVR sample application. The File and Window accelerators are missing from the in-place table and exact copies of them are in the embedded table.

String Table Additions

Only one string table addition is necessary in a server application—a string to signify that the OLE initialization failed. As an example, here is the string-table entry AppWizard generates:

```
STRINGTABLE DISCARDABLE
BEGIN
    IDP_OLE_INIT_FAILED      "OLE initialization failed.  Verify
    that the OLE libraries are the correct version."
END
```

Note   In the above example, the string literal has been split over two lines. Be sure to enter this text on one line. Using the Visual C++ string editor will ensure these are entered on one line.

Mini-Server Additions

The same additions apply for mini-servers as those listed above for full-servers. Because a mini-server can't be run in stand-alone mode, its main menu is much smaller. The main menu created by AppWizard has only a File menu, containing only the items Exit and About. Embedded and in-place menus for mini-servers are exactly the same as those for full-servers.

See Also   Article: "Menus and Resources: Menu Merging"

Menus and Resources: Menu Merging

This article details the steps necessary for Microsoft Foundation Class Library applications to handle Visual Editing and in-place activation properly. In-place activation poses a challenge for both container and server applications. The user remains in the same starting frame window, but is actually running another application. This requires coordination between the resources of the container and server applications.

Topics covered in this article include:

- Menu layouts
- Toolbars and status bars

Menu Layouts

The first step is to coordinate menu layouts. Container applications should create a new menu to be used only when embedded items are activated in place. At the minimum, this menu should consist of the following, in the order listed:

1. File menu identical to the one used when files are open. (Usually no other menu items are placed before the next item.)
2. Two consecutive separators.
3. Window menu identical to the one used when files are open. Some applications may have other menu items, such as an Options menu, that belong in the group that remains on the menu when an embedded item is activated in place. For example, the Scribble application built in the Scribble tutorial has a Pen menu that remains on the menu bar when items are activated in place.

Server applications should also create a new menu specifically for in-place activation. It should be exactly like the menu used when files are open, but without menu items, such as File and Window, that manipulate the server application instead of the data. This menu should also contain two consecutive separators to indicate where the container's second group of menu items should go.

For an example, take a look at the layout of some sample in-place menus for a container and a server. The details of each menu item have been removed to make the example clearer. The container's in-place menu has the following entries:

```
IDR_CONTAINERTYPE_CNTR_IP MENU PRELOAD DISCARDABLE
BEGIN
    POPUP "&File C1"
    MENUITEM SEPARATOR
    MENUITEM SEPARATOR
    POPUP "&Options C2"
    POPUP "&Window C2"
END
```

The consecutive separators indicate where the first part of the server's menu should go. Now look at the server's in-place menu:

```
IDR_SERVERTYPE_SRVR_IP MENU PRELOAD DISCARDABLE
BEGIN
    POPUP "&Edit S1"
    POPUP "&Format S1"
    MENUITEM SEPARATOR
    MENUITEM SEPARATOR
    POPUP "&Help S2"
END
```

The separators here indicate where the second group of container menu items should go. The resulting menu structure when an object from this server is activated in place inside this container looks like this:

```
BEGIN
    POPUP "&File C1"
    POPUP "&Edit S1"
    POPUP "&Format S1"
    POPUP "&Options C2"
    POPUP "&Window C2"
    POPUP "&Help S2"
END
```

As you can see, the separators have been replaced with the different groups of each application's menu.

Accelerator tables associated with the in-place menu should also be supplied by the server application. The container will incorporate them into its own accelerator tables.

When an embedded item is activated in place, the framework loads the in-place menu. It then asks the server application for its menu for in-place activation and inserts it where the separators are. This is how the menus combine. You get menus from the container for operating on the file and window placement, and you get menus from the server for operating on the item.

Toolbars and Status Bars

Server applications should create a new toolbar and store its bitmap in a separate file. AppWizard-generated applications store this bitmap in a file called ITOOLBAR.BMP. The new toolbar replaces the container application's toolbar when your server's item is activated in place, and should contain the same items as your normal toolbar, but remove icons representing items on the File and Window menus.

This toolbar is loaded in your **COleIPFrameWnd**-derived class, created for you by AppWizard. The status bar is handled by the container application. For more information on the implementation of in-place frame windows, see the article "Servers: Implementing a Server."

See Also   Articles: "Activation," "Servers," "Containers"

Message Map

The Microsoft Foundation Class Library (MFC) uses a mechanism called the "message map" to route Windows messages and commands to the windows, documents, views, and other objects in an MFC application. Message maps map Windows messages; commands from menus, toolbar buttons, and accelerators; and control-notification messages.

The standard Windows message loop is encapsulated in the **Run** member function of class **CWinApp**. The message loop gets messages representing mouse clicks, keystrokes, and other events from Windows and dispatches them to particular windows or other "command targets." Each object derived from class **CCmdTarget**, including objects derived from class **CWnd**, has a message map. This includes windows, dialog boxes, documents, views, threads, and the application itself.

Message maps connect messages to message handler functions, or "handlers," in the target object. For example, a **WM_LBUTTONDOWN** message might be mapped to an **OnLButtonDown** handler function in a view object. When the message is received, the message map calls the handler function.

Message maps, command targets, message handlers, and other components of the message-handling architecture of MFC are described in detail in Chapter 2, "Working with Messages and Commands."

See Also   Article: "Message Map: Ranges of Messages"

In the *Class Library Reference*: **CCmdTarget**

Message Map: Ranges of Messages

This article explains how to map a range of messages to a single message handler function (instead of mapping one message to only one function).

There are times when you need to process more than one message or control notification in exactly the same way. At such times, you might wish to map all of the messages to a single handler function. Message-map ranges allow you to do this for a contiguous range of messages:

- You can map ranges of command IDs to:
    - A command handler function.
    - A command update handler function.
- You can map control-notification messages for a range of control IDs to a message handler function.

Topics covered in this article include:

- Writing the message-map entry
- Declaring the handler function
- Example for a range of command IDs
- Example for a range of control IDs

Important   ClassWizard does not support message-map ranges, so you must write the message-map entries and handler function declarations yourself, as described in this article.

Writing the Message-Map Entry

In the .CPP file, add your message-map entry, as shown in the following example:

```
...
BEGIN_MESSAGE_MAP(CMyApp, CWinApp)
    //{{AFX_MSG_MAP(CMyApp)
    ...
        ON_COMMAND_RANGE(ID_MYCMD_ONE, ID_MYCMD_TEN, OnDoSomething)
    //}}AFX_MSG_MAP
END_MESSAGE_MAP( )
...
```

The message-map entry consists of the following items:

- The message-map range macro:
  - **ON_COMMAND_RANGE**
  - **ON_UPDATE_COMMAND_UI_RANGE**
  - **ON_CONTROL_RANGE**
- Parameters to the macro:

  The first two macros take three parameters:
  - The command ID that starts the range.
  - The command ID that ends the range.
  - The name of the message handler function.

  The range of command IDs must be contiguous.

  The third macro, **ON_CONTROL_RANGE**, takes an additional first parameter: a control-notification message, such as **EN_CHANGE**.

Declaring the Handler Function

In the .H file, add your handler function declaration outside the //{{AFX_MSG comment brackets. The following code shows how this might look, as shown in the next-to-last line below:

```
// Generated message-map functions
protected:
    //{{AFX_MSG(CMyView)
        ...
    //}}AFX_MSG
    afx_msg void OnDoSomething( UINT nID );
    DECLARE_MESSAGE_MAP()
```

Handler functions for single commands normally take no parameters. Handler functions for message-map ranges require an extra parameter, *nID*, of type **UINT**. This parameter is the first parameter. The extra parameter accommodates the extra command ID needed to specify which command the user actually chose.

Example for a Range of Command IDs

When might you use ranges? One example is in handling commands like the "zoom" command in the HIERSVR sample. This command zooms the view, scaling it between 25% and 300% of its normal size. HIERSVR's view class uses a range to handle the zoom commands with a message-map entry resembling this:

```
ON_COMMAND_RANGE(ID_VIEW_ZOOM25, ID_VIEW_ZOOM300, OnZoom)
```

When you write the message-map entry, you specify:

- Two command IDs, beginning and ending a contiguous range.

  Here they're ID_VIEW_ZOOM25 and ID_VIEW_ZOOM300.

- The name of the handler function for the commands.

  Here it's OnZoom.

The function declaration would resemble this:

```
afx_msg void OnZoom(UINT nID);
```

The case of update handler functions is similar, and likely to be more widely useful. It's quite common to write **ON_UPDATE_COMMAND_UI** handlers for a number of commands and find yourself writing, or copying, the same code over and over. The solution is to map a range of command IDs to one update handler function using the **ON_UPDATE_COMMAND_UI_RANGE** macro. The command IDs must form a contiguous range. For an example, see the **OnUpdateZoom** handler and its **ON_UPDATE_COMMAND_UI_RANGE** message-map entry in the HIERSVR sample's view class.

Example for a Range of Control IDs

Another interesting case is mapping control-notification messages for a range of control IDs to a single handler. Suppose the user can click any of 10 buttons. To map all 10 buttons to one handler, your message-map entry would look like this:

```
ON_CONTROL_RANGE(BN_CLICKED, IDC_BUTTON1, IDC_BUTTON10, OnButtonClicked)
```

When you write the **ON_CONTROL_RANGE** macro in your message map, you specify:

- A particular control-notification message.

  Here it's **BN_CLICKED**.

- The control ID values associated with the contiguous range of controls.

  Here these are `IDC_BUTTON1` and `IDC_BUTTON10`.

- The name of the message handler function.

  Here it's `OnButtonClicked`.

When you write the handler function, specify the extra **UINT** parameter, as shown in the following:

```
...
void CMyDialog::OnButtonClicked( UINT nID )
{
    int nButton = nID - IDC_BUTTON1;
    ASSERT( nButton >= 0 && nButton < 10 );
    // ...
}
```

The `OnButtonClicked` handler for a single **BN_CLICKED** message takes no parameters. The same handler for a range of buttons takes one **UINT**. The extra parameter allows for identifying the particular control responsible for generating the **BN_CLICKED** message.

The code shown in the example is typical: converting the value passed to an **int** within the message range and asserting that this is the case. Then you might take some different action depending on which button was clicked.

MFC

The Microsoft Foundation Class Library (MFC) is an "application framework" (often called the "framework" in this documentation) for writing applications for Microsoft Windows and other platforms that support the Win32 API. The framework is implemented as a group of C++ classes, many of which represent common objects such as documents, windows, dialog boxes, toolbars, and so on.

This article presents an overview of MFC, lists articles describing various components of MFC and MFC tools, and lists articles describing changes from previous versions of MFC.

For an Overview of MFC

Part 1 of *Programming with the Microsoft Foundation Class Library* presents an overview of MFC:

- Chapter 1, "Using the Classes to Write Applications for Windows"
- Chapter 2, "Working with Messages and Commands"
- Chapter 3, "Working with Frame Windows, Documents, and Views"
- Chapter 4, "Working with Dialog Boxes, Controls, and Control Bars"
- Chapter 5, "Working with Object Linking and Embedding"
- Chapter 6, "Working with Databases"
- Chapter 7, "Using the General-Purpose Classes"

Encyclopedia Articles About Aspects of MFC

The following main articles in Part 2 explain specific areas in more detail. Some articles describe how a component or feature of MFC works. Others describe how to carry out a procedure in programming with MFC. Each of these articles is typically the "main" article in a group of related "child" articles.

- AppWizard
- ClassWizard
- Clipboard
- CObject Class
- Collections
- COMMON.RC Sample Resources
- Database Overview
- Date and Time
- Debugging
- Diagnostics
- Dynamic-Link Libraries (DLLs)
- Exceptions
- Files
- Help
- Library Versions
- Memory Management
- Message Map
- Multithreading
- OLE Overview
- Printing
- Property Sheets
- Serialization (Object Persistence)

- Strings
- Toolbars
- Tools for MFC Programming

If MFC is new to you, begin with the overview in Part 1. If you need information in a specific area, try Part 2. You can also access specific topics in either part easily using the search capabilities in Books Online.

Differences from Other Versions of MFC

For details about how this version of MFC has changed from previous versions, and for information about porting your applications from previous versions of MFC to this version, see the following articles:

- MFC: Changes from MFC Versions 2.0 and 2.5
- MFC: Changes from MFC Version 2.0 32-Bit Edition
- MFC: Features No Longer Available
- MFC: 32-Bit Programming Issues
- MFC: Porting MFC Applications to 32 Bit
- MFC: MFC Porting Tips
- MFC: Using the MFC Source Files

MFC: Changes from MFC Versions 2.0 and 2.5

You may be upgrading to version 3.0 of the Microsoft Foundation Class Library from one of the previous 16-bit versions: either MFC version 2.0 or 2.5, which are part of Visual C++ versions 1.0 and 1.5, respectively.

This article covers the following topics:

- Upgrading from MFC Version 2.5
- Upgrading from MFC Version 2.0

Upgrading from MFC Version 2.5

- Support for 32-bit programming.

  MFC version 3.0 targets Win32 platforms, including Intel Win32s™, Windows NT, and "Chicago," as well as MIPS® Windows NT and the Macintosh®. The same MFC code works for all of the different targets.

- Extended Win32 API coverage.

  The coverage includes new GDI functionality such as Beziers and Paths and a number of other Win32 "USER" APIs.

- Support for C++ exceptions.

MFC uses C++ exceptions. The MFC exception handling macros are also provided for backward compatibility and compiler portability.

- Collection classes based on C++ templates.

   These classes make it easier to derive your own type-safe collection classes.

- Support for creating property sheets, also referred to as "tab dialog boxes," in your programs.

   You can create property sheets containing tabs like those found in Microsoft Word for Windows version 6.0 and Visual C++. This support is in classes **CPropertyPage** and **CPropertySheet**.

- Support for creating "dockable" tool bars in your programs.

   You can create toolbars that the user can drag to various parts of the main frame window. API member functions for dockable toolbars are in classes **CToolBar** and **CFrameWnd**.

- Support for "tool tips" like those in Microsoft Excel.

   When the user moves the mouse over a toolbar button in your application, a small box is shown on top of the button to describe the action that would be performed.

- Support for Unicode and Double-Byte Character Sets (DBCS).

   Your applications can be more easily internationalized using Unicode or DBCS strings.

- Support for 3D controls.

   Simply call **CWinApp::Enable3dControls** from your `InitInstance` function to get a three-dimensional appearance in your dialog boxes.

- Support for frame windows with thin caption bars, such as those used for Visual C++ property windows.

   See class **CMiniFrameWnd** in the *Class Library Reference*.

- Message-map support for ranges of command IDs and control IDs.

   For example, you can map a range of command IDs to a single message handler.

- New **CString** member functions, such as **Format**, which resembles the **sprintf** run-time function.

- Automatic linking of the correct version of the MFC library and any other required libraries, such as the Win32 libraries, OLE libraries, or ODBC libraries.

Upgrading from MFC Version 2.0

If you're upgrading from version 2.0, you get the following support in addition to the features listed under "Upgrading from MFC Version 2.5" above:

- Support for Object Linking and Embedding (OLE) version 2.0.

MFC OLE classes make it easier to write OLE Visual Editing servers and containers and to implement OLE Automation in your applications. See Chapter 5, "Working with Object Linking and Embedding," and the article "OLE Overview."

- Support for data access with Open Database Connectivity (ODBC).

  MFC database classes help you manipulate data in databases for which you have the appropriate 32-bit ODBC driver. See Chapter 6, "Working with Databases," and the article "Database Overview."

To complete your picture of what's new in this version, also see the article "MFC: Changes from MFC Version 2.0 32-Bit Edition."

See Also   Articles: "Dynamic-Link Libraries (DLLs)," "MFC: 32-Bit Programming Issues," "Toolbars: Docking and Floating," "Toolbars: Tool Tips," "Strings: Unicode and Multibyte Character Set (MBCS) Support," "Property Sheets," "Collections," "Exceptions," "Message Map: Ranges of Messages"

In *Programming Techniques*: Chapter 12, "Developing for International Markets"

MFC: Changes from MFC Version 2.0 32-Bit Edition

This article discusses changes in version 3.0 of the Microsoft Foundation Class Library for users of the 32-bit version of MFC version 2.0 (sometimes called MFC version 2.1), which is part of Visual C++ 1.0 32-Bit Edition. Changes include:

- Full support for writing multithreaded applications.

  You can use MFC functionality in both the primary thread of execution and in secondary threads.

- Support for Object Linking and Embedding (OLE) version 2.0.

  MFC OLE classes make it easier to write OLE servers and containers and to implement OLE Automation in your applications. See Chapter 5, "Working with Object Linking and Embedding," and the article "OLE Overview."

- Support for data access with Open Database Connectivity (ODBC).

  MFC database classes help you manipulate data in databases for which you have the appropriate 32-bit ODBC driver. See Chapter 6, "Working with Databases," and the article "Database Overview."

- Support for MFC packaged in a shared DLL, called AFXDLL.

  To use AFXDLL, a set of DLLs that contains the entire 32-bit Microsoft Foundation Class Library, use "/D_AFXDLL" in your compiler options and one of the "MFC30" DLLs in your linker options.

  Using AFXDLL results in smaller executable files than statically linking the class library with your application. This is particularly useful if you have several applications that run at the same time; they can share the DLL.

- **WIN32_LEAN_AND_MEAN**.

  To improve build times and reduce the size of your application's precompiled header, MFC defines the symbol **WIN32_LEAN_AND_MEAN**. This definition lists a group of less commonly used header files that MFC does not automatically include through including AFXWIN.H.

  To see the list of header files specifically excluded from MFC builds, look at the definition of **WIN32_LEAN_AND_MEAN** in WINDOWS.H. If you need the definitions provided by any of those files, you must explicitly include the appropriate file yourself.

  WIN32_LEAN_AND_MEAN was not defined in MFC version 2.1, and all of the extra headers were included.

For a more detailed accounting of these differences, see the article "MFC: 32-Bit Programming Issues." To complete your picture of what's new in this version, see the article "MFC: Changes from MFC Versions 2.0 and 2.5."

See Also   Articles: "MFC: Changes from MFC Versions 2.0 and 2.5," "Multithreading," "Dynamic-Link Libraries (DLLs)," "Library Versions," "MFC: 32-Bit Programming Issues," "OLE Overview," "Database Overview"

MFC: Features No Longer Available

This article describes features of MFC that are not available in this Win32 version. These include:

- VBX controls (not supported on 32-bit platforms).
- Microsoft Windows for Pen Computing classes (not supported under Windows NT).
- The **UnrealizeObject** function has been deleted in Win32.

  Since calls to **CGdiObject::UnrealizeObject** are common in programs written for Windows version 3.*x*, yet are now unnecessary, this member function is retained for backward compatibility. It now always returns a nonzero value, without making an underlying Win32 function call. Calls to **CGdiObject::UnrealizeObject** should not be made in new Win32 programs and should be removed from existing programs eventually.

- The **QueryAbort** function has been deleted in Win32; the **CDC::QueryAbort** member function has also been deleted.

  If your program needs this functionality, you should create a member function that calls your AbortProc callback function directly.

- The console library variants, NAFXCR.LIB and NAFXCRD.LIB, are no longer available.

You should now link with NAFXCW.LIB or NAFXCWD.LIB with no loss in capability or content from projects that previously used NAFXCR.LIB or NAFXCRD.LIB.

See Also   Articles: "MFC: Changes from MFC Version 2.0 32-Bit Edition," "MFC: Changes from MFC Versions 2.0 and 2.5"

MFC: 32-Bit Programming Issues

This article summarizes issues that arise when programming in the 32-bit environment.

Version 3.0 of the Microsoft Foundation Class Library (MFC) uses the Win32 application programming interface (API). Many of the Win32 API functions are encapsulated in MFC class member functions. However, one of the fundamental tenets of programming with MFC is that you can always make direct calls to the Windows API.

Issues include:

- Applications created with the 32-bit version of MFC version 3.0 can run on Windows NT, Windows version 3.1 (using Win32s), and other Win32 platforms. To write portable applications, you must avoid using Win32 API functions that are not supported on all of your target platforms.

  (OLE applications on Windows NT require Windows NT version 3.5 or later.)

- Visual C++ version 2.0 cannot load and save executable (.EXE) files, compiled resource script (.RES) files, or dynamic-link libraries, and it does not directly support new Win32 resource types (the message table resource type or Unicode strings in resources).

- Differences between the 16-bit versions of MFC and version 3.0 (32-bit) are:

  - The packing of *lParam* and *wParam* in the **CWnd** members **OnCommand** and **OnParentNotify** has changed from 16-bit MFC. For more information, see "Changing Message Handlers" in the article "MFC: Porting Tips."

  - The **CTime** class has constructors that accept system and file times from Win32. For more information, see the article "Date and Time: SYSTEMTIME Support."

  - The class library provides new member functions that wrap many Win32 API functions, including many Win32 GDI functions.

  - Class **CWinThread** supports multithreaded programming. For more information, see the article "Multithreading."

  - Most of the class library is enabled for Unicode and for Double-Byte Character Set (DBCS) programming. The database classes are the exception. This enabling means that many class member functions now take character and string parameters of types based on type **TCHAR**. For more information, see Chapter 12 in *Programming Techniques*.

- The 32-bit MFC static link and dynamic-link libraries are named differently from the 16-bit libraries. See the article "Library Versions."

Some features of the class library are no longer available in the 32-bit environment. See the article "MFC: Features No Longer Available."

See Also   Articles: "MFC: Porting MFC Applications to 32-Bit," "MFC: Porting Tips"

MFC: Porting MFC Applications to 32-Bit

This article describes how to port a 16-bit Microsoft Foundation Class Library application to 32-bit. For more general information on writing 32-bit applications, see the article "MFC: 32-Bit Programming Issues."

Well-written MFC 2.0 and 2.5 applications that don't use 16-bit features (such as VBX controls, inline assembler, 16-bit ints, or Win32 API functions) can usually be migrated to Win32 with no changes.

This article describes:

- A porting procedure.
- General tips for porting to Win32.

Porting Procedure

The following procedure uses the same top-down approach advocated in Chapter 1 of *Programming Techniques*.

▶ **To port a 16-bit framework application to 32 bits**

1. Import your application files into a new Visual C++ project.

    Simply open your old project. Projects created with Visual C++ versions 1.0 and 1.5 are converted automatically to version 2.0 format.

2. Remove VBX controls.

    VBX controls are not supported in a 32-bit application. Thus, the **CVBControl** class, the **AfxRegisterVBEvent**, **AfxGetPict**, **AfxSetPict**, and **AfxReferencePict** global functions, and the **ON_VBXEVENT** macro are unavailable with Win32. If you use VBX controls in your application, you must replace them with standard Windows controls, redesigning your application as necessary.

3. Remove Windows for Pens extensions.

    The 32-bit version of MFC does not currently include the **CHEdit** and **CBEdit** classes, which implement 16-bit extensions for Windows for Pens. Thus, if your existing application supports pen extensions, it will not compile as a 32-bit application. If you want to run with Win32, you will need to substitute another form of user input, most likely keyboard input, for the pen class input.

4. Replace difficult-to-port code, such as assembly-language functions and MS-DOS calls, with stubs.

   Win32 is designed to be portable, and your applications should follow suit. If your 16-bit application makes calls to an assembly-language module, you should rewrite it in C or C++ if possible. Otherwise, you will be faced with rewriting the assembly-language portion for each hardware platform that can run Win32.

   If you've used any MS-DOS services for file I/O, including those used by Windows version 3.x, you will have to rewrite the code using the new Win32 file I/O set that replaces these services. If you've used the **CFile** class for file I/O, you are shielded from this change because **CFile** uses the new function calls even though its member function interface remains unchanged.

   If you need to write custom file I/O functions, see the Win32 Software Development Kit documentation for more information.

5. Build your application with Visual C++ version 2.0 and note any 32-bit related problems.

6. Use the information in "General Tips for Porting to Win32" below to fix any problems. Rebuild until the main body of your program is running correctly.

7. Implement each function you stubbed in step 4 with portable code until the entire application runs correctly.

8. Remove MFC libraries from the link input list.

   Let the MFC header files automatically link in the correct version of MFC, as described in the article "Library Versions."

Note If you want your application to support Unicode, follow the guidelines in Chapter 12 of *Programming Techniques*.

General Tips for Porting to Win32

Moving to 32 bits means changing from a 16-bit segmented architecture to a 32-bit flat address space. What will this change in architecture mean when you port your existing 16-bit application? Different memory models, near and far pointers, and the limitations of 64K segments do not exist under Win32.

Certain fundamental Windows parameters also change in Win32:

- Handles to windows and to GDI objects such as pens, brushes, and menus are now 32 bits wide.

- System metrics have changed (screen dimensions and colors are now 32-bit values), and thus many graphics and other functions have changed.

- A **WPARAM** is now 32 bits wide, which means that message packing and window procedures change.

- The **WinMain** function parameters have changed (this is handled for you in the **CWinApp** class).

For more general information about porting to Win32, see Chapter 1 of *Programming Techniques*.

See Also   Articles: "MFC: 32-Bit Programming Issues," "MFC: Porting Tips"

MFC: Porting Tips

This article gives tips for porting your application from 16-bit to 32-bit.

Although most of the changes in Windows parameters are handled for you within the framework, there are some changes you will have to make manually. They are described in this article, which covers:

- Changing message handlers
- Using the collection classes

The **CTime** class has also changed. See the article "Date and Time: SYSTEMTIME Support."

Changing Message Handlers

Window handles in the Win32 API are now 32-bit values; consequently, the **WPARAM** type has been widened from 16 to 32 bits to accommodate this change. This widening often necessitates repacking the values carried by the *wParam* and *lParam* parameters.

A 16-bit application, written for Windows without using the framework, requires a considerable amount of code rewriting to port successfully to 32-bit. Each window procedure declaration must be modified, as well as the message-handling code within the procedure.

The class library accommodates most of these changes internally. The framework hides the window procedure from you, unpacks *wParam* and *lParam*, and passes the properly unpacked values to you in message handlers. The only two instances that require your attention are functions that override the **CWnd::OnCommand** and **CWnd::OnParentNotify** message handlers, where the framework passes *wParam* or *lParam* directly from Windows to you.

The framework also unpacks the *wParam* and *lParam* values associated with a **WM_COMMAND** message to implement message-map entries. The framework properly unpacks the values as appropriate for Windows version 3.*x* or Win32 with no attention from you.

CWnd::OnCommand

If your application overrides **OnCommand**, check the code carefully and modify it so that it unpacks *wParam* and *lParam* correctly. Your 16-bit override of **OnCommand** may compile successfully, but will not execute correctly.

When the framework receives a **WM_COMMAND** message, it calls the **CWnd::OnCommand** member function with the following arguments:

virtual BOOL OnCommand(WPARAM *wParam*, **LPARAM** *lParam* **);**

A command ID, a control handle, and a notification message can be packed in *wParam* and *lParam*, depending on the circumstances of the call.

You don't need to change the way you extract the command ID; it is packed the same way in both environments. You can extract it this way:

```
UINT nID = LOWORD(wParam);
```

You extract the remaining two values in this way in the 16-bit framework:

```
HWND hWndCtrl = (HWND)LOWORD(lParam);      //Control handle
int nCode = HIWORD(lParam);                //Notification code
```

You extract them this way in the 32-bit framework:

```
HWND hWndCtrl = (HWND)lParam;              //Control handle
int nCode = HIWORD(wParam);                //Notification code
```

In both the 16-bit and 32-bit versions, if the **OnCommand** message is from an accelerator, the value retrieved in nCode is 1. If the message is from a menu, the value in nCode is 0.

CWnd::OnParentNotify

As with **OnCommand**, carefully check any code in your application that overrides **OnParentNotify** and modify it so that it unpacks values from *lParam* correctly. Your 16-bit override of **OnParentNotify** will compile successfully, but will not execute correctly.

The framework calls the **CWnd::OnParentNotify** member function with the following arguments:

afx_msg void OnParentNotify(UINT *message*, **LPARAM** *lParam* **);**

The **OnParentNotify** member function is called for the parent of a child window in two cases: when the mouse is clicked over a child window, and when a child window is created or destroyed.

When the *message* parameter is equal to **WM_CREATE** or **WM_DESTROY**, the framework's 16-bit packing of *lParam* puts the child window handle in the low-order word and the identifier of the child window in the high-order word. For the

32-bit framework, the child window handle has been widened and now takes up all of *lParam*; the child window identifier is unavailable.

If your Win32 code in **OnParentNotify** requires the child ID, retrieve it like this:

```
CWnd* pChild = FromHandle( (HWND)lParam );
int nID = pChild->GetDlgCtrlID();
```

In this example, **FromHandle** returns the **CWnd** object attached to the child window handle. The **GetDlgCtrlID** member function returns the child window ID. You could also retrieve the child ID by passing the child handle directly to the Windows **GetDlgCtrlID** function, but the code above also retrieves a pointer to the child **CWnd** object.

The pointer returned in pChild is temporary and should not be stored for use beyond the scope of **OnParentNotify**.

Using the Collection Classes

With Windows version 3.*x*, the **CObArray** class and all related array collection classes are constrained by 16-bit memory models and must fit within a single 64K segment.

With Win32, the number of elements that can fit within a framework array collection is limited only by the amount of available memory. The maximum number of collection elements is the largest possible value of a **UINT**, which is much larger than a typical computer's memory. The increase in maximum collection size should have little effect upon your code because a framework collection simply throws a **CMemoryException** when it reaches its memory limit in both the 16-bit version and the 32-bit version of the framework.

See Also   Articles: "MFC: 32-Bit Programming Issues," "MFC: Porting MFC Applications to 32-Bit," "Date and Time: SYSTEMTIME Support"

MFC: Using Database Classes with Documents and Views

You can use the MFC database classes with or without the document/view architecture. This article emphasizes working with documents and views. It explains:

- How to write a form-based application using a **CRecordView** object as the main view on your document.
- How to use **CRecordset** objects in your documents and views.
- Other considerations.

For alternatives, see the article "MFC: Using Database Classes Without Documents and Views."

Writing a Form-Based Application

Many data-access applications are based on forms. The user interface is a form containing controls in which the user examines, enters, or edits data. To make your application form-based, use class **CRecordView**. You can specify **CRecordView** for your view class when you run AppWizard, or you can use ClassWizard later to create a **CRecordView**-derived class.

In a form-based application, each record view object stores a pointer to a **CRecordset** object. The framework's record field exchange (RFX) mechanism exchanges data between the recordset and the data source. The dialog data exchange (DDX) mechanism exchanges data between the field data members of the recordset object and the controls on the form. **CRecordView** also provides default command handler functions for navigating from record to record on the form.

▶ **To create a form-based application with AppWizard**

- See the article "AppWizard: Database Support."

▶ **To add a database form to your application with ClassWizard**

- See the article "ClassWizard: Creating a Database Form."

For a full discussion of forms, see the article "Record Views." For an example of an application with multiple record views on a database, see the Enroll tutorial application, Step 4, in \MSVC20\SAMPLES\MFC\ENROLL\STEP4. The step is not covered in the tutorial, but you can examine the code.

Using Recordsets in Documents and Views

Many simple form-based applications don't need "documents." If your application is more complex, you'll probably want to use a document as a proxy for the database, storing a **CDatabase** object that connects to the data source. Form-based applications usually store a pointer to a recordset object in the view. Other kinds of database applications store recordsets and **CDatabase** objects in the document. Here are some possibilities for using documents in database applications:

- If you're accessing a recordset in a local context, create **CRecordset** objects locally in member functions of the document or the view, as needed.

  Declare a recordset object as a local variable in a function. Pass **NULL** to the constructor, which causes the framework to create and open a temporary **CDatabase** object for you. As an alternative, pass a pointer to a **CDatabase** object. Use the recordset within the function and let it be destroyed automatically when the function exits.

  When you pass **NULL** to a recordset constructor, the framework uses information returned by the recordset's **GetDefaultConnect** member function to create a **CDatabase** object and open it. The wizards implement **GetDefaultConnect** for you.

- If you're accessing a recordset during the lifetime of your document, embed one or more **CRecordset** objects in your document.

  Construct the recordset objects either when you initialize the document or as needed. You might write a function that returns a pointer to the recordset if it already exists, or constructs and opens the recordset if it doesn't exist yet. Close, delete, and re-create the recordset as needed, or call its **Requery** member function to refresh the records.

- If you're accessing a data source during the lifetime of your document, embed a **CDatabase** object or store a pointer to a **CDatabase** object in it.

  The **CDatabase** object manages a connection to your data source. The object is constructed automatically during document construction, and you call its **Open** member function when you initialize the document. When you construct recordset objects in document member functions, you pass a pointer to the document's **CDatabase** object. This associates each recordset with its data source. The **CDatabase** object is usually destroyed when the document closes. The recordset objects are typically destroyed when they exit the scope of a function.

Other Considerations

Form-based applications often do not have any use for the framework's document serialization mechanism, so you might want to remove, disable, or replace the New and Open commands on the File menu. See the article "Serialization: Serialization vs. Database Input/Output."

You might also want to make use of the many user-interface possibilities that the framework can support. For example, you could use multiple **CRecordView** objects in a splitter window, open multiple recordsets in different multiple document interface (MDI) child windows, and so on.

You might want to implement printing of whatever is in your view—whether it's a form implemented with **CRecordView** or something else. As a class derived from **CFormView**, **CRecordView** doesn't support printing, but you can override the **OnPrint** member function. For more information, see class **CFormView**, and see the VIEWEX sample application.

You might not want to use documents and views at all. In that case, see the article "MFC: Using Database Classes Without Documents and Views."

See Also   Article: "Serialization: Serialization vs. Database Input/Output"

MFC: Using Database Classes Without Documents and Views

Although in many cases you will want to use the framework's document/view architecture in your database applications, sometimes you might not want to use them. This article explains:

- When you don't need to use document/view functionality such as document serialization.
- AppWizard support for applications without serialization and without document-related File menu commands such as New, Open, Save, and Save As.
- How to work with an application that uses a minimal document.
- How to structure an application with no document or view.

When You Don't Need Documents

For some applications, there is a distinct concept of a "document." These applications typically load all or most of a file from storage into memory with a File Open command. They write the updated file back to storage all at once with a File Save or Save As command. What the user sees is a data file.

Some categories of applications, however, don't require a document. Database applications operate in terms of "transactions." The application selects records from a database and presents them to the user, often one at a time. What the user sees is usually a single current record, which may be the only one in memory.

If your application doesn't require a document for storing data, you can dispense with some or all of the framework's document/view architecture. How much you dispense with depends on the approach you prefer. You might:

- Use a minimal document as a place to store a connection to your data source but dispense with normal document features such as serialization. This is advantageous especially when you want several views of the data and would like to synchronize all of the views, updating them all at once and so on.
- Use a frame window, into which you draw directly rather than using a view. Omit the document. Store any data or data connections in the frame-window object.

AppWizard Options for Documents and Views

If you use AppWizard to create your application, all of the database options produce applications with documents and views. Some of the options provide documents and views without document functionality you won't need for your database application. Table 1 shows the kinds of document/view support for each option.

Table 1   AppWizard Options for Documents and Views

Option	View	Document
None (no database support).	Derived from **CView**.	Full document support including serialization and New, Open, Save, and Save As commands on the File menu.
Only include header files.	Derived from **CView**.	Same. You can store **CDatabase** and/or **CRecordset** objects in your document or your view.
A database view, without file support.	Derived from **CRecordView**.	Document does not support serialization or the New, Open, Save, and Save As commands. You can use it to store your **CRecordset** and to coordinate multiple views.
Both a database view and file support.	Derived from **CRecordView**.	Full document support, including serialization and document-related File menu commands. Use serialization for special purposes, such as storing user profile information.

For a discussion of using the AppWizard options "A database view, without file support" and "Both a database view and file support," see "Applications with Minimal Documents" below.

For a discussion of writing applications with no document, see "Applications with No Document" later in this article.

For a discussion of alternatives to serialization, and alternative uses for serialization, see the article "Serialization: Serialization vs. Database Input/Output."

Applications with Minimal Documents

AppWizard has two options that support form-based data-access applications. Each option creates a **CRecordView**-derived view class and a document. They differ in what they leave out of the document.

A Document Without File Support

Select the AppWizard database option "A database view, without file support" if you don't need document serialization. The document still serves the following useful purposes:

- It's a convenient place to store a **CRecordset**.

This usage parallels ordinary document concepts: the document "stores" the data —or, in this case, a set of records—and the view is a view of the document.

- If your application presents multiple views (such as multiple record views), a document supports coordinating the views.

  If multiple views show the same data, you can use the **CDocument::UpdateAllViews** member function to coordinate updates to all views when any view changes the data.

You'll usually use this option for simple form-based applications such as the Enroll tutorial application. AppWizard supports a convenient structure for such applications automatically.

A Document with File Support

Select the AppWizard database option "Both a database view and file support" when you have an alternative use for the document-related File menu commands and document serialization. For the data-access portion of your program, you can use the document in the same way as described in "A Document Without File Support" above. You can use the document's serialization capability, for example, to read and write a serialized user profile document that stores the user's preferences or other useful information. For more ideas, see the article "Serialization: Serialization vs. Database Input/Output."

AppWizard supports this option, but you must write the code that serializes the document. Store the serialized information in document data members.

Applications With No Document

You might sometimes want to write an application that uses neither documents nor views. Without documents, you store your data (such as a **CRecordset** object) in your frame-window class or your application class. Any additional requirements depend on whether the application presents a user interface.

Database Support with a User Interface

If you have a user interface (other than, say, a console command-line interface), your application draws directly into the frame window's client area rather than into a view. Such an application doesn't use **CRecordView**, **CFormView**, or **CDialog** for its main user interface (but it will normally use **CDialog** for ordinary dialogs).

Writing Applications Without Documents

Applications without documents resemble applications written with the Microsoft Foundation Class Library version 1.0. AppWizard doesn't support creating this kind of application, so you must write your own **CWinApp**-derived class and, if needed, also create a **CFrameWnd** or **CMDIFrameWnd** class. Override **CWinApp::InitInstance** and declare an application object as

```
CYourNameApp NEAR theApp;
```

The framework still supplies the message-map mechanism and many other features.

Database Support Separate from the User Interface

Some applications need either no user interface or only a minimal one. For example, suppose you're writing:

- An intermediate data-access object that other applications (clients) call for special processing of data between the application and the data source.

- An application that processes data without user intervention, such as an application that moves data from one database format to another, or one that does calculations and performs batch updates.

Because there is no document that owns the **CRecordset** object, you'll probably want to store it as an embedded data member in your **CWinApp**-derived application class. Alternatives include:

- Not keeping a permanent **CRecordset** object at all. You can pass **NULL** to your **CRecordset** class constructors. In that case, the framework creates a temporary **CDatabase** object using the information in the recordset's **GetDefaultConnect** member function. This is the most likely alternative approach.

- Making the **CRecordset** object a global variable. This variable should be a pointer to a **CRecordset** object that you create dynamically in your **CWinApp::InitInstance** override. (This avoids attempting to construct the object before the framework is initialized.)

- Using recordset objects as you would within the context of a document or a view. Create recordsets in the member functions of your application or frame-window objects.

See Also   Article: "Serialization: Serialization vs. Database Input/Output"

MFC: Using the MFC Source Files

Full source code is supplied with the Microsoft Foundation Class Library (MFC). Header files (.H) are in the \MSVC20\MFC\INCLUDE directory; implementation files (.CPP) are in the \MSVC20\MFC\SRC directory.

Note The \MSVC20\MFC\SRC directory contains a makefile you can use with NMAKE to build MFC library versions, including a browse version. A browse version of MFC is useful for tracing through the calling structure of MFC itself. The file README.TXT in that directory explains how to use this makefile.

This article explains the convention that MFC uses to comment the various parts of each class, what these comments mean, and what you should expect to find in each section. ClassWizard and AppWizard use a similar convention for the classes they create for you, and you will probably find these conventions useful for your own code.

You might be familiar with the **public**, **protected**, and **private** C++ keywords. When looking at the MFC header files, you'll find that each class may have several of each of these. For example, public member variables and functions might be under more than one **public** keyword. This is because MFC separates member variables and functions based on their use, not by the type of access allowed. MFC uses **private** sparingly—even items considered implementation details are generally protected and many times are public. Even though access to the implementation details is discouraged, MFC leaves the decision to you.

In both the MFC source files and the files that AppWizard creates, you will find comments like these within class declarations (usually in this order):

```
// Constructors
// Attributes
// Operations
// Overridables
// Implementation
```

Topics covered in this article include:

- An example of the comments
- The // Implementation comment
- The // Constructors comment
- The // Attributes comment
- The // Operations comment
- The // Overridables comment

An Example of the Comments

The following partial listing of class **CStdioFile** uses most of the comments:

```
class CStdioFile : public CFile
{
    DECLARE_DYNAMIC(CStdioFile)

public:
// Constructors
    CStdioFile();
...

// Attributes
    FILE* m_pStream;      // stdio FILE
...

// Operations
    virtual void WriteString(LPCTSTR lpsz);
...
    virtual LPTSTR ReadString(LPTSTR lpsz, UINT nMax);
...

// Implementation
public:
...
};
```

These comments consistently mark sections of the class declaration that contain similar kinds of class members. Keep in mind that these are MFC conventions, not hard and fast rules.

The // Implementation Comment

The most important section is the // Implementation section.

This section houses all implementation details. Both member variables and member functions can appear in this section. Everything below this line could change in a future release of MFC. Unless you can't avoid it, you should not rely on details below the // Implementation line. In addition, members declared below the implementation line are not documented, although some implementation is discussed in technical notes. Overrides of virtual functions in the base class reside in this section, regardless of which section the base class function is defined in, since the fact that a function overrides the base class implementation is considered an implementation detail. Typically these members are protected, but not always.

Notice from the **CStdioFile** listing under "An Example of the Comments" earlier in this article that members declared below the // Implementation comment may be declared as **public**, **protected**, or **private**. The point is that you should only use these members with caution, because they might change in the future. Declaring a group of members as **public** may be necessary for the class library implementation to work correctly. However, this does not imply that you may safely use the members so declared.

Note You may find comments of the remaining types either above or below the //
Implementation comment. In either case, they describe the kinds of members
declared below them. If they occur below the // Implementation comment, you
should assume that the members might change in future versions of MFC.

The // Constructors Comment

This section declares constructors (in the C++ sense) as well as any initialization
functions required to really use the object. For example, **CWnd::Create** is in the
constructors section because before you use the **CWnd** object it must be "fully
constructed" by first calling the C++ constructor and then calling the **Create**
function. Typically these members are public.

CStdioFile has three constructors, one of which is shown in the listing under "An
Example of the Comments" earlier in this article.

The // Attributes Comment

This section contains the public attributes (or properties) of the object. Usually
these are member variables, or Get/Set functions. The "Get" and "Set" functions
may or may not be virtual. The "Get" functions are usually **const**, since they don't
usually have side effects. These members are usually public; protected and private
attributes are typically found in the implementation section.

In the sample listing from class **CStdioFile**, under "An Example of the Comments"
earlier in this article, the list includes one member variable, **m_pStream**. Class
CDC lists nearly 20 members under this comment.

Note Large classes, such as **CDC** and **CWnd**, may have so many members that
simply listing all of the attributes in one group would not add much to clarity. In
such cases, the class library uses other comments as headings to further delineate
the members. For example, **CDC** uses // Device-Context Functions, //
Drawing Tool Functions, // Drawing Attribute Functions, and
more. Groups that represent attributes will follow the usual syntax described above.
Many of the OLE classes have an implementation section called // Interface
Maps.

The // Operations Comment

This section contains member functions that you can call on the object to make it do
things or perform actions (perform operations). These functions are typically non-
const since they usually have side effects. They may be virtual or nonvirtual
depending on the needs of the class. Typically these members are public.

In the sample listing from class **CStdioFile**, under "An Example of the Comments"
earlier in this article, the list includes two member functions under this comment:
ReadString and **WriteString**.

As with attributes, operations may be further subdivided.

The // Overridables Comment

This section contains virtual functions that you can override in a derived class when you need to modify the base class behavior. They are usually named starting with "On", although it is not strictly necessary. Functions here are designed to be overridden, and often implement or provide some sort of "callback" or "hook." Typically these members are protected.

In MFC itself, pure virtual functions are always placed in this section. A pure virtual function in C++ is one of the form:

```
virtual void OnDraw( ) = 0;
```

In the sample listing from class **CStdioFile**, under "An Example of the Comments" earlier in this article, the list includes no overridables section. Class **CDocument**, on the other hand, lists approximately 10 overridable member functions.

In some classes, you may also see the comment `// Advanced Overridables`. These are functions that only advanced programmers should attempt to override. You will probably never need to override them.

Note The conventions described in this article also work well, in general, for OLE Automation methods and properties. Automation methods are similar to MFC operations. Automation properties are similar to MFC attributes. Automation events (supported for OLE Controls) are similar to MFC overridable member functions.

Multithreading

The Microsoft Foundation Class Library (MFC) provides support for multithreaded applications. This article describes what processes and threads are, and MFC's approach to multithreading.

A "process" is an executing instance of an application. For example, when you double-click the Notepad icon in Program Manager, you start a process that runs Notepad.

A "thread" is a path of execution within a process. When you start Notepad, the operating system creates a process and begins executing the primary thread of that process. When this thread terminates, so does the process. This primary thread is supplied to the operating system by the startup code in the form of a function address. Usually, it is the address of the **main** or **WinMain** function that is supplied.

You can create additional threads in your application if you wish. You may want to do this to handle background or maintenance tasks when you don't want the user to wait for them to complete. All threads in MFC applications are represented by **CWinThread** objects. In most situations, you don't even have to explicitly create these objects; instead call the framework helper function **AfxBeginThread**, which creates the **CWinThread** object for you.

MFC distinguishes two types of threads: user-interface threads and worker threads. User-interface threads are commonly used to handle user input and respond to events and messages generated by the user. Worker threads are commonly used to complete tasks, such as recalculation, that do not require user input. The Win32 API does not distinguish between types of threads; it just needs to know the thread's starting address so it can begin to execute the thread. MFC handles user-interface threads specially by supplying a message pump for events in the user interface. **CWinApp** is an example of a user-interface thread object, as it derives from **CWinThread** and handles events and messages generated by the user.

Special attention should be given to situations where more than one thread may require access to the same object. The article "Multithreading: Programming Tips" describes techniques you can use to get around problems that may arise in these situations.

MFC encompasses only a small portion of the available Win32 multithreading functions. Win32 APIs such as critical sections, mutexes, semaphores, and events are not covered by MFC. You need to refer to and use the Win32 API directly for these objects.

Writing and debugging multithreaded programming is inherently a complicated and tricky undertaking, as you must ensure that objects are not accessed by more than one thread at a time. The articles in the Multithreading group do not teach the basics of multithreaded programming, only how to use MFC in your multithreaded program. The multithreaded MFC samples included in Visual C++ illustrate a few multithreaded programming techniques and Win32 APIs not encompassed by MFC, but are only intended to be a starting point.

For more information on how the operating system handles processes and threads, see Chapter 43, "Processes and Threads," in the *Win32 Programmer's Reference, Volume 2*.

To gain an understanding of how to write a multithreaded program, you should refer to a book such as Jeffrey Richter's *Advanced Windows NT* (Microsoft Press, 1994).

For more details on MFC multithreading support, see the following articles:

- Multithreading: Creating User-Interface Threads
- Multithreading: Creating Worker Threads
- Multithreading: Terminating Threads
- Multithreading: Programming Tips

Multithreading: Creating User-Interface Threads

A user-interface thread is commonly used to handle user input and respond to user events independently of threads executing other portions of the application. The main application thread (provided in your **CWinApp**-derived class) is already created and started for you. This article describes the steps necessary to create additional user-interface threads.

The first thing you must do when creating a user-interface thread is derive a class from **CWinThread**. You must declare and implement this class using the **DECLARE_DYNCREATE** and **IMPLEMENT_DYNCREATE** macros. This class must override some functions, and can override others. These functions and what they should do are presented in Table 1.

Table 1   Functions to Override When Creating a User-Interface Thread

Function name	Purpose
ExitInstance	Perform cleanup when thread terminates. Usually overridden.
InitInstance	Perform thread instance initialization. Must be overridden.
OnIdle	Perform thread-specific idle-time processing. Not usually overridden.
PreTranslateMessage	Filter messages before they are dispatched to **TranslateMessage** and **DispatchMessage**. Not usually overridden.

Table 1 Functions to Override When Creating a User-Interface Thread (*continued*)

Function name	Purpose
ProcessWndProcException	Intercept unhandled exceptions thrown by the thread's message and command handlers. Not usually overridden.
Run	Controlling function for the thread. Contains the message pump. Rarely overridden.

MFC provides two versions of **AfxBeginThread** through parameter overloading: one for user-interface threads and the other for worker threads. To start your user-interface thread, call **AfxBeginThread** providing the following information:

- The **RUNTIME_CLASS** of the class you derived from **CWinThread**.
- (Optionally) The desired priority level. The default is normal priority. For more information on the available priority levels, see **::SetThreadPriority** in the *Win32 Programmer's Reference, Volume 4*.
- (Optionally) The desired stack size for the thread. The default is the same size stack as the creating thread.
- (Optionally) **CREATE_SUSPENDED** if you want the thread to be created in a suspended state. The default is 0, or start the thread normally.
- (Optionally) The desired security attributes. The default is the same access as the parent thread. For more information on the format of this security information, see **SECURITY_ATTRIBUTES** in the *Win32 Programmer's Reference, Volume 5*.

AfxBeginThread does most of the work for you. It creates a new object of your class, initializes it with the information you supply, and calls **CWinThread::CreateThread** to start executing the thread. Checks are made throughout the procedure to make sure all objects are deallocated properly should any part of the creation fail.

See Also Articles: "Multithreading: Terminating Threads," "Multithreading: Creating Worker Threads"

In the *Class Library Reference*: **CWinThread**

In the *Win32 Programmer's Reference, Volume 2*: Chapter 43, "Processes and Threads"

Multithreading: Creating Worker Threads

A worker thread is commonly used to handle background tasks that the user shouldn't have to wait for to continue using your application. Tasks such as recalculation and background printing are good examples of worker threads. This article details the steps necessary to create a worker thread. Topics include:

- Starting the thread
- Implementing the controlling function
- Example

Creating a worker thread is a relatively simple task. Only two steps are required to get your thread running: implementing the controlling function and starting the thread. It is not necessary to derive a class from **CWinThread**. You can if you need a special version of **CWinThread**, but it is not required for most simple worker threads. You can use **CWinThread** without modification.

Starting the Thread

There are two overloaded versions of **AfxBeginThread**: one for user-interface threads and one for worker threads. To begin execution of your worker thread, call **AfxBeginThread** providing the following information:

- The address of the controlling function.
- The parameter to be passed to the controlling function.
- (Optionally) The desired priority of the thread. The default is normal priority. For more information on the available priority levels, see **::SetThreadPriority** in the *Win32 Programmer's Reference, Volume 4.*
- (Optionally) The desired stack size for the thread. Default is the same size stack as the creating thread.
- (Optionally) **CREATE_SUSPENDED** if you want the thread to be created in a suspended state. The default is 0, or start the thread normally.
- (Optionally) The desired security attributes. The default is the same access as the parent thread. For more information on the format of this security information, see **SECURITY_ATTRIBUTES** in the *Win32 Programmer's Reference, Volume 5.*

AfxBeginThread creates and initializes a **CWinThread** object for you, starts it, and returns its address so you can refer to it later. Checks are made throughout the procedure to make sure all objects are deallocated properly should any part of the creation fail.

Implementing the Controlling Function

The controlling function defines the thread. When this function is entered, the thread starts, and when it exits, the thread terminates. This function should have the following prototype:

```
UINT MyControllingFunction( LPVOID pParam );
```

The parameter is a single 32-bit value. The value the function receives in this parameter is the value that was passed to the constructor when the thread object was created. The controlling function can interpret this value in any manner it chooses. It can be treated as a scalar value, or a pointer to a structure containing multiple parameters, or it can be ignored. If the parameter refers to a structure, the structure can be used not only to pass data from the caller to the thread, but also to pass data back from the thread to the caller. If you use such a structure to pass data back to the caller, the thread will need to notify the caller when the results are ready. For information on communicating from the worker thread to the caller, see the article "Multithreading: Programming Tips."

When the function terminates, it should return a **DWORD** value indicating the reason for termination. Typically, this exit code is 0 to indicate success with other values indicating different types of errors. This is purely implementation dependent. Some threads may maintain usage counts of objects, and return the current number of uses of that object. To see how applications can retrieve this value, see the article "Multithreading: Terminating Threads."

There are some restrictions on what you can do in a multithreaded program written with the Microsoft Foundation Class Library. For descriptions of these restrictions and other tips on using threads, see the article "Multithreading: Programming Tips."

Example

This example shows how to define a controlling function and use it from another portion of the program.

```
DWORD MyThreadProc( LPVOID pParam )
{
    CMyObject* pObject = (CMyObject*)pParam;

    if (pObject == NULL ||
        !pObject->IsKindOf(RUNTIME_CLASS(CMyObject)))
    return -1;  // illegal parameter

    // do something with 'pObject'
    return 0;   // thread completed successfully
}

// inside a different function in the program
.
.
.
pNewObject = new CMyObject;
AfxBeginThread(MyThreadProc, pNewObject);
.
.
.
```

See Also Articles: "Multithreading: Creating User-Interface Threads," "Multithreading: Terminating Threads," "Multithreading: Programming Tips"

Multithreading: Terminating Threads

Two normal situations cause a thread to terminate: the controlling function exits or the thread should not be allowed to run to completion. If a word processor used a thread for background printing, the controlling function would terminate normally if printing completed successfully. Should the user wish to cancel the printing, however, the background printing thread would have to be terminated prematurely. This article explains both how to implement each situation, and how to get the exit code of a thread after it terminates.

Normal Thread Termination

For a worker thread, normal thread termination is simple: exit the controlling function and return a value that signifies the reason for termination. You can use either the **AfxEndThread** function or a **return** statement. Typically, 0 signifies successful completion, but that is up to the programmer.

For a user-interface thread, the process is just as simple: from within the user-interface thread, call **::PostQuitMessage** in the *Win32 Programmer's Reference, Volume 4*. The only parameter that **::PostQuitMessage** takes is the exit code of the thread. As for worker threads, 0 typically signifies successful completion.

Premature Thread Termination

Terminating a thread prematurely is almost as simple: call **AfxEndThread** from within the thread. Pass the desired exit code as the only parameter. This stops execution of the thread, deallocates the thread's stack, detaches all DLLs attached to the thread, and deletes the thread object from memory.

AfxEndThread must be called from within the thread to be terminated. If you wish to terminate a thread from another thread, you must set up a communication method between the two threads.

Retrieving the Exit Code of a Thread

To get the exit code of either the worker or the user-interface thread, call the **::GetExitCodeThread** function in the *Win32 Programmer's Reference, Volume 3*. This function takes the handle to the thread (stored in the m_hThread data member of **CWinThread** objects) and the address of a **DWORD**.

If the thread is still active, **::GetExitCodeThread** will place **STILL_ACTIVE** in the supplied **DWORD** address; otherwise, the exit code is placed in this address.

Retrieving the exit code of **CWinThread** objects takes an extra step. By default, when a **CWinThread** thread terminates, the thread object is deleted. This means that you cannot access the m_hThread data member since the **CWinThread** object no longer exists. To avoid this situation, do one of the following two things:

- Set the m_bAutoDelete data member to **FALSE**. This allows the **CWinThread** object to survive after the thread has been terminated. You can then access the m_hThread data member after the thread has been terminated. If you use this technique, however, you are responsible for destroying the **CWinThread** object as the framework will not automatically delete it for you. This is the preferred method.

  −Or−

- Store the thread's handle separately. After the thread is created, copy its m_hThread data member (using **::DuplicateHandle**) to another variable and access it through that variable. This way the object is deleted automatically upon termination and you can still find out why the thread terminated. Be careful that the thread does not terminate before you can duplicate the handle. The safest way to do this is to pass **CREATE_SUSPENDED** to **AfxBeginThread**, store the handle, and then resume the thread by calling **ResumeThread**.

Either method allows you to determine why a **CWinThread** object terminated.

See Also   In the *Class Library Reference*: **CWinThread, AfxEndThread**

In the *Run-Time Library Reference*: **_endthreadex, _beginthreadex**

In the *Win32 Programmer's Reference, Volume 3*: **::GetExitCodeThread, ::ExitThread**

Multithreading: Programming Tips

Multithreaded applications require stricter care than single-threaded applications when accessing data. Since there are multiple, independent paths of execution in use simultaneously in multithreaded applications, either the algorithms, the data, or both must be aware that data could be used by more than one thread at a time. This article explains techniques for avoiding potential problems when programming multithreaded applications with the Microsoft Foundation Class Library (MFC).

Accessing Objects from Multiple Threads

For size and performance reasons, MFC objects are not thread safe at the object level, only at the class level. This means that you can have two separate threads manipulating two different **CString** objects, but not two threads manipulating the same **CString** object. If you absolutely must have multiple threads manipulating the same object, protect such access with appropriate Win32 synchronization mechanisms, such as critical sections. For more information on critical sections and other related objects, see Chapter 44, "Synchronization," in the *Win32 Programmer's Reference, Volume 2*.

The class library uses critical sections internally to protect global data structures, such as those used by the debug memory allocator.

Accessing MFC Objects from Non-MFC Threads

If you have a multithreaded application that creates a thread in a way other than using a **CWinThread** object, you cannot access other MFC objects from that thread. In other words, if you want to access any MFC object from a secondary thread, you must create that thread with one of the methods described in the "Multithreading: Creating User-Interface Threads" or "Multithreading: Creating Worker Threads" articles. These methods are the only ones that allow the class library to initialize the internal variables necessary to handle multithreaded applications.

Windows Handle Maps

As a general rule, a thread can only access MFC objects that it created. This is because temporary and permanent Windows handle maps are kept in thread local storage to ensure protection from simultaneous access from multiple threads. For example, a worker thread cannot perform a calculation and then call a document's **UpdateAllViews** member function to have the windows that contain views on the new data modified. This will have no effect at all, since the map from **CWnd** objects to **HWND**s is local to the primary thread. What this means is that one thread may have a mapping from a Windows handle to a C++ object, but another thread may map that same handle to a different C++ object. Changes made in one thread would not be reflected in the other.

There are several ways around this problem. The first is to pass individual handles (such as an **HWND**) rather than C++ objects to the worker thread. The worker thread then adds these objects to its temporary map by calling the appropriate **FromHandle** member function. You could also add the object to the thread's permanent map by calling **Attach**, but this should only be done if you are guaranteed that the object will exist longer than the thread.

Another method is to create new user-defined messages corresponding to the different tasks your worker threads will be performing and post these messages to the application's main window using **::PostMessage**. This method of communication is similar to two different applications conversing except that both threads are executing in the same address space.

For more information on handle maps, see Technical Note 3 under MFC in Books Online. For more information on thread local storage, see sections 43.1.7, "Thread Local Storage," and 43.2.4, "Using Thread Local Storage," in the *Win32 Programmer's Reference, Volume 2*.

Communicating Between Threads

MFC does not explicitly provide class member functions for any interthread communication mechanisms such as mutexes, semaphores, and critical sections. It is encouraged that you use the Win32 APIs for these mechanisms in your MFC applications. Information on these topics can be found in Chapter 44, "Synchronization," in the *Win32 Programmer's Reference, Volume 2*.

See Also   In the *Class Library Reference*: **CWinThread**

ODBC

In addition to an overview of Open Database Connectivity (ODBC), this article explains:

- How ODBC works with the database classes.
- How ODBC drivers work with dynasets.
- What ODBC components you need to redistribute with your applications.

You will also want to read the related article "ODBC: The ODBC Cursor Library."

ODBC is a call-level interface that allows applications to access data in any database for which there is an ODBC driver. Using ODBC, you can create database applications with access to any database for which your end-user has an ODBC driver. ODBC provides an API that allows your application to be independent of the source database management system (DBMS).

ODBC is the database portion of the Microsoft Windows Open Services Architecture (WOSA), an interface which allows Windows-based desktop applications to connect to multiple computing environments without rewriting the application for each platform.

The following are components of ODBC:

- ODBC API

  A library of function calls, a set of error codes, and a standard Structured Query Language (SQL) syntax for accessing data on DBMSs.
- ODBC Driver Manager

  A dynamic-link library (ODBC32.DLL) that loads ODBC database drivers on behalf of an application. This DLL is transparent to your application.
- ODBC database drivers

  One or more DLLs that process ODBC function calls for specific DBMSs.
- ODBC Cursor Library

  A dynamic-link library (ODBCCR32.DLL) that resides between the ODBC Driver Manager and the drivers and handles scrolling through the data.
- ODBC Administrator

  A tool used for configuring a DBMS to make it available as a data source for an application.

An application achieves independence from DBMSs by working through an ODBC driver written specifically for a DBMS rather than working directly with the DBMS. The driver translates the calls into commands its DBMS can use, simplifying the developer's work, and making it available for a wide range of data sources.

The database classes support any data source for which you have an ODBC driver. This might, for example, include a relational database, an Indexed Sequential Access Method (ISAM) database, a Microsoft Excel spreadsheet, or a text file. The ODBC drivers manage the connections to the data source, and SQL is used to select records from the database.

Visual C++ version 2.0 provides an ODBC driver for the following remote database:

- SQL Server

Parts of the ODBC Software Development Kit (SDK) are included with this product. For a list of ODBC drivers available from Microsoft and other companies, call 1-800-227-4679 and request an ODBC Driver Catalog.

For more information on ODBC, see the ODBC SDK *Programmer's Reference*, and the ODBC API Reference Help system.

ODBC and the Database Classes

The database classes encapsulate the ODBC API function calls you would normally make yourself in the member functions of the **CDatabase** and **CRecordset** classes. For example, the complex ODBC call sequences, binding of returned records to storage locations, handling of error conditions, and other operations are managed for you by the database classes. As a result, you use a considerably simpler class interface to manipulate records through a recordset object.

Although the database classes encapsulate ODBC functionality, they do not provide a one-to-one mapping of ODBC API functions. The database classes provide a higher level of abstraction, modeled after data-access objects found in Microsoft Access and Microsoft Visual Basic. For more information, see "Similarity to the Microsoft Access and Visual Basic Data-Access API" on page 107 in Chapter 6.

ODBC Driver Requirements for Dynasets

In the MFC database classes, dynasets are recordsets with dynamic properties— they remain synchronized with the data source in certain ways. MFC dynasets (but not forward-only recordsets) require an Open Database Connectivity (ODBC) driver with Level 2 API conformance. If the driver for your data source conforms to the Level 1 API set, you can still use both updatable and read-only snapshots and forward-only recordsets, but not dynasets. However, a Level 1 driver can support dynasets if it supports extended fetch and keyset-driven cursors.

In ODBC terminology, dynasets and snapshots are referred to as "cursors." A cursor is a mechanism used for keeping track of its position in a recordset. For more information about driver requirements for dynasets, see the article "Dynaset." For more information about cursors, see the ODBC SDK *Programmer's Reference*.

Note For updatable recordsets, your ODBC driver must support either positioned update statements or the **::SQLSetPos** ODBC API function. If both are supported, MFC uses **::SQLSetPos** for efficiency. Alternatively, for snapshots, you can use the cursor library, which provides the required support for updatable snapshots (static cursors and positioned update statements).

Redistributing ODBC Components to Your Customers

If you incorporate the functionality of the ODBC Setup and ODBC Administrator programs into your application, you must also distribute to your users the files which run these programs. These ODBC files reside in the \MSVC20\REDIST directory of the Visual C++ version 2.0 CD-ROM disc. The REDISTRB.WRI file and the license agreement both contain the list of ODBC files that you may redistribute.

Consult the documentation for any ODBC drivers you plan to ship. You'll need to determine which DLLs and other files to ship.

In addition, you need to include one other file in most cases. The ODBCCR32.DLL is the ODBC Cursor Library. This library gives Level 1 drivers the capability of forward and backward scrolling. It also provides the capability of supporting snapshots. For more information on the ODBC Cursor Library, see the article "ODBC: The ODBC Cursor Library."

The following articles provide more information on using ODBC with the database classes:

- ODBC: The ODBC Cursor Library
- ODBC: Configuring an ODBC Data Source
- ODBC: Calling ODBC API Functions Directly

See Also   Article: "ODBC Administrator"

ODBC: The ODBC Cursor Library

This article describes the ODBC Cursor Library and explains how to use it. Topics include:

- The Cursor Library and Level 1 ODBC drivers
- Positioned updates and timestamp columns
- Using the Cursor Library

The ODBC Cursor Library is a dynamic-link library (DLL) that resides between the ODBC Driver Manager and the driver. In ODBC terms, a driver maintains a "cursor" to keep track of its position in the recordset. The cursor marks the position in the recordset to which you have already scrolled — the current record.

The Cursor Library and Level 1 ODBC Drivers

The ODBC Cursor Library gives Level 1 drivers the following new capabilities:

- Forward and backward scrolling. Level 2 drivers don't need the cursor library because they are already scrollable.

- Support for snapshots. The cursor library manages a buffer containing the snapshot's records. This buffer reflects your program's deletions and edits to records but not the additions, deletions, or edits of other users, so the snapshot is only as current as the cursor library's buffer. The buffer also does not reflect your own additions until you call **Requery**. Dynasets do not use the cursor library.

The cursor library will give you snapshots (static cursors) even if they are not normally supported by your driver. If your driver already supports static cursors, you don't need to load the cursor library to get snapshot support. If you do use the cursor library, you can use only snapshots and forward-only recordsets. If your driver supports dynasets (KEYSET_DRIVEN cursors) and you want to use dynasets, you must not use the cursor library. If you want to use both snapshots and dynasets, you must base them on two different **CDatabase** objects (two different connections) unless your driver supports both.

Positioned Updates and Timestamp Columns

Note If your ODBC driver supports **SQLSetPos**, which MFC uses if available, this topic does not apply to you.

Most Level 1 drivers do not support positioned updates. Such drivers rely on the cursor library to emulate the capabilities of Level 2 drivers in this regard. The cursor library emulates positioned update support by doing a searched update on the unchanging fields.

In some cases, a recordset may contain a timestamp column as one of those unchanging fields. Two issues arise in using MFC recordsets with tables that contain timestamp columns.

The first issue concerns updatable snapshots on tables with timestamp columns. If the table to which your snapshot is bound contains a timestamp column, you should call **Requery** after you call **Edit** and **Update**. If not, you may not be able to edit the same record again. When you call **Edit** and then **Update**, the record is written to the data source and the timestamp column is updated. If you don't call **Requery**, the timestamp value for the record in your snapshot no longer matches the corresponding timestamp on the data source. When you try to update the record again, the data source may disallow the update because of the mismatch.

The second issue concerns limitations of class **CTime** when used with the **RFX_Date** function to transfer time and date information to or from a table. Processing the **CTime** object imposes some overhead in the form of extra intermediate processing during the data transfer. The date range of **CTime** objects may also be too limiting for some applications. A new version of the **RFX_Date** function takes an ODBC **TIMESTAMP_STRUCT** parameter instead of a **CTime** object. For more information, see **RFX_Date** in "Macros and Globals" in the *Class Library Reference*.

Using the Cursor Library

When you connect to a data source—by calling **CDatabase::Open**—you can specify whether to use the cursor library for the data source. If you will be creating snapshots on that data source, specify **TRUE** for the **bUseCursorLib** parameter to **Open** (or rely on the default value of **TRUE**). However, if your ODBC driver supports dynasets and you want to open dynasets on the data source, the cursor library must not be used (it masks some driver functionality needed for dynasets). In that case, specify **FALSE** for the **bUseCursorLib** parameter.

ODBC: Configuring an ODBC Data Source

To use a data source with an application you've developed, you must use ODBC Administrator to configure it. ODBC Administrator keeps track of available data sources and their connection information in the Windows NT registry. You use ODBC Administrator to add, modify, and delete data sources in the Data Sources dialog box, and to add and delete ODBC drivers.

ODBC Administrator is automatically installed with the Microsoft Foundation Class Library database support. For more information about the ODBC Administrator program, see the article "ODBC Administrator" and the online ODBC API Reference help system.

Technical Note 48, available under MFC in Books Online, describes how to write ODBC Setup and Administration programs for MFC database applications.

See Also   Article: "ODBC: Calling ODBC API Functions Directly"

ODBC: Calling ODBC API Functions Directly

The database classes provide a simpler interface to a data source than does ODBC. As a result, the classes don't encapsulate all of the ODBC API. For any functionality that falls outside the abilities of the classes, you must call ODBC API functions directly. For example, you must call the ODBC catalog functions

(**::SQLColumns**, **::SQLProcedures**, **::SQLTables**, and others) directly. Samples of direct ODBC function calls used with the classes can be found in the \MSVC20\SAMPLES\MFC\CATALOG directory of your Visual C++ CD-ROM disc.

To call an ODBC API function directly, you must take the same steps you'd take if you were making the calls without the framework. You must:

- Allocate storage for any results the call returns.
- Pass an ODBC **HDBC** or **HSTMT** handle, depending on the parameter signature of the function.

  Member variables **CDatabase::m_hdbc** and **CRecordset::m_hstmt** are available so that you do not need to allocate and initialize these yourself.
- Perhaps call additional ODBC functions to prepare for or follow up the main call.
- Deallocate storage when you finish.

For more information about these steps, see the ODBC SDK *Programmer's Reference*.

In addition to these steps, you need to take extra steps to check function return values, assure that your program isn't waiting for an asynchronous call to finish, and so on. You can simplify these last steps by using the **AFX_SQL_ASYNC** and **AFX_SQL_SYNC** macros. See "Macros and Globals" in the *Class Library Reference* for information.

See Also   Article: "ODBC"

ODBC Administrator

ODBC Administrator is used to register and configure the data sources available to you either locally or across a network. ClassWizard uses information supplied by ODBC Administrator to create code in your applications that connects your users to data sources.

You must use ODBC Administrator to add and remove data sources. Depending on the ODBC driver, you can also create new data sources.

During Setup, you select the ODBC drivers you want to install. You can later install additional drivers using ODBC Administrator.

Note ODBC Administrator is installed during Setup. If you chose Custom Installation and did not select the "Database (ODBC) files" check box, you need to run Setup again to install the necessary files.

▶ **To install or remove ODBC drivers**

1. Open ODBC Administrator by double-clicking its icon in the Control Panel.

   This displays a Data Sources dialog box.

2. Select the Drivers button.

   - To add drivers, choose Add, then specify the path to the ODBC drivers. Select one or more ODBC drivers to install, then choose OK. ODBC Administrator copies the files to your disk.

   - To remove drivers, select the driver you want to delete, then choose Delete. If you answer Yes to the subsequent message box, ODBC Administrator deletes the driver and the data sources associated with it from the Data Sources dialog box. ODBC Administrator does not delete the files from your disk.

3. Choose Close to return to the Data Sources dialog box, and Close again to exit ODBC Administrator.

Tip For information about a driver, highlight the driver and choose About.

For information about configuring a data source with ODBC Administrator, see Chapter 3 in the ODBC *SDK Guide*.

See Also   Article: "Data Source (ODBC)"

OLE Overview

Object Linking and Embedding (OLE) is a mechanism that allows users to create and edit documents containing data created by multiple applications. These documents, called "compound documents" seamlessly integrate various types of data, or "items." Sound clips, spreadsheets, and bitmaps are typical examples of items found in compound documents. Supporting OLE in your application allows you to use compound documents without worrying about switching between the different applications; OLE does the switching for you.

You use a "container application" to create compound documents and a "server application" to create the items within the container application. Any application you write can be a container, a server, or both.

OLE incorporates many different concepts that all work toward the goal of seamless interaction between applications. These areas include the following:

Linking and Embedding

Linking and Embedding are the two methods for storing items inside a compound document that were created in another application. For general information on the differences between the two, see the "OLE Overview:

Linking and Embedding" article. For more detailed information, see the "Containers" and "Servers" articles.

In-Place Activation

Activating an embedded item in the context of the container application is called "in-place activation." Your container application's interface changes to incorporate the features of the application that created the embedded item. Linked items are never activated "in-place" because the actual data for the item is contained in a separate file, out of the context of the application containing the link. For more information on in-place activation, see the "Activation" article.

Note Linking and embedding and in-place activation provide the main features of OLE Visual Editing.

Automation

OLE Automation allows one application to drive another application. The driving application is known as an "automation client," and the application being driven is known as an "automation server." For more information on automation, see the "Automation Clients" and "Automation Servers" articles.

Compound Files

Compound files provide a standard file format that simplifies structured storing of compound documents for OLE applications. Within a compound file, "storages" have many features of directories and "streams" have many features of files. For more information on compound files, see the "Containers: Compound Files" article.

Uniform Data Transfer

Uniform Data Transfer (UDT) is a set of interfaces that allow data to be sent and received in a standard fashion, regardless of the actual method chosen to transfer the data. UDT forms the basis for data transfers by using the Clipboard and drag and drop. For more information on UDT, see the "Data Objects and Data Sources (OLE)" article.

Drag and Drop

Drag and drop is an easy-to-use, direct-manipulation technique to transfer data between applications, between windows within an application, or even within a single window in an application. The data to be transferred is simply selected and dragged to the desired destination. For more information on drag and drop, see the "Drag and Drop" article.

Component Object Model

The Component Object Model (COM) provides the infrastructure used when OLE objects communicate with each other. The Microsoft Foundation Class Library OLE classes simplify COM for the programmer. For more information about the COM, see Chapter 1 in the *OLE 2 Programmer's Reference, Volume 1*.

Some of the more important general OLE topics are covered in the following articles:

- OLE Overview: Linking and Embedding
- OLE Overview: Containers and Servers
- OLE Overview: Implementation Strategies
- OLE Overview: Microsoft Foundation Class Library Implementation

For information about handling context-sensitive help in OLE applications, see the article "Help: OLE Support for Help."

For general OLE information not found in the above articles, see the *OLE 2 Programmer's Reference, Volume 1*. Another good source of information is Kraig Brockschmidt's book *Inside OLE 2* (Microsoft Press, 1994).

OLE Overview: Linking and Embedding

This article defines the OLE terms "linking" and "embedding."

Using the Paste command in an OLE application creates an "embedded item." An embedded item is stored as part of the compound document that contains it. In this way, a document file for a word processor document can contain not only text, but also bitmaps, graphs, formulas, or any other type of data.

OLE provides another way to incorporate data from another application: creating a "linked item." The steps for creating a linked item are similar to those for creating an embedded item, except that you use the Paste Link command instead of the Paste command. Unlike an embedded item, a linked item stores its data in a separate file.

For example, if you are working in a word processor document and create a linked item of some spreadsheet cells, the data for the linked item is stored in the original spreadsheet document. The word processor document contains only the information specifying where the item can be found; that is, it contains a link to the original spreadsheet document. When you double-click the cells, the spreadsheet application is launched and the original spreadsheet document is loaded from where it was stored.

Every OLE item, whether embedded or linked, has a type associated with it based on the application that created it. For example, a Microsoft Paintbrush™ item is one type of item, while a Microsoft Excel item is another type. However, some applications can create more than one item type; for example, Microsoft Excel can create worksheet items, chart items, and macrosheet items. Each of these items can be uniquely identified by the system using a "Class Identifier" or **CLSID**.

For more information on the kind of data stored in embedded and linked items, see the *OLE 2 Programmer's Reference, Volume 1*.

See Also   Articles: "OLE Overview: Containers and Servers," "Containers: Client Items," "Servers: Server Items"

OLE Overview: Containers and Servers

This article explains and defines container and server applications.

A "Visual Editing container application" is an application that can incorporate embedded or linked items into its own documents. The documents managed by a container application must be able to store and display OLE items as well as the data created by the application itself. A container application must also allow users to insert new items or edit existing items by activating server applications when necessary. The user-interface requirements of a container application are listed in the "Containers: User-Interface Issues" article.

A "Visual Editing server application" is an application that can create OLE items for use by container applications. Server applications usually support copying their data to the Clipboard or drag and drop so that a container application can paste the data as an embedded or linked item. An application can be both a container and a server.

Most servers are stand-alone applications or "full-servers"; they can either be run as stand-alone applications or can be launched by a container application. A "mini-server" is a special type of server application that can be launched only by a container; it cannot be run as a stand-alone application. The Microsoft Draw and Microsoft Graph servers are examples of mini-servers.

Containers and servers do not communicate directly. Instead, they communicate through the OLE system DLLs. These DLLs provide functions that containers and servers call, and the containers and servers provide callback functions that the DLLs call.

Using this means of communication, a container doesn't need to know the implementation details of the server application. It allows a container to accept items created by any server without having to define the types of servers with which it can work. As a result, the user of a container application can take advantage of future applications and data formats. As long as these new applications are OLE servers, a compound document will be able to incorporate items created by those applications.

See Also   Articles: "OLE Overview: Microsoft Foundation Class Library Implementation," "Containers," "Servers," "Containers: Client Items," "Servers: Server Items"

OLE Overview: Implementation Strategies

Depending on your application, there are four possible implementation strategies
for adding OLE support:

- You are writing a new application.

  This situation usually requires the least work. You simply run AppWizard and
  select OLE options to create a skeleton application. For information on the OLE
  options in AppWizard and what they do, see the article "AppWizard: OLE
  Support."

- You have a program written with the Microsoft Foundation Class Library
  version 2.0 or higher that does not support OLE.

  Create a new application with AppWizard as above, then copy and paste the
  code from the new application into your existing application. This will work for
  servers, containers, or automated applications. See step 7 of the Scribble tutorial
  in *Introducing Visual C++* for an example of this strategy.

- You have a Microsoft Foundation Class Library program that implements OLE
  version 1.0 support.

  See Technical Note 41 under MFC in Books Online for this conversion strategy.

- You have an application that was not written using the Microsoft Foundation
  classes and that may or may not have implemented OLE support.

  This situation requires the most work. One approach is to create a new
  application, as in the first strategy, then copy and paste your existing code into
  it. If your existing code is written in C, you may need to modify it so it can
  compile as C++ code. If your C code calls the Windows API, you do not have to
  change it to use the Microsoft Foundation classes. This approach likely will
  require some restructuring of your program to support the document/view
  architecture used by versions 2.0 and higher of the Microsoft Foundation
  classes. For more information on this architecture, see Technical Note 25 under
  MFC in Books Online.

Once you have decided on a strategy, you should either read the "Containers" or
"Servers" family of articles (depending on the type of application you are writing),
or examine the sample programs installed on your disk, or both. The OCLIENT and
HIERSVR samples show how to implement the various aspects of containers and
servers, respectively. These samples are in the
\MSVC20\SAMPLES\MFC\OCLIENT and
\MSVC20\SAMPLES\MFC\HIERSVR directories. At various points throughout
this encyclopedia, you will be referred to certain functions in these samples as
examples of the techniques being discussed.

See Also   Articles: "Containers: Implementing a Container," "Servers: Implementing a
Server," "AppWizard: OLE Support"

OLE Overview: Microsoft Foundation Class Library Implementation

Because of the size and complexity of the raw OLE API, calling it directly to write OLE applications can be very time-consuming. The goal of the Microsoft Foundation Class Library implementation of OLE is to reduce the amount of work you have to do to write full-featured, OLE-capable applications.

This article explains the parts of the OLE API that have *not* been implemented inside MFC. The discussion also explains how what is implemented maps to the OLE 2 SDK.

Portions of OLE Not Implemented by the Class Library

There are a few interfaces and features of OLE not directly provided by the Microsoft Foundation Class Library. If you want to use these features, you can call the OLE API directly.

IMoniker Interface

The **IMoniker** interface is implemented by the class library (for example, the **COleServerItem** class), but is not exposed to the programmer. For more information about this interface, see Chapter 8 in the *OLE 2 Programmer's Reference, Volume 1.*

IUnknown and **IMarshal** Interfaces

The **IUnknown** interface is implemented by the class library, but is not exposed to the programmer. The **IMarshal** interface is not implemented by the class library, but is used internally. OLE Automation servers built using the class library already have marshalling capabilities built in. For more information about these interfaces, see Chapter 5 in the *OLE 2 Programmer's Reference, Volume 1.*

Docfiles (Compound Files)

Compound files are partially supported by the class library. None of the functions that directly manipulate compound files beyond creation are supported. MFC uses class **COleFileStream** to support manpulation of streams with standard file functions. For more information, see the article "Containers: Compound Files."

In-Process Servers and Object Handlers

In-process servers and object handlers allow implementing Visual Editing data or full component object model (COM) objects in a DLL. To do this, you can implement your DLL by calling the OLE API directly. These two features are not fully supported by the class library. If you are writing an OLE Automation server and your server has no user interface, it is possible to make your server an in-process server and put it completely into a DLL. For more information about these topics, see the article "Automation Servers" and see Chapters 1 and 5 in the *OLE 2 Programmer's Reference, Volume 1.*

Tip The easiest way to implement an OLE Automation server is to place it in a DLL. MFC supports this approach.

For detailed information on how the Microsoft Foundation OLE classes implement OLE interfaces, see Technical Notes 38, 39, and 40 under MFC in Books Online.

See Also   Articles: "OLE Overview: Implementation Strategies," "OLE Overview"

Porting

See the articles "MFC: Porting MFC Applications to 32-Bit" and "MFC: Porting Tips."

See Also

In *Programming Techniques*: Chapter 1, "Porting 16-Bit Code to 32-Bit Windows"

Under MFC in Books Online: Technical Note 19, "Updating Existing MFC Applications to MFC 3.0." This note describes migration to MFC version 2.0 and above.

Print Preview

See the article "Printing."

See Also

Article: "Printing: The Print Preview Architecture"

Printing

This group of articles explains how printing is implemented in the Microsoft Foundation Class Library (MFC) and how to advantage of the printing architecture already built into the framework. The articles also explain how MFC supports easy implementation of print preview functionality and how you can use and modify that functionality.

Microsoft Windows implements device-independent display. In MFC, this means that the same drawing calls, in the OnDraw member function of your view class, are responsible for drawing on the display and on other devices, such as printers. For print preview, the target device is a simulated printer output to the display.

Your Role in Printing vs. the Framework's Role

Your view class has the following responsibilities:

- Inform the framework how many pages are in the document.
- When asked to print a specified page, draw that portion of the document.
- Allocate and deallocate any fonts or other GDI resources needed for printing.
- If necessary, send any escape codes needed to change the printer mode before printing a given page; for example, to change the printing orientation on a per-page basis.

The framework's responsibilities are as follows:

- Display the Print dialog box.

- Create a **CDC** object for the printer.
- Call the **StartDoc** and **EndDoc** member functions of the **CDC** object.
- Repeatedly call the **StartPage** member function of the **CDC** object, inform the view class which page should be printed, and call the **EndPage** member function of the **CDC** object.
- Call overridable functions in the view at the appropriate times.

The following articles discuss how the framework supports printing and print preview:

- Printing: How Default Printing Is Done
- Printing: Multipage Documents
- Printing: Headers and Footers
- Printing: Allocating GDI Resources
- Printing: The Print Preview Architecture

See Also   In *Introducing Visual C++*: Chapter 14, "Enhancing Printing"

Printing: How Default Printing Is Done

This article explains the default printing process in Windows in terms of the MFC framework.

In MFC applications, the view class has a member function named OnDraw which contains all the drawing code. OnDraw takes a pointer to a **CDC** object as a parameter. That **CDC** object represents the device context to receive the image produced by OnDraw. When the window displaying the document receives a **WM_PAINT** message, the framework calls OnDraw and passes it a device context for the screen (a **CPaintDC** object, to be specific). Accordingly, OnDraw's output goes to the screen.

In programming for Windows, sending output to the printer is very similar to sending output to the screen. This is because the Windows graphics device interface (GDI) is hardware-independent; you can use the same GDI functions for screen display or for printing simply by using the appropriate device context. If the **CDC** object that OnDraw receives represents the printer, OnDraw's output goes to the printer.

This explains how MFC applications can perform simple printing without requiring extra effort on your part. The framework takes care of displaying the Print dialog box and creating a device context for the printer. When the user selects the Print command from the File menu, the view passes this device context to OnDraw, which draws the document on the printer.

However, there are some significant differences between printing and screen display. When you print, you have to divide the document into distinct pages and display them one at a time, rather than display whatever portion is visible in a window. As a corollary, you have to be aware of the size of the paper (whether it's letter size, legal size, or an envelope). You may want to print in different orientations, such as landscape or portrait mode. The Microsoft Foundation Class Library can't predict how your application will handle these issues, so it provides a protocol for you to add these capabilities.

That protocol is described in the article "Printing: Multipage Documents."

See Also   In the *Class Library Reference*: **CDC**

Printing: Multipage Documents

This article describes the Windows printing protocol and explains how to print documents that contain more than one page. The article covers the following topics:

- The Printing Protocol
- Overriding View Class Functions
- Pagination
- Printer Pages vs. Document Pages
- Print-Time Pagination

The Printing Protocol

To print a multipage document, the framework and view interact in the following manner. First the framework displays the Print dialog box, creates a device context for the printer, and calls the **StartDoc** member function of the **CDC** object. Then, for each page of the document, the framework calls the **StartPage** member function of the **CDC** object, instructs the view object to print the page, and then calls the **EndPage** member function. If the printer mode must be changed before starting a particular page, the view object sends the appropriate escape code by calling the **Escape** member function of the **CDC** object. When the entire document has been printed, the framework calls the **EndDoc** member function.

Overriding View Class Functions

The **CView** class defines several member functions that are called by the framework during printing. By overriding these functions in your view class, you provide the connections between the framework's printing logic and your view class's printing logic. Table 1 lists these member functions.

Table 1   CView's Overridable Functions for Printing

Name	Reason for overriding
OnPreparePrinting	To insert values in the Print dialog box, especially the length of the document
OnBeginPrinting	To allocate fonts or other GDI resources
OnPrepareDC	To adjust attributes of the device context for a given page, or to do print-time pagination
OnPrint	To print a given page
OnEndPrinting	To deallocate GDI resources

You can do printing-related processing in other functions as well, but these functions are the ones that drive the printing process.

Figure 1 illustrates the steps involved in the printing process and shows where each of **CView**'s printing member functions are called. The rest of this article explains most of these steps in more detail. Additional parts of the printing process are described in the article "Printing: Allocating GDI Resources."

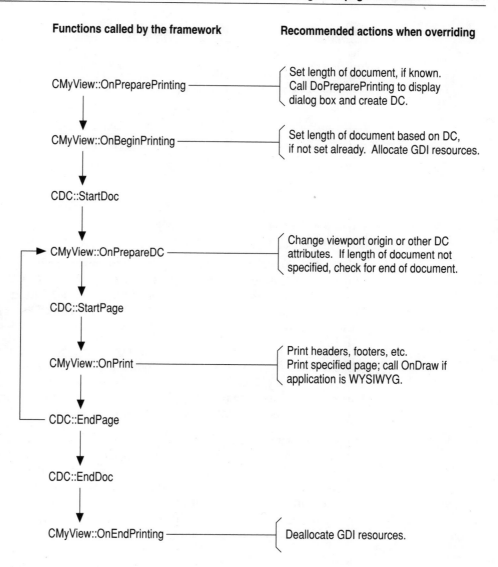

Functions called by the framework	Recommended actions when overriding
CMyView::OnPreparePrinting	Set length of document, if known. Call DoPreparePrinting to display dialog box and create DC.
CMyView::OnBeginPrinting	Set length of document based on DC, if not set already. Allocate GDI resources.
CDC::StartDoc	
CMyView::OnPrepareDC	Change viewport origin or other DC attributes. If length of document not specified, check for end of document.
CDC::StartPage	
CMyView::OnPrint	Print headers, footers, etc. Print specified page; call OnDraw if application is WYSIWYG.
CDC::EndPage	
CDC::EndDoc	
CMyView::OnEndPrinting	Deallocate GDI resources.

Figure 1   The Printing Loop

Pagination

The framework stores much of the information about a print job in a **CPrintInfo** structure. Several of the values in **CPrintInfo** pertain to pagination; these values are accessible as shown in Table 2.

Table 2   Page Number Information Stored in CPrintInfo

Member variable or function name(s)	Page number referenced
GetMinPage / SetMinPage	First page of document
GetMaxPage / SetMaxPage	Last page of document
GetFromPage	First page to be printed
GetToPage	Last page to be printed
m_nCurPage	Page currently being printing

Page numbers start at 1; that is, the first page is numbered 1, not 0. For more information about these and other members of **CPrintInfo**, see the *Class Library Reference*.

At the beginning of the printing process, the framework calls the view's **OnPreparePrinting** member function, passing a pointer to a **CPrintInfo** structure. AppWizard provides an implementation of **OnPreparePrinting** that calls **DoPreparePrinting**, another member function of **CView**. **DoPreparePrinting** is the function that displays the Print dialog box and creates a printer device context.

At this point the application doesn't know how many pages are in the document; it uses the default values 1 and 0xFFFF for the numbers of the first and last page of the document. If you know how many pages your document has, override **OnPreparePrinting** and call **SetMaxPage** for the **CPrintInfo** structure before you send it to **DoPreparePrinting**; this lets you specify the length of your document.

DoPreparePrinting then displays the Print dialog box; when it returns, the **CPrintInfo** structure contains the values specified by the user. If the user wishes to print only a selected range of pages, he or she can specify the starting and ending page numbers in the Print dialog box; the framework retrieves these values using the **GetFromPage** and **GetToPage** functions. If the user doesn't specify a page range, the framework calls **GetMinPage** and **GetMaxPage** and uses the values returned to print the entire document.

For each page of a document to be printed, the framework calls two member functions in your view class, **OnPrepareDC** and **OnPrint**, and passes each function two parameters: a pointer to a **CDC** object and a pointer to a **CPrintInfo** structure. Each time the framework calls **OnPrepareDC** and **OnPrint**, it passes a different value in the **m_nCurPage** member of the **CPrintInfo** structure. In this way the framework tells the view which page should be printed.

The **OnPrepareDC** member function is also used for screen display; it makes adjustments to the device context before drawing takes place. **OnPrepareDC** serves a similar role in printing, but there are a couple of differences: first, the **CDC** object represents a printer device context instead of a screen device context, and second, a **CPrintInfo** object is passed as a second parameter. (This parameter is **NULL** when **OnPrepareDC** is called for screen display.) Override **OnPrepareDC** to make adjustments to the device context based on which page is being printed; for example, you can move the viewport origin and the clipping region to ensure that the appropriate portion of the document gets printed.

The **OnPrint** member function performs the actual printing of the page. The article "Printing: How Default Printing Is Done" shows how the framework calls **OnDraw** with a printer device context to perform printing. More precisely, the framework calls **OnPrint** with a **CPrintInfo** structure and a device context, and **OnPrint** passes the device context to **OnDraw**. Override **OnPrint** to perform any rendering that should be done only during printing and not for screen display; for example, to print headers or footers (see the article "Printing: Headers and Footers" for more information). Then call **OnDraw** from the override of **OnDraw** to do the rendering common to both screen display and printing.

The fact that **OnDraw** does the rendering for both screen display and printing means that your application is WYSIWYG: "What you see is what you get." However, suppose you aren't writing a WYSIWYG application. For example, consider a text editor that uses a bold font for printing but displays control codes to indicate bold text on the screen. In such a situation, you use **OnDraw** strictly for screen display. When you override **OnPrint**, substitute the call to **OnDraw** with a call to a separate drawing function. That function draws the document the way it appears on paper, using the attributes that you don't display on the screen.

Printer Pages vs. Document Pages

When you refer to page numbers, it's sometimes necessary to distinguish between the printer's concept of a page and a document's concept of a page. From the point of view of the printer, a page is one sheet of paper. However, one sheet of paper doesn't necessarily equal one page of the document. For example, if you're printing a newsletter, where the sheets are to be folded, one sheet of paper might contain both the first and last pages of the document, side by side. Similarly, if you're printing a spreadsheet, the document doesn't consist of pages at all; instead, one sheet of paper might contain rows 1 through 20, columns 6 through 10.

All the page numbers in the **CPrintInfo** structure refer to printer pages. The framework calls **OnPrepareDC** and **OnPrint** once for each sheet of paper that will pass through the printer. When you override the **OnPreparePrinting** function to specify the length of the document, you must use printer pages. If there is a one-to-one correspondence (that is, one printer page equals one document page), then this is easy. If, on the other hand, document pages and printer pages do not directly correspond, you must translate between them. For example, consider printing a spreadsheet. When overriding **OnPreparePrinting**, you must calculate how many sheets of paper will be required to print the entire spreadsheet and then use that value when calling the **SetMaxPage** member function of **CPrintInfo**. Similarly, when overriding **OnPrepareDC**, you must translate **m_nCurPage** into the range of rows and columns that will appear on that particular sheet and then adjust the viewport origin accordingly.

Print-Time Pagination

In some situations, your view class may not know in advance how long the document is until it has actually been printed. For example, suppose your application isn't WYSIWYG, so a document's length on the screen doesn't correspond to its length when printed.

This causes a problem when you override **OnPreparePrinting** for your view class: you can't pass a value to the **SetMaxPage** function of the **CPrintInfo** structure, because you don't know the length of a document. If the user doesn't specify a page number to stop at using the Print dialog box, the framework doesn't know when to stop the print loop. The only way to determine when to stop the print loop is to print out the document and see when it ends; your view class must check for the end of the document while it is being printed, and then inform the framework when the end is reached.

The framework relies on your view class's **OnPrepareDC** function to tell it when to stop. After each call to **OnPrepareDC**, the framework checks a member of the **CPrintInfo** structure called **m_bContinuePrinting**. Its default value is **TRUE**; as long as it remains so, the framework continues the print loop. If it is set to **FALSE**, the framework stops. To perform print-time pagination, override **OnPrepareDC** to check whether the end of the document has been reached, and set **m_bContinuePrinting** to **FALSE** when it has.

The default implementation of **OnPrepareDC** sets **m_bContinuePrinting** to **FALSE** if the current page is greater than 1. This means that if the length of the document wasn't specified, the framework assumes the document is one page long. One consequence of this is that you must be careful if you call the base class version of **OnPrepareDC**; do not assume that **m_bContinuePrinting** will be **TRUE** after calling the base class version.

See Also   Articles: "Printing: Headers and Footers," "Printing: Allocating GDI Resources"

In the *Class Library Reference*: **CView**, **CDC**

Printing: Headers and Footers

This article explains how to add headers and footers to a printed document.

When you look at a document on the screen, the name of the document and your current location in the document are commonly displayed in a title bar and a status bar. When looking at a printed copy of a document, it's useful to have the name and page number shown in a header or footer. This is a common way in which even WYSIWYG programs differ in how they perform printing and screen display.

The **OnPrint** member function is the appropriate place to print headers or footers because it is called for each page, and because it is called only for printing, not for screen display. You can define a separate function to print a header or footer, and pass it the printer device context from **OnPrint**. You may need to adjust the window origin or extent before calling **OnDraw** to avoid having the body of the page overlap the header or footer. You might also have to modify **OnDraw** because the amount of the document that fits on the page could be reduced.

One way to compensate for the area taken by the header or footer is to use the **m_rectDraw** member of **CPrintInfo**. Each time a page is printed, this member is initialized with the usable area of the page. If you print a header or footer before printing the body of the page, you can reduce the size of the rectangle stored in **m_rectDraw** to account for the area taken by the header or footer. Then **OnPrint** can refer to **m_rectDraw** to find out how much area remains for printing the body of the page.

You cannot print a header, or anything else, from **OnPrepareDC**, because it is called before the **StartPage** member function of **CDC** has been called. At that point, the printer device context is considered to be at a page boundary. You can perform printing only from the **OnPrint** member function.

See Also   Articles: "Printing: Multipage Documents," "Printing: Allocating GDI Resources"

Printing: Allocating GDI Resources

This article explains how to allocate and deallocate the Windows graphics device interface (GDI) objects needed for printing.

Suppose you need to use certain fonts, pens, or other GDI objects for printing, but not for screen display. Because of the memory they require, it's inefficient to allocate these objects when the application starts up. When the application isn't printing a document, that memory might be needed for other purposes. It's better to allocate them when printing begins, and then delete them when printing ends.

To allocate these GDI objects, override the **OnBeginPrinting** member function. This function is well suited to this purpose for two reasons: the framework calls this function once at the beginning of each print job and, unlike **OnPreparePrinting**, this function has access to the **CDC** object representing the printer device driver. You can store these objects for use during the print job by defining member variables in your view class that point to GDI objects (for example, **CFont *** members, and so on).

To use the GDI objects you've created, select them into the printer device context in the **OnPrint** member function. If you need different GDI objects for different pages of the document, you can examine the **m_nCurPage** member of the **CPrintInfo** structure and select the GDI object accordingly. If you need a GDI object for several consecutive pages, Windows requires that you select it into the device context each time **OnPrint** is called.

To deallocate these GDI objects, override the **OnEndPrinting** member function. The framework calls this function at the end of each print job, giving you the opportunity to deallocate printing-specific GDI objects before the application returns to other tasks.

See Also   Article: "Printing: How Default Printing Is Done"

Printing: The Print Preview Architecture

This article explains how the MFC framework implements print preview functionality. Topics covered include:

- The Print Preview Process
- Modifying Print Preview

Print preview is somewhat different from screen display and printing because, instead of directly drawing an image on a device, the application must simulate the printer using the screen. To accommodate this, the Microsoft Foundation Class Library defines a special class derived from **CDC**, called **CPreviewDC**. All **CDC** objects contain two device contexts, but usually they are identical. In a **CPreviewDC** object, they are different: the first represents the printer being simulated, and the second represents the screen on which output is actually displayed.

The Print Preview Process

When the user selects the Print Preview command from the File menu, the framework creates a **CPreviewDC** object. Whenever your application performs an operation that sets a characteristic of the printer device context, the framework also performs a similar operation on the screen device context. For example, if your application selects a font for printing, the framework selects a font for screen display that simulates the printer font. Whenever your application would send output to the printer, the framework instead sends the output to the screen.

Print preview also differs from printing in the order that each draws the pages of a document. During printing, the framework continues a print loop until a certain range of pages has been rendered. During print preview, one or two pages are displayed at any time, and then the application waits; no further pages are displayed until the user responds. During print preview, the application must also respond to **WM_PAINT** messages, just as it does during ordinary screen display.

The **OnPreparePrinting** function is called when preview mode is invoked, just as it is at the beginning of a print job. The **CPrintInfo** structure passed to the function contains several members whose values you can set to adjust certain characteristics of the print preview operation. For example, you can set the **m_nNumPreviewPages** member to specify whether you want to preview the document in one-page or two-page mode.

Modifying Print Preview

You can modify the behavior and appearance of print preview in a number of ways rather easily. For example, you can, among other things:

- Cause the print preview window to display a scroll bar for easy access to any page of the document.

- Cause print preview to maintain the user's position in the document by beginning its display at the current page.

- Cause different initialization to be performed for print preview and printing.

- Cause print preview to display page numbers in your own formats.

If you know how long the document is and call **SetMaxPage** with the appropriate value, the framework can use this information in preview mode as well as during printing. Once the framework knows the length of the document, it can provide the preview window with a scroll bar, allowing the user to page back and forth through the document in preview mode. If you haven't set the length of the document, the framework cannot position the scroll box to indicate the current position, so the framework doesn't add a scroll bar. In this case, the user must use the Next Page and Previous Page buttons on the preview window's control bar to page through the document.

For print preview, you may find it useful to assign a value to the **m_nCurPage** member of **CPrintInfo**, even though you would never do so for ordinary printing. During ordinary printing, this member carries information from the framework to your view class; this is how the framework tells the view which page should be printed.

By contrast, when print preview mode is started, the **m_nCurPage** member carries information in the opposite direction: from the view to the framework. The framework uses the value of this member to determine which page should be previewed first. The default value of this member is 1, so the first page of the document is displayed initially. You can override **OnPreparePrinting** to set this member to the number of the page being viewed at the time the Print Preview command was invoked. This way, the application maintains the user's current position when moving from normal display mode to print preview mode.

Sometimes you may want **OnPreparePrinting** to perform different initialization depending on whether it is called for a print job or for print preview. You can determine this by examining the **m_bPreview** member variable in the **CPrintInfo** structure; this member is set to **TRUE** when print preview is invoked.

The **CPrintInfo** structure also contains a member named **m_strPageDesc**, which is used to format the strings displayed at the bottom of the screen in single-page and multiple-page modes. By default these strings are of the form "Page *n*" and "Pages *n - m*," but you can modify **m_strPageDesc** from within **OnPreparePrinting** and set the strings to something more elaborate. See **CPrintInfo** in the *Class Library Reference* for more information.

See Also   Article: "Printing"

In the *Class Library Reference*: **CView**, **CDC**

Property Sheets

The Microsoft Foundation Class Library (MFC) contains support for property sheets, also known as "tab dialog boxes." This article explains how and when to use property sheets in your MFC applications. Topics include:

- Using property sheets in your application
- Adding controls to a property sheet

A property sheet is a special kind of dialog box that is generally used to modify the attributes of some external object, such as the current selection in a view. The property sheet has three main parts: the containing dialog box, one or more property pages shown one at a time, and a tab at the top of each page that the user clicks to select that page. Property sheets are useful for situations where you have a number of similar groups of settings or options to change. An example of a property sheet is the Project Settings dialog box in Visual C++. In this case, there are a number of different groups of options that need to be set. The property sheet allows a large amount of information to be grouped in an easily understood fashion.

Using Property Sheets in Your Application

To use a property sheet in your application, complete the following steps:

1. Create a dialog template resource for each property page. Keep in mind that the user may be switching from one page to another, so lay out each page as consistently as possible.

   The dialog templates for all pages do not have to be the same size. The first page you add to the property sheet should be the largest, as the framework uses the size of the first page to determine how much space to allocate in the property sheet for the property pages.

   When you create the dialog template resource for a property page, you must specify the following styles in the Dialog Properties property sheet:

   - Set the Style list box on the Styles page to Child.
   - Set the Border list box on the Styles page to Thin.
   - Ensure that the Disabled and Titlebar check boxes on the Styles page are checked.
   - Set the Caption edit box on the General page to the text you wish to appear in the tab for this page.

2. Use ClassWizard to create a **CPropertyPage**-derived class corresponding to each property page dialog template. To do this, choose ClassWizard from the Project menu while the focus is on a particular property page dialog box. Choose **CPropertyPage** as the base class in ClassWizard.

3. Using ClassWizard, create member variables to hold the values for this property page. The process for adding member variables to a property page is exactly the same as adding member variables to a dialog box, since a property page is a specialized dialog box.

4. Implement a **CPropertySheet** object in your source code. Usually, you implement the **CPropertySheet** object in the handler for the command that displays the property sheet. This object represents the entire property sheet. If you implement a modal property sheet with the **DoModal** function, the framework supplies four pushbuttons by default: OK, Cancel, Apply Now, and Help. The framework creates no pushbuttons for modeless property sheets created with the **Create** function. You do not need to derive a class from **CPropertySheet** unless you want to either add other controls (such as a preview window) or display a modeless property sheet. This step is necessary for modeless property sheets since they do not contain any default controls that could be used to close the property sheet.

5. For each page to be added to the property sheet, do the following:

   - Construct one object for each **CPropertyPage**-derived class that you created using ClassWizard earlier in this process.

   - Call **CPropertySheet::AddPage** for each page.

   Typically, the object that creates the **CPropertySheet** also creates the **CPropertyPage** objects in this step. However, if you implement a **CPropertySheet**-derived class, you can embed the **CPropertyPage** objects in the **CPropertySheet** object and call **AddPage** for each page from the **CPropertySheet**-derived class constructor. **AddPage** adds the **CPropertyPage** object to the property sheet's list of pages but does not actually create the window for that page. Therefore, it is not necessary to wait until creation of the property sheet window to call **AddPage**; you can call **AddPage** from the property sheet's constructor.

6. Call **CPropertySheet::DoModal** or **Create** to display the property sheet. Call **DoModal** to create a property sheet as a modal dialog box. Call **Create** to create the property sheet as a modeless dialog box.

7. Exchange data between property pages and the owner of the property sheet. This is explained in the article "Property Sheets: Exchanging Data."

For an example of how to use property sheets, see the PROPDLG sample under MFC Samples in Books Online.

Adding Controls to a Property Sheet

By default, a property sheet allocates window area for the property pages, the tab index, and the OK, Cancel, Apply Now, and Help buttons. (A modeless property sheet does not have the OK, Cancel, Apply Now, and Help buttons.) You can add other controls to the property sheet. For example, you can add a preview window to the right of the property page area, to show the user what the current settings would look like if applied to an external object.

You can add controls to the property sheet dialog in the **OnCreate** handler. Accommodating additional controls usually requires expanding the size of the property sheet dialog. After calling the base class **CPropertySheet::OnCreate**, call **GetWindowRect** to get the width and height of the currently allocated property sheet window, expand the rectangle's dimensions, and call **MoveWindow** to change the size of the property sheet window.

For more information on property sheets, see the following articles:

- Property Sheets: Exchanging Data
- Property Sheets: Creating a Modeless Property Sheet
- Property Sheets: Handling the Apply Now Button

See Also   In the *Class Library Reference*: **CPropertyPage**, **CPropertySheet**

Property Sheets: Exchanging Data

As with most dialog boxes, the exchange of data between the property sheet and the application is one of the most important functions of the property sheet. This article describes how to accomplish this task.

Exchanging data with a property sheet is actually a matter of exchanging data with the individual property pages of the property sheet. The procedure for exchanging data with a property page is the same as for exchanging data with a dialog box, since a **CPropertyPage** object is just a specialized **CDialog** object. The procedure takes advantage of the framework's dialog data exchange (DDX) facility, which exchanges data between controls in a dialog box and member variables of the dialog box object.

The important difference between exchanging data with a property sheet and with a normal dialog box is that the property sheet has multiple pages, so you must exchange data with all the pages in the property sheet. For more information on DDX, see "Dialog Data Exchange and Validation" on page 87 in Chapter 4.

The following example illustrates exchanging data between a view and two pages of a property sheet:

```
void CMyView::DoModalPropertySheet()
{
    CPropertySheet propsheet;
    CMyFirstPage pageFirst; // derived from CPropertyPage
    CMySecondPage pageSecond; // derived from CPropertyPage
```

```
        // Move member data from the view (or from the currently
        // selected object in the view, for example).
        pageFirst.m_nMember1 = m_nMember1;
        pageFirst.m_nMember2 = m_nMember2;

        pageSecond.m_strMember3 = m_strMember3;
        pageSecond.m_strMember4 = m_strMember4;

        propsheet.AddPage(&pageFirst);
        propsheet.AddPage(&pageSecond);

        if (propsheeet.DoModal() == IDOK)
        {
            m_nMember1 = pageFirst.m_nMember1;
            m_nMember2 = pageFirst.m_nMember2;
            m_nMember3 = pageSecond.m_strMember1;
            m_nMember4 = pageSecond.m_strMember2;
            GetDocument()->SetModifiedFlag();
            GetDocument()->UpdateAllViews(NULL);
        }
    }
```

See Also   Article: "Property Sheets"

Property Sheets: Creating a Modeless Property Sheet

Normally, the property sheets you create will be modal. When using a modal property sheet, the user must close the property sheet before using any other part of the application. This article describes methods you can use to create a modeless property sheet that allows the user to keep the property sheet open while using other parts of the application.

To display a property sheet as a modeless dialog box instead of as a modal dialog box, call **CPropertySheet::Create** instead of **DoModal**. However, there are some extra tasks that you must implement to support a modeless property sheet.

One of the additional tasks is exchanging data between the property sheet and the external object it is modifying when the property sheet is open. This is generally the same task as for standard modeless dialog boxes. Part of this task is implementing a channel of communication between the modeless property sheet and the external object to which the property settings apply. This implementation is far easier if you derive a class from **CPropertySheet** for your modeless property sheet. This article assumes you have done so.

One method for communicating between the modeless property sheet and the external object (the current selection in a view, for example) is to define a pointer from the property sheet to the external object. Define a function (called something like SetMyExternalObject) in the **CPropertySheet**-derived class to change the pointer whenever the focus changes from one external object to another. The SetMyExternalObject function needs to reset the settings for each property page to reflect the newly selected external object. To accomplish this, the SetMyExternalObject function must be able to access the **CPropertyPage** objects belonging to the **CPropertySheet** class.

The most convenient way to provide access to property pages within a property sheet is to embed the **CPropertyPage** objects in the **CPropertySheet**-derived object. Embedding **CPropertyPage** objects in the **CPropertySheet**-derived object differs from the typical design for modal dialog boxes, where the owner of the property sheet creates the **CPropertyPage** objects and passes them to the property sheet via **CPropertySheet::AddPage**.

There are many user-interface alternatives for determining when the settings of the modeless property sheet should be applied to an external object. One alternative is to apply the settings of the current property page whenever the user changes any value. Another alternative is to provide an Apply Now button, which allows the user to accumulate changes in the property pages before committing them to the external object. For information on ways to handle the Apply Now button, see the article "Property Sheets: Handling the Apply Now Button."

See Also   Articles: "Property Sheets," "Property Sheets: Exchanging Data," "Life Cycle of a Dialog Box" (in Chapter 4)

Property Sheets: Handling the Apply Now Button

Property sheets have a capability that standard dialog boxes do not: they allow the user to apply changes they have made before closing the property sheet. This is done using the Apply Now button. This article discusses methods you can use to properly implement this feature.

Modal dialog boxes usually apply the settings to an external object when the user clicks OK to close the dialog box. The same is true for a property sheet: when the user clicks OK, the new settings in the property sheet take effect.

However, you may want to allow the user to save settings without having to close the property sheet dialog box. This is the function of the Apply Now button. The Apply Now button applies the current settings in all of the property pages to the external object, as opposed to applying only the current settings of the currently active page.

By default, the Apply Now button is always disabled. You must write code to enable the Apply Now button at the appropriate times, and you must write code to implement the effect of Apply Now, as explained below.

If you do not wish to offer the Apply Now functionality to the user, it is not necessary to remove the Apply Now button. You can leave it disabled, as will be common among applications that use standard property sheet support available in future versions of Windows.

To report a page as being modified and enable the Apply Now button, call **CPropertyPage::SetModified(TRUE)**. If any of the pages report being modified, the Apply Now button will remain enabled, regardless of whether the currently active page has been modified.

You should call **CPropertyPage::SetModified** whenever the user changes any settings in the page. One way to detect when a user changes a setting in the page is to implement change notification handlers for each of the controls in the property page, such as **EN_CHANGE** or **BN_CLICKED**.

To implement the effect of the Apply Now button, the property sheet must tell its owner, or some other external object in the application, to apply the current settings in the property pages. At the same time, the property sheet should disable the Apply Now button by calling **CPropertyPage::SetModified(FALSE)** for all pages that applied their modifications to the external object.

For an example of this process, see the PROPDLG sample under MFC Samples in Books Online.

See Also   Article: "Property Sheets"

Record

A record is a collection of data about a single entity, such as an account or a customer, stored in a table (a "row" of the table). A record consists of a group of contiguous columns (sometimes called fields) that contain data of various types. A set of records selected from a data source—often called a "result set" in database terms—is called a "recordset" in MFC. See the article "Recordset" for more details.

Record Field Exchange

The MFC database classes automate moving data between the data source and a recordset using a mechanism called "record field exchange" (RFX). RFX is similar to dialog data exchange (DDX). Moving data between a data source and the field data members of a recordset requires multiple calls to the recordset's **DoFieldExchange** function and considerable interaction between the framework and ODBC. The RFX mechanism is type-safe and saves you the work of calling ODBC functions such as **::SQLBindCol**. (For more information about DDX, see Chapter 12 in the *Visual C++ User's Guide*.)

RFX is mostly transparent to you. If you declare your recordset classes with AppWizard or ClassWizard, RFX is built into them automatically. All recordset classes are derived from the base class **CRecordset** supplied by the framework. AppWizard lets you create an initial recordset class. ClassWizard lets you add other recordset classes as you need them. You use ClassWizard to map recordset field data members to table columns on the data source. For more information and examples, see the article "ClassWizard: Creating a Recordset Class."

You must manually add a small amount of RFX code in three cases—when you want to:

- Use parameterized queries. See the article "Recordset: Parameterizing a Recordset."
- Perform joins—using one recordset for columns from two or more tables. See the article "Recordset: Performing a Join."
- Bind data columns dynamically. This is less common than parameterization. See the article "Recordset: Dynamically Binding Data Columns."

If you need a more advanced understanding of RFX, see the article "Record Field Exchange: How RFX Works."

The following articles explain the details of using recordset objects:

- Record Field Exchange: Using RFX
- Record Field Exchange: Using the RFX Functions

■ Record Field Exchange: How RFX Works

See Also Articles: "Recordset," "ClassWizard: Creating a Recordset Class," "AppWizard: Database Support"

In the *Class Library Reference*: **CRecordset**

Record Field Exchange: Using RFX

This article explains what you do to use RFX in relation to what the framework does. The related article, "Record Field Exchange: Working with the Wizard Code," continues the discussion. That article introduces the main components of RFX and explains the code that AppWizard and ClassWizard write to support RFX and how you might want to modify the wizard code.

Writing calls to the RFX functions in your **DoFieldExchange** override is explained in the article "Record Field Exchange: Using the RFX Functions."

Table 1 shows your role in relation to what the framework does for you.

Table 1   Using RFX: You and the Framework

You...	The framework...
Declare your recordset classes with ClassWizard. Specify names and data types of field data members.	ClassWizard derives a **CRecordset** class and writes a **DoFieldExchange** override for you, including an RFX function call for each field data member.
(Optional) Manually add any needed parameter data members to the class. Manually add an RFX function call to **DoFieldExchange** for each parameter data member, add a call to **CFieldExchange::SetFieldType** for the group of parameters, and specify the total number of parameters in **m_nParams**. See "Recordset: Parameterizing a Recordset."	
(Optional) Manually bind additional columns to field data members. Manually increment **m_nFields**. See "Recordset: Dynamically Binding Data Columns."	
Construct an object of your recordset class. Before using the object, set the values of its parameter data members, if any.	For efficiency, the framework prebinds the parameters, using ODBC. When you pass parameter values, the framework passes them to the data source. Only the parameter values are sent for requeries, unless the sort and/or filter strings have changed.

Table 1   Using RFX: You and the Framework (*continued*)

You...	The framework...
Open a recordset object using **CRecordset::Open**.	Executes the recordset's query, binds columns to field data members of the recordset, and calls **DoFieldExchange** to exchange data between the first selected record and the recordset's field data members.
Scroll in the recordset using **CRecordset::Move** or a menu or toolbar command.	Calls **DoFieldExchange** to transfer data to the field data members from the new current record.
Add, update, and delete records.	Calls **DoFieldExchange** to transfer data to the data source.

See Also

Articles: "Record Field Exchange: How RFX Works," "Recordset: Obtaining SUMs and Other Aggregate Results"

In the *Class Library Reference*: **CRecordset**, **CFieldExchange**, "Macros and Globals"

Record Field Exchange: Working with the Wizard Code

This article explains the code that AppWizard and ClassWizard write to support RFX and how you might want to alter that code.

When you create a recordset class with ClassWizard (or with AppWizard), the wizard writes the following RFX-related elements for you, based on the data source, table, and column choices you make in the wizard:

- Declarations of the recordset field data members in the recordset class.
- An override of **CRecordset::DoFieldExchange**.
- Initialization of recordset field data members in the recordset class constructor.

The Field Data Member Declarations

The wizards write a recordset class declaration in an .H file that resembles the following for class `CSections`:

```
class CSections : public CRecordset
{
public:
    CSections(CDatabase* pDatabase);
    CSections::~CSections();

// Field/Param Data
    //{{AFX_FIELD(CSections, CRecordset)
    CString m_strCourseID;
    CString m_strInstructorID;
    CString m_strRoomNo;
    CString m_strSchedule;
    CString m_strSectionNo;
    //}}AFX_FIELD

// Implementation
protected:
    virtual CString GetDefaultConnect(); // Default connection string
    virtual CString GetDefaultSQL();     // Default SQL for Recordset
    virtual void DoFieldExchange(CFieldExchange* pFX);  // RFX support
    DECLARE_DYNAMIC(CSections)
};
```

Notice the following key features about the class above:

- Special "//{{AFX_FIELD" comments that bracket the field data member declarations. ClassWizard uses these to update your source file.

- The wizard overrides the **DoFieldExchange** member function of class **CRecordset**.

Caution Never edit the code inside "//{{AFX" brackets. Always use ClassWizard. If you add parameter data members or new field data members that you bind yourself, add them outside the brackets.

The DoFieldExchange Override

DoFieldExchange is the heart of RFX. The framework calls **DoFieldExchange** any time it needs to move data either from data source to recordset or from recordset to data source. **DoFieldExchange** also supports obtaining information about field data members through the **IsFieldDirty** and **IsFieldNull** member functions.

The following **DoFieldExchange** override is for the CSections class. ClassWizard writes the function in the .CPP file for your recordset class.

```
void CSections::DoFieldExchange(CFieldExchange* pFX)
{
    //{{AFX_FIELD_MAP(CSections)
    pFX->SetFieldType(CFieldExchange::outputColumn);
    RFX_Text(pFX, "CourseID", m_strCourseID);
    RFX_Text(pFX, "InstructorID", m_strInstructorID);
    RFX_Text(pFX, "RoomNo", m_strRoomNo);
    RFX_Text(pFX, "Schedule", m_strSchedule);
    RFX_Text(pFX, "SectionNo", m_strSectionNo);
    //}}AFX_FIELD_MAP
}
```

Notice the following key features of the function:

- The special "//{{AFX_FIELD_MAP" comments. ClassWizard uses these to update your source file. This section of the function is called the "field map."

- A call to **CFieldExchange::SetFieldType**, through the *pFX* pointer. This call specifies that all RFX function calls up to the end of **DoFieldExchange** or the next call to **SetFieldType** are "output columns." See **CFieldExchange::SetFieldType** in the *Class Library Reference* for more information.

- Several calls to the **RFX_Text** global function—one per field data member (all of which are **CString** variables in the example). These calls specify the relationship between a column name on the data source and a field data member. The RFX functions do the actual data transfer. The class library supplies RFX functions for all of the common data types. For more information about RFX functions, see the article "Record Field Exchange: Using the RFX Functions."

Note The order of the columns in your result set must match the order of the RFX function calls in `DoFieldExchange`.

- The *pFX* pointer to a **CFieldExchange** object that the framework passes when it calls **DoFieldExchange**. The **CFieldExchange** object specifies the operation that **DoFieldExchange** is to perform, the direction of transfer, and other context information.

The Recordset Constructor

The recordset constructor that the wizards write contains two things related to RFX:

- An initialization for each field data member.

- An initialization for the **m_nFields** data member, which contains the number of field data members.

The constructor for the `CSections` recordset example looks like this:

```
CSections::CSections(CDatabase* pdb)
    : CRecordset(pdb)
{
    //{{AFX_FIELD_INIT(CSections)
    m_strCourseID = "";
    m_strInstructorID = "";
    m_strRoomNo = "";
    m_strSchedule = "";
    m_strSectionNo = "";
    m_nFields = 5;
    //}}AFX_FIELD_INIT
}
```

Important If you add any field data members manually, as you might if you bind new columns dynamically, you must increment **m_nFields**. Do so with another line of code outside the "//{{AFX_FIELD_INIT" brackets:

```
m_nFields += 3;
```

This is the code for adding three new fields. If you add any parameter data members, you must initialize the **m_nParams** data member, which contains the number of parameter data members. Put the **m_nParams** initialization outside the brackets.

See Also   Article: "Record Field Exchange: Using the RFX Functions"

Record Field Exchange: Using the RFX Functions

This article explains how to use the RFX function calls that make up the body of your **DoFieldExchange** override.

The RFX global functions exchange data between columns on the data source and field data members in your recordset. Normally you use ClassWizard to write the RFX function calls in your recordset's **DoFieldExchange** member function. This article describes the functions briefly and shows the data types for which RFX functions are available. Technical Note 43 under MFC in Books Online describes how to write your own RFX functions for additional data types.

RFX Function Syntax

Each RFX function takes three parameters (and some take an optional fourth or fifth parameter):

- A pointer to a **CFieldExchange** object. You simply pass along the *pFX* pointer passed to **DoFieldExchange**.
- The name of the column as it appears on the data source.

- The name of the corresponding field data member or parameter data member in the recordset class.

- (Optional) In some of the functions, the maximum length of the string or array being transferred. This defaults to 255 bytes, but you might want to change it. The maximum size is based on the maximum size of a **CString** object— **INT_MAX** (2,147,483,647) bytes—but you will probably encounter driver limits before that size.

- (Optional) In the **RFX_Text** function, you sometimes use a fifth parameter to specify the data type of a column.

For more information, see the RFX functions under "Macros and Globals" in the *Class Library Reference*. For an example of when you might make special use of the parameters, see the article "Recordset: Obtaining SUMs and Other Aggregate Results."

RFX Data Types

The class library supplies RFX functions for transferring many different data types between the data source and your recordsets. The following list summarizes the RFX functions by data type. In cases where you must write your own RFX function calls, select from these functions by data type.

Function	Data Type
RFX_Bool	**BOOL**
RFX_Byte	**BYTE**
RFX_Binary	**CByteArray**
RFX_Double	**double**
RFX_Single	**float**
RFX_Int	**int**
RFX_Long	**long**
RFX_LongBinary	**CLongBinary**
RFX_Text	**CString**
RFX_Date	**CTime**

For more information, see the RFX function documentation under "Macros and Globals" in the *Class Library Reference*. For information about how C++ data types map to SQL data types, see Table 1 in the article "SQL: SQL and C++ Data Types."

See Also   Articles: "Record Field Exchange: How RFX Works," "Recordset: Parameterizing a Recordset," "Recordset: Dynamically Binding Data Columns," "Recordset: Obtaining SUMs and Other Aggregate Results"

In the *Class Library Reference*: **CRecordset**, **CFieldExchange**

Record Field Exchange: How RFX Works

This article explains the RFX process. This is a fairly advanced topic, covering:

- RFX and the recordset
- The RFX process

RFX and the Recordset

The recordset object's field data members, taken together, constitute an "edit buffer" that holds the selected columns of one record. When the recordset is first opened and is about to read the first record, RFX binds (associates) each selected column to the address of the appropriate field data member. When the recordset updates a record, RFX calls ODBC API functions to send an SQL **UPDATE** or **INSERT** statement to the driver. RFX uses its knowledge of the field data members to specify the columns to write.

The framework backs up the edit buffer at certain stages so it can restore its contents if necessary. RFX backs up the edit buffer before adding a new record and before editing an existing record. It restores the edit buffer in some cases—for example, after an **Update** call following **AddNew**, but not if you abandon a newly changed edit buffer by, for example, moving to another record before calling **Update**.

Besides exchanging data between the data source and the recordset's field data members, RFX manages binding parameters. When the recordset is opened, any parameter data members are bound in the order of the "?" placeholders in the SQL statement that **CRecordset::Open** constructs. For more information, see the article "Recordset: Parameterizing a Recordset."

Your recordset class's override of **DoFieldExchange** does all the work, moving data in both directions. Like dialog data exchange (DDX), RFX needs information about the data members of your class. ClassWizard provides the necessary information by writing a recordset-specific implementation of **DoFieldExchange** for you, based on the field data member names and data types you specify with the wizard.

The Record Field Exchange Process

This section describes the sequence of RFX events as a recordset object is opened and as you add, update, and delete records. Table 1 in the article "Record Field Exchange: Using RFX" shows the process at a high level, illustrating operations as a recordset is opened. Table 1 and Table 2 in this article show the process as RFX processes a **Move** command in the recordset and as RFX manages an update. During these processes, **DoFieldExchange** is called to perform many different operations. The **m_nOperation** data member of the **CFieldExchange** object determines which operation is requested. You might find it helpful to read the articles "Recordset: How Recordsets Select Records" and "Recordset: How Recordsets Update Records" before you read this material.

RFX: Initial Binding of Columns and Parameters

The following RFX activities occur, in the order shown, when you call a recordset object's **Open** member function:

- If the recordset has parameter data members, the framework calls **DoFieldExchange** to "bind" the parameters to parameter placeholders in the recordset's SQL statement string. A data type-dependent representation of the value of the parameter is used for each placeholder found in the **SELECT** statement. This occurs after the SQL statement is "prepared" but before it is executed. (For information about statement preparation, see the **::SQLPrepare** function in the ODBC *Programmer's Reference*.)

- The framework calls **DoFieldExchange** a second time to bind the values of selected columns to corresponding field data members in the recordset. This establishes the recordset object as an edit buffer containing the columns of the first record.

- The recordset executes the SQL statement and the data source selects the first record. The record's columns are loaded into the recordset's field data members.

Table 1 shows the sequence of RFX operations when you open a recordset.

Table 1   Sequence of RFX Operations During Recordset Open

Your operation	DoFieldExchange operation	Database/SQL operation
1. Open recordset.		
	2. Build an SQL statement.	
		3. Send the SQL.
	4. Bind parameter data member(s).	
	5. Bind field data member(s) to column(s).	
		6. ODBC does the move and fills in the data.
	7. Fix up the data for C++.	

Recordsets use ODBC's "prepared execution" to allow for fast requerying with the same SQL statement. For more information about prepared execution, see the ODBC SDK *Programmer's Reference*.

RFX: Scrolling

When you scroll from one record to another, the framework calls **DoFieldExchange** to replace the values previously stored in the field data members with values for the new record.

Table 2 shows the sequence of RFX operations when the user moves from record to record.

Table 2   Sequence of RFX Operations During Scrolling

Your operation	DoFieldExchange operation	Database/SQL operation
1. Call **MoveNext** or one of the other Move functions.		
		2. ODBC does the move and fills in the data.
	3. Fix up the data for C++.	

RFX: Adding New Records and Editing Existing Records

If you add a new record, the recordset operates as an edit buffer to build up the contents of the new record. As with adding records, editing records involves changing the values of the recordset's field data members. From the RFX perspective, the sequence is as follows:

1. Your call to the recordset's **AddNew** or **Edit** member function causes RFX to store the current edit buffer so it can be restored later.

2. **AddNew** or **Edit** prepares the fields in the edit buffer so RFX can detect changed field data members.

   Since a new record has no previous values to compare new ones with, **AddNew** sets the value of each field data member to a **PSEUDO_NULL** value. Later, when you call **Update**, RFX compares each data member's value with the **PSEUDO_NULL** value; if there's a difference, the data member has been set. (**PSEUDO_NULL** is not the same thing as a record column with a true Null value; nor is either the same as C++ **NULL**.)

   Unlike the **Update** call for **AddNew**, the **Update** call for **Edit** compares updated values with previously stored values rather than using **PSEUDO_NULL**. The difference is that **AddNew** has no previous stored values for comparison.

3. You directly set the values of field data members whose values you want to edit or that you want filled for a new record. (This can include calling **SetFieldNull**.)

4. Your call to **Update** checks for changed field data members, as described in step 2 (see Table 2 above). If none have changed, **Update** returns 0. If some

field data members have changed, **Update** prepares and executes an SQL **INSERT** statement that contains values for all updated fields in the record.

5. For **AddNew**, **Update** concludes by restoring the previously stored values of the record that was current before the **AddNew** call. For **Edit**, the new, edited values remain in place.

Table 3 shows the sequence of RFX operations when you add a new record or edit an existing record.

Table 3   Sequence of RFX Operations During AddNew and Edit

Your operation	DoFieldExchange operation	Database/SQL operation
1. Call **AddNew** or **Edit**.		
	2. Back up the edit buffer.	
	3. For **AddNew**, mark field data members as "clean" and Null.	
4. Assign values to recordset field data members.		
5. Call **Update**.		
	6. Check for changed fields.	
	7. Build SQL **INSERT** statement for **AddNew** or **UPDATE** statement for **Edit**.	
		8. Send the SQL.
	9. For **AddNew**, restore the edit buffer to its backed-up contents. For **Edit**, delete the backup.	

RFX: Deleting Existing Records

When you delete a record, RFX sets all the fields to **NULL** as a reminder that the record is deleted and you must move off it. You won't need any other RFX sequence information.

See Also   Article: "ClassWizard"

In the *Class Library Reference*: **CFieldExchange**, **CRecordset::DoFieldExchange**, "Macros and Globals"

Recordset

A **CRecordset** object represents a set of records selected from a data source. The records can be from:

- A table.
- A query.
- A stored procedure that accesses one or more tables.

An example of a recordset based on a table is "all customers," which accesses a Customer table. An example of a query is "all invoices for Joe Smith." An example of a recordset based on a stored procedure (sometimes called a predefined query) is "all of the delinquent accounts," which invokes a stored procedure in the back-end database. A recordset can join two or more tables from the same data source, but not from different data sources.

Note Some ODBC drivers support "views" of the database. A view in this sense is a query originally created with the SQL **CREATE VIEW** statement. AppWizard and ClassWizard don't currently support views, but it is possible to code this support yourself.

Recordset Capabilities

All recordset objects share the following capabilities:

- If the data source is not read-only, you can specify that your recordset be updatable, appendable, or read-only. If the recordset is updatable, you can choose either pessimistic or optimistic locking methods, provided the driver supplies the appropriate locking support. If the data source is read-only, the recordset will be read-only.
- You can call member functions to scroll through the selected records.
- You can filter the records to constrain which records are selected from those available.
- You can sort the records in ascending or descending order, based on one or more columns.
- You can parameterize the recordset in order to qualify the recordset selection at run time.

Snapshots and Dynasets

There are two principal kinds of recordsets: snapshots and dynasets, both supported by class **CRecordset**. Each shares the common characteristics of all recordsets, but each also extends the common functionality in its own specialized way. Snapshots provide a static view of the data and are useful for reports and other situations in which you want a view of the data as it existed at a particular time. Dynasets provide a dynamic view of the data and are necessary if you want records to reflect updates made by other users or via other recordsets in your own application (without having to "requery" or "refresh" the recordset, except that you must requery to see records added by other users). Both can be updatable or read-only.

CRecordset also allows for a third kind of recordset, a "forward-only recordset." If you do both of the following

- Pass the option **CRecordset::forwardOnly** as the *nOpenType* parameter of the **Open** member function

- Pass **CRecordset::readOnly** as the *dwOptions* parameter to **Open**

you get a recordset that doesn't allow updates or backward scrolling. Use this kind of recordset for less program overhead when you don't need backward scrolling. For example, you might use a forward-only recordset to migrate data from one data source to another, where you only need to move through the data in a forward direction.

Important For information about ODBC driver requirements for dynaset support, see the article "ODBC." Currently the ODBC drivers supplied with Visual C++ do not support dynasets.

Your Recordsets

For every distinct table, view, or stored procedure you wish to access, you must define a class derived from **CRecordset**, normally with the help of ClassWizard. (The exception is a database join, in which one recordset represents columns from two or more tables.) When you declare a recordset class with ClassWizard, you also enable the record field exchange (RFX) mechanism. RFX simplifies transfer of data from the data source into your recordset and from your recordset to the data source, much as the dialog data exchange (DDX) mechanism does.

A recordset object gives you access to all the selected records. You scroll through the multiple selected records using **CRecordset** member functions, such as **MoveNext** and **MovePrev**. At the same time, a recordset object represents only one of the selected records, the "current record." You can examine the fields of the current record by declaring recordset class member variables that correspond to columns of the table or of the records that result from the database query. ClassWizard helps you declare these recordset class data members. You update a record by scrolling to it—making it the current record—and changing the values of these data members. For details about recordset data members, see the article "Recordset: Architecture."

ISAM Database Support

Visual C++ does not provide ODBC drivers capable of accessing Indexed Sequential Access Method (ISAM) data formats. However, you can obtain the Microsoft ODBC Driver Fulfillment Kit (32-Bit), which contains 32-bit ODBC drivers for many common data formats, including:

- Microsoft Access
- dBASE®
- Microsoft FoxPro®
- BTrieve®
- Paradox™

Other drivers are also available from other sources. You can create MFC recordsets using any of these drivers. For information about obtaining ODBC Driver Pack version 2.0, see the article "Database Overview"

The articles listed below explain the details of using recordset objects. The articles are listed in functional categories and a natural browse order to permit sequential reading.

Articles about the mechanics of opening, reading, and closing recordsets:

- Recordset: Architecture
- Recordset: Declaring a Class for a Table
- Recordset: Creating and Closing Recordsets
- Recordset: Scrolling
- Recordset: Filtering Records
- Recordset: Sorting Records
- Recordset: Parameterizing a Recordset

Articles about the mechanics of modifying recordsets:

- Recordset: Adding, Updating, and Deleting Records
- Recordset: Locking Records
- Recordset: Requerying a Recordset

Articles about somewhat more advanced techniques:

- Recordset: Performing a Join
- Recordset: Declaring a Class for a Predefined Query
- Recordset: Dynamically Binding Data Columns
- Recordset: Working with Large Data Items

- Recordset: Obtaining SUMs and Other Aggregate Results

Articles about how recordsets work:

- Recordset: How Recordsets Select Records
- Recordset: How Recordsets Update Records

See Also   Articles: "Recordset: Declaring a Class for a Table," "ClassWizard: Creating a Recordset Class," "Record Field Exchange," "Transaction"

Recordset: Architecture

This article describes the data members that comprise the architecture of a recordset object:

- Field data members
- Parameter data members
- **m_nFields** and **m_nParams** data members

A Sample Class

When you use ClassWizard to declare a recordset class derived from **CRecordset**, the resulting class has the general structure shown in the following simple class:

```
class CCourse : CRecordset
{
    //{{AFX_FIELD(CCourse, CRecordset)
    CString m_strCourseID;
    CString m_strCourseTitle;
    //}}AFX_FIELD
    CString m_strIDParam;
};
```

At the beginning of the class, ClassWizard writes a set of "field data members." When you create the class with ClassWizard, you must specify one or more field data members. If the class is parameterized, as the sample class is (with the data member m_strIDParam), you must manually add parameter data members. ClassWizard doesn't support adding parameters to a class.

Field Data Members

The most important members of your recordset class are the field data members. For each column you select from the data source, the class contains a data member of the appropriate data type for that column. For example, the sample class shown at the beginning of this article has two field data members, both of type **CString**, called m_strCourseID and m_strCourseTitle.

When the recordset selects a set of records, the framework automatically "binds" the columns of the "current" record (after the **Open** call, the first record is current) to the field data members of the object. That is, the framework uses the appropriate field data member as a buffer in which to store the contents of a record column.

As the user scrolls to a new record, the framework uses the field data members to represent the current record. The framework refreshes the field data members, replacing the previous record's values. The field data members are also used for updating the current record and for adding new records. As part of the process of updating a record, you specify the update values by assigning values directly to the appropriate field data member(s).

Parameter Data Members

If the class is "parameterized," it has one or more parameter data members. A parameterized class lets you base a recordset query on information obtained or calculated at run time.

Note You must manually place these data members outside the "//{{AFX_FIELD" comment brackets.

Typically, the parameter helps narrow the selection, as in the following example. Based on the sample class at the beginning of this article, the recordset object might execute the following SQL statement:

```
SELECT CourseID, CourseTitle FROM Course WHERE CourseID = ?
```

The "?" is a placeholder for a parameter value that you supply at run time. When you construct the recordset and set its m_strIDParam data member to "MATH101", the effective SQL statement for the recordset becomes:

```
SELECT CourseID, CourseTitle FROM Course WHERE CourseID = MATH101
```

By defining parameter data members, you tell the framework about parameters in the SQL string. The framework binds the parameter, which lets ODBC know where to get values to substitute for the placeholder. In the example, the resulting recordset contains only the record from the Course table with a CourseID column whose value is "MATH101". All specified columns of this record are selected. You can specify as many parameters (and placeholders) as you need.

Note MFC does nothing itself with the parameters—in particular, it doesn't perform a text substitution. Instead, MFC tells ODBC where to get the parameter; ODBC retrieves the data and performs the necessary parameterization.

Important The order of parameters is important. For details about this and more information about parameters, see the article "Recordset: Parameterizing a Recordset."

Using m_nFields and m_nParams

When ClassWizard writes a constructor for your class, it also initializes the **m_nFields** data member, which specifies the number of field data members in the class. If you add any parameters to your class, you must also add an initialization for the **m_nParams** data member, which specifies the number of parameter data members. The framework uses these values to work with the data members.

For more information and examples, see the article "Record Field Exchange: Using RFX."

See Also   Articles: "Recordset: Declaring a Class for a Table," "Record Field Exchange"

Recordset: Declaring a Class for a Table

The most common recordset class opens a single table. To declare a recordset class for a single table, use ClassWizard. In ClassWizard, choose each column you want by naming a corresponding recordset field data member. See the article "ClassWizard: Creating a Recordset Class."

Other uses for recordsets include:

- Joining two or more tables.
- Containing the results of a predefined query.

See Also   Articles: "Recordset: Creating and Closing Recordsets," "Recordset: Declaring a Class for a Predefined Query," "Recordset: Performing a Join"

Recordset: Creating and Closing Recordsets

To use a recordset, you must construct a recordset object, then call its **Open** member function to run the recordset's query and select records. When you finish with the recordset, you must close and destroy the object.

This article explains:

- When and how to create a recordset object.
- When and how you can qualify the recordset's behavior by parameterizing, filtering, sorting, or locking it.
- When and how to close a recordset object.

Creating Recordsets at Run Time

Before you can create recordset objects in your program, you must write application-specific recordset classes. For more information on this preliminary step, see the article "ClassWizard: Creating a Recordset Class."

Open a dynaset or snapshot object when you need to select records from a data source. The type of object to create depends on what you need to do with the data in your application and on what your ODBC driver supports. For more information, see the articles "Dynaset" and "Snapshot."

▶   **To open a recordset**

1. Construct an object of your **CRecordset**-derived class.

   You can construct the object on the heap or on the stack frame of a function.

2. Optionally modify the default recordset behavior. For the available options, see "Setting Recordset Options" later in this article.

3. Call the object's **Open** member function.

In the constructor, pass a pointer to a **CDatabase** object, or pass **NULL** to use a temporary database object that the framework will construct and open based on the connection string returned by the **GetDefaultConnect** member function. The **CDatabase** object may or may not already be connected to a data source.

The call to **Open** uses SQL to select records from the data source. The first record selected (if any) is the "current record." The values of this record's fields are stored in the recordset object's field data members. If any records were selected, both the **IsBOF** and **IsEOF** member functions return 0.

In your **Open** call, you can:

- Specify whether the recordset is a dynaset or snapshot. Recordsets open as snapshots by default. Or you can specify a forward-only recordset, which allows only forward scrolling, one record at a time.

- Specify a string to replace the default SQL **SELECT** statement that the recordset constructs.

- Specify whether the recordset is read-only or append-only. Recordsets allow full updating by default, but you can limit that to adding new records only or you can disallow all updates.

The following example shows how to open a read-only snapshot object, of class CStudentSet, an application-specific class:

```
// Construct the snapshot object
CStudentSet rsStudent( NULL );
// Set options if desired, then open the recordset
if(!rsStudent.Open(CRecordset::snapshot, NULL, CRecordset::readOnly))
    return FALSE;
// Use the snapshot to operate on its records...
```

After you call **Open**, use the member functions and data members of the object to work with the records. In some cases, you may want to "requery" or "refresh" the recordset to include changes that have occurred on the data source. See the article "Recordset: Requerying a Recordset."

Tip   The connect string you use during development might not be the same connect string that your eventual users need. For ideas about generalizing your application in this regard, see the article "Data Source: Managing Connections."

Setting Recordset Options

After you construct your recordset object but before you call **Open** to select records, you may want to set some options to control the recordset's behavior. For all recordsets, you can:

- Specify a filter to constrain record selection. See the article "Recordset: Filtering Records."

- Specify a sort order for the records. See the article "Recordset: Sorting Records."

- Specify parameters so you can select records using information obtained or calculated at run time. See the article "Recordset: Parameterizing a Recordset."

You can also set the following option if conditions are right:

- If the recordset is updatable and supports locking options, specify the locking method used for updates. See the article "Recordset: Locking Records."

Important   To affect record selection, you must set these options before you call the **Open** member function.

Closing a Recordset

When you finish with your recordset, you must dispose of it and deallocate its memory.

▶ **To close a recordset**

1. Call its **Close** member function.
2. Destroy the recordset object.

If you declared it on the stack frame of a function, the object is destroyed automatically when the object goes out of scope. Otherwise, use the **delete** operator.

Close frees the recordset's **HSTMT** handle. It doesn't destroy the C++ object.

See Also   Articles: "Recordset: Scrolling," "Recordset: Adding, Updating, and Deleting Records," "Dynaset," "Snapshot"

Recordset: Scrolling

After you select records, you need to access each record to display it or to use it for calculations, report writing, and so on. Scrolling lets you move from record to record within your recordset.

This article explains:

- How to scroll from one record to another in a recordset.
- Under what circumstances scrolling is and is not supported.

Scrolling from One Record to Another

Recordsets provide several member functions you can use to "scroll" or move from one record to the next, previous, first, or last record, or move *n* records relative to the current position. You can also test whether you have scrolled beyond the first or the last record.

To determine whether scrolling is possible in your recordset, call the **CanScroll** member function of class **CRecordset**.

▶ **To scroll**

- Forward one record: call the **MoveNext** member function.
- Backward one record: call the **MovePrev** member function.
- To the first record in the recordset: call the **MoveFirst** member function.
- To the last record in the recordset: call the **MoveLast** member function.
- *N* records relative to the current position: call the **Move** member function.

▶ **To test for the end or the beginning of the recordset**

- Have you scrolled past the last record? Call the **IsEOF** member function.
- Have you scrolled past the first record (moving backward)? Call the **IsBOF** member function.

For example, the following code uses **IsBOF** and **IsEOF** to detect the limits of a recordset as the code scrolls through it in both directions.

```
// Open a snapshot; first record is current
CEnrollmentSet rsEnrollmentSet( NULL );
rsEnrollmentSet.Open( );
// Deal with empty recordset
if( rsEnrollmentSet.IsEOF( ) )
    return FALSE;
// Scroll to the end of the snapshot
while ( !rsEnrollmentSet.IsEOF( ) )
    rsEnrollmentSet.MoveNext( );
// Past last record, so no record is current
// Move to the last record
rsEnrollmentSet.MoveLast( );
// Scroll to beginning of the snapshot
while( !rsEnrollmentSet.IsBOF( ) )
    rsEnrollmentSet.MovePrev( );
// Past first record, so no record is current
rsEnrollmentSet.MoveFirst( );
// First record (if any) is current again
```

IsEOF returns a nonzero value if the recordset is positioned past the last record. **IsBOF** returns a nonzero value if the recordset is positioned past the first record (before all records). In either case, there is no current record to operate on. If you call **MovePrev** when **IsBOF** is already true, or call **MoveNext** when **IsEOF** is already true, the framework throws a **CDBException**.

Tip In the general case, where records may be deleted by you or by other users (other recordsets), check that both **IsEOF** and **IsBOF** return a nonzero value to detect an empty recordset.

When Scrolling Is Supported

As originally designed, SQL provided only forward scrolling, but ODBC extends scrolling capabilities. The available level of support for scrolling depends on the ODBC driver(s) your application will work with, your driver's ODBC API conformance level, and whether the ODBC Cursor Library is loaded into memory. For more information, see the articles "ODBC" and "ODBC: The ODBC Cursor Library."

Tip You can control whether the cursor library is used. See the *bUseCursorLib* parameter to **CDatabase::Open**.

Note Unlike Microsoft Access and Microsoft Visual Basic, the MFC database classes don't provide a set of **Find** functions for locating the next (or previous) record that meets specified criteria.

See Also Article: "Recordset: Filtering Records"

Recordset: Filtering Records

This article explains how to "filter" a recordset so that it selects only a particular subset of the available records. For example, you might want to select only the class sections for a particular course, such as MATH101. A filter is a "search condition" defined by the contents of an SQL **WHERE** clause. When the framework appends it to the recordset's SQL statement, the **WHERE** clause constrains the selection.

You must establish a recordset object's filter after you construct the object but before you call its **Open** member function (or before you call the **Requery** member function for an existing recordset object whose **Open** member function has been called previously).

▶   **To specify a filter for a recordset object**

1. Construct a new recordset object (or prepare to call **Requery** for an existing object).

2. Set the value of the object's **m_strFilter** data member.

   The filter is a null-terminated string. It contains the contents of the SQL **WHERE** clause but not the keyword **WHERE**. For example, use

   ```
   m_pSet->m_strFilter = "CourseID = 'MATH101'";
   ```

   not

   ```
   m_pSet->m_strFilter = "WHERE CourseID = 'MATH101'";
   ```

   Note The literal string "MATH101" is shown with single quotation marks above. In the ODBC SQL specification, single quotes are used to denote a character string literal. Check your ODBC driver documentation for the quoting requirements of your DBMS in this situation. This syntax is also discussed further near the end of this article.

   ---

3. Set any other options you need, such as sort order, locking mode, or parameters. Specifying a parameter is especially useful. For information on parameterizing your filter, see the article "Recordset: Parameterizing a Recordset."

4. Call **Open** for the new object (or **Requery** for a previously opened object).

Tip Using parameters in your filter is potentially the most efficient method for retrieving records.

Tip Recordset filters are useful for joining tables and for using parameters based on information obtained or calculated at run time.

The recordset selects only those records that meet the search condition you specified. For example, to specify the course filter described above (assuming a variable strCourseID currently set, for instance, to "MATH101"), do the following:

```
// Using the recordset pointed to by m_pSet
// Set the filter
m_pSet->m_strFilter = "CourseID = " + strCourseID;
// Run the query with the filter in place
if( m_pSet->Open( snapshot, NULL, CRecordset::readOnly ) )
    // Use the recordset
```

The recordset contains records for all class sections for MATH101.

Notice how the filter string was set in the example above, using a string variable. This is the typical usage. But suppose you wanted to specify the literal value 100 for the course ID. The following code shows how to set the filter string correctly with a literal value:

```
m_strFilter = "StudentID = '100'";    // correct
```

Note the use of single quote characters; if you set the filter string directly, the filter string is *not*:

```
m_strFilter = "StudentID = 100";    // incorrrect for some drivers
```

The quoting shown above conforms to the ODBC specification, but some DBMSs may require other quote characters. For more information, see the article "SQL: Customizing Your Recordset's SQL Statement."

Note If you choose to override the recordset's default SQL string by passing your own SQL string to **Open**, you should not set a filter if your custom string has a **WHERE** clause. For more information about overriding the default SQL, see the article "SQL: Customizing Your Recordset's SQL Statement."

See Also Articles: "Recordset: Sorting Records," "Recordset: How Recordsets Select Records," "Recordset: Parameterizing a Recordset," "Recordset: How Recordsets Update Records," "Recordset: Locking Records"

Recordset: Sorting Records

This article explains how to sort your recordset. You can specify one or more columns on which to base the sort, and you can specify ascending or descending order (**ASC** or **DESC**; **ASC** is the default) for each specified column. For example, if you specify two columns, the records are sorted first on the first column named, then on the second column named. An SQL **ORDER BY** clause defines a sort.

When the framework appends the **ORDER BY** clause to the recordset's SQL query, the clause controls the selection's ordering.

You must establish a recordset's sort order after you construct the object but before you call its **Open** member function (or before you call the **Requery** member function for an existing recordset object whose **Open** member function has been called previously).

▶ **To specify a sort order for a recordset object**

1. Construct a new recordset object (or prepare to call **Requery** for an existing one).

2. Set the value of the object's **m_strSort** data member.

   The sort is a null-terminated string. It contains the contents of the **ORDER BY** clause but not the keyword **ORDER BY**. For example, use:

   ```
   recordset.m_strSort = "LastName DESC, FirstName DESC";
   ```

   not

   ```
   recordset.m_strSort = "ORDER BY LastName DESC, FirstName DESC";
   ```

3. Set any other options you need, such as a filter, locking mode, or parameters.

4. Call **Open** for the new object (or **Requery** for an existing object).

The selected records are ordered as specified. For example, to sort a set of student records in descending order by last name, then first name, do the following:

```
// Construct the recordset
CStudentSet rsStudent( NULL );
// Set the sort
rsStudent.m_strSort = "LastName DESC, FirstName DESC";
// Run the query with the sort in place
rsStudent.Open( );
```

The recordset contains all of the student records, sorted in descending order (Z to A) by last name, then by first name.

Note If you choose to override the recordset's default SQL string by passing your own SQL string to **Open**, do not set a sort if your custom string has an **ORDER BY** clause.

See Also   Articles: "Recordset: Parameterizing a Recordset," "Recordset: Filtering Records"

Recordset: Parameterizing a Recordset

Sometimes you'd like to be able to select records at run time, using information you've calculated or obtained from your end-user. Recordset parameters let you accomplish that goal.

This article explains:

- The purpose of a parameterized recordset.
- When and why you might want to parameterize a recordset.
- How to declare parameter data members in your recordset class.
- How to pass parameter information to a recordset object at run time.

Parameterized Recordsets

A parameterized recordset lets you pass parameter information at run time. This has two valuable effects:

- It may result in better execution speed.
- It lets you build a query at run time, based on information not available to you at design time, such as information obtained from your user or calculated at run time.

When you call **Open** to run the query, the recordset uses the parameter information to complete its SQL **SELECT** statement. You can parameterize any recordset.

When to Use Parameters

Typical uses for parameters include:

- Passing run-time arguments to a predefined query.

   To pass parameters to a stored procedure, you must specify a complete custom ODBC **CALL** statement—with parameter placeholders—when you call **Open**, overriding the recordset's default SQL statement. See **CRecordset::Open** in the *Class Library Reference* and the articles "SQL: Customizing Your Recordset's SQL Statement" and "Recordset: Declaring a Class for a Predefined Query."

- Efficiently performing numerous requeries with different parameter information.

   For example, each time your end-user looks up information for a particular student in the student registration database, you can specify the student's name or ID as a parameter obtained from the user. Then, when you call your recordset's **Requery** member function, the query selects only that student's record.

   Your recordset's filter string, stored in **m_strFilter**, might look like this:

   ```
   "StudentID = ?"
   ```

Suppose you obtain the student ID in the variable `strInputID`. When you set a parameter to `strInputID` (for example, the student ID 100) the value of the variable is bound to the parameter placeholder represented by the "?" in the filter string.

Assign the parameter value as follows:

```
strInputID = "100";
...
m_strParam = strInputID;
```

Note that you would *not* want to set up a filter string this way:

```
m_strFilter = "StudentID = 100";    // 100 is incorrectly quoted
                                    // for some drivers
```

For a discussion of how to use quotes correctly for filter strings, see the article "Recordset: Filtering Records."

The parameter value is different each time you requery the recordset for a new student ID.

Tip Using a parameter is more efficient than simply a filter. For a parameterized recordset, the database must process an SQL **SELECT** statement only once. For a filtered recordset without parameters, the **SELECT** statement must be processed each time you **Requery** with a new filter value.

For more information about filters, see the article "Recordset: Filtering Records."

Parameterizing Your Recordset Class

Before you create your recordset class, determine what parameters you need, what their data types are, and how the recordset will use them.

▶ **To parameterize a recordset class**

1. Run ClassWizard and create the class. See the article "ClassWizard: Creating a Recordset Class."

2. Specify field data members for the recordset's columns.

3. After ClassWizard writes the class to a file in your project, go to the .H file and manually add one or more parameter data members to the class declaration. The addition might look something like the following example, part of a snapshot class designed to answer the query "Which students are in the senior class?"

```
class CStudentSet : public CRecordset
{
// Field/Param Data
    //{{AFX_FIELD(CStudentSet, CRecordset)
    CString m_strFirstName;
    CString m_strLastName;
    CString m_strStudentID;
    CString m_strGradYear;
    //}}AFX_FIELD
    CString m_strGradYrParam;
};
```

ClassWizard writes field data members inside the "//{{AFX_FIELD" comment brackets. You add your parameter data members outside the comment brackets. The convention is to append the word "Param" to each name.

4. Modify the **DoFieldExchange** member function definition in the .CPP file. Add an RFX function call for each parameter data member you added to the class. For information on writing your RFX functions, see the article "Record Field Exchange: How RFX Works." Precede the RFX calls for the parameters with a single call to

```
pFX->SetFieldType( CFieldExchange::param );
// RFX calls for parameter data members
```

5. In the constructor of your recordset class, increment the count of parameters, **m_nParams**.

   For information, see "The Recordset Constructor" in the article "Record Field Exchange: Working with the Wizard Code."

6. When you write the code that creates a recordset object of this class, place a "?" (question mark) symbol in each place in your SQL statement string(s) where a parameter is to be replaced.

   At run time, "?" placeholders are filled, in order, by the parameter values you pass. The first parameter data member set after the **SetFieldType** call replaces the first "?" in the SQL string, the second parameter data member replaces the second "?", and so on.

Important Parameter order is important: the order of RFX calls for parameters in your DoFieldExchange function must match the order of the parameter placeholders in your SQL string.

Tip The most likely string to work with is the string you specify (if any) for the class's **m_strFilter** data member, but some ODBC drivers may allow parameters in other SQL clauses.

Passing Parameter Values at Run Time

You must specify parameter values before you call **Open** (for a new recordset object) or **Requery** (for an existing one).

▶ **To pass parameter values to a recordset object at run time**

1. Construct the recordset object.

2. Prepare a string or strings, such as the **m_strFilter** string, containing the SQL statement, or part(s) of it. Put "?" placeholders where the parameter information is to go.

3. Assign a run-time parameter value to each parameter data member of the object.

4. Call the **Open** member function (or **Requery**, for an existing recordset).

For example, suppose you want to specify a filter string for your recordset using information obtained at run time. Assume you have constructed a recordset of class CStudentSet earlier—called rsStudents—and now want to requery it for a particular kind of student information.

```
// Set up a filter string with parameter placeholders
rsStudents.m_strFilter = "GradYear <= ?";
// Obtain or calculate parameter values to pass--simply assigned here
CString strGradYear = GetCurrentAcademicYear( );
// Assign the values to parameter data members
rsStudents.m_strGradYrParam = strGradYear;
// Run the query
if( !rsStudents.Requery( ) )
    return FALSE;
```

The recordset contains records for those students whose records meet the conditions specified by the filter, which was constructed from run-time parameters. In this case, the recordset contains records for all senior students.

Note If needed, you can set the value of a parameter data member to Null, using **SetFieldNull**. You can likewise check whether a parameter data member is Null, using **IsFieldNull**.

See Also   Articles: "Recordset: Adding, Updating, and Deleting Records," "Recordset: Filtering Records," "Recordset: How Recordsets Select Records"

Recordset: Adding, Updating, and Deleting Records

Updatable snapshots and dynasets allow you to add, edit (update), and delete records. This article explains:

- How to determine whether your recordset is updatable.

- How to add a new record.
- How to edit an existing record.
- How to delete a record.

For more information about how updates are carried out and how your updates appear to other users, see the article "Recordset: How Recordsets Update Records." Normally, when you add, edit, or delete a record, the recordset changes the data source immediately. You can instead batch groups of related updates into "transactions." If a transaction is in progress, the update doesn't become final until you "commit" the transaction. This allows you to "take back" or "roll back" the changes. For information about transactions, see the article "Transaction."

Table 1 summarizes the options available for recordsets with different update characteristics.

Table 1   Recordset Read/Update Options

Type	Read	Edit records	Delete records	Add new (append)
read-only	Y	N	N	N
append-only	Y	N	N	Y
fully updatable	Y	Y	Y	Y

Determining Whether Your Recordset is Updatable

A recordset object is updatable if (a) the data source is updatable, and (b) you opened the recordset as updatable. Its updatability also depends on (c) the SQL statement you use, (d) the capabilities of your ODBC driver, and (e) whether the ODBC Cursor Library is in memory or not. You can't update a read-only recordset or data source.

▶ **To determine whether your recordset is updatable**

- Call the recordset object's **CanUpdate** member function.

    CanUpdate returns a nonzero value if the recordset is updatable.

By default, recordsets are fully updatable (you can perform **AddNew**, **Edit**, and **Delete** operations). But you can also use the **appendOnly** option to open updatable recordsets. A recordset opened this way allows only the addition of new records with **AddNew**. You can't edit or delete existing records. You can test whether a recordset is open only for appending by calling the **CanAppend** member function. **CanAppend** returns a nonzero value if the recordset is either fully updatable or open only for appending.

The following code shows how you might use **CanUpdate** for a recordset object called `rsStudentSet`:

```
if( !rsStudentSet.Open( ) )
    return FALSE;
if( !rsStudentSet.CanUpdate( ) )
{
    AfxMessageBox( "Unable to update the Student recordset." );
    return;
}
```

Caution When you prepare to update a recordset by calling **Update**, take care that your recordset includes all columns making up the primary key of the table (or all of the columns of any unique index on the table). In some cases, the framework can use only the columns selected in your recordset to identify which record in your table to update. Without all the necessary columns, multiple records may be updated in the table, possibly damaging the referential integrity of the table. In this case, the framework will throw exceptions when you call **Update**.

Adding a New Record

You can add new records to a recordset if its **CanAppend** member function returns a nonzero value.

▶ **To add a new record to a recordset**

1. Make sure the recordset is appendable.

2. Call the recordset object's **AddNew** member function.

    AddNew prepares the recordset to act as an edit buffer. All field data members are set to the special value Null (having no value) and marked as unchanged so only changed ("dirty") values will be written to the data source when you call **Update**.

3. Set the values of the new record's field data members.

    Assign values to the field data members. Those you don't assign will not be written to the data source.

4. Call the recordset object's **Update** member function.

    Update completes the addition by writing the new record to the data source. For what happens if you fail to call **Update**, see the article "Recordset: How Recordsets Update Records."

For information about how adding records works and about when added records are visible in your recordset, see the article "Recordset: How AddNew, Edit, and Delete Work."

The following example shows how to add a new record:

```
if( !rsStudent.Open( ) )
    return FALSE;
if( !rsStudent.CanAppend( ) )
    return FALSE;                          // no field values were set
rsStudent.AddNew( );
rsStudent.m_strName = strName;
rsStudent.m_strCity = strCity;
rsStudent.m_strStreet = strStreet;
if( !rsStudent.Update( ) )
{
    AfxMessageBox( "Record not added; no field values were set." );
    return FALSE;
}
```

For additional information, see "How AddNew Works" in the article "Recordset: How AddNew, Edit, and Delete Work."

Tip To cancel an **AddNew** or **Edit** call, simply make another call to **AddNew** or **Edit** or call **Move** with the **AFX_MOVE_REFRESH** parameter. Data members will be reset to their previous values and you will still be in **Edit** or **Add** mode.

Editing an Existing Record

You can edit existing records if your recordset's **CanUpdate** member function returns a nonzero value.

▶ **To edit an existing record in a recordset**

1. Make sure the recordset is updatable.
2. Scroll to the record you want to update.
3. Call the recordset object's **Edit** member function.

   Edit prepares the recordset to act as an edit buffer. All field data members are marked so that the recordset can tell later whether they were changed. The new values for changed field data members are written to the data source when you call **Update**.

4. Set the values of the new record's field data members.

   Assign values to the field data members. Those you don't assign values will remain unchanged.

5. Call the recordset object's **Update** member function.

   Update completes the edit by writing the changed record to the data source. For what happens if you fail to call **Update**, see the article "Recordset: How Recordsets Update Records."

After you edit a record, the edited record remains the current record.

The following example shows an **Edit** operation. It assumes the user has moved to a record he or she wants to edit.

```
rsStudent.Edit( );
rsStudent.m_strStreet = strNewStreet;
rsStudent.m_strCity = strNewCity;
rsStudent.m_strState = strNewState;
rsStudent.m_strPostalCode = strNewPostalCode;
if( !rsStudent.Update( ) )
{
    AfxMessageBox( "Record not updated; no field values were set." );
    return FALSE;
}
```

For more information, see "How Edit Works" in the article "Recordset: How AddNew, Edit, and Delete Work."

Tip To cancel an **AddNew** or **Edit** call, simply make another call to **AddNew** or **Edit** or call **Move** with the **AFX_MOVE_REFRESH** parameter. Data members will be reset to their previous values and you will still be in **Edit** or **Add** mode.

Deleting a Record

You can delete records if your recordset's **CanUpdate** member function returns a nonzero value.

▶ **To delete a record**

1. Make sure the recordset is updatable.

2. Scroll to the record you want to update.

3. Call the recordset object's **Delete** member function.

   Delete immediately marks the record as deleted, both in the recordset and on the data source.

   Unlike **AddNew** and **Edit**, **Delete** has no corresponding **Update** call.

4. Scroll to another record.

Important After a **Delete** call, there is no current record and **IsDeleted** returns a nonzero value. An error occurs if you call **Delete** again, or another update operation, before you scroll to another record. Once you have scrolled off the record, MFC will skip over that record the next time you scroll to it.

The following example shows a **Delete** operation. It assumes the user has moved to a record he or she wants to delete. After **Delete** is called, it's important to move to a new record.

```
rsStudent.Delete( );
rsStudent.MoveNext( );
```

For more information about the effects of the **AddNew**, **Edit**, and **Delete** member functions, see the article "Recordset: How Recordsets Update Records."

See Also   Article: "Recordset: Locking Records"

Recordset: Locking Records

This article explains:

- The kinds of record locking available.
- How to lock records in your recordset during updates.

When you use a recordset to update a record on the data source, your application can lock the record so no other user can update the record at the same time. The state of a record updated by two users at "the same time" is undefined unless the system can guarantee that two users can't update a record simultaneously.

Record-Locking Modes

The database classes provide two record-locking modes:

- Optimistic locking (the default)
- Pessimistic locking

Updating a record occurs in three steps:

1. You begin the operation by calling the **Edit** member function.
2. You change the appropriate fields of the current record.
3. You end the operation—and normally commit the update—by calling the **Update** member function.

Optimistic locking locks the record on the data source only during the **Update** call. If you use optimistic locking in a multiuser environment, the application should handle an **Update** failure condition. Pessimistic locking locks the record as soon as you call **Edit** and doesn't release it until you call **Update** (failures are indicated via the **CDBException** mechanism, not by a value of **FALSE** returned by **Update**). Pessimistic locking has a potential performance penalty for other users, since concurrent access to the same record may have to wait until completion of your application's **Update** process.

Locking Records in Your Recordset

If you want to change a recordset object's locking mode from the default, you must change the mode before you call **Edit**.

▶ **To change the current locking mode for your recordset**

• Call the **SetLockingMode** member function, specifying either
  CRecordset::pessimistic or **CRecordset::optimistic**.

The new locking mode remains in effect until you change it again or the recordset is closed.

Note Relatively few ODBC drivers currently support pessimistic locking.

See Also   Articles: "Recordset: Performing a Join," "Recordset: Adding, Updating, or Deleting Records"

Recordset: Performing a Join

This article explains:

- What a join is.
- How to perform a join of multiple tables.

What a Join Is

The join operation—a common data-access task—lets you work with data from more than one table using a single recordset object. Joining two or more tables yields a recordset that can contain columns from each table, but appears as a single table to your application. Sometimes the join uses all columns from all tables, but sometimes the SQL **SELECT** clause in a join uses only some of the columns from each table. The database classes support read-only joins but not updatable joins.

The key to a join operation is one or more columns that the tables have in common. For example, suppose there is a "CourseID" column in both the Course table and the Section table for an application such as the ENROLL tutorial. In the Course table, the CourseID column contains a unique ID value for each possible course. In the Section table, the CourseID column probably doesn't contain unique values, since each course usually has more than one section.

To select records containing columns from joined tables, you need the following items:

- A table list containing the names of all tables being joined.
- A column list containing the names of all participating columns. Columns with the same name but from different tables are qualified by the table name.
- A filter (SQL **WHERE** clause) that specifies the column(s) on which the tables are joined. This filter takes the form "Table1.KeyCol = Table2.KeyCol" and actually accomplishes the join. For the ENROLL example above, the filter is:

```
Course.CourseID = Section.CourseID
```

Performing the Join

The following procedure shows a join of two tables but can apply to joins of any number of tables (all on the same data source). The procedure involves first binding columns from multiple tables with ClassWizard, then directly modifying source code to complete the join.

Binding the Table Columns

▶ **To bind columns from both tables to a single recordset**

1. Use ClassWizard to create a recordset class for the join. In ClassWizard choose Data Sources to open the Data Sources dialog box and bind columns from the first table to recordset field data members.

    See the article "ClassWizard: Creating a Recordset Class."

2. Choose ClassWizard's Update Columns button to open the Data Sources dialog box a second time.

3. Select a data source and choose OK to close the Data Sources dialog box.

4. In the Tables dialog box, select the name of the second table and choose OK to close the dialog box.

5. Bind columns from the second table to additional recordset field data members.

    If any column names from the second table duplicate column names from the first table, be sure to give the corresponding recordset field data members unique names. For example, if you're joining Instructor and Section tables, each table might contain a column named RoomNo; you might bind one column to m_strInstrOffice and the other to m_strClassRoom.

6. Close ClassWizard.

Modifying the Source Files

Once you create the recordset class with ClassWizard, you must customize two parts of the class code. First, edit the class's table list, then qualify any columns with the same name but from different tables. You'll need to edit the calls in your DoFieldExchange override to insert table names.

For example, the student registration database for the ENROLL tutorial sample contains Instructor and Section tables. The Instructor table contains the following columns:

-   InstructorID
-   Name
-   RoomNo (the instructor's office)

The Section table contains the following columns:

- InstructorID
- Schedule
- RoomNo (where the class is held)
- SectionNo
- CourseID
- Capacity (maximum size of the section)

▶ **To modify the recordset's table list**

- Rewrite the recordset's `GetDefaultSQL` member function to return a string containing a comma-delimited list of table names.

For example, if your `CJoinSet` recordset joins a Course table to a Section table, you should rewrite your `GetDefaultSQL` function to look something like this:

```
CString CJoinSet::GetDefaultSQL()
{
    return "SECTION, INSTRUCTOR";
}
```

Tip As an alternative, you can pass a string containing a comma-delimited list of table names in the *lpszSQL* parameter when you call the recordset's **Open** member function. The string has the same form as the string returned in the example above.

▶ **To qualify columns with the same name from different tables**

- Edit the RFX function calls in the recordset's **DoFieldExchange** member function.

    For each duplicate column name, edit the second parameter in the RFX call to prefix a table name to the column name already there. Separate the table name and the column name with a period.

For example, because `CJoinSet` binds a `RoomNo` column from each table, you must modify the two RFX calls for these columns as shown in the following code:

```
void CJoinSet::DoFieldExchange(CFieldExchange* pFX)
{
    //{{AFX_FIELD_MAP(CJoinSet)
    SetFieldType(pFX, CFieldExchange::outputColumn);
    RFX_Text(pFX, "Section.RoomNo", m_strClassRoom);
    RFX_Text(pFX, "Instructor.RoomNo", m_strInstructorOffice);
    // ...
    //}}AFX_FIELD_MAP
}
```

In the second parameter of each RFX function call above, the name `RoomNo` is prefixed by the table name. The two items are separated by a period.

Setting the Join Conditions with a Filter

When you construct a `CJoinSet` object in your program, set its filter to specify which columns constitute the join. Then call the recordset's **Open** member function as shown in the following example, which joins the Instructor and Section tables on their common InstructorID column:

```
CJoinSet ssJoin( NULL );
ssJoin.m_strFilter = "Instructor.InstructorID = Section.InstructorID";
if( !ssJoin.Open( ) )
    return FALSE;          // recordset could not be opened
```

The filter supplies the connection between two columns that makes it possible to view two tables as if they were one.

You can join more than two tables in the same way by equating multiple pairs of columns, each pair joined by the SQL keyword **AND**.

See Also   Articles: "Recordset: Declaring a Class for a Predefined Query," "Recordset: Declaring a Class for a Table," "Recordset: Requerying a Recordset"

Recordset: Declaring a Class for a Predefined Query

This article explains how to create a recordset class for a predefined query (sometimes called a "stored procedure," as in Microsoft SQL Server).

Some database management systems (DBMSs) allow you to create a predefined query and call it from your programs like a function. The query has a name, may or may not take parameters, and may or may not return records. The procedure in this article describes how to call a predefined query that returns records (and perhaps takes parameters).

The database classes don't support updating predefined queries. The difference between a snapshot predefined query and a dynaset predefined query is not updatability but whether changes made by other users (or other recordsets in your program) are visible in your recordset.

Tip You don't need a recordset to call a predefined query that doesn't return records. Prepare the SQL statement as described below, but execute it by calling the **CDatabase** member function **ExecuteSQL**.

You can create a single recordset class to manage calling a predefined query, but you must do some of the work yourself. ClassWizard doesn't support creating a class specifically for this purpose.

▶ **To create a class for calling a predefined query (stored procedure)**

1. Use ClassWizard to create a recordset class for the table that contributes the most columns returned by the query. This gives you a head start.

2. Manually add field data members for any columns of any tables that the query returns but that ClassWizard didn't create for you. Add them outside the "//{{AFX_FIELD" comments.

   For example, if the query returns three columns each from two additional tables, add six field data members (of the appropriate data types) to the class.

3. Manually add RFX function calls in the `DoFieldExchange` member function of the class, one corresponding to the data type of each added field data member.

   Add these function calls outside the "//{{AFX_FIELD_MAP" comments. Immediately before these RFX calls, call **SetFieldType**, as shown here:

   ```
   pFX->SetFieldType( CFieldExchange::outputColumn );
   ```

   Note You must know the data types and the order of columns returned in the result set. The order of RFX function calls in `DoFieldExchange` must match the order of result set columns.

---

4. Manually add initializations for the new field data members in the recordset class constructor.

   You must also increment the initialization value for the **m_nFields** data member. ClassWizard writes the initialization, but it only covers the field data members it adds for you. Put the increment statement outside the comment brackets. For example:

   ```
   m_nFields += 6;
   //{{AFX_FIELD(CDelinquents, CRecordset)
   ...
   //}}AFX_FIELD
   ```

   Some data types shouldn't be initialized here—for example, **CLongBinary** or byte arrays.

5. If the query takes parameters, add a parameter data member for each parameter, an RFX function call for each, and an initialization for each.

   You must increment **m_nParams** for each added parameter, as you did **m_nFields** for added fields in step 4 above. See the article "Recordset: Parameterizing a Recordset" for details.

6. Manually write an SQL statement string with the following form:

   ```
   {CALL proc-name [(? [, ?]...)]}
   ```

   where **CALL** is an ODBC keyword, *proc-name* is the name of the query as it is known on the data source, and the "?" items are placeholders for the parameter values you supply to the recordset at run time (if any). The following example prepares a placeholder for one parameter:

```
CString mySQL = "{CALL Delinquent_Accts (?)}";
```

7. In the code that opens the recordset, first set the values of the recordset's parameter data members, then call the **Open** member function, passing your SQL string for the *lpszSQL* parameter. Or, instead, replace the string returned by the GetDefaultSQL member function in your class.

The following examples illustrate the procedure for calling a predefined query, named Delinquent_Accts, which takes one parameter for a sales district number. This query returns three columns: Acct_No, L_Name, Phone. All columns are from the Customers table.

The recordset below specifies field data members for the columns the query returns and a parameter for the sales district number requested at run time.

```
class CDelinquents : public CRecordset
{
// Field/Param Data
    //{{AFX_FIELD(CDelinquents, CRecordset)
    LONG m_lAcct_No;
    CString m_strL_Name;
    CString m_strPhone;
    //}}AFX_FIELD
    LONG m_lDistParam;
    // ...
};
```

This class declaration is as ClassWizard writes it, except for the m_lDistParam member added manually outside the "//{{AFX_FIELD" comment. Other members below the comments aren't shown here.

The next example shows the initializations for the data members in the CDelinquents constructor. You add the two lines outside the comment brackets.

```
CDelinquents::CDelinquents(CDatabase* pdb)
    : CRecordset(pdb)
{
    //{{AFX_FIELD_INIT(CDelinquents)
    m_lAcct_No = 0;
    m_strL_Name = "";
    m_strPhone = "";
    m_nFields = 3;
    //}}AFX_FIELD_INIT
    m_nParams = 1;
    m_lDistParam = 0;
}
```

Note the initializations for **m_nFields** and **m_nParams**. ClassWizard initializes **m_nFields**; you initialize **m_nParams**.

The next example shows the RFX functions in `CDelinquents::DoFieldExchange`:

```
void CDelinquents::DoFieldExchange(CFieldExchange* pFX)
{
//{{AFX_FIELD_MAP(CDelinquents)
    pFX->SetFieldType(CFieldExchange::outputColumn);
    RFX_Long(pFX, "Acct_No", m_lAcct_No);
    RFX_Text(pFX, "L_Name", m_strL_Name);
    RFX_Text(pFX, "Phone", m_strPhone);
//}}AFX_FIELD_MAP
    pFX->SetFieldType(CFieldExchange::param);
    RFX_Long(pFX, "Dist_No", m_lDistParam);
}
```

Besides making the RFX calls for the three returned columns, this code manages binding the parameter you pass at run time. The parameter is keyed to the `Dist_No` (district number) column.

The next example shows how to set up the SQL string and how to use it to open the recordset.

```
// Construct a CDelinquents recordset object
CDelinquents rsDel( NULL );
CString strSQL = "{CALL Delinquent_Accts (?)}"
// Specify a parameter value (obtained earlier from the user)
rsDel.m_lDistParam = lDistrict;
// Open the recordset and run the query
if( rsDel.Open( CRecordset::snapshot, strSQL ) )
    // Use the recordset ...
```

This code constructs a snapshot, passes it a parameter obtained earlier from the user, and calls the predefined query. When the query runs, it returns records for the specified sales district. Each record contains columns for the account number, customer's last name, and customer's phone number.

Tip You might want to handle a return value (output parameter) from a stored procedure. The MFC database classes don't support output parameters, but see the **::SQLProcedures** example code in the ODBC *Programmer's Reference* for information.

See Also   Articles: "Recordset: Requerying a Recordset," "Recordset: Declaring a Class for a Table," "Recordset: Performing a Join"

Recordset: Requerying a Recordset

This article explains how you can use a recordset object to "requery"—refresh—itself from the database, and when you might want to do that with the **Requery** member function.

The principal reasons for requerying a recordset are to:

- Bring the recordset up to date with respect to records added by you or by other users and records deleted by other users (those you delete are already reflected in the recordset).

- Refresh the recordset based on changing parameter values.

Bringing the Recordset Up to Date

Frequently you will want to requery your recordset object to bring it up to date. In a multiuser database environment, other users can make changes to the data during the life of your recordset. For more information about when your recordset reflects changes made by other users and when other users' recordsets reflect your changes, see the articles "Recordset: How Recordsets Update Records" and "Dynaset."

Requerying Based on New Parameters

Another frequent—and equally important—use of **Requery** is to select a new set of records based on changing parameter values. For example, step 2 in the ENROLL tutorial application illustrates using a combo box in a record view to select from a list of all available college courses. When the user selects a different course from the combo box, ENROLL requeries a Section table to select only those class sections for the course the user chose in the combo box. See the `CSectionForm::OnSelendokCourseList` member function in "Requerying the CSectionSet Recordset" in Chapter 26 of *Introducing Visual C++*.

Tip Query speed is probably significantly faster if you call **Requery** with changing parameter values than if you call **Open** again.

Requerying Dynasets vs. Snapshots

Because dynasets are meant to present a set of records with dynamic, up-to-date data, you'll want to requery dynasets often if you want to reflect other users' additions. Snapshots, on the other hand, are useful because you can safely rely on their static contents while you prepare reports, calculate totals, and so on. Still, you may sometimes want to requery a snapshot as well. In a multiuser environment, snapshot data may lose synchronization with the data source as other users change the database.

▶ **To requery a recordset object**

- Call the **Requery** member function of the object.

Alternatively, you can simply close and reopen the original recordset. In either case, the new recordset represents the current state of the data source.

For an example, see the article "Record Views: Filling a List Box from a Second Recordset."

Tip To optimize **Requery** performance, avoid changing the recordset's filter or sort. Change only the parameter value before calling **Requery**.

If the **Requery** call fails, you can retry the call; otherwise, your application should terminate gracefully. A call to **Requery** or **Open** might fail for any of a number of reasons. Perhaps a network error occurs; or, during the call, after the existing data is released but before the new data is obtained, another user might get exclusive access; or the table on which your recordset depends could be deleted.

See Also   Articles: "Recordset: Dynamically Binding Data Columns," "Recordset: Creating and Closing Recordsets"

Recordset: Dynamically Binding Data Columns

Recordsets manage binding table columns that you specify at design time, but there are cases when you may want to bind columns that were unknown to you at design time. This article explains:

- When you might want to bind columns dynamically to a recordset.
- How to bind columns dynamically at run time.

When You Might Bind Columns Dynamically

At design time, ClassWizard creates recordset classes based on the known tables and columns on your data source. Databases can change between when you design them and later when your application uses those tables and columns at run time. You or another user might add or drop a table or add or drop columns from a table that your application's recordset relies upon. This probably isn't a concern for all data-access applications, but if it is for yours, how can you cope with changes in the database schema, other than by redesigning and recompiling? The purpose of this article is to answer that question.

This article describes the most common case in which you might bind columns dynamically—having begun with a recordset based on a known database schema, you want to handle additional columns at run time. The article further assumes that the additional columns map to **CString** field data members, the most common case, although suggestions are supplied to help you manage other data types.

With a small amount of extra code, you can:

- Determine what columns are available at run time.

- Bind additional columns to your recordset dynamically, at run time.

Your recordset still contains data members for the columns you knew about at design time. It also contains a small amount of extra code that dynamically determines whether any new columns have been added to your target table and, if so, binds these new columns to dynamically allocated storage (rather than to recordset data members).

This article doesn't cover other dynamic binding cases, such as dropped tables or columns. For those, you'll need to use ODBC API calls more directly. See the ODBC *Programmer's Reference*.

Example code for this article comes from the DYNABIND and CATALOG samples. For information about MFC samples, see MFC Samples under MFC in Books Online.

How to Bind Columns Dynamically

To bind columns dynamically in a case like that of the DYNABIND example, you must know (or be able to determine) the names of the additional columns. You must also allocate storage for the additional field data members, specify their names and their types, and specify the number of columns you're adding.

The following discussion mentions two different recordsets. The first is the "main recordset" that selects records from the target table. The second is a special "column recordset" used to get information about the columns in your target table.

The General Process

At the most general level, you follow these steps:

1. Construct your main recordset object.

   Optionally, pass a pointer to an open **CDatabase** object, or be able to supply connection information to the column recordset in some other way.

2. Take steps to add columns dynamically.

   See the process described in "Adding the Columns" below.

3. Open your main recordset.

   The recordset selects records and uses record field exchange (RFX) to bind both the "static" columns (those mapped to recordset field data members) and the dynamic columns (mapped to extra storage that you allocate).

Adding the Columns

Dynamically binding added columns at run time requires the following steps:

1. Determine at run time what columns are in the target table. Extract from that information a list of the columns that have been added to the table since your recordset class was designed.

A good approach is to use a "column recordset" class designed to query the data source for column information for the target table—such as column name, data type, and so on. The CATALOG sample program (in \MSVC20\SAMPLES\MFC\CATALOG) provides a recordset class called `CColumns` that you can use to build a list of the new columns' names.

2. Provide storage for the new field data members. Your main recordset class doesn't have field data members for unknown columns, so you must provide a place to store the names, result values, and possibly data type information (if the columns are of different data types).

   One approach is to build one or more dynamic lists: one for the new columns' names, another for their result values, and a third for their data types (if necessary). These lists, particularly the value list, provide the information and the necessary storage for binding.

   Figure 1 illustrates building the lists.

Figure 1   Building Lists of Columns to Bind Dynamically

3. Add an RFX function call in your main recordset's **DoFieldExchange** function for each added column. These RFX calls do the work of fetching a record, including the additional columns, and binding the columns to recordset data members or to your dynamically supplied storage for them.

   One approach is to add a loop to your main recordset's **DoFieldExchange** function that loops through your list of new columns, calling the appropriate RFX function for each column in the list. On each RFX call, pass a column name from the column name list and a storage location in the corresponding member of the result value list.

Lists of Columns

The four lists you need to work with are named as follows throughout this article:

Current-Table-Columns (List 1 in Figure 1)
   A list of the columns currently in the table on the data source. This list may or may not match the list of columns currently bound in your recordset.

Bound-Recordset-Columns (List 2 in Figure 1)

A list of the columns bound in your recordset (usually set up with ClassWizard). These columns already have RFX statements in your **DoFieldExchange** function.

Columns-To-Bind-Dynamically (List 3 in Figure 1)

A list of columns in the table but not in your recordset. These are the columns you want to bind dynamically.

Dynamic-Column-Values (List 4 in Figure 1)

A list containing storage for the values retrieved from the columns you bind dynamically. Elements of this list correspond to those in Columns-to-Bind-Dynamically, one to one.

Building Your Lists

With a general strategy in mind, you can turn to the details. The procedures in the rest of this article show you how to build the lists shown in "Lists of Columns." The procedures guide you through:

- Determining the columns in your table at run time
- Determining the names of columns not in your recordset
- Providing dynamic storage for columns newly added to the table
- Dynamically adding RFX calls for new columns

Determining the Columns in Your Table at Run Time

First, build Current-Table-Columns (as in Figure 1): a list of the columns in the table on the data source.

▶   **To determine the columns in a table at run time (Current-Table-Columns)**

1. Borrow the files COLUMNST.H/.CPP from \MSVC20\SAMPLES\MFC\CATALOG. Add the .CPP file to your project and include the .H file as needed.

2. At run time, construct a "column recordset" object of class `CColumn`, passing a pointer to an open **CDatabase** object.

3. Before you call **Open**, set one or more of the column recordset's parameters. The following table describes what these parameters specify.

Parameter	Description
`m_strQualifierParam`	Identifies the database containing the table for ODBC. You usually don't need to specify this value.
`m_strOwnerParam`	Identifies the person who created the target table.

Parameter	Description
m_strTableNameParam	Identifies the target table by name.
m_strColumnNameParam	Identifies a specific column by name.

In most cases, you need only the table name, although some data sources might require the owner name as well, and others might require even more information. In addition to table name, use the column name parameter if you need information for only a single column in the table. For information about these parameters, see **::SQLColumns** in the ODBC SDK *Programmer's Reference*.

4. Call **Open** for the column recordset.

   The recordset returns a record for each column in the specified table (unless you specify **m_strColumnNameParam**).

5. Construct Current-Table-Columns, a collection object that can hold **CString** objects.

   For example, you might use a **CStringList**.

6. Scroll through the object's records, loading column names into Current-Table-Columns as you go.

This procedure results in a collection object that contains the names of all columns in a specified table. For example, Figure 1 shows Current-Table-Columns (List 1) with four elements. The last element is "Phone." For descriptions of the lists, see "Lists of Columns" above.

Determining Which Table Columns Are Not in Your Recordset

Next, build a list (Bound-Recordset-Columns, as in List 2 in Figure 1) that contains a list of the columns already bound in your main recordset. Then build a list (Columns-to-Bind-Dynamically, derived from Current-Table-Columns and Bound-Recordset-Columns) that contains column names that are in the table on the data source but not in your main recordset.

▶ **To determine the names of columns not in the recordset (Columns-to-Bind-Dynamically)**

1. Build a list (Bound-Recordset-Columns) of the columns already bound in your main recordset.

   One approach is to create Bound-Recordset-Columns at design time. You can visually examine the RFX function calls in the recordset's **DoFieldExchange** function to get these names. Then set up your list as an array initialized with the names.

   For example, Figure 1 shows Bound-Recordset-Columns (List 2) with three elements. Bound-Recordset-Columns is missing the Phone column shown in Current-Table-Columns (List 1).

2. Compare Current-Table-Columns and Bound-Recordset-Columns to build a list (Columns-to-Bind-Dynamically) of the columns not already bound in your main recordset.

    One approach is to loop through your list of columns in the table at run time (Current-Table-Columns) and your list of columns already bound in your recordset (Bound-Recordset-Columns) in parallel. Into Columns-to-Bind-Dynamically put any names in Current-Table-Columns that don't appear in Bound-Recordset-Columns.

    For example, Figure 1 shows Columns-to-Bind-Dynamically (List 3) with one element: the Phone column found in Current-Table-Columns (List 1) but not in Bound-Recordset-Columns (List 2).

3. Build a list of Dynamic-Column-Values (as in List 4 in Figure 1) in which to store the data values corresponding to each column name stored in your list of columns to bind dynamically (Columns-to-Bind-Dynamically).

    The elements of this list play the role of new recordset field data members. They are the storage locations to which the dynamic columns are bound. For descriptions of the lists, see "Lists of Columns" above.

Providing Storage for the New Columns

Next, set up storage locations for the columns to be bound dynamically. The idea is to provide a list element in which to store each column's value. These storage locations parallel the recordset member variables, which store the normally bound columns.

▶ **To provide dynamic storage for new columns (Dynamic-Column-Values)**

- Build Dynamic-Column-Values, parallel to Columns-to-Bind-Dynamically, to contain the value of the data in each column.

    For example, Figure 1 shows Dynamic-Column-Values (List 4) with one element: a **CString** object containing the actual phone number for the current record: "555-1212".

    In the most common case, Dynamic-Column-Values has elements of type **CString**. If you're dealing with columns of varying data types, you'll need a list that can contain elements of a variety of types.

The result of the preceding procedures is two main lists: Columns-to-Bind-Dynamically containing the names of columns and Dynamic-Column-Values containing the values in the columns for the current record.

Tip If the new columns aren't all of the same data type, you might want an extra parallel list containing items that somehow define the type of each corresponding element in the column list. (You can use the values **AFX_RFX_BOOL**, **AFX_RFX_BYTE**, and so on, for this if you wish. These constants are defined in AFXDB.H.) Choose a list type based on how you represent the column data types.

Adding RFX Calls to Bind the Columns

Finally, arrange for the dynamic binding to occur by placing RFX calls for the new columns in your `DoFieldExchange` function.

▶ **To dynamically add RFX calls for new columns**

- In your main recordset's **DoFieldExchange** member function, add code that loops through your list of new columns (Columns-to-Bind-Dynamically). In each loop, extract a column name from Columns-to-Bind-Dynamically and a result value for the column from Dynamic-Column-Values. Pass these items to an RFX function call appropriate to the data type of the column. For descriptions of the lists, see "Lists of Columns" above.

In the common case, in your **RFX_Text** function calls you extract **CString** objects from the lists, as in the following lines of code, where Columns-to-Bind-Dynamically is a **CStringList** called `m_listName` and Dynamic-Column-Values is a **CStringList** called `m_listValue`:

```
RFX_Text( pFX,
            m_listName.GetNext( posName ),
            m_listValue.GetNext( posValue ));
```

For an example of such a loop added to **DoFieldExchange**, see `CSections::DoFieldExchange` in the file SECTIONS.CPP in the DYNABIND sample program. For more information about RFX functions, see "Macros and Globals" in the *Class Library Reference*.

Tip If the new columns are of different data types, use a switch statement in your loop to call the appropriate RFX function for each type.

When the framework calls **DoFieldExchange** during the **Open** process to bind columns to the recordset, the RFX calls for the static columns bind those columns. Then your loop repeatedly calls RFX functions for the dynamic columns.

See the complete source code in the DYNABIND sample program.

See Also   Article: "Recordset: Working with Large Data Items"

Recordset: Working with Large Data Items

Suppose your database can store large pieces of data, such as bitmaps (employee photographs, maps, pictures of products, and so on). This kind of data is often referred to as a Binary Large Object (or BLOB) because:

- Each field value is large.

- Unlike numbers and other simple data types, it has no predictable size.

- The data is formless from the perspective of your program.

This article explains what support the database classes provide for working with such objects.

Managing Large Objects

Recordsets solve the special difficulty of managing binary large objects through a class called **CLongBinary**. By giving a field data member of your recordset the type **CLongBinary**, you provide a fixed base from which RFX can manage the transfer of such an object between your recordset and the data source and through which you can manipulate the data inside the object. RFX needs a specific site for retrieved data, and you need a handle to the underlying data.

The CLongBinary Class

A **CLongBinary** object is a simple shell around an **HGLOBAL** handle to a block of storage allocated on the heap. When it binds a table column containing a binary large object, RFX allocates the **HGLOBAL** handle when it needs to transfer the data to the recordset and stores the handle in the **CLongBinary** field of the recordset.

In turn, you use the **HGLOBAL** handle, **m_hData**, to work with the data itself, operating on it as you would on any handle data.

Caution **CLongBinary** objects can't be used as parameters in function calls. In addition, their implementation, which calls **::SQLGetData**, necessarily slows scrolling performance for a scrollable snapshot. This may also be true when you use an **::SQLGetData** call yourself to retrieve dynamic schema columns.

See Also   Articles: "Recordset: Obtaining SUMs and Other Aggregate Results," "Record Field Exchange"

Recordset: Obtaining SUMs and Other Aggregate Results

This article explains how to obtain aggregate results using the following SQL keywords:

- **SUM**   Calculates the total of the values in a column with a numeric data type.
- **MIN**   Extracts the smallest value in a column with a numeric data type.
- **MAX**   Extracts the largest value in a column with a numeric data type.
- **AVG**   Calculates an average value of all the values in a column with a numeric data type.
- **COUNT**   Counts the number of records in a column of any data type.

You use these SQL functions to obtain statistical information about the records in a data source rather than to extract records from the data source. The recordset that is created usually consists of a single record (if all columns are aggregates) that contains a value. (There might be more than one record if you used a **GROUP BY** clause.) This value is the result of the calculation or extraction performed by the SQL function.

Tip   To add an SQL **GROUP BY** clause (and possibly a **HAVING** clause) to your SQL statement, append it to the end of **m_strFilter**. For example:

```
m_strFilter = "sales > 10 GROUP BY SALESPERSON_ID";
```

You can limit the number of records you use to obtain aggregate results by filtering and sorting the columns.

Caution   Some aggregation operators return a different data type from the column(s) over which they are aggregating.

- **SUM** and **AVG** may return the next larger data type (for example, calling with **int** returns **LONG** or **double**).
- **COUNT** usually returns **LONG** regardless of target column type.
- **MAX** and **MIN** return the same data type as the columns they calculate.

For example, ClassWizard creates `long m_lSales` to accommodate a Sales column, but you'll need to replace this with a `double m_dblSumSales` data member to accommodate the aggregate result. See the example that follows.

▶ **To obtain an aggregate result for a recordset**

1. Create a recordset containing the column(s) from which you want to obtain aggregate results.

2. Modify the **DoFieldExchange** function for the recordset. Replace the string representing the column name (the second argument of the RFX function call(s)) with a string representing the aggregation function on the column. For example, replace

```
RFX_Long(pFX, "Sales", m_lSales);
```

with

```
RFX_Double(pFX, "Sum(Sales)", m_dblSumSales)
```

3. Open the recordset. The result of the aggregation operation will be left in m_dblSumSales.

Note ClassWizard actually assigns data member names without Hungarian prefixes. For example, the wizard would produce m_Sales for a Sales column, rather than the m_lSales name used earlier for illustration.

If you're using a **CRecordView** class to view the data, you'll have to change the DDX function call to display the new data member value; in this case, changing it from

```
DDX_FieldText(pDX, IDC_SUMSALES, m_pSet->m_lSales, m_pSet);
```

to

```
DDX_FieldText(pDX, IDC_SUMSALES, m_pSet->m_dblSumSales, m_pSet);
```

See Also   Article: "Recordset: How Recordsets Select Records"

Recordset: How Recordsets Select Records

This article explains:

- Your role and your options in selecting records.
- How a recordset constructs its SQL statement and selects records.
- What you can do to customize the selection.

Recordsets select records from a data source through an ODBC driver by sending SQL statements to the driver. The SQL sent depends on how you design and open your recordset class.

Your Options in Selecting Records

Table 1 shows your options in selecting records.

Table 1   How and When You Can Affect a Recordset

When you ...	You can ...
Declare your recordset class with ClassWizard...	Specify which table to select from.
	Specify which columns to include.
	See "ClassWizard: Creating a Recordset Class."
Complete your recordset class implementation...	Override member functions such as **OnSetOptions** (advanced) to set application-specific options or to change defaults. Specify parameter data members if you want a parameterized recordset.
Construct a recordset object (before you call **Open**) and then...	Specify a search condition (possibly compound) for use in a **WHERE** clause that filters the records. See "Recordset: Filtering Records."
	Specify a sort order for use in an **ORDER BY** clause that sorts the records. See "Recordset: Sorting Records."
	Specify parameter values for any parameters you added to the class. See "Recordset: Parameterizing a Recordset."
Run the recordset's query by calling **Open**...	Specify a custom SQL string to replace the default SQL string set up by ClassWizard. See **CRecordset::Open** in the *Class Library Reference* and "SQL: Customizing Your Recordset's SQL Statement."
Call **Requery** to requery the recordset with the latest values on the data source...	Specify new parameters, filter, or sort. See "Recordset: Requerying a Recordset."

How a Recordset Constructs Its SQL Statement

When you call a recordset object's **Open** member function, **Open** constructs an SQL statement using some or all of the following ingredients:

- The *lpszSQL* parameter passed to **Open**. If not **NULL**, this parameter specifies a custom SQL string, or part of one. The framework parses the string. If the string is an SQL **SELECT** statement or an ODBC **CALL** statement, the framework uses the string as the recordset's SQL statement. If the string does not begin with "SELECT" or "{CALL", the framework uses what's supplied to construct an SQL **FROM** clause.

- The string returned by **GetDefaultSQL**. By default, this is the name of the table you specified for the recordset in ClassWizard, but you can change what the function returns. The framework calls **GetDefaultSQL**—if the string doesn't begin with "SELECT" or "{CALL", it is assumed to be a table name, which is used to construct an SQL string.

- The field data members of the recordset, which are to be bound to specific columns of the table. The framework binds record columns to the addresses of these members, using them as buffers. The framework determines the correlation of field data members to table columns from the RFX function calls in the recordset's **DoFieldExchange** member function.

- The filter for the recordset, if any, contained in the **m_strFilter** data member. The framework uses this string to construct an SQL **WHERE** clause.

  See the article "Recordset: Filtering Records."

- The sort order for the recordset, if any, contained in the **m_strSort** data member. The framework uses this string to construct an SQL **ORDER BY** clause.

  See the article "Recordset: Sorting Records."

Tip To use the SQL **GROUP BY** clause (and possibly the **HAVING** clause), append the clause(s) to the end of your filter string.

- The values of any parameter data members you specify for the class. You set parameter values just before you call **Open** or **Requery**. The framework binds the parameter values to "?" placeholders in the SQL string. At compile time, you specify the string with placeholders; at run time, the framework fills in the details based on the parameter values you pass.

  See the article "Recordset: Parameterizing a Recordset."

Open constructs an SQL **SELECT** statement from these ingredients. See "Customizing the Selection" below for details about how the framework uses the ingredients.

After constructing the statement, **Open** sends the SQL to the ODBC Driver Manager (and the ODBC Cursor Library if it is in memory), which sends it on to the ODBC driver for the specific DBMS. The driver communicates with the DBMS to carry out the selection on the data source and fetches the first record. The framework loads the record into the field data members of the recordset.

You can use a combination of these techniques to open tables and to construct a query based on a join of multiple tables. With additional customization, you can call predefined queries (stored procedures), select table columns not known at design time and bind them to recordset fields, or perform most other data-access tasks. Tasks you can't accomplish by customizing recordsets can still be accomplished by calling ODBC API functions or directly executing SQL statements with **CDatabase::ExecuteSQL**.

Customizing the Selection

Besides supplying a filter, a sort order, or parameters, you can take the following actions to customize your recordset's selection:

- Pass a custom SQL string in *lpszSQL* when you call **Open** for the recordset. Anything you pass in *lpsqSQL* takes precedence over what the **GetDefaultSQL** member function returns.

  See the article "SQL: Customizing Your Recordset's SQL Statement." That article describes the kinds of SQL statements (or partial statements) you can pass to **Open** and what the framework does with them.

  Note   If the custom string you pass does not begin with "SELECT" or "{CALL", MFC assumes it contains a table name. This also applies to the next bulleted item below.

- Alter the string that ClassWizard writes in your recordset's **GetDefaultSQL** member function. Edit the function's code to change what it returns. By default, ClassWizard writes a **GetDefaultSQL** function that returns a single table name.

  You can have **GetDefaultSQL** return any of the items that you can pass in the *lpszSQL* parameter to **Open**. If you don't pass a custom SQL string in *lpszSQL*, the framework uses the string that **GetDefaultSQL** returns. At a minimum, **GetDefaultSQL** must return a single table name. But you can have it return multiple table names, a full **SELECT** statement, an ODBC **CALL** statement, and so on. For a list of what you can pass to *lpszSQL*—or have **GetDefaultSQL** return—see the article "SQL: Customizing Your Recordset's SQL Statement."

  If you're performing a join of two or more tables, rewrite **GetDefaultSQL** to customize the table list used in the SQL **FROM** clause. See the article "Recordset: Performing a Join."

- Manually bind additional field data members, perhaps based on information you obtain about the schema of your data source at run time. You add field data members to the recordset class, RFX function calls for them to the **DoFieldExchange** member function, and initializations of the data members in the class constructor.

  See the article "Recordset: Dynamically Binding Data Columns."

- Override recordset member functions, such as **OnSetOptions**, to set application-specific options or to override defaults.

If you want to base the recordset on a complex SQL statement, you'll need to use some combination of these customization techniques. For example, perhaps you want to use SQL clauses and keywords not directly supported by recordsets, or perhaps you're joining multiple tables.

See Also   Articles: "Recordset: How Recordsets Update Records," "ODBC," "SQL,"
"Recordset: Filtering Records," "Recordset: Sorting Records," "Recordset:
Locking Records"

Recordset: How Recordsets Update Records

Besides their ability to select records from a data source, recordsets can (optionally)
update or delete the selected records or add new records. Three factors determine a
recordset's updatability: whether the connected data source is updatable, the options
you specify when you create a recordset object, and the SQL that is created.

Note   The SQL upon which your **CRecordset** object is based can affect your
recordset's updatability. For example, if your SQL contains a join or a **GROUP
BY** clause, MFC sets the updatability to **FALSE**.

This article explains:

- Your role in recordset updating and what the framework does for you.
- The recordset as an "edit buffer" and the differences between dynasets and
  snapshots.

The article "Recordset: How AddNew, Edit, and Delete Work" describes the
actions of these functions from the point of view of the recordset.

The article "Recordset: More About Updates" completes the recordset update story
by explaining how transactions affect updates, how closing a recordset or scrolling
affects updates in progress, and how your updates interact with the updates of other
users.

Your Role in Recordset Updating

Table 1 shows your role in using recordsets to add, edit, or delete records, along
with what the framework does for you.

Table 1   Recordset Updating: You and the Framework

You...	The framework...
Determine whether the data source is updatable (or appendable).	Supplies **CDatabase** member functions for testing the data source's updatability or appendability.
Open an updatable recordset (of any type).	
Determine whether the recordset is updatable by calling **CRecordset** update functions such as **CanUpdate** or **CanAppend**.	

Table 1   Recordset Updating: You and the Framework (*continued*)

You...	The framework...
Call recordset member functions to add, edit, and delete records.	Manages the mechanics of exchanging data between your recordset object and the data source.
Optionally, use transactions to control the update process.	Supplies **CDatabase** member functions to support transactions.

For more information about transactions, see the article "Transaction."

The Edit Buffer

Taken collectively, the field data members of a recordset serve as an "edit buffer" that contains one record—the "current" record. Update operations use this buffer to operate on the current record.

- When you add a record, the edit buffer is used to build a new record. When you finish adding the record, the record that was previously current becomes current again.

- When you update (edit) a record, the edit buffer is used to set the field data members of the recordset to new values. When you finish updating, the updated record is still current.

When you call **AddNew** or **Edit**, the current record is stored so it can be restored later as needed. When you call **Delete**, the current record is not stored but is marked as deleted, and you must scroll to another record.

Note   The edit buffer plays no role in record deletion. When you delete the current record, the record is marked as deleted, and the recordset is "not on a record" until you scroll to a different record.

Dynasets and Snapshots

Dynasets refresh a record's contents as you scroll to the record. Snapshots are static representations of the records, so a record's contents are not refreshed unless you call **Requery**. To use all the functionality of dynasets, you must be working with an ODBC driver that conforms to the correct level of ODBC API support. For more information, see the articles "ODBC" and "Dynaset."

See Also   Article: "Recordset: How AddNew, Edit, and Delete Work"

Recordset: How AddNew, Edit, and Delete Work

This article explains how the **AddNew**, **Edit**, and **Delete** member functions of class **CRecordset** work. Topics covered include:

- How adding records works
- Visibility of added records
- How editing records works
- How deleting records works

As a supplement, you might want to read the article "Record Field Exchange: How RFX Works," which describes the corresponding role of RFX in update operations.

How AddNew Works

Adding a new record to a recordset involves calling the recordset's **AddNew** member function, setting the values of the new record's field data members, and calling the **Update** member function to write the record to the data source.

As a precondition for calling **AddNew**, the recordset must not have been opened as read-only. The **CanUpdate** and **CanAppend** member functions let you determine these conditions.

When you call **AddNew**:

1. The record in the edit buffer is stored, so its contents can be restored if the operation is canceled.
2. The field data members are flagged so it will be possible to detect changes in them later. The field data members are also marked "clean" (unchanged) and set to a Null value. (C++ **NULL** is not the same as Null, which in database terminology means "having no value.")

After you call **AddNew**, the edit buffer represents a new, empty record, ready to be filled in with values. To do this, you manually set the values by assigning to them. Instead of specifying an actual data value for a field, you can call **SetFieldNull** to specify the value Null—the field "has no value."

To commit your changes, you call **Update**.

When you call **Update** for the new record:

- If your ODBC driver supports the **::SQLSetPos** ODBC API function, MFC uses the function to add the record on the data source. With **::SQLSetPos**, MFC can add a record more efficiently because it doesn't have to construct and process an SQL statement.

  –Or–

- If **::SQLSetPos** can't be used, MFC does the following:

1. If no changes are detected, **Update** does nothing and returns 0.

2. If there are changes, **Update** constructs an SQL **INSERT** statement. The columns represented by all dirty field data members are listed in the **INSERT** statement. To force a column to be included, call the **SetFieldDirty** member function:

   ```
   SetFieldDirty( &m_dataMember, TRUE );
   ```

3. **Update** commits the new record—the **INSERT** statement is executed and the record is committed to the table on the data source (and the recordset, if not a snapshot) unless a transaction is in progress (see "How Transactions Affect Updates" in the article "Recordset: More About Updates").

4. The stored record is restored to the edit buffer. The record that was current before the **AddNew** call is current again regardless of whether the **INSERT** statement was successfully executed.

Tip For complete control of a new record, take the following approach: (a) set the values of any fields that will have values; (b) explicitly set any fields that will remain Null by calling **SetFieldNull** with a pointer to the field and the parameter **TRUE** (the default). If you want to ensure that a field is not written to the data source, call **SetFieldDirty** with a pointer to the field and the parameter **FALSE**, and do not modify the field's value. To determine whether a field is allowed to be Null, call **IsFieldNullable**.

Tip *Advanced*: To detect when recordset data members change value, MFC uses a **PSEUDO_NULL** value appropriate to each data type that you can store in a recordset. If you must explicitly set a field to the **PSEUDO_NULL** value and the field happens already to be marked Null, you must also call **SetFieldNull**, passing the address of the field in the first parameter and **FALSE** in the second parameter.

Visibility of Added Records

When is an added record visible to your recordset? Added records sometimes show up and sometimes aren't visible, depending on two things:

- What your driver is capable of.
- What the framework can take advantage of.

If your ODBC driver supports the **::SQLSetPos** ODBC API function, MFC uses the function to add records. With **::SQLSetPos**, added records are visible to any updatable MFC recordset. Without support for the function, added records are not visible, and you must call **Requery** to see them. Using **::SQLSetPos** is also more efficient.

How Edit Works

Editing an existing record in a recordset involves scrolling to the record, calling the recordset's **Edit** member function, setting the values of the new record's field data members, and calling the **Update** member function to write the changed record to the data source.

As a precondition for calling **Edit**, the recordset must be updatable and on a record. The **CanUpdate** and **IsDeleted** member functions let you determine these conditions. The current record also must not already have been deleted, and there must be records in the recordset (both **IsBOF** and **IsEOF** return 0).

When you call **Edit**, the record in the edit buffer (the current record) is stored. The stored record's values are later used to detect whether any fields have changed.

After you call **Edit**, the edit buffer still represents the current record but is now ready to accept changes to the field data members. To change the record, you manually set the values of any field data members you want to edit. Instead of specifying an actual data value for a field, you can call **SetFieldNull** to specify the value Null—the field "has no value." (Don't confuse Null with C++ **NULL**.) To commit your changes, you call **Update**.

Tip To get out of **AddNew** or **Edit** mode, call **Move** with the parameter **AFX_MOVE_REFRESH**.

As a precondition for calling **Update**, the recordset must not be empty and the current record must not have been deleted. **IsBOF**, **IsEOF**, and **IsDeleted** should all return 0.

When you call **Update** for the edited record:

- If your ODBC driver supports the **::SQLSetPos** ODBC API function, MFC uses the function to update the record on the data source. With **::SQLSetPos**, the driver compares your edit buffer with the corresponding record on the server, updating the record on the server if the two are different. With **::SQLSetPos**, MFC can update a record more efficiently because it doesn't have to construct and process an SQL statement.

    −Or−

- If **::SQLSetPos** can't be used, MFC does the following:

    1. If there have been no changes, **Update** does nothing and returns 0.

    2. If there are changes, **Update** constructs an SQL **UPDATE** statement. The columns listed in the **UPDATE** statement are based on the field data members that have changed.

    3. **Update** commits the changes—executes the **UPDATE** statement—and the record is changed on the data source, but not committed if a transaction is in progress (see the article "Transaction: Performing a Transaction in a

Recordset" for details about how the transaction affects the update). ODBC keeps a copy of the record, which also changes.

4. Unlike the process for **AddNew**, the **Edit** process does not restore the stored record. The edited record remains in place as the current record.

Caution When you prepare to update a recordset by calling **Update**, take care that your recordset includes all columns making up the primary key of the table (or all of the columns of any unique index on the table, or enough columns to uniquely identify the row). In some cases, the framework can use only the columns selected in your recordset to identify which record in your table to update. Without all the necessary columns, multiple records may be updated in the table. In this case, the framework will throw exceptions when you call **Update**.

Tip If you call **AddNew** or **Edit** after having called either function previously but before you call **Update**, the edit buffer is refreshed with the stored record, replacing the new or edited record in progress. This behavior gives you a way to abort an **AddNew** or **Edit** and begin a new one: if you determine that the record-in-progress is faulty, simply call **Edit** or **AddNew** again.

How Delete Works

Deleting a record from a recordset involves scrolling to the record and calling the recordset's **Delete** member function. Unlike **AddNew** and **Edit**, **Delete** does not require a matching call to **Update**.

As a precondition for calling **Delete**, the recordset must be updatable and it must be on a record. The **CanUpdate**, **IsBOF**, **IsEOF**, and **IsDeleted** member functions let you determine these conditions.

When you call **Delete**:

- If your ODBC driver supports the **::SQLSetPos** ODBC API function, MFC uses the function to delete the record on the data source. Using **::SQLSetPos** is usually more efficient than using SQL.

  –Or–

- If **::SQLSetPos** can't be used, MFC does the following:

  1. The current record in the edit buffer is not backed up as in **AddNew** and **Edit**.
  2. **Delete** constructs an SQL **DELETE** statement that will remove the record.

     The current record in the edit buffer is not stored as in **AddNew** and **Edit**.
  3. **Delete** commits the deletion—executes the **DELETE** statement. The record is marked deleted on the data source and, if the record is a snapshot, in ODBC.

4. The deleted record's values are still in the field data members of the recordset, but the field data members are marked Null and the recordset's **IsDeleted** member function will return a nonzero value.

Important After deleting a record, you should scroll to another record to refill the edit buffer with the new record's data. It's an error to call **Delete** again, or to call **Edit**.

For information about the SQL statements used in update operations, see the article "SQL."

See Also   Articles: "Recordset: More About Updates," "Record Field Exchange"

Recordset: More About Updates

This article explains:

- How other operations, such as transactions, affect updates.
- Your updates and those of other users.
- More about the **Update** and **Delete** member functions.

How Other Operations Affect Updates

Your updates are affected by transactions in effect at the time of the update, by closing the recordset before completing a transaction, and by scrolling before completing a transaction.

How Transactions Affect Updates

Beyond understanding how **AddNew**, **Edit**, and **Delete** work, it's important to understand how the **BeginTrans**, **CommitTrans**, and **Rollback** member functions of **CDatabase** work with the update functions of **CRecordset**.

By default, calls to **AddNew** and **Edit** affect the data source immediately when you call **Update**. **Delete** calls take effect immediately. But you can establish a transaction and execute a batch of such calls. The updates are not permanent until you commit them. If you change your mind, you can roll back the transaction instead of committing it.

Tip The MFC transaction model is, by design, rather restrictive. If it is too restrictive for your application, see Technical Note 47 under MFC in Books Online.

For more information about transactions, see the article "Transaction."

How Closing the Recordset Affects Updates

If you close a recordset, or its associated **CDatabase** object, with a transaction in progress (you haven't called **CommitTrans** or **Rollback**), the transaction is rolled back automatically. "How Rollback Affects Transactions" in the article "Transaction: How Transactions Affects Update" describes the effect this has on **AddNew**, **Edit**, or **Delete** operations in progress.

How Scrolling Affects Updates

When you scroll in a recordset, the edit buffer is filled with each new current record (the previous record is not stored first). Scrolling skips over records previously deleted. If you scroll after an **AddNew** or **Edit** call without calling **Update**, **CommitTrans**, or **Rollback** first, any changes are lost (with no warning to you) as a new record is brought into the edit buffer. The edit buffer is filled with the record scrolled to, the stored record is freed, and no change occurs on the data source. This applies to both **AddNew** and **Edit**.

Your Updates and the Updates of Other Users

When you use a recordset to update data, your updates affect other users. Similarly, the updates of other users during the lifetime of your recordset affect you.

In a multiuser environment, other users can open recordsets that contain some of the same records you have selected in your recordset. Changes to a record before you retrieve it are reflected in your recordset. Dynasets retrieve a record each time you scroll to it, so dynasets reflect changes each time you scroll to a record. Snapshots retrieve a record the first time you scroll to it, so snapshots reflect only those changes that occur before you scroll to the record initially.

Records added by other users after you open the recordset don't show up in your recordset unless you requery. If your recordset is a dynaset, edits to existing records by other users do show up in your dynaset when you scroll to the affected record. If your recordset is a snapshot, edits don't show up until you requery the snapshot. If you want to see records added or deleted by other users in your snapshot, or records added by other users in your dynaset, call **Requery** to rebuild the recordset. (Note that the deletions of other users show up in your dynaset.) You may also call **Requery** to see records you add, but not to see your deletions.

Tip   To force caching of an entire snapshot at once, call **MoveLast** immediately after you open the snapshot. Then call **MoveFirst** to begin working with the records. **MoveLast** is equivalent to scrolling over all the records, but it retrieves them all at once. Note, however, that this can lower performance and may not be required for some drivers.

The effects of your updates on other users are similar to their effects on you.

More About Update and Delete

This section provides additional information to help you work with **Update** and **Delete**.

Update Success and Failure

If **Update** succeeds, the **AddNew** or **Edit** mode ends. To begin an **AddNew** or **Edit** mode again, call **AddNew** or **Edit**.

If **Update** fails (returns **FALSE** or throws an exception), you remain in **AddNew** or **Edit** mode, depending on which function you called last. You can then do one of the following:

- Modify a field data member and try the **Update** again.

- Call **AddNew** to reset the field data members to Null, set the values of the field data members, then call **Update** again.

- Call **Edit** to reload the values that were in the recordset before the first call to **AddNew** or **Edit**, then set the values of the field data members, then call **Update** again. After a successful **Update** call (except after an **AddNew** call), the field data members retain their new values.

- Call **Move** (including **Move** with a parameter of **AFX_MOVE_REFRESH**, or 0), which flushes any changes and ends any **AddNew** or **Edit** mode in effect.

Update and Delete

On an **Update** or **Delete** operation, one and only one record should be updated. That record is the current record, which corresponds to the data values in the fields of the recordset. If for some reason no records are affected or more than one record is affected, an exception is thrown containing one of the following **RETCODE** values:

- **AFX_SQL_ERROR_NO_ROWS_AFFECTED**
- **AFX_SQL_ERROR_MULTIPLE_ROWS_AFFECTED**

When these exceptions are thrown, you remain in the **AddNew** or **Edit** state you were in when you called **Update** or **Delete**. Here are the most common scenarios in which you would see these exceptions. You're most likely to see:

- **AFX_SQL_ERROR_NO_ROWS_AFFECTED** when you're using optimistic locking mode and another user has modified the record in a way that prevents the framework from identifying the correct record to update or delete.

- **AFX_SQL_ERROR_MULTIPLE_ROWS_AFFECTED** when the table you're updating has no primary key or unique index, and you don't have enough columns in the recordset to uniquely identify a table row.

See Also   Articles: "Recordset: How Recordsets Select Records," "Record Field Exchange," "Transaction," "SQL," "Exceptions: Database Exceptions"

Record Views

To support form-based data-access applications, the class library provides class **CRecordView**. A "record view" is a form view object whose controls are mapped directly to the field data members of a recordset object (and indirectly to the corresponding columns in a query result or table on the data source). Like its base class **CFormView**, **CRecordView** is based on a dialog template resource.

Topics covered in this article include:

- Uses for database forms
- Features of class CRecordView
- Data exchange for record views
- Your role in working with a record view
- Designing and creating a record view

Form Uses

Forms are useful for a variety of data-access tasks:

- Data entry
- Read-only examination of data
- Updating data

Features of Class CRecordView

You can do form-based data-access programming with class **CFormView**, but **CRecordView** is generally a better class to derive from. In addition to its **CFormView** features, **CRecordView**:

- Provides dialog data exchange (DDX) between the form controls and the associated recordset object.
- Handles Move First, Move Next, Move Previous, and Move Last commands for navigating through the records in the associated recordset object.
- Updates changes to the current record when the user moves to another record.

For more information about navigation, see the article "Record Views: Supporting Navigation in a Record View."

Data Exchange for Record Views

When you use ClassWizard to map the controls in a record view's dialog template resource to the fields of a recordset, the framework manages exchanging data in both directions—from recordset to controls and from controls to recordset. Using the DDX mechanism means you don't have to write the code to transfer data back and forth yourself. Make a few connections in ClassWizard and you're done.

DDX for record views works in conjunction with RFX for recordsets. RFX moves data between the current record of the data source and the field data members of a recordset object. DDX moves the data from the field data members to the controls in the form. This combination fills the form controls initially and as the user moves from record to record. It can also move updated data back to the recordset and then the data source.

Figure 1 shows the relationship between DDX and RFX for record views.

Figure 1   Dialog Data Exchange and Record Field Exchange

For more information about DDX, see Chapter 12 in the *Visual C++ User's Guide*. For more information about RFX, see the article "Record Field Exchange."

Your Role in Working with a Record View

Table 1 shows what you typically must do to work with a record view and what the framework does for you.

Table 1   Working with a Record View: You and the Framework

You...	The framework...
Use the Visual C++ dialog editor to design the form.	The dialog editor makes it easy to create a dialog template resource with controls.
Use ClassWizard to create classes derived from **CRecordView** and **CRecordset**.	ClassWizard writes the classes for you.
Use ClassWizard to map record view controls to recordset field data members.	Provides DDX between the controls and the recordset fields.
	Provides default command handlers for Move First, Move Last, Move Next, and Move Previous commands from menus or toolbar buttons.
	Updates changes to the data source.

Table 1   **Working with a Record View: You and the Framework (*continued*)**

You...	The framework...
[Optional] Write code to fill list boxes or combo boxes or other controls with data from a second recordset.	
[Optional] Write code for any special validations.	
[Optional] Write code to add or delete records.	

Form-based programming is only one approach to working with a database. For information on applications using some other user interface, or no user interface, see the articles "MFC: Using Database Classes with Documents and Views" and "MFC: Using Database Classes Without Documents and Views."

Designing and Creating a Record View

You can create your record view class with either AppWizard or ClassWizard. If you use AppWizard, the wizard creates the record view class and a dialog template resource for it (without controls). You must use the Visual C++ dialog editor to add controls to the dialog template resource. On the other hand, if you use ClassWizard, you must first create the dialog template resource in the dialog editor, then open ClassWizard and create the record view class.

▶   **To create your record view with AppWizard**

- See the article "AppWizard: Database Support."

▶   **To design your form**

- See Chapter 5, "Using the Dialog Editor," in the *Visual C++ User's Guide*.

▶   **To create your record view class with ClassWizard**

- See the article "ClassWizard: Creating a Database Form."

Tip   For an example of an application with multiple record views on a database, see the ENROLL tutorial application, Step 4. The step is described in "ENROLL" in the MFC Samples under MFC in Books Online rather than in the ENROLL tutorial; you can examine the code in \MSVC20\SAMPLES\MFC\ENROLL\STEP4.

The following articles explain additional details of using record views:

- Record Views: Supporting Navigation in a Record View
- Record Views: Using a Record View
- Record Views: Filling a List Box from a Second Recordset

See Also   Articles: "Record Views: Supporting Navigation in a Record View," "AppWizard: Database Support," "ClassWizard: Creating a Database Form," "ClassWizard: Mapping Form Controls to Recordset Fields," "Recordset"

Record Views: Supporting Navigation in a Record View

This article explains how to support movement from record to record in your record view. The article covers:

- Command handling for record scrolling commands.
- User-interface update handlers for scrolling commands.

Command Handlers for Record Scrolling

Class **CRecordView** provides default command handling for the following standard commands:

- **ID_RECORD_MOVE_FIRST**
- **ID_RECORD_MOVE_LAST**
- **ID_RECORD_MOVE_NEXT**
- **ID_RECORD_MOVE_PREV**

The **OnMove** member function of class **CRecordView** provides default command handling for all four commands, which move from record to record. As these commands are issued, RFX loads the new record into the recordset's fields and DDX moves the values into the record form's controls. (For information about RFX, see the article "Record Field Exchange.")

Important Be sure to use these standard command IDs for any user-interface objects associated with the standard record navigation commands.

User-Interface Updating for Record Views

CRecordView also provides default user-interface update handlers for the navigation commands. These handlers automate enabling and disabling the user-interface objects—menu items and toolbar buttons. AppWizard supplies standard menus and, if you choose the AppWizard "Initial Toolbar" option, a set of toolbar buttons for the commands. If you create a record view class with ClassWizard, you may want to add similar user-interface objects to your application.

▶ **To create menu resources with the menu editor**
- Using the information in Chapter 6, "Using the Menu Editor," in the *Visual C++ User's Guide*, create your own menu with the same four commands.

▶ **To create toolbar buttons with the graphics editor**

1. Using the information in Chapter 9, "Using the Graphic Editor," in the *Visual C++ User's Guide*, edit the toolbar bitmap resource to add toolbar buttons for your record navigation commands.

2. In your project's MAINFRM.CPP file, edit the **buttons** array to add command IDs for the toolbar buttons.

For an example of these steps, see Chapter 10, "Constructing the User Interface," in *Introducing Visual C++*.

See Also   Article: "Record Views: Using a Record View"

Record Views: Using a Record View

This article explains how you might commonly customize the default code that the wizard writes for you. Typically, you'll want to constrain the record selection with a filter or parameters, perhaps sort the records, or customize the SQL statement.

Using **CRecordView** is much the same as using **CFormView**. The basic approach is to use the record view to display and perhaps update the records of a single recordset. Beyond that, you might want to use other recordsets as well, as discussed in the article "Record Views: Filling a List Box from a Second Recordset."

Record View Code Created by AppWizard

ClassWizard (or AppWizard) overrides the view's **OnInitialUpdate** and **OnGetRecordset** member functions. After the framework creates the frame window, document, and view, it calls OnInitialUpdate to initialize the view. OnInitialUpdate obtains a pointer to the recordset from the document. A call to the base class **CRecordView::OnInitialUpdate** function opens the recordset. The following code shows this process:

```
void CSectionForm::OnInitialUpdate()
{
    m_pSet = &GetDocument()->m_sectionSet;
    CRecordView::OnInitialUpdate();
}
```

When the recordset opens, it selects records. **CRecordset::Open** makes the first record the current record, and DDX moves data from the recordset's field data members to the corresponding form controls in the view. For more information about RFX, see the article "Record Field Exchange." For more information about DDX, see Chapter 12 in the *Visual C++ User's Guide*. For details of the document/view creation process, see Chapter 1 in this book.

Important You should give your end users the capability to "refresh" the record view controls from the recordset. Without this capability, if a user changes a control's value to an illegal value, he or she could be permanently stuck on the current record. To refresh the controls, you call **UpdateData** with a parameter of **FALSE**. For an example, see Step 3 in the ENROLL tutorial—look at the OnRecordAdd member function in file SECTFORM.CPP. The tutorial begins in Chapter 24 in *Introducing Visual C++*.

Changes You Might Make to the Default Code

ClassWizard writes a recordset class for you that simply selects all records in a single table. You'll often want to modify that behavior in one or more of the following ways:

- Set a filter and/or a sort order for the recordset. Do this in OnInitialUpdate after the recordset object is constructed but before its **Open** member function is called. See the articles "Recordset: Filtering Records" and "Recordset: Sorting Records" for details. For an example, see the OnInitialUpdate member function in the file \MSVC20\SAMPLES\MFC\ENROLL\STEP2\SECTFORM.CPP.

- Parameterize the recordset. Specify the actual run-time parameter value after the filter. See the article "Recordset: Parameterizing a Recordset" for details.

- Pass a customized SQL string to the **Open** member function. For a discussion of what you can accomplish with this technique, see the article "SQL: Customizing Your Recordset's SQL Statement."

See Also   Article: "Record Views: Filling a List Box from a Second Recordset"

Record Views: Filling a List Box from a Second Recordset

By default, a record view is associated with a single recordset object, whose fields are mapped to the record view's controls. Sometimes you will want to put a list box or combo box control in your record view and fill it with values from a second recordset object. The user can use the list box to select a new category of information to display in the record view. This article explains how and when to do that.

For example, the ENROLL tutorial in *Introducing Visual C++* uses a record view, CSectionForm, to display information about sections of college courses. ENROLL binds the form's controls to the field data members of a recordset of class CSectionSet. CSectionForm's combo box control is filled from a second recordset of class CCourseSet that contains a record for each course offered at the school. When the user selects a new course in the combo box, the record view requeries the `CSectionSet` recordset to get the sections for the selected course. See the ENROLL tutorial sample under MFC Samples in Books Online. Step 2 adds the combo box.

The model for this article, then, consists of a primary recordset that fills the controls of your form, while a secondary recordset fills a list box or combo box. Selecting a string from the list box causes your program to requery the primary recordset based on what was selected.The procedure below uses a combo box but applies equally to a list box.

▶ **To fill a list box or combo box from a second recordset**

1. Create the recordset object.
2. Obtain a pointer to the **CComboBox** object for the combo box control.
3. Empty the combo box of any previous contents.
4. Move through all records in the recordset, calling **CComboBox::AddString** for each string from the current record you want to add to the combo box.
5. Initialize the selection in the combo box.

The code in the `OnInitialUpdate` member function of class `CSectionForm` in the ENROLL tutorial sample illustrates the procedure. The following excerpt shows how the combo box is filled by extracting a course ID value from each record in the recordset pointed to by `pCourses`.

```
void CSectionForm::OnInitialUpdate()
{
    // ...

    // Fill the combo box with all of the courses
    CENROLLDoc* pDoc = GetDocument();
    if (!pDoc->m_courseSet.Open())
        return;

    // ...

    m_ctlCourseList.ResetContent();
    if (pDoc->m_courseSet.IsOpen())
    {
        while (!pDoc->m_courseSet.IsEOF() )
        {
            m_ctlCourseList.AddString(
                pDoc->m_courseSet.m_CourseID);
            pDoc->m_courseSet.MoveNext();
        }
    }
    m_ctlCourseList.SetCurSel(0);
}
```

This function uses a second recordset, m_courseSet, which contains a record for each course offered, and a **CComboBox** control, m_ctlCourseList, which is stored in the record view class.

The function gets m_courseSet from the document and opens it. Then it empties m_ctlCourseList and scrolls through m_courseSet. For each record, the function calls the combo box's **AddString** member function to add the course ID value from the record. Finally, the code sets the combo box's selection.

Registration

When a user wants to insert an OLE item into an application, OLE presents a list of object types to choose from. OLE gets this list from the system registration database, which contains information provided by all server applications. When a server registers itself, the entries it puts into the system registration database describe each type of object it supplies, file extensions, and the path to itself, among other information.

The framework and the OLE system DLLs use this registry to determine what types of OLE items are available on the system. The OLE system DLLs also use this registry to determine how to launch a server application when a linked or embedded object is activated.

This article describes what each server application needs to do when it is installed and each time it is executed.

For detailed information about the system registration database and the format of the .REG files used to update it, see the *OLE 2 Programmer's Reference, Volume 1*.

Server Installation

When you first install your server application, it should register all the types of OLE items that it supports. You can also have the server update the system registration database every time it executes as a stand-alone application. This keeps the registration database up-to-date if the server's executable file is moved.

If you want to register your application during installation, use the REGEDT32.EXE program found in your Windows directory. If you include a setup program with your application, you should have the setup program run "REGEDT32 /S *appname*.REG". Otherwise, instruct the user to run REGEDT32 manually.

REGEDT32 merges the contents of the .REG text file into the registration database. To actually verify the database or to repair it, use REGEDT32 /V. Exercise care to avoid deleting essential OLE entries.

Server Initialization

When you create a server application with AppWizard, the wizard completes all initialization tasks for you automatically. This section describes what you must do if you write a server application manually.

When a server application is launched by a container application, the OLE system DLLs add the "/Embedding" option to the server's command line. A server application's behavior differs depending on whether it was launched by a container, so the first thing an application should do when it begins execution is check for the "/Embedding" or "-Embedding" option on the command line. If this switch exists, you should load a different set of resources that show the server as being either in-place active or fully open. For more information, see the article "Menus and Resources: Server Additions."

Your server application should also call its **CWinApp::RunEmbedded** function to parse the command line. If it returns a nonzero value, the application should not show its window because it has been run from a container application, not as a stand-alone application. This function updates the server's entry in the system registration database and calls the **RegisterAll** member function for you, performing instance registration.

When your server application is starting, you must ensure that it can perform instance registration. Instance registration does not add an entry to the registration database. Instead, it informs the OLE system DLLs that the server is active and ready to receive requests from containers. Perform instance registration of the server by calling the **ConnectTemplate** member function defined by **COleTemplateServer**. This connects the **CDocTemplate** object to the **COleTemplateServer** object.

The **ConnectTemplate** function takes three parameters: the server's **CLSID**, a pointer to the **CDocTemplate** object, and a flag indicating whether the server supports multiple instances. A mini-server must be able to support multiple instances; that is, it must be possible for multiple instances of the server to run simultaneously, one for each container. Consequently, you should pass **TRUE** for this flag when launching a mini-server.

If you are writing a mini-server, by definition it will always be launched by a container. You should still parse the command line to check for the "/Embedding" option. The absence of this option on the command line means that the user has tried to launch the mini-server as a stand-alone application. If this occurs, you should register the server with the system registration database and then display a message box informing the user to launch the mini-server from a container application.

See Also   Article: "Servers"

In the *Class Library Reference*: **CWinApp::RunAutomated**, **CWinApp::RunEmbedded**, **COleTemplateServer**

Result Set

See the article "Recordset."

RFX

See the article "Record Field Exchange."

Rollback

See the article "Transaction."

Schema

A database schema describes the current structure of the tables and database views in the database. In general, ClassWizard assumes that the schema for the table(s) accessed by a recordset will not change, but the database classes can deal with some schema changes, such as adding, reordering, or deleting unbound columns. If a table changes, you can "refresh" your recordset for the table using ClassWizard's Update Columns button and then recompile your application.

You can also supplement the code ClassWizard produces to deal with a database whose schema is not entirely known at compile time. For more information, see the article "Recordset: Dynamically Binding Data Columns."

See Also   Articles: "SQL," "Recordset," "ClassWizard"

Serialization (Object Persistence)

This article explains the serialization mechanism provided in the Microsoft Foundation Class Library (MFC) to allow objects to persist between runs of your program.

"Serialization" is the process of writing or reading an object to or from a persistent storage medium, such as a disk file. MFC supplies built-in support for serialization in the class **CObject**. Thus, all classes derived from **CObject** can take advantage of **CObject**'s serialization protocol.

The basic idea of serialization is that an object should be able to write its current state, usually indicated by the value of its member variables, to persistent storage. Later, the object can be re-created by reading, or deserializing, the object's state from the storage. Serialization handles all the details of object pointers and circular references to objects that are used when you serialize an object. A key point is that the object itself is responsible for reading and writing its own state. Thus, for a class to be serializable, it must implement the basic serialization operations. As shown in the Serialization group of articles, it is easy to add this functionality to a class.

MFC uses an object of the **CArchive** class as an intermediary between the object to be serialized and the storage medium. This object is always associated with a **CFile** object, from which it obtains the necessary information for serialization, including the filename and whether the requested operation is a read or write. The object that performs a serialization operation can use the **CArchive** object without regard to the nature of the storage medium.

A **CArchive** object uses overloaded insertion (<<) and extraction (>>) operators to perform writing and reading operations. For more information, see "Storing and

Loading CObjects via an Archive" in the article "Serialization: Serializing an Object."

Note Do not confuse the **CArchive** class with general-purpose iostream classes, which are for formatted text only. The **CArchive** class is for binary-format serialized objects.

The following articles cover the two main tasks required for serialization:

- Serialization: Making a Serializable Class
- Serialization: Serializing an Object

The article "Serialization: Serialization vs. Database Input/Output" is part of the group of articles on database topics. The article describes when serialization is an appropriate input/output technique in database applications.

Serialization: Making a Serializable Class

Five main steps are required to make a class serializable. They are listed below and explained in the following sections:

1. Deriving your class from **CObject** (or from some class derived from **CObject**).
2. Using the **DECLARE_SERIAL** macro in the class declaration.
3. Overriding the **Serialize** member function.
4. Defining a constructor that takes no arguments.
5. Using the **IMPLEMENT_SERIAL** macro in the implementation file for your class.

If you call **Serialize** directly rather than through the >> and << operators of **CArchive**, the last three steps are not required for serialization.

Deriving Your Class from CObject and Using the DECLARE_SERIAL Macro

The basic serialization protocol and functionality are defined in the **CObject** class. By deriving your class from **CObject** (or from a class derived from **CObject**), as shown in the following declaration of class CPerson, you gain access to the serialization protocol and functionality of **CObject**.

The **DECLARE_SERIAL** macro is required in the declaration of classes that will support serialization, as shown here:

```
class CPerson : public CObject
{
    DECLARE_SERIAL( CPerson )
    // rest of declaration follows...
};
```

Overriding the Serialize Member Function

The **Serialize** member function, which is defined in the **CObject** class, is
responsible for actually serializing the data necessary to capture an object's current
state. The **Serialize** function has a **CArchive** argument that it uses to read and
write the object data. The **CArchive** object has a member function, **IsStoring**,
which indicates whether **Serialize** is storing (writing data) or loading (reading
data). Using the results of **IsStoring** as a guide, you either insert your object's data
in the **CArchive** object with the insertion operator (**<<**) or extract data with the
extraction operator (**>>**).

Consider a class that is derived from **CObject** and has two new member variables,
of types **CString** and **WORD**. The following class declaration fragment shows the
new member variables and the declaration for the overridden **Serialize** member
function:

```
class CPerson : public CObject
{
public:
    DECLARE_SERIAL( CPerson, )
    // empty constructor is necessary
    CPerson(){};

    CString m_name;
    WORD    m_number;

    void Serialize( CArchive& archive );

    // rest of class declaration
};
```

▶   **To override the Serialize member function**

1. Call your base class version of **Serialize** to make sure that the inherited portion
   of the object is serialized.

2. Insert or extract the member variables specific to your class.

   The insertion and extraction operators interact with the archive class to read and
   write the data. The following example shows how to implement **Serialize** for the
   CPerson class declared above:

```
void CPerson::Serialize( CArchive& archive )
{
    // call base class function first
    // base class is CObject in this case
    CObject::Serialize( archive );

    // now do the stuff for our specific class
    if( archive.IsStoring() )
        archive << m_name << m_number;
    else
        archive >> m_name >> m_number;
}
```

You can also use the **CArchive::Read** and **CArchive::Write** member functions to read and write large amounts of untyped data.

Defining a Constructor with No Arguments

MFC requires a default constructor when it re-creates your objects as they are deserialized (loaded from disk.) The deserialization process will fill in all member variables with the values required to re-create the object.

This constructor can be declared public, protected, or private. If you make it protected or private, you ensure that it will only be used by the serialization functions. The constructor must put the object in a state that allows it to be safely deleted if necessary.

Note If you forget to define a constructor with no arguments in a class that uses the **DECLARE_SERIAL** and **IMPLEMENT_SERIAL** macros, you will get a "no default constructor available" compiler warning on the line where the **IMPLEMENT_SERIAL** macro is used.

Using the IMPLEMENT_SERIAL Macro in the Implementation File

The **IMPLEMENT_SERIAL** macro is used to define the various functions needed when you derive a serializable class from **CObject**. You use this macro in the implementation file (.CPP) for your class. The first two arguments to the macro are the name of the class and the name of its immediate base class.

The third argument to this macro is a schema number. The schema number is essentially a version number for objects of the class. Use an integer greater than or equal to 0 for the schema number. (Don't confuse this schema number with database terminology.)

The MFC serialization code checks the schema number when reading objects into memory. If the schema number of the object on disk does not match the schema number of the class in memory, the library will throw a **CArchiveException**, preventing your program from reading an incorrect version of the object.

If you want your `Serialize` member function to be able to read multiple versions —that is, files written with different versions of the application—you can use the value **VERSIONABLE_SCHEMA** as an argument to the **DECLARE_SERIAL** macro. For usage information and an example, see the **GetObjectSchema** member function of class **CArchive**.

The following example shows how to use **IMPLEMENT_SERIAL** for a class, `CPerson`, that is derived from **CObject**:

```
IMPLEMENT_SERIAL( CPerson, CObject, 1 )
```

Once you have a serializable class, you can serialize objects of the class, as discussed in the article "Serialization: Serializing an Object."

See Also   In the *Class Library Reference*: **CArchive**

Serialization: Serializing an Object

The article "Serialization: Making a Serializable Class" shows how to make a class serializable. Once you have a serializable class, you can serialize objects of that class to and from a file via a **CArchive** object. This article explains:

- What a CArchive object is.
- Two ways to create a CArchive.
- How to use the CArchive << and >> operators.
- Storing and loading CObjects via an archive.

You can let the framework create the archive for your serializable document or explicitly create the **CArchive** object yourself. You can transfer data between a file and your serializable object by using the << and >> operators for **CArchive** or, in some cases, by calling the `Serialize` function of a **CObject**-derived class.

What Is a CArchive Object

A **CArchive** object provides a type-safe buffering mechanism for writing or reading serializable objects to or from a **CFile** object. Usually the **CFile** object represents a disk file; however, it can also be a memory file (**CMemFile** object), perhaps representing the Clipboard.

A given **CArchive** object either stores (writes, serializes) data or loads (reads, deserializes) data, but never both. The life of a **CArchive** object is limited to one pass through writing objects to a file or reading objects from a file. Thus, two successively created **CArchive** objects are required to serialize data to a file and then deserialize it back from the file.

When an archive stores objects to a file, the archive attaches the **CRuntimeClass** name to the objects. Then, when another archive loads objects from a file to memory, the **CObject**-derived objects are dynamically reconstructed based on the **CRuntimeClass** of the objects. A given object may be referenced more than once as it is written to the file by the storing archive. The loading archive, however, will reconstruct the object only once. The details about how an archive attaches **CRuntimeClass** information to objects and reconstructs objects, taking into account possible multiple references, are described in Technical Note 2 under MFC in Books Online.

As data is serialized to an archive, the archive accumulates the data until its buffer is full. Then the archive writes its buffer to the **CFile** object pointed to by the **CArchive** object. Similarly, as you read data from an archive, it reads data from the file to its buffer and then from the buffer to your deserialized object. This buffering reduces the number of times a hard disk is physically read, thus improving your application's performance.

Two Ways to Create a CArchive Object

There are two ways to create a **CArchive** object:

- Implicit creation of a **CArchive** object via the framework
- Explicit creation of a **CArchive** object

Implicit Creation of a CArchive Object via the Framework

The most common, and easiest, way is to let the framework create a **CArchive** object for your document on behalf of the Save, Save As, and Open commands on the File menu.

Here is what the framework does when the user of your application issues the Save As command from the File menu:

1. Presents the File Save As dialog box and gets the filename from the user.
2. Opens the file named by the user as a **CFile** object.
3. Creates a **CArchive** object that points to this **CFile** object. In creating the **CArchive** object, the framework sets the mode to "store" (write, serialize), as opposed to "load" (read, deserialize).
4. Calls the Serialize function defined in your **CDocument**-derived class, passing it a reference to the **CArchive** object.

Your document's Serialize function then writes data to the **CArchive** object, as explained shortly. Upon return from your Serialize function, the framework destroys the **CArchive** object and then the **CFile** object.

Thus, if you let the framework create the **CArchive** object for your document, all you have to do is implement the document's Serialize function that writes and reads to and from the archive. You also have to implement `Serialize` for any **CObject**-derived objects that the document's `Serialize` function in turn serializes directly or indirectly.

Explicit Creation of a CArchive Object

Besides serializing a document via the framework, there are other occasions when you may need a **CArchive** object. For example, you might want to serialize data to and from the Clipboard, represented by a **CMemFile** object. Or, you may want to use a user interface for saving a file that is different from the one offered by the framework. In this case, you can explicitly create a **CArchive** object. You do this the same way the framework does, using the following procedure.

▶ **To explicitly create a CArchive object**

1. Construct a **CFile** object or an object derived from **CFile**.

2. Pass the **CFile** object to the constructor for **CArchive**, as shown in the following example:

```
CFile theFile;
theFile.Open(..., CFile::modeWrite);
CArchive archive(&theFile, CArchive::store);
```

The second argument to the **CArchive** constructor is an enumerated value that specifies whether the archive will be used for storing or loading data to or from the file. The `Serialize` function of an object checks this state by calling the **IsStoring** function for the archive object.

When you are finished storing or loading data to or from the **CArchive** object, close it. Although the **CArchive** (and **CFile**) objects will automatically close the archive (and file), it is good practice to explicitly do so since it makes recovery from errors easier. For more information about error handling, see the article "Exceptions: Catching and Deleting Exceptions."

▶ **To close the CArchive object**

• The following example illustrates how to close the **CArchive** object:

```
archive.Close();
theFile.Close();
```

Using the CArchive << and >> Operators

CArchive provides << and >> operators for writing and reading simple data types as well as **CObject**s to and from a file.

▶ **To store an object in a file via an archive**

  • The following example shows how to store an object in a file via an archive:

```
CArchive ar(&theFile, CArchive::store);
WORD wEmployeeID;
...
ar << wEmployeeID;
```

▶ **To load an object from a value previously stored in a file**

  • The following example shows how to load an object from a value previously stored in a file:

```
CArchive ar(&theFile, CArchive::load);
WORD wEmployeeID;
...
ar >> wEmployeeID;
```

Usually, you store and load data to and from a file via an archive in the Serialize functions of **CObject**-derived classes, which you must have declared with the **DECLARE_SERIALIZE** macro. A reference to a **CArchive** object is passed to your Serialize function. You call the **IsLoading** function of the **CArchive** object to determine whether the Serialize function has been called to load data from the file or store data to the file.

The Serialize function of a serializable **CObject**-derived class typically has the following form:

```
void CPerson::Serialize(CArchive& ar)
{
    CObject::Serialize(ar);
    if (ar.IsStoring())
    {
        // TODO:  add storing code here
    }
    else
    {
    // TODO:  add loading code here
    }
}
```

The above code template is exactly the same as the one AppWizard creates for the Serialize function of the document (a class derived from **CDocument**). This code template helps you write code that is easier to review, because the storing code and the loading code should always be parallel, as in the following example:

```
void CPerson:Serialize(CArchive& ar)
{
    if (ar.IsStoring())
    {
        ar << m_strName;
        ar << m_wAge;
    }
    else
    {
        ar >> m_strName;
        ar >> m_wAge;
    }
}
```

The library defines **<<** and **>>** operators for **CArchive** as the first operand and the following data types and class types as the second operand:

CObject*	**SIZE** and **CSize**	**float**
WORD	**CString**	**POINT** and **CPoint**
DWORD	**BYTE**	**RECT** and **CRect**
double	**LONG**	**CTime** and **CTimeSpan**

Note Storing and loading **CObject**s via an archive requires extra consideration. For more information see "Storing and Loading CObjects via an Archive" below.

The **CArchive** **<<** and **>>** operators always return a reference to the **CArchive** object, which is the first operand. This enables you to chain the operators, as illustrated below:

```
BYTE bSomeByte;
WORD wSomeWord;
DWORD wSomeDoubleWord;
...
ar << bSomeByte << wSomeWord << wSomeDoubleWord;
```

Storing and Loading CObjects via an Archive

Storing and loading **CObject**s via an archive requires extra consideration. In certain cases, you should call the Serialize function of the object, where the **CArchive** object is a parameter of the Serialize call, as opposed to using the **<<** or **>>** operator of the **CArchive**. The important fact to keep in mind is that the **CArchive** **>>** operator constructs the **CObject** in memory based on **CRuntimeClass** information previously written to the file by the storing archive.

Therefore, whether you use the **CArchive** **<<** and **>>** operators, versus call Serialize, depends on whether you *need* the loading archive to dynamically reconstruct the object based on previously stored **CRuntimeClass** information. Use the `Serialize` function in the following cases:

- When deserializing the object, you know the exact class of the object beforehand.
- When deserializing the object, you already have memory allocated for it.

Caution If you load the object using the `Serialize` function, you must also store the object using the `Serialize` function. Don't store using the **CArchive <<** operator and then load using the `Serialize` function, or store using the `Serialize` function and then load using **CArchive >>** operator.

The following example illustrates the cases:

```
class CMyObject : public CObject
{
    // ...Member functions
    CMyObject();
    virtual void Serialize( CArchive& ar );

// Implementation
protected:
    DECLARE_SERIAL( CMyObject )
};

class COtherObject : public CObject
{
    // ...Member functions
    COtherObject();
    virtual void Serialize( CArchive& ar );

// Implementation
protected:
    DECLARE_SERIAL( COtherObject )
};

class CCompoundObject : public CObject
{
    // ...Member functions
    CCompoundObject();
    virtual void Serialize( CArchive& ar );

// Implementation
protected:
    CMyObject m_myob;      // Embedded object
    COtherObject* m_pOther;    // Object allocated in constructor
    CObject* m_pObDyn;     // Dynamically allocated object
```

```
                    //..Other member data and implementation

                    DECLARE_SERIAL( CCompoundObject )
            };

            CCompoundObject::CCompoundObject()
            {
                m_pOther = new COtherObject; // Exact type known and object already
                            //allocated.
                m_pObDyn = NULL;    // Will be allocated in another member function
                            // if needed, could be a derived class object.
            }

            void CCompundObject::Serialize( CArchive& ar )
            {
                CObject::Serialize( ar );    // Always call base class Serialize.
                m_myob.Serialize( ar );    // Call Serialize on embedded member.
                m_pOther->Serialize( ar );    // Call Serialize on objects of known
                            exact type.

                // Serialize dynamic members and other raw data
                if ( ar.IsStoring() )
                {
                    ar << m_pObDyn;
                    // Store other members
                }
                else
                {
                    ar >> m_pObDyn; // Polymorphic reconstruction of persistent
                            // object
                            //load other members
                }
            }
```

In summary, if your serializable class defines an embedded **CObject** as a member, you should *not* use the **CArchive** << and >> operators for that object, but should call the Serialize function instead. Also, if your serializable class defines a pointer to a **CObject** (or an object derived from **CObject**) as a member, but constructs this other object in its own constructor, you should also call Serialize.

See Also   In the *Class Library Reference*: **CArchive**

Serialization: Serialization vs. Database Input/Output

This article explains when to use document objects and serialization for file-based input/output (I/O) and when other I/O techniques are appropriate—because the application reads and writes data on a per-transaction basis, as in database applications. If you don't use serialization, you also won't need the File Open, Save, and Save As commands. Topics covered include:

- Deciding how your application will handle input/output
- Handling the File menu in database applications

Deciding How to Handle Input/Output

Whether you use file-based I/O or not depends on how you respond to the questions in the following decision tree, which begins with the question:

Does the primary data in your application reside in a disk file?

1. Yes, the primary data resides in a disk file.

   Does the application read the whole file into memory on File Open and write the whole file back to disk on File Save?

   1.1 Yes—this is the default MFC document case.

   Use **CDocument** serialization.

   1.2 No—this is typically the case of transaction-based updating of the file.

   The CHKBOOK sample is an example of this case. You update the file on a per-transaction basis and don't need **CDocument** serialization.

2. No, the primary data doesn't reside in a disk file.

   Does the data reside in an ODBC data source?

   2.1 Yes, the data resides in an ODBC data source.

   Use MFC's database support. The standard MFC implementation for this case includes a **CDocument** object that stores a **CDatabase** object, as discussed in the article "Database Overview." The application might also read and write an auxiliary file—the purpose of the AppWizard "both a database view and file support" option. In this case, you'd use serialization for the auxiliary file.

   2.2 No, the data doesn't reside in an ODBC data source.

   Examples of this case: the data resides in a non-ODBC DBMS; the data is read via some other mechanism, such as OLE or DDE.

   In such cases, you won't use serialization, and your application won't have Open and Save menu items. You might still want to use a **CDocument** as a "home base," just as an MFC ODBC application uses the document to store **CRecordset** objects. But you won't use the framework's default File Open/Save document serialization.

To support the Open, Save, and Save As commands on the File menu, the framework provides document serialization. Serialization reads and writes data, including objects derived from class **CObject**, to permanent storage, normally a disk file. Serialization is easy to use and serves many of your needs, but it may be inappropriate in many data-access applications. Data-access applications typically update data on a "per-transaction" basis. They update the records affected by the transaction rather than reading and writing a whole data file at once.

For general information about serialization, see the article "Serialization (Object Persistence)." For information on MFC sample programs, such as CHKBOOK, see the name of the sample under MFC Samples in Books Online.

The File Menu in an MFC Database Application

If you create an MFC database application and don't use serialization, how should you interpret the Open, Close, Save, and Save As commands on the File menu? While there are no style guidelines for this question, here are a few suggestions:

- Eliminate the File menu's Open command entirely.
- Interpret the Open command as "open database" and show the user a list of data sources your application recognizes.
- Interpret the Open command as, perhaps, "open profile." Retain Open for opening a serialized file, but use the file to store a serialized document containing "user profile" information, such as the user's preferences, including his or her login ID (optionally excluding the password) and the data source he or she most recently worked with.

AppWizard supports creating an application with no document-related File menu commands. Select the "A database view, without file support" option on the database options page.

To interpret a File menu command in a special way, you must override one or more command handlers, mostly in your **CWinApp**-derived class. For example, if you completely override **OnFileOpen** (which implements the **ID_FILE_OPEN** command) to mean "open database":

- Don't call the base class version of **OnFileOpen**, since you're completely replacing the framework's default implementation of the command.
- Use the handler instead to display a dialog box listing data sources. You can display such a dialog by calling **CDatabase::Open** with the parameter **NULL**. This opens an ODBC dialog box that displays all available data sources on the user's machine.
- Because database applications typically don't save a whole document, you'll probably want to remove the Save and Save As implementations unless you use a serialized document to store profile information. Otherwise, you might implement the Save command as, for example, "commit transaction." See Technical Note 22 under MFC in Books Online for more information about overriding these commands.

Servers

A "Visual Editing server application" creates Object Linking and Embedding (OLE) items for use by container applications. Some server applications only support the creation of embedded items; others support the creation of both embedded and linked items. Some support linking only, although this is rare. All server applications must support activation by container applications when the user wants to edit an item. If a server application supports linked items, it must also be able to copy its data, using the Clipboard or drag and drop, so that a container can paste in new OLE items. An application can be both a container and a server; that is, it can both incorporate data into its documents, and create data that can be incorporated as items into other applications' documents.

A "mini-server" is a special type of server application that can only be launched by a container. The Microsoft Draw and Microsoft Graph servers are examples of mini-servers. A mini-server does not store documents as files on disk; instead, it reads its documents from and writes them to items in documents belonging to containers. As a result, a mini-server only supports embedding, not linking.

A "full-server" can be run either as a stand-alone application or launched by a container application. A full-server can store documents as files on disk. It can support embedding only, both embedding and linking, or only linking. The user of a container application creates an embedded item by choosing the Cut or Copy command in the server and the Paste command in the container. A linked item is created by choosing the Copy command in the server and the Paste Link command in the container.

Table 1 summarizes characteristics of different types of servers:

Table 1   Server Characteristics

Type of server	Supports multiple instances	Items per document	Documents per instance
Mini-server	Yes	1	1
SDI full-server	Yes	1 (if linking is supported, 1 or more)	1
MDI full-server	No (not required)	1 (if linking is supported, 1 or more)	0 or more

A server application should support multiple containers simultaneously, in the event that more than one container wants to edit an embedded or linked item. If the server is an SDI application (or a mini-server with a dialog box interface), multiple instances of the server must be able to run simultaneously. This allows a separate instance of the application to handle each container's requests.

If the server is an MDI application, it can simply create a new MDI child window each time a container needs to edit an item. In this way, a single instance of the application can support multiple containers.

Your server application must tell the OLE system DLLs what to do if one instance of the server is already running when another container requests its services: whether it should launch a new instance of the server or direct all containers' requests to one instance of the server.

For more details on servers, see the following articles:

- Servers: Implementing a Server
- Servers: Implementing Server Documents
- Servers: Implementing In-Place Frame Windows
- Servers: Server Items
- Servers: User-Interface Issues

See Also   Articles: "Containers," "Containers: Advanced Features," "Menus and Resources," "Registration"

Servers: Implementing a Server

This article explains the code AppWizard creates for a Visual Editing server application. If you are not using AppWizard, this article lists the areas where you must write code to implement a server application.

If you are using AppWizard to create a new server application, AppWizard provides a significant amount of server-specific code for you. If you are adding Visual Editing server functionality to an existing application, you must duplicate the code that AppWizard would have provided before adding the rest of the necessary server code.

The server code that AppWizard provides falls into several categories:

- Defining server resources:
    - The menu resource used when the server is editing an embedded item in its own window.
    - The menu and toolbar resources used when the server is active in place.

  For more information on these resources, see the article "Menus and Resources: Server Additions."
- Defining an item class derived from **COleServerItem**. For further details on server items, see the article "Servers: Server Items."
- Changing the base class of the document class to **COleServerDoc**. For further details, see the article "Servers: Implementing Server Documents."

- Defining a frame-window class derived from **COleIPFrameWnd**. For further details, see the article "Servers: Implementing In-Place Frame Windows."
- Creating an entry for the server application in the Windows registration database and registering the new instance of the server with the OLE system. For information on this topic, see the article "Registration."
- Initializing and launching the server application. For information on this topic, see the article "Registration."

See Also   Articles: "Containers," "Menus and Resources," "Registration"

Servers: Implementing Server Documents

This article explains the steps you must take to successfully implement a server document if you did not specify the OLE Server option in AppWizard.

▶ **To define a server document class**

1. Derive your document class from **COleServerDoc** instead of **CDocument**.
2. Create a server item class derived from **COleServerItem**.
3. Implement the **OnGetEmbeddedItem** member function of your server document class.

   OnGetEmbeddedItem is called when the user of a container application creates or edits an embedded item. It should return an item representing the entire document. This should be an object of your **COleServerItem**-derived class.

4. Override the **Serialize** member function to serialize the contents of the document. You do not need to serialize the list of server items unless you are using them to represent the native data in your document. For more information, see "Implementing Server Items" in the article "Servers: Server Items."

When a server document is created, the framework automatically registers the document with the OLE system DLLs. This allows the DLLs to identify the server documents.

See Also   Articles: "Servers: Server Items," "Servers: Implementing a Server," "Servers: Implementing In-Place Frame Windows"

Servers: Implementing In-Place Frame Windows

This article explains what you must do to implement in-place frame windows in your Visual Editing server application if you do not use AppWizard to create your server application automatically. In place of following the procedure outlined in this article, you could use an existing in-place frame-window class from either an

AppWizard-generated application or a sample provided with Visual C++ version 2.0.

▶ **To declare an in-place frame-window class**

1. Derive an in-place frame-window class from **COleIPFrameWnd**; use the **DECLARE_DYNCREATE** macro in your class header file.

   −Or−

   Use the **IMPLEMENT_DYNCREATE** macro in your class implementation (.CPP) file. This allows objects of this class to be created by the framework.

2. Declare a **COleResizeBar** member in the frame-window class. This is needed if you want to support in-place resizing in server applications. If you have a toolbar, declare a **CToolBar** member in the frame-window class.

   −Or−

   Declare an **OnCreate** message handler (using ClassWizard); call **Create** for your **COleResizeBar** member, if you've defined it.

   −Or−

   Override the **OnCreateControlBars** member function to create a toolbar when the server is active in place. For example:

```
BOOL CInPlaceFrame::OnCreateControlBars(CWnd* pWndFrame,
    CWnd* pWndDoc)
{
    // create toolbar on client's frame window
    if (!m_wndToolBar.Create(pWndFrame) ||
        !m_wndToolBar.LoadBitmap(IDR_PROJECTTYPE_SRVR_IP) ||
        !m_wndToolBar.SetButtons(buttons,
          sizeof(buttons)/sizeof(UINT)))
    {
        TRACE("Failed to create toolbar\n");
        return FALSE;
    }

    // set this window as owner, so messages are
    // delivered to proper app
    m_wndToolBar.SetOwner(this);
    return TRUE;
}
```

   See the discussion of this code following step 3.

3. Include the header file for this in-place frame-window class in your main .CPP file.

The *buttons* parameter to the **SetButtons** member function called in step 2 above is an array of toolbar button IDs. The series of function calls in the **if** statement creates the toolbar from the resources the server provided. At this point, the toolbar is part of the container's window hierarchy. Because this toolbar is derived from **CToolBar**, it will pass its messages to its owner, the container application's frame window, unless you change the owner. That is why the call to **SetOwner** is necessary. This call changes the window where commands are sent to be the server's in-place frame window, causing the messages to be passed to the server. This allows the server to react to operations on the toolbar that it provides.

The ID for the toolbar bitmap should be the same as the other in-place resources defined in your server application. See the article "Menus and Resources: Server Additions" for details.

Tip A new form of **OnCreateControlBars** supports dockable toolbars for in-place editing. This form of the function takes a **CFrameWnd** pointer as a parameter rather than a **CWnd** pointer. Overriding this function allows you, for example, to call **EnableDocking**.

See Also   Articles: "Servers: Implementing a Server," "Servers: Implementing Server Documents," "Servers: Server Items"

Servers: Server Items

When a container launches a server so that a user can edit an embedded or linked OLE item, the server application creates a "server item." The server item, which is an object of a class derived from **COleServerItem**, provides an interface between the server document and the container application.

The **COleServerItem** class defines several overridable member functions that are called by the OLE system, usually in response to requests from the container. Server items, which typically are created by the server application, can represent part of the server document or the entire document. When an OLE item is embedded in the container document, the server item represents the entire server document. When the OLE item is linked, the server item can represent a part of the server document or the whole document, depending on whether the link is to a part or to the whole.

In the HIERSVR sample, for example, the server-item class, **CServerItem**, has a member that is a pointer to an object of the class **CServerNode**. The **CServerNode** object is a node in the HIERSVR application's document, which is a tree. When the **CServerNode** object is the root node, the **CServerItem** object represents the whole document. When the **CServerNode** object is a child node, the **CServerItem** object represents a part of the document. See HIERSVR in MFC Samples under MFC in Books Online.

Implementing Server Items

If you use AppWizard to produce "starter" code for your application, all you have to do to include server items in your starter code is to choose one of the server options from the OLE Options page. If you're adding server items to an existing application, perform the following steps:

▶ **To implement a server item**

1. Derive a class from **COleServerItem**.

2. Implement your derived class's override of the **OnDraw** member function.

   The framework calls **OnDraw** to render the OLE item into a metafile; the container application uses this metafile to render the item. Your application's view class also has an **OnDraw** member function, which is used to render the item when it is fully open in the server application. (An OLE item is "fully open" when it is displayed in the server application's main window; by contrast, an item is "active in place" when it is open in the container application's document window.)

3. Implement an override of **OnGetEmbeddedItem** for your server-document class. For further information, see the article "Servers: Implementing Server Documents" and the HIERSVR sample application in MFC Samples under MFC in Books Online.

4. Implement your server-item class's **OnGetExtent** member function. The framework calls this function to retrieve the size of the item; the default implementation does nothing.

A Tip for Server-Item Architecture

As noted in "Implementing Server Items" above, server applications must be able to render items both in the server's view and in a metafile used by the container application. In the Microsoft Foundation Class Library's application architecture, the view class's **OnDraw** member function renders the item when it is being edited (see **CView::OnDraw** in the *Class Library Reference*); the server item's **OnDraw** renders the item into a metafile in all other cases (see **COleServerItem::OnDraw**).

You can avoid duplication of code by writing helper functions in your server-document class and calling them from the **OnDraw** functions in your view and server-item classes. The HIERSVR sample application uses this strategy: the functions **CServerView::OnDraw** and **CServerItem::OnDraw** both call **CServerDoc::DrawTree** to render the item.

The view and the item both have **OnDraw** member functions because they draw under different conditions. The view must take into account such factors as zooming, selection size and extent, clipping, and user-interface elements such as scroll bars. The server item, on the other hand, always draws the entire OLE object.

See Also   In the *Class Library Reference*: **CView::OnDraw**, **COleServerItem**, **COleServerDoc::OnGetEmbeddedItem**

Servers: User-Interface Issues

A server application has a number of features that must be added to the user interface to supply OLE items to container applications. For further information on the menus and additional resources that need to be added to a server application, see the article "Menus and Resources: Server Additions."

See Also   Article: "Menus and Resources"

Snapshot

A snapshot is a recordset that reflects a static view of the data as it existed at the time the snapshot was created. Once you open the snapshot and move to all the records, the set of records it contains and their values don't change until you rebuild the snapshot by calling **Requery**. You can create updatable or read-only snapshots with the database classes. Unlike a dynaset, an updatable snapshot doesn't reflect changes to record values made by other users but does reflect updates and deletions made by your program. Records added to a snapshot don't become visible to the snapshot until you call **Requery**.

Tip A snapshot is an ODBC "static cursor." Static cursors don't actually get a row of data until you scroll to that record. To ensure that all records are immediately retrieved, you can scroll to the end of your recordset, then scroll to the first record you're interested in. Note, however, that scrolling to the end entails extra overhead and can lower performance.

Snapshots are most valuable when you need the data to remain fixed during your operations, as when you're generating a report or performing calculations. Even so, the data source can diverge considerably from your snapshot, so you may want to rebuild it from time to time.

Snapshot support is based on the ODBC Cursor Library, which provides static cursors and positioned updates (needed for updatability) for any Level 1 driver. The cursor library DLL must be loaded in memory for this support. By default, the cursor library is loaded when you construct a **CDatabase** object and call its **Open** member function. (If you are using dynasets instead of snapshots, you'll want to cause the cursor library *not* to be loaded.)

Snapshots are available only if the ODBC Cursor Library was loaded when the **CDatabase** object was constructed or the ODBC driver you're using supports static cursors.

Important For some ODBC drivers, snapshots (static cursors) may not be updatable. Check your driver documentation for cursor types supported and the concurrency types they support. To guarantee updatable snapshots, make sure you load the cursor library into memory when you create a **CDatabase** object. See the article "ODBC: The ODBC Cursor Library."

Note If you want to use both snapshots and dynasets, you must base them on two different **CDatabase** objects (two different connections).

For more information about the properties snapshots share with all recordsets, see the article "Recordset." For more information about ODBC and snapshots, including the ODBC Cursor Library, see the article "ODBC."

SQL

Structured Query Language (SQL) is a way to communicate with a relational database that lets you define, query, modify, and control the data. Using SQL syntax, you can construct a statement that extracts records according to criteria you specify.

SQL statements begin with a keyword "verb" such as **CREATE** or **SELECT**. It is a very powerful language; a single statement can affect an entire table.

Many versions of SQL exist, each developed with a particular DBMS in mind. The MFC database classes recognize a set of SQL statements that corresponds to the X/Open and SQL Access Group Common Applications Environment (CAE) SQL draft specification (1991). For details on the syntax of these statements, see Appendix C in the ODBC SDK *Programmer's Reference*.

This article explains:

- The relationship between ODBC and SQL.
- The most common SQL keywords used by the database classes.
- How the database classes use SQL.

Open Database Connectivity (ODBC)

The database classes are implemented with ODBC, which uses SQL in a call-level interface rather than embedding SQL commands in the code. ODBC uses SQL to communicate with a data source through ODBC drivers. These drivers interpret the SQL and translate it, if necessary, for use with a particular database format, such as Microsoft Access. For more information about how ODBC uses SQL, see the article "ODBC" and the ODBC SDK *Programmer's Reference*.

The Database Classes

The database classes are designed to let you manipulate and update data in an existing data source. ClassWizard and the database classes construct most of the SQL statements for you.

The database classes use a portion of SQL known as the Data Manipulation Language (DML). These commands let you work with all or part of the data source, add new records, edit records, and delete records. Table 1 lists the most common SQL keywords and the ways the database classes use them.

Table 1   Some Common SQL Keywords

SQL keyword	ClassWizard and database classes use it ...
SELECT	To identify which tables and columns in the data source are to be used.
WHERE	To apply a filter which narrows the selection.
ORDER BY	To apply a sort order to the recordset.
INSERT	To add new records to a recordset.
DELETE	To delete records from a recordset.
UPDATE	To modify the fields of a record.

In addition, the database classes recognize ODBC **CALL** statements, which you can use to call a predefined query (or stored procedure) on some data sources. The ODBC database driver interprets these statements and substitutes the command appropriate for each DBMS.

Note Not all DBMSs support **CALL** statements.

If the classes cannot recognize a user-supplied statement in **CRecordset::Open**, it is interpreted as a table name.

For an explanation of how the framework constructs SQL statements, see the articles "Recordset: How Recordsets Select Records" and "SQL: Customizing Your Recordset's SQL Statement."

SQL databases use data types similar to those used in C and C++. For a discussion of these similarities, see the article "SQL: SQL and C++ Data Types."

You can find more information about SQL, including a list of supported SQL statements, data types, SQL core grammar, and a reading list of recommended publications about SQL, in the ODBC SDK *Programmer's Reference*.

How the Database Classes Use SQL

The recordsets you derive from the database classes use ODBC to communicate with a data source, and ODBC retrieves records from the data source by sending SQL statements. This article explains the relationship between the database classes and SQL.

A recordset constructs an SQL statement by building up the pieces of an SQL statement into a **CString**. The string is constructed as a **SELECT** statement, which returns a set of records.

When the recordset calls ODBC to send an SQL statement to the data source, the ODBC Driver Manager passes the statement to the ODBC driver, and the driver sends it to the underlying DBMS. The DBMS returns a result set of records, and the ODBC driver returns the records to the application. The database classes let your program access the result set in a type-safe C++ class derived from **CRecordset**.

The following articles provide more information about how the database classes use SQL:

- SQL: Customizing Your Recordset's SQL Statement
- SQL: SQL and C++ Data Types
- SQL: Making Direct SQL Calls

See Also   Article: "ODBC"

SQL: Customizing Your Recordset's SQL Statement

This article explains

- How the framework constructs an SQL statement.
- How to override the SQL statement.

SQL Statement Construction

Your recordset bases record selection primarily on an SQL **SELECT** statement. When you declare your class with ClassWizard, the wizard writes an overriding version of the **GetDefaultSQL** member function that looks something like this (for a recordset class called CAuthors).

```
CString CAuthors::GetDefaultSQL()
{
    return "AUTHORS";
}
```

By default, this override returns the table name you specified with ClassWizard—in the example, the table name is "AUTHORS." When you later call the recordset's **Open** member function, **Open** constructs a final **SELECT** statement of the form:

```
SELECT rfx-field-list FROM table-name [WHERE m_strFilter]
       [ORDER BY m_strSort]
```

where `table-name` is obtained by calling **GetDefaultSQL** and `rfx-field-list` is obtained from the RFX function calls in **DoFieldExchange**. This is what you get for a **SELECT** statement unless you replace it with an overriding version at run time, although you can also modify the default statement with parameters or a filter.

Important If you specify a column name that contains (or could contain) spaces, you must enclose the name in square brackets. For example, the name "First Name" should be "[First Name]".

To override the default **SELECT** statement, pass a string containing a complete **SELECT** statement when you call **Open**. Instead of constructing its own default string, the recordset uses the string you supply. If your replacement statement contains a **WHERE** clause, don't specify a filter in **m_strFilter** because you would then have two filter statements. If your replacement statement contains an **ORDER BY** clause, don't specify a sort in **m_strSort** so that you will not have two sort statements.

Caution In the ENROLL tutorial application, filter strings typically use a parameter placeholder, "?", rather than assigning a specific literal value, such as "MATH101", at compile time. If you do use literal strings in your filters (or other parts of the SQL statement), you may have to "quote" such strings with a DBMS-specific "literal prefix" and "literal suffix" character (or characters). For example, the code in the ENROLL tutorial uses a single quote character to bracket the value assigned as the filter, "MATH101". You may also encounter special syntactic requirements for operations such as outer joins, depending on your DBMS. Use ODBC functions to obtain this information from your driver for the DBMS. For example, call **::SQLGetTypeInfo** for a particular data type, such as **SQL_VARCHAR**, to request the **LITERAL_PREFIX** and **LITERAL_SUFFIX** characters. If you are writing database-independent code, see Appendix C in the ODBC *Programmer's Reference* for detailed syntax information.

A recordset object "constructs" the SQL statement that it uses to select records unless you pass a custom SQL statement. How this is done depends mainly on the value you pass in the *lpszSQL* parameter of the **Open** member function.

The general form of an SQL **SELECT** statement is:

```
SELECT [ALL | DISTINCT] column-list FROM table-list
    [WHERE search-condition][ORDER BY column-list [ASC | DESC]]
```

One way to add the **DISTINCT** keyword to your recordset's SQL statement is to embed the keyword in the first RFX function call in **DoFieldExchange**. For example:

```
. . .
    RFX_Text(pFX, "DISTINCT CourseID", m_strCourseID);
. . .
```

Warning   Use this technique only with a recordset opened as read-only.

Overriding the SQL Statement

Table 1 shows the possibilities for the *lpszSQL* parameter to **Open**. The cases in the table are explained following the table.

Table 1   The *lpszSQL* Parameter and the SQL String Constructed

Case	What you pass in *lpszSQL*	The resulting SELECT statement
1	**NULL**	**SELECT** *rfx-field-list* **FROM** *table-name*
		CRecordset::Open calls **GetDefaultSQL** to get the table name. The resulting string is one of Cases 2 through 5, depending on what **GetDefaultSQL** returns.
2	A table name	**SELECT** *rfx-field-list* **FROM** *table-name*
		The field list is taken from the RFX statements in **DoFieldExchange**. If **m_strFilter** and **m_strSort** are not empty, adds the **WHERE** and/or **ORDER BY** clauses.
3 *	A complete **SELECT** statement but without a **WHERE** or **ORDER BY** clause	As passed. If **m_strFilter** and **m_strSort** are not empty, adds the **WHERE** and/or **ORDER BY** clauses.
4 *	A complete **SELECT** statement with a **WHERE** and/or **ORDER BY** clause	As passed. **m_strFilter** and/or **m_strSort** must remain empty, or two filter and/or sort statements will be produced.
5 *	A call to a stored procedure	As passed.

* **m_nFields** must be less than or equal to the number of columns specified in the **SELECT** statement. The data type of each column specified in the **SELECT** statement must be the same as the data type of the corresponding RFX output column.

Case 1   *lpszSQL* = NULL

The recordset selection depends on what **GetDefaultSQL** returns when **CRecordset::Open** calls it. Cases 2 through 5 describe the possible strings.

Case 2   *lpszSQL* = a Table Name

The recordset uses record field exchange (RFX) to build the column list from the column names provided in the RFX function calls in the recordset class's override of **DoFieldExchange**. If you used ClassWizard to declare your recordset class, this case has the same result as Case 1 (provided that you pass the same table name you specified in ClassWizard). If you don't use ClassWizard to write your class, this is the simplest way to construct the SQL statement.

The following example constructs an SQL statement that selects records from the ENROLL database sample in MFC Samples under MFC in Books Online. When the framework calls the **GetDefaultSQL** member function, the function returns the name of the table, SECTION.

```
CString CEnrollSet::GetDefaultSQL()
{
    return "SECTION";
}
```

To obtain the names of the columns for the SQL **SELECT** statement, the framework calls the **DoFieldExchange** member function.

```
void CEnrollSet::DoFieldExchange(CFieldExchange* pFX)
{
    pFX->SetFieldType(CFieldExchange::outputColumn);
    //{{AFX_FIELD_MAP(CEnrollSet)
    RFX_Text(pFX, "CourseID", m_strCourseID);
    RFX_Text(pFX, "InstructorID", m_strInstructorID);
    RFX_Text(pFX, "RoomNo", m_strRoomNo);
    RFX_Text(pFX, "Schedule", m_strSchedule);
    RFX_Text(pFX, "SectionNo", m_strSectionNo);
    //}}AFX_FIELD_MAP
}
```

When complete, the SQL statement looks like this:

```
SELECT CourseID, InstructorID, RoomNo, Schedule, SectionNo
    FROM SECTION
```

Case 3   *lpszSQL* = a SELECT/FROM Statement

You specify the column list by hand rather than relying on RFX to construct it automatically. You might want to do this when:

- You want to specify the **DISTINCT** keyword following **SELECT**.

    Your column list should match the column names and types in the same order as they are listed in **DoFieldExchange**.

- You have reason to manually retrieve column values using the ODBC function **::SQLGetData** rather than relying on RFX to bind and retrieve columns for you.

    You might, for example, want to accommodate new columns a customer of your application added to the database tables after the application was distributed. You need to add these extra field data members not known at the time you declared the class with ClassWizard.

    Your column list should match the column names and types in the same order as they are listed in **DoFieldExchange**, followed by the names of the manually bound columns. The CATALOG sample program provides classes called **CTable** and **CColumn** which you can use to retrieve column information from the data source. For more information, see the article "Recordset: Dynamically Binding Data Columns" and CATALOG in MFC Samples under MFC in Books Online.

- You want to join tables by specifying multiple tables in the **FROM** clause.

    For information and an example, see the article "Recordset: Performing a Join."

Case 4   *lpszSQL* = SELECT/FROM Plus WHERE and/or ORDER BY

You specify everything: the column list (based on the RFX calls in **DoFieldExchange**), the table list, and the contents of a **WHERE** and/or an **ORDER BY** clause. If you specify your **WHERE** and/or **ORDER BY** clauses this way, be sure not to use **m_strFilter** and/or **m_strSort**.

Case 5   *lpszSQL* = a Stored Procedure Call

If you need to call a predefined query (such as a stored procedure in a Microsoft SQL Server database), you must write a **CALL** statement in the string you pass to *lpszSQL*. ClassWizard doesn't support declaring a recordset class for calling a predefined query. Not all predefined queries return records.

If a predefined query doesn't return records, you can use the **CDatabase** member function **ExecuteSQL** directly. For a predefined query that does return records, you must also manually write the RFX calls in **DoFieldExchange** for any columns the procedure returns. The RFX calls must be in the same order, and return the same types, as the predefined query. For more information, see the article "Recordset: Declaring a Class for a Predefined Query."

See Also   Articles: "SQL: SQL and C++ Data Types," "SQL: Making Direct SQL Calls"

SQL: SQL and C++ Data Types

Table 1 maps ANSI SQL data types to C++ data types. This augments the C language information given in Appendix D of the ODBC SDK *Programmer's Reference*. ClassWizard manages most data-type mapping for you. If you don't use

ClassWizard, you can use the mapping information to help you write the field exchange code manually.

Table 1   ANSI SQL Data Types Mapped to C++ Data Types

ANSI SQL data type	C++ data type
CHAR	CString
DECIMAL	CString [1]
SMALLINT	int
REAL	float
INTEGER	long
FLOAT	double
DOUBLE	double
NUMERIC	CString [1]
VARCHAR	CString
LONGVARCHAR	CLongBinary, CString [2]
BIT	BOOL
TINYINT	BYTE
BIGINT	CString [1]
BINARY	CByteArray
VARBINARY	CByteArray
LONGVARBINARY	CLongBinary, CByteArray [3]
DATE	CTime, CString
TIME	CTime, CString
TIMESTAMP	CTime, CString

[1] ANSI **DECIMAL** and **NUMERIC** map to **CString** because **SQL_C_CHAR** is the default ODBC transfer type.

[2] Character data beyond 255 characters is truncated by default when mapped to **CString**. You can extend the truncation length by explicitly setting the *nMaxLength* argument of **RFX_Text**.

[3] Binary data beyond 255 characters is truncated by default when mapped to **CByteArray**. You can extend the truncation length by explicitly setting the *nMaxLength* argument of **RFX_Binary**.

See Also   Article: "SQL: Making Direct SQL Calls"

SQL: Making Direct SQL Calls

This article explains:

- When to use direct SQL calls.
- How you make direct SQL calls to the data source.

When to Call SQL Directly

To create new tables, drop tables, alter existing tables, create indexes, and perform other SQL functions which change the data source schema, you must issue an SQL statement directly to the data source using Database Design Language (DDL). When you use ClassWizard to create a recordset for a table — at design time — you can choose which columns of the table to represent in the recordset. This doesn't allow for columns you or another user of the data source add to the table later, after your program has been compiled. The database classes don't support DDL directly, but you can still write code to bind a new column to your recordset dynamically, at run time. For information on how to do this binding, see the article "Recordset: Dynamically Binding Data Columns."

You can use the DBMS itself to alter the schema, or another tool which lets you perform DDL functions.

You can also use ODBC function calls for sending SQL statements, such as calling a predefined query (stored procedure) that doesn't return records.

Making Direct SQL Function Calls

You can directly execute an SQL call using a **CDatabase** object. Set up your SQL statement string (usually in a **CString**) and pass it to the **ExecuteSQL** member function of your **CDatabase** object. If you use ODBC function calls to send an SQL statement that normally returns records, the records are ignored. For more information, see the member function **CDatabase::ExecuteSQL** of class **CDatabase** in the *Class Library Reference*.

See Also   In the *Class Library Reference*: **CDatabase::ExecuteSQL**

Stored Procedure

A predefined query stored in a data source and activated by an ODBC CALL statement.

See the articles "Recordset: Declaring a Class for a Table" and "SQL: Making Direct SQL Calls."

Strings

This article describes the general-pupose services that the class library provides related to string manipulation.

The **CString** class provides support for manipulating strings. It is intended to replace and extend the functionality normally provided by the C run-time library string package. The **CString** class supplies member functions and operators for simplified string handling, similar to those found in Basic. The class also provides constructors and operators for constructing, assigning, and comparing **CStrings** and standard C++ string data types. Because **CString** is not derived from **CObject**, you can use **CString** objects independently of most of the Microsoft Foundation Class Library (MFC).

CString objects follow "value semantics." A **CString** object represents a unique value. Think of a **CString** as an actual string, not as a pointer to a string.

A **CString** object represents a sequence of a variable number of characters. **CString** objects can be thought of as arrays of characters.

Unicode and MBCS Provide Portability

With MFC version 3.0, MFC, including **CString**, is enabled for both Unicode and Multibyte Character Sets (MBCS). This support makes it easier for you to write portable applications that you can build for either Unicode or ANSI characters. To enable this portability, each character in a **CString** object is of type **TCHAR**, which is defined as **wchar_t** if you define the symbol **_UNICODE** when you build your application, or as **char** if not. A **wchar_t** character is 16 bits wide. (Unicode is available only under Windows NT.) MBCS is enabled if you build with the symbol **_MBCS** defined. MFC itself is built with either the **_MBCS** symbol (for the NAFX libraries) or the **_UNICODE** symbol defined (for the UAFX libraries).

Note The **CString** examples in this and the accompanying articles on strings show literal strings properly formatted for Unicode portability, using the **_T** macro, which translates the literal string to the form

```
L"literal string"
```

which the compiler treats as a Unicode string. For example, the following code:

```
CString strName = _T("Name");
```

is translated as a Unicode string if **_UNICODE** is defined or as an ANSI string if not. For more information, see the article "Strings: Unicode and Multibyte Character Set (MBCS) Support."

A **CString** object can store up to **INT_MAX** (2,147,483,647) characters. The **TCHAR** data type is used to get or set individual characters inside a **CString** object. Unlike character arrays, the **CString** class has a built-in memory allocation capability. This allows **CString** objects to automatically grow as needed (that is, you don't have to worry about growing a **CString** object to fit longer strings).

CStrings and const char Pointers

A **CString** object also can act like a literal C-style string (an **LPCTSTR**, which is the same as **const char*** if not under Unicode). The **LPCTSTR** conversion operator allows **CString** objects to be freely substituted for character pointers in function calls. The **CString(LPCTSTR** *lpsz*) constructor allows character pointers to be substituted for **CString** objects.

No attempt is made to fold **CString** objects. If you make two **CString** objects containing `Chicago`, for example, the characters in `Chicago` are stored in two places. (This may not be true of future versions of MFC, so you should not depend on it.)

Tips Use the **GetBuffer** and **ReleaseBuffer** member functions when you need to directly access a **CString** as a nonconstant pointer to a character (**LPTSTR** instead of a **const** character pointer, **LPCTSTR**).

Use the **AllocSysString** and **SetSysString** member functions to allocate and set **BSTR** objects used in OLE Automation.

Where possible, allocate **CString** objects on the frame rather than on the heap. This saves memory and simplifies parameter passing.

The **CString** class is not implemented as a Microsoft Foundation Class Library collection class, although **CString** objects can certainly be stored as elements in collections.

The following articles provide more information about **CString**:

- Strings: Basic CString Operations
- Strings: CString Semantics
- Strings: CString Operations Relating to C-Style Strings
- Strings: CString Exception Cleanup
- Strings: CString Argument Passing
- Strings: Unicode and Multibyte Character Set (MBCS) Support

See Also   In the *Class Library Reference*: **CString**

Strings: Basic CString Operations

This article explains basic **CString** operations, including:

- Creating CString objects from standard C literal strings
- Accessing individual characters in a CString
- Concatenating two CString objects
- Comparing CString objects

The **CString** class provides member functions and overloaded operators that duplicate and, in some cases, surpass the string services of the C run-time libraries (for example, **strcat**). This article describes some of the main operations of the **CString** class.

Creating CString Objects from Standard C Literal Strings

You can assign C-style literal strings to a **CString** just as you can assign one **CString** object to another:

- Assign the value of a C literal string to a **CString** object:

```
CString myString = "This is a test";
```

- Assign the value of one **CString** to another **CString** object:

```
CString oldString = "This is a test";
CString newString = oldString;
```

  The contents of a **CString** object are copied when one **CString** object is assigned to another. Thus, the two strings do not share a reference to the actual characters that make up the string. For more information on using **CString** objects as values, see the article "Strings: CString Semantics."

Tip To write your application so that it can be compiled for Unicode or for ANSI, code literal strings using the **_T** macro. For more information, see the article "Strings: Unicode and Multibyte Character Set (MBCS) Support."

Accessing Individual Characters in a CString

You can access individual characters within a **CString** object with the **GetAt** and **SetAt** member functions. You can also use the array element, or subscript, operator (**[ ]**) instead of **GetAt** to get individual characters (this is similar to accessing array elements by index, as in standard C-style strings). Index values for **CString** characters are zero-based.

Concatenating Two CString Objects

To concatenate two **CString** objects, use the concatenation operators (**+** or **+=**) as follows:

```
CString s1 = "This ";          //Cascading concatenation
s1 += "is a ";
CString s2 = "test";
CString message = s1 + "big " + s2;
//Message contains "This is a big test".
```

At least one of the arguments to the concatenation operators (+ or +=) must be a **CString** object, but you can use a constant character string (such as **"big"**) or a **char** (such as **'x'**) for the other argument.

Comparing CString Objects

The **Compare** member function and the **==** operator for **CString** are equivalent. **Compare**, **operator==**, and **CompareNoCase** are MBCS- and Unicode-aware; **CompareNoCase** is also case insensitive. The **Collate** member function of **CString** is locale-sensitive and is often slower than **Compare**. **Collate** should be used only where it is necessary to abide by the sorting rules as specified by the current locale.

The following list shows the available **CString** comparison functions and their equivalent Unicode/MBCS-portable functions in the C run-time library:

CString function	MBCS function	Unicode function
Compare	**_mbscmp**	**wcscmp**
CompareNoCase	**_mbsicmp**	**_wcsicmp**
Collate	**strcoll**	**wcscoll**

The **CString** class overrides the relational operators (**<, <=, >=, >, ==,** and **!=**). You can compare two **CStrings** using these operators, as shown here:

```
CString s1( "Tom" );
CString s2( "Jerry" );
if( s1 < s2 )
    ...
```

Strings: CString Semantics

Even though **CString** objects are dynamically growable objects, they act like built-in primitive types and simple classes. Each **CString** object represents a unique value. **CString** objects should be thought of as the actual strings rather than as pointers to strings.

The most obvious consequence of using **CString** objects as values is that the string contents are copied when you assign one **CString** to another. Thus, even though two **CString** objects may represent the same sequence of characters, they do not share those characters. Each **CString** has its own copy of the character data. When you modify one **CString** object, the copied **CString** object is not modified, as shown by the following example:

```
CString s1, s2;
s1 = s2 = "hi there";

if( s1 == s2 )              // TRUE - they are equal
    ...

s1.MakeUpper();        // Does not modify s2
if( s2[0] == 'h' )          // TRUE - s2 is still "hi there"
```

Notice in the example that the two **CString** objects are considered to be "equal" because they represent the same character string. The **CString** class overloads the equality operator (**==**) to compare two **CString** objects based on their value (contents) rather than their identity (address).

Strings: CString Operations Relating to C-Style Strings

It is often useful to manipulate the contents of a **CString** object as if it were a C-style null-terminated string. This article covers the following topics:

- Converting to C-style null-terminated strings
- Working with standard run-time library string functions
- Modifying CString contents directly
- Using CString objects with variable argument functions
- Specifying CString formal parameters

Converting to C-Style Null-Terminated Strings

Consider the following two cases:

- In the simplest case, you can cast a **CString** object to be an **LPCTSTR**. The **LPCTSTR** type conversion operator returns a pointer to a read-only C-style null-terminated string from a **CString** object.

  The pointer returned by **LPCTSTR** points into the data area used by the **CString**. If the **CString** goes out of scope and is automatically deleted or something else changes the contents of the **CString**, the **LPCTSTR** pointer will no longer be valid. Treat the string to which the pointer points as being temporary.

- You can use **CString** functions, such as **SetAt**, to modify individual characters in the string object. However, if you need a copy of a **CString** object's characters that you can modify directly, use **strcpy** (or the Unicode/MBCS-portable **_tcscpy**) to copy the **CString** object into a separate buffer where the characters can be safely modified, as shown by the following example:

```
CString theString( "This is a test" );
LPCTSTR lpsz = new TCHAR[theString.GetLength()+1];
strcpy( lpsz, theString );
//... modify lpsz as much as you want
```

Note The second argument to **strcpy** (or the Unicode/MBCS-portable **_tcscpy**) is either a **const wchar_t*** (Unicode) or a **const char*** (ANSI). The example above passes a **CString** for this argument. The C++ compiler automatically applies the conversion function defined for the **CString** class that converts a **CString** to an **LPCTSTR**. The ability to define casting operations from one type to another is one of the most useful features of C++.

Working with Standard Run-Time Library String Functions

In most situations, you should be able to find **CString** member functions to perform any string operation for which you might consider using the standard C run-time library string functions, such as **strcmp** (or the Unicode/MBCS-portable **_tcscmp**).

If you need to use the C run-time string functions, you can use the techniques described in "Converting to C-Style Null-Terminated Strings" above to copy the **CString** object to an equivalent C-style string buffer, perform your operations on the buffer, and then assign the resulting C-style string back to a **CString** object.

Modifying CString Contents Directly

In most situations, you should use **CString** member functions to modify the contents of a **CString** object or to convert the **CString** to a C-style character string.

However, there are certain situations, such as working with operating-system functions that require a character buffer, where it is advantageous to directly modify the **CString** contents.

The **GetBuffer** and **ReleaseBuffer** member functions allow you to gain access to the internal character buffer of a **CString** object and modify it directly. The following steps show how to use these functions for this purpose:

1. Call **GetBuffer** for a **CString** object, specifying the length of the buffer you require.

2. Use the pointer returned by **GetBuffer** to write characters directly into the **CString** object.

3. Call **ReleaseBuffer** for the **CString** object to update all the internal **CString** state information (such as the length of the string). After modifying a **CString** object's contents directly, you must call **ReleaseBuffer** before calling any other **CString** member functions.

Using CString Objects with Variable Argument Functions

Some C functions take a variable number of arguments. A notable example is **printf**. Because of the way this kind of function is declared, the compiler cannot be sure of the type of the arguments and cannot determine which conversion operation to perform on the argument. Therefore, it is essential that you use an explicit type cast when passing a **CString** object to a function that takes a variable number of arguments.

▶ **To use a CString object in a variable argument function**

- Explicitly cast the **CString** to an **LPCTSTR** string, as shown here:

```
CString kindOfFruit = "bananas";
int     howmany = 25;
printf( "You have %d %s\n", howmany, (LPCTSTR)kindOfFruit );
```

Specifying CString Formal Parameters

For most functions that need a string argument, it is best to specify the formal parameter in the function prototype as a **const** pointer to a character (**LPCTSTR**) instead of a **CString**. When a formal parameter is specified as a **const** pointer to a character, you can pass either a pointer to a **TCHAR** array, a literal string ["hi there"], or a **CString** object. The **CString** object will be automatically converted to an **LPCTSTR**. Any place you can use an **LPCTSTR**, you can also use a **CString** object.

You can also specify a formal parameter as a constant string reference (that is, **const CString&**) if the argument will not be modified. Drop the **const** modifier if the string will be modified by the function. If a default null value is desired, initialize it to the null string [""], as shown below:

```
void AddCustomer( const CString& name,
                  const CString& address,
                  const CString& comment = "" );
```

For most function results, you can simply return a **CString** object by value.

See Also   Article: "Strings: CString Argument Passing"

In the *Class Library Reference*: **CString**

Strings: CString Exception Cleanup

In previous versions of MFC, it was important that you clean up **CString** objects after use. With MFC version 3.0, explicit cleanup is no longer necessary.

Under the C++ exception handling mechanism that MFC now uses, you don't have to worry about cleanup after an exception. For a description of how C++ "unwinds" the stack after an exception is caught, see Chapter 7, "C++ Exception Handling," in *Programming Techniques*. Even if you use the MFC **TRY/CATCH** macros instead of the C++ keywords **try** and **catch**, MFC uses the C++ exception mechanism underneath, so you still don't need to clean up explicitly.

See Also   Article: "Exceptions"

Strings: CString Argument Passing

This article explains how to pass **CString** objects to functions and how to return **CString** objects from functions.

Argument-Passing Conventions

When you define a class interface, you must determine the argument-passing convention for your member functions. There are some standard rules for passing and returning **CString** objects. If you follow the rules described in "Strings as Function Inputs" and "Strings as Function Outputs" below, you will have efficient, correct code.

Strings as Function Inputs

If a string is an input to a function, in most cases it is best to declare the string function parameter as **LPCTSTR**. Convert to a **CString** object as necessary within the function using constructors and assignment operators. If the string contents are to be changed by a function, declare the parameter as a nonconstant **CString** reference (**CString&**).

Strings as Function Outputs

Normally you can return **CString** objects from functions since **CString** objects follow value semantics like primitive types. To return a read-only string, use a constant **CString** reference (**const CString&**). The following example illustrates the use of **CString** parameters and return types:

```
class CName : public CObject
{
private:
    CString m_firstName;
    char m_middleInit;
    CString m_lastName;
public:
    CName() {}
    void SetData( LPCTSTR fn, const char mi, LPCTSTR ln )
    {
        m_firstName = fn;
        m_middleInit = mi;
        m_lastName = ln;
    }
    void GetData( CString& cfn, char mi, CString& cln )
    {
        cfn = m_firstName;
        mi = m_middleInit;
        cln = m_lastName;
    }
```

```
        CString GetLastName()
        {
            return m_lastName;
        }
};
...
CName name;
CString last, first;
TCHAR middle;
name.SetData( "John", 'Q', "Public" );
ASSERT( name.GetLastName() == "Public" );
name.GetData( first, middle, last );
ASSERT( ( first == "John" ) && ( last == "Public" ) );
...
```

Strings: Unicode and Multibyte Character Set (MBCS) Support

Some international markets use languages, such as Japanese and Chinese, with large character sets. To support programming for these markets, the Microsoft Foundation Class Library (MFC) is enabled for two different approaches to handling large character sets:

- Unicode
- Multibyte Character Sets (MBCS)

MFC Support for Unicode Strings

The entire class library (except the database classes) is conditionally enabled for Unicode characters and strings. In particular, class **CString** is Unicode-enabled.

CString is based on the **TCHAR** data type. If the symbol **_UNICODE** is defined for a build of your program, **TCHAR** is defined as type **wchar_t**, a 16-bit character encoding type; otherwise, it is defined as **char**, the normal 8-bit character encoding. Under Unicode, then, **CString**s are composed of 16-bit characters. Without Unicode, they are composed of characters of type **char**.

To complete the Unicode picture for your application, you must also:

- Use the **_T** macro to conditionally code literal strings to be portable to Unicode.
- When you pass strings, pay attention to whether function arguments require a length in characters or a length in bytes. The difference is important if you're using Unicode strings.
- Use portable versions of the C run-time string-handling functions.

- Use the following data types for characters and character pointers:

  TCHAR
  Where you would use **char**.

  LPTSTR
  Where you would use **char***.

  LPCTSTR
  Where you would use **const char***. **CString** provides the **operator LPCTSTR** to convert between **CString** and **LPCTSTR**.

CString also supplies Unicode-aware constructors, assignment operators, and comparison operators.

For more information on Unicode programming, see Chapter 12 in *Programming Techniques*. The *Run-Time Library Reference* defines portable versions of all of its string-handling functions. See the category "Internationalization" in Chapter 1 of the *Run-Time Library Reference*.

MFC Support for MBCS Strings

The class library is also enabled for multibyte character sets (except for the database classes)—specifically for double-byte character sets (DBCS).

Note The version of ODBC shipped with Visual C++ version 2.0 is not MBCS enabled. Subsequent versions of ODBC will be MBCS enabled (specifically DBCS enabled).

Under this scheme, a character can be either one or two bytes wide. If it is two bytes wide, its first byte is a special "lead byte," chosen from a particular range depending on which code page is in use. Taken together, the lead and "trail bytes" specify a unique character encoding.

If the symbol _MBCS is defined for a build of your program, type **TCHAR**, on which **CString** is based, maps to **char**. It's up to you to determine which bytes in a **CString** are lead bytes and which are trail bytes. The C run-time library supplies functions to help you determine this.

Under DBCS, a given string can contain all single-byte ANSI characters, all double-byte characters, or a mixture of the two. These possibilities require special care in parsing strings, including **CString** objects.

Note Unicode string serialization in MFC can read both Unicode and MBCS strings regardless of which version of the application you are running. Because of this, your data files are portable between Unicode and MBCS versions of your program.

CString member functions use special "generic text" versions of the C run-time functions they call, or they use Unicode-aware functions such as **lstrlen** or **lstrcpy**. Thus, for example, if a **CString** function would normally call **strcmp**, it calls the corresponding generic-text function **_tcscmp** instead. Depending on how the symbols **_MBCS** and **_UNICODE** are defined, **_tcscmp** maps as follows:

_MBCS defined
   _mbscmp

_UNICODE defined
   wcscmp

Neither symbol defined
   strcmp

Note   **_MBCS** and **_UNICODE** are mutually exclusive symbols.

Generic-text function mappings for all of the run-time string-handling routines are detailed in the *Run-Time Library Reference*. See the category "Internationalization."

Similarly, **CString** member functions are implemented using "generic" data type mappings. To enable both MBCS and Unicode, MFC uses **TCHAR** for **char**, **LPTSTR** for **char***, and **LPCTSTR** for **const char***. These result in the correct mappings for either MBCS or Unicode.

For more information about MFC support for MBCS (DBCS), see Chapter 12 in *Programming Techniques*.

Structured Query Language

See the article "SQL."

Table

A table is the fundamental structure of a relational database management system. It is typically a data structure composed of records (rows) and fields (columns) with data stored in each cell formed by the record and field intersection.

A table in a database for which there is an ODBC driver can be accessed via a **CRecordset** object. The recordset object can select some or all of the records, and some or all of the columns.

See Also   Articles: "Record," "Recordset"

Toolbars

A toolbar is a form of control bar—a child window that can contain buttons, edit boxes, check boxes, or other kinds of Windows controls. Some kinds of control bars, such as dialog bars, can contain a wide variety of controls, but a toolbar is based on a bitmap that contains a row of button images. These buttons can act like pushbuttons, check boxes, or radio buttons.

Toolbars are usually aligned to the top of a frame window, but a toolbar in an application created with the Microsoft Foundation Class Library (MFC) can, if you choose, be "docked" to any side (or sides) of its parent window that you specify. MFC toolbars can also be made to "float" in draggable "mini-frame windows."

You can also have your toolbars show "tool tips" as the user moves the mouse over the toolbar buttons. A tool tip is a small popup window that appears near a toolbar button to explain its purpose to the user.

For general information about toolbars and other control bars, see Chapter 4, "Working with Dialog Boxes, Controls, and Control Bars."

For information about docking and floating toolbars and about tool tips, see the following articles:

- Toolbars: Docking and Floating
- Toolbars: Tool Tips

See Also   In the *Class Library Reference*: **CToolbar**, **CControlBar**

Toolbars: Docking and Floating

The Microsoft Foundation Class Library adds a new capability to existing toolbar support: dockable toolbars. A dockable toolbar can be attached, or "docked," to any side of its parent window, or it can be "floated" in its own mini-frame window (using **CMiniFrameWnd**). This article explains how to use dockable toolbars in your applications.

If you use AppWizard to generate the skeleton of your application, you are asked to choose whether you want dockable toolbars. By default, AppWizard generates the code that performs the three actions necessary to place a dockable toolbar in your application:

- Enable docking for the frame window.
- Enable docking for the toolbar.
- Dock the toolbar to the frame window.

If any of these steps are missing, your application will display a standard toolbar. The last two steps must be performed for each dockable toolbar in your application.

Enabling Docking in a Frame Window

To dock toolbars to a frame window, the frame window (or destination) must be enabled to allow docking. This is done using the **CFrameWnd::EnableDocking** function, which takes one **DWORD** parameter that is a set of style bits indicating which side of the frame window accepts docking. If a toolbar is about to be docked and there are multiple sides that it could be docked to, the sides indicated in the parameter passed to **EnableDocking** are used in the following order: top, bottom, left, right. If you want to be able to dock control bars anywhere, pass **CBRS_ALIGN_ANY** to **EnableDocking**.

Enabling Docking for a Toolbar

After you have prepared the destination for docking, you must prepare the toolbar (or source) in a similar fashion. Call **CControlBar::EnableDocking** for each toolbar you want to dock, specifying the destination sides to which the toolbar should dock. If none of the sides specified in the call to **CControlBar::EnableDocking** match the sides enabled for docking in the frame window, the toolbar cannot dock—it will float. Once it has been floated, it remains a floating toolbar, unable to dock to the frame window.

Docking and Floating the Toolbar

To actually dock the toolbar to the frame window, you must call **CFrameWnd::DockControlBar**. This is normally called by the framework when the user attempts to drop the toolbar on a side of the frame window that allows docking.

In addition, you can call this function at any time to dock control bars to the frame window. This is normally done during initialization, when restoring settings from the previous execution of the application. More than one toolbar can be docked to a particular side of the frame window.

Detaching a dockable toolbar from the frame window is called "floating" the toolbar. Call **CFrameWnd::FloatControlBar** to do this. Specify the toolbar to be floated, the point where it should be placed, and an alignment style that determines whether the floating toolbar is horizontal or vertical.

This function is normally called when a user drags a toolbar off its docked location and drops it in a location where docking is not enabled. This can be anywhere inside or outside the frame window. As with **DockControlBar**, this function can also be called during initialization, when restoring settings from the previous execution of the application.

The MFC implementation of dockable toolbars does not provide some of the extended features found in some applications that support dockable toolbars. Features such as customizable toolbars or dynamic layout of toolbars are not provided.

If you wish to retain the state of dockable toolbars (whether docked or floating) between invocations of your application, use the functions **CControlBar::SetBarStyle** and **CControlBar::GetBarStyle** to retrieve and restore the settings of any particular control bar. Normally, you would store this information in the application's .INI file using **CFrameWnd::SaveBarState** and retrieve it using **CFrameWnd::LoadBarState**.

See Also   Article: "Toolbars: Tool Tips"

Toolbars: Tool Tips

Tool tips are the tiny popup windows that present short descriptions of a toolbar button's purpose when you position the mouse over a button for a period of time. When you create an application with AppWizard that has a toolbar, tool tip support is provided for you. This article both explains the tool tip support created by AppWizard and how to add tool tip support to your application.

To activate tool tips in your application, you must do two things:

- Add the **CBRS_TOOLTIPS** style to the other styles (such as **WS_CHILD**, **WS_VISIBLE**, and other **CBRS_** styles) passed as the dwStyle parameter to the **CToolBar::Create** function.

- Append the toolbar tip text, separated by a newline character ('\n'), to the string resource containing the command-line prompt for the toolbar command. The string resource shares the ID of the toolbar button.

▶ **To add the tool tip text to your string table**

1. Open the string table in the project's .RC file.

2. Find the string table entry with the same ID as the toolbar button. For example, a string-table entry identified with **ID_FILE_NEW** provides the command-line prompt and optional tool tip for the New File toolbar button.

3. Add a newline character and the desired text to the existing string. For example, change the string for the New File button from

```
"Create a new document"
```
to
```
"Create a new document\nNew"
```

This will put the text "New" in the tool tip popup window when the mouse is positioned over the New File button in the toolbar.

If a control bar with tool tips enabled has child controls placed on it, the control bar will display a tool tip for every child control on the control bar as long as it meets the following criteria:

- The ID of the control is not −1.

- The string-table entry with the same ID as the child control in the resource file has a tool tip string.

A feature related to tool tips is "fly by" status bar updating. By default, the message on the status bar only describes a particular toolbar button when the button is activated. By including **CBRS_FLYBY** in your list of styles passed to **CToolBar::Create**, you can have these messages updated when the mouse cursor passes over the toolbar without actually activating the button.

See Also   Article: "Toolbars: Docking and Floating"

Tools for MFC Programming

Visual C++ supplies a number of tools that help you build applications for Windows using the Microsoft Foundation Class Library (MFC). These tools include:

- AppWizard
- Resource editors
- ClassWizard

The final topic in this article, "Using the Tools To Create an Application," highlights the roles of these tools in combination. Other articles explore the details of each wizard. The *Visual C++ User's Guide* details the resource editors in Chapters 4 through 11.

AppWizard Creates Skeleton Code

AppWizard creates the starter files for a new application. The starter files consist of C++ source files, resource files, header files, and a project file. They include the code necessary to implement basic features for applications for Windows. These basic features include such things as window management, a basic menu structure, and basic menu commands. They also include skeleton code for features that you need to implement for your specific application. In the course of developing your application, you add the code required to flesh out the skeleton fully. For instance, you need to add code that loads a file for your application properly, or saves a document in the appropriate file format on disk. AppWizard marks these locations in the source files it creates as "// TODO" comments.

Resource Editors Create Resources

Visual C++ has a number of integrated editors for various kinds of Windows resources. These include menus, dialogs, string tables, accelerator tables, version resources, and graphical objects, such as icons, cursors, and bitmaps.

AppWizard creates an .RC file containing basic resources: standard menus, an About dialog box, a string table containing predefined strings, and so on. Other files contain a default icon, a version resource, and, if you choose the option to include an initial toolbar, a bitmap containing images for toolbar buttons.

As you program, you'll usually need to add more menus, additional dialog boxes, new strings and accelerators, and so on. Typically, you invoke the appropriate editor to create or edit these resources. In some cases, such as menus, toolbar buttons, and dialog boxes, you first create the resource, specifying its ID, then use ClassWizard to connect the resource to code.

ClassWizard Fills Out Implementation Details

ClassWizard allows you to create new classes or member functions and variables to implement the details of your application's operation. It also works with the resource editors to implement user-interface objects, such as dialog boxes, in your application.

You use the resource editors to create these user-interface objects. You then use ClassWizard to generate functions and message maps for each user-interface object. For example, you might use the dialog editor to create an edit control in a dialog box. Later, in ClassWizard, you can create a class member function to handle input to the edit box and the member variables to validate and store the entered information. You can also use ClassWizard to connect a menu command or a toolbar button to the dialog box to display it.

Using the Tools To Create an Application

The development phase of any Windows-based application typically includes a number of passes, involving editing source and resource files, building the project, and testing and debugging. Because these activities are iterative and interwoven during a normal development cycle, they don't follow one another in a strict sequential order.

The following steps, nonetheless, describe the general procedure for beginning application development using AppWizard, ClassWizard, and the Visual C++ resource editors.

▶ **To use the tools together**

1. Choose the File New command and select Project and then select the MFC AppWizard project type. Use AppWizard to select the location for your project and the characteristics of your project.

2. Use ClassWizard to create classes, member functions, and member variables for the skeleton code in your application. ClassWizard also displays the locations in the source files where you need to add code specific to your implementation.

3. Use the Visual C++ resource editors to create resources for your application.

4. Use ClassWizard to create the classes and member functions to handle those resources.

5. Build the application with the Build command on the Project menu.

See Also   Articles: "AppWizard," "ClassWizard"

Trackers

The **CRectTracker** class provides a user interface between Object Linking and Embedding (OLE) items and your user by providing a variety of display styles. These styles include: solid, hatched, or dashed borders; a hatched pattern that covers the OLE item; and resize handles that can be located on the outside or inside of a border. Trackers can be used in conjunction with objects derived from **COleClientItem** to give visual cues on the current status of the item.

The OCLIENT sample demonstrates a common interface using trackers and OLE client items from the viewpoint of a container application. For a demonstration of the different styles and abilities of a tracker object, see the TRACKER sample. For information about these samples, see MFC Samples under MFC in Books Online.

For more information on implementing trackers in your OLE application, see the following article:

- Trackers: Implementing Trackers in Your OLE Application

See Also   Article: "Trackers: Implementing Trackers in Your OLE Application"

In the *Class Library Reference*: **COleClientItem**, **CRectTracker**

Trackers: Implementing Trackers in Your OLE Application

Trackers provide a graphical interface to enable users to interact with OLE client items. By using different tracker styles, OLE client items can be displayed with hatched borders, resize handles, or a variety of other visual effects. This article describes:

- Tracking and how to implement it in your code.
- The rubber-band effect and trackers.

The article also covers the use of styles with trackers.

This article makes several references to the OCLIENT sample. This sample is described in MFC Samples under MFC in Books Online.

How to Implement Tracking in Your Code

To track an OLE item, you must handle certain events related to the item, such as clicking the item or updating the view of the document. In all cases, it is sufficient to declare a temporary **CRectTracker** object and manipulate the item by means of this object.

When a user selects an item or inserts an object with a menu command, you must initialize the tracker with the proper styles to represent the state of the OLE item. Table 1 outlines the convention used by the OCLIENT sample. For more information on these styles, see **CRectTracker** in the *Class Library Reference*.

Table 1   Container Styles and State of the OLE Item

Style displayed	State of OLE item
Dotted border	Item is linked
Solid border	Item is embedded in your document
Resize handles	Item is currently selected
Hatched border	Item is currently in-place active
Hatching pattern overlays item	Item's server is open

You can handle this initialization easily using a procedure that checks the state of the OLE item and sets the appropriate styles. The SetupTracker function found in the OCLIENT sample demonstrates tracker initialization. The parameters for this function are the address of the tracker, *pTracker*; a pointer to the client item that is related to the tracker, *pItem*; and a pointer to a rectangle, *pTrueRect*. For a more complete example of this function, see the OCLIENT sample.

The SetupTracker code example below presents a single function; lines of the function are interspersed with discussion of the function's features:

```
void CMainView::SetupTracker( CRectTracker* pTracker,
                              CRectItem* pItem, CRect* pTrueRect )
{
```

The tracker is initialized by setting the resize handle size and clearing the style of the tracker.

```
    pTracker->m_sizeMin.cx = 8;
    pTracker->m_sizeMin.cy = 8;

    pTracker->m_nStyle = 0;
```

The following code sample checks to see whether the item is currently selected and whether the item is linked to the document or embedded in it. Resize handles located on the inside of the border are added to the style, indicating that the item is currently selected. If the item is linked to your document, the dotted border style is used. A solid border is used if the item is embedded.

```
    if ( pItem == m_pSelection )
        pTracker->m_nStyle |= CRectTracker::resizeInside;

    if ( pItem->GetType( ) == OT_LINK )
        pTracker->m_nStyle |= CRectTracker::dottedLine;
    else
        pTracker->m_nStyle |= CRectTracker::solidLine;
```

The following code overlays the item with a hatched pattern if the item is currently open.

```
    if ( pItem->GetItemState( ) == COleClientItem::openState ||
        pItem->GetItemState( ) == COleClientItem::activeUIState )
        pTracker->m_nStyle |= CRectTracker::hatchInside;
}
```

You can then call this function whenever the tracker has to be displayed. For example, call this function from the **OnDraw** function of your view class. This updates the tracker's appearance whenever the view is repainted. For a complete example, see the **CMainView::OnDraw** function of the OCLIENT sample.

Events will occur in your application that require tracker code, such as resizing, moving, or hit detecting. These actions usually indicate that an attempt is being made to grab or move the item. In these cases you will need to decide what was grabbed: a resize handle or a portion of the border between resize handles. The **OnLButtonDown** message handler is a good place to test the position of the mouse in relation to the item. Make a call to **CRectTracker::HitTest**. If the test returns something besides **CRectTracker::hitOutside**, the item is being resized or moved.

Therefore, you should make a call to the **Track** member function. See the **CMainView::OnLButtonDown** function located in the OCLIENT sample for a complete example.

The **CRectTracker** class provides several different cursor shapes used to indicate whether a move, resize, or drag operation is taking place. To handle this event, check to see whether the item currently under the mouse is selected. If it is, make a call to **CRectTracker::SetCursor**, or call the default handler. The following example is from the OCLIENT sample:

```
BOOL CMainView::OnSetCursor( CWnd* pWnd, UINT nHitTest, UINT message )
{
    if ( pWnd == this && m_pSelection != NULL )
    {
        // give the tracker for the selection a chance
        CRectTracker tracker;
        SetupTracker( &tracker, m_pSelection );
        if ( tracker.SetCursor( this, nHitTest ))
            return TRUE;
    }
    return CScrollView::OnSetCursor( pWnd, nHitTest, message );
}
```

Rubber-Banding and Trackers

Another feature supplied with trackers is the "rubber-band" selection, which allows a user to select multiple OLE items by dragging a sizing rectangle around the items to be selected. When the user releases the left mouse button, items within the region selected by the user are selected and can be manipulated by the user. For instance, the user might drag or drop the selection into another container application.

Implementing this feature requires some additional code in your application's **WM_LBUTTONDOWN** handler function.

The following code sample implements rubber-band selection and additional features and is taken from the **WM_LBUTTONDOWN** handler function of TRACKER.

```
if (pDoc->m_tracker.HitTest(point) < 0)
{
    // just to demonstrate CRectTracker::TrackRubberBand
    CRectTracker tracker;
    if (tracker.TrackRubberBand(this, point, pDoc->m_bAllowInvert))
    {
        MessageBeep(0); // beep indicates TRUE
        // see if rubber band intersects with the doc's tracker
        CRect rectT;
        tracker.m_rect.NormalizeRect(); // so intersect rect works
        if (rectT.IntersectRect(tracker.m_rect, pDoc->m_tracker.m_rect))
```

```
                    {
                        // if so, put resize handles on it (i.e. select it)
                        if (pDoc->m_tracker.m_nStyle & CRectTracker::resizeInside)
                        {
                            // swap from resize inside to resize outside for effect
                            pDoc->m_tracker.m_nStyle &= ~CRectTracker::resizeInside;
                            pDoc->m_tracker.m_nStyle |= CRectTracker::resizeOutside;
                        }
                        else
                        {
                        // just use inside resize handles on first time
                        pDoc->m_tracker.m_nStyle &= ~CRectTracker::resizeOutside;
                        pDoc->m_tracker.m_nStyle |= CRectTracker::resizeInside;
                        }
                        pDoc->SetModifiedFlag();
                        pDoc->UpdateAllViews(NULL, (LPARAM)(LPCRECT)rectSave);
                        pDoc->UpdateAllViews(NULL);
                    }
                }
            }
```

If you want to allow reversible orientation of the tracker during rubber-banding, you should call **CRectTracker::TrackRubberBand** with the third parameter set to **TRUE**. Remember that allowing reversible orientation will sometimes cause **CRectTracker::m_rect** to become inverted. This can be corrected by a call to **CRect::NormalizeRect**.

See Also   Articles: "Containers: Client Items," "Drag and Drop: Customizing"

In the *Class Library Reference*: **CRectTracker**

Transaction

A transaction is a way to "batch" a series of updates to a data source so that all are committed at once, or none are committed if you roll back the transaction. If you do not use a transaction, changes to the data source are committed automatically rather than committed on demand.

Note Not all ODBC database drivers support transactions to the level required by the database classes. Call the **CanTransact** member function of your **CDatabase** or **CRecordset** object to determine whether your driver supports transactions for a given database. **CanTransact** tells you whether transaction support on the data source is sufficient for the database classes; it does not tell you whether the data source provides full transaction support. For more information about required transaction levels and the MFC transaction model, see Technical Note 47 under MFC in Books Online.

Calls to the **AddNew** and **Edit** member functions of a **CRecordset** object affect the data source immediately when you call **Update**. **Delete** calls also take effect immediately. In contrast, you can use a transaction consisting of multiple calls to **AddNew**, **Edit**, **Update**, and **Delete**, which are performed but not committed until you call **CommitTrans** explicitly. By establishing a transaction, you can execute a series of such calls while retaining the ability to roll them back. If a critical resource is unavailable or some other condition prevents the entire transaction from being completed, you can roll back the transaction instead of committing it. In that case, none of the changes belonging to the transaction affect the data source.

Note   Besides affecting your recordset, transactions affect SQL statements that you execute directly as long as you use the ODBC **HDBC** associated with your **CDatabase** object or an ODBC **HSTMT** based on that **HDBC**.

Transactions are particularly useful when you have multiple records that must be simultaneously updated. In this case, you want to avoid a half-completed transaction, such as might happen if an exception were thrown before the last update was made. Grouping such updates into a transaction allows a recovery (rollback) from the changes, and returns the records to the pretransaction state. For example, if a bank transfers money from account A to account B, both the withdrawal from A and the deposit to B must succeed to process the funds correctly, or the whole transaction must fail.

In the database classes, you perform transactions through **CDatabase** objects. A **CDatabase** object represents a connection to a data source, and one or more recordsets associated with that **CDatabase** object operate on tables of the database through recordset member functions.

Note   Only one level of transactions is supported; you cannot nest transactions, nor can a transaction span multiple database objects.

Note   The MFC transaction model, which is recordset-centered, requires that the cursor be preserved on commit and on rollback. If this requirement is too restrictive for your application, see Technical Note 47 under MFC in Books Online.

The following articles provide more information about how transactions are performed:

- Transaction: Performing a Transaction in a Recordset
- Transaction: How Transactions Affect Updates

See Also   In the *Class Library Reference*: **CDatabase**, **CRecordset**

Transaction: Performing a Transaction in a Recordset

This article explains how to perform a transaction in a recordset.

Note   Only one level of transactions is supported; you cannot nest transactions.

▶ **To perform a transaction in a recordset**

1. Call the **CDatabase** object's **BeginTrans** member function.
2. Call the **AddNew/Update**, **Edit/Update**, and **Delete** member functions of one or more recordset objects of the same database as many times as needed. See the article "Recordset: Adding, Updating, and Deleting Records."
3. Finally, call the **CDatabase** object's **CommitTrans** member function. Or, if an error occurs in one of the updates, or you decide to cancel the changes, call its **Rollback** member function.

The following example uses two recordsets to delete a student's enrollment from a school registration database, removing the student from all classes in which the student is enrolled. The **Delete** calls in both recordsets must succeed, so a transaction is required. The example assumes the existence of m_dbStudentReg, a member variable of type **CDatabase** already connected to the data source, and the recordset classes CEnrollmentSet and CStudentSet. The strStudentID function contains a value obtained from the user.

```
BOOL CEnrollDoc::RemoveStudent(CString strStudentID)
{
    // remove student from all the classes student is enrolled in
    CEnrollmentSet  rsEnrollmentSet(&m_dbStudentReg);
    rsEnrollmentSet.m_strFilter = "StudentID = " + strStudentID;
    if ( !rsEnrollmentSet.Open(CRecordset::dynaset) )
        return FALSE;
    CStudentSet  rsStudentSet(&m_dbStudentReg);
    rsStudentSet.m_strFilter = "StudentID = " + strStudentID;
    if ( !rsStudentSet.Open(CRecordset::dynaset) )
        return FALSE;
    if ( !m_dbStudentReg.BeginTrans())
        return FALSE;
    TRY
    {
        while (!rsEnrollmentSet.IsEOF())
        {
            rsEnrollmentSet.Delete();
            rsEnrollmentSet.MoveNext();
        }
```

```
        // delete the student record
        rsStudentSet.Delete();

        m_dbStudentReg.CommitTrans();
    }
    CATCH_ALL(e)
    {
        m_dbStudentReg.Rollback();
        return FALSE;
    }
    return TRUE;
}
```

Warning Calling **BeginTrans** again without calling **CommitTrans** or **Rollback** is an error.

See Also

Articles: "Transaction: How Transactions Affect Updates," "Transaction"

In the *Class Library Reference*: **CDatabase**, **CRecordset**

Transaction: How Transactions Affect Updates

Updates to the data source are managed during transactions through the use of an "edit buffer" (the same method used outside of transactions). The field data members of a recordset collectively serve as an edit buffer that contains the current record, which the recordset backs up temporarily during an **AddNew** or **Edit**. During a **Delete** operation, the current record is not backed up within a transaction. For more information about the edit buffer and how updates store the current record, see the article "Recordset: How Recordsets Update Records."

During transactions, **AddNew**, **Edit**, and **Delete** operations can be committed or rolled back. The effects of **CommitTrans** and **Rollback** may cause the current record to not be restored to the edit buffer. To make sure that the current record is properly restored, it is important to understand how the **CommitTrans** and **Rollback** member functions of **CDatabase** work with the update functions of **CRecordset**.

How CommitTrans Affects Updates

Table 1 explains the effects of **CommitTrans** on transactions.

Table 1   How CommitTrans Affects Updates

Operation	Status of data source
AddNew and **Update**, then **CommitTrans**	New record added to data source.
AddNew (without **Update**), then **CommitTrans**	New record is lost. Record not added to data source.
Edit and **Update**, then **CommitTrans**	Edits committed to data source.
Edit (without **Update**), then **CommitTrans**	Edits to the record are lost. Record remains unchanged on the data source.
Delete then **CommitTrans**	Records deleted from data source.

How Rollback Affects Transactions

Table 2 explains the effects of **Rollback** on transactions.

Table 2   How Rollback Affects Transactions

Operation	Status of current record	You must also:	Status of data source
AddNew and **Update**, then **Rollback**	Content of the current record is stored temporarily to make room for new record. New record is entered into edit buffer. After **Update** is called, the current record is restored to the edit buffer.		Addition to data source made by **Update** is reversed.
AddNew (without **Update**), then **Rollback**	Content of the current record is stored temporarily to make room for new record. Edit buffer contains new record.	Call **AddNew** again to restore the edit buffer to an empty, new record. Or call **Move**(0) to restore the old values to the edit buffer.	Because **Update** was not called, there were no changes made to the data source.
Edit and **Update**, then **Rollback**	An unedited version of the current record is stored temporarily. Edits are made to the content of the edit buffer. After **Update** is called, the unedited version of the record is still temporarily stored.	*Dynaset*: Scroll off the current record then back to restore the unedited version of the record to the edit buffer. *Snapshot*: Call **Requery** to refresh the recordset from the data source.	Changes to data source made by **Update** are reversed.

Table 2   How Rollback Affects Transactions (*continued*)

Operation	Status of current record	You must also:	Status of data source
Edit (without **Update**), then **Rollback**	An unedited version of the current record is stored temporarily. Edits are made to the content of the edit buffer.	Call **Edit** again to restore the unedited version of the record to the edit buffer.	Because **Update** was not called, there were no changes made to the data source.
Delete then **Rollback**	Content of the current record is deleted.	Call **Requery** to restore the content of the current record from the data source.	Deletion of data from data source is reversed.

See Also   Articles: "Transaction," "Transaction: Performing a Transaction in a Recordset"

In the *Class Library Reference*: **CDatabase**, **CRecordset**

Type Library

See the article "Automation Clients: Using Type Libraries."

Unicode

On Windows NT platforms, MFC supports the Unicode standard for encoding wide characters.

For information on using Unicode with MFC, see Chapter 12 in *Programming Techniques*.

Verbs, OLE

See the article "Activation: Verbs."

Visual Editing

See the article "Servers: Implementing In-Place Frame Windows."

Wizards

See the articles "AppWizard" and "ClassWizard."

PART 3

Appendix

APPENDIX A

Microsoft Education and Certification

As a computer professional, you face the challenge of keeping up with the accelerated pace of technological advances. To maximize the potential of new technologies, you need to constantly expand your knowledge and skills, and find a reliable way to indicate to others that you have current—and validated—education and skills.

Microsoft® Education and Certification is designed to assist you in not only keeping up with, but staying ahead of the competition. We provide the knowledge, skills, and validation to help you get ahead—and stay ahead. You can attend training at Microsoft Solution Provider Authorized Technical Education Centers, taking Microsoft Education Courses delivered by Microsoft Certified Trainers. And the Microsoft Certified Professional program enables you to validate and promote your technical expertise as an expert with the skills needed to build, implement, and support solutions with Microsoft products.

Your Direct Route to Knowledge

Microsoft offers courses on Microsoft Visual C++™ and the Microsoft Foundation Class Library (MFC) that are available through Microsoft Solution Provider Authorized Technical Education Centers located around the world:

- The "Introduction to Microsoft Visual C++ 1.5 and Object-Oriented Programming" course provides COBOL programmers with the fundamental skills needed to write code for implementing simple classes. It teaches the key constructs of C++, the fundamentals of object-oriented analysis and design, and the basic skills needed to use the integrated development environment within the Microsoft Visual C++ development system.

- "Programming in Microsoft C++" is a Microsoft-developed course designed to introduce the basic concepts of object-oriented design. It presents in detail major concepts of object-oriented programming and discusses usage and implementation issues of the Microsoft C++ programming language. The course ends with an overview of the major object-oriented languages and advanced object-oriented features.

- The "Programming with Microsoft Win32® in C Using Visual C++ 32-bit Edition" course provides developers with lab-based instruction that focuses on the processes and procedures needed to develop 32-bit applications for the Microsoft Windows NT™ operating system using the Microsoft Visual C++ development system for Windows NT.

- "Windows-based Programming Using Microsoft Foundation Class Library 2.0" is a Microsoft-developed course that teaches skilled C++ programmers how to use MFC version 2.0 and the Microsoft Visual C++ development system to create programs for the Microsoft Windows™ operating system.

- The "Programming for Microsoft Windows Environment" course instructs students on the fundamentals of developing a Windows-based application. The initial steps involve creating a basic application that displays a window. As the course progresses, increasing functionality is added to the application, such as menus, dialog boxes, and text. Instruction is a mix of lecture and hands-on lab work, designed to provide a broad-based foundation of Windows-based programming skills.

- The "User-Interface Design Workshop" is a one-day course that introduces students to the fundamental principles behind user-interface design. The basic user-interface design process is discussed, as well as information on graphics design and usability testing.

For more information about these and other Microsoft courses, and a referral to a Microsoft Solution Provider Authorized Technical Education Center near you, please call Microsoft at (800) SOLPROV. Outside the United States and Canada, please contact your local Microsoft Subsidiary.

Get Ahead with the Right Education

Microsoft education gives you the competitive edge to design and implement new systems faster, so you can take full advantage of the potential of new technologies and products.

Microsoft Education Courses are developed straight-from-the-source in conjunction with Microsoft product developers and support engineers. These courses:

- Offer timely, in-depth, and accurate training that's based on real-world experience.

- Use hands-on labs to provide the key knowledge and skills you need to build, implement, and support effective solutions with Microsoft products.

- Help you efficiently and effectively prepare for Microsoft Certified Professional exams.

You can learn where and how you like, with:

- Instructor-led classes delivered by Microsoft Certified Trainers at Microsoft Solution Provider Authorized Technical Education Centers.

- Self-study courses (available in video, workbook, or computer-based training formats—all with hands-on labs) that give you the flexibility to learn in your own location and at your convenience.

You can choose the Microsoft-course curriculum that meets your specific career needs:

The systems engineer curriculum helps you gain the skills to implement information systems and support Microsoft applications and operating systems.

The developer curriculum provides the skills you need to build applications for Microsoft Windows operating systems, using a variety of Microsoft tools and products.

The information systems manager curriculum includes senior management seminars that help you gain a clear understanding of the new, complex world of client-server computing and learn proven strategies for implementation.

Microsoft Solution Provider Authorized Technical Education Centers meet Microsoft's high standards for excellence in instruction and facilities. They provide you with:

- Straight-from-the-source courseware that's developed by Microsoft, so you know you're getting the most-accurate, in-depth, and timely training available.

- Microsoft Certified Trainers who bring the most-current Microsoft product information to the classroom; Microsoft Certified Trainers have proven instructional skills and expertise with the courseware.

- Training classes conveniently located in your area to save you the time and expense of travel.

No matter what type of Microsoft training you choose, you gain the hands-on skills you need to make technology decisions, and to build, implement, and support solutions that take full advantage of Microsoft technology.

To Pass the Competition, Prove You're the Best in Your Field

The Microsoft Certified Professional program is the recognized way to assure employers and clients that you have the knowledge and skills to help them build, implement, and support effective solutions. And that you have the validated expertise to help them get the most out of their technology investment. When you're a Microsoft Certified Professional, you have earned your credibility with Microsoft technology.

518   **Programming with the Microsoft Foundation Class Library**

The Microsoft Certified Professional program is designed to identify your proven expertise and help you gain new career and business opportunities in an increasingly competitive marketplace. As a Microsoft Certified Professional, you are *recognized and promoted by Microsoft* as an expert with the technical skills and knowledge Microsoft recommends to implement and support solutions with Microsoft products. You receive:

- **Recognition** of your knowledge and proficiency with Microsoft products. (Microsoft helps build this recognition by promoting the expertise of the Microsoft Certified Professional community to the industry and potential clients.)
- **Access to technical information** directly from Microsoft, including a prepaid trial membership in the Microsoft TechNet technical information network (which provides valuable information via monthly CD-ROM disks and a dedicated CompuServe® forum) and special invitations to Microsoft conferences and technical training events.
- **Microsoft Certified Professional logos** and other materials to let you identify your Microsoft Certified Professional status to colleagues or clients.

The Microsoft Certified Professional program provides your organization:

- **An excellent return on training investments** by providing a standard method to determine training needs and measure results.
- **Increased customer satisfaction and decreased costly support costs** through improved service, increased productivity, and greater technical self-sufficiency.
- **A reliable benchmark** for hiring, promotions, and career planning.
- **An assurance of quality** when outsourcing computer services.

To become a Microsoft Certified Professional, you must pass rigorous certification exams that provide a valid and reliable measure of technical proficiency and expertise. These exams are developed with the input of professionals in the industry and reflect how Microsoft products are used in actual organizations. The exams are conducted by an independent organization—Drake Training and Technologies—at more than 375 Drake Authorized Testing Centers around the world.

Microsoft Certified Professional certification validates your specific area of expertise:

Microsoft Certified Product Specialists are qualified to provide installation, configuration, and support for users of Microsoft desktop products.

Microsoft Certified Systems Engineers are qualified to effectively implement, maintain, and support information systems with Microsoft Windows NT and other Microsoft advanced systems and workgroup products.

Microsoft Certified Trainers are instructionally and technically qualified to deliver Microsoft Education Courses through Microsoft authorized sites. Call **(800) 688-0496** for more information on becoming a Microsoft Certified Trainer. Outside the United States and Canada, contact your local Microsoft Subsidiary.

Future Microsoft Certification for Developers is to be formally announced in the third quarter of calendar year 1994. Exam development for this certification is already in progress, and we will be releasing individual exams as they become available. Although passing an individual exam does not, by itself, qualify an individual for Microsoft certification, it does provide an opportunity to get an early start on completing the developer certification requirements. Individuals will receive transcripts from Microsoft stating the successful completion of these certification exams.

Map Your Route to Success

Use the Microsoft Education and Certification Roadmap to quickly map your personal training and certification plan. This easy-to-use, Microsoft Windows-based application guides you through the process of determining your goals and mapping the route that enables you to quickly achieve them. The roadmap:

- Enables you to map a customized education and certification plan and print a to-do list.

- Includes detailed outlines and prerequisites of Microsoft Education Courses that meet your needs.

- Provides comprehensive information on the requirements for the Microsoft Certified Professional certifications, with detailed exam topic outlines and preparation guidelines.

- Helps you relate Microsoft Education Courses to specific certification exams, so you know which courses can help you gain the skills to meet your certification goals.

- Includes information on related Microsoft products and services.

Contacting Microsoft

Call (800) 636-7544 to have a Microsoft Education and Certification Roadmap sent to you. Outside the United States and Canada, contact your local Microsoft Subsidiary.

Index

T

Contributors to
Programming with the Microsoft Foundation Class Library

Gail Brown, Editor
Samuel G. Dawson, Index Editor
Mike Eddy, Production
Jonathan Kagle, Writer
Eric Landes, Writer
Seth Manheim, Writer
Bill Nolan, Writer
Mark Olson, Art Director
Chuck Sphar, Writer
Rod Wilkinson, Editor

Programming Techniques

Microsoft® Visual C++™

Development System for Windows™ and Windows NT™
Version 2.0

Microsoft Corporation

Contents

Figures and Tables

Introduction

The Windows NT™ operating system provides many new challenges for programmers. You may need to port Windows 3.*x* applications, or want to explore new areas of functionality provided by Windows NT.

Visual C++™ for Windows NT is designed to make these new features easy to use. The product includes language elements that support areas of functionality such as templates, exception handling, DLLs, and multithread applications.

Programming Techniques is a guide to these advanced language features. Most are directly relevant to services provided by Windows NT, or are at least different from Windows 3.*x*. Therefore, most of the chapters in this manual deal with porting or use of advanced features for Windows NT.

Development Strategies for Windows NT

Windows NT is a complete operating system, not just a graphical user interface (GUI), so you can use it to run simple console applications. In fact, you can use any technique described in this manual without writing for a graphical user interface, as long as no GUI objects are involved. The rest of this section describes how to approach development when porting a traditional program for Windows, which does involve GUI objects such as window handles, window procedures, and messages.

You can begin using Visual C++ for Windows NT without using new areas of functionality. Instead, you can concentrate on adapting code for Windows 3.*x* to compile and run correctly with Windows NT. (Chapters 1-4 contain information on porting issues for applications written for Windows and the new programming model for DLLs.) However, you may want to start using new features that are most useful to your application. For example, you can use threads if your application has many operations that would be best handled as background tasks.

Note The term Win32® is used in this manual to refer to the *common* feature-set and architecture of the Win32 API. Certain features are not supported by some implementations of the Win32 API (such as multithread operations not supported by Win32s™).

Using this Manual

To understand the basic use of Visual C++, you should refer to other manuals in this documentation set. Despite its name, *Programming Techniques* does not attempt to teach the basics of C, C++, or programming in Windows. Instead, it covers advanced topics.

However, the first few chapters may be immediately useful if you port existing applications from Windows 3.*x*. The order of information in the manual reflects the different ways you can use it. The following table suggests which chapters you should turn to for various topics.

To do this	Refer to chapters
Port 16-bit applications to Win32™	1–3
Create a 32-bit DLL	4
Create a multithread application	5
Use new language features of Visual C++	6–8
Learn about advanced topics, such as new calling conventions, programming with mixed languages, advanced profiling, and developing for international markets	9–12

Note For information on Microsoft product support, see "Using Microsoft Support Services" in *Introducing Visual C++*.

Document Conventions

This book uses the following typographic conventions:

Example	Description
STDIO.H	Uppercase letters indicate filenames, segment names, registers, and terms used at the operating-system command level.
char, _setcolor, __int32	Bold type indicates C and C++ keywords, operators, language-specific characters, and library routines. Within discussions of syntax, bold type indicates that the text must be entered exactly as shown.
	Many functions and constants begin with either a single or double underscore. These are part of the name and are mandatory. For example, to have the **__cplusplus** manifest constant be recognized by the compiler, you must enter the leading double underscore.

Example	Description
expression	Words in italics indicate placeholders for information you must supply, such as a filename. Italic type is also used occasionally for emphasis in the text.
[[*option*]]	Items inside double square brackets are optional.
**#pragma pack {1	2}**	Braces and a vertical bar indicate a choice among two or more items. You must choose one of these items unless double square brackets ([[ ]]) surround the braces.
`#include <io.h>`	This font is used for examples, user input, program output, and error messages in text.
CL [[*option...*]] *file...*	Three dots (an ellipsis) following an item indicate that more items having the same form may appear.

`while()`
`{`
   .
   .
   .
`}`
	A column or row of three dots tells you that part of an example program has been intentionally omitted.

CTRL+ENTER	Small capital letters are used to indicate the names of keys on the keyboard. When you see a plus sign (+) between two key names, you should hold down the first key while pressing the second.
	The carriage-return key, sometimes marked as a bent arrow on the keyboard, is called ENTER.
"argument"	Quotation marks enclose a new term the first time it is defined in text.
`"C string"`	Some C constructs, such as strings, require quotation marks. Quotation marks required by the language have the form `"  "` and `'  '` rather than " " and ' '.
Color Graphics Adapter (CGA)	The first time an acronym is used, it is usually spelled out.

C H A P T E R   1

Porting 16-Bit Code to 32-Bit Windows

This chapter describes how to create a 32-bit version of an application written for Windows 3.*x* in C, and how to make the code portable *between* versions of Windows. Portable code can be recompiled as a 16-bit application or a 32-bit application.

Overview of 32-Bit Programming

The 32-bit API was designed to minimize the impact on existing code so that 16-bit applications could be adapted as easily as possible. However, some changes were mandated by the larger address space. Pointers are all 32 bits wide and no longer **near** or **far**, and your code cannot make assumptions based on segmented memory.

Items which have increased to 32 bits include:

- Window handles
- Handles to other objects, such as pens, brushes, and menus
- Graphics coordinates

These size differences are generally resolved in WINDOWS.H or by the C language, but some changes to source code are necessary. Because the different sizes can change the way information is packed in some message parameters, you must rewrite code that handles these messages. The larger size of graphics coordinates also affects a number of function calls.

Some source code changes are required because Win32 uses higher-level mechanisms for certain operations, such as MS-DOS calls. With these mechanisms, the 32-bit API is adaptable to many platforms, and it supports powerful new features such as multiple threads of execution.

Although Windows 3.x and Win32 were designed to be as compatible as possible, you may need to carefully review large amounts of source code. Where do you start? The top-down approach is recommended:

1. Compile the application for 32 bits, and note the compiler-generated errors.
2. Replace complex procedures that are difficult to port, and procedures written in assembly language, with stub procedures (which do nothing except return).
3. Fix errors in the main portion of the application, using the techniques described in this chapter.
4. Individually fill each stub procedure with portable code after the main portion of the application compiles and runs correctly.

Using PORTTOOL to Automate Porting

You can use the PORTTOOL utility (PORTTOOL.EXE) to port applications more easily. This utility finds locations in your code, such as references to certain API functions and messages, that are likely to need revision.

Use the following steps to start using the PORTTOOL utility:

1. Run PORTTOOL and load a Windows 3.x source file.
2. From the Search menu, select the SearchAPI option to search for problematic API functions and messages.

When a problem is found, a dialog box is displayed specifying the message or function and suggesting what change is needed. Although the porting tool is not intended to replace your primary editor, it does support basic editing capabilities (such as Cut, Paste, and Search).

PORTTOOL uses settings in the file PORT.INI to determine what items to look for. This file is based on the "Summary of API and Message Differences" table on page 20.

Note The source code for the PORTTOOL utility is in the following directory: \MSVC20\SAMPLES\SDKTOOLS\PORTTOOL. You can examine this code to better understand how PORTTOOL works, or modify it and rebuild it for your own needs. An executable version of the PORTTOOL utility is included in the \MSVC20\BIN directory.

Porting Applications

The following sections describe general areas of code you need to modify when porting a 16-bit application to Win32. These areas include the following:

- Window procedure declarations
- Near and far type declarations
- Data types
- Messages
- Calls to API functions
- WinMain function

If your application uses advanced techniques, such as manipulating the WIN.INI file, focus, and mouse capture, you may need to consult the section, "Special Considerations for Advanced Applications," on page 16.

Revising the Window Procedure Declaration

To port a Windows 3.*x* application, you must revise the declaration of the window procedure. The following is a declaration of a window procedure for a Windows 3.*x* application.

```
LONG FAR PASCAL MainWndProc( HWND hWnd,
    unsigned message,
    WORD wParam,
    LONG lParam)
```

To revise the declaration for Win32, replace the data types used in Windows 3.*x* as shown in Table 1.1. The following code can be compiled as a 32-bit application, but it can still be used to compile 16-bit applications as before:

```
LRESULT CALLBACK MainWndProc(  HWND hWnd,
    UINT message,
    WPARAM wParam,
    LPARAM lParam)
```

Table 1.1 summarizes the changes to the declaration noted in the previous example.

Table 1.1   Changes to the Window Procedure Declaration

Windows 3.x	Win32 (portable code)	Reason for changing
FAR PASCAL	**CALLBACK**	**CALLBACK** is guaranteed to use whatever calling convention is appropriate for windows and dialog procedures.
unsigned	**UINT**	Meaning is the same, but **UINT** guarantees portability for future platforms.
WORD	**WPARAM**	**WORD** is always 16 bits. The **WPARAM** type grows to 32 bits.
LONG	**LPARAM**	Meaning is the same, but **LPARAM** guarantees portability for future platforms.

A significant difference between the Windows 3.x declaration and the portable version involves the *wParam* parameter, which grows to 32 bits under Win32. Therefore, replacing the **WORD** type with **WPARAM** is critical. The **WPARAM** type varies with the operating system, as does **UINT**: these types are 16 bits wide under Windows 3.x and 32 bits wide under Win32.

The other changes shown in Table 1.1 are recommended for code clarity and portability. For example, **WPARAM** and **LPARAM** are automatically defined to be the correct types for message parameters, and **CALLBACK** will always be the correct declaration for window procedures.

A 32-bit *wParam* message parameter combined with the addresses and handles that grow to 32 bits, means that some messages must be repacked, as described in the section "Handling 32-Bit Messages" on page 5.

Removing Near and Far Type Declarations

Windows NT does not distinguish between near and far addresses. Because the types **NEAR** and **FAR** are defined in WINDEF.H, they are automatically handled by the include file, which redefines them as empty strings for Windows NT. Thus, **NEAR** and **FAR** are ignored. A convenient solution is to use the /D command-line option to replace the keywords by empty strings. For example:

```
/D_near=   /D_far= /D__near=   /D__far=
```

Using Proper Data Types

Windows 3.x source code often uses the type **WORD** interchangeably with types such as **HWND** and **HANDLE**. For example, the type cast **(WORD)** might be used to cast a data type to a handle:

```
hWnd = (WORD) SendMessage( hWnd, WM_GETMDIACTIVATE, 0, 0 );
```

This code compiles Windows 3.x applications correctly because both the **WORD** type and handles are 16 bits. But the code produces errors when compiled for Win32 because handles (such as **HWND** types) grow to 32 bits while the **WORD** type is still 16 bits.

Examine each occurrence of **WORD** casts and data definitions in your code, and revise as follows:

- If a variable or expression is to hold a handle, replace **WORD** with **HWND**, **HPEN**, **HINSTANCE**, or another handle type.

- If a variable or expression is a graphics coordinate or some other integer value that grows from 16 to 32 bits, replace **WORD** with **UINT**, and **short** with **int.**

- Continue to use the **WORD** type only if the data type needs to be 16 bits for all versions of Windows (usually because it is a function argument or structure member).

In the portable version of the previous example, the **(WORD)** cast is replaced by **(HWND)**:

```
hWnd = (HWND) SendMessage( hWnd, WM_GETMDIACTIVATE, 0, 0 );
```

In general, it is best to use the most specific type possible. Avoid using a generic handle type such as **HANDLE**, and use a more specific type such as **HPEN**. You should also define specific types for application-specific objects you create.

Handling 32-Bit Messages

Handles grow to 32 bits under Win32, so they can no longer be combined with other information and still fit into a 32-bit parameter (*lParam*). The handle now occupies all of *lParam*, so information formerly in the high or low word of *lParam* must now move to *wParam*.

Because the *wParam* message parameter also grows to 32 bits, it can hold the information that can no longer be held in *lParam*.

Figure 1.1 illustrates how the parameter sizes change, and how information is repacked for WM_COMMAND, one of the messages affected.

Figure 1.1   Parameter Sizes

Extracting Data from Messages with Portable Code

The cleanest way to handle a repacked message is to revise your code so that it extracts needed information and stores it in local variables. This localizes message-packing issues to a few lines of your code.

For example, you can use the following code to handle the WM_COMMAND message:

```
case WM_COMMAND:
    id = LOWORD(wParam);
    hwndChild = (HWND)(UINT)lParam;
    cmd = HIWORD(wParam);
```

Summary of Windows Messages Affected

Use Table 1.2 to reference the packing of Windows messages affected by porting.

Except for WM_CTLCOLOR, each message in Table 1.2 lists both 16-bit Windows packing and Win32 packing for messages.

Table 1.2   Windows Messages Affected by Porting

Message	Windows	wParam	lParam
WM_ACTIVATE	16-bit	state	fMinimized, hwnd
	Win32	state, fMinimized	hwnd (32 bits)
WM_CHARTOITEM	16-bit	char	pos, hwnd
	Win32	char, pos	hwnd (32 bits)

Table 1.2   Windows Messages Affected by Porting (*continued*)

Message	Windows	wParam	lParam
WM_COMMAND	16-bit	id	hwnd, cmd
	Win32	id, cmd	hwnd (32 bits)
WM_CTLCOLOR	16-bit	hdc	hwnd, type
WM_CTLCOLOR*type*[1]	Win32	hdc (32 bits)	hwnd (32 bits)
WM_MENUSELECT	16-bit	cmd	flags, hMenu
	Win32	cmd, flags	hMenu (32 bits)
WM_MDIACTIVATE	16-bit	fActivate	hwndDeactivate, hwndActivate
	Win32	hwndActivate (32 bits)	hwndDeactivate (32 bits)
WM_MDISETMENU	16-bit	0	hMenuFrame, hMenuWindow
	Win32	hMenuFrame (32 bits)	hMenuWindow (32 bits)
WM_MENUCHAR	16-bit	char	hMenu, fMenu
	Win32	char, fMenu	hMenu (32 bits)
WM_PARENTNOTIFY	16-bit	msg	id, hwndChild
	Win32	msg, id	hwndChild (32 bits)
WM_VKEYTOITEM	16-bit	code	item, hwnd
	Win32	code, item	hwnd (32 bits)
EM_GETSEL (returns wStart, wEnd)	16-bit	0	0
	Win32	0 or lpdwStart	0 or lpdwEnd
EM_LINESCROLL	16-bit	0	nLinesVert, nLinesHorz
	Win32	mLinesHorz (32 bits)	nLinesVert (32 bits)
EM_SETSEL	16-bit	0	wStart, wEnd
	Win32	wStart (32 bits)	wEnd (32 bits)
WM_HSCROLL, WM_VSCROLL	16-bit	code	pos, hwnd
	Win32	code, pos	hwnd (32 bits)

[1] Under Win32, WM_CTLCOLOR is replaced by a series of messages, each corresponding to a different type. To write portable code, use **#ifdef** statements to handle this difference.

Summary of DDE Messages Affected

DDE messages are packed differently for Win32 and Windows 3.*x.*, as shown in Table 1.3.

Table 1.3   DDE Messages Affected by Porting

Message	Windows	wParam	lParam
WM_DDE_ACK (posted form only)	16-bit	hwnd	wStatus, aItem or wStatus, hCommands
	Win32	hwnd (32 bits)	hDDEAck (see following paragraph)
WM_DDE_ADVISE	16-bit	hwnd	hOptions, aItem
	Win32	hwnd (32 bits)	hDDEAdvise (see following paragraph)
WM_DDE_DATA	16-bit	hwnd	hData, aItem
	Win32	hwnd (32 bits)	hDDEData (see following paragraph)
WM_DDE_POKE	16-bit	hwnd	hData, aItem
	Win32	hwnd (32 bits)	hDDEPoke (see following paragraph)

Because of storage limitations, some of the information is stored in a structure, which is accessed through the handle in *lParam*. You can use the following API functions to extract information from these structures: **PackDDElParam**, **UnPackDDElParam**, and **FreeDDElParam**.

For information on how to use these structures and API functions, consult the Win32 API reference.

Adjusting Calls to API Functions

Most of your source code is not affected by differences between the APIs of Windows 3.*x* and Win32. The underlying definitions in WINDOWS.H automatically adjust data to the correct size. But you may need to revise code if you call API functions in any of the following categories:

- Graphics functions
- Functions accessing "extra" window data
- MS-DOS system calls
- Far-pointer functions
- Functions getting list and combo box contents

Graphics Functions

Most of the Windows 3.x API functions that must be replaced return packed x- and y-coordinates.

In Windows 3.x, the x- and y-coordinates are 16 bits each and are packed into the 32-bit (**DWORD**) function return value, the largest valid size. In Win32, the coordinates are 32 bits each, totaling 64 bits, and are thus too large to fit into a single return value. Each Windows 3.x function is replaced by a Win32 function with the same name, but with an **Ex** suffix added. The **Ex** functions pass the x- and y-coordinates using an additional parameter instead of a return value. Both Win32 and Windows 3.x support these new functions.

The problematic graphics functions fall into two groups. The first group, functions that set coordinates, are shown in the following table with the Win32 versions.

Windows 3.x function	Portable version of function
MoveTo	MoveToEx
OffsetViewportOrg	OffsetViewportOrgEx
OffsetWindowOrg	OffsetWindowOrgEx
ScaleViewportExt	ScaleViewportExtEx
ScaleWindowExt	ScaleWindowExtEx
SetBitmapDimension	SetBitmapDimensionEx
SetMetaFileBits	SetMetaFileBitsEx
SetViewportExt	SetViewportExtEx
SetWindowExt	SetWindowExtEx
SetWindowOrg	SetWindowOrgEx

Each of the functions in the first column returns a value, although application code frequently ignores it. However, even if you do not care about the return value, you must replace the old function call with the new form. The old functions are not supported under Win32.

Each **Ex** function includes an additional parameter that points to a location to receive data. After the function call, this data provides the same information as the corresponding function's return value. If you do not need this information, you can pass **NULL** to this parameter.

Under Windows 3.x, a call to the **MoveTo** function can be written as follows:

```
MoveTo( hDC, x, y );
```

In the portable version supported by both versions of Windows, the call to **MoveTo** is rewritten as follows. Note that the information returned by **MoveTo** under Windows 3.*x* is still ignored:

```
MoveToEx( hDC, x, y, NULL );
```

As a general rule, pass **NULL** as the last parameter unless you need to use the x- and y-coordinates returned by the Windows 3.*x* version. In the latter case, use the procedure outlined in the next few paragraphs for the **Get** functions.

The second group consists of functions in which the application code normally does use the return value. They are listed in the following table.

Windows 3.*x* function	Portable version of function
GetAspectRatioFilter	GetAspectRatioFilterEx
GetBitmapDimension	GetBitmapDimensionEx
GetBrushOrg	GetBrushOrgEx
GetCurrentPosition	GetCurrentPositionEx
GetTextExtent	GetTextExtentPoint
GetTextExtentEx	GetTextExtentExPoint
GetViewportExt	GetViewportExtEx
GetViewportOrg	GetViewportOrgEx
GetWindowExt	GetWindowExtEx
GetWindowOrg	GetWindowOrgEx

The **GetTextExtent** function uses the **Point** suffix because there is already a Windows 3.1 extended function **GetTextExtentEx**. Therefore, the **Point** suffix is added to the functions **GetTextExtent** and **GetTextExtentEx**, to name the portable versions for each.

As with the first group of functions, each **Ex** (and **Point**) version adds an additional parameter: a pointer to a **POINT** or **SIZE** structure to receive x- and y-coordinates. Because this structure is always the appropriate size for the environment, you can write portable code by:

- Declaring a local variable of type **POINT** or **SIZE**, as appropriate.
- Passing a pointer to this structure as the last parameter to the function.
- Calling the function. The function responds by filling the structure with the appropriate information.

For example, the Windows 3.*x* version call to **GetTextExtent** extracts the x- and y-coordinates from a **DWORD** return value (stored in a temporary variable, dwXY):

```
DWORD    dwXY;

dwXY = GetTextExtent( hDC, szLabel1, strlen( szLabel1 ) );
rect.left = 0; rect.bottom = 0;
rect.right = LOWORD(dwXY);
rect.top = HIWORD(dwXY);
InvertRect( hDC, &rect );
```

The portable version passes a pointer to a temporary **SIZE** structure, and then it extracts data from the structure:

```
SIZE sizeRect;

GetTextExtentPoint( hDC, szLabel1, strlen( szLabel1 ), &sizeRect );
rect.left = 0; rect.bottom = 0;
rect.right = sizeRect.cx;
rect.top = sizeRect.cy;
InvertRect( hDC, &rect );
```

Functions That Access the Extra Window Data

The functions described in this section manipulate the "extra" data area of a window structure. This structure can contain system information and user-defined data. You specify the size of this data area by using the **cbClsExtra** and **cbWndExtra** members of the **WNDCLASS** structure when you register the window class.

The following Windows 3.*x* functions get or set 16 bits during each call: **GetClassWord**, **GetWindowWord**, **SetClassWord**, and **SetWindowWord**.

In Win32, each of these system-information items grows to 32 bits. Therefore, in Win32, you would use the following functions which access 32 bits at a time: **GetClassLong**, **GetWindowLong**, **SetClassLong**, and **SetWindowLong**.

Each of these functions takes two parameters: a window handle and an offset into the data area. These offsets differ depending on whether you are compiling for Windows 3.*x* or Win32.

The index values specifying these offsets correspond to each other as follows:

Windows 3.x	Win32 (nonportable)
GCW_CURSOR	GCL_CURSOR
GCW_HBRBACKGROUND	GCL_HBRBACKGROUND
GCW_HICON	GCL_HICON
GWW_HINSTANCE	GWL_HINSTANCE
GWW_HWNDPARENT	GWL_HWNDPARENT
GWW_ID	GWL_ID
GWW_USERDATA	GWL_USERDATA

In the case of **GWW_HWNDPARENT**, you can avoid calls to **GetWindowLong** and **GetWindowWord**, and instead use a single call to a new API function, **GetParent**. This API function returns a handle of the appropriate size. The following example illustrates a call to **GetParent** that has the same results as the **#ifdef** statements shown in the previous example:

```
hwndParent = GetParent( hWnd );
```

Remember that offsets may change for private data that you store in the window structure. You should review this code carefully and recalculate offsets for Win32, noting that some data types, such as handles, increase in size.

Porting MS-DOS System Calls

The **DOS3Call** API function in Windows 3.x must be called from assembly language. It is typically used to perform file I/O. In Win32, you should replace assembly language code that calls **DOS3Call** with the appropriate Win32 file I/O calls. Other (non-file) INT 21H functions should be replaced with the portable Windows API call as shown in the following table.

INT 21H subfunction	MS-DOS operation	Win32 API equivalent
0EH	Select Disk	**SetCurrentDirectory**
19H	Get Current Disk	**GetCurrentDirectory**
2AH	Get Date	**GetDateAndTime**
2BH	Set Date	**SetDateAndTime**
2CH	Get Time	**GetDateAndTime**
2DH	Set Time	**SetDateAndTime**
36H	Get Disk Free Space	**GetDiskFreeSpace**
39H	Create Directory	**CreateDirectory**
3AH	Remove Directory	**RemoveDirectory**
3BH	Set Current Directory	**SetCurrentDirectory**

INT 21H subfunction	MS-DOS operation	Win32 API equivalent
3CH	Create Handle	**CreateFile**
3DH	Open Handle	**CreateFile**
3EH	Close Handle	**CloseHandle**
3FH	Read Handle	**ReadFile**
40H	Write Handle	**WriteFile**
41H	Delete File	**DeleteFile**
42H	Move File Pointer	**SetFilePointer**
43H	Get File Attributes	**GetAttributesFile**
43H	Set File Attributes	**SetAttributesFile**
47H	Get Current Directory	**GetCurrentDirectory**
4EH	Find First File	**FindFirstFile**
4FH	Find Next File	**FindNextFile**
56H	Change Directory Entry	**MoveFile**
57H	Get Date/Time of File	**GetDateAndTimeFile**
57H	Set Date/Time of File	**SetDataAndTimeFile**
59H	Get Extended Error	**GetLastError**
5AH	Create Unique File	**GetTempFileName**
5BH	Create New File	**CreateFile**
5CH	Lock	**LockFile**
5CH	Unlock	**UnlockFile**
67H	Set Handle Count	**SetHandleCount**

File Operations

You may need to increase the size of fixed-length buffers for filenames and environment strings. Windows NT (one of the forms of Win32) supports filenames of up to 256 characters, rather than the 8.3 format supported by MS-DOS. You can make code more portable by allocating longer buffers or by using dynamic memory allocation. If you want to conserve memory under Windows 3.*x*, you can use **#ifdef** statements to allocate buffers of the proper length for the environment. You can also use macros such as _MAX_PATH and _MAX_FNAME, defined in STDLIB.H.

Windows NT requires a stricter use of file open and close operations than Windows 3.*x*. There are some combinations of open and close functions (for example, mixing **_open** with **_lclose**) that may work in code for Windows 3.*x*, but require revision to work correctly with Windows NT.

You may also need to make changes in low-level file I/O. In porting Windows 3.*x* code, some developers change from using the Windows API file I/O functions (such as **_lopen** and **_lread**) to using the C run-time low-level I/O functions (such as **_open** and **_read**). All versions of the Windows API support only binary mode, not text mode, but the C run-time calls use text mode by default. Therefore, when changing from the Windows file I/O to the C run-time versions, open files in binary mode by doing one of the following:

- Link with BINMODE.OBJ, which changes the default mode for all file-open operations.
- Open the individual files with _O_BINARY flag set.
- Use **setmode** to change an open file to _O_BINARY.

Far-Pointer Functions

Windows 3.*x* provides functions for memory and file manipulation using far pointers, which have the form **_f***xxxx*. In Win32, these functions are replaced by similarly-named functions of the form *xxxx*, because there is no need for far pointers in Win32. (The **_f** prefix is dropped from the name.)

The WINDOWSX.H file defines the **_f***xxxx* function names so that in Win32, the **_f***xxxx* function names are equated to corresponding functions that are still supported. This means that as long as you include WINDOWSX.H, you don't have to rewrite calls to these functions. Some of the definitions are:

```
#define _fmemcpy    memcpy
#define _fstrcpy    strcpy
#define _fstrcmp    strcmp
#define _fstrcat    strcat
```

Functions Getting List and Combo Box Contents

The Win32 API contains two new functions, shown in the following table, that provide an improved means of extracting list and combo box contents. In each case, you use the portable version of the function to specify a buffer size for a string that receives the information.

Windows 3.*x* function	Portable version of the function
DlgDirSelect	**DlgDirSelectEx**
DlgDirSelectComboBox	**DlgDirSelectComboBoxEx**

For example, Windows 3.*x* code might contain the following function call:

```
DlgDirSelect( hDlg, lpString, nIDListBox );
```

This line of code should be replaced by the following call to **DlgDirSelectEx**:

```
DlgDirSelectEx( hDlg, lpString, strlen(lpString), nIDListBox );
```

Revising the WinMain Function

You need to revise the **WinMain** function if either of the following is true:

- Your application needs to know when another instance of the application is running, or
- You need to access the command line.

Otherwise, the code in this function generally needs no change.

The parameter list for **WinMain** is the same for Win32 and Windows 3.*x*:

```
int PASCAL WinMain(hInstance, hPrevInstance, lpCmdLine, nCmdShow)
```

However, under Win32, there are two differences in the values passed through these parameters:

- The *hPrevInstance* parameter is always passed NULL.
- The *lpCmdLine* parameter points to a string containing the entire command line.

The following two sections discuss each of these differences.

Initializing Instances

The *hPrevInstance* parameter is always passed NULL in Win32. This causes each instance of an application to act as though it were the only instance running. The application must register the window class, and it cannot access data used by other instances, except through standard interprocess communication techniques such as shared memory or DDE. Calls to **GetInstanceData** must be replaced with these techniques.

Before registering a window class, source code for Windows 3.*x* normally tests *hPrevInstance* to see another instance of the application is already running. This code needs no change, because under Win32, it will always register the window class.

Some applications must know whether other instances are running. Sometimes this is because data sharing is required. More frequently, it is because only one instance of the application should run at a time. Examples of this latter case include Control Panel and Task Manager.

Applications cannot use *hPrevInstance* to test for previous instances under Win32. An alternative method must be used, such as creating a unique named pipe, creating or testing for a named semaphore, broadcasting a unique message, or calling **FindWindow**.

Accessing the Command Line Through lpCmdLine

In Windows 3.*x*, the *lpCmdLine* parameter points to a string containing the command line starting with the first parameter. The name of the application is not included. In Win32, *lpCmdLine* points to a string containing the entire command line, including the application itself.

Special Considerations for Advanced Applications

Additional revisions may sometimes be necessary for applications that use advanced API calls or coding tricks. If your application is fairly complex, you should scan this section to make sure that you don't need to make additional changes.

Revising Advanced API Calls

Applications may need further revision if they use API calls dealing with any of the following: accessing .INI files, setting focus and active window, capturing the mouse, and sharing graphical objects.

Profile Strings and .INI Files

Although Windows NT and Win32s are both examples of Win32, Windows NT has some features not present in Win32s.

Windows 3.*x* applications can access .INI files directly. In Windows NT, however, such code doesn't work because the information in .INI files is replaced by a registration database. This database offers some advantages, including security controls that prevent an application from corrupting system information, error logging, remote software updating, and remote administration of workstation software.

You can write portable code by using the profile API supported by Windows 3.*x* and all versions of Win32, including Windows NT. Call the **GetProfileString** and **WriteProfileString** API functions instead of accessing .INI files directly. These functions use whichever underlying mechanism (.INI file or registration database) is supported by the environment you are compiling for.

Focus, Mouse Capture, and Localized Input

The Windows NT environment differs from Windows 3.*x* in that each thread of execution has its own message pump. This change affects window focus and mouse capture.

Window Focus

In Windows NT, each thread of execution can set or get the focus only to windows created by the current thread. This prevents applications from interfering with each other. One application's delay in responding cannot cause other applications to suspend their response to user actions, as often happens in Windows 3.*x*.

Consequently, the following API functions work differently under Windows NT:

GetActiveWindow(VOID)	**SetActiveWindow(HWND)**
GetCapture(VOID)	**SetCapture(HWND)**
GetFocus(VOID)	**SetFocus(HWND)**
ReleaseCapture(VOID)	

The **Get** functions listed above can now return NULL, which could not happen in Windows 3.*x*. Therefore, it's important to test the return value of **GetFocus** before using it. Instead of returning the window handle of another thread, the function returns NULL. For example, you call **GetFocus** and another thread has the focus. Note that it's possible for a call to **GetFocus** to return NULL even though an earlier call to **SetFocus** successfully set the focus. Similar considerations apply to **GetCapture** and **GetActiveWindow**.

The **Set** functions can only specify a window created by the current thread. If you attempt to pass a window handle created by another thread, the call to the **Set** function fails.

Mouse Capture

Mouse capture is also affected by the Windows NT localized input queues. If the mouse is captured on mouse down, the window capturing the mouse receives mouse input until the mouse button is released, as in Windows 3.*x*. But if the mouse is captured while the mouse button is up, the window receives mouse input only as long as the mouse is over that window or another window created by the same thread.

Shared Graphical Objects

Win32 applications run in separate address spaces. Graphical objects are specific to the application and cannot be manipulated by other processes as in Windows 3.*x*. A handle to a bitmap passed to another process cannot be used because the original process retains ownership.

Each process should create its own pens and brushes. A cooperative process may access the bitmap data in shared memory (by way of standard interprocess communications) and create its own copy of the bitmap. Bitmap alterations must be communicated between the cooperative processes by way of interprocess communication, such as DDE.

Win32 adds an explicit ownership transfer API function for graphical objects to explicitly allow cooperative applications to share graphical objects.

Solving Problems Due to C Coding Techniques

Some portability problems can be caused by coding techniques that do not translate successfully to other memory models and processors. You can avoid these problems by not using segmented memory. The header files will then handle standard pointers and manage memory correctly.

Memory and Pointers

To be portable, source code must avoid any techniques that rely on the 16-bit *segment*:*offset* address structure, because all pointers are 32 bits in size under Win32 and use flat rather than segmented memory.

This difference in pointer structure is usually not a problem unless the code uses **HIWORD**, **LOWORD**, or similar macros to manipulate portions of the pointer.

For example, in Windows 3.*x*, memory is allocated to align on a segment boundary, which makes memory allocation functions return a pointer with an offset of 0x0000. The following code exploits this fact to run successfully under Windows 3.*x*:

```
ptr2 = ptr1 = malloc();              // ptr2 = xxxx:0000
LOWORD( ptr2 ) = index * elementsize;  // Place offset of array element
                                     //   into ptr2 low word
```

Such code does not work properly under Win32. But standard pointer constructs, such as the following, always result in portable code:

```
ptr1 = malloc();            // Set ptr1 to start of memory block
ptr2 = &ptr1[i];            // Place offset of array element
```

Here are some other guidelines for dealing with pointers:

- All pointers, including those that access the local heap, are 32 bits under Win32.

- Addresses never wrap, as they can with the low word in segmented addressing. For example, in Windows 3.x, an address can wrap from 1000:FFFF to 1000:0000.

- Structures that hold near pointers in Windows 3.x must be revised because all pointers are 32 bits in Win32. This may affect code that uses constants to access structure members, and it may also affect alignment.

Structure Alignment

Applications should generally align structure members at addresses that are "natural" for the data type and the processor involved. For example, a 4-byte data member should have an address that is a multiple of four.

This principle is especially important when you write code for porting to multiple processors. A misaligned 4-byte data member, which is on an address that is not a multiple of four, causes a performance penalty with an 80386 processor and a hardware exception with a MIPS® RISC processor. In the latter case, although the system handles the exception, the performance penalty is significantly greater.

The following guidelines ensure proper alignment for processors targeted by Win32:

Type	Alignment
char	Align on byte boundaries
short (16-bit)	Align on even byte boundaries
int and **long** (32-bit)	Align on 32-bit boundaries
float	Align on 32-bit boundaries
double	Align on 64-bit boundaries
structures	Largest alignment requirement of any member
unions	Alignment requirement of the first member

The compiler automatically aligns data in accordance with these requirements, inserting padding in structures up to the limit (default pack size) specified by the /Zp option or **#pragma pack**. For example, /Zp2 permits up to 1 byte of padding, /Zp4 permits up to 3 bytes of padding, and so on. The default pack size for Windows 3.x is 2, whereas the default for Win32 is 8. As a consequence:

- If you have specified a packing limit with /Zp or **#pragma pack**, you may not get the proper alignment (the default value) for Win32.

- The different default setting for Win32 can impact your source code by changing the offsets of some structure members. Examine your code closely to see whether you have hard-coded these offsets, or whether your code makes assumptions based on a certain default pack size.

Ranges and Promotions

Occurrences of **int**, **unsigned**, and **unsigned int** indicate potential portability problems because size and range are not constant. Data that would not exceed its range in Win32 could exceed range in Windows 3.*x*. Sign extension also works differently, so exercise caution in performing bitwise manipulation of this data.

Source code that relies on wrapping often presents portability problems and should be avoided. For example, a loop should not rely on an **unsigned** variable wrapping at 65535 (the maximum value in Windows 3.*x*) back down to 0.

Summary of API and Message Differences

Table 1.4 provides a complete list of API calls and messages that require implementation changes for Win32.

Table 1.4   API and Message Implementation Changes for Win32

API/Message	Support	Comments
AccessResource	Dropped	No Win32 API equivalent (resource API in progress)
AddFontResource	Enhanced	Must use string, not handle, for filename
AllocDSToCSAlias	Dropped	No Win32 API equivalent
AllocResource	Dropped	No Win32 API equivalent (resource API in progress)
AllocSelector	Dropped	No Win32 API equivalent
ChangeSelector	Dropped	No Win32 API equivalent
CloseComm	Dropped	Replaced by **CloseFile**
CloseSound	Dropped	Replaced by multimedia sound support
CountVoiceNotes	Dropped	Replaced by multimedia sound support
DeviceCapabilities	Dropped	Replaced by portable **DeviceCapabilitiesEx**
DeviceMode	Dropped	Replaced by portable **DeviceModeEx**
DlgDirSelect	Dropped	Replaced by portable **DlgDirSelectEx**
DlgDirSelectComboBox	Dropped	Replaced by portable **DlgDirSelectComboBoxEx**
DOS3Call	Dropped	Replaced by named, portable Win32 API
ExtDeviceMode	Dropped	Replaced by portable **ExtDeviceModeEx**
FlushComm	Dropped	Replaced by **PurgeComm**

Table 1.4   API and Message Implementation Changes for Win32 (*continued*)

API/Message	Support	Comments
FreeSelector	Dropped	No Win32 API equivalent
GetAspectRatioFilter	Dropped	Replaced by portable **GetAspectRatioFilterEx**
GetBitmapDimension	Dropped	Replaced by portable **GetBitmapDimensionEx**
GetBrushOrg	Dropped	Replaced by portable **GetBrushOrgEx**
GetClassWord	Enhanced	Use **GetClassLong** for values that grow to 32 bits in Win32
GetCodeHandle	Dropped	No Win32 API equivalent
GetCodeInfo	Dropped	No Win32 API equivalent
GetCommError	Dropped	Replaced by **GetCommState**
GetCurrentPDB	Dropped	No Win32 API equivalent
GetCurrentPosition	Dropped	Replaced by portable **GetCurrentPositionEx**
GetEnvironment	Dropped	No Win32 API equivalent
GetInstanceData	Dropped	No equivalent; use alternative supported IPC mechanism
GetKBCodePage	Dropped	No Win32 API equivalent
GetMetaFileBits	Dropped	Replaced by portable **GetMetaFileBitsEx**
GetModuleUsage	Enhanced	Always returns 1 on Win32
GetTempDrive	Dropped	Not applicable to Win32
GetTextExtent	Dropped	Replaced by portable **GetTextExtentPoint**
GetTextExtentEx	Dropped	Replaced by portable **GetTextExtentExPoint**
GetThresholdEvent	Dropped	Replaced by multimedia sound support
GetThresholdStatus	Dropped	Replaced by multimedia sound support
GetViewportExt	Dropped	Replaced by portable **GetViewportExtEx**
GetViewportOrg	Dropped	Replaced by portable **GetViewportOrgEx**
GetWindowExt	Dropped	Replaced by portable **GetWindowExtEx**
GetWindowOrg	Dropped	Replaced by portable **GetWindowOrgEx**
GetWindowWord	Enhanced	Use **GetWindowLong** for values that grow to 32 bits on Win32

Table 1.4   API and Message Implementation Changes for Win32 (*continued*)

API/Message	Support	Comments
GlobalDosAlloc	Dropped	No Win32 API equivalent
GlobalDosFree	Dropped	No Win32 API equivalent
GlobalPageLock	Dropped	No Win32 API equivalent
GlobalPageUnlock	Dropped	No Win32 API equivalent
LimitEMSPages	Dropped	No Win32 API equivalent
LocalNotify	Dropped	No Win32 equivalent
MoveTo	Dropped	Replaced by portable **MoveToEx**
NetBIOSCall	Dropped	Replaced by named, portable Win32 API
OffsetViewportOrg	Dropped	Replaced by portable **OffsetViewportOrgEx**
OffsetWindowOrg	Dropped	Replaced by portable **OffsetWindowOrgEx**
OpenComm	Dropped	Replaced by **OpenFile**
OpenSound	Dropped	Replaced by multimedia sound support
ProfClear	Dropped	Replaced by Win32 profile-string API
ProfFinish	Dropped	Replaced by Win32 profile-string API
ProfFlush	Dropped	Replaced by Win32 profile-string API
ProfInsChk	Dropped	Replaced by Win32 profile-string API
ProfSampRate	Dropped	Replaced by Win32 profile-string API
ProfSetup	Dropped	Replaced by Win32 profile-string API
ProfStart	Dropped	Replaced by Win32 profile-string API
ProfStop	Dropped	Replaced by Win32 profile-string API
ReadComm	Dropped	Replaced by ReadFile
RemoveFontResource	Enhanced	Must use string, not handle, for filename
ScaleViewportExt	Dropped	Replaced by portable **ScaleViewportExtEx**
ScaleWindowExt	Dropped	Replaced by portable **ScaleWindowExtEx**
SetBitmapDimension	Dropped	Replaced by portable **SetBitmapDimensionEx**
SetClassWord	Enhanced	Use **SetClassLong** for values that grow to 32 bits on Win32
SetCommEventMask	Dropped	Replaced by **SetCommMask**
SetEnvironment	Dropped	No Win32 API equivalent

Table 1.4   API and Message Implementation Changes for Win32 (*continued*)

API/Message	Support	Comments
SetMetaFileBits	Dropped	Replaced by portable **SetMetaFileBitsEx**
SetResourceHandler	Dropped	No Win32 API equivalent (resource API in progress)
SetSoundNoise	Dropped	Replaced by multimedia sound support
SetViewportExt	Dropped	Replaced by portable **SetViewportExtEx**
SetViewportOrg	Dropped	Replaced by portable **SetViewportOrgEx**
SetVoiceAccent	Dropped	Replaced by multimedia sound support
SetVoiceEnvelope	Dropped	Replaced by multimedia sound support
SetVoiceNote	Dropped	Replaced by multimedia sound support
SetVoiceQueueSize	Dropped	Replaced by multimedia sound support
SetVoiceSound	Dropped	Replaced by multimedia sound support
SetVoiceThreshold	Dropped	Replaced by multimedia sound support
SetWindowExt	Dropped	Replaced by portable **SetWindowExtEx**
SetWindowOrg	Dropped	Replaced by portable **SetWindowOrgEx**
SetWindowWord	Enhanced	Use **SetWindowLong** for values that grow to 32 bits on Win32
StartSound	Dropped	Replaced by multimedia sound support
StopSound	Dropped	Replaced by multimedia sound support
SwitchStackBack	Dropped	No Win32 API equivalent
SwitchStackTo	Dropped	No Win32 API equivalent
SyncAllVoices	Dropped	Replaced by multimedia sound support
UngetCommChar	Dropped	No Win32 equivalent
ValidateCodeSegments	Dropped	No Win32 API equivalent
ValidateFreeSpaces	Dropped	No Win32 API equivalent
WaitSoundState	Dropped	Replaced by multimedia sound support
WriteComm	Dropped	Replaced by **WriteFile**
EM_GETSEL	Enhanced	*wParam/lParam* packing changed
EM_LINESCROLL	Enhanced	*wParam/lParam* packing changed
EM_SETSEL	Enhanced	*wParam/lParam* packing changed
WM_ACTIVATE	Enhanced	*wParam/lParam* packing changed
WM_CHANGECBCHAIN	Enhanced	*wParam/lParam* packing changed

Table 1.4   API and Message Implementation Changes for Win32 (*continued*)

API/Message	Support	Comments
WM_CHARTOITEM	Enhanced	*wParam/lParam* packing changed
WM_COMMAND	Enhanced	*wParam/lParam* packing changed
WM_CTLCOLOR	Replaced	Replaced by WM_CTLCOLOR*type* messages; *wParam/lParam* packing changed
WM_DDE_ACK	Enhanced	*wParam/lParam* packing changed
WM_DDE_ADVISE	Enhanced	*wParam/lParam* packing changed
WM_DDE_DATA	Enhanced	*wParam/lParam* packing changed
WM_DDE_EXECUTE	Enhanced	*wParam/lParam* packing changed
WM_DDE_POKE	Enhanced	*wParam/lParam* packing changed
WM_HSCROLL	Enhanced	*wParam/lParam* packing changed
WM_MDIACTIVATE	Enhanced	*wParam/lParam* packing changed
WM_MDISETMENU	Enhanced	*wParam/lParam* packing changed
WM_MENUCHAR	Enhanced	*wParam/lParam* packing changed
WM_MENUSELECT	Enhanced	*wParam/lParam* packing changed
WM_PARENTNOTIFY	Enhanced	*wParam/lParam* packing changed
WM_VKEYTOITEM	Enhanced	*wParam/lParam* packing changed
WM_VSCROLL	Enhanced	*wParam/lParam* packing changed
(**WORD**)	16-bit	Check if incorrect cast of 32-bit value; **WORD** is unsigned 16-bit int
GCW_CURSOR	Dropped	Replaced by **Get|SetClassCursor**
GCW_HBRBACKGROUND	Dropped	Replaced by **Get|SetClassBrBackground**
GCW_HICON	Dropped	Replaced by **Get|SetClassIcon**
GWW_HINSTANCE	Dropped	Replaced by GWL_HINSTANCE
GWW_HWNDPARENT	Dropped	Replaced by GWL_HWNDPARENT
GWW_ID	Dropped	Replaced by GWL_ID
GWW_USERDATA	Dropped	Replaced by GWL_USERDATA
HIWORD	16-bit	Check if HIWORD target is 16-bit or 32-bit
LOWORD	16-bit	Check if LOWORD target is 16-bit or 32-bit
WndProc	Widened	Define Window procedures: **WndProc** (**HWND** hwnd, **UINT** msg, **UINT** *wParam*, **UINT** *lParam*)

Table 1.4   API and Message Implementation Changes for Win32 (*continued*)

API/Message	Support	Comments
wndproc	Widened	Define Window procedures: **WndProc** (**HWND** hwnd, **UINT** msg, **UINT** *wParam*, **UINT** *lParam*)
DCB	Enhanced	Changes to bitfields and additional structure members
MAKEPOINT	Dropped	Replaced by LONG2POINT

CHAPTER 2

Handling Messages with Portable Macros

Instead of taking the case-by-case approach shown in Chapter 1, you can use message-cracking macros to write message handlers similar to those you'd write when using Microsoft Foundation Classes. These message handlers use the same parameter list regardless of operating system, thereby solving message-packing issues. This chapter describes these and other macros defined in WINDOWSX.H (or WINDOWSX.H16 in the case of 16-bit applications).

Using Message Crackers

Message crackers are a set of macros that extract useful information from the *wParam* and *lParam* parameters of a message and hide the details of how information is packed.

Using message crackers initially requires that you revise some of your code. Message crackers also have a minor impact on performance by involving an additional function call. However, they offer the following advantages:

- Portability. Message crackers free you from packing issues and guarantee proper extraction of information, regardless of which environment you're compiling for.

- Readability. With message crackers, you can understand source code because message parameters are translated into data with meaningful names.

- Ease of use. In addition to decoding *wParam* and *lParam*, message crackers place message-handling code in separate functions. Instead of a long **switch** statement, you have a separate handler for each message.

Overview of Message Crackers

You use message crackers in your code by writing a separate message handler function for each message. Then you use a macro to call each of those functions from within your window procedure.

Use of message crackers for all messages is recommended, but you can optionally combine code that uses message crackers for some messages with code that responds directly to other messages.

Note To use message crackers, make sure you include the file WINDOWSX.H (or WINDOWSX.H16, in the case of 16-bit applications).

Suppose you have a message, WM_THIS. The code to handle this message would look like this:

```
LRESULT CALLBACK My_WndProc( HWND hwnd, UINT msg, UINT wParam, LONG
lParam )
    .
    .
    .
switch( msg ) {
    case WM_THIS:
        // Place code to handle message here
```

To use message crackers, write a message handler, then call it from the **switch** statement. Suppose that there are two pieces of information contained in the WM_THIS message: *thisHdc* and *thisData*. Message crackers unpack this information from *wParam* and *lParam*, and pass it as parameters to your message handler, MyWnd_OnThis, as depicted in Figure 2.1.

```
switch( msg ) {
    case WM_THIS:
        return HANDLE_WM_THIS( hwnd, wParam, lParam, MyWnd_OnThis );


BOOL MyWnd_OnThis( HWND hwnd, HDC thisHdc, WORD thisData )
{
// Place code to handle message here
}
```

Figure 2.1 Passing Parameters to Message Handlers with Message Crackers

Note that the parameters to MyWnd_OnThis (after *hwnd*, which is always the first parameter) consist of information directly usable by your code: *thisHdc* and *thisData*. The macro HANDLE_WM_THIS translates *wParam* and *lParam* into *thisHdc* and *thisData* as it makes the function call.

The following general steps summarize how to use message crackers:

- Declare a prototype for each message-handling function.
- In the window procedure, call the message handler. Use either a message decoder (such as HANDLE_WM_CREATE) or the HANDLE_MSG macro.
- Write the message handler. Use a message forwarder such as FORWARD_WM_CREATE to call the default message procedure.

Declaring Message-Handler Prototypes

To use message crackers, first declare a prototype for the message handling function ("message handler" for short). Although you can give your message handlers any name you want, a recommended convention is:

*WndClass_***On***Msg*

in which *WndClass* is the name of the window class, and *Msg* is the name of the message in mixed case, with the "WM" dropped. For example, the following code contains prototypes for functions handling WM_CREATE, WM_PAINT, and WM_MOUSEMOVE:

```
BOOL MyWnd_OnCreate( HWND hwnd, CREATESTRUCT FAR* lpCreateStruct );
void MyWnd_OnPaint( HWND hwnd );
void MyWnd_OnMouseMove( HWND hwnd, int x, int y, UINT keyFlags );
```

The first parameter to each function is always *hwnd*, which is a handle to the window that received the message. The rest of the parameters vary; each message handler has its own customized parameter list. To declare the appropriate parameters for a message, see the corresponding definitions in WINDOWSX.H.

Calling the Message Handler

In your window procedure, you call a message handler by using a message-decoder macro such as HANDLE_WM_CREATE or HANDLE_WM_PAINT. The general form for using these macros is:

case *msg***:**
 return HANDLE_*msg* **(hwnd, wParam, lParam,** *handler* **);**

You should always return the value of the macro, even if no return value is expected and the corresponding message handler has **void** return type.

For example, you could place the following macros in your code:

```
switch( msg ) {
    case WM_CREATE:
        return HANDLE_WM_CREATE( hwnd, wParam, lParam, MyWnd_OnCreate );
    case WM_PAINT:
        return HANDLE_WM_PAINT( hwnd, wParam, lParam, MyWnd_OnPaint );
    case WM_MOUSEMOVE:
        return HANDLE_WM_MOUSEMOVE( hwnd, wParam, lParam,
                                    MyWnd_OnMouseMove );

        .
        .
        .
```

Alternatively, you can use the generic HANDLE_MSG macro, which generates the same code as the previous example, but saves space:

```
switch( msg ) {
    HANDLE_MSG( hwnd, WM_CREATE, MyWnd_OnCreate );
    HANDLE_MSG( hwnd, WM_PAINT, MyWnd_OnPaint );
    HANDLE_MSG( hwnd, WM_MOUSEMOVE, MyWnd_OnMouseMove );

    .
    .
    .
```

HANDLE_MSG assumes that you use the names *wParam* and *lParam* in the window procedure parameter list. You cannot use this macro if you have given these parameters other names.

Writing the Message Handler

In the message-handling function, you respond to the message using parameters that have been translated from *wParam* and *lParam* and passed to the function. In the following example, *lpCreateStruct* is an example of a parameter translated from *wParam* and *lParam*:

```
BOOL MyCls_OnCreate(HWND hwnd, CREATESTRUCT FAR* lpCreateStruct)
{
    // Place message-handling code here

    return FORWARD_WM_CREATE(hwnd, lpCreateStruct, DefWindowProc);
}
```

Message-handling code often finishes by calling **DefWindowProc** or some other default message procedure. You make this function call by using a "message forwarder," which uses the following form:

return FORWARD_*msg*(*parmlist*, *defaultMsgProc*);

The *parmlist* is the same list of parameters in the message handler, and *defaultMsgProc* is the default message procedure, typically **DefWindowProc**. The message forwarder repacks the information in the parameter list into the appropriate *wParam/lParam* format (depending on target environment) and forwards the message to the default message procedure.

Putting it Together: An Example

In the following example, several message handlers are used in a window procedure to show where the various prototypes and macros fit into the code.

The header file, MYAPP.H, consists of function prototypes, including prototypes for the message handlers. Note how each message handler has its own parameter list, which is customized to represent the information packed in the corresponding message:

```
// MYAPP.H

// Window procedure prototype

LRESULT CALLBACK MyWnd_WndProc(HWND hwnd, UINT msg, WPARAM wParam, LPARAM lParam);

// Default message handler

#define MyWnd_DefProc     DefWindowProc

// MyWnd class message handler functions, declared in a .h file:
//
void MyWnd_OnMouseMove(HWND hwnd, int x, int y, UINT keyFlags);
void MyWnd_OnLButtonDown(HWND hwnd, BOOL fDoubleClick, int x, int y, UINT keyFlags);
void MyWnd_OnLButtonUp(HWND hwnd, int x, int y, UINT keyFlags);
```

The rest of the code in this example is in MYAPP.C, which contains the window procedure and the individual message handlers. With message crackers, the function of the window procedure is principally to route each message to the appropriate handler.

Both the WM_LBUTTONDOWN and WM_LBUTTONDBLCLK messages map to the MyWnd_OnLButtonDown procedure. This mapping is one of the special cases of message handling described in the next section.

```c
// MYAPP.C    --------------------------------------------------------------

// MyWnd window procedure implementation.
//
LRESULT CALLBACK MyWnd_WndProc(HWND hwnd, UINT msg, WPARAM wParam, LPARAM Param)
{
    switch (msg)
    {
        HANDLE_MSG(hwnd, WM_MOUSEMOVE,MyWnd_OnMouseMove);
        HANDLE_MSG(hwnd, WM_LBUTTONDOWN, MyWnd_OnLButtonDown);
        HANDLE_MSG(hwnd, WM_LBUTTONDBLCLK, MyWnd_OnLButtonDown);
        HANDLE_MSG(hwnd, WM_LBUTTONUP, MyWnd_OnLButtonUp);
    default:
        return MyWnd_DefProc(hwnd, msg, wParam, lParam);
    }
}

// Message handler function implementations:
//
void MyWnd_OnMouseMove(HWND hwnd, int x, int y, UINT keyFlags)
{
    .
    .
    .
    return FORWARD_WM_MOUSEMOVE( hwnd, x, y, keyFlags, MyWnd_DefProc);
}

void MyWnd_OnLButtonDown(HWND hwnd, BOOL fDoubleClick, int x, int y, UINT keyFlags)
{
    .
    .
    .
    return FORWARD_WM_LBUTTONDOWN( hwnd, fDoubleClick, x, y, keyFlags, MyWnd_DefProc);
}

void MyWnd_OnLButtonUp(HWND hwnd, int x, int y, UINT keyFlags)
{
    .
    .
    .
    return FORWARD_WM_LBUTTONUP( hwnd, x, y, keyFlags, MyWnd_DefProc);
}
```

Note that the symbol `MyWnd_DefProc` is defined to represent **DefWindowProc** to make code more reusable. This approach assumes you have a similar definition in each application. For example, in an MDI child control procedure, you would have this definition:

```
#define MyWnd_DefProc    DefMDIChildProc
```

If you then copied your message handler to the MDI procedure, you would only need to change the prefix in `MyWnd_DefProc` to make the copied code work correctly. Conversely, if your code used the explicit call to **DefWindowProc**, it could create a bug that would be difficult to find when copied to the MDI code.

Handling Special Cases of Messages

As a general rule, there is one set of message crackers for each message: a message decoder and a message forwarder. Another rule is that each message handler you write should return the same value that your code would normally return for that message. The following messages present exceptions to these rules.

Message handler	Comment
OnCreate, OnNCCreate	**BOOL** return type: returns TRUE if there are no errors. If FALSE is returned, a window will not be created.
OnKey	Handles both key up and key down messages. The extra parameter *fDown* indicates whether the key is down or up.
OnLButtonDown, OnRButtonDown	Handles both click (button down) and double-click messages. The extra parameter *fDoubleClick* indicates whether the message received is a double-click message.
OnChar	This handler is passed only by character, and not the virtual key or key flags information.

Writing Message Crackers for User-Defined Messages

You can use message crackers with window messages that you define, but you must write your own macros. The easiest way to do this is to copy and modify existing macros from WINDOWSX.H.

To understand how to write these macros, consider some of the message crackers defined in WINDOWSX.H:

```
/* BOOL Cls_OnCreate(HWND hwnd, CREATESTRUCT FAR* lpCreateStruct) */
```

```
#define HANDLE_WM_CREATE(hwnd, wParam, lParam, fn) \
    ((fn)(hwnd, (CREATESTRUCT FAR*)lParam) ? 0L : (LRESULT)-1L)

#define FORWARD_WM_CREATE(hwnd, lpCreateStruct, fn) \
    (BOOL)(DWORD)(fn)(hwnd, WM_CREATE, 0, (LPARAM)lpCreateStruct)
```

The message decoder (**HANDLE_***msg*) should be defined as a function call, (fn), followed by *hwnd* and other parameters derived from *wParam* and *lParam*. The message forwarder (**FORWARD_***msg*) performs the reverse operation on the parameters, putting information back together to restore *wParam* and *lParam* before making the function call (fn). Each of these macros must cast the return value so that the correct type is returned.

When calling the message crackers you write, be careful about variable message values. If your message value is a constant (such as WM_USER+100), you can use HANDLE_MSG with the message in a **switch** statement. However, if the message is registered with **RegisterWindowMessage**, it assigns a number at run time. In this situation, you can't use HANDLE_MSG, because variables cannot be used as **case** values. You must handle the message separately, in an **if** statement:

```
// In MyWnd class initialization code:
//
UINT WM_NEWMESSAGE= 0;

WM_NEWMESSAGE= RegisterWindowMessage("WM_NEWMESSAGE");
    .
    .
    .
// In MyWnd_WndProc(): window procedure:
//
LRESULT CALLBACK MyWnd_WndProc(HWND hwnd, WORD msg, WPARAM wParam,
                        LPARAM lParam)
{
    if (msg == WM_NEWMESSAGE)
        HANDLE_WM_NEWMESSAGE(hwnd, wParam, lParam, MyWnd_OnNewMessage);

    switch (msg)
    {
        HANDLE_MSG(hwnd, WM_MOUSEMOVE, MyWnd_OnMouseMove);
        .
        .
        .
    }
}
```

Adapting Message Crackers for Special Cases

Generally, you can use message crackers with all types of application code. However, certain situations require modifications in coding style.

The next few sections show how to adapt message-cracker coding techniques for dialog procedures, window subclassing, and window instance data.

Dialog Procedures

Dialog procedures return a **BOOL** value to indicate whether the message was processed. (Window procedures, in contrast, return a **LONG** value rather than a **BOOL**.) Therefore, to adapt a message cracker to dialog-procedure code, you must call the message handler and cast the value to **BOOL**.

Because you have to insert the **(BOOL)** cast, you can't use HANDLE_MSG. You must invoke the message-decoder macro explicitly. Here's an example that shows how you'd use message crackers in a dialog procedure:

```
BOOL MyDlg_OnInitDialog(HWND hwndDlg, HWND hwndFocus, LPARAM lParam);
void MyDlg_OnCommand(HWND hwnd, int id, HWND hwndCtl, UINT codeNotify);

BOOL CALLBACK MyDlg_DlgProc(HWND hwndDlg, UINT msg, WPARAM wParam, LPARAM lParam)
{
    switch (msg)
    {
    //
    // Since HANDLE_WM_INITDIALOG returns an LRESULT,
    // we must cast it to a BOOL before returning.
    //
    case WM_INITDIALOG:
        return (BOOL)HANDLE_WM_INITDIALOG(hwndDlg, wParam, lParam, MyDlg_OnInitDialog);

    case WM_COMMAND:
        HANDLE_WM_COMMAND(hwndDlg, wParam, lParam, MyDlg_OnCommand);
        return TRUE;
        break;

    default:
        return FALSE;
    }
}
```

Window Subclassing

When you use message crackers with a subclassed window procedure, the strategy described earlier for using message forwarders does not work. Recall that this strategy involves the following macro call:

return FORWARD_*msg***(** *parmlist***,** *defaultMsgProc* **);**

This use of a message forwarder (**FORWARD_***msg*) calls *defaultMsgProc* directly. But in a subclassed window procedure, you must call the window procedure of the superclass by using the API function **CallWindowProc**. The problem is that **FORWARD_***msg* calls *defaultMsgProc* with four parameters, but **CallWindowProc** needs five parameters.

The solution is to write an intermediate procedure. For example, the intermediate procedure could be named test_DefProc:

```
FORWARD_WM_CHAR(hwnd, ch, cRepeat, test_DefProc);
```

The test_DefProc function calls **CallWindowProc** and prepends the address of the superclass function (in this case, test_lpfnwpDefProc) to the parameter list:

```
LRESULT test_DefProc( HWND hwnd, UINT msg, WPARAM wParam, LPARAM lParam)
{
    return CallWindowProc(test_lpfnwpDefProc, hwnd, msg, wParam,
lParam);
}
```

You need to write one such procedure for each subclassed window in your application. Each time you use a message forwarder, you give this intermediate procedure as the function address instead of **DefWindowProc**. The following example code shows the complete context:

```
// Global variable that holds the previous window proc address of
// the subclassed window:
//
WNDPROC test_lpfnwpDefProc = NULL;

// Code fragment to subclass a window and store previous wndproc value:
//
void Subclasstest(HWND hwndtest)
{
    extern HINSTANCE g_hinsttest;    // Global application instance handle
```

```
// SubclassWindow() is a macro API that calls SetWindowLong()
    // as appropriate to change the window proc of hwndtest.
    //
    test_lpfnwpDefProc = SubclassWindow(hwndtest,
            (WNDPROC)MakeProcInstance( (FARPROC)test_WndProc, g_hinsttest));
    .
    .
    .
}


// Default message handler function
//
// This function invokes the superclasses' window procedure.  It
// must be declared with the same signature as any window proc,
// so it can be used with the FORWARD_WM_* macros.
//
LRESULT test_DefProc( HWND hwnd, UINT msg, WPARAM wParam, LPARAM lParam)
{
    return CallWindowProc(test_lpfnwpDefProc, hwnd, msg, wParam, lParam);
}
// test window procedure.  Everything here is the same as in the
// normal non-subclassed case: the differences are encapsulated in
// test_DefProc.
//
LRESULT CALLBACK test_WndProc(HWND hwnd, UINT msg, WPARAM wParam, LPARAM lParam)
{
    switch (msg)
    {
        HANDLE_MSG(hwnd, WM_CHAR, test_OnChar);
        .
        .
        .
    default:
        //
        // Be sure to call test_DefProc(), NOT DefWindowProc()!
        //
        return test_DefProc(hwnd, msg, wParam, lParam);
    }
}


// Message handlers
//
```

```
void test_OnChar(HWND hwnd, UINT ch, int cRepeat)
{
    if (ch == testvalue)
    {
        // handle it here
    }
    else
    {
        // Forward the message on to test_DefProc
        //
        FORWARD_WM_CHAR(hwnd, ch, cRepeat, test_DefProc);
    }
}
```

Window Instance Data

It is common for a window to keep user-declared state variables (or "instance data") in a separate data structure allocated by the application. You associate this data structure with its corresponding window by storing a pointer to the structure in a specially named window property or in a window word (allocated by setting the **cbWndExtra** field of the WNDCLASS structure when the class is registered).

You can adapt message crackers to work with this use of instance data. Place the *hwnd* of the window in the first member of the structure. Then, in the message decoders (**HANDLE_***msg* macros), pass the address of the structure instead of the *hwnd*. The message handler now gets a pointer to the structure instead of the *hwnd*, but it can access the *hwnd* through indirection. You may need to rewrite some of the message handler to make it use indirection to access the window handle.

The following example illustrates this technique:

```
// Window instance data structure.  Must include window handle field.
//
typedef struct _test
{
    HWND hwnd;
    int otherStuff;
} test;

// "test" window class was registered with cbWndExtra = sizeof(test*), so we
// can use a window word to store back pointer.  Window properties can also
// be used.
//
```

```
// These macros get and set the pointer to the instance data corresponding to the
// window.  Use GetWindowWord or GetWindowLong as appropriate based on the default
// size of data pointers.
//
#ifdef _WIN32
#define test_GetPtr(hwnd)        (test*)GetWindowLong((hwnd), 0)
#define test_SetPtr(hwnd, ptest) (test*)SetWindowLong((hwnd), 0, (LONG)(ptest))
#else
#define test_GetPtr(hwnd)        (test*)GetWindowWord((hwnd), 0)
#define test_SetPtr(hwnd, ptest) (test*)SetWindowWord((hwnd), 0, (WORD)(ptest))
#endif


// Default message handler

#define test_DefProc DefWindowProc

// Message handler functions, declared with a test* as their first argument,
// rather than an HWND.  Other than that, their signature is identical to
// that shown in WINDOWSX.H.
//
BOOL test_OnCreate(test* ptest, CREATESTRUCT FAR* lpcs);
void test_OnPaint(test* ptest);
//
// Code to register the test window class:
//
BOOL test_Init(HINSTANCE hinst)
{
    WNDCLASS cls;

    cls.hCursor         = ...;
    cls.hIcon           = ...;
    cls.lpszMenuName    = ...;
    cls.hInstance       = hinst;
    cls.lpszClassName   = "test";
    cls.hbrBackground   = ...;
    cls.lpfnWndProc     = test_WndProc;
    cls.style           = CS_DBLCLKS;
    cls.cbWndExtra      = sizeof(test*);  // room for instance data ptr
    cls.cbClsExtra      = 0;

    return RegisterClass(&cls);
}


// The window proc for class "test".  This demonstrates how instance data is
// attached to a window and passed to the message handler functions.
//
```

```
LRESULT CALLBACK test_WndProc(HWND hwnd, UINT msg, WPARAM wParam, LPARAM lParam)
{
    test* ptest = test_GetPtr(hwnd);

    if (ptest == NULL)
    {
    // If we're creating the window, try to allocate it.
    //
        if (msg == WM_NCCREATE)
        {
        // Create the instance data structure, set up the hwnd backpointer
        // field, and associate it with the window.
        //
        ptest = (test*)LocalAlloc(LMEM_FIXED | LMEM_ZEROINIT, sizeof(test));

        // If an error occurred, return 0L to fail the CreateWindow call.
        // This will cause CreateWindow() to return NULL.
        //
        if (ptest == NULL)
            return 0L;
        ptest->hwnd = hwnd;
        test_SetPtr(hwnd, ptest);

        // NOTE: the rest of the test structure should be initialized
        // inside Template_OnCreate() (or Template_OnNCCreate()).  Further
        // creation data may be accessed through the CREATESTRUCT FAR* parameter.
        //
        }
        else
        {
        // It turns out WM_NCCREATE is NOT necessarily the first message
        // received by a top-level window (WM_GETMINMAXINFO is).
        // Pass messages that precede WM_NCCREATE on through to
        // test_DefProc
        //
        return test_DefProc(hwnd, msg, wParam, lParam);
        }
    }

    if (msg == WM_NCDESTROY)
    {
        LocalFree((HLOCAL)ptest);

        ptest = NULL;
        test_SetPtr(hwnd, NULL);

    }

    switch (msg)
    {
```

```
HANDLE_MSG(ptest, WM_CREATE, test_OnCreate);
HANDLE_MSG(ptest, WM_PAINT, test_OnPaint);
...

default:
    return test_DefProc(hwnd, msg, wParam, lParam);
}
}
```

Using Control Message Functions

The role of the control message API functions is the opposite of message crackers: instead of handling messages sent to your window, they send messages to other windows (controls).

Each of the control message functions packs parameters into the appropriate *wParam/lParam* format and then calls **SendMessage**. These functions offer the same portability advantages as message crackers; they free you from having to know how the current operating system packs *wParam* and *lParam*.

The function calls also improve code readability and support better type checking. When used with the STRICT enhancements, the control message functions help prevent incorrect passing of message parameters.

To see how the control message functions work, first look at the following source code, which makes two calls to **SendMessage** to print all the lines in an edit control:

```
void PrintLines(HWND hwndEdit, WHND hwndDisplay)
{
    int line;
    int lineLast = (int)SendMessage(hwndEdit, EM_GETLINECOUNT, 0, 0L);

    for (line = 0; line < lineLast; line++)
    {
        int cch;
        char ach[80];

        *((LPINT)ach) = sizeof(ach);
        cch = (int)SendMessage(hwndEdit, EM_GETLINE,
                line, (LONG)(LPSTR)ach);

        PrintInWindow(ach, hwndDisplay);
    }
}
```

The following source code uses two control message functions, **Edit_GetLineCount** and **Edit_GetLine**, to perform the same task. This version of the code is shorter, easier to read, doesn't generate compiler warnings, and doesn't have any non-portable casts:

```
void PrintLines(HWND hwndEdit, WHND hwndDisplay)
{
    int line;
    int lineLast = Edit_GetLineCount(hwndEdit);

    for (line = 0; line < lineLast; line++)
    {
        int cch;
        char ach[80];

        cch = Edit_GetLine(hwndEdit, line, ach, sizeof(ach));

        PrintInWindow(ach, hwndDisplay);
    }
}
```

The control message API functions are listed in Table 2.1. For more information, refer to the macro definitions in WINDOWSX.H and the documentation for the corresponding window message.

Table 2.1 Control Message API Functions

Control group	Functions
Static Text Controls:	**Static_Enable**(*hwnd*, *fEnable*)
	Static_GetIcon(*hwnd*, *hIcon*)
	Static_GetText(*hwnd*, *lpch*, *cchMax*)
	Static_GetTextLength(*hwnd*)
	Static_SetIcon(*hwnd*, *hIcon*)
	Static_SetText(*hwnd*, *lpsz*)
Button Controls:	**Button_Enable**(*hwnd*, *fEnable*)
	Button_GetCheck(*hwnd*)
	Button_GetState(*hwnd*)
	Button_GetText(*hwnd*, *lpch*, *cchMax*)
	Button_GetTextLength(*hwnd*)
	Button_SetCheck(*hwnd*, *check*)
	Button_SetState(*hwnd*, *state*)
	Button_SetStyle(*hwnd*, *style*, *fRedraw*)
	Button_SetText(*hwnd*, *lpsz*)
Edit Controls:	**Edit_CanUndo**(*hwnd*)

Table 2.1   Control Message API Functions (*continued*)

Control group	Functions
Edit Controls:	**Edit_EmptyUndoBuffer**(*hwnd*)
	Edit_Enable(*hwnd*, *fEnable*)
	Edit_FmtLines(*hwnd*, *fAddEOL*)
	Edit_GetFirstVisible(*hwnd*)
	Edit_GetHandle(*hwnd*)
	Edit_GetLine(*hwnd*, *line*, *lpch*, *cchMax*)
	Edit_GetLineCount(*hwnd*)
	Edit_GetModify(*hwnd*)
	Edit_GetRect(*hwnd*, *lprc*)
	Edit_GetSel(*hwnd*)
	Edit_GetText(*hwnd*, *lpch*, *cchMax*)
	Edit_GetTextLength(*hwnd*)
	Edit_LimitText(*hwnd*, *cchMax*)
	Edit_LineFromChar(*hwnd*, *ich*)
	Edit_LineIndex(*hwnd*, *line*)
	Edit_LineLength(*hwnd*, *line*)
	Edit_ReplaceSel(*hwnd*, *lpszReplace*)
	Edit_Scroll(*hwnd*, *dv*, *dh*)
	Edit_SetHandle(*hwnd*, *h*)
	Edit_SetModify(*hwnd*, *fModified*)
	Edit_SetPasswordChar(*hwnd*, *ch*)
	Edit_SetRect(*hwnd*, *lprc*)
	Edit_SetRectNoPaint(*hwnd*, *lprc*)
	Edit_SetSel(*hwnd*, *ichStart*, *ichEnd*)
	Edit_SetTabStops(*hwnd*, *cTabs*, *lpTabs*)
	Edit_SetText(*hwnd*, *lpsz*)
	Edit_SetWordBreak(*hwnd*, *lpfnWordBreak*)
	Edit_Undo(*hwnd*)
Scroll Bar Controls:	**ScrollBar_Enable**(*hwnd*, *flags*)
	ScrollBar_GetPos(*hwnd*)
	ScrollBar_GetRange(*hwnd*, *lpposMin*, *lpposMax*)
	ScrollBar_SetPos(*hwnd*, *pos*, *fRedraw*)
	ScrollBar_SetRange(*hwnd*, *posMin*, *posMax*, *fRedraw*)
	ScrollBar_Show(*hwnd*, *fShow*)

Table 2.1   Control Message API Functions (*continued*)

Control group	Functions
List Box Controls:	**ListBox_AddFile**(*hwnd*, *lpszFilename*)
	ListBox_AddItemData(*hwnd*, *data*)
	ListBox_AddString(*hwnd*, *lpsz*)
	ListBox_DeleteString(*hwnd*, *index*)
	ListBox_Dir(*hwnd*, *attrs*, *lpszFileSpec*)
	ListBox_Enable(*hwnd*, *fEnable*)
	ListBox_FindItemData(*hwnd*, *indexStart*, *data*)
	ListBox_FindString(*hwnd*, *indexStart*, *lpszFind*)
	ListBox_GetAnchorIndex(*hwnd*)
	ListBox_GetCaretIndex(*hwnd*)
	ListBox_GetCount(*hwnd*)
	ListBox_GetCurSel(*hwnd*)
	ListBox_GetHorizontalExtent(*hwnd*)
	ListBox_GetItemData(*hwnd*, *index*)
	ListBox_GetItemHeight(*hwnd*, *index*)[1]
	ListBox_GetItemRect(*hwnd*, *index*, *lprc*)
	ListBox_GetSel(*hwnd*, *index*)
	ListBox_GetSelCount(*hwnd*)
	ListBox_GetSelItems(*hwnd*, *cItems*, *lpIndices*)
	ListBox_GetText(*hwnd*, *index*, *lpszBuffer*)
	ListBox_GetTextLen(*hwnd*, *index*)
	ListBox_GetTopIndex(*hwnd*)
	ListBox_InsertItemData(*hwnd*, *lpsz*, *index*)
	ListBox_InsertString(*hwnd*, *lpsz*, *index*)
	ListBox_ResetContent(*hwnd*)
	ListBox_SelectItemData(*hwnd*, *indexStart*, *data*)
	ListBox_SelectString(*hwnd*, *indexStart*, *lpszFind*)
	ListBox_SelItemRange(*hwnd*, *fSelect*, *first*, *last*)
	ListBox_SetAnchorIndex(*hwnd*, *index*)
	ListBox_SetCaretIndex(*hwnd*, *index*)
	ListBox_SetColumnWidth(*hwnd*, *cxColumn*)
	ListBox_SetCurSel(*hwnd*, *index*)
	ListBox_SetHorizontalExtent(*hwnd*, *cxExtent*)
	ListBox_SetItemData(*hwnd*, *index*, *data*)

Table 2.1   Control Message API Functions (*continued*)

Control group	Functions
List Box Controls:	**ListBox_SetItemHeight**(*hwnd, index, cy*)[1]
	ListBox_SetSel(*hwnd, fSelect, index*)
	ListBox_SetTabStops(*hwnd, cTabs, lpTabs*)
	ListBox_SetTopIndex(*hwnd, indexTop*)
Combo Box Controls:	**ComboBox_AddItemData**(*hwnd, data*)
	ComboBox_AddString(*hwnd, lpsz*)
	ComboBox_DeleteString(*hwnd, index*)
	ComboBox_Dir(*hwnd, attrs, lpszFileSpec*)
	ComboBox_Enable(*hwnd, fEnable*)
	ComboBox_FindItemData(*hwnd, indexStart, data*)
	ComboBox_FindString(*hwnd, indexStart, lpszFind*)
	ComboBox_GetCount(*hwnd*)
	ComboBox_GetCurSel(*hwnd*)
	ComboBox_GetDroppedControlRect(*hwnd, lprc*)[1]
	ComboBox_GetDroppedState(*hwnd*)[1]
	ComboBox_GetEditSel(*hwnd*)
	ComboBox_GetExtendedUI(*hwnd*)[1]
	ComboBox_GetItemData(*hwnd, index*)
	ComboBox_GetItemHeight(*hwnd*)
	ComboBox_GetLBText(*hwnd, index, lpszBuffer*)
	ComboBox_GetLBTextLen(*hwnd, index*)
	ComboBox_GetText(*hwnd, lpch, cchMax*)
	ComboBox_GetTextLength(*hwnd*)
	ComboBox_InsertItemData(*hwnd, index, data*)
	ComboBox_InsertString(*hwnd, index, lpsz*)
	ComboBox_LimitText(*hwnd, cchLimit*)
	ComboBox_ResetContent(*hwnd*)
	ComboBox_SelectItemData(*hwnd, indexStart, data*)
	ComboBox_SelectString(*hwnd, indexStart, lpszSelect*)
	ComboBox_SetCurSel(*hwnd, index*)
	ComboBox_SetEditSel(*hwnd, ichStart, ichEnd*)
	ComboBox_SetExtendedUI(*hwnd, flags*)[1]
	ComboBox_SetItemHeight(*hwnd, cyItem*)[1]

Table 2.1   Control Message API Functions (*continued*)

Control group	Functions
Combo Box Controls:	**ComboBox_SetText**(*hwnd*, *lpsz*)
	ComboBox_ShowDropdown(*hwnd*, *fShow*)

1 Supported only for Win32, not for Windows 3.*x*. These APIs are not available if you define the symbol WINVER as equal to 0x0300, on the command line or with a **#define** statement.

C H A P T E R   3

WINDOWS.H and STRICT Type Checking

The WINDOWS.H file contains definitions, macros, and structures to help you write source code that is portable between versions of Microsoft Windows. Some of the WINDOWS.H features are enabled when you define the STRICT symbol on the command line or in a makefile. This chapter explains the advantages of STRICT features and how using them affects the writing of code.

New Types and Macros

Chapter 1, "Porting 16-Bit Code to 32-Bit Windows," introduced some new standard types for programming in Windows. The old types, such as **FAR PASCAL** for declaring window procedures, may work in existing code but are not guaranteed to work in all future versions of Windows. Therefore, you should convert your code to use the new standards wherever appropriate.

General Data Types

The following table summarizes the new standard types defined in WINDOWS.H. These types are polymorphic (they can contain different kinds of data) and are generally useful throughout applications. Other new types, handles, and function pointers also are introduced in following sections.

Typedef	Description
WINAPI	Use in place of **FAR PASCAL** in API declarations. If you are writing a DLL with exported API entry points, you can use this for your own APIs.
CALLBACK	Use in place of **FAR PASCAL** in application callback routines such as window procedures and dialog procedures.
LPCSTR	Same as **LPSTR**, except used for read-only string pointers. Defined as (**const char FAR***).

Typedef	Description
UINT	Portable unsigned integer type whose size is determined by host environment (32 bits for Windows NT). Synonym for **unsigned int**. Used in place of **WORD** except in the rare cases where a 16-bit unsigned quantity is desired even on 32-bit platforms.
LRESULT	Type used for return value of window procedures.
LPARAM	Type used for declaration of lParam, the fourth parameter of a windows procedure.
WPARAM	Type used for declaration of wParam, the third parameter of a windows procedure (a polymorphic data type).
LPVOID	Generic pointer type, equivalent to (**void ***). Should be used instead of **LPSTR**.

Utility Macros

WINDOWS.H provides a series of utility macros that are useful for working with the types listed in General Data Types in the previous section. The utility macros listed in the following table help create and extract data from these types. The **FIELDOFFSET** macro is particularly useful when you need to give the numeric offset of a structure member as an argument.

Utility	Description
MAKELPARAM(*low*, *high*)	Combines two 16-bit quantities into an **LPARAM**.
MAKELRESULT(*low*, *high*)	Combines two 16-bit quantities into an **LRESULT**.
MAKELP(*sel*, *off*)	Combines a selector and an offset into a **FAR VOID*** pointer. Useful only for Windows 3.*x*.
SELECTOROF(*lp*)	Extracts the selector part of a far pointer. Returns a **UINT**. Useful only for Windows 3.*x*.
OFFSETOF(*lp*)	Extracts the offset part of a far pointer. Returns a **UINT**. Useful only for Windows 3.*x*.
FIELDOFFSET(*type*, *field*)	Calculates the offset of a member of a data structure. The *type* is the type of structure, and *field* is the name of the structure member or field.

New Handle Types

In addition to the existing Windows handle types such as **HWND, HDC, HBRUSH,** and so on, WINDOWS.H defines the following new handle types. They are particularly important if STRICT type checking is enabled, but you can use them even if you do not define STRICT.

Handle	Description
HINSTANCE	Instance handle type
HMODULE	Module handle type
HBITMAP	Bitmap handle type
HLOCAL	Local handle type
HGLOBAL	Global handle type
HTASK	Task handle type
HFILE	File handle type
HRSRC	Resource handle type
HGDIOBJ	Generic GDI object handle type (except HMETAFILE)
HMETAFILE	Metafile handle type
HDWP	**DeferWindowPos( )** handle
HACCEL	Accelerator table handle
HDRVR	Driver handle (Windows NT only)

Using STRICT to Improve Type Checking

When you define the STRICT symbol, you enable features that require more care in declaring and using types. This helps you write more portable code. This extra care will also reduce your debugging time. Enabling STRICT redefines certain data types so that the compiler won't permit assignment from one type to another without an explicit cast. This is especially helpful with Windows code. Errors in passing data types are reported at compile time instead of causing fatal errors at run time.

When STRICT is defined, WINDOWS.H type definitions change as follows:

- Specific handle types are defined to be mutually exclusive; for example, you won't be able to pass an **HWND** where an **HDC** type argument is required. Without STRICT, all handles are defined as integers, so the compiler doesn't prevent you from using one type of handle where another type is expected.

- All callback function types (dialog procedures, window procedures, and hook procedures) are defined with full prototypes. This prevents you from declaring callback functions with incorrect parameter lists.

- Parameter and return value types that should use a generic pointer are declared correctly as **LPVOID** instead of as **LPSTR** or another pointer type.

- The **COMSTAT** structure is declared according to the ANSI standard.

Enabling STRICT Type Checking

To enable STRICT type checking, define the symbol name "STRICT." You can specify this definition on the command line or in a makefile by giving /DSTRICT as a compiler option.

To define STRICT on a file-by-file basis (supported by C but not C++ as explained in the note that follows), insert a **#define** statement before including WINDOWS.H in files where you want to enable STRICT:

```
#define STRICT
#include WINDOWS.H
```

For best results, you should also set the warning level for error messages to at least /W3. This is always advisable with applications for Windows, because a coding practice that causes a warning (for example, passing the wrong number of parameters) usually causes a fatal error at run time if it is not corrected.

Note If you are writing a C++ application, you don't have the option of applying STRICT to only some of your source files. Because of the way C++ "type safe linking" works, mixing STRICT and non-STRICT source files in your application can cause linking errors.

Making Your Application STRICT Compliant

Some source code that in the past compiled successfully might produce error messages when you enable STRICT type checking. The following sections describe the minimal requirements for making your code compile when STRICT is enabled. Additional steps are recommended, especially if you want to produce portable code. These are covered in the section "Using STRICT Type Checking," on page 52.

General Requirements

The principal requirement is that you must declare correct handle types and function pointers instead of relying on more general types such as **unsigned int** and **FARPROC**. You cannot use one handle type where another is expected. This also means that you may have to change function declarations and use more type casts.

For best results, the generic **HANDLE** type should be used only when necessary. Consult the preceding section "New Types and Macros," on page 47, for a list of new specific handle types.

Using Function Pointers

Always declare function pointers with the proper function type (such as **DLGPROC** or **WNDPROC**) rather than **FARPROC**. You'll need to cast function pointers to and from the proper function type when using **MakeProcInstance**, **FreeProcInstance**, and other functions that take or return a **FARPROC**, as shown in the following code:

```
BOOL CALLBACK DlgProc(HWND hwnd, UINT msg, WPARAM wParam,
                        LPARAM lParam);
DLGPROC lpfnDlg;

lpfnDlg = (DLGPROC)MakeProcInstance((FARPROC)DlgProc, hinst);
...
FreeProcInstance((FARPROC)lpfnDlg);
```

Declaring Functions Within Your Application

Make sure all application functions are declared. Placing all function declarations in an include file is recommended because you can easily scan your declarations and look for parameter and return types that should be changed.

If you use the /Zg compiler option to create header files for your functions, remember that you'll get different results depending on whether you have enabled STRICT type checking. With STRICT disabled, all handle types generate the same base type (**unsigned short** in Windows 3.*x*). With STRICT enabled, they generate base types such as **HWND __near *** or **HDC __near ***. To avoid conflict, you need to recreate the header file each time you disable, enable STRICT, or edit the header file to use the types **HWND, HDC, HANDLE**, and so on, instead of the base types.

Any API function declarations that you copied from WINDOWS.H into your source code may have changed, and your local declaration may be out of date. Remove your local declaration.

Functions That Require Casts

Some API functions have generic return types or parameters. For example, a function like **SendMessage** returns data that may be any number of types, depending on the context. When you see any of these functions in your source code, make sure that you use the correct type cast and that it is as specific as possible.

The following table summarizes these functions.

API Function	Comment
LocalLock	Cast result to the proper kind of data pointer.
GlobalLock	Cast result to the proper kind of data pointer.
GetWindowWord	Cast result to appropriate data type.

API Function	Comment
GetWindowLong	Cast result to appropriate data type
SetWindowWord	Cast argument as it is passed to function.
SetWindowLong	Cast argument as it is passed to function.
SendMessage	Cast result to appropriate data type; cast to **UINT** before casting to a handle type.
DefWindowProc	See comment for **SendMessage**.
SendDlgItemMsg	See comment for **SendMessage**.

When you call **SendMessage**, **DefWindowProc**, or **SendDlgItemMessage**, you should first cast the result to type **UINT**. You need to take similar steps for any API function that returns **LRESULT** or **LONG**, where the result contains a handle. This is necessary for writing portable code because the size of a handle is either 16 bits or 32 bits, depending on the version of Windows. The **(UINT)** cast ensures proper conversion. The following code shows an example in which **SendMessage** returns a handle to a brush:

```
HBRUSH hbr;

hbr = (HBRUSH)(UINT)SendMessage(hwnd, WM_CTLCOLOR, ..., ...);
```

The CreateWindow Function

The **CreateWindow** and **CreateWindowEx** *hmenu* parameter is sometimes used to pass an integer control ID. In this case, you must cast this to an **HMENU** type:

```
HWND hwnd;
int id;

hwnd = CreateWindow("Button", "Ok", BS_PUSHBUTTON,
        x, y, cx, cy, hwndParent,
        (HMENU)id,       // Cast required here
        hinst,
        NULL);
```

Using STRICT Type Checking

To get the most benefit from STRICT type checking, there are additional guidelines you should follow. Your code will be more portable in future versions of Windows if you make the following changes:

Change	To
HANDLE	A specific handle such as **HINSTANCE, HMODULE, HGLOBAL, HLOCAL**, and so on
WORD	**UINT**, except where you want a 16-bit value even when the platform is 32 bits
WORD	**WPARAM**, where *wParam* is declared
LONG	**LPARAM** or **LRESULT** as appropriate

Anytime you need an integer data type, you should declare it as **UINT** except where a 16-bit value is specifically required (as in a structure or parameter). Even if a variable never exceeds the range of a 16-bit integer, it can be more efficiently handled by the processor if it is 32 bits.

The types **WPARAM, LPARAM, LRESULT**, and **void *** are "polymorphic data types." They hold different kinds of data at different times, even when STRICT type checking is enabled. To get the benefit of type checking, you should cast values of these types as soon as possible. Note that message crackers (as well as the Microsoft Foundation Classes) automatically recast *wParam* and *lParam* for you in a portable way.

Take special care to distinguish **HMODULE** and **HINSTANCE** types. Even with STRICT enabled, they are defined as the same base type. Most kernel module management functions use **HINSTANCE** types, but there are a few API functions that return or accept only **HMODULE** types.

Accessing the New COMSTAT Structure

The Windows 3.*x* declaration of the **COMSTAT** structure is not compatible with ANSI standards. WINDOWS.H now defines the **COMSTAT** structure, for compatibility with ANSI compilers, so that the /W4 option does not issue warnings.

To support backward compatibility of source code, WINDOWS.H does not use the new structure definition unless the version of Windows (as indicated by WINVER) is 3.*x* or later, or if STRICT is defined. When you enable STRICT, the presumption is that you are trying to write portable code. Therefore, WINDOWS.H uses the new **COMSTAT** structure for all versions of Windows if STRICT is enabled.

The new structure definition replaces the bit fields with flags which access bits in a single field, named **status**, as shown in the following table. Each flag turns on a different bit.

Windows 3.x field name	Flag accessing the status field
fCtsHold	CSTF_CTSHOLD
fDsrHold	CSTF_DSRHOLD
fEof	CSTF_EOF
fRlsdHold	CSTF_RLSDHOLD
fTxim	CSTF_TXIM
fXoffHold	CSTF_XOFFHOLD
fXoffSent	CSTF_XOFFSENT

If your code accesses any of these status fields, you need to change your code as appropriate. For example, suppose you have the following code written for Windows 3.x:

```
if (comstat.fEof || fCondition)
    comstat.fCtsHold = TRUE;
    comstat.fTxim = FALSE;
```

This code should be replaced by code that accesses individual bits of the **status** field by using flags. Note the use of bitwise operators:

```
if ((comstat.status & CSTF_EOF) || fCondition)
    comstat.status |= CSTF_CTSHOLD;
    comstat.status &= ~CSTF_TXIM;
```

Interpreting Error Messages Affected by STRICT

Enabling STRICT type checking may affect the kind of error messages you receive. With STRICT enabled, all handle types are defined as pointer types. When you incorrectly use these types (for example, passing an **int** where an **HDC** is expected), you will get warning messages referring to errors in pointer indirection.

STRICT also requires that **FARPROC** function pointers be recast as more specific function pointer types such as **DLGPROC**. However, **MakeProcInstance** and **FreeProcInstance** still work with the **FARPROC** type. If you do not cast between **FARPROC** and the appropriate function pointer type, the compiler will warn about an error in function parameter lists.

Note that using **MakeProcInstance** is useful for portability, if you want to use the same source to compile for Windows 3.x. Under Win32, however, **MakeProcInstance** performs no operation, but returns the function name.

C H A P T E R   4

Creating DLLs for Windows NT

Microsoft Visual C++ for Windows NT offers full support for creating dynamic-link libraries (DLLs) as well as applications. Technically, a DLL is an executable file, but it usually functions as a library for applications. Multiple applications can access the contents of a single copy of a DLL in memory.

The compiler supports placement of data symbols and C++ objects in DLLs and in functions. The compiler's run-time library initializes global C++ objects as needed.

The compiler, run-time library, and Microsoft Foundation Class Library (MFC) support DLL creation in other important ways as well. If you are porting DLL source code written for Windows 3.x, you may need to revise it as described in this chapter. If you are building a DLL using MFC, read the article "Dynamic Link Libraries (DLLs)" in *Programming with the Microsoft Foundation Class Library* after reading this chapter. It contains information specific to building DLLs with MFC.

This chapter covers the following topics:

- Overview of differences
- Run-time library behavior
- The **DllMain** function
- The **dllexport** and **dllimport** attributes
- Exporting C++ functions
- Building the DLL
- Special issues with DLLs

Overview of Differences

If you have built 16-bit DLLs for Windows 3.*x*, you should find that building DLLs for Windows NT is more convenient. The compiler offers more direct support, which can save you several steps in DLL creation. The specific differences are:

- There is no separate startup module. The DLL startup sequence is handled directly by C/C++ run-time library code linked into your DLL.

- The run-time library code initializes any static non-local C++ objects by calling the appropriate constructors. (Each process gets its own copy of all the DLL's static data, including objects.)

- Other initialization and termination are handled through the single user-defined function, **DllMain**. You can write or choose not to include this function.

- You import and export symbols directly in your source code. Using the **dllexport** attribute (similar to **__export** in Windows 3.*x*) saves you from having to use a separate module-definition file. Using **dllimport** improves efficiency and enables you to import data and objects as well as code.

- The timing of calls to routines registered with **atexit** can differ.

The most fundamental difference is that code from the C/C++ run-time library is linked into your DLL (or linked at run time if you are using the DLL version of the run-time library), which minimizes some coding problems. The run-time library code calls the constructors and destructors as appropriate for static, non-local C++ objects in the DLL.

The run-time code also calls the user-defined **DllMain** function for both initialization and termination, so that you have an opportunity to allocate or release additional resources, as needed. These calls are made in four situations: process attach, process detach, thread attach, and thread detach. If you don't need initialization or termination, you can omit **DllMain** from source code.

The rest of this chapter describes how to build a DLL, and how to write a **DllMain** function and use the **dllexport** and **dllimport** attributes.

Run-time Library Behavior

As explained in the previous section, the C/C++ run-time library code performs the DLL startup sequence, eliminating the need for a separate module; it also calls constructors and destructors as appropriate for global C++ objects.

For example, in the following DLL source code, Equus and Sugar are two static, non-local objects of class CHorse, defined in HORSES.H. There is no function in source code that contains calls to a constructor function for CHorse or to the destructor function, because these objects are defined outside of any function.

Therefore, calls to these constructors and destructors must be performed by the run-time code. (The run-time library code for applications also performs this function.)

```
#include "horses.h"

CHorse  Equus( ARABIAN, MALE );
CHorse  Sugar( THOROUGHBRED, FEMALE );

BOOL    WINAPI   DllMain (HANDLE hInst,
                         ULONG ul_reason_for_call,
                         LPVOID lpReserved)
...
```

Each time a new process attempts to use the DLL, the operating system creates a separate copy of the DLL's data: this is called *process attach*. The run-time library code for the DLL calls the constructors for all the global objects, if any, and then calls your **DllMain** function with process attach selected. The opposite situation is process detach: the run-time library code calls **DllMain** with process detach selected and then calls a list of termination functions including **atexit** functions, destructors for the global objects, and destructors for the **static** objects. Note that the order of events in process attach is the reverse of that in process detach.

The run-time library code is also called during thread attach and thread detach (explained later in this chapter), but the run-time code does no initialization or termination on its own.

The DllMain Function

Unlike Windows 3.*x* DLLs, Windows NT calls one function, **DllMain,** for both initialization and termination. It also makes calls on both a per-process and per-thread basis, so several initialization calls can be made if a process is multithreaded. The function is optional; if you don't provide it in source code, the compiler links its own version, which does nothing but return TRUE.

If you are building a DLL with MFC, **DllMain** may need to perform additional tasks. For more information, see the article "DLLs: Initialization and Termination" in *Programming with the Microsoft Foundation Class Library*.

DllMain uses the **WINAPI** convention and three parameters. The following code shows the first line in a **DllMain** definition:

```
BOOL    WINAPI   DllMain (HANDLE hInst,
                         ULONG ul_reason_for_call,
                         LPVOID lpReserved)
```

The function returns TRUE (1) to indicate success. If, during per-process initialization, the function returns zero, the system cancels the process.

The *ul_reason_for_call* parameter indicates the reason **DllMain** was called: initialization or termination, for a process or a thread. The following table describes the meaning of the four possible values.

Value of *ul_reason_for_call*	Description
DLL_PROCESS_ATTACH	A new process is attempting to access the DLL; one thread is assumed.
DLL_THREAD_ATTACH	A new thread of an existing process is attempting to access the DLL; this call is made beginning with the *second thread* of a process attaching to the DLL.
DLL_PROCESS_DETACH	A process is detaching from the DLL.
DLL_THREAD_DETACH	One of the additional threads (not the first thread) of a process is detaching from the DLL.

The *lpReserved* parameter is reserved for the system's use and should not be manipulated by your source code.

Windows 3.*x* DLL initialization functions are passed the following information:

- The DLL's instance handle
- The DLL's data segment (DS)
- The heap size specified in the DLL's .DEF file
- The command line

Win32 DLL initialization functions are passed the following information:

- The *hModule* parameter, a module handle.
- The *ul_reason_for_call* parameter, an enumerated type that indicates which of four reasons the LibMain procedure is being called: process attach, thread attach, thread detach, or process detach.
- The *lpReserved* parameter, which is unused.

The following code presents a basic skeleton showing what the definition of **DllMain** might look like:

```
BOOL APIENTRY DllMain( HANDLE hModule,
                       DWORD ul_reason_for call,
                       LPVOID lpReserved )
{
    switch( dwReason) {
    case DLL_PROCESS_ATTACH:
    ...
    case DLL_THREAD_ATTACH:
    ...
    case DLL_THREAD_DETACH:
    ...
```

```
    case DLL_PROCESS_DETACH:
    ...
    }
    return TRUE;
}
```

The Win32 module handle has the same purpose as the Windows 3.*x* instance
handle. Otherwise, Win32 DLL initialization functions do not include the
parameters for Windows 3.*x* initialization, as described in the following table.

Parameter	Comment
DLL data segment	Not needed in Win32; memory model is flat, not segmented.
Size of DLL's local heap	All calls to local memory management functions operate on the default heap.
Pointer to command line	The command line can be obtained through a call to the **GetCommandLine** API function.

The dllexport and dllimport Attributes

The DLL model for Windows NT is different from that for Windows 3.*x*. To write
the most efficient DLL code and to make the transition as smooth as possible, use
the **dllexport** and **dllimport** import attributes.

As you write a DLL, you can use **dllexport** to declare that a symbol (function, data,
or object) is being exported to applications and other DLLs. The compiler produces
the most efficient code as a result, and you no longer need a module-definition
(.DEF) file to export your symbols.

When you create header files for use with your DLLs, you should include
dllimport declarations for each symbol, so applications properly declare each
DLL symbol to be used. The DLL users still need an import library, but use of
dllimport produces more efficient code. Also, **dllimport** must be used to import
data items and objects.

Because they are attributes and not keywords, **dllexport** and **dllimport** must be
used in conjunction with the __**declspec** keyword. The following procedure is
recommended:

1. Use the __**declspec** keyword, along with **dllexport** and **dllimport**, to define
   import and export macros for your source code.
2. Use these macros you've defined to declare symbols as export or import.

For more information on **dllexport** and **dllimport**, see "The dllexport and dllimport
Attributes" in Appendix B in the *C++ Language Reference*.

The __declspec Keyword

The Visual C++ language (including C source modules) uses the **__declspec** keyword to extend storage class attributes. Storage class determines how a given symbol is accessed by the compiler. For example, **static**, a storage class attribute in standard C/C++, specifies that a variable is not stored on the stack.

This version of Visual C++ defines four extended storage class attributes: **dllexport**, **dllimport**, **thread**, and **naked**. These are not supported directly as keywords. Instead, these Microsoft-specific extended class storage attributes are used with **__declspec** to reduce the number of reserved words. This chapter introduces the **dllexport** and **dllimport** attributes. Chapter 5, "Creating Multithread Applications for Windows NT ," discusses the **thread** attribute and Chapter 9, "Using Calling Conventions," discusses the **naked** attribute.

The syntax for using **__declspec** is:

__declspec(*attribute* **)** *variable-declaration*

For example, the following definition exports an integer, using **dllexport** as the attribute:

```
__declspec( dllexport ) int SumInterest = 0;
```

Exporting Symbols

The use of **dllexport** (when used with **__declspec** as explained in the previous section) replaces the **__export** keyword supported in Windows 3.*x*. To port DLL source code, you should replace each instance of **__export**. The **dllexport** attribute eliminates the need for a .DEF file.

To export symbols, the recommended approach is to define a macro for **__declspec(dllexport)** and then use the macro with each symbol:

```
#define DllExport   __declspec( dllexport )

DllExport    int i = 10;        // Definition, because initialized
DllExport    int j;             // Definition, because of DllExport
DllExport    void func();       // Declaration
```

With uninitialized data, **dllexport** causes the statement to be a definition unless it is combined with **extern**, in which case it is a declaration. The difference is important: a definition tells the compiler to create a symbol; a declaration informs the compiler that the symbol is created somewhere else. Thus, in the previous example, j is defined rather than declared, because of **DllExport**. The nature of the other two statements is already clear from syntax.

When you combine the **extern** keyword with **dllexport**, it tells the compiler that the symbol is defined and exported by the DLL, but not necessarily in this source-code module. For example, the following is a data declaration, not definition:

```
extern  DllExport  j;            // Symbol j is declared
```

It should be clear that exporting a symbol is inconsistent with automatic ("stack" or "local") storage class. Therefore, the following code produces an error, because it attempts to export a symbol Sum defined on the stack:

```
void func()
{
b    DllExport   int   Sum;      // Error: cannot export local variable
```

However, the following code compiles correctly because Sum is only declared, not defined, within the function. This code enables Sum to be used within the scope of func, but the code does not create it:

```
void func()
{
    extern   DllExport   int   Sum;    // Ok, because extern means Sum
                                       // is defined in another
                                       // module of this DLL.
```

For information on exporting symbols from DLLs built with MFC, see the article "DLLs: Importing and Exporting" in *Programming with the Microsoft Foundation Class Library.*

Importing Symbols

A program that uses public symbols defined by a DLL is said to *import* them. Windows 3.*x* required only the use of an import library, normally supplied by the DLL author, to handle the mechanics of importing. In Windows NT, the DLL user must still link with the import library, but needs to use **dllimport** as well.

As a DLL author, you should accommodate this requirement by using **dllimport** in the header files you supply. If you don't, DLL users can still access DLL functions, but their code will be less efficient, and they will not have access to DLL public data symbols and objects.

To import symbols, the recommended approach is to define a macro for **__declspec(import)** and then use the macro to declare each imported symbol:

```
#define DllImport   __declspec( dllimport )

DllImport   int   j;
DllImport   void func();
```

The **dllimport** attribute must be used in a declaration, not a definition, because you obviously cannot define a new symbol and at the same time import it from another program. You also cannot declare an imported symbol as **static**, which implies that the symbol is defined in the current module.

```
DllImport    int  j = 2;        // Error: initialization implies definition

void func()
{
    static DllImport int  i;  // Error: static
```

It is valid to give the same symbol both the **dllexport** and **dllimport** attributes. This could happen if you are sharing header files between different programs. Otherwise, it should not happen. When both attributes are used, the **dllexport** attribute takes precedence:

```
DllImport    int     i;
DllExport    int     i;   // Warning issued, but dllexport takes
                          //  precedence
```

If you are compiling your program as a C language module, you cannot use the address of an imported symbol to initialize a global or static variable. However, in C++, you can use the address of an imported symbol to initialize any variable or object.

For information on importing symbols from or into DLLs built with MFC, see the article "DLLs: Importing and Exporting" in *Programming with the Microsoft Foundation Class Library*.

Exporting C++ Functions

If you have functions in a DLL written in C++ that you want to access from a C language module, you will probably want to declare these functions with C linkage instead of C++ linkage. Unless otherwise specified, the C++ compiler uses C++ type-safe naming (also known as name decoration) and C++ calling conventions, which can be difficult to call from C.

To specify C linkage, specify `extern "C"` for your function declarations, for example:

```
extern "C"__declspec( dllexport ) int MyFunc(long parm1);
```

For more information on linkage specification, see "Linkage Specifications" in Chapter 6 of the *C++ Language Reference*.

Importing and Exporting Inline Functions

Imported functions can be defined as inline. The effect is roughly the same as defining a standard function inline; calls to the function are expanded into inline code, much like a macro. This is principally useful as a way of supporting C++ classes in a DLL that may inline some of their member functions for efficiency.

One feature of an imported inline function is that in C++, you can take its address. The compiler returns the address of the copy of the inline function residing in the DLL. Another feature of imported inline functions is that unlike global imported data, you can initialize static local data of the imported function.

You should exercise care when providing imported inline functions, because they can create the possibility of version conflicts. An inline function gets expanded into the application code; therefore, if you later rewrite the function, it does not get updated unless the application itself is recompiled. (Normally, DLL functions can be updated without rebuilding the applications that use them.)

Building the DLL

There are two categories of compiler options you should know about when you build a DLL. The /LD option causes the compiler to build a DLL instead of an application. You can select it automatically by using the Visual C++ environment to build a DLL, or by specifying /LD on the command line. The other options that can affect building of a DLL are /MD, /MT, and /ML, which select run-time library type.

Using Visual C++ to Build DLLs

To build a DLL from within the Visual C++ environment, make sure that you select "Windows dynamic-link library" as the program type when you create a new project. Visual C++ uses a dialog box to offer a choice of program types when you choose New from the Project menu. If you have already created the project and it does not have DLL program type, you can change the program type by choosing Project from the Options menu.

To debug a DLL, you must run an application that calls your DLL. Choose the Debug menu command from the Options menu. A dialog box appears for you to specify which application to run while debugging.

The /LD Option

The Visual C++ environment automatically sets the /LD option when you choose "Windows dynamic-link library" as the program type. You can also specify /LD directly when using the command line to invoke the compiler.

When the /LD option is specified, the compiler passes the –DLL option to the linker, causing a DLL to be built. The compiler also does the following:

- Looks for the **DllMain** function in the source code.
- Links with DLL startup code that performs some initialization for you.
- Produces an import library to be linked to applications that call your DLL.
- Interprets /Fe as naming a DLL rather than an EXE file; the default program name becomes *basename*.DLL instead of *basename*.EXE.
- Changes default for C run-time library support, as explained in the next section.

Multithread Support and /M Options

The /MD, /ML, and /MT options determine whether the program being built has single-thread support, multithread support, or uses a dynamic-link version of the run-time library (MSVCRT10.DLL). The following table shows the purpose of each option.

Option	Links to
/MD	MSVCRT10.DLL, a dynamic-link library that is multithread aware
/ML	Single-thread-aware library (default for applications)
/MT	Multithread-aware library (default for DLLs)

It is usually best to use the /MD or /MT option when building a DLL. These options support multithread applications. When you specify /ML, your DLL will work reliably only when called by single-thread applications. A multithread application that calls a DLL without multithread awareness is likely to fail. Therefore, don't specify /ML unless you know that it will be used only by single-thread applications.

The compiler chooses /MT by default when you build a DLL.

Note that deciding whether to use MSVCRT10.DLL and whether to build an application or DLL are largely independent choices. You could, for example, choose to build an application that uses the DLL version of the run-time library (/MD); conversely, you could build a DLL that is statically linked to the C run-time library (/MT or /ML).

Special Issues with DLLs

The following sections discuss issues that occur occasionally in special situations: mutual DLL imports and the effect of dynamic loading on thread-local storage. You can write a simple DLL without worrying about these issues. However, if you use any of these features, it is helpful to be aware of the issues.

Mutual Imports

Exporting or importing to another executable file presents complications when the imports are mutual (or "circular"). For example, two DLLs import symbols from each other, similar to mutually-recursive functions.

The problem with mutually-importing executable files (usually DLLs) is that neither can be built without building the other first. Each build process requires, as input, an import library produced by the *other* build process.

The solution is to use the LIB utility with the /DEF option, which produces an import library without building the executable file. Using this utility, you can build all the import libraries you need, no matter how many DLLs are involved or how complicated the dependencies are.

The general solution is:

1. Take each DLL in turn. (Any order is feasible, although some orders are more optimal.) If all the needed import libraries exist and are current, run LINK to build the executable file (DLL). This produces an import library. Otherwise, run LIB to produce an import library.

   Running LIB with the /DEF option produces an additional file with an .EXP extension. The .EXP file must be used later to build the executable file.

2. After using either LINK or LIB to build all the import libraries, go back and run LINK to build any executable files that were not built in the previous step. Note that the corresponding .EXP file must be specified on the LINK line.

   If you had run the LIB utility earlier to produce an import library for DLL1, LIB produced the file DLL1.EXP as well. You must use DLL1.EXP as input to LINK when building DLL1.DLL.

Figure 4.1 illustrates a solution for two mutually-importing DLLs, DLL1 and DLL2. The first step is to run LIB, with the /DEF option set, on DLL1. This step produces DLL1.LIB, an import library, and DLL1.EXP. The import library is used to build DLL2, which in turn produces an import library for DLL2's symbols. The final step builds DLL1, by using DLL1.EXP and DLL2.LIB as input. Note that an .EXP file for DLL2 is *not* necessary, because LIB was not used to build DLL2's import library.

Figure 4.1   Linking Two DLLs with Mutual Imports

For more information on the LIB utility and the /DEF option, see Appendix D in the *Visual C++ User's Guide*.

DLL Loading and Thread-Local Storage

An executable file loads a DLL in one of two ways: statically or dynamically. The exported contents of a DLL are *always* dynamically bound, regardless of how it is loaded. Furthermore, these mechanisms are not mutually exclusive, as one application can statically load a DLL and another can attach to it dynamically. A statically-loaded DLL is "static" only in the sense that an application sets up imports to it at build time.

- Static loading is the standard mechanism, invoked when a program is built with import libraries referring to the DLL. When the application builder is relatively sure that a particular DLL will be used, this method is most efficient because symbols can be accessed with the **dllimport** attribute.

- Dynamic loading attaches to a DLL specified at run time. This mechanism uses **LoadLibrary** and other API functions such as **GetProcAddress**, bypassing use of imports. Use this technique when you don't know at build time whether a DLL will be accessed. This way the DLL is not initialized until it is accessed.

If a DLL declares static-extent data as **__declspec(thread)**, it can cause a protection fault if dynamically loaded. After the DLL is loaded with **LoadLibrary**, it causes system failure whenever the code references this data. (Static-extent data includes both global and local **static** items.)

Therefore, when you create a DLL, you should either avoid this use of thread-local storage, or inform DLL users about potential pitfalls, in case they attempt dynamic loading.

C H A P T E R   5

Creating Multithread Applications for Windows NT

Microsoft Visual C++ for Microsoft Windows NT provides support for creating multithread applications with Windows NT. You should consider using more than one thread if your application needs to manage multiple activities, such as simultaneous keyboard and mouse input. One thread can process keyboard input while a second thread filters mouse activities. A third thread can update the display screen based on data from the mouse and keyboard threads. At the same time, other threads can access disk files or get data from a communications port.

With Visual C++, there are two ways to program with multiple threads: use the Microsoft Foundation Class library (MFC) or the C run-time library and the Win32 API. For information on creating multithread applications with MFC, read the "Multithreading" articles in *Programming with the Microsoft Foundation Class Library* after reading this chapter.

This chapter explains the features in Visual C++ that support the creation of multithread programs.

Note Win32s does not support multithreading. Calls to the Win32 APIs and C run-time library functions mentioned in this chapter will return an error.

Multithread Programs

A thread is basically a path of execution through a program. It is also the smallest unit of execution that Windows NT schedules. A thread consists of a stack, the state of the CPU registers, and an entry in the execution list of the system scheduler. Each thread shares all of the process's resources.

A process consists of one or more threads and the code, data, and other resources of a program in memory. Typical program resources are open files, semaphores, and dynamically allocated memory. A program executes when the system scheduler gives one of its threads execution control. The scheduler determines which threads should run and when they should run. Threads of lower priority may have to wait while higher priority threads complete their tasks. On multiprocessor machines, the scheduler can move individual threads to different processors to "balance" the CPU load.

Each thread in a process operates independently. Unless you make them visible to each other, the threads execute individually, and are unaware of the of other threads in a process. Threads sharing common resources, however, must coordinate their work by using semaphores or another method of interprocess communication. See "Writing a Multithread Program" later in this chapter for more information about synchronizing threads.

Library Support

If one thread is suspended by the Windows NT scheduler while executing the **printf** function, one of the program's other threads might start executing. If the second thread also calls **printf**, data might be corrupted. To avoid this, access to static data used by the function must be restricted to one thread at a time.

You do not need to serialize access to stack-based (automatic) variables because each thread has a different stack. Therefore, a function that uses only automatic (stack) variables is re-entrant. The standard C run-time libraries, such as LIBCE, have a limited number of re-entrant functions. A multithread program needing to use C run-time library functions that are normally not re-entrant should be built with the multithread library LIBCMT.LIB.

The Multithread C Libraries: LIBCMT.LIB and MSVCRT.LIB

The support library LIBCMT.LIB is a re-entrant library for creating multithread programs. The MSVCRT.LIB library, which calls code in the shared MSVCRT10.DLL, is also re-entrant. When your application calls functions in these libraries, the following rules may apply:

- All library calls must use the C (**__cdecl**) calling convention; programs compiled using other calling conventions (such as **__fastcall** or **__stdcall**) must use the standard include files for the run-time library functions they call.

- Variables passed to library functions must be passed by value or cast to a pointer.

Programs built with LIBCMT.LIB do not share C run-time library code or data with any dynamic-link libraries they call.

Alternatives to LIBCMT.LIB and MSVCRT.LIB

If you build a multithread program without using LIBCMT.LIB, you must do the following:

- Use the standard C libraries and limit library calls to the set of re-entrant functions.

- Use the Windows NT API thread management functions, such as **CreateThread**.

- Provide your own synchronization for functions that are not re-entrant by using Windows NT services such as semaphores and the **EnterCriticalSection** and **LeaveCriticalSection** functions.

Warning   The multithread library LIBCMT.LIB includes the **_beginthread** and **_endthread** functions. The **_beginthread** function performs initialization without which many C run-time functions will fail. You must use **_beginthread** instead of **CreateThread** in C programs built with LIBCMT.LIB if you intend to call C run-time functions.

The Multithread Libraries Compile Option

To build a multithread application that uses the C run-time libraries, you must tell the compiler to use a special version of the libraries. To select these libraries, first choose Project from the Options menu, then click the Compiler button. From the compiler options dialog box, choose Runtime Libraries, and then select Multithread Libraries (LIBCMT.LIB). Choose OK to return to editing.

From the command line, the Multithread Library compiler option (/MT) is the best way to build a multithread program with LIBCMT.LIB. This option, which is automatically set when you specify a multithreaded application when creating a new project, embeds the LIBCMT library name in the object file.

Include Files

The Microsoft Visual C++ for Windows NT include files contain conditional sections for multithread applications using LIBCMT.LIB. To compile your application with the appropriate definitions, you can:

- Compile with the Multithread Library compiler option described in the previous section.

- Define the symbolic constant **_MT** in your source file or on the command line with the /D option.

Standard include files declare C run-time library functions as they are implemented in the libraries. If you used the Maximum Optimization (/Ox) or Register Calling Convention (/Gr) option, the compiler assumes that all functions should be called using the register calling convention. The run-time library functions were compiled using the C calling convention, and the declarations in the standard include files tell the compiler to generate correct external references to these functions.

See "Compiling and Linking" on page 79 for examples of how to use the **_MT** constant.

C Run-Time Library Functions for Thread Control

All Windows NT programs have at least one thread. Any thread can create additional threads. A thread can complete its work quickly and then terminate, or it can stay active for the life of the program.

The LIBCMT and MSVCRT C run-time libraries provide two functions for thread creation and termination: the **_beginthread** and **_endthread** functions.

The **_beginthread** function creates a new thread and returns a thread identifier if the operation is successful. The thread terminates automatically if it completes execution, or it can terminate itself with a call to **_endthread**.

Warning If you are going to call C run-time routines from a program built with LIBCMT.LIB, you must start your threads with the **_beginthread** function. Do not use the Windows NT functions **ExitThread** and **CreateThread**. Using **SuspendThread** can lead to a deadlock when more than one thread is blocked waiting for the suspended thread to complete its access to a C run-time data structure.

The _beginthread Function

The **_beginthread** function creates a new thread. A thread shares the code and data segments of a process with other threads in the process, but has its own unique register values, stack space, and current instruction address. The system gives CPU time to each thread, so that all threads in a process can execute concurrently. You can find a complete description of **_beginthread** and its arguments in Help.

The **_beginthread** function is similar to the **CreateThread** function in the Windows NT API but has these differences:

- The **_beginthread** function lets you pass multiple arguments to the thread.
- The **_beginthread** function initializes certain C run-time library variables. This is important only if you use the C run-time library in your threads.
- **CreateThread** provides control over security attributes. You can use this function to start a thread in a suspended state.

The **_beginthread** function returns a handle to the new thread if successful or−1 if there was an error.

The _endthread Function

The **_endthread** function terminates a thread created by **_beginthread**. Threads terminate automatically when they complete. The **_endthread** function is useful for conditional termination from within a thread. A thread dedicated to communications processing, for example, can quit if it is unable to get control of the communications port. You can find a complete description of **_endthread** in Help.

Sample Multithread C Program

BOUNCE.C is a sample multithread program that creates a new thread each time the letter 'a' or 'A' is entered at the keyboard. Each thread bounces a "happy face" of a different color around the screen. Up to 32 threads can be created. The program's normal termination occurs when 'q' or 'Q' is entered. See "Compiling and Linking" for details on compiling and linking BOUNCE.C.

```
/*  Bounce - Creates a new thread each time the letter 'a' is typed.
 *  Each thread bounces a happy face of a different color around the screen.
 *  All threads are terminated when the letter 'Q' is entered.
 *
 *  This program requires the multithread library. For example, compile
 *  with the following command line:
 *      CL /MT BOUNCE.C
 */

#include <windows.h>
#include <stdlib.h>
#include <string.h>
#include <stdio.h>
#include <conio.h>
#include <process.h>

#define MAX_THREADS  32

/* getrandom returns a random number between min and max, which must be in
 * integer range.
 */
#define getrandom( min, max ) ((rand() % (int)(((max) + 1) - (min))) + (min))

void main( void );                      /* Thread 1: main */
void KbdFunc( void  );                  /* Keyboard input, thread dispatch */
void BounceProc( char * MyID );         /* Threads 2 to n: display */
void ClearScreen( void );               /* Screen clear */
void ShutDown( void );                  /* Program shutdown */
```

```
void WriteTitle( int ThreadNum );          /* Display title bar information */
HANDLE  hConsoleOut;                        /* Handle to the console */
HANDLE  hRunMutex;                          /* "Keep Running" mutex */
HANDLE  hScreenMutex;                       /* "Screen update" mutex  */
int     ThreadNr;                           /* Number of threads started */
CONSOLE_SCREEN_BUFFER_INFO csbiInfo;        /* Console information */


void main()                                 /* Thread One */
{
    /* Get display screen information & clear the screen.*/
    hConsoleOut = GetStdHandle( STD_OUTPUT_HANDLE );
    GetConsoleScreenBufferInfo( hConsoleOut, &csbiInfo );
    ClearScreen();
    WriteTitle( 0 );
    /* Create the mutexes and reset thread count. */
    hScreenMutex = CreateMutex( NULL, FALSE, NULL );   /* Cleared */
    hRunMutex = CreateMutex( NULL, TRUE, NULL );       /* Set */
    ThreadNr = 0;

    /* Start waiting for keyboard input to dispatch threads or exit. */
    KbdFunc();

    /* All threads done. Clean up handles. */
    CloseHandle( hScreenMutex );
    CloseHandle( hRunMutex );
    CloseHandle( hConsoleOut );
}

void ShutDown( void )                       /* Shut down threads */
{
    while ( ThreadNr > 0 )
    {
            /* Tell thread to die and record its death. */
            ReleaseMutex( hRunMutex );
            ThreadNr--;
    }
    /* Clean up display when done */
    WaitForSingleObject( hScreenMutex, INFINITE );
    ClearScreen();
}

void KbdFunc( void )                        /* Dispatch and count threads. */
{
    int         KeyInfo;

    do
    {
```

```
KeyInfo = _getch();
        if( tolower( KeyInfo ) == 'a' && ThreadNr < MAX_THREADS )
        {
            ThreadNr++;
            _beginthread( BounceProc, 0, &ThreadNr );
            WriteTitle( ThreadNr );
        }
    } while( tolower( KeyInfo ) != 'q' );

    ShutDown();
}


void BounceProc( char *MyID )
{
    char        MyCell, OldCell;
    WORD        MyAttrib, OldAttrib;
    char        BlankCell = 0x20;
    COORD       Coords, Delta;
    COORD       Old = {0,0};
    DWORD       Dummy;

/* Generate update increments and initial display coordinates. */
    srand( (unsigned) *MyID * 3 );
    Coords.X = getrandom( 0, csbiInfo.dwSize.X - 1 );
    Coords.Y = getrandom( 0, csbiInfo.dwSize.Y - 1 );
    Delta.X = getrandom( -3, 3 );
    Delta.Y = getrandom( -3, 3 );

    /* Set up "happy face" & generate color attribute from thread number.*/
    if( *MyID > 16)
        MyCell = 0x01;                  /* outline face */
    else
        MyCell = 0x02;                  /* solid face */
    MyAttrib = *MyID & 0x0F;            /* force black background */

    do
    {
        /* Wait for display to be available, then lock it. */
        WaitForSingleObject( hScreenMutex, INFINITE );

        /* If we still occupy the old screen position, blank it out. */
        ReadConsoleOutputCharacter( hConsoleOut, &OldCell, 1, Old, &Dummy );
        ReadConsoleOutputAttribute( hConsoleOut, &OldAttrib, 1, Old, &Dummy );
        if (( OldCell == MyCell ) && (OldAttrib == MyAttrib))
            WriteConsoleOutputCharacter( hConsoleOut, &BlankCell, 1, Old, &Dummy );

        /* Draw new face, then clear screen lock */
        WriteConsoleOutputCharacter( hConsoleOut, &MyCell, 1, Coords, &Dummy );
        WriteConsoleOutputAttribute( hConsoleOut, &MyAttrib, 1, Coords, &Dummy );
        ReleaseMutex( hScreenMutex );
```

```
        /* Increment the coordinates for next placement of the block. */
        Old.X = Coords.X;
        Old.Y = Coords.Y;
        Coords.X += Delta.X;
        Coords.Y += Delta.Y;

        /* If we are about to go off the screen, reverse direction */
        if( Coords.X < 0 || Coords.X >= csbiInfo.dwSize.X )
        {
            Delta.X = -Delta.X;
            Beep( 400, 50 );
        }
        if( Coords.Y < 0 || Coords.Y > csbiInfo.dwSize.Y )
        {
            Delta.Y = -Delta.Y;
            Beep( 600, 50 );
        }
    }
    /* Repeat while RunMutex is still taken. */
    while ( WaitForSingleObject( hRunMutex, 75L ) == WAIT_TIMEOUT );

}

void WriteTitle( int ThreadNum )
{
    char    NThreadMsg[80];

    sprintf( NThreadMsg, "Threads running: %02d.  Press 'A' to start a thread,'Q' to
quit.", ThreadNum );
    SetConsoleTitle( NThreadMsg );
}

void ClearScreen( void )
{
    DWORD   dummy;
    COORD   Home = { 0, 0 };
    FillConsoleOutputCharacter( hConsoleOut, ' ', csbiInfo.dwSize.X * csbiInfo.dwSize.Y,
Home, &dummy );
}
```

Writing a Multithread Program

When you write a program with multiple threads, you must coordinate their behavior and use of the program's resources. You must also make sure that each thread receives its own stack.

Sharing Common Resources

Each thread has its own stack and its own copy of the CPU registers. Other resources, such as files, static data, and heap memory, are shared by all threads in the process. Threads using these common resources must be synchronized. Windows NT provides several ways to synchronize resources, including semaphores, critical sections, events, and mutexes.

When multiple threads are accessing static data, your program must provide for possible resource conflicts. Consider a program where one thread updates a static data structure containing x,y coordinates for items to be displayed by another thread. If the update thread alters the x coordinate and is preempted before it can change the y coordinate, the display thread may be scheduled before the y coordinate is updated. The item would be displayed at the wrong location. You can avoid this problem by using semaphores to control access to the structure.

A mutex (short for *mut*ual *ex*clusion) is a way of communicating among threads or processes that are executing asynchronously of one another. This communication is usually used to coordinate the activities of multiple threads or processes, typically by controlling access to a shared resource by "locking" and "unlocking" the resource. To solve this x,y coordinate update problem, the update thread would set a mutex indicating that the data structure is in use before performing the update. It would clear the mutex after both coordinates had been processed. The display thread must wait for the mutex to be clear before updating the display. This process of waiting for a mutex is often called "blocking" on a mutex because the process is blocked and cannot continue until the mutex clears.

The BOUNCE.C program shown in the previous section uses a mutex named ScreenMutex to coordinate screen updates. Each time one of the display threads is ready to write to the screen, it calls **WaitForSingleObject** with the handle to ScreenMutex and constant **INFINITE** to indicate that the **WaitForSingleObject** call should block on the mutex and not time out. If ScreenMutex is clear, the wait function sets the mutex so other threads cannot interfere with the display and continues executing the thread. Otherwise, the thread blocks until the mutex clears. When the thread completes the display update, it releases the mutex by calling **ReleaseMutex**.

Screen displays and static data are only two of the resources requiring careful management. For example, your program may have multiple threads accessing the same file. Because another thread may have moved the file pointer, each thread must reset the file pointer before reading or writing. In addition, each thread must make sure that it is not preempted between the time it positions the pointer and the time it accesses the file. These threads should use a semaphore to coordinate access to the file by bracketing each file access with **WaitForSingleObject** and **ReleaseMutex** calls. The following code fragment illustrates this technique:

```
HANDLE    hIOMutex= CreateMutex (NULL, FALSE, NULL);

WaitForSingleObject( hIOMutex, INFINITE );
fseek( fp, desired_position, 0L );
fwrite( data, sizeof( data ), 1, fp );
ReleaseMutex( hIOMutex);
```

Thread Stacks

All of an application's default stack space is allocated to the first thread of execution, which is known as thread 1. As a result, you must specify how much memory to allocate for a separate stack for each additional thread your program needs. The operating system will allocate additional stack space for the thread, if necessary, but you must specify a default value.

The first argument in the **_beginthread** call is a pointer to the **BounceProc** function, which will execute the threads. The second argument specifies the default stack size for the thread. The last argument is an ID number that is passed to **BounceProc**. **BounceProc** uses the ID number to seed the random number generator and to select the thread's color attribute and display character.

Threads that make calls to the C run-time library or to the Windows NT API must allow sufficient stack space for the library and API functions they call. The C **printf** function requires more than 500 bytes of stack space, and you should have 2K of stack space available when calling Windows NT API routines.

Because each thread has its own stack, you can avoid potential collisions over data items by using as little static data as possible. Design your program to use automatic stack variables for all data that can be private to a thread. The only global variables in the BOUNCE.C program are either mutexes or variables that never change after they are initialized.

Windows NT also provides Thread-Local Storage (TLS) to store per-thread data. See "Thread Local Storage" on page 80.

Compiling and Linking

The steps for compiling and linking the multithread program BOUNCE.C using the Visual Workbench are:

1. Create a new project. Choose Console Application (.EXE) from the Project Type list, and turn off the Use Microsoft Foundation Classes box.

2. Add the file containing the C source code to the project.

3. In the Project Options dialog box, choose Compiler and set the Runtime Libraries to Multithread Libraries (LIBCMT.LIB).

4. Build the project by choosing Build from the Project menu.

Note The BOUNCE.C program appears as a sample on the Visual C++ CD-ROM. See the Sample help file for more information.

The steps for compiling and linking the multithread program BOUNCE.C from the command line are:

1. Ensure that the Win32 library files and LIBCMT.LIB are in the directory specified in your LIB environment variable.

2. Compile and link the program with the CL command-line option /MT:

```
CL /MT BOUNCE.C
```

3. If you choose not to use the /MT option, you must take these steps:

   - Define the _MT symbol before including header files. You can do this by specifying /D _MT on the command line.

   - Specify the multithread library and suppress default library selection.

   The multithread include files are used when you define the symbolic constant _MT. You can do this with the CL command line option /D _MT or within the C source file before any include statements, as follows:

```
#define _MT
#include <stdlib.h>
```

Avoiding Problem Areas

There are several problems you might encounter in creating, linking, or executing a multithread C program. Some of the more common ones are described here.

Problem	Probable cause
You get a message box showing that your program caused a protection violation.	Many Windows NT programming errors cause protection violations. A common cause of protection violations is the indirect assignment of data to null pointers. This results in your program trying to access memory that does not "belong" to it, so a protection violation is issued.
	An easy way to detect the cause of a protection violation is to compile your program with debugging information, and then run it through the debugger in Visual Workbench. When the protection fault occurs, Windows NT transfers control to the debugger, and the cursor is positioned on the line that caused the problem.
Your program generates numerous compile and link errors.	If you attempt to compile and link a multithread program without defining the symbolic constant _MT, many of the definitions required for the multithread library will be missing. If you are using the Visual Workbench, make sure that the C/C++ Compiler Options dialog box specifies multithread libraries. From the command line, define _MT to CL with /MT or /D _MT, or use #define _MT in your program.
	You can eliminate many potential problems by setting the compiler's warning level to one of its highest values and heeding the warning messages. By using the /W3 or /W4 warning level options, you can detect unintentional data conversions, missing function prototypes, and use of non-ANSI features.

Thread Local Storage (TLS)

Thread Local Storage (TLS) is the method by which each thread in a given multi-threaded process may allocate locations in which to store thread-specific data. Dynamically bound (run-time) thread-specific data is supported by way of the TLS API (TlsAlloc, TlsGetValue, TlsSetValue, TlsFree). Windows NT and the Visual C++ compiler now support statically bound (load-time) per-thread data in addition to the existing API implementation.

API Implementation

Thread Local Storage is implemented through the Win32 API layer as well as the compiler. For details, see the Win32 API documentation for TlsAlloc, TlsGetValue, TlsSetValue, and TlsFree.

The Visual C++ compiler includes a keyword to make thread local storage operations more automatic, rather than through the API layer. This syntax is described in the next section.

Compiler Implementation

To support TLS, a new attribute, **thread**, has been added to the C and C++ languages and is supported by the Visual C++ compiler. This attribute is an extended storage class modifier, as described in the previous section. Use the **__declspec** keyword to declare a **thread** variable. For example, the following code declares an integer thread local variable and initializes it with a value:

```
__declspec( thread ) int tls_i = 1;
```

Rules and Limitations

The following guidelines must be observed when declaring statically-bound thread local objects and variables:

- The **thread** attribute can be applied only to data declarations and definitions. It cannot be used on function declarations or definitions. For example, the following code will generate a compiler error:

```
#define Thread  __declspec( thread )
Thread void func();     // This will generate an error.
```

- The **thread** modifier may be specified only on data items with **static** extent. This includes global data objects (both **static** and **extern**), local static objects, and static data members of C++ classes. Automatic data objects may not be declared with the **thread** attribute. The following code will generate compiler errors:

```
#define Thread  __declspec( thread )
void func1()
{
    Thread int tls_i;           // This will generate an error.
}

int func2( Thread int tls_i )   // This will generate an error.
{
    return tls_i;
}
```

- The declarations and the definition of a thread local object must all specify the **thread** attribute. For example, the following code will generate an error:

```
#define Thread  __declspec( thread )
extern int tls_i;      // This will generate an error, since the
int Thread tls_i;      // declaration and definition differ.
```

- The **thread** attribute cannot be used as a type modifier. For example, the following code will generate a compiler error:

```
char __declspec( thread ) *ch;      // Error
```

- C++ classes cannot use the **thread** attribute. However, C++ class objects may be instantiated with the **thread** attribute. For example, the following code will generate a compiler error:

```
#define Thread  __declspec( thread )
class Thread C      // Error: classes cannot be declared Thread.
{
// Code
};
C CObject;
```

Because the declaration of C++ objects that utilize the **thread** attribute is permitted, the following two examples are semantically equivalent:

```
#define Thread  __declspec( thread )
Thread class B
{
// Code
} BObject;          // OK--BObject is declared thread local.

class B
{
// Code
}
Thread B BObject;   // OK--BObject is declared thread local.
```

- Because C++ objects with constructors and destructors (as well as any object that utilizes some form of initialization semantics) may be allocated as thread local objects, an associated initialization routine (such as the constructor) is called to initialize that object. For example:

```
class tlsClass
{
    private:
        int x;
    public:
        tlsClass() { x = 1; } ;
        ~tlsClass();
}
```

```
__declspec( thread ) tlsClass tlsObject;
extern int func();
__declspec( thread ) int y = func();
```

In this case, data or objects initialized by the `func` routine do not necessarily belong to the same thread into which `tlsObject` is instantiated.

- The address of a thread local object is not considered constant, and any expression involving such an address is not considered a constant expression. In standard C, the effect of this is to forbid the use of the address of a thread local variable as an initializer for an object or pointer. For example, the following code will be flagged as an error by the C compiler:

```
#define Thread   __declspec( thread )
Thread int tls_i;
int *p = &tls_i;      //This will generate an error in C.
```

This restriction does not apply in C++, however. Because C++ permits dynamic initialization of all objects, you can initialize an object with an expression that uses the address of a thread local variable. This is accomplished in the same way as the construction of thread local objects. For example, the code shown previously will not generate an error when compiled as a C++ source file. Note that the address of a thread local variable is only valid as long as the thread in which the address was taken still exists.

- Standard C permits the initialization of an object or variable with an expression involving a reference to itself, but only for objects of non-static extent. Although C++ normally permits such dynamic initialization of objects with an expression involving a reference to itself, this type of initialization is not permitted with thread local objects. For example:

```
#define Thread   __declspec( thread )
Thread int tls_i = tls_i;              // Error in C and C++
int j = j;                             // OK in C++, error in C
Thread int tls_i = sizeof( tls_i )     // Legal in C and C++
```

Note that a `sizeof` expression that includes the object being initialized does not constitute a reference to itself, and is legal in both C and C++.

C++ does not allow such dynamic initialization of thread data because of possible future enhancements to the thread local storage facility.

- If a DLL declares any non-local data or object as __**declspec**(thread), it can cause a protection fault if dynamically loaded. After the DLL is loaded with LoadLibrary, it causes system failure whenever the code references the non-local __**declspec**(thread) data.

For More Information

You can find more information on:

- Creating multithreaded programs using MFC in *Programming with the Microsoft Foundation Class Library*.
- C run-time functions in *C Run-Time Library Reference*.
- Win32 APIs covering threads and synchronization in *Win32 Programmer's Guide*.

More information is also available through Help.

C H A P T E R   6

Templates

Templates enable you to define a family of functions or classes that can operate on different types of information. This chapter describes the Microsoft implementation of C++ templates, which is based on the ISO WG21/ANSI X3J16 working papers towards the evolving standard for C++.

For more information on templates, see Chapter 6, "Declarations," of the *C++ Language Reference*.

What Are Templates?

Templates are a mechanism for generating functions and classes based on type parameters (templates are sometimes called "parameterized types"). By using templates, you can design a single class that operates on data of many types, instead of having to create a separate class for each type.

For example, to create a type-safe function that returns the minimum of two parameters without using templates, you would have to write a set of overloaded functions like this:

```
// min for ints
int min( int a, int b )
    return ( a < b ) ? a : b;

// min for longs
long min( long a, long b )
    return ( a < b ) ? a : b;

// min for chars
char min( char a, char b )
    return ( a < b ) ? a : b;

//etc...
```

By using templates you can reduce this duplication to a single templated function:

```
template <class T> T min( T a, T b )
    return ( a < b ) ? a : b;
```

Templates can significantly reduce source code size and increase code flexibility without reducing type safety.

Function Templates

With function templates, you can specify a set of functions that are based on the same code, but act on different types or classes. For example:

```
template <class T> void MySwap( T& a, T& b )
{
    T c( a );
    a = b; b = c;
}
```

This code defines a family of functions that swap their parameters. From this template you can generate functions that will swap not only **int** and **long** types, but also user-defined types. MySwap will even swap classes if the class's copy constructor and assignment operator are properly defined.

In addition, the function template will prevent you from swapping objects of different types, since the compiler knows the types of the a and b parameters at compile time. Note that all of the template parameters inside the angle brackets must be used as parameters for the templated function.

You call a templated function as you would a nontemplated function; no special syntax is needed. For example:

```
int i, j;
char k;
MySwap( i, j );     //OK
MySwap( i, k );     //Error, different types.
```

Function Template Instantiation

When a templated function is first called for each type, the compiler creates an "instantiation," a specialized version of the templated function for the type. This instantiation will be called every time the function is used for the type. If you have several identical instantiations, even in different modules, only one copy of the instantiation will end up in the executable.

Standard type conversions are not applied to templated functions. Instead, the compiler first looks for an "exact match" for the parameters supplied. If this fails, it tries to create a new instantiation to create an "exact match." Finally, the compiler attempts to apply overloading resolution to find a match for the parameters. If this fails, the compiler generates an error.

Microsoft Specific →

Trivial type conversions, but not promotions, are applied when trying to match template types. This behavior is disabled by turning on "Disable Language Extensions" (/Za) C++ compiler option.

END Microsoft Specific

Function Template Overrides

With a templated function, you can define special behavior for a specific type by providing a non-templated function for that type. For example:

```
void MySwap( double a, double b);
```

This declaration enables you to define a different function for **double** variables. Like other non-templated functions, standard type conversions (such as promoting a variable of type **float** to **double**) are applied.

Class Templates

You can use class templates to create a family of classes that operate on a type.

```
template <class T, int i> class TempClass
{
public:
    TempClass( void );
    ~TempClass( void );
    int MemberSet( T a, int b );
private:
    T Tarray[i];
    int arraysize;
};
```

In this example, the templated class uses two parameters, a type T and an int i. The T parameter can be passed any type, including structures and classes. The i parameter has to be passed an integer constant. Since i is a constant defined at compile time, you can define a member array of size i using a standard automatic array declaration.

Unlike function templates, you do not need to use all template parameters in the definition of a templated class.

Member Functions

Members of classes are defined slightly differently than those of nontemplated classes. Continuing the preceding example:

```
template <class T, int i>
    int TempClass< T, i >::MemberSet( T a, int b )
    {
        if( ( b >= 0 ) && (b < i) )
        {
            Tarray[b++] = a;
            return sizeof( a );
        }
        else
            return -1;
    }
```

Constructors and Destructors

Although constructors and destructors reference the name of the templated class twice, the template parameters should be referenced only once in the fully specified name.

```
template <class T, int i>
TempClass< T, i >::TempClass( void )
{
    TRACE( "TempClass created.\n" );
}

template <class T, int i>
TempClass< T, i >::~TempClass( void )
{
    TRACE( "TempClass destroyed.\n" );
}
```

Class Template Instantiation

Unlike function templates, when instantiating a class template, you must explicitly instantiate the class by giving the parameters for the templated class. To create an instance of TempClass:

```
TempClass< float, 6 > test1;       // OK
TempClass< char, items++ > test2;  // Error, second parameter
                                   // must be constant.
```

No code is generated for a templated class (or function) until it is instantiated. Moreover, member functions are instantiated only if they are called. This can cause problems if you are building a library with templates for other users. See "Explicit Instantiation" in Chapter 6 of the *C++ Language Reference* for more information.

Angle Bracket Placement

Bad placement of angle brackets (<>) causes many template syntax errors. Make sure that you use proper spacing and parenthesis to distinguish angle brackets from operators such as >> and ->. For example:

```
TempClass< float, a > b ? a : b > test1;
```

should be rewritten as

```
TempClass< float, (a > b ? a : b) > test1;
```

Similarly, pay extra attention when using macros that use angle brackets as template arguments.

When Should You Use Templates?

Templates are often used to:

- Create a type-safe collection class (for example, a stack) that can operate on data of any type.
- Add extra type checking for functions that would otherwise take **void** pointers.
- Encapsulate groups of operator overrides to modify type behavior (such as smart pointers).

Most of these uses can be implemented without templates; however templates offer several advantages:

- Templates are easier to write. You create only one generic version of your class or function instead of manually creating specializations.
- Templates can be easier to understand, since they can provide a straightforward way of abstracting type information.
- Templates are type safe. Since the types that templates act upon are known at compile-time, the compiler can perform type checking before errors occur.

Templates vs. Macros

In many ways, templates work like preprocessor macros, replacing the templated variable with the given type. However, there are many differences between a macro like this:

```
#define min(i, j) (((i) < (j)) ? (i) : (j))
```

and a template:

```
template<class T> T min (T i, T j) { return ((i < j) ? i : j) }
```

Here are some problems with the macro:

- There is no way for the compiler to verify that the macro parameters are of compatible types. The macro is expanded without any special type checking.

- The i and j parameters are evaluated twice. For example, if either parameter has a postincremented variable, the increment is performed two times.

- Since macros are expanded by the preprocessor, compiler error messages will refer to the expanded macro, rather than the macro definition itself. Also the macro will show up in expanded form during debugging.

Templates vs. Void Pointers

Many functions that are now implemented with void pointers can be implemented with templates. Void pointers are often used to allow functions to operate on data of an unknown type. When using void pointers, the compiler cannot distinguish types, so it cannot perform type checking or type-specific behavior such as using type-specific operators, operator overloading, or constructors and destructors.

With templates, you can create functions and classes that operate on typed data. The type looks abstracted in the template definition. However, at compile-time the compiler creates a separate version of the function for each specified type. This enables the compiler to treat templated classes and functions as if they acted on specific types. Templates can also improve coding clarity, since you don't need to create special cases for complex types such as structures.

Collection Classes

Templates are a good way of implementing collection classes. Version 3.0 of the Microsoft Foundation Classes uses templates to implement six new collection classes: **CArray**, **CMap**, **CList**, **CTypedPtrArray**, **CTypedPtrList**, and **CTypedPtrMap**. For information on these classes, see the *Class Library Reference*. For additional information on using and customizing these classes, see the "Collections" articles in *Programming with the Microsoft Foundation Class Library*.

The MyStack collection is a simple implementation of a stack. The two template parameters, T and i, specify the type of elements in the stack and the maximum number of that item in the stack. The push and pop member functions add and remove items on the stack, with the stack growing from the bottom of the stack.

```
template <class T, int i> class MyStack
{
    T StackBuffer[i];
    int cItems;
```

```
public:
    void MyStack( void ) : cItems( i ) {};
    void push( const T item );
    T pop( void );
};

template <class T, int i> void MyStack< T, i >::push( const T item )
{
    if( cItems > 0 )
     StackBuffer[--cItems] = item;
    else
     throw "Stack overflow error.";
    return;
}

template <class T, int i> T MyStack< T, i >::pop( void )
{
    if( cItems < i )
     return StackBuffer[cItems++]
    else

     throw "Stack underflow error.";
}
```

Smart Pointers

C++ allows you to create "smart pointer" classes that encapsulate pointers and override pointer operators to add new functionality to pointer operations. Templates allow you to create generic wrappers to encapsulate pointers of almost any type.

The following code outlines a simple reference count garbage collector. The template class Ptr<T> implements a garbage collecting pointer to any class derived from RefCount.

```
class RefCount {
    int crefs;
public:
    RefCount(void) { crefs = 0; }
    void upcount(void) { ++crefs; }
    void downcount(void) { if (--crefs == 0) delete this; }
};

class Sample : public RefCount {
public:
    void doSomething(void) { TRACE("Did something\n");}
};
```

```
template <class T> class Ptr {
    T* p;
public:
    Ptr(T* p_) : p(p_) { p->upcount(); }
    ~Ptr(void) { p->downcount(); }
    operator T*(void) { return p; }
    T& operator*(void) { return *p; }
    T* operator->(void) { return p; }
    Ptr& operator=(T* p_) {
        p->upcount(); p = p_; p->downcount(); return *this;
    }
};

int main() {
    Ptr<Sample> p  = new Sample; // sample #1
    Ptr<Sample> p2 = new Sample; // sample #2
    p = p2; // #1 has 0 refs, so it is destroyed; #2 has two refs
    p->doSomething();
    return 0;
    // As p2 and p go out of scope, their destructors call
    // downcount. The cref variable of #2 goes to 0, so #2 is
    // destroyed
}
```

Classes RefCount and Ptr<T> together provide a simple garbage collection solution for any class that can afford the int per instance overhead to inherit from RefCount. Note that the primary benefit of using a parametric class like Ptr<T> instead of a more generic class like Ptr is the former is complete type-safe. The preceding code ensures that a Ptr<T> can be used almost anywhere a T* is used; in contrast, a generic Ptr would only provide implicit conversions to void*.

For example, if this class is used to create and manipulate garbage collected files, symbols, strings, and so forth. From the class template Ptr<T>, the compiler will create template classes Ptr<File>, Ptr<Symbol>, Ptr<String>, and so on, and their member functions: Ptr<File>::~Ptr(), Ptr<File>::operator File*(), Ptr<String>::~Ptr(), Ptr<String>::operator String*(), and so on.

CHAPTER 7

C++ Exception Handling

The C++ language provides built-in support for handling anomalous situations, known as "exceptions," which may occur during the execution of your program. With C++ exception handling, your program can communicate unexpected events to a higher execution context that is better able to recover from such abnormal events. These exceptions are handled by code which is outside the normal flow of control.

Note In this chapter, the terms "structured exception handling" and "structured exception" (or "C exception") refer exclusively to the Win32 structured exception handling mechanism provided by Windows NT. All other references to exception handling (or "C++ exception") refer to the C++ exception handling mechanism.

Unlike the Win32 structured exception handling mechanism, the language itself provides support for C++ exception handling. This chapter describes the Microsoft implementation of C++ exception handling, which is based on the ISO WG21/ANSI X3J16 working papers towards the evolving standard for C++.

Exception Handling Overview

For C++ programs, you should use C++ exception handling rather than structured exception handling. While structured exception handling works in C++ programs, you can ensure that your code is more portable by using C++ exception handling. The C++ exception handling mechanism is more flexible, in that it can handle exceptions of any type. C exceptions are always of type **unsigned int**.

In C++, the process of raising an exception is called "throwing" an exception. A designated exception handler then "catches" the thrown exception.

To enable C++ exception handling in your code, select Enable Exception Handling in the Customize (C++ Specific) section of the Advanced C++ Compiler Options dialog box, or use the /GX compiler option. The default is /GX-, which disables exception handling unwind semantics.

Note   Version 3.0 of the Microsoft Foundation Classes, which is included with Visual C++, uses the C++ exception handling mechanism. Although you are encouraged to use C++ exception handling in new code, version 3.0 retains the macros from previous versions of MFC so that old code will not be broken. The macros and the new mechanism can be combined, as well. For information on mixing macros and C++ exception handling and on converting old code to use the new mechanism, see the articles "Exceptions: Macros and C++," and "Exceptions: Converting Old Code," in *Programming with the Microsoft Foundation Class Library*.

Exception Handling Syntax

The structure for C++ exception handling is represented by the following syntax:

Syntax

try-block :
  try *compound-statement handler-list*

handler-list :
  *handler handler-list*_{opt}

handler :
  catch (*exception-declaration*) *compound-statement*

exception-declaration :
  type-specifier-list declarator
  type-specifier-list abstract-declarator
  type-specifier-list
  ...

throw-expression :
  throw *assignment-expression*_{opt}

The *compound-statement* after the **try** clause is the guarded section of code. The *throw-expression* throws an exception. The *compound-statement* after the **catch** clause is the exception handler, and catches the exception thrown by the **throw**-expression. The *exception-declaration* statement after the **catch** clause indicates the type of exception the clause handles. The type can be any valid data type, including a C++ class.

If the exception-declaration statement is an ellipsis (**...**), the **catch** clause handles any type of exception, including a C exception. Such a handler must be the last handler for its **try** block.

The operand of **throw** is syntactically similar to the operand of a **return** statement.

Microsoft Specific →

Microsoft C++ does not support the function **throw** signature mechanism, as described in section 15.5 of the ANSI C++ draft.
END Microsoft Specific

Type-Safe Exception Handling

C++ exception handling supports type-safe exception handlers. C exceptions are always identified by an **unsigned int**. With C++ exception handling, you can specify that exceptions of a particular type (including C++ objects) are caught by a handler that matches the type of the exception being thrown.

How It Works

Exceptions are typically thrown inside a guarded section of code known as a **try** block. Directly below the **try** block are a series of associated **catch** handlers. The C++ exception handling model is known as "non-resumable." Once the flow of program control has left the **try** block, it never returns to that block.

For example, this program detects failure of a memory allocation operation using the **new** operator. If **new** is successful, the **catch** handler is never executed:

```
#include <iostream.h>

int main()
{
    char *buf;
    try
    {
        buf = new char[512];
        if( buf == 0 )
            throw "Memory allocation failure!";
    }
    catch( char * str )
    {
        cout << "Exception raised: " << str << endl;
    }
    // ...
    return 0;
}
```

The operand of the **throw** expression specifies that an exception of type char * is being thrown. It is handled by a **catch** handler that expresses the ability to catch an exception of type char *. In the event of a memory allocation failure, this is the output from the preceding example:

```
Exception raised: Memory allocation failure!
```

If no exception is thrown during execution of a **try** block, the **catch** clause(s) that follow the **try** block are not executed. Execution continues at the statement after the last **catch** clause following the **try** block in which the exception was thrown. Control can only enter a **catch** handler through a thrown exception; never via a **goto** statement or a **case** label in a **switch** statement.

C++ Exceptions

The real power of C++ exception handling lies not only in its ability to deal with exceptions of varying types, but also in its ability to automatically call destructor functions during stack unwinding for all local objects constructed before the exception was thrown.

The context which exists between the **throw** site and the **catch** handler is referred to as the "exception stack frame." This frame may contain objects with destructor semantics. If an exception is thrown during execution of the guarded section or in any routine the guarded section calls (directly or indirectly), an exception object is created from the object created by the **throw** operand. (This implies that a copy constructor may be involved.) At this point, the compiler looks for a **catch** clause in a higher execution context that can handle an exception of the type thrown, or a **catch** handler that can handle any type of exception. The **catch** handlers are examined in order of their appearance following the **try** block. If no appropriate handler is found, the next dynamically enclosing **try** block is examined. This process continues until the outermost enclosing **try** block is examined.

If a matching handler is still not found, or if an exception occurs while unwinding, but before the handler gets control, the predefined run-time function **terminate** is called. If an exception occurs after throwing the exception, but before the unwind begins, the **terminate** function is called. You can install a custom termination function to handle such situations. For more information, see "Unhandled Exceptions" on page 100.

The following example demonstrates C++ exception handling using classes with destructor semantics. It declares two C++ classes; one (class CTest) for defining the exception object itself, and the second (class CDtorDemo) for demonstrating the destruction of a separate frame object during stack unwinding:

```
#include <iostream.h>

void MyFunc( void );
```

```
class CTest
{
public:
    CTest(){};
    ~CTest(){};
    const char *ShowReason() const { return "Exception in CTest class.";
}

};

class CDtorDemo
{
public:
    CDtorDemo();
    ~CDtorDemo();
};

CDtorDemo::CDtorDemo()
{
    cout << "Constructing CDtorDemo." << endl;
}

CDtorDemo::~CDtorDemo()
{
    cout << "Destructing CDtorDemo." << endl;
}

void MyFunc()
{

    CDtorDemo D;
    cout<< "In MyFunc(). Throwing CTest exception." << endl;
    throw CTest();
}

int main()
{
    cout << "In main." << endl;
    try
    {
        cout << "In try block, calling MyFunc()." << endl;
        MyFunc();
    }
    catch( CTest E )
    {
        cout << "In catch handler." << endl;
        cout << "Caught CTest exception type: ";
        cout << E.ShowReason() << endl;
    }
```

```
catch( char *str )
    {
        cout << "Caught some other exception: " << str << endl;
    }
    cout << "Back in main. Execution resumes here." << endl;
    return 0;

}
```

If a matching **catch** handler is found, and it catches by value, its formal parameter is initialized by copying the exception object. If it catches by reference, the parameter is initialized to refer to the exception object. After the formal parameter is initialized, the process of "unwinding the stack" begins. This involves the destruction of all automatic objects that were constructed (but not yet destructed) between the beginning of the **try** block associated with the **catch** handler and the exception's throw site. Destruction occurs in reverse order of construction. The **catch** handler is executed and the program resumes execution following the last handler (that is, the first statement or construct which is not a **catch** handler).

This is the output from the preceding example:

```
In main.
In try block, calling MyFunc().
Constructing CDtorDemo.
In MyFunc(). Throwing CTest exception.
Destructing CDtorDemo.
In catch handler.
Caught CTest exception type: Exception in CTest class.
Back in main. Execution resumes here.
```

Note the declaration of the exception parameter in both **catch** handlers:

```
catch( CTest E )
{ // ... }
catch( char *str )
{ // ... }
```

You do not need to declare this parameter; in many cases it may be sufficient to notify the handler that a particular type of exception has occurred. However, if you do not declare an exception object in the exception declaration, you will not have access to the object in the **catch** handler clause. For example:

```
catch( CTest )
{
    // No access to a CTest exception object in this handler.
}
```

A **throw** expression with no operand re-throws the exception currently being handled. Such an expression should appear only in a **catch** handler or in a function called from within a **catch** handler. The re-thrown exception object is the original exception object (not a copy). For example:

```
try
{
    throw CSomeOtherException();
}
catch(...)        // Handle all exceptions
{
    // Respond (perhaps only partially) to exception
    //...

    throw;        // Pass exception to some other handler
}
```

Catchable Types

Because C++ enables you to throw exceptions of any type, you need to determine which **catch** handlers can catch an exception of a specific class type. A C++ exception can be caught by a **catch** handler that specifies the same type as the thrown exception, or by a handler that can catch any type of exception. An exception can also be caught by a **catch** handler that uses a reference to the same type as the thrown exception.

If the type of thrown exception is a class, which also has a base class (or classes), it can be caught by handlers that accept base classes of the exception's type, as well as references to bases of the exception's type. Note that when an exception is caught by a reference, it is bound to the actual thrown exception object; otherwise, it is a copy (much the same as an argument to a function).

When an exception is thrown, it may be caught by the following types of **catch** handlers:

- A handler that can accept any type (using the ellipsis syntax).
- A handler that accepts the same type as the exception object; since it is a copy, **const** and **volatile** modifiers are ignored.
- A handler that accepts a reference to the same type as the exception object.
- A handler that accepts a reference to a **const** or **volatile** form of the same type as the exception object.
- A handler that accepts a base class of the same type as the exception object; since it is a copy, **const** and **volatile** modifiers are ignored. The **catch** handler for a base class must not precede the **catch** handler for the derived class.

- A handler that accepts a reference to a base class of the same type as the exception object.

- A handler that accepts a reference to a **const** or **volatile** form of a base class of the same type as the exception object.

- A handler that accepts a pointer to which a thrown pointer object can be converted via standard pointer conversion rules.

Unhandled Exceptions

If a matching **catch** handler (or ellipsis **catch** handler) cannot be found for the current exception, the predefined **terminate** run-time function is called. (You can also explicitly call **terminate** in any of your handlers.) The default action of **terminate** is to call **abort**. If you want `terminate` to call some other function in your program before exiting the application, call the **set_terminate** function with the name of the function to be called as its single argument. You can call **set_terminate** at any point in your program. The **terminate** routine always calls the last function given as an argument to **set_terminate**.

The following example code throws a `char *` exception, but does not contain a handler designated to catch exceptions of type `char *`. The call to `set_terminate` instructs `terminate` to call `term_func`:

```
#include <eh.h>        // For function prototypes
#include <iostream.h>
#include <process.h>

void term_func()
{
    //...
    cout << "term_func was called by terminate." << endl;
    exit( -1 );
}
int main()
{
    try
    {
        // ...
        set_terminate( term_func );
        // ...
        throw "Out of memory!"; // No catch handler for this exception
    }
    catch( int )
    {
        cout << "Integer exception raised." << endl;
    }
    return 0;
}
```

After performing any desired cleanup tasks, the term_func function should terminate the program or current thread, ideally by calling exit. If it doesn't, and instead returns to its caller, abort is called.

Order of Handlers

The order in which **catch** handlers appear is significant, because handlers for a given **try** block are examined in order of their appearance. For example, it is an error to place the handler for a base class before the handler for a derived class. Once a matching **catch** handler is found, subsequent handlers are not examined. As a result, an ellipsis **catch** handler must be the last handler for its **try** block. For example:

```
// ...
try
{
    // ...
}
catch( ... )
{
    // Handle exception here.
}
// Error: the next two handlers are never examined.
catch( const char * str )
{
    cout << "Caught exception: " << str << endl;
}
catch( CExcptClass E )
{
    // Handle CExcptClass exception here.
}
```

In this example, the ellipsis **catch** handler is the only handler that is examined.

Mixing C and C++ Exceptions

If you want to write more portable code, using structured exception handling in a C++ program is not recommended. However, you may sometimes want to mix C and C++ source code, and need some facility for handling both kinds of exceptions. Because a structured exception handler has no concept of objects or typed exceptions, it cannot handle exceptions thrown by C++ code; however, C++ **catch** handlers can handle C exceptions. As such, C++ exception handling syntax (**try**, **throw**, **catch**) is not accepted by the C compiler, but structured exception handling syntax (**__try**, **__except**, **__finally**) is supported by the C++ compiler.

If you mix C and C++ exceptions, note the following:

1. C++ exceptions and C exceptions cannot be mixed within the same function.
2. Termination handlers (**_ _finally** blocks) are always executed, even during unwinding after an exception is thrown.
3. C++ exception handling can catch and preserve unwind semantics in all modules compiled with the /GX compiler option (this option enables unwind semantics).
4. There may be some situations in which destructor functions are not called for all objects. For example, if a C exception occurs while attempting to make a function call through an uninitialized function pointer, and that function takes as parameters objects that were constructed before the call, those objects will not be destructed during stack unwind.

Exception Handling Differences

The major difference between structured exception handling and C++ exception handling is that the C++ exception handling model deals in types, while the C structured exception handling model deals with exceptions of one type; specifically, **unsigned int**. That is, C exceptions are identified by an unsigned integer value, whereas C++ exceptions are identified by data type. When an exception is raised in C, each possible handler executes a filter, which examines the C exception context and determines whether to accept the exception, pass it to some other handler, or ignore it. When an exception is thrown in C++, it may be of any type.

A second difference is that the C structured exception handling model is referred to as "asynchronous," in that exceptions occur secondary to the normal flow of control. The C++ exception handling mechanism is fully "synchronous," which means that exceptions occur only when they are thrown.

If a C exception is raised in a C++ program, it can be handled by a structured exception handler with its associated filter, or by a C++ **catch** handler, whichever is dynamically nearest to the exception context. For example, the following C++ program raises a C exception inside a C++ **try** context:

```
#include <iostream.h>

void SEHFunc( void );

int main()
{
    try
    {
        SEHFunc();
    }
    catch( ... )
    {
        cout << "Caught a C exception."<< endl;
    }
```

```
        return 0;
}
void SEHFunc()
{
    __try
    {
        int x, y = 0;
        x = 5 / y;
    }
    __finally
    {
        cout << "In finally." << endl;
    }
}
```

This is the output from the preceding example:

```
In finally.
Caught a C exception.
```

C Exception Wrapper Class

In a simple example like this, the C exception can be caught only by an ellipsis (...) **catch** handler. No information about the type or nature of the exception is communicated to the handler. While this method works, in some cases you may need to define a transformation between the two exception handling models so that each C exception is associated with a specific class. To do this, you can define a C exception "wrapper" class, which can be used or derived from to attribute a specific class type to a C exception. By doing so, each C exception can be handled by a C++ **catch** handler in more discrete ways than the preceding example.

Your wrapper class might have an interface consisting of some member functions that determine the value of the exception, and for accessing the extended exception context information provided by the C exception model. You might also want to define a default constructor and a constructor that accepts an unsigned int argument (to provide for the underlying C exception representation), and a bitwise copy constructor. The following is a possible implementation of a C exception wrapper class:

```
class SE_Exception
{
private:
    unsigned int nSE;
protected:
    SE_Exception( unsigned int n ) : nSE( n ) {}
```

```
public:
    SE_Exception() {}
    SE_Exception( SE_Exception& ) {}
    ~SE_Exception() {}
    unsigned int getSeNumber() { return nSE; }
};
```

To use this class, you install a custom C exception translator function which is called by the internal exception handling mechanism each time a C exception is thrown. Within your translator function, you can throw any typed exception (perhaps an SE_Exception type, or a class type derived from SE_Exception), which can be caught by an appropriate matching C++ **catch** handler. The translator function can simply return, which indicates that it did not handle the exception. If the translator function itself raises a C exception, **terminate** is called.

To specify a custom translation function, call the **_set_se_translator** function with the name of your translation function as its single argument. The translator function that you write is called once for each function invocation on the stack that has **try** blocks. There is no default translator function; if you do not specify one by calling **_set_se_translator**, the C exception can only be caught by an ellipsis **catch** handler.

For example, the following code installs a custom translation function, then raises a C exception which is wrapped by the SE_Exception class:

```
#include <stdio.h>
#include <eh.h>
#include <windows.h>

class SE_Exception {
private:
    unsigned int nSE;
protected:
    SE_Exception(unsigned int n) : nSE(n) {}
public:
    SE_Exception() {}
    SE_Exception( SE_Exception& ) {}
    ~SE_Exception() {}
    unsigned int getSeNumber() { return nSE; }
};

void SEFunc(void);
void trans_func( unsigned, _EXCEPTION_POINTERS*);

int main()
{
    _set_se_translator( trans_func );
    try
    {
        SEFunc();
```

```
        }
        catch( SE_Exception e )
        {
            printf( "Caught a __try exception with SE_Exception.\n" );
            printf( "nSE = 0x%x\n", e.getSeNumber() );
        }
        return 0;
}
void SEFunc()
{
    __try
    {
        int x, y=0;
        x = 5 / y;
    }
    __finally
    {
        printf( "In finally\n" );
    }
}
void trans_func( unsigned int u, _EXCEPTION_POINTERS* pExp )
{
    printf( "In trans_func.\n" );
    throw SE_Exception( u );
}
```

Exception Handling Overhead

There is a certain amount of extra overhead associated with the C++ exception handling mechanism, which may increase the size of executable files and slow program execution time. The /GX compiler option enables C++ exception handling and unwind semantics. If you are not using C++ exception handling in your program and you want to eliminate the associated overhead, you can use the /GX- compiler option to turn off exception handling and unwind semantics. Note that /GX- is the default.

Due to the nature of exception handling and the extra overhead involved, exceptions should be used only to signal the occurrence of unusual or unanticipated program events. Exception handlers should not be used to redirect the program's normal flow of control. For example, an exception should not be thrown in cases of potential logic or user input errors, such as the overflow of an array boundary. In these cases, simply returning an error code may be cleaner and more concise. Judicious use of exception handling constructs makes your program easier to maintain, and your code more readable.

For more information about C++ exception handling, see the *C++ Annotated Reference Manual* by Margaret Ellis and Bjarne Stroustrup.

CHAPTER 8

Structured Exception Handling

Windows NT supports a robust approach to handling exceptions, called structured exception handling, which involves cooperation of the operating system but also has direct support in the programming language.

You can write more reliable code with structured exception handling. You can ensure that resources, such as memory blocks and files, are properly closed in the event of unexpected termination. You can also handle specific problems, such as insufficient memory, with concise, structured code that doesn't rely on **goto** statements or elaborate testing of return codes.

Note This chapter describes structured exception handling for the C programming language. Although structured exception handling can also be used with C++, the new C++ exception handling method should be used for C++ programs. See the section, "Using Structured Exception Handling with C++" for information on special considerations. For more information on C++ exception handling, see Chapter 7, "C++ Exception Handling".

Overview of Structured Exception Handling

An "exception" is an event that is unexpected or disrupts the ability of the process to proceed normally. Exceptions can be detected by both hardware and software. Hardware exceptions include dividing by zero and overflow of a numeric type. Software exceptions include those you detect and signal to the system by calling the **RaiseException** function, and special situations detected by Windows NT.

How Structured Exception Handling Works

The traditional approach to exception handling involves passing error codes: one function detects an error and passes an error code to its caller. This process may continue through many levels, until the error is communicated to the function that can properly respond to the error. If there is a weak link in the chain of function calls, the whole procedure fails.

Structured exception handling avoids this propagation of error codes. Its distinctive feature is that after an exception handler is installed, it can handle the exception no matter how many other functions are called. Thus, function A can handle an exception raised inside a function called by A.

Exception Handlers and Termination Handlers

The previous section used the term "exception handlers" in a generic sense, but there are actually two kinds:

- Exception handlers, which can respond to or dismiss the exception.
- Termination handlers, which are called when an exception causes termination inside a block of code.

These two types of handlers are distinct, yet they are closely related through a process called "unwinding the stack." When an exception occurs, Windows NT looks for the most recently installed exception handler that is currently active. The handler can do one of three things:

- Pass control to other handlers (fail to recognize exception).
- Recognize but dismiss the exception.
- Recognize and handle the exception.

The exception handler that recognizes the exception may not be in the function that was running when the exception occurred. In some cases it may be in a function much higher on the stack. The currently running function, as well as all functions on the stack frame, are terminated. During this process, the stack is "unwound": local variables of terminated functions, unless they are **static**, are cleared from the stack.

As it unwinds the stack, the operating system calls any termination handlers you've written for each function. Use of a termination handler gives you a chance to clean up resources that otherwise would remain open due to abnormal termination. If you've entered a critical section, you can exit in the termination handler. If the program is going to shut down, you can perform other housekeeping tasks such as closing and removing temporary files.

Writing an Exception Handler

Exception handlers are typically used to respond to specific errors. You can use the exception-handling syntax to filter out all exceptions other than those you know how to handle. Other exceptions should be passed to other handlers (possibly in the run-time library or the operating system) written to look for those specific exceptions.

Syntax of Exception Handlers

The structure for C exception handlers is shown in the following syntax:

__try {
  statement-block-1
}
__except (*filter*) {
  statement-block-2
}

The statements in *statement-block-1* are executed unconditionally. During execution of *statement-block-1*, the exception handler defined by *filter* and *statement-block-2* is active (it becomes the current exception handler).

If an exception occurs during execution of *statement-block-1*, including any function called directly or indirectly, the system gives control to the current exception handler—unless a handler with higher precedence takes control.

For example, in the following code, the first exception is handled by the outer block, because it is outside the scope of the inner **__try** block. The second exception is handled by the inner block, which takes precedence.

```
__try {
    float x, y=0;
    x = 5 / y;        // This exception handled by outer block
    __try {
        x = 0;
        y = 27 / x; // This exception handled by inner block
    }
    __except( GetExceptionCode() == STATUS_FLOATING_DIVIDE_BY_ZERO) {
        printf("handled by inner block");
    }
}
__except( GetExceptionCode() == STATUS_FLOATING_DIVIDE_BY_ZERO ) {
    printf( "handled by outer block" );
}
```

This code shows an example of nested exception handlers. Note that calling a function that has a **try-except** block has the same effect as nesting; the **try-except** block in the most recently called function takes precedence.

When an exception handler takes control, the system first evaluates the *filter*. One of the powerful features of structured exception handling is that although *filter* is evaluated out of normal program sequence (often during execution of another function), *filter* can refer to local variables within its scope just as any C expression. After *filter* is evaluated, the next action depends on the value returned.

Value of filter	Description
EXCEPTION_CONTINUE_SEARCH (0)	Passes control to exception handler with next highest precedence. The handler has declined to recognize the exception.
EXCEPTION_CONTINUE_EXECUTION(−1)	Dismisses exception, and continues execution at the location where the exception was raised.
EXCEPTION_EXECUTE_HANDLER (1)	Handles exception by executing statements in *statement-block-2*. Execution then falls through to the end of this statement block.

If the value of *filter* is EXCEPTION_EXECUTE_HANDLER, execution does not resume where the exception was raised, but falls through to the end of *statement-block-2* after it is executed. All blocks and function calls nested inside *statement-block-1* are terminated before *statement-block-2* is entered.

Writing an Exception Filter

You can handle an exception either by jumping to the level of the exception handler or by continuing execution. Instead of using *statement-block-2* to handle the exception and falling through, you can use *filter* to clean up the problem and then, by returning−1, resume normal flow without clearing the stack.

Note Some exceptions cannot be continued. If *filter* evaluates to −1 for such an exception, the system raises a new exception. When you call **RaiseException**, you determine whether the exception will continue.

For example, the following code uses a function call in the *filter* expression: this function handles the problem and then returns −1 to resume normal flow of control:

```
main ()
{
    int Eval_Exception( void );

    __try {
    ...
    }
    __except ( Eval_Exception( GetExceptionCode( ))) {
        // No code; this block never executed.
}
...
}

int Eval_Exception ( int n_except )
{
```

```
        if ( n_except != STATUS_INTEGER_OVERFLOW &&
            n_except != STATUS_FLOATING_OVERFLOW )      // Pass on most
            return EXCEPTION_CONTINUE_SEARCH;              //  exceptions

        // Execute some code to clean up problem

        ResetVars( 0 );     // ResetVars -- example function to initialize
                            //  data to 0
        return EXCEPTION_CONTINUE_EXECUTION;
}
```

It's a good idea to use a function call in the *filter* expression whenever *filter* needs to do anything complex. Evaluating the expression causes execution of the function, in this case, Eval_Exception.

Note the use of **GetExceptionCode** to determine the exception. You must call this function inside the filter itself. Eval_Exception cannot call **GetExceptionCode**, but it must have the exception code passed to it.

This handler passes control to another handler unless the exception is an integer or floating-point overflow. If it is, the handler calls a function (ResetVars is only an example, not an API function) to reset some global variables. *Statement-block-2*, which in this example is empty, can never be executed because Eval_Exception never returns EXCEPTION_EXECUTE_HANDLER (1).

Using a function call is a good general-purpose technique for dealing with complex filter expressions. Two other C language features that are useful are:

- The conditional operator
- The comma operator

The conditional operator is frequently useful, because it can be used to check for a specific return code and then return one of two different values. For example, the filter in the following code recognizes the exception only if the exception is STATUS_INTEGER_OVERFLOW:

```
__except( GetExceptionCode() == STATUS_INTEGER_OVERFLOW ? 1 : 0 ) {
```

The purpose of the conditional operator in this case is mainly to provide clarity, because the following code produces the same results:

```
__except( GetExceptionCode() == STATUS_INTEGER_OVERFLOW ) {
```

The conditional operator is more useful in situations where you might want the filter to evaluate to −1, EXCEPTION_CONTINUE_EXECUTION.

Another useful C language feature is the comma operator, which enables you to perform multiple, independent operations inside a single expression. The effect is roughly that of executing multiple statements and then returning the value of the last expression. For example, the following code stores the exception code in a variable and then tests it:

```
__except( nCode = GetExceptionCode(), nCode == STATUS_INTEGER_OVERFLOW )
```

Raising Software Exceptions

Some of the most common sources of program errors are not flagged as exceptions by the system. For example, if you attempt to allocate a memory block but there is insufficient memory, the run-time or API function does not raise an exception but returns an error code.

However, you can treat any condition as an exception by detecting that condition in your code and then reporting it by calling the **RaiseException** function. By flagging errors this way, you can bring the advantages of structured exception handling to any kind of run-time error.

To use structured exception handling with errors you define:

- Define your own exception code for the event.

- Call **RaiseException** when you detect a problem.

- Use exception-handling filters to test for the exception code you defined.

The WINERROR.H file shows the format for exception codes. To make sure that you do not define a code that conflicts with an existing exception code, set the third most significant bit to 1. The four most-significant bits should be set as shown in the following table.

Bits	Recommended binary setting	Description
31-30	11	These two bits describe the basic status of the code: 11 = error, 00 = success, 01 = informational, 10 = warning.
29	1	Client bit. Set to 1 for user-defined codes.
28	0	Reserved bit. (Leave set to 0.)

You can set the first two bits to a setting other than 11 binary if you want, although the "error" setting is appropriate for most exceptions. The important thing to remember is to set bits 29 and 28 as shown in the table.

The resulting error code should therefore have the highest four bits set to hexadecimal E. For example, the following definitions define exception codes that do not conflict with any Windows NT exception codes. (You may, however, need to check which codes are used by third-party DLLs.)

```
#define STATUS_INSUFFICIENT_MEM     0xE0000001
#define STATUS_FILE_BAD_FORMAT      0xE0000002
```

After you have defined an exception code, you can use it to raise an exception. For example, the following code raises the STATUS_INSUFFICIENT_MEM exception in response to a memory allocation problem:

```
lpstr = _malloc( nBufferSize );
if (lpstr == NULL)
    RaiseException( STATUS_INSUFFICIENT_MEM, 0, 0, 0);
```

If you want to simply raise an exception, you can set the last three parameters to 0. The three last parameters are useful for passing additional information and setting a flag that prevents handlers from continuing execution. See the *Windows NT Programmer's Reference* for more information on the **RaiseException** function.

In your exception-handling filters, you can then test for the codes you've defined. For example:

```
__try {
    ...
}
__except (GetExceptionCode() == STATUS_INSUFFICIENT_MEM ||
        GetExceptionCode() == STATUS_FILE_BAD_FORMAT )
```

Hardware Exceptions

Most of the standard exceptions recognized by the operating system are hardware-defined exceptions. Windows NT recognizes a few low-level software exceptions, but these are usually best handled by Windows NT.

Windows NT maps the hardware errors of different processors to the exception codes in this section. In some cases, a processor may generate only a subset of these exceptions. Windows NT preprocesses information about the exception and issues the appropriate exception code.

The hardware exceptions recognized by Windows NT are summarized in the following table:

Exception code	Cause of exception
STATUS_ACCESS_VIOLATION	Reading or writing to an inaccessible memory location.
STATUS_BREAKPOINT	Encountering a hardware-defined breakpoint; used only by debuggers.
STATUS_DATATYPE_MISALIGNMENT	Reading or writing to data at an address that is not properly aligned; for example, 16-bit entities must be aligned on 2-byte boundaries. (Not applicable to Intel 80x86 processors.)
STATUS_FLOATING_DIVIDE_BY_ZERO	Dividing floating-point type by 0.0.
STATUS_FLOATING_OVERFLOW	Exceeding maximum positive exponent of floating-point type.
STATUS_FLOATING_UNDERFLOW	Exceeding magnitude of lowest negative exponent of floating-point type.
STATUS_FLOATING_RESEVERED_OPERAND	Using a reserved floating-point format (invalid use of format).
STATUS_ILLEGAL_INSTRUCTION	Attempting to execute an instruction code not defined by the processor.
STATUS_PRIVILEGED_INSTRUCTION	Executing an instruction not allowed in current machine mode.
STATUS_INTEGER_DIVIDE_BY_ZERO	Dividing an integer type by 0.
STATUS_INTEGER_OVERFLOW	Attempting an operation that exceeds the range of the integer.
STATUS_SINGLE_STEP	Executing one instruction in single-step mode; used only by debuggers.

Many of the exceptions listed in this table are intended to be handled by debuggers, the operating system, or other low-level code. With the exception of integer and floating-point errors, your code should not handle these errors. Thus, you should usually use the exception-handling filter to ignore exceptions (evaluate to 0). Otherwise, you may prevent lower-level mechanisms from responding appropriately.

You can, however, take appropriate precautions against the potential effect of these low-level errors by writing termination handlers as described later in this chapter.

Restrictions on Exception Handlers

The principal limitation to using exception handlers in code is that you cannot use a **goto** statement to jump into a **__try** statement block. Instead, you must enter the statement block through normal flow of control. You can jump out of a **__try** statement block and nest exception handlers as you choose.

You also cannot nest an exception handler or termination handler inside an **__except** block.

Writing a Termination Handler

Unlike an exception handler, a termination handler is always executed, regardless of whether the protected block of code terminated normally. The sole purpose of the termination handler should be to ensure that resources, such as memory, handles, and files, are properly closed regardless of how a section of code finishes executing.

Syntax of Termination Handlers

The structure of a termination handler is shown in the following syntax:

```
__try {
    statement-block-1
}
__finally {
    statement-block-2

}
```

The statements in *statement-block-1* are executed unconditionally. The statements in *statement-block-2* are always executed, in one of two ways:

- If *statement-block-1* finishes execution normally, *statement-block-2* is then executed.

- If *statement-block-1* is prematurely terminated for any reason, including a jump out of the block, the system executes *statement-block-2* as a part of the process of unwinding the stack.

In the second case, the **AbnormalTermination** function returns TRUE if called from within *statement-block-2*; otherwise, it returns FALSE.

If *statement-block-1* was abnormally terminated, the termination handler is executed as a part of the process of unwinding the stack. If control jumps outside of several blocks of code at once, the system clears the stack frame for each block of code or function exited, starting with the lowest (most deeply-nested) stack frame. As each frame is cleared, the system executes its termination handler.

For example, suppose a series of function calls links function A to function D, as shown in Figure 8.1. Each function has one termination handler. If an exception is raised in function D and handled in A, the termination handlers are called in this order as the system unwinds the stack: D, C, B.

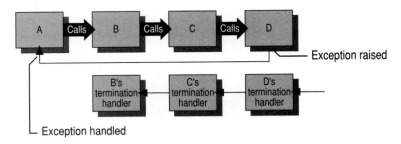

Figure 8.1   Order of Termination-Handler Execution

Cleaning up Resources

During termination-handler execution, you may not know which resources are actually allocated before the termination handler was called. It is possible that the _ _**try** statement block was interrupted before all resources were allocated, so that not all resources were opened.

Therefore, to be safe, you should check to see which resources are actually open before proceeding with termination-handling clean-up. A recommended procedure is to:

1. Initialize handles to NULL.

2. In the _ _**try** statement block, allocate resources. Handles are set to positive values as the resource is allocated.

3. In the _ _**finally** statement block, release each resource whose corresponding handle or flag variable is nonzero or not NULL.

For example, the following code uses a termination handler to close three files and a memory block that were allocated in the **__try** statement block. Before cleaning up a resource, the code first checks to see if the resource was allocated.

```
void    FileOps()
{
    FILE *fp1, *fp2, *fp3;
    LPVOID lpvoid;

    lpvoid = fp1 = fp2 = fp3 = NULL;
    __try {
        lpvoid = malloc( BUFFERSIZE );
        fp1 = fopen( "ADDRESS.DAT", "w+" );
        fp2 = fopen( "NAMES.DAT", "w+" );
        fp3 = fopen( "CARS.DAT", "w+" );
        .
        .
        .
    }
    __finally {
        if ( fp1 ) fclose( fp1 );
        if ( fp2 ) fclose( fp2 );
        if ( fp3 ) fclose( fp3 );
        if ( lpvoid ) free( lpvoid );
    }
}
```

Timing of Exception Handling: A Summary

A termination handler is executed no matter how the **__try** statement block is terminated. Causes include jumping out of the **__try** block, a **longjmp** statement that transfers control out of the block, and unwinding the stack due to exception handling.

Note   Visual C++ for Windows NT supports two forms of the **setjmp** and **longjmp** statements. The fast version bypasses termination handling but is more efficient. To use this version, include the file SETJMP.H. The other version supports termination handling as described in the previous paragraph. To use this version, include the file SETJMPEX.H. The increase in performance of the fast version depends on hardware configuration.

The operating system executes all termination handlers in the proper order before any other code can be executed, including the body of an exception handler.

When the cause for interruption is an exception, the system must first execute the filter portion of one or more exception handlers before deciding what to terminate. The order of events is:

1. An exception is raised.
2. The system looks at the hierarchy of active exception handlers and executes the filter of the handler with highest precedence; this is the exception handler most recently installed and most deeply nested, in terms of blocks and function calls.
3. If this filter passes control (returns 0), the process continues until a filter is found that does not pass control.
4. If this filter returns −1, execution continues where the exception was raised, and no termination takes place.
5. If the filter returns 1, the following events occur:
    *   The system unwinds the stack, clearing all stack frames between the currently executing code (where the exception was raised) and the stack frame that contains the exception handler gaining control.
    *   As the stack is unwound, each termination handler on the stack is executed.
    *   The exception handler itself is executed.
    *   Control passes to the line of code after the end of this exception handler.

Restrictions on Termination Handlers

You cannot use a **goto** statement to jump into a __**try** statement block or a __**finally** statement block. Instead, you must enter the statement block through normal flow of control. (You can, however, jump out of a __**try** statement block.) Also, you cannot nest an exception handler or termination handler inside a __**finally** block.

In addition, some kinds of code permitted in a termination handler produce questionable results, so you should use them with caution, if at all. One is a **goto** statement that jumps out of a __**finally** statement block. If the block is executing as part of normal termination, nothing unusual happens. But if the system is unwinding the stack, that unwinding stops, and the current function gains control as if there were no abnormal termination.

A **return** statement inside a __**finally** statement block presents roughly the same situation. Control returns to the immediate caller of the function containing the termination handler. If the system was unwinding the stack, this process is halted, and the program proceeds as if there had been no exception raised.

Using Structured Exception Handling with C++

Structured exception handling described in this chapter works with both C and C++ source files. However, it is not specifically designed for C++, and is not recommended. You can ensure that your code is more portable by using C++ exception handling. Also, the C++ exception handling mechanism is more flexible, in that it can handle exceptions of any type.

Microsoft C++ now supports the C++ exception handling model, based on the ISO WG21/ANSI X3J16 working papers towards the evolving standard for C++. This mechanism automatically handles destruction of local objects during stack unwind. If you are writing fault-tolerant C++ code, and you want to implement exception handling, it is strongly recommended that you use C++ exception handling, rather than structured exception handling. (Note that while the C++ compiler supports structured exception handling constructs as described in this chapter, the standard C compiler does not support the C++ exception handling syntax.) For detailed information about C++ exception handling, see Chapter 7, "C++ Exception Handling," Chapter 5 of the *C++ Language Reference*, and the *Annotated C++ Reference Manual* by Margaret Ellis and Bjarne Stroustrup.

C H A P T E R   9

Using Calling Conventions

The Visual C/C++ compiler provides several ways to call internal and external functions. The information in this chapter can help you debug your program and interface your code with assembly-language routines.

This chapter covers the differences between the calling conventions, how arguments are passed, and how values are returned by functions. It also discusses naked function calls, an advanced feature that enables you to write your own prolog and epilog code.

Argument Passing and Naming Conventions

All arguments are widened to 32 bits when they are passed. Return values are also widened to 32 bits and returned in the EAX register, except for 8-byte structures, which are returned in the EDX:EAX register pair. Larger structures are returned in the EAX register as pointers to hidden return structures. Parameters are pushed onto the stack from right to left.

The compiler generates prolog and epilog code to save and restore the ESI, EDI, EBX, and EBP registers, if they are used in the function.

Note For information on how to define your own function prolog and epilog code see "Naked Functions" on page 126.

The following calling conventions are supported by the Visual C/C++ compiler.

Keyword	Stack clean-up	Parameter passing
__cdecl	Caller	Pushes parameters on the stack, in reverse order (right to left)
__stdcall	Callee	Pushes parameters on the stack, in reverse order (right to left)
__fastcall	Callee	Stored in registers, then pushed on stack
thiscall (not a keyword)	Callee	Pushed on stack; **this** pointer stored in ECX

__cdecl

This is the default calling convention for C and C++ programs. Because the stack is cleaned up by the caller, it can do **vararg** functions. The **__cdecl** calling convention creates larger executables than **__stdcall**, because it requires each function call to include stack clean-up code.

All function arguments are pushed on the stack. In C, the **__cdecl** function names are prefixed by an underscore when decorated.

Note For more information on decorated names, see your C++ compiler documentation and Appendix J of the *Visual C++ User's Guide*.

__stdcall

The **__stdcall** calling convention is used to call Win32 API functions. The callee cleans the stack, so the compiler makes **vararg** functions **__cdecl**. Functions that use this calling convention require a function prototype.

All function arguments are pushed on the stack. In C, the **__stdcall** function names are prefixed by an underscore and suffixed with **@***number* when decorated, where *number* is the number of bytes (in decimal) used by the widened arguments pushed to the stack.

__fastcall

The **__fastcall** calling convention is similar to the **__stdcall** calling convention, but **__fastcall** speeds function calling by storing up to two arguments in the ECX and EDX registers. Any additional arguments are pushed to the stack as in the other calling conventions.

In C, the __**fastcall** function names are prefixed by the at sign (@) and suffixed with **@*number*** when decorated, where *number* is the number of bytes (in decimal) used by the widened arguments pushed to the stack plus the number of bytes taken by the widened arguments passed in registers.

Note Future compiler versions may use different registers to store parameters.

thiscall

This is the default calling convention used by C++ member functions that do not use variable arguments. The callee cleans the stack, so the compiler makes **vararg** functions __**cdecl,** and pushes the **this** pointer on the stack last. The *thiscall* calling convention cannot be explicitly specified in a program, because *thiscall* is not a keyword.

All function arguments are pushed on the stack. Because this calling convention applies only to C++, there is no C name decoration scheme.

Obsolete Calling Conventions

The __**pascal**, __**fortran**, and __**syscall** calling conventions are no longer supported. You can emulate their functionality by using one of the supported calling conventions and appropriate linker options.

WINDOWS.H now supports the **WINAPI** macro, which translates to the appropriate calling convention for the target. Use **WINAPI** where you previously used **PASCAL** or __**far** __**pascal**.

Calling Example: Function Prototype and Call

The following example shows the results of making a function call using various calling conventions.

This example is based on the following function skeleton. Replace *calltype* with the appropriate calling convention.

```
void    calltype MyFunc( char c, short s, int i, double f );
    .
    .
    .
```

```
void    MyFunc( char c, short s, int i, double f )
    {
     .
     .
     .
    }
 .
 .
 .
MyFunc ('x', 12, 8192, 2.7183);
```

Results

__cdecl

The C decorated function name is "_MyFunc." See your compiler documentation for the C++ decorated name.

Figure 9.1   The __cdecl calling convention

__stdcall and *thiscall*

The C decorated name (__**stdcall**) is "_MyFunc@20." See your compiler documentation for the C++ decorated name.

Figure 9.2   The __stdcall and *thiscall* calling conventions

__fastcall

The C decorated name (**__stdcall**) is "@MyFunc@20." See your compiler documentation for the C++ decorated name.

Figure 9.3   The __fastcall calling convention

Naked Functions

Functions declared with the **naked** attribute are emitted without prolog or epilog code, enabling you to write your own custom prolog/epilog sequences using inline assembler. Naked functions are provided as an advanced feature. They enable you to declare a function that is being called from a context other than C/C++, and thus make different assumptions about where parameters are, or which registers are preserved. Examples include routines such as MS-DOS interrupt handlers. This feature is particularly useful for writers of virtual device drivers (VxDs).

Syntax

Because the **naked** attribute is not a type modifier, naked functions use the extended attribute syntax, as described previously. For example, the following code defines a function with the **naked** attribute:

```
__declspec( naked ) int func( formal_parameters )
{
    // Function body
}
```

Or, alternatively:

```
#define Naked  __declspec( naked )
Naked int func( formal_parameters )
{
    // Function body
}
```

The **naked** modifier affects only the nature of the compiler's code generation for the function's prolog and epilog sequences. It does not affect the code that is generated for calling such functions. Thus, the **naked** attribute is not considered part of the function's type. As such, function pointers cannot have the **naked** attribute. Furthermore, the **naked** attribute has no meaning when applied to a data definition. Any attempt to apply it to a data definition will generate a compiler error. For example, the following code samples will generate errors:

```
__declspec( naked ) int i;  // Error--naked attribute not permitted on
                            // data declarations.

extern __declspec( naked ) int i;   // Error--naked attribute not
                                    // permitted on data declarations.
```

The **naked** attribute is relevant only to the definition of the function. Thus it cannot be specified on the function's prototype. The following declaration will generate a compiler error:

```
__declspec( naked ) int func();  // Error--naked attribute not permitted
                                 // on function declarations.
```

A new symbolic argument for use in the inline assembler block of function prolog code is provided by the compiler. This symbol, **__LOCAL_SIZE**, is used to allocate space for local variables on the stack frame in your custom prolog code. This constant contains a value determined by the compiler, and represents the number of bytes of local variables.

__LOCAL_SIZE includes all user-defined locals as well as compiler-generated temporary variables. **__LOCAL_SIZE** may be used as an immediate operand or in an expression. For example:

```
mov     eax, __LOCAL_SIZE        /* Immediate operand */
mov     eax, __LOCAL_SIZE + 4    /* Expression */
mov     eax, [ebp - __LOCAL_SIZE]   /* Expression */
```

Rules and Limitations

The following rules and limitations apply to naked functions:

- The **return** statement is not permitted.
- Structured Exception Handling constructs are not permitted because they must unwind across the stack frame.
- For the same reason, any form of **setjmp** is prohibited.
- Use of the **_alloca** function is prohibited.
- To ensure that no initialization code for local variables appears before the prolog sequence, initialized local variables are not permitted at function scope. In particular, the declaration of C++ objects is not permitted at function scope. There may, however, be initialized data in a nested scope.
- Frame pointer optimization (the /Oy compiler option) is not recommended, but it is automatically suppressed for a naked function.
- You cannot declare C++ class objects at the function lexical scope. You can, however, declare objects in a nested block.

Naked Function Example

The following is a minimal example of a naked function containing custom prolog and epilog sequences:

```
__declspec ( naked ) func()
{
    int i;
    int j;

    _asm
        {
        push ebp
        mov     ebp, esp
        sub     esp, __LOCAL_SIZE
        }

    /* C and/or _asm code */

    _asm
        {
        mov     esp, ebp
        pop     ebp
        ret
        }
}
```

C H A P T E R   1 0

Programming with Mixed Languages

Mixed-language programming is the process of building programs in which the source code is written in two or more languages. Although mixed-language programming presents some additional challenges, it is worthwhile because it enables you to call existing code that may be written in another language.

Microsoft provides 32-bit versions of C, C++, MASM, and Fortran, and mixed-language programming is possible between all these languages. Mixed-language programming for Win32 is not the same as for 16-bit environments, but in many respects it is simpler.

Overview of Mixed-Language Issues

This section reviews basic concepts of mixed-language programming, and introduces relevant new Win32 features. For example, the **__stdcall** keyword replaces the **fortran** and **pascal** keywords in C modules. Another important aspect of Win32 is that all addresses are the same size, simplifying pass by reference. Thus, you may want to review this section even if you have written mixed-language programs extensively for MS-DOS.

Mixed-language programming is possible with Microsoft languages because each language implements functions, subroutines, and procedures in approximately the same way. Table 10.1 shows how different kinds of routines from each language equate to each other. For example, a C main program could call an external **void** function, which is actually implemented as a Fortran subroutine.

Table 10.1   Language Equivalents for Calls to Routines

Language	Call with return value	Call with no return value
Assembly language	Procedure	Procedure
C and C++	function	(**void**) function
Fortran	**FUNCTION**	**SUBROUTINE**

In this chapter, the term "routine" refers to functions, subroutines, and procedures from different languages. This definition does not include macros or inline functions, which are not implemented using the stack.

There are some important differences in the way languages implement these routines, however. This chapter presents a series of keywords, attributes, and techniques to reconcile these differences, which fall into three categories:

- Adjusting calling conventions
- Adjusting naming conventions
- Passing by value or by reference

In addition, you need to reconcile differences in the way individual data types (strings, arrays, common blocks, and so on) may be treated. This important and complex topic is discussed in the last section.

Adjusting Calling Conventions

The calling convention determines how a program makes a call and where the parameters are passed. In a single-language program, calling conventions are nearly always correct, because there is one default for all modules and because header files enforce consistency between the caller and the called routine. In a mixed-language program, different languages cannot share the same header files. It's easy to link Fortran and C modules that use different calling conventions, and the error isn't apparent until the bad call is made at run time, causing immediate program failure. Therefore, you should check calling conventions carefully for each mixed-language call.

Table 10.2 summarizes how C and Fortran calling conventions work.

Table 10.2   C and Fortran Calling Conventions

Calling convention	Parameter passing	Stack cleared by
C/C++	Pushes parameters on the stack, in reverse order (right to left)	Caller
Fortran (__stdcall)	Pushes parameters on the stack, in reverse order (right to left)	Called function

In C and C++ modules, you can specify the Fortran calling convention by using the **__stdcall** keyword in a function prototype or definition. The **__stdcall** convention is also used by window procedures and API functions. For example, the following C language prototype sets up a function call to a subroutine using the Fortran calling convention:

```
extern void __stdcall fortran_routine (int n);
```

Instead of changing the calling convention of the C code, you can adjust the Fortran source code by using the **C** attribute, enclosed in brackets ([ ]). For example, the following declaration assumes the subroutine is called with the C calling convention:

```
SUBROUTINE CALLED_FROM_C [C] (A)
INTEGER*4 A
```

It should be clear that calling conventions need only agree between individual calls and the called routines, and that the conventions must be the same: both caller and called routine must use the C/C++ convention or both must use the **_ _stdcall** convention (the Fortran default).

Note In programs written for the graphical user interface of Windows, **PASCAL**, **WINAPI**, and **CALLBACK** are all defined with **_ _stdcall**. But the C language default is still **cdecl**.

Table 10.3 summarizes how to specify calling conventions. You can always specify calling conventions explicitly rather than relying on the default, which is a good technique for mixed-language programming.

Table 10.3   Specifying Calling Conventions

Language	C calling convention	Fortran calling convention
C/C++	**cdecl** (default)	**_ _stdcall**
Fortran	**C** attribute	**STDCALL** attribute (default)

Adjusting Naming Conventions

The naming convention determines how a language alters a symbol name as it places the name in a .OBJ file. This is an issue for external data symbols shared between modules as well as external routines. Parameter names are never affected. The reasons for altering the name include case sensitivity or lack thereof, type decoration, and other issues. Note that you can always see exactly how a name has been placed in a .OBJ file by using the DUMPBIN utility with the–SYMBOLS option. If naming conventions are not reconciled, the program cannot successfully link. You will receive an "unresolved external" error.

Naming conventions are closely related to calling conventions because the keywords that specify calling conventions affect naming conventions as well. However, C/C++ preserves case sensitivity in its symbol tables and Fortran does not, which can necessitate some additional work on your part. Fortunately, you can use the Fortran **ALIAS** attribute to resolve any discrepancy in names.

Table 10.4 summarizes how C, Fortran, and C++ handle public names.

Table 10.4   Naming Conventions in C, Fortran, and C++

Language	Name translated as	Case of name in OBJ file
C, **cdecl** (default)	_name	Mixed case preserved
C, **__stdcall**	_name@nn	Mixed case preserved
Fortran [C]	_name	All lowercase
Fortran [STDCALL]	_name@nn	All lowercase
Fortran default	_name@nn	All uppercase
C++	_name@@decoration	Mixed case preserved

In Table 10.4, *nn* represents the stack space, in decimal notation, occupied by parameters. For example, assume a function is declared in C as

```
extern int __stdcall Sum_Up( int a, int b, int c );
```

Each integer occupies 4 bytes, so the symbol name placed in the .OBJ file is:

```
_Sum_Up@12
```

Case sensitivity can present a problem. The 32-bit linker always distinguishes case. The strategy you use to handle a discrepancy due to case depends on whether the situation involves:

- Calls from C to Fortran, where Fortran cannot be recompiled
- Symbol names that are all lowercase
- Mixed-case names

C Calls Using Fortran Names

If you call a Fortran routine from C and cannot recompile the Fortran code, and if the routine uses Fortran defaults, then you must use an all-uppercase name to make the call. Use of the **__stdcall** convention is not enough, because **__stdcall** (unlike the **fortran** keyword in 16-bit code) always preserves case. Fortran generates all-uppercase names by default and the C code must match it.

For example, this prototype sets up a call to a Fortran function ffarctan:

```
extern float __stdcall FFARCTAN( float angle );
```

All-Lowercase Names

If the name of the routine appears as all lowercase in C, then naming conventions are automatically correct when the **C** or **STDCALL** attribute is applied to the Fortran declaration. Any case may be used in the Fortran source code, including mixed case; the **C** and **STDCALL** attributes change the name to all lowercase. Note that this is a way in which **STDCALL** differs from the Fortran default behavior.

Mixed Case Names

If the name of the routine appears as mixed-case in C, and you cannot change the name, you can only resolve naming conflicts by using the Fortran **ALIAS** attribute. **ALIAS** is required in this situation so that Fortran will generate mixed-case names.

To use the **ALIAS** attribute, place the name in quotation marks exactly as it is to appear in the .OBJ file. For example, suppose you are calling a C function that has the following prototype:

```
extern void My_Proc (int i);
```

The Fortran call to this function should be declared with the following **INTERFACE** block:

```
INTERFACE TO SUBROUTINE My_Proc [C, ALIAS:'_My_Proc'] (I)
INTEGER*4 I
END
```

Note   When using the _ _stdcall convention, both Fortran and C should calculate parameter-space size by rounding each parameter upward to multiples of four (because it is more efficient to keep the stack-pointer aligned on 4-byte boundaries). Thus, the function Print_Nums which is passed a byte, a short, and a long integer should be translated as _Print_Nums@12. However, there is an early version of 32-bit Fortran that translates this as _Print_Nums@7, not rounding upward. To correct the discrepancy, use the **ALIAS** attribute.

Passing By Value or By Reference

Each individual parameter can be passed by value or by reference (which places the address of the parameter on the stack). In Fortran, C, and C++, all addresses are the same size (4 bytes), so there is no passing by near or far reference. You need to make sure that for every call, the calling program and the called routine agree on how each parameter is passed. Otherwise, the called routine receives bad data.

The C/C++ technique for passing parameters is always the same, regardless of calling convention: all parameters are passed by value, except for arrays, which are translated into the address of the first member. To pass data by reference, pass a pointer to it.

The Fortran technique for passing parameters changes depending on the calling convention specified. By default, Fortran passes all data by reference (except the hidden length argument of strings, which is a special case). If the **C** or **STDCALL** attribute is used, the default changes to passing all data by value.

In Fortran, use the **VALUE** and **REFERENCE** attributes to specify pass by value or pass by reference. In mixed-language programming, it is a good idea to always specify passing technique explicitly rather than relying on defaults. For example, the following C declaration sets up a call to a Fortran subroutine:

```
extern void __stdcall TESTPROC( int ValParm, int *RefParm );
```

In the following example, the definition of TESTPROC in Fortran declares how each parameter is passed. The **REFERENCE** attribute is not strictly necessary in this example, but using it is a good idea, in case you later change the calling convention.

```
SUBROUTINE TESTPROC( VALPARM, REFPARM )
INTEGER*4 VALPARM [VALUE]
INTEGER*4 REFPARM [REFERENCE]
END
```

Table 10.5 summarizes parameter-passing defaults. Note that an array name in C is equated to its starting address. Therefore arrays are passed by reference. To pass an array by value, declare a structure with the array as its only member.

Table 10.5   C/C++ and Fortran Defaults for Passing Parameters

Language	By value	By reference
C/C++	*variable*	* *variable*
Fortran	*variable* **[VALUE]**	*variable* **[REFERENCE]**, or *variable*
Fortran [C or STDCALL]	*variable* **[VALUE]**, or *variable*	*variable* **[REFERENCE]**
C/C++ arrays	**struct** { *type* } *variable*	*variable*

C Calls to Fortran

This section applies the principles in the section "Overview of Mixed-Language Issues" to a typical case involving one function call and one subroutine call from C to Fortran. Default conventions are assumed for Fortran, so adjustments are made to the C code.

The C main program uses the **__stdcall** keyword to call the Fortran routines with the correct calling convention. The C source must use all-uppercase names for the routines, because this Fortran code does not use the **C**, **STDCALL**, or **ALIAS** attributes. Finally, pass by value and pass by reference are specified explicitly, though pass by reference would have been assumed by default for Fortran.

```c
/*      File CMAIN.C   */

#include <stdio.h>

extern int __stdcall FACT (int n);
extern void __stdcall PYTHAGORAS (float a, float b, float *c);

main()
{
    float c;
    printf("Factorial of 7 is: %d\n", FACT(7));
    PYTHAGORAS (30, 40, &c);
    printf("Hypotenuse if sides 30, 40 is: %f\n", c);
}
```

```fortran
C    File FORSUBS.FOR
C
      INTEGER*4 FUNCTION Fact (n)
      INTEGER*4 n [VALUE]
      INTEGER*4 i, amt
      amt = 1
      DO i = 1, n
        amt = amt * i
      END DO
      Fact = amt
      END

      SUBROUTINE Pythagoras (a, b, c)
      REAL*4 a [VALUE]
      REAL*4 b [VALUE]
      REAL*4 c [REFERENCE]
      c = SQRT (a * a + b * b)
      END
```

Fortran Calls to C

This section applies the principles in the section "Overview of Mixed-Language Issues" to a typical case involving one function call and one subroutine call from Fortran to C. Default conventions are assumed for C, so adjustments are made to the Fortran code. The example in this section is the converse of that in the previous section.

The Fortran main program uses the **C** attribute to call the C functions with the correct calling convention. The **C** attribute causes Fortran to generate all-lowercase names, so the **ALIAS** attribute must be used to preserve mixed case. Finally, pass by value and pass by reference are specified explicitly, though pass by value would have been assumed because of the **C** attribute.

```
C   File FORMAIN.FOR
C
      INTERFACE TO INTEGER*4 FUNCTION Fact [C,ALIAS:'_Fact'] (n)
      INTEGER*4 n [VALUE]
      END

      INTERFACE TO SUBROUTINE Pythagoras [C,ALIAS:'_Pythagoras'] (a,b,c)
      REAL*4 a [VALUE]
      REAL*4 b [VALUE]
      REAL*4 c [REFERENCE]
      END

      INTEGER*4 Fact
      REAL*4 c
      WRITE (*,*) 'Factorial of 7 is ', Fact (7)
      CALL Pythagoras (30, 40, c)
      WRITE (*,*) 'Hypotenuse if sides 30, 40 is ', c
      END

/*  File CSUBS.C  */

#include <math.h>

int Fact( int n )
{
    if (n > 1)
        return( n * Fact( n - 1 ));
    return 1;
}

void Pythagoras( float a, float b, float *c)
{
    *c = sqrt( a * a + b * b );
}
```

Building the Mixed-Language Program

In Win32, the choice of libraries is much simpler than it is in 16-bit environments. Consequently, it is easier to build a mixed-language program. To link C and Fortran modules, use the Fortran linker; the linker should find the correct default libraries.

For example, the simple console applications featured in the previous sections require no special options. The CMAIN application can be created with the following commands:

```
cl /c cmain.c
fl32 cmain.obj forsubs.for
```

The FORMAIN application can be created with the following commands:

```
cl /c csubs.c
fl32 formain.for cmain.obj
```

Multithread applications should have full multithread support, so if you use LIBFMT.LIB, make sure that LIBCMT.LIB is specified as a default library as well.

Mixed-Language Programming with C++

C++ uses the same calling convention and parameter-passing techniques as C, but naming conventions are different because of C++ decoration of external symbols. The **extern "C"** syntax makes it possible for a C++ module to share data and routines with other languages, by causing C++ to drop name decoration.

The following example declares prn as an external function using the C naming convention. This declaration appears in C++ source code.

```
extern "C"
{
    void prn();
}
```

To call functions written in Fortran (or MASM), declare the function as you would in C and use a **"C"** linkage specification. For example, to call the Fortran function FACT from C++, declare it as follows:

```
extern "C" {    int __stdcall FACT( int n ); }
```

The **extern "C"** syntax can be used to adjust a call from C++ to other languages, or to change the naming convention of C++ routines called from other languages. However, **extern "C"** can only be used from within C++. If the C++ code does not use **extern "C"** and cannot be changed, you can call C++ routines only by determining the name decoration and generating it from the other language. You can always determine the decoration by using the DUMPBIN utility. Use this approach only as a last resort, because the decoration scheme is not guaranteed to remain the same between versions.

Use of **extern "C"** has some restrictions:

- You cannot declare a member function with **extern "C"**.
- You can specify **extern "C"** for only one instance of an overloaded function; all other instances of an overloaded function have C++ linkage.

For more information on the **extern "C"** linkage specification, see the *C++ Language Reference*.

Handling Data Types

Even when you've reconciled calling conventions, naming conventions, and parameter passing technique (pass by value or pass by reference), it is still possible to pass data incorrectly, because each language has different ways of handling data types. The following sections describe how to pass each type of data between languages.

Numeric Data Types

Normally, passing numeric data does not present a problem. The most important thing to keep in mind when passing numeric types is that in Win32, the C **int** type is 4 bytes, not 2 bytes, and therefore is equivalent to the Fortran **INTEGER*4** type. The **COMPLEX** type is a special case and is discussed in a later section. Table 10.6 summarizes equivalent numeric data types for Fortran, MASM, and C/C++.

Table 10.6   Equivalent Fortran, MASM, and C/C++ Numeric Data Types

Fortran	MASM	C/C++
CHARACTER*1	**BYTE**	**unsigned char**
INTEGER*1	**SBYTE**	**char**
(none)	**WORD**	**unsigned short**

Table 10.6   Equivalent Fortran, MASM, and C/C++ Numeric Data Types (*continued*)

Fortran	MASM	C/C++
INTEGER*2	SWORD	short
(none)	DWORD	unsigned long, unsigned int
INTEGER, INTEGER*4	SDWORD	long, int
REAL, REAL*4	REAL4	float
DOUBLE PRECISION, REAL*8	REAL8	double

If a C program passes an unsigned data type to a Fortran routine, the routine can accept the argument as the equivalent signed data type, but you should be careful that the range of the signed type is not exceeded.

Pointers (Address Variables)

In Fortran, you use the **LOC** function to extract the address of a variable. (In Win32, all addresses are 4 bytes, so there is no separate **LOCFAR** function as for 16-bit environments.) Because Fortran does not have a pointer type, the result of the **LOC** function must be stored in an **INTEGER*4** variable or passed as a parameter of type **INTEGER*4**. Generally, a pointer should be passed by value.

Passing a pointer by value is equivalent to passing what it points to by reference. In the following example, the two subroutine calls push identical data on the stack, and in each case the C routine called should expect an address. The two functions require different parameter declarations.

```
INTERFACE TO SUBROUTINE pass_addr1 [C] (addr_data)
REAL*8 addr_data [REFERENCE]
END

INTERFACE TO SUBROUTINE pass_addr2 [C] (addr_data)
INTEGER*4 addr_data [VALUE]
END

REAL*8 x
INTEGER*4 ptr
CALL pass_addr1 (x)
ptr = LOC(x)
CALL pass_addr2 (ptr)
```

Arrays

Each language varies in the way that arrays are declared and indexed. Array indexing is a source-level consideration and involves no difference in the underlying data. There are two differences in the way elements are indexed by each language:

- The value of the lower array bound is different.

  By default, Fortran indexes the first element of an array as 1. C and C++ index it as 0. Fortran subscripts should therefore be 1 higher. (Fortran also provides the option of specifying another integer lower bound.)

- C varies subscripts in row-major order, Fortran in column-major order.

The differences in how subscripts are varied only affect arrays with more than one dimension. With row-major order (C and C++), the rightmost dimension changes fastest. With column-major order (Fortran), the leftmost dimension changes fastest. Thus, in C, the first four elements of an array declared as X[3][3] are

```
X[0][0]    X[0][1]    X[0][2]    X[1][0]
```

In Fortran, the four elements are

```
X(1,1)    X(2,1)    X(3,1)    X(1,2)
```

The preceding C and Fortran arrays illustrate the difference between row-major and column-major order, and also the difference in the assumed lower bound between C and Fortran. Table 10.7 shows equivalencies for array declarations in each language. In this table, r is the number of elements of the row dimension (which changes the slowest), and c is the number of elements of the column dimension (which changes the fastest).

Table 10.7   Equivalent Array Declarations

Language	Array declaration	Array reference
C/C++	*type x[r][c]*, or **struct** { *type x[r][c];* } *x* [1]	*x[r][c]*
Fortran	*type x(c, r)*	*x(c+1, r+1)*

[1] Use a structure to pass an array by value in C and C++.

The order of indexing extends to any number of dimensions you declare. For example, the C declaration

```
int arr1[2][10][15][20];
```

is equivalent to the Fortran declaration

```
INTEGER*2 ARR1( 20, 15, 10, 2 )
```

The constants used in a C array declaration represent dimensions, not upper bounds as they do in other languages. Therefore, the last element in the C array declared as int arr[5][5] is arr[4][4], not arr[5][5].

The following code provides a complete example, showing how arrays are passed as arguments to a routine.

```
C      File FORARRS.FOR
C

       INTERFACE TO SUBROUTINE Pass_Arr [C,ALIAS:'_Pass_Arr'] ( Array )
       INTEGER*4 Array( 10, 10 )
       END

       INTEGER*4 Arr( 10, 10 )
       CALL Pass_Arr( Arr )
       write (*,*) 'Array values: ', Arr(1, 10), Arr(2, 10)
       END

/*      File CF.C  */

#include <stdio.h>

void Pass_Arr ( int arr[10][10] )
{
    arr[9][0] = 10;
    arr[9][1] = 20;
}
```

Character Strings

In Win32, Fortran by default passes a hidden length argument for strings. This argument is easily accessible to other languages, unlike the string-length information passed in 16-bit versions of Fortran. The hidden length argument consists of an unsigned 4-byte integer, always passed by value, immediately following the character string argument.

For example, if a Fortran program sets up the following call to a routine, Pass_Str, implemented in C:

```
       INTERFACE TO SUBROUTINE Pass_Str (string)
       CHARACTER*(*) string
       END
```

Then the C routine must expect two arguments:

```
void __stdcall PASS_STR (char *string, unsigned int length_arg )
```

Another important difference is in the format of the strings themselves. C strings are null-terminated. For example, given the following assignment:

```
Char *cstring="C text string";
```

The string data is stored as shown in the following figure.

Fortran strings are not null-terminated, and they are padded with blank spaces when assigned string data that is shorter than the declared length. For example, given the following assignment:

```
CHARACTER*14 forstring
DATA FORSTRING /"Fortran STRING'/
```

The string data is stored as follows. Note that if the string were any longer, it would be padded with trailing blanks.

A more efficient approach, wherever possible, is to adopt C string behavior. When the **C** or **STDCALL** attribute is applied to a routine, Fortran does not pass a hidden length argument. Furthermore, you can use the C-string feature to assign null-terminated string data in Fortran, as follows:

```
CHARACTER*20 forstring
DATA forstring /'This is a string'C/
```

The string variable, `forstring`, can then be passed to a C routine. If the **C** or **STDCALL** attribute is used, Fortran passes forstring just as C does: pushing the address of a null-terminated string onto the stack, with no hidden length argument.

Note Fortran functions of type **CHARACTER*(*)** place a hidden string argument at the beginning of the parameter list; this may include both string address and length, as appropriate. C functions that implement such a call from Fortran must declare this hidden string argument explicitly and use it to return a value. However, you are more likely to avoid errors by not using character-string return types. Use subroutines whenever possible.

The following example demonstrates how a Fortran main program calls a C function that translates a string to all-uppercase. Because the string is passed by reference, there is no need to use a string return type. Note that the **C** attribute stops Fortran from passing a hidden string-length argument, and the **DATA** statement uses a "C" to specify null termination.

```
C     File FORMAIN.FOR
C
      INTERFACE TO SUBROUTINE Ucase [C,ALIAS:'_Ucase'] (text)
      CHARACTER*(*) text [REFERENCE]
      END

      CHARACTER*40 forstring
      DATA forstring /'This is a sample string.'C/
      WRITE (*, *) forstring
      CALL Ucase (forstring)
      WRITE (*, *) forstring
      END

/*    File CSTR.C    */

#include <ctype.h>

void Ucase( char *string )
{
    char *ptr;

    for (ptr = string; *ptr; ptr++)
        *ptr = toupper( *ptr );
}
```

This use of C strings is usually the best approach, because most C library functions, as well as API functions, assume null-termination. However, if you use C to write string-manipulation functions, it is a good idea to translate null-terminated strings back into blank-padded strings after the C function returns. The following code performs this operation:

```
      SUBROUTINE Fix_C_Str (text, length)
      CHARACTER*(*) text
      INTEGER*4 length

      INTEGER*4 i

C  Find the first null ('\0')

      i = 1
      DO WHILE ((i .LE. length) .AND. (text(i:i) .NE. '\0'))
        i = i + 1
      END DO

C  Pad with blanks to the end of the string

      DO WHILE (i .LE. length)
        text (i:i) = ' '
      END DO
      END
```

Structures, COMPLEX, and LOGICAL Types

The Fortran structure variable, defined with the **STRUCTURE** keyword and declared with the **RECORD** statement, is equivalent to C **struct** declarations. You can pass structures by value or by reference. Be careful, however, about the effect of structure alignment if you are going to share structures.

C, C++, and MASM do not directly implement the Fortran types **COMPLEX*8** and **COMPLEX*16**. However, you can write structures that are equivalent. The type **COMPLEX*8** has two fields, both of which are 4-byte floating-point numbers; the first contains the real-number component, and the second contains the imaginary-number component. The type **COMPLEX** is equivalent to the type **COMPLEX*8**. The type **COMPLEX*16** is similar to **COMPLEX*8**. The only difference is that each field of **COMPLEX*16** contains an 8-byte floating-point number.

Note Fortran functions of type **COMPLEX** place a hidden **COMPLEX** argument at the beginning of the parameter list. C functions that implement such a call from Fortran must declare this hidden string argument explicitly, and use it to return a value. The C return type should be **void**.

Here are the C/C++ structure definitions for the Fortran **COMPLEX** types.

```
struct complex8 {
    float    real, imag;
};

struct complex16 {
    double   real, imag;
};
```

A Fortran **LOGICAL*2** is stored as a 1-byte indicator value (1=true, 0=false) followed by one unused byte. A Fortran **LOGICAL*4** is stored as a 1-byte indicator value followed by three unused bytes. The type **LOGICAL** is equivalent to **LOGICAL*4**.

To pass or receive a Fortran **LOGICAL** type, use an integer. Note that only the low byte is tested or used by Fortran.

The C++ **class** type has the same layout as the corresponding C **struct** type, unless the class defines virtual functions or has base classes. Classes that lack those features can be passed in the same way as C structures.

Common Blocks

You can pass individual members of a Fortran common block in an argument list, just as you can any data item. However, you can also give a different language module access to the entire common block.

C or C++ modules can reference the items of a common block by first declaring a structure with fields that correspond to the common-block variables. Having defined a structure with the appropriate fields, the C or C++ module must then connect with the common block. The next two sections present methods for gaining access to common blocks.

Passing the Address of a Common Block

To pass the address of a common block, simply pass the address of the first variable in the block. (In other words, pass the first variable by reference.) The receiving C or C++ module should expect to receive a structure by reference.

In the following example, the C function initcb receives the address of the variable N, which it considers to be a pointer to a structure with three fields:

```
C       Fortran SOURCE CODE
C

        COMMON /CBLOCK/N, X, Y
        INTEGER*4 N
        REAL*8     X, Y
    .
    .
    .

        CALL INITCB( N )

/* C source code */

struct block_type
{
    long   n;
    double x;
    double y;
};

initcb( struct block_type * block_hed )
{
    block_hed->n = 1;
    block_hed->x = 10.0;
    block_hed->y = 20.0;
}
```

Accessing Common Blocks Directly

You can access Fortran common blocks directly by defining a structure with the appropriate fields and then declaring the structure as an external data symbol. For example, the following code defines a structure named CBLOCK, which the C code can use to directly access items in the Fortran common block named CBLOCK:

```
struct block_type
{
    int     n;
    double x;
    double y;
};

extern struct block_type CBLOCK;
```

C H A P T E R   1 1

Advanced Profiling

The Microsoft 32-Bit Source Profiler is a powerful analysis tool for examining the run-time behavior of your programs. You can use information generated by the profiler to identify which sections of code work efficiently and which need to be examined more carefully. (For basic information on the profiler, see Chapter 15 of the *Visual C++ User's Guide*.)

Note For complete syntax and command-line options for PREP, PROFILE and PLIST see Appendix C in the *Visual C++ User's Guide*.

Combining PROFILE Sessions

With the profiler's modular design, you can make several profiling runs without having to run PREP each time (see Figure 11.1). After PREP has created .PBI and .PBT files, you can reuse these files with PROFILE to create multiple .PBO files. You can then merge the .PBO files using the PREP /IO command-line option with multiple .PBO files. The Visual Workbench Profile dialog box contains a Merge option button that automates this process.

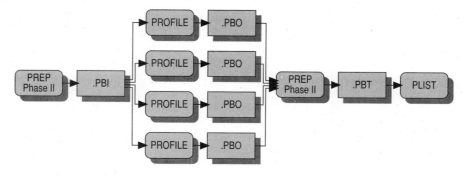

Figure 11.1   Combining PROFILE Sessions

Using the Profile Dialog Box Merge Option

The .PBI, .PBO, and .PBT files for your project are generated the first time you run profile. After that, you can use the Merge option button in the Profile dialog box (shown in Figure 11.2). PROFILE executes each time you choose the Merge button, and PREP Phase II adds the result to the existing .PBT file. PLIST prints the cumulative results each time the profiled program exits.

Figure 11.2   Profile dialog box

Using Batch Files

If you use the Merge button, you will get a PLIST report each time you invoke PROFILE. If, instead, you need a single PLIST report from multiple profile runs, you must write and execute a batch file like this:

```
PREP /LV myprog.exe myfuncs.dll
PROFILE /O myprog1 myprog.exe
PROFILE /O myprog2 myprog.exe
PROFILE /O myprog3 myprog.exe
PREP /IT myprog /IO myprog1 /IO myprog2 /IO myprog3 /OT myprog
PLIST myprog >myprog.out
```

Or, alternatively, because PREP Phase II adds data to an existing .PBT file:

```
PREP /LV myprog.exe myfuncs.dll
PROFILE myprog
PREP /M myprog
PROFILE myprog
PREP /M myprog
PROFILE myprog
PREP /M myprog
PLIST myprog >myprog.out
```

> **Note** You can merge only eight .PBO files from the command line with each PREP invocation. To overcome this limitation, use PREP Phase II to merge groups of .PBO files into .PBT files. Then, merge the resulting .PBT files to yield a single .PBT file that contains statistics from the constituent .PBO files.

You cannot merge .PBO or .PBT files from different .PBI files. PREP can combine information only from profiling sessions that use the same .EXE and .PBI files (and therefore have identical profiling characteristics). You cannot, for example, merge the results of a timing session with the results of a coverage session.

Reusing .PBT and .PBI Files

For a large program, it can take a lot of time for PREP to create .PBT and .PBI files from scratch. You must rebuild these files if you change your source code or the profiling method, but you can reuse the files if you only need another profile run with different program input data. Just copy the .PBT file after the initial Phase I PREP run. The .PBI file is never changed, so you don't need to copy it.

Profiling Dynamic-Link Libraries

Profiling a dynamic-link library (DLL) is similar to profiling an .EXE file. When you profile a DLL, you follow the same steps and use the same commands that you would for an .EXE file. The same profiling rules that apply to .EXE files (such as the need to include debugging information and to supply a .MAP file) apply to DLLs.

For function profiling, the DLL is typically renamed with a _LL extension, but the .EXE file looks for a file with a .DLL extension when it executes. Therefore the prepared DLL must be renamed prior to profiling.

The following batch file (PROFDLL.BAT) profiles a DLL with the assumption that the .EXE file has not been prepared for profiling:

```
COPY %1.dll save
PREP /OM %1.dll
COPY %1._ll %1.dll
PROFILE /I %1 /O %1 %2 %3 %4 %5 %6
COPY save %1.dll
PREP /M %1
PLIST %1
```

> **Note** The preceding batch generates a message warning you that the main program has not been prepared for profiling.

If you had a main program HEARTS.EXE that used a DLL called CARDS.DLL, and you wanted to profile only CARDS.DLL, you would run the preceding batch as:

```
PROFDLL cards hearts
```

Profiling Multiple .DLL and .EXE Files

The profiler can profile several DLLs and their calling executable file in a single profiler run. With phase I PREP command-line options, you can specify more than one .DLL or .EXE.

The following commands demonstrate how to profile an executable file and two DLLs from the command line:

```
PREP /OM /FC wingame.exe aliens.dll hiscore.dll
PROFILE wingame.exe
PREP /M  wingame
PLIST wingame >wingame.out
```

The first line causes PREP to create WINGAME.PBI and WINGAME.PBT files that include information on WINGAME.EXE, ALIENS.DLL, and HISCORE.DLL. The next line causes PROFILE to run WINGAME.EXE (actually WINGAME._XE, as generated by PREP Phase I). During the execution of WINGAME, PROFILE collects statistics for WINGAME.EXE as well as ALIENS.DLL and HISCORE.DLL, if they are called. The final two lines process the information from the profiling session and store the results in WINGAME.OUT.

Program Statistics vs. Module Statistics

PLIST reports always start with a "Program Statistics" section followed by a "Module Statistics" section. If there are several DLLs involved, as in the previous example, there is one "Module Statistics" section per .EXE or .DLL. The "Program Statistics" section lists totals for the entire program, including DLLs. Total time includes time in functions and modules not being profiled.

Profiling Inlined Code

If you specify, the Visual C++ compiler will perform inlining, which replaces a function call with an actual copy of the code. Profiling inlined code requires special attention.

Function Profiling for Inlined Functions

Because inlined functions don't generate .MAP file entries or CALL instructions, the profiler cannot tell when the computer is executing one of these functions. The time, hit, and coverage data will be attributed to the "calling" function.

Note In many cases there are .MAP file entries for "inlined" functions because the functions are not necessarily inlined everywhere in the application. Take this into account when you analyze profiler results.

Line Profiling for Inlined Functions

The profiler can provide line-level hit count and coverage information for inlined functions. Be sure to include the source lines in the Phase I PREP command-line options, just as you would include source lines in the calling program.

Profiling Windows NT Console Applications

Windows NT console applications do not use the graphical user interface; they run from the command line, often doing console input/output. You can easily use the profiler with these applications. If the application does do console I/O, you should run the profiling batch from the command prompt rather than from the Profile dialog box.

Profiling Multithreaded Applications

For multithreaded applications, profiler behavior depends on the profiling method.

For line counting and line coverage, the profiler does not discriminate among threads. The hit counts encompass all the program's threads.

For function timing, function counting, and function coverage, profiling is thread-dependent. You can profile an individual thread by (1) declaring the thread's main function as the starting function (PREP /SF option), and (2) including all functions in the program (don't use the PREP/EXC option).

The profile results will be difficult to interpret if you do not specify a starting function, if you specify a starting function that is called from multiple threads, or if you don't include all functions.

Profiling on a "Quiet" Computer

For maximum profiler accuracy, close as many other applications as possible during profiling. In particular, do not run programs such as electronic mail that execute at random intervals.

Miscellaneous Profiler Restrictions

Function-level profiling works only with ordinary functions that return with the stack pointer unchanged. Profiling should be turned off for functions that change the stack pointer or store the return address for later use. The profiler automatically turns off profiling for the functions **alloca** and **setjmp**. If you write your own similar functions, you must write them in assembly language. By default, assembly-language functions are excluded from profiling. Do not use these functions with the PREP /INC option.

C H A P T E R   1 2

Developing for International Markets

An important aspect of developing applications for international markets is the adequate representation of local character sets. The ASCII character set defines characters in the range 0x00 to 0x7F. There are other character sets, primarily European, that define the characters within the range 0x00 to 0x7F identically to the ASCII character set and also define an extended character set from 0x80 to 0xFF. Thus an 8-bit, single-byte–character set (SBCS) is sufficient to represent the ASCII character set as well as the character sets for many European languages. However, some non-European character sets, such as Japanese Kanji, include many more characters than can be represented in a single-byte coding scheme, and therefore require multibyte-character set (MBCS) encoding.

Unicode and MBCS

The Microsoft Foundation Class Library (MFC) and the C run-time library for Visual C++ are enabled in two ways to assist your international programming:

- Support for the Unicode standard on Windows NT.

  Unicode is a 16-bit character encoding, providing enough encodings for all languages. All ASCII characters are included in Unicode as "widened" characters.

- Support for a form of Multibyte Character Set (MBCS) called Double Byte Character Set (DBCS) on all platforms.

  DBCS characters are composed of one or two bytes. Some ranges of bytes are set aside for use as "lead bytes." A lead byte specifies that it and the following "trail byte" comprise a single two-byte-wide character. You must keep track of which bytes are lead bytes. In a particular multibyte-character set, the lead bytes fall within a certain range, as do the trail bytes. When these ranges overlap, it may be necessary to evaluate the context to determine whether a given byte is functioning as a lead byte or a trail byte.

Note In this documentation, "MBCS" is used to describe all non-Unicode support for wide characters. In Visual C++, MBCS always means DBCS. Character sets wider than two bytes are not supported.

By definition, the ASCII character set is a subset of all multibyte-character sets. In many multibyte character sets, each character in the range 0x00–0x7F is identical to the character that has the same value in the ASCII character set. For example, in both ASCII and MBCS character strings, the one-byte **NULL** character ('\0') has value 0x00 and indicates the terminating null character.

International Enabling

Most traditional C and C++ code makes assumptions about character and string manipulation that do not work well for international applications. While both MFC and the run-time library support Unicode or MBCS, there is still work for you to do. To guide you, this section explains the meaning of "international enabling" in Visual C++:

- Both Unicode and MBCS are enabled by means of portable data types in MFC function parameter lists and return types. These types are conditionally defined in the appropriate ways, depending on whether your build defines the symbol **_UNICODE** or the symbol **_MBCS** (which means DBCS). Different variants of the MFC libraries are automatically linked with your application, depending on which of these two symbols your build defines.

- Class library code uses portable run-time functions and other means to ensure correct Unicode or MBCS behavior.

- You still must handle certain kinds of internationalization tasks in your code:

  - Use the same portable run-time functions that make MFC portable under either environment.

  - Make literal strings and characters portable under either environment using the **_T** macro. For more information, see "Generic-Text Mappings in TCHAR.H" on page 166.

  - Take precautions when parsing strings under MBCS. These precautions are not needed under Unicode.

  - Take care if you mix ANSI (8-bit) and Unicode (16-bit) characters in your application. It's possible to use ANSI characters in some parts of your program and Unicode characters in others, but you cannot mix them in the same string.

Note European and MBCS character sets have some characters, such as accented letters, with character codes greater than 0x80. Since most code uses signed characters, these characters greater than 0x80 are sign extended when converted to **int**. This is a problem for array indexing because the sign-extended characters, being negative, will index outside the array.

Languages that use MBCS, such as Japanese, are also unique. Since a character may consist of one or two bytes, you should always manipulate both bytes at the same time.

Locales and Code Pages

A "locale" reflects the local conventions and language for a particular geographical region. A given language may be spoken in more than one country; for example, Portuguese is spoken in Brazil as well as Portugal. Conversely, a country may have more than one official language. For example, Canada has two: English and French. Thus, Canada has two distinct locales: Canadian-English and Canadian-French. Some locale-dependent categories include the formatting of dates and the display format for monetary values.

The language determines the text and data formatting conventions, while the country determines the national conventions. Every language has a unique mapping, represented by "code pages," which includes characters other than those in the alphabet (such as punctuation marks and numbers). A code page is a character set and is related to the current locale and language. As such, a locale is a unique combination of language, country, and code page. The code page setting can determine the locale setting and can be changed at run-time by calling the **setlocale** run-time function.

Different languages may use different code pages. For example, the ANSI code page 1252 is used for American English and most European languages, and the ANSI code page 932 is used for Japanese Kanji. Virtually all code pages share the ASCII character set for the lowest 128 characters (0x00 to 0x7F).

Any single-byte code page can be represented in a table (with 256 entries) as a mapping of byte values to characters (including numbers and punctuation marks), or glyphs. Any multibyte code page can also be represented as a very large table (with 64K entries) of double-byte values to characters. In practice, however, they are usually represented as a table for the first 256 (single-byte) characters and as ranges for the double-byte values.

The C run-time library has two types of internal code pages: locale and multi-byte. You can change the current code page during program execution (see the documentation for the **setlocale** and **setmbcp** functions). Also, the run-time library may obtain and use the value of the operating system code page. In Windows NT, the operating system code page is the "system default ANSI" code page. This code page is constant for the duration of the program's execution.

When the locale code page changes, the behavior of the locale-dependent set of functions changes to that dictated by the chosen code page. By default, all locale-dependent functions begin execution with a locale code page unique to the "C" locale. You can change the internal locale code page (as well as other locale-specific properties) by calling the **setlocale** function. A call to **setlocale**(LC_ALL, "") will set the locale to that indicated by the operating system's default code page.

Similarly, when the multibyte code page changes, the behavior of the multibyte functions changes to that dictated by the chosen code page. By default, all multi-byte functions begin execution with a multibyte code page corresponding to the operating system's default code page. You can change the internal multibyte code page by calling the **setmbcp** function.

The C run-time function **setlocale** sets, changes, or queries some or all of the current program's locale information. The **_wsetlocale** routine is a wide-character version of **setlocale**; the arguments and return values of **_wsetlocale** are wide-character strings. For more information, see the documentation for **setlocale** in the *Run-Time Library Reference*.

Benefits of Character Set Portability

You can benefit from using MFC and C run-time portability features even if you don't currently intend to internationalize your application:

- Coding portably makes your code base flexible. You can later move it easily to Unicode or MBCS.

- Using Unicode makes your applications for Windows NT more efficient. Windows NT uses Unicode, so non-Unicode strings passed to and from the operating system must be translated, incurring overhead.

- Using MBCS enables you to support international markets on Win32 platforms other than Windows NT, including future 32-bit versions of Microsoft Windows.

Internationalization Strategies

Depending on your target operating system(s) and markets, you have several internationalization strategies:

- Your application uses Unicode and therefore runs on Windows NT.

  You use Unicode-specific programming techniques and all characters are 16 bits wide (although you can use ANSI characters in some parts of your program for special purposes). The C run-time library provides functions, macros, and data types for Unicode-only programming. MFC is fully Unicode-enabled.

- Your application uses MBCS and can be run on any Win32 platform.

  You use MBCS-specific programming techniques. Strings can contain single-byte characters, double-byte characters, or both. The C run-time library provides functions, macros, and data types for MBCS-only programming. MFC is fully MBCS-enabled.

- The source code for your application is written for complete portability—by recompiling with the symbol **_UNICODE** or the symbol **_MBCS** defined, you can produce versions that use either.

  You use fully portable C run-time functions, macros, and data types. MFC's flexibility supports any of these strategies.

Most of this chapter focuses on writing completely portable code that you can build as Unicode or as MBCS.

Support for Unicode

A "wide character" is a two-byte multilingual character code. Any character used in modern computing worldwide, including technical symbols and special publishing characters, can be represented according to the Unicode specification as a wide character. Because each wide character is always represented in a fixed size of 16 bits, using wide characters simplifies programming with international character sets.

A wide-character string is represented as a **wchar_t[]** array and is pointed to by a **wchar_t*** pointer. Any ASCII character can be represented as a wide character by prefixing the letter L to the character. For example, L'\0' is the terminating wide (16-bit) **NULL** character. Similarly, any ASCII string literal can be represented as a wide-character string literal by prefixing the letter L to the ASCII literal (L"Hello").

Generally, wide characters take more space in memory than multibyte characters but are faster to process. In addition, only one locale can be represented at a time in multibyte encoding, whereas all character sets in the world are represented simultaneously by the Unicode representation.

The MFC framework is Unicode-enabled throughout, except for the database classes. (ODBC is not Unicode enabled.) MFC accomplishes Unicode enabling by using "portable" macros throughout, as shown in Table 12.1:

Table 12.1   Portable Data Types in MFC

Non-portable Data Type(s)	Replaced by This Macro
char	_TCHAR
char*, LPSTR (Win32 data type)	LPTSTR
const char*, LPCSTR (Win32 data type)	LPCTSTR

Class **CString** uses **_TCHAR** as its base and provides constructors and operators for easy conversions. Most string operations for Unicode can be written by using the same logic used for handling the Windows ANSI character set, except that the basic unit of operation is a 16-bit character instead of an 8-bit byte. Unlike working with multibyte character sets (MBCS), you do not have to (and should not) treat a Unicode character as if it were two distinct bytes.

Using wmain

Microsoft Specific →

Visual C++ supports defining a **wmain** function and passing wide-character arguments to your Unicode application. You declare formal parameters to **wmain** using a format similar to **main**. You can then pass wide-character arguments and, optionally, a wide-character environment pointer to the program. The *argv* and *envp* parameters to **wmain** are of type **wchar_t***.
For example:

wmain(int *argc***, wchar_t ***argv***[ ], wchar_t ***envp***[ ])**

Note   MFC Unicode applications use **wWinMain** as the entry point. In this case, **CWinApp::m_lpCmdLine** is a Unicode string. Be sure to set **wWinMainCRTStartup** as the Entry Point symbol in the Output category of the Project Settings Link dialog box.

If your program uses a **main** function, the multibyte-character environment is created by the run-time library at program startup. A wide-character copy of the environment is created only when needed (for example, by a call to the **_wgetenv** or **_wputenv** functions). On the first call to **_wputenv**, or on the first call to **_wgetenv** if an MBCS environment already exists, a corresponding wide-character string environment is created. The environment is then pointed to by the **_wenviron** global variable, which is a wide-character version of the **_environ** global variable. At this point, two copies of the environment (MBCS and Unicode) exist simultaneously and are maintained by the run-time system throughout the life of the program.

Similarly, if your program uses a **wmain** function, a wide-character environment is created at program startup and is pointed to by the **_wenviron** global variable. An MBCS (ASCII) environment is created on the first call to **_putenv** or **getenv**, and is pointed to by the **_environ** global variable.

END Microsoft Specific

Unicode Programming Summary

To take advantage of the MFC and C run-time support for Unicode, you need to:

- Define _UNICODE.

  Define the symbol **_UNICODE** before you build your program.

- Specify entry point.

  In the Output category of the Link field in the Project Settings dialog box, set the Entry Point Symbol to **wWinMainCRTStartup**.

- Use "portable" run-time functions and types.

  Use the proper C run-time functions for Unicode string handling. You can use the *wcs* family of functions, but you may prefer the fully "portable" (internationally enabled) **_TCHAR** macros. These macros are all prefixed with *_tcs*; they substitute, one for one, for the *str* family of functions. These functions are described in detail in the "Internationalization" section in the *Run-Time Library Reference*. For more information, see "Generic-Text Mappings in TCHAR.H" on page 166.

  Use **_TCHAR** and the related portable data types described in "Support for Unicode" on page 157.

- Handle literal strings properly.

  The Visual C++ compiler interprets a literal string coded as

  ```
  L"this is a literal string"
  ```

  to mean a string of Unicode characters. You can use the same prefix for literal characters. Use the **_T** macro to code literal strings generically, so they compile as Unicode strings under Unicode or as ANSI strings (including MBCS) without Unicode. For example, instead of:

  ```
  pWnd->SetWindowText( "Hello" );
  ```

  use:

  ```
  pWnd->SetWindowText( _T("Hello") );
  ```

  With **_UNICODE** defined, **_T** translates the literal string to the L-prefixed form; otherwise, **_T** translates the string without the L prefix.

Tip The **_T** macro is identical to the **_TEXT** macro.

- Be careful passing string lengths to functions.

  Some functions want the number of characters in a string; others want the number of bytes. For example, if **_UNICODE** is defined, the following call to a **CArchive** object will not work (`str` is a **CString**):

  ```
  archive.Write( str, str.Length( ) );     // invalid
  ```

  In a Unicode application, the length gives you the number of characters but not the correct number of bytes, since each character is two bytes wide. Instead, you must use:

  ```
  archive.Write( str, str.Length( ) * sizeof( _TCHAR ) );     // valid
  ```

  which specifies the correct number of bytes to write.

  However, MFC member functions that are character-oriented, rather than byte-oriented, work without this extra coding:

  ```
  pDC->TextOut( str, str.Length( ) );
  ```

  CDC::TextOut takes a number of characters, not a number of bytes.

To summarize, MFC and the run-time library provide the following support for Unicode programming under Windows NT:

- Except for database class member functions, all MFC functions are Unicode enabled, including **CString**. **CString** also provides Unicode/ANSI conversion functions.
- The run-time library supplies Unicode versions of all string-handling functions. (The run-time library also supplies "portable" versions suitable for Unicode or for MBCS. These are the _tcs_ macros.)
- TCHAR.H supplies portable data types and the **_T** macro for translating literal strings and characters. See "Generic-Text Mappings in TCHAR.H" on page 166.
- The run-time library provides a wide-character version of **main**. Use **wmain** to make your application "Unicode aware."

Support for Multibyte Character Sets (MBCS)

For platforms used in markets whose languages use large character sets, the best alternative to Unicode is MBCS. MFC supports MBCS by using "internationalizable" data types and C run-time functions. You should do the same in your code.

Under MBCS, characters are encoded in either one or two bytes. In two-byte characters, the first, or "lead-byte" signals that both it and the following byte are to be interpreted as one character. The first byte comes from a range of codes reserved for use as lead bytes. Which ranges of bytes can be lead bytes depends on the code page in use. For example, Japanese code page 932 uses the range 0x81 through 0x9F as lead bytes, but Korean code page 949 uses a different range.

Consider all of the following in your MBCS programming:

MBCS characters in the environment
    MBCS characters can appear in strings such as file and directory names.

Editing operations
    Editing operations in MBCS applications should operate on characters, not bytes. The caret should not split a character, the RIGHT ARROW key should move right one character, and so on. Delete should delete a character; Undo should reinsert it.

String handling
    In an application that uses MBCS, string handling poses special problems. Characters of both widths are mixed in a single string; therefore you must remember to check for lead bytes.

Run-time library support
    The C run-time library and MFC support single-byte, MBCS, and Unicode programming. Single-byte strings are processed with the *str* family of run-time functions; MBCS strings are processed with corresponding *_mbs* functions; and Unicode strings are processed with corresponding *wcs* functions. MFC class member function implementations use portable run-time functions that map, under the right circumstances, to the normal *str* family of functions, the MBCS functions, or the Unicode functions, as described in "MBCS/Unicode portability."

MBCS/Unicode portability
    Using the header file TCHAR.H, you can build single-byte, MBCS, and Unicode applications from the same sources. TCHAR.H defines macros prefixed with *_tcs* , which map to *str*, *_mbs*, or *wcs* functions as appropriate. To build MBCS, define the symbol **_MBCS**. To build Unicode, define the symbol **_UNICODE**. By default, **_MBCS** is defined for MFC applications. For more information, see "Generic-Text Mappings in TCHAR.H" on page 166.

Note   Behavior is undefined if you define both **_UNICODE** and **_MBCS**.

The MBCTYPE.H and MBSTRING.H header files define MBCS-specific functions and macros, which you may need in some cases. For example, **_ismbblead** tells you whether a specific byte in a string is a lead byte.

MBCS Programming Tips

This section supplies tips for successful multibyte character set (MBCS) programming. The advice applies to MFC applications and applications written without MFC. Topics include:

- General MBCS programming advice
- Incrementing and decrementing pointers
- Byte indices
- Last character in a string
- Character assignment
- Character comparison
- Buffer overflow

General MBCS Programming Advice

Use the following tips:

- MFC, including its **CString** class, is MBCS-enabled.
- For flexibility, use run-time macros such as **_tcschr** and **_tcscpy** when possible. For more information, see "Generic-Text Mappings in TCHAR.H" on page 166.
- Use the C run-time **_getmbcp** function to get information about the current code page.

Incrementing and Decrementing Pointers

Use the following tips:

- Point to lead bytes, not trail bytes. It is usually unsafe to have a pointer to a trail byte. It's usually safest to scan a string forward rather than in reverse.
- There are pointer increment/decrement functions and macros available which move over a whole character:

  ```
  sz1++;
  ```

  becomes

  ```
  sz1 = _mbsinc( sz1 );
  ```

  The **_mbsinc** and **_mbsdec** functions correctly increment and decrement in *character* units, regardless of the character size.

- For decrements, you need a pointer to the head of the string, as in the following:

```
sz2--;
```

becomes

```
sz2 = _mbsdec( sz2Head, sz2 );
```

Alternatively, your "head" pointer could be to a valid character in the string, such that

```
sz2Head < sz2
```

You must have a pointer to a known valid lead byte.

- You may want to maintain a pointer to the previous character for faster calls to **_mbsdec**.

Byte Indices

Use the following tips:

- Working with a bytewise index into a string presents problems similar to those posed by pointer manipulation. Consider this example, which scans a string for a backslash character:

```
while ( rgch[ i ] != '\\' )
    i++;
```

This may index a trail byte, not a lead byte, and thus it may not point to a *character*.

- Use the **_mbslen** function to solve the preceding problem:

```
while ( rgch[ i ] != '\\' )
    i += _mbslen( rgch + i );
```

This correctly indexes to a lead byte, hence to a *character*. The **_mbslen** function determines the size of a character (one or two bytes).

The Last Character in a String

Use the following tips:

- Trail byte ranges overlap the ASCII character set in many cases. You can safely use bytewise scans for any control characters (less than 32).

- Consider the following line of code, which might be checking to see if the last character in a string is a backslash character:

```
if ( sz[ strlen( sz ) - 1 ] == '\\' )      // Is last character a '\'?
    // . . .
```

Since **strlen** is not "MBCS-aware," it will return the number of bytes, not the number of characters, in a multibyte string. Also, note that in some code pages (932, for example), '\' (0x5c) is a valid trail byte (sz is a C string).

One possible solution is to code it this way:

```
char *pLast;
pLast = _mbsrchr( sz, '\\' );    // find last occurence of '\' in sz
if ( pLast && ( *_mbsinc( pLast ) == '\0' ) )
    // . . .
```

This code uses the MBCS functions **_mbsrchr** and **_mbsinc**. Since these functions are MBCS-aware, they can distinguish between a '\' character and a trail byte '\'. The code performs some action if the last character in the string is a null ('\0').

Character Assignment

Consider the following example, in which the while loop scans a string, copying all characters except 'X' into another string:

```
while( *sz2 )
{
    if( *sz2 != 'X' )
        *sz1++ = *sz2;
    else
        sz2++;
}
```

The code copies the byte at sz2 to the location pointed to by sz1, then increments sz1 to receive the next byte. But if the next character in sz2 is a double-byte character, the assignment to sz1 will copy only the first byte. The following code uses a portable function to copy the character safely and another to increment sz1 and sz2 correctly:

```
while( *sz2 )
{
    if( *sz2 != 'X' )
    {
        _mbscpy( sz1, sz2 );
        sz1 = _mbsinc( sz1 );
    }
    else
        sz2 = _mbsinc( sz2 );
}
```

Character Comparison

Use the following tips:

- Comparing a known lead byte with an ASCII character works correctly:

```
if( *sz1 == 'A' )
    // ...
```

- Comparing two unknown characters requires the use of one of the macros defined in TCHAR.H:

```
if( !_mbccmp( sz1, sz2) )
    // ...
```

This ensures that both bytes of a double-byte character are compared for equality.

Buffer Overflow

Varying character sizes can cause problems when you put characters into a buffer. Consider the following code, which copies characters from a string, sz, into a buffer, rgch:

```
cb = 0;
while( cb < sizeof( rgch ) )
    rgch[ cb++ ] = *sz++;
```

The question is: was the last byte copied a lead byte? The following does not solve the problem because it can potentially overflow the buffer:

```
cb = 0;
while( cb < sizeof( rgch ) )
{
    _mbccpy( rgch + cb, sz );
    cb += _mbclen( sz );
    sz = _mbsinc( sz );
}
```

The **_mbccpy** call is an attempt to do the right thing—copy the full character, whether it's one or two bytes. But it doesn't take into account that the last character copied may not fit the buffer if the character is two bytes wide. The correct solution is:

```
cb = 0;
while( (cb + _mbclen( sz )) <= sizeof( rgch ) )
{
    _mbccpy( rgch + cb, sz );
    cb += _mbclen( sz );
    sz = _mbsinc( sz );
}
```

This code tests for possible buffer overflow in the loop test, using **_mbclen** to test the size of the current character pointed to by s z. By making a call to the **_mbsnbcpy** function, you can replace the code in the **while** loop with a single line of code. For example:

```
cb = 0;
while( (cb + _mbclen( sz )) <= sizeof( rgch ) )
{
    _mbsnbcpy( rgch, sz, sizeof( rgch ) );
}
```

Generic-Text Mappings in TCHAR.H

To simplify transporting code for international use, the Microsoft run-time library provides Microsoft-specific "generic-text" mappings for many data types, routines, and other objects. You can use these mappings, which are defined in TCHAR.H, to write generic code that can be compiled for single byte, multibyte, or Unicode, depending on a manifest constant you define using a **#define** statement. Generic-text mappings are Microsoft extensions that are not ANSI compatible.

Using the header file TCHAR.H, you can build single-byte, MBCS, and Unicode applications from the same sources. TCHAR.H defines macros prefixed with _tcs, which, with the correct preprocessor definitions, map to *str*, _mbs, or *wcs* functions as appropriate. To build MBCS, define the symbol **_MBCS**. To build Unicode, define the symbol **_UNICODE**. To build a single-byte application, define neither (the default). By default, **_MBCS** is defined for MFC applications.

The _**TCHAR** data type is defined conditionally in TCHAR.H. If the symbol **_UNICODE** is defined for your build, **_TCHAR** is defined as **wchar_t**; otherwise, for single-byte and MBCS builds, it is defined as **char**. (**wchar_t**, the basic Unicode wide character data type, is the 16-bit counterpart to an 8-bit signed **char**.) For international applications, use the _tcs family of functions, which operate in _**TCHAR** units, not bytes. For example, _**tcsncopy** copies *n* _**TCHAR**s, not *n* bytes.

Table 12.2   Preprocessor Directives for Generic-Text Mappings

# define	Compiled Version	Example
_UNICODE	Unicode (wide-character)	**_tcsrev** maps to **_wcsrev**
_MBCS	Multibyte-character	**_tcsrev** maps to **_mbsrev**
None (the default: neither **_UNICODE** nor **_MBCS** defined)	SBCS (ASCII)	**_tcsrev** maps to **strrev**

For example, the generic-text function **_tcsrev**, defined in TCHAR.H, maps to **_mbsrev** if you defined **_MBCS** in your program, or to **_wcsrev** if you defined **_UNICODE**. Otherwise **_tcsrev** maps to **strrev**. Other data type mappings are provided in TCHAR.H for programming convenience, but **_TCHAR** is the most useful.

Table 12.3   Generic-Text Data Type Mappings

Generic-Text Data Type Name	SBCS (_UNICODE, _MBCS Not Defined)	_MBCS Defined	_UNICODE Defined
_TCHAR	char	char	wchar_t
_TINT	int	int	wint_t
_TSCHAR	signed char	signed char	wchar_t
_TUCHAR	unsigned char	unsigned char	wchar_t
_TXCHAR	char	unsigned char	wchar_t
_T or **_TEXT**	No affect (removed by preprocessor)	No affect (removed by preprocessor)	**L** (converts following character or string to its Unicode counterpart)

For a complete list of generic-text mappings of routines, variables, and other objects, see Appendix B in the *Run-Time Library Reference*.

Note   Do not use the *str* family of functions with Unicode strings, which are likely to contain embedded null bytes. Similarly, do not use the *wcs* family of functions with MBCS (or SBCS) strings.

The following code fragments illustrate the use of **_TCHAR** and **_tcsrev** for mapping to the MBCS, Unicode, and SBCS models.

```
_TCHAR *RetVal, *szString;
RetVal = _tcsrev(szString);
```

If **_MBCS** has been defined, the preprocessor maps this fragment to the code:

```
char *RetVal, *szString;
RetVal = _mbsrev(szString);
```

If **_UNICODE** has been defined, the preprocessor maps the fragment to the code:

```
wchar_t *RetVal, *szString;
RetVal = _wcsrev(szString);
```

If neither **_MBCS** nor **_UNICODE** has been defined, the preprocessor maps the fragment to single-byte ASCII code:

```
char *RetVal, *szString;
RetVal = strrev(szString);
```

Thus you can write, maintain, and compile a single source code file to run with routines that are specific to any of the three kinds of character sets.

Using TCHAR.H Data Types with _MBCS Code

When the manifest constant **_MBCS** is defined, a given generic-text routine maps to one of the following kinds of routines:

- An SBCS routine that handles multibyte bytes, characters, and strings appropriately. In this case, the string arguments are expected to be of type **char***. For example, **_tprintf** maps to **printf**; the string arguments to **printf** are of type **char***. If you use the **_TCHAR** generic-text data type for your string types, the formal and actual parameter types for **printf** match because **_TCHAR*** maps to **char***.

- An MBCS-specific routine. In this case, the string arguments are expected to be of type **unsigned char***. For example, **_tcsrev** maps to **_mbsrev**, which expects and returns a string of type **unsigned char***. Again, if you use the **_TCHAR** generic-text data type for your string types, there is a potential type conflict because **_TCHAR** maps to type **char**.

Following are three solutions for preventing this type conflict (and the C compiler warnings or C++ compiler errors that would result).

- Use the default behavior. TCHAR.H provides generic-text routine prototypes for routines in the run-time libraries, as in the following example.

```
char * _tcsrev(char *);
```

In the default case, the prototype for **_tcsrev** maps to **_mbsrev** through a thunk in LIBC.LIB. This changes the types of the **_mbsrev** incoming parameters and outgoing return value from **_TCHAR *** (i.e., **char ***) to **unsigned char ***. This method ensures type matching when you are using **_TCHAR**, but it is relatively slow due to the function call overhead.

- Use function inlining by incorporating the following preprocessor statement in your code.

```
#define _USE_INLINING
```

This method causes an inline function thunk, provided in TCHAR.H, to map the generic-text routine directly to the appropriate MBCS routine. The following code excerpt from TCHAR.H provides an example of how this is done.

```
__inline char *_tcsrev(char *_s1)
{return (char *)_mbsrev((unsigned char *)_s1);}
```

If you can use inlining, this is the best solution, because it guarantees type matching and has no additional time cost.

- Use "direct mapping" by incorporating the following preprocessor statement in your code.

```
#define _MB_MAP_DIRECT
```

This approach provides a fast alternative if you do not want to use the default behavior or cannot use inlining. It causes the generic-text routine to be mapped by a macro directly to the MBCS version of the routine, as in the following example from TCHAR.H.

```
#define _tcschr _mbschr
```

When you take this approach, you must be careful to ensure use of appropriate data types for string arguments and string return values. You can use type casting to ensure proper type matching or you can use the **_TXCHAR** generic-text data type. **_TXCHAR** maps to type **char** in SBCS code but maps to type **unsigned char** in MBCS code. For more information about generic-text macros, see Appendix B in the *Run-Time Library Reference*.

For More Information

For more information on developing for international markets, see the following:

- In the *Run-Time Library Reference*: "Internationalization."
- In the *Win32 Programmer's Reference, Volume 2*: Chapter 53, "String Manipulation and Unicode."
- In *Advanced Windows NT*, Microsoft Press, 1994, by Jeffrey Richter: Chapter 11, "Unicode."
- The Unicode™ Standard: Worldwide Character Encoding, Version 1.0, Volumes 1 and 2, Addison-Wesley, 1992.

Index

H

HANDLE data type 50
Handle types 48
HANDLE_MSG macro 30, 34–35
HANDLE_WM_ macros 28
Handlers, message 27
Handles
    and WORD data type 5
    increased to 32 bits 1
Handling exceptions *See* Structured exception handling
Hardware exceptions 113
Header (.H) files
    and DLL imports 59–62
    effect of STRICT on 51
HINSTANCE data type 53
HIWORD macro 18
HMENU data type 52
HMODULE data type 53
hPrevInstance parameter 15
HWND type, porting to 32 bits 5

I

Import libraries 64–65
Importing
    inline functions 63
    symbols 61
Imports, mutual 65
#include files, #define _MT and 71
Include files. #define _MT and 71
Indexing arrays, mixed-language programming 140–141
Indirection errors, and STRICT 54
.INI files 16
Initialization (.INI) files 16
Initialization of DLLs 57–58
Initializing application instance 15
Inline functions 63
Input queues, localized 17
Input/output, file 14
Installing exception handlers 109
Instance
    application 15
    data, Window 11
    handle 48
Instantiation
    class template 88
    discussed 86
    explicit 88
INT 21H functions 12
Integer data types in mixed languages 138
Integers in Win32 5
Integers, size and range 20

K

Keyboard messages 33

L

/LD compiler option 64
LIB utility, and building DLLs 65
LIBCMT.LIB
    alternatives to 71
    compiler options 71
    /MT compiler option 71
    using 70
Libraries
    run-time DLL 64
    run-time, and DLLs 56
Linking multithread applications 79
List box functions 14
ListBox_ control message functions 42
Loading DLLs 66
LoadLibrary API function 67
LOC function in Fortran 139
Local data, stack usage 79
Local handle 48
Local heap, and pointers 18–19
Local variables, __LOCAL_SIZE symbolic constant 127
__LOCAL_SIZE symbolic constant 127
Locales
    defined 155
    setlocale function 156
    setmbcp function 156
Localized input queues 17
LocalLock function 51
LockFile function 12
LOGICAL type in Fortran 144
Long filenames 13
longjmp function 117
_lopen and _lread functions 14
Low-level file I/O 14
Lower bounds of arrays 140
Lowercase, names in Fortran 133
LOWORD macro 18
LPARAM data type 47
lParam message parameter 5
lParam, and message crackers 30
lParam, and sending messages 41
lpCmdLine parameter 15
LPCSTR data type 47
LPSTR data type 49

Internationalization
    discussed 153
    development strategies 156
Interprocess communication 18

Contributors to *Programming Techniques*

Samuel G. Dawson, Index Editor
Barbara Haerer, Editor
Jonathan Kagle, Writer
Matt LaBelle, Production
Seth Manheim, Writer
Mark Olson, Art Director
Chuck Sphar, Writer

Tools of the Trade

Inside Visual C++,™ 2nd ed.
David J. Kruglinski

Now updated to cover Visual C++ version 1.5, this book covers
OLE, ODBC enhancements, and Microsoft Foundation Class (MFC)
Library version 2.5. This is the foundation book for Visual C++ developers programming in Windows. Through fast-paced examples, this book takes readers from the basics through the advanced capabilities of this rich programming environment, while explaining the methodologies and the tools. The CD-ROM includes all the source code files necessary to create the sample programs in the book.

768 pages, softcover with one CD-ROM
$39.95 ($53.95 Canada)   ISBN 1-55615-661-8

Inside OLE 2
Kraig Brockschmidt

Here's the inside scoop on how to build powerful object-oriented applications for Windows. Written by a leading OLE expert, this guide shows experienced programmers how to take advantage of OLE 2 to develop next-generation applications that will take Windows to a new level. Brockschmidt explains how to build OLE 2 applications from scratch as well as how to convert existing applications. The disks contain 44 source code examples that demonstrate how to implement objects and how to integrate OLE 2 features in your applications.

1008 pages, softcover with two 1.44-MB 3.5-inch disks
$49.95 ($67.95 Canada)   ISBN 1-55615-618-9

Code Complete
Steve McConnell

"We were impressed.... A pleasure to read, either straight through or as a reference."   **PC Week**

This practical handbook of software construction covers the art and science of software development, from design to testing. Examples are provided in C, Pascal, Basic, FORTRAN, and Ada—but the focus is on programming techniques. Topics include up-front planning, applying good design techniques to construction, using data effectively, reviewing for errors, managing construction activities, and relating personal character to superior software.

880 pages, softcover $35.00 ($44.95 Canada)   ISBN 1-55615-484-4

Microsoft *Press*®